MORALE FOR A FREE WORLD

America and Not America Only

*I see not America only—I see not only Liberty's
nation, but other nations . . .*

I see this day the People beginning their landmarks.

MORALE

FOR A FREE WORLD

America and Not America Only

★

TWENTY-SECOND YEARBOOK

★

AMERICAN ASSOCIATION OF SCHOOL ADMINISTRATORS

A DEPARTMENT OF THE NATIONAL EDUCATION ASSOCIATION OF THE UNITED STATES
(formerly the Department of Superintendence)

1201 SIXTEENTH STREET, NORTHWEST, WASHINGTON 6, D. C.

COPYRIGHT, FEBRUARY 1944   PRICE $2.00

COMMISSION ON EDUCATION FOR MORALE

CARROLL R. REED
First Assistant Superintendent of Schools, Washington, D. C.
CHAIRMAN

JOHN E. ANDERSON
*Director, Institute of Child Welfare, University of Minnesota,
Minneapolis, Minnesota*

WINIFRED E. BAIN
President, Wheelock College, Boston, Massachusetts

FRANK S. FREEMAN
Professor of Education and Psychology, Cornell University, Ithaca, New York

ROY W. HATCH
*Formerly Head, Department of the Social Studies, New Jersey State Teachers
College, Montclair, New Jersey*

LAURA E. KELLAR
Principal, Atwater Elementary School, Shorewood, Milwaukee, Wisconsin

J. CAYCE MORRISON
*Assistant Commissioner for Research, State Education Department,
Albany, New York*

RALPH BARTON PERRY
Professor of Philosophy, Harvard University, Cambridge, Massachusetts

J. W. RAMSEY
Superintendent of Schools, Fort Smith, Arkansas

JAMES M. SPINNING
Superintendent of Schools, Rochester, New York

FOREWORD

To our surprise we find ourselves in an age of heroism. After two decades of sophistication, depression, and intellectual cynicism, we learn that there was a sound substratum of child rearing and child teaching and that a race of heroes was growing up among us. The forces of evil have evoked the spirit of valor among American youth.

A wounded soldier, sick and shaken from a torpedo explosion, face and hands severely burned, is ready to take his place on a safety raft. Instead of leaving, he makes two trips to a partially submerged life-belt locker of the sinking ship to get belts for the badly wounded who otherwise may have no chance at all for escape.

Army nurses and doctors on Bataan and Corregidor continue their work of mercy regardless of bombardment, fatigue, and hunger. They choose to risk capture or death rather than leave their posts of service.

Three men drag themselves ashore on a South Sea island, miraculously still alive after thirty-four days on a raft without food or water. Starved, exhausted, covered with blistering sores from the tropic sun, they pull their naked bodies erect and *march* inland, because they are Americans. "If any Japs were there, we did not want to be crawling."

An army officer says: "Our kids, American boys, are just kind of automatically wonderful. Just thru our own way of life they get something that makes them superior fighters. They don't have to be indoctrinated and have it hammered in for months or years. The fighter pilot flies with his heart. The thing that makes him superior in combat is inside him all the time. Our kids have it, and I think it is something they get naturally, something they get just by growing up in this country. I think that the thing that makes them better fighters is an individual sense of responsibility to what they are doing and a capacity to think for themselves."

Could an educator have said it better? "An individual sense of responsibility to what they are doing and a capacity to think for themselves"—these are what the schools want to teach. These are among the qualities basic to democratic morale, the morale that makes it possible for a person to give fully of his best efforts on behalf of the highest ideals of his country.

The past two years have shown again that this country in war can count on its armed forces for selfless devotion to duty. Civilians have shared in the sacrifices and services that total war demands. We built better than we knew in preparation for wartime morale. How can the schools lay foundations for morale that will be equally high in the transition to peace and in the long years that lie ahead? This book is an effort to answer that question.

When danger was greatest our minds were clear to see the value of what was at stake. In passionate conviction we dedicated our lives to freedom and all the ideals of democracy. As we begin to come out of the crisis, there will come the danger of mental and moral exhaustion —a relapse to a new cynicism. But the real war goes on so long as truth, freedom, fellow feeling, and human dignity are under attack in this country or anywhere in the world.

The physical heroism of war must be matched by the moral heroism of informed and devoted citizens. The United States and the world need men and women of character and courage who are capable of sustained and driving service in the common cause of building a better way of life for humanity. When schools and colleges, public and private, have done all that they can do in education for morale, there will be greater recognition given to the heroes of peace. In public service, in business and industry, and in other walks of life, there must be brave choices between personal advantage and the general good. Old prejudices and injustices still must be opposed in every community and in every nation. Citizens everywhere need an education that will give them strength to align themselves with the forces that promote the growth and freedom of the human spirit.

The Commission which prepared the 1944 yearbook was appointed early in 1942 by President W. Howard Pillsbury. Chapters prepared by individual members have been revised in the light of discussion at successive meetings, so that the final draft represents the judgment of the Commission as a whole.

Acknowledgment is made of assistance rendered by the staff in Washington, D. C. The executive secretary of the American Association of School Administrators, S. D. Shankland, helped in all phases of the Commission's work. Hazel Davis, assistant director of the NEA Research Division, supervised the editing of the volume, with the assistance of Beryl Evans of the Research Division and Katherine Lichliter of the NEA Division of Publications.

CONTENTS

OFFICIAL RECORDS

LIST OF FIGURES

LIST OF TABLES

End papers from photograph by Long Beach, California, Public Schools

YEARS OF THE UNPERFORMED

★ *Years of the unperformed! Your horizon rises—I see it parting away
for more august dramas;
I see not America only—I see not only Liberty's nation, but other
nations preparing;
I see tremendous entrances and exits—I see new combinations—I see
the solidarity of races;
(Have the old forces played their parts, are the acts suitable to them
closed?)*

*I see Freedom, completely armed, and victorious, with Law on one
side and Peace on the other, issuing forth against the idea of caste.
I see men marching and countermarching by swift millions;
I see the frontiers and boundaries of the old aristocracies broken;
I see the landmarks of European kings removed;
I see this day the People beginning their landmarks (all others give
way).*

*Never were such sharp questions asked as this day;
Never was average man, his soul, more energetic, more like a God.
Lo, how he urges and urges, leaving the masses no rest;
His daring foot is on land and sea everywhere—he colonizes the
Pacific, the archipelagoes;
—What whispers are these, O lands, running ahead of you, passing
under the seas?
Are all nations communing? Is there going to be but one heart to the
Globe?
Is humanity forming, en-masse? For lo! tyrants tremble, crowns grow
dim;
The earth, restive, confronts a new era, perhaps a general divine war.*

*Years prophetical! The space ahead as I walk, as I vainly try to pierce
it, is full of phantoms;
Unborn deeds, things soon to be, project their shapes around me;
Your dreams, O years, how they penetrate through me!
The performed America and Europe grow dim, retiring in shadow
behind me,
The unperformed, more gigantic than ever, advance, advance upon me.*

—WALT WHITMAN, *Drum Taps*, 1865

CHAPTER I

For a Thousand Years

MORALE IS RELATIVELY A NEW WORD in American life. It came into general use in the United States in 1917-18 and was treated in various publications which appeared shortly after the close of the first World War. Then, so far as the general public was concerned, the concept lay dormant for nearly two decades. Only after Munich did it again attract the attention of American writers and thinkers.

With the fall of France, morale became a key word in American thought and discussion.[1] With America's entrance into the second World War, the word "morale" was on every tongue. It appeared in advertising, governmental publications, the daily press, reports of learned societies, educational periodicals, magazines for lay readers, and conference reports of national organizations. There was a voluntary Committee for National Morale with fourteen subcommittees. More than six hundred different organizations were promoting morale in one form or another. There were books and reports on civilian morale, psychological factors in morale, the psychiatry of civilian morale, the psychology of war, and war morale.

The word "morale" symbolizes a new trend in American thought. It names a quality essential to the successful prosecution of war, vital to the soldier in the field and to the civilian on the home front. It reflects the inescapable fact that under the conditions of modern warfare the entire people are participants and that how they feel powerfully affects what they do. Like "democracy," the concept of "morale" holds great significance for the future.

Morale in War

Morale is a war word. Military writers take as their text Napoleon's statement that "the moral is to the physical as three to one." In 1917 the United States government was suddenly confronted with converting millions of civilians into an effective fighting force. This transition had to be accomplished in the shortest possible time.

---

[1] During the two years 1917 and 1918, the *Readers' Guide to Periodical Literature* listed two articles a year on morale. During the next twenty years only eight articles were listed. For the past three years the record was as follows: 1940, 38; 1941, 99; and 1942, 156.

Moreover this army had to fight on European soil, thereby breaking traditions ingrained in American thought thru three centuries of physical separation from the Old World.

This citizen army consisted of free men, men who had been taught to think, men who had grown up in the traditions of freedom. It was not enough to put them into uniform, to teach them to use the weapons of war, and to develop their powers of physical endurance. More important than all these was their understanding of the issues for which they were to fight, their health, their spirit, their courage, and their confidence in their own powers.

President Wilson and his Secretary of War, Newton D. Baker, understood these needs. Both were especially capable in voicing the moral concepts of the American people. Both understood the inter-relations of morals and morale and the importance of psychology as a powerful factor in an army's achievement. Thru their leadership the American people became acquainted with the concept of morale as a necessary quality of the soldier.

To develop morale in its new army the federal government, thru its War Department and related agencies, took practical steps. It initiated studies of the moral conditions surrounding army camps and the effect of those conditions upon the men.[2] It provided lectures on the psychology of war for officers in training and for enlisted men.[3] A morale division was organized in the Army and a morale officer was placed in every camp. The government enlisted the services of the Y.M.C.A., Y.M.H.A., Knights of Columbus, Salvation Army, and other similar agencies, to establish centers near every training camp, every embarkation center, and on every fighting front. Thru these agencies provision was made for entertainment and special services that would keep men's spirits high. For the most part these were distinctive additions to the realm of war.

Even as the government centered its efforts on developing the morale of its citizen soldiers and their leaders, individuals sensed the importance of the spirit of those behind the lines—the civilians in all walks of life. The issue was well stated by Hocking:

> For behind the army lies the nation; and the whole unwieldy mass, army and nation, is much more a mental unit than in any previous war, each dependent on the courage and good-will of the other. . . .

[2] Gulick, Luther H. *Morals and Morale.* New York: Association Press, 1919. 192 p.
[3] Miller, Arthur Harrison. *Leadership.* New York: G. P. Putnam's Sons, 1920. 174 p.

For war, completely seen, is no mere collision of physical forces: it is a collision of will against will. It is, after all, the mind and will of a nation—a thing intangible and invisible—that assembles the materials of war, the fighting forces, the ordnance, the whole physical array. It is this invisible thing that wages the war; it is this same invisible thing that on one side or other must admit the finish and so end it. As things are now, it is the element of "morale" that controls the outcome.[4]

The Committee on Public Information was formed. Its chairman was a student of the work of Thomas Paine.[5] He followed the lead of the President who appealed to the "verdict of mankind." While frankly working in the realm of propaganda, the Committee's varied experience in molding public opinion proved a rich source for later research in the technics of building morale.[6]

Before the close of the first World War the importance of psychological factors—the will to win, the lack of mental reservation, and belief in the rightness of one's cause—in both civil and military life, was generally recognized. Thru the studied efforts of governments to enlist the spirit of their total populations in war had evolved a new word, "morale." Of all the nations that had participated in the war of 1914-18, Germany was first to comprehend the full significance of morale as a psychological weapon of war.

With the signing of the Armistice, German military leaders turned at once to the study of the psychological factors inherent in their defeat and essential to their preparation for the next war.[7] Out of their multitudinous and critical study of military psychology evolved their advocacy of the mobilization of the entire nation and "the use of psychology as an instrument of politics, diplomacy and military strategy." The first stage of Germany's rearmament program was morale building in the nation as a whole. As one of their writers expressed it, "morale building agencies were not hit by the disarmament imposed on us by the Versailles Treaty; thus propaganda replaced military considerations and became a political weapon."[8]

The Germans' entire program was predicated on the principle that .

[4] Hocking, William Ernest. *Morale and Its Enemies.* New Haven, Conn.: Yale University Press, 1918. p. 7, 8.
[5] Creel, George. "Propaganda and Morale." *American Journal of Sociology* 47: 340-51; November 1941.
[6] Lasswell, Harold D. *Propaganda Technique in the World War.* New York: Peter Smith, 1938. 233 p.
[7] Farago, Ladislas, and Gittler, L. Frederick, editors. *German Psychological Warfare.* New York: Committee for National Morale (51 East 42d St.), 1941. p. 2.
[8] Farago, Ladislas, and Gittler, L. Frederick, editors, *op. cit.*, p. 3.

"military service is the highest expression of the 'Germanic way of life.' " Its driving motive was "to produce a new type of militant young German . . . and to make one militarized corporate body of the whole nation." It aimed at "the indoctrination of the German people with traditional soldierly virtues."[9] To prepare the whole people for the "hour" when the next war would break, the Nazis replaced all existing education with a form of military education aimed at the mental, spiritual, and physical preparation of the whole people for war. Total education was directed to fulfilling the Nazis' plan. All school subjects were adapted to the specific requirements of military upbringing. Education was extended to include all organizations of youth and areas of life not previously considered within the realm of planned education. Service in the Army was made the climax of youth's total education.

In the German Army's educational program, the ideological conditioning of soldiers was considered of equal and often of greater importance than technical training. Among the methods of indoctrination used were discussion of daily political events, patriotic education thru presentation of historic military examples, social evenings of comradeship, weekly lectures and community singing, festive hours commemorating historic events, daily ten-minute periods to stimulate front-line spirit, and planned recreation of various types.

The Germans conceived of the maintenance and nursing of morale as the most precious of military tools and the essential aim of educational policy. They employed artists to paint historic scenes from the past history of the regiment to embellish the officers' mess hall. Medical officers and psychologists collaborated with combat officers in designing uniforms. Much emphasis was placed on symbols. All instruction was pointed toward combat with the emphasis on offense. They studied the causes and means of reducing the effects of negative factors such as fear, isolation, adverse weather conditions, defeat, and reorientation of the state's ideology. Thru experiment and otherwise they studied how to make negative factors more demoralizing in the enemy's troops or population. For example, they "conducted large-scale experiments of artificial panics among soldiers, civilians, and school-children."[10]

Beyond the fact that every youth thru military education would

[9] Farago, Ladislas, and Gittler, L. Frederick, editors, *op. cit.*, p. 23.
[10] Farago, Ladislas, and Gittler, L. Frederick, editors. *op. cit.*, p. 35-44.

develop morale, the Germans consciously sought to develop feelings of security and invincibility in the civilian population, to appeal to the people's faith in Germany's "historic world mission," and to cultivate a feeling of superiority. They attempted to develop a civilian morale that would withstand every test of war. But the Nazis also took precautions against possible defections and defeat. Just as Hitler later boasted that his first victory was against the German people themselves,[11] so his party realized that their last defense might be made against German uprising. The dependence of the Nazi leadership upon enforced discipline and intimidation is now a matter of historic record. The Nazi concept of maintaining civilian morale thru force was an outgrowth of Hartman's thesis that "terrorism is a relatively gentle means of keeping the masses in a state of permanent obedience."

The success of German arms in the battles of Poland and France forced not only the government but the people of the United States to study the character of the forces that challenged the American way of life. From the fall of France to Pearl Harbor the debate was heated and the outcome not altogether certain. The United States being a democracy, leadership in developing morale sprang spontaneously from the people. Voluntary organizations developed on every side. Established organizations turned their attention to analyzing the meaning of the American way and to educating their own membership. Not since the great debates upon the federal Constitution or the debates on slavery had the American people engaged in such analyses and discussions of the basic principles of American political philosophy. With the advent of war the government itself created organizations to promote public understanding and support.

Those interested in developing American morale reviewed America's experience in the first World War. The experience of that war, crystallized by such writers as Hocking, Gulick, and Hall, took on new meaning. Publications of European writers were analyzed. The nature of morale was examined in terms of psychology, psychiatry, religion, and morals. Analysis was made of the development of morale thru education, propaganda, radio, news, movies, recreation, youth groups, labor organizations, industry, and advertising. Research was undertaken by individuals and by groups to discover the

[11] New York Times. "Excerpts From the Speech Made by Reichsfuehrer Hitler at Munich." *New York Times*, November 9, 1942. p. 13.

problems and to improve the methods of morale building among students, minority groups, and various elements of the civilian population. The published record on morale in the United States was chiefly a product of civilian initiative. For the most part the contribution of government was in response to civilian stimulus. Everywhere the emphasis was upon developing understanding, upon voluntary sacrifice to a common end. Nowhere does the difference between the United States and Germany stand out more clearly than in the development of civilian morale for total war.

Obviously the contrasting experience of Germany and the United States between 1918 and 1942 contributes much to man's understanding of developing morale for war. But there is more to learn from the experience of the several nations participating in the second World War.

America's experience with the Japanese armed forces indicates that Japan has been not altogether unmindful of the educational procedures that produce morale. Back of its army's outstanding emphasis on training in morale is the fundamental principle of Japanese education in general, which fuses moral and national education. In Japan moral education is not based upon religion as in western European countries but rather upon the good of the state.[12] In the process of borrowing and integrating ideas from Western civilization, Japan apparently has blended its ancient moral code with promotion of national progress based on Western cultures. From the evidence available the moral code of the Japanese is in no way affected by the ethical principles of the Christian faith.[13] The meaning of this in the light of current and future developments may well be pondered.

There are other questions for educators, scientists, and statesmen to pursue. What relations, if any, are to be found between the acts of government, the processes of education, and the morale of the Russian people? What caused the difference in the morale of the French and the English in 1940? Was it geographical location only, or inherited racial characteristics, or the effects of systems of education, or qualities of leadership? How can education develop that moral spirit which survives the crisis of war and makes a people strong in

---

[12] *Encyclopaedia Britannica*, Vol. 12, p. 922.

[13] Yoshida, Kumaji. "The Philosophy Underlying the National System of Education in Japan." *Educational Yearbook, 1929.* International Institute, Teachers College, Columbia University. New York: Teachers College, Columbia University, 1929. p. 427-60.

war or in peace? Thru the crucible of war it is possible that democracy may be forging an instrument for ultimate peace.

Morale in Peace

"Peace" in military mouths to-day is a synonym for "war expected." The word has become a pure provocative, and no government wishing peace sincerely should allow it ever to be printed in a newspaper. Every up-to-date dictionary should say that "peace" and "war" mean the same thing, now *in posse,* now *in actu.* It may even reasonably be said that the intensely sharp competitive *preparation* for war by the nations *is the real war,* permanent, unceasing; and that the battles are only a sort of public verification of the mastery gained during the "peace"-interval.[14]

So wrote William James in 1910. How well events since then have confirmed his analysis of peace and war! James paid his respects to a "sheep's paradise." He made it clear that "the moral equivalent of war" will not be obtained thru merely running away from war, that peace is not merely the absence of physical combat.

James argued that to attain peace permanently on this globe the states must preserve some of the elements of army discipline. He would have them cultivate in all youth the martial virtues—"intrepedity, contempt of softness, surrender of private interest, obedience to command." These he accepted as "absolute and permanent human goods." Whether James selected the best elements of discipline to illustrate his thesis may be debated, but the thesis itself is basic to the morale of an enduring peace.

As one means of attaining the *moral equivalent* of war, James proposed "a conscription of the whole youthful population to form for a certain number of years a part of the army enlisted against *Nature.*" Thru such a measure he saw the military ideals of hardihood and discipline "wrought into the growing fibre of the people" and the attainment of certain manly virtues—"toughness without callousness, authority with as little criminal cruelty as possible, and painful work done cheerily because the duty is temporary."[15] After thirty years of alternating war and peace it is clear that peace which is merely the absence of war is no peace at all.

The great challenging problem of democracy is to develop morale for peace. One of the earlier students of American education to rec-

---

[14] James, William. "The Moral Equivalent of War." *McClure's Magazine* 35: 463-68; August 1910. See also: *Memories and Studies.* New York: Longmans, Green and Co., 1917. Chapter 11, "The Moral Equivalent of War," p. 267-96.
[15] James, William, *op. cit.*

ognize the importance of this problem was G. Stanley Hall. Having during the war turned his vast abilities to the study of morale, with the war's ending he summarized his work in a textbook for use in college instruction.[16] In addition to his treatment of morale for war, Hall examined morale in its relations to labor, prohibition, profiteering, feminism, education, statesmanship, communism, and religion. In his last eight chapters he laid a foundation for consideration of the morale of peace. It was a crystallization of ideas to which the present and the future may well refer, for in morale Hall found the supreme standard of life and conduct.

During the twenty years from 1920 to 1940, concepts of morale were kept alive in the United States largely by the schools and by students of labor and social welfare. By far the greater number of published articles dealt with morale in the schools and with methods of attaining it.[17] During two decades the schools kept alive something of the ideals generated by the first World War but directed their efforts in morale building toward the objectives of social enterprise. In a word, the schools experimented with the development of morale for peaceful ends, more precisely for the development of better schools. Their experience may hold a key to the future.

During the depression of the 1930's, students of unemployment began to write and speak of the morale of the unemployed. Many positive measures were taken by society thru both governmental action and private endeavor. Among the efforts of government on a national scale were the establishment of the Civilian Conservation Corps, the Work Projects Administration, the National Youth Administration, the Farm Security Administration, and the Social Security Board. One of the chief claims for the WPA nursery schools was that thru care of young children and association with parents they contributed to maintaining the morale of the home. The National Youth Administration contributed to maintaining the morale of youth thru helping them to learn a skill or obtain remunerative employment. The Civilian Conservation Corps was an experiment illustrating James's proposal to enlist youth in the continuing war against nature. It provided training for youth in some of the elements of army discipline that would help youth in the pursuits of

---

[16] Hall, G. Stanley. *Morale, the Supreme Standard of Life and Conduct.* New York: D. Appleton and Co., 1920. 378 p.

[17] During the ten-year period 1930-39, the *Education Index* listed twenty-five articles on morale.

peace. Whatever the merits or demerits of these adventures of government, thru them American democracy experimented with processes in building and maintaining the integrity and dignity of human beings. Thru the darkest and longest economic depression the United States has known, bringing as it did discouragement and disillusionment to millions, the people as a whole did not lose faith in the principles of American democracy. How much of this faith retained was due to the work of specially created administrative agencies and how much to the accumulated effects of a century of public education is not known, but the outcome begets confidence that democracy may build morale for peace quite as effectively as for war.

The concept of morale in civil life is permeating the realm of industry and labor management. With the ever increasing industrialization of civilized life there is growing recognition of the need for study and research on the problems of human collaboration in business and industry. The literature of industrial relations more and more gives attention to morale—to consideration of why people act, feel, and believe as they do. The essence of morale building in business management has been aptly summarized by a student of industrial relations in the following:

Maintaining internal equilibrium within the social organization of the plant involves keeping the channels of communication free and clear so that orders are transmitted downward without distortion and so that relevant information regarding situations at the work level is transmitted upward without distortion to those levels at which it can be best made use of. This involves getting the bottom of the organization to understand the economic objectives of the top; it also means getting the top of the organization to understand the feelings and sentiments of the bottom. It involves moving people about in the organization— transferring, upgrading, downgrading, promoting, demoting, placing, and selecting—in a manner that will be in accordance with the social values of the human situation and hence in a manner that will preserve morale.[18]

In the positive efforts of schools and colleges to develop morale in their own institutional life, in the great national experiments for maintaining morale during the depression, and in the experimental research of business and industry to determine the value of morale among employees, one perceives the beginning of the search for the moral equivalent of war, advocated by James several years before the first World War.

---

[18] Roethlisberger, F. J. *Management and Morale*. Cambridge, Mass.: Harvard University Press, 1942. p. 192-93.

In discussing the lessons of twenty years, Hocking calls attention to "the growing recognition of morale as a factor in every social enterprise" and especially to "the extraordinary social movements which have filled the interval, both in Europe and in Asia." He draws the significant conclusion that in both the student movement in China and the nationalist movement in India morale was high without the strained accompaniments of morale building observed in Germany or Italy. From the Chinese movement Hocking deduces the further idea that there is a "morale for *being* as well as for doing." And finally he points out that "the best morale is only obtainable with those who would form the group for the given enterprise on their own initiative, and this requires that they have the idea and the disposition to create."[19]

Review of the two decades between the two world wars shows that in Germany morale building was consciously directed toward the next war; in the United States it was a sporadic groping toward the improvement of various social enterprises. Even the dictators must borrow the words of democracy to promote morale among their own people.[20] Out of the experience of world movements is being evolved the principles on which free men may build in creating the morale of peace.

The Transition from War to Peace

In 1917-18, the government of the United States built morale on a basis of high idealism. We entered "a war to end war." We fought to make the world safe for democracy. We offered the world a League of Nations designed to enforce the peace and to solve at the conference table future differences between nations.

With the signing of the Armistice political passions rose to the surface. The high idealism of the war period faded into the background. The American people took the road back to "normalcy." The morale developed during the heat of war disappeared. The United States settled back into isolationism, pacifism, and disregard of its obligations to the remainder of the world.

Entering the second World War, people began to say of the first that we had won the war and lost the peace. Gradually there has

---

[19] Hocking, William Ernest. "The Nature of Morale." *American Journal of Sociology* 47: 302-20; November 1941.

[20] Mann, Thomas. *The Coming Victory of Democracy.* New York: Alfred A. Knopf, 1938. 70 p.

developed the belief that this present war is an outgrowth of the
failure of the United States to carry thru following the last war.
There is a growing belief that we must stay with the job this time
until our enemy nations have demonstrated their willingness and
capacity to live within the company of free peoples. This brings us
squarely to the fact that morale for winning the war is not enough,
nor will the development of morale for an isolated peace bring aught
but misery in its wake.

Even in the heat of war, the people of the United States begin to
perceive the need to evolve a clear vision of the part this country
should play in the world following the cessation of hostilities. Should
we help keep the peace thruout the world? Should we maintain the
principles of the lend-lease program? What guarantees should we
exact of our enemies? What reciprocal arrangements should we
make for education and exchange of ideas? What has each of our
allies to contribute to the further progress of free men? These are
typical of the questions asked by the people of the United States as
they become more fully involved in the prosecution of the war.

Assuming that the war will continue thru 1944 or longer, our people will be tired, even weary, of welldoing. There will be great and
difficult domestic issues to settle. Old national ideals will demand a
rehearing. There will be the call to put our own house in order before
we undertake to serve as our brothers' keeper. And abroad there may
be those, erstwhile friends, who will want no more of us or at least
only a generous share of our charity. To them our faults, now submerged in the crucible of war, will again loom large. Even should
we operate only on the highest level of selfless idealism, there will
be many an issue on which our efforts will seem a hopeless task. How
then can we take thought for the days of transition and steel our
hearts for the harder task that must be done when the fighting is
ended? How envisage the greater adventure of reshaping a disor-
dered world?

First, we can begin now to consider the issues that will confront
the peoples of the world when the fighting ends. It is essential that
the right questions be asked. It is important that they be asked in
every school and college and that they be discussed in every forum,
in the press, in club programs, at the country store, wherever the
people meet. In developing the understanding of all our people
teachers are in a position to play a leading role. Their education

should give them a background to understand the issues. Thru their teaching they shape the attitudes and the thinking of youth. Thru their civic and social relationships they influence the attitudes and the understanding of their own generation.

Successful transition from war to peace will require a better understanding of the peoples of other lands than we have yet gained in the United States. Complete understanding between Russia and the United States will be as essential to keeping the peace as it is to winning the war. The people of China have great gifts to contribute to mankind. The people of India seek a place in the concourse of free nations. Every nation in the world has something to contribute to the peace of the world. It is important that we understand and appreciate the gifts they can make. In the schools of the United States are found the children of every race and of every nation. What has each of these racial or national groups contributed to the making of the United States? What has each gained here that he would like to make available to his distant cousins in the old home-land? In the American school should begin the development of that sympathetic understanding that should be reflected in the councils of all free peoples.[21]

In the conduct of the war teachers will discover principles operating and procedures being tried that may prove the basis of a sound transition from war to peace. An outstanding illustration is seen in the provision of the lend-lease program. The work of the Office of the Coordinator of Inter-American Affairs affords another illustration of a sound basis for postwar international relations. Thru various agencies men and women are being trained to administer the difficult problems we shall meet in helping the stricken nations— friend and enemy—to make the transition to the new goals for which the United Nations fight.

Nor is the history of the United Nations lacking in illustration of practice and principle to guide the reshaping of the world to the ways of peace. America's administration of the Boxer indemnity netted large returns to both the United States and China. The role of the Filipinos in the present war is proof that the United States built better than we knew in the Philippines. The role of South Africa, Canada, New Zealand, and Australia shows that a people may gain

---

[21] Adamic, Louis. *Two-Way Passage.* New York: Harper and Brothers, 1941. 328 p.

and exercise all the rights and privileges of a free nation within the framework of a commonwealth of free peoples. Russia's success in welding peoples speaking more than a hundred different languages and dialects into one powerful whole proves that language and custom need be no barrier to achieving a union of diverse peoples.

". . . never before has a conflict between nations had so many distinct traces of an international civil war." [22] The people of the United States might well take as their motto the words of William Lloyd Garrison: "My country is the world; my countrymen are mankind."

The Long Future

Morale for the war is not enough. Neither will morale for the transition from war to peace be enough.

> Wert capable of war—its tug and trials? Be capable of peace, its trials;
> For the tug and mortal strain of nations come at last in peace—not war.
> —WALT WHITMAN, "Thou Mother with Thy Equal Brood"

War settles some issues. The American Revolution not only made the colonies "free and independent states" but gave a mighty impulse to the principles of freedom thruout the world. In the United States the Civil War settled the question as to whether a state had the right to secede from the Union. At Tours Charles Martel turned back the Mohammedan invasion of western Europe and made it possible for Christianity to influence the course of Western civilization. The Punic Wars determined that Rome, not Carthage, should rule the ancient world, and Rome kept the peace longer than has any power before or since.

Voicing the ambitions of his people, Hitler has said repeatedly that the present war is to settle the dominion of the world for a thousand years. It lies within the power of the United Nations to make Hitler's prophecy wiser than he knew. But the decision will not be gained alone by feat of arms, nor would a peace based on physical force prove more than a structure built on shifting sand.

Following 1918 the German Republic was launched with high hopes and an idealistic constitution. Even hard-headed American business poured millions of dollars into the redevelopment of Germany's industry. For fifteen years the republic maintained the out-

[22] Fortune. "Steam from the Melting Pot." *Fortune* 26: 75-76, 128, 130, 132, 134, 137; September 1942.

ward semblance of control. Meanwhile, in both Germany and the other Western nations, opposing forces were undermining democracy. National, group, and individual selfishness prevailed. The outcomes were pacifism, isolationism, glorification of the strong man, and appeasement. After twenty years the morale of the democratic nations was dormant, to say the least. Using the fine phrases of democracy, the Nazis took over the control of Germany and the Weimar republic disappeared. It is not enough to develop morale for a decade or a generation.

The United Nations have stated their ideals. With the winning of the war these ideals may be made available to all peoples and may be implemented according to their respective needs and desires. As the war has demonstrated so clearly, many elements of the ideals expressed in the Atlantic Charter and the Four Freedoms are common to men everywhere. From the viewpoint of the United States we have the task of making democracy safe for the world. Our task is to refine both its principles and its practices. Herein lies the moral equivalent of war.

Just as American boys are being called to every land where the fortunes of free men are at stake, so will American youth be needed in every land to carry America's contributions to the building of a better world. Just as America's machines are flowing to every nook and corner of the world, so in the days to come will the ideals and concepts of free men nurtured here for three hundred years flow out to strengthen the efforts of all men in their ever continuing striving for the self-evident rights of life, liberty, and the pursuit of happiness. This is a function of education.

The way to universal freedom will not be an easy road. The building of a total world of free men will be infinitely more difficult than winning the total war. The future is to be achieved, not retained. More than once in modern times has plain humanity risen to new heights, seen visions of a new day, and achieved miracles. As in the French Revolution and again in the Russian, spectacular gains have been made. In more recent times the same upsurge of the common man has taken place in Mexico and Spain. Back of all the excesses of revolution were countless humble people in pursuit of a dream.[23] The student movement of China, the nationalist movement of India, the

---

[23] Saunders, D. A. "The Failure of Propaganda." *Harper's* 183: 648-55; November 1941.

clarification of the concepts of democracy, and the striving to improve its practice the world over demonstrate that the plain people of the world are on the march. To help them build a better world is an adventure challenging the best qualities of mankind. The task will not be easy. As was written in 1918, so it may be written again:

> Democracy is not a fact accomplished. Democracy is an ideal. The freest nation on earth . . . has taken but a few steps along the road that leads to the true Commonwealth of Man.
>
> The war to make the world safe for that crude beginning of the democratic experiment . . . has been well fought. And now a new conflict looms before us— the war for the carrying through of that experiment.[24]

To assist the schools and colleges in developing the morale of generations of free men ever seeking the greater fulfilment of their dreams this book is prepared.

---

[24] Goddard, Harold. *Morale*. New York: George H Doran Co., 1918. p. 117.

★ *If there is to be a world order there must be a world morale. The words "man," "humanity," and "mankind" must be invested with the same power to allegiance as the word "American." All men must be encouraged to dwell upon the great achievements that demonstrate the levels to which human nature is capable of rising. All men can take pride in their kinship with the best men.*

CHAPTER II

Democratic Morale in a Free World

MORALE is the backbone of the soul.
Morale is the will to carry thru against all obstacles what the heart approves.

Morale is faith plus courage plus discipline.

Morale is the factor that enables people as individuals or as groups to live up to their highest possibilities; it is the catalyzing agent which stirs the soul to work out and to keep on working out its purpose.

Morale is what makes us continue to fight on when courage is gone and faith is only something remembered.

Morale is knowing where you want to go and going there.

Morale is purpose with vitamins in it.

Morale is living your faith gladly or at least relentlessly.

Morale is the determination not to let yourself or your comrades down.

Morale is sticking to the job for the job's sake.

Morale is damning the torpedoes.

Morale is being a man.

Morale is what keeps you going after your knees give out.

Morale is Browning's "Prospice."

Morale is the spirit of Valley Forge, Gettysburg, and Chateau-Thierry. It is the spirit of Winston Churchill when he announced to his cabinet that France was out of the war and Britain stood alone: "Gentlemen, to tell the truth, I find it rather exhilarating."

Morale is not knowing when you're licked, and then you aren't.

Morale is one for all and all for one—right thru to the end.

These lay definitions of morale sum up what the public thinks it is. Despite their diversity and the vernacular in which they are expressed, they convey a common idea. Assuming human capacity, innate or acquired, and assuming a task to be performed, there are different degrees to which the given capacity may be realized and converted into performance. In other words, relatively to any given work a man may be at "his best" or he may fall short of his best in varying degrees. This variable is called "morale." A man's morale is "high" when he gives all and "low" when he gives only a small fraction of what he has to give. Altho the term "morale" may be applied to the isolated individual, it is more commonly applied, and hereinafter is applied, to men living and acting in a group—to collective capacity, a common task, and the degree to which the members of a group devote their collective capacity to the common task. In the collective form of morale the elements of cooperation and agreement play a primary role. The group and its members have high morale when they act together with goodwill and when their acceptance of leadership is not a mere passive obedience based on habit or fear but a voluntary and hearty concert of action.

The importance of morale is proportional to the difficulty of the task, that is, the extent to which successful performance requires the utmost use of all latent capacities. This topic receives special emphasis in time of war or crisis, when there are unusual obstacles to overcome and hardships to be endured and when internal rivalries and conflicts are clearly fatal to collective effort. But morale is a factor in all social life, and its neglect in normal times is a serious defect in modern democracies.

The need for high morale is more evident in war than in peace because the consequences of low morale are more immediately felt and more easily traceable to this cause. The slow disintegration of French political life might have been fatal in the long run even had there been no war, but the military catastrophe accelerated and dramatized this consequence. As the effects of morale are more immediately evident in time of war, so it is easier to direct attention to it and persuade men of its importance. The common task of defeating the enemy and the need of extreme exertion and of concerted effort are then in the plain view of all. Peace also has its common tasks, of infinite difficulty, requiring the working together of diverse individuals and groups, but their success or failure is slow and the causes are obscure. Hence when men wish to call attention to the factor of morale in peacetime they use the metaphors of war and speak of the "army" of citizens, the political "campaign," or the "battle" for good government.

The Problem of Motivation

Morale is a characteristic of human behavior and its seat is the human will. Hence the problem of morale is a problem of motivation. If morale is to be high, there must be strong incentives to vigorous and concerted action. Men's impulses to action must be directed and intensified so that they will prevail over inertia, pain, or selfish desires. The technic of morale depends, then, on controlling the conditions which affect human motivation. No attempt is made in this yearbook to employ a rigidly consistent terminology.[1] There is, however, among the several authors, together with other contemporary writers on the same subject, a broad agreement upon a series of levels in human nature, and a corresponding grouping of the basic factors of morale. As an animal organism man is subject to the play of biochemical forces and governed and impelled by physical needs and appetites. Man's mental life is governed by psychological propensities, or drives, and determined by the forces which unite individual with individual in society. Beyond this it is characteristic of man to integrate his life, individual and social, thru adherence to ideas, goals, or purposes. There is no sharp line of demarcation between these levels. Unanswerable proof of this is afforded by the example of sex, which rests on biochemical forces and physical appetites, exhibits the play of nearly every psychological and social force, and is, in romantic love or the familial virtues, swayed by mystical forces and directed to ideal values. But these distinctions provide nonetheless a convenient classification of those factors of human nature which are involved in human behavior and which provide the underlying conditions of that powerful motivation which constitutes high morale.

PHYSICAL FACTORS

Health, nutrition, protection from excessive heat and cold, and all the physical factors which enhance satisfaction and cheerfulness enable individuals or groups to respond more fully to any demand which may be made upon them. If physical conditions are too severe, the effect is depressing, while if they are made too easy the effect is relaxing. Men can be prepared to deal with obstacles and continued strain only by being inured to them. But if hardships are

---

[1] A recent writer (Kurt Lewin) proposes to use the expression "tension system" for the dynamics of human behavior. The variable terminology, however, reflects the fact that there is as yet no agreement among psychologists as to the underlying explanation.

deliberately created for the purpose of training, this purpose must be made plain; otherwise they will provoke resentment. There is a balance of physical conditions, of satisfactions and privations, which conduces to what is called "fitness," signifying the maximum of alertness, responsiveness, and vital energy of which men are capable.

PSYCHOLOGICAL FACTORS

The psychological conditions of high morale consist of effective stimuli to primary impulses, together with the formation of habits which provide for routine performances and release effort for action requiring conscious regulation and choice. Especially important in the creation of morale are the social dispositions of gregariousness, participation, emulation, combativeness, and suggestibility. These and other deep-seated springs of action combine to create the prestige of leadership, the potency of symbols, and above all *esprit de corps*.

IDEATIONAL FACTORS

Men exert themselves to the utmost when they believe, and believe *in*, an idea. An ideal goal serves to unify the activities of an individual and keep him steadily on the same course of action despite the solicitations of his diverse and momentary desires. When the members of the group share the same idea, it serves to bind them together and enables them to subordinate diverse and conflicting interests to a "common cause."

The major factors in morale, then, are fitness (physical), *esprit de corps* (psychological), and the common cause (ideational). In all these factors there is a blend of heredity and environment. Even the physical or biological factors are modified by experience and reflect social and historical influence. All men need food, for example, but the satisfaction of this need varies from one social group to another in terms of habit and usage. A man will starve for lack of nourishment, but he will also feel frustrated if he is deprived of the kind of food to which he is accustomed, or if he is unable to have his "three meals a day" accompanied by the amenities characteristic of his social group. The biological need of sex is broadened by social usage into taboos against forms of unchastity or promiscuity, forms of courtship and marriage, and all in values associated in any given

society with the institutions of the family. The social and other
psychological forces which govern human behavior are all translated into specific compulsions, such as military honor, the pride of
status, or the coercions of custom which vary from group to group.

But the effect of social environment is most pronounced on the
ideational levels. The further one departs from the basic animal
needs, the more pronounced is this variability. The causes and technics of fitness and *esprit de corps* will be largely the same in totalitarian and democratic societies. Ideational morale in these two societies, on the other hand, will have comparatively little in common.
The capacity for ideas and the function of ideas as giving life unity
of goal and direction are no doubt hereditary. Ideas themselves are
not "innate" but are the products of experience accumulated thru
generations, recorded and communicated and showing almost limit-
less variability. It is here that we shall find the most marked pecu-
liarities in the morale of those societies which by history and conviction are democratic.

It is obvious that morale is related to and dependent upon body,
mind, and spirit. Mind and spirit may triumph over weakness of the
flesh, but there must be an adequate physical envelope furnished
with adequate food, clothing, and shelter, as well as with the conditions of health, including rest and recreation. There is need for
companionship, the regard of others, and acceptance by the group.
Morale is concerned with the degree to which the economic and social system enables a man to attain the creature satisfactions. But
to sleep and to feed is not enough. A spark disturbs the clod. Having
a soul, man demands spiritual satisfactions. It is a part of the task
of leadership and institutions to meet this demand—to provide temptations upward.

A man's idea of what he could and should be, of what he could
and should do, his willingness to strive and fail, and his will to strive
and not fail—these are what make him in the fullest sense a man.
Whence come his aspirations? From himself, from others, and from
books he learns to measure his powers and to frame his ideals. He
imagines the possession of this, the accomplishment of that. From
the seeking as well as from the finding he draws his sense of the
worth of life. Growth and development are the law of his being. One
conquest made, a new one beckons, the reach always exceeding the
grasp.

Methods of Developing Ideational Morale

The remainder of this chapter is devoted to morale upon the ideational level, with special reference to those unifying goals which operate in a society committed to democracy.

It is essential to a modern nation that its members should be bound together by common beliefs. These beliefs do not and should not embrace the whole of the lives of the members, but they create the framework of a "common cause" within which private individuals and groups may develop their more detailed beliefs and their special interests without destroying the public order. In a democracy, with its emphasis on liberty and tolerance, these private spheres are made as wide as possible, but this must not blind us to the fact that a democracy is no exception to the rule. No organized society whatever, whether totalitarian or democratic, is possible unless its members share certain fundamental beliefs. Indeed since they are broader the beliefs of democracy must be all the stronger. More strain is put upon them by the vigor and autonomy of the private spheres. The failure to recognize this need is one of the reasons for the weakness and instability of so-called "liberal" societies.

The "common cause" is grasped intellectually and adhered to emotionally. In implanting it neither of these elements can be neglected. Democracy—its meaning, its conditions, its forms, and its effects—can be *understood* by a totalitarian society, that is, by a society which seeks to understand democracy in order to destroy it. A democratic society is distinguished by its *attachment* to democracy—by its being in favor of democracy, as distinguished from taking a neutral or hostile attitude.[2] Democracy must be an "ideal" and not merely an "idea"; the letter "l" makes all the difference.

The common cause known as "democracy" may be divided into five ideals, each of which must be rooted in both the understanding and the affections: love of truth, freedom under law, fellow feeling, respect for human dignity, and personal responsibility.

LOVE OF TRUTH

This idea must first be *understood*, by recognizing the difference between truth and mere opinion. Truth is belief supported by reasons or evidence, as exemplified by the proofs of mathematics or the

---

[2] For a discussion of the central place of "attitudes" in morale, see Chapter XI.

verifications of experimental science. It is to be distinguished not
only from unsupported or dogmatic belief but also from unbelief or
skepticism. To understand truth implies, furthermore, a knowledge
of the conditions by which truth may be attained and the knowledge
of its effects upon human life. But a democracy will be distinguished
by a love of truth and by a faith in its beneficence. To achieve this
result truth must be made attractive, thru being connected directly
with the satisfaction of intellectual curiosity and indirectly with
the various social and personal goods of which it is the condition.

FREEDOM UNDER LAW

To understand freedom is to grasp the extent to which human
action is governed by the will, the psychological and social conditions by which the control of the will is impeded and enhanced, the
forms of social organization thru which personal freedom is raised
to its maximum, and the effects of freedom in human life. It is especially important to see that the freedom of one person or group impinges upon the freedom of others and that freedom must therefore
be restrained and regulated. But, being understood, freedom can then
be either loved or hated, desired or feared. The crucial test of the
love of freedom is not the desire to be free oneself but the desire for
the freedom of others and the enjoyment of the social relationship
of mutual respect in an orderly society of free persons.

FELLOW FEELING

Fellow feeling is that sense of compassion and impulse to mutual
aid which unites a man to others of his kind. It is sometimes called
humanity. Here the role of understanding is to overcome the effect
of the comparative immediacy and warmth of one's own interests.
To understand one's fellow man it is necessary to put oneself in his
place, as prescribed by the Golden Rule. The lesson to be learned is
objectivity and universality as opposed to the bias of a single person
or group. This is the substance of justice, which is the impartial
recognition of all interests and persons concerned and is reflected in
that sense of fairness, or a "square deal," thru which each man is
brought to substitute "we" for "I" and thru which this first person
plural is extended to include larger and larger aggregates of men
until none is omitted.

In this case a feeling, namely the feeling of sympathy, is essential
even to understanding, and the cultivation of this feeling is the most

important part of moral education. It tends to be overlaid and inhibited by calculating self-interest and by various forms of narrow group solidarities. But the fellow feeling and sympathy, together with the sentiment of humanity and the ideal of justice, may be despised as weaknesses or they may be praised and exalted. A person or society is not democratic until these attitudes gain the supreme place in human relations. They must be excited and strengthened by appropriate stimuli and, at the same time, linked by habit to certain specific objects.

RESPECT FOR HUMAN DIGNITY

All men possess in some degree what are called "higher faculties," such as thought, creative imagination, and reflective choice. This fact has first to be understood by an analysis of human nature, in which these faculties are distinguished from other human characteristics, such as reflexes, instincts, emotions, and habits. When the distinction is made there.is created an option in one's attitude toward man between respect and contempt, both having their basis in human nature. Respect for the dignity of man is an emotional attitude in which the emphasis is put on those faculties which distinguish man as "created in the image of God," rather than on those traits which man shares with other animals. To cultivate this democratic attitude of respect it is necessary to dwell upon the great achievements of statesmanship, morals, science, art, and religion as demonstrating the levels to which human nature is capable of rising. All men are encouraged to take pride in their kinship with the best men.

The people of the United States embrace many races and nationalities. While this fact creates difficulties of friction and prejudice, it may be turned to advantage, as providing a schooling in world democracy. A democratic American, if he is true to his creed, will have learned to esteem men for their essential human qualities rather than for their externals. He does not have to go abroad to discover mankind but is confronted with it at home.

PERSONAL RESPONSIBILITY

The social group is a more or less organized aggregate of individuals. The socialization of man results in mass behavior and in institutions, in which the individual tends to be submerged. The fact is that there are two grades of human entities: individuals and groups. Individualism as a democratic sentiment means that the emphasis is put on the individuals rather than on the group. To cultivate this emphasis and the corresponding emotional attitudes and sentiments it is necessary to recognize that institutions exist for men, rather than men for institutions. A political democracy depends on the creation among its individual members of a sense that the government is their government; that it exists in order to promote their good; and that the power which it exerts is in their hands if, as they should, they are resolved to use it. The higher activities of men—moral, intellectual, and esthetic—are essentially functions of an individual rather than of the group. It is true that the individual is in large measure the product of the group and that his life and attainments are inconceivable without his social relations, organized or unorganized. It is to be pointed out that it is the individual and not the group that enjoys happiness or suffers sorrow, acts from a sense of duty, loves God and fellow man, draws conclusions from premises, exercises the creative imagination, and performs the acts of choice and deliberate will for which men are held morally responsible. The term "personality" may be used to signify the higher forms of life, in which the individual realizes these distinctively human possibilities.

The five ideas enumerated in the preceding paragraphs are all interrelated. Without freedom men cannot exercise their higher faculties, and a man whose higher faculties are developed will not be content with slavery or submergence in the group. The development of personality will beget a just recognition of its presence or potentiality in other men. A developed man will love truth and will wish it to be spread abroad, both for its own sake and for its contribution to the other values of life.

Democracy is the name which it is customary to give to that form of life which is founded on these five elements—love of truth, freedom under law, fellow feeling, respect for human dignity, and personal responsibility. It signifies these values as the purposes for which society is organized and, at the same time, the methods of organization and control, such as popular government and legal rights, by which these values are best achieved.

In order that democracy shall be adopted as a common cause and served with ardor and fidelity, these five ideas must be both elucidated to the understanding and endeared to the affections. The first part of this educative process involves instruction in the facts of history, psychology, and the social sciences; the second involves the presentation of these facts in such manner as will stimulate the feeling dispositions, whether original or acquired. Each idea must be not only analyzed but given concrete embodiments and symbols, associated with objects already held dear and grafted on impulses which have their roots deep in human nature. Democracy has, in short, to be both described and loved. To learn democracy one has both to know about it and to care about it.

Limiting Factors of Education for Morale

Democracies hesitate to employ the methods necessary to inculcate a love of democracy among their own peoples because of certain scruples represented by the evil associations of the word "propaganda." It is desirable to know just what these scruples are and to distinguish those which are legitimate from those that rest on misunderstanding. The guiding principle here is that in a democracy the methods employed for building morale must not violate its own democratic standards. Using this principle there are two common scruples which rest on misunderstanding and can be dismissed: namely, the scruple against indoctrination and the scruple against emotional appeal.

There is nothing in democracy which forbids indoctrination. A democracy must hope that its own democratic creed will be acquired by social inheritance, by the early domestic influences which form the mind before it is wholly matured, and by the unconscious atmospheric influences of the total environment. If when his critical powers are developed the individual finds himself already a lover of truth and freedom, humane in his feelings, a respecter of his fellow man, and an individualist, there can be no complaint—on democratic grounds. It is impossible for the individual to be reared in a social vacuum, free from indoctrinating influences; nor, even if it were desirable, could the capacity for doubt, for criticism, or for independent inquiry be developed in their place. If this inevitable indoctrination is not to be left to accident, it must be recognized as a function of education. The only question is whether indoctrination shall be left to irresponsible agencies, motivated by profit or political demagoguery, or to the agencies of home, school, church, and other recognized institutions. Indoctrination should be consciously and methodically brought into line with the basic tenets of democracy.

Nor is there anything in the democratic creed which forbids emotional appeal. As has been pointed out, a creed does not consist merely in beliefs concerning matters of fact or in an intellectual grasp of meanings or proofs but involves an alignment of will and feeling. Ideas must become ideals. There is no such thing as ideational morale without bias. Hopes, aspirations, duties, and the hierarchy of values, in which first things are put first and means are subordinated to ends, are all forms of bias. They cannot be implanted by cultivating an attitude of neutral detachment. *A mind can be filled with facts and theorems on any subject whatsoever, including democracy itself, and still remain completely undemocratic.*

Granting, then, that the building of morale requires, and may legitimately employ, both indoctrination and emotional appeal, there remains the task of determining what, in a democracy, are the scruples which should be retained. The answer is to be found in the same ideals of democracy which have been enumerated. In building morale a democracy must remain faithful to its own principles. It must not practice deception or exploit ignorance, for this would weaken the love of truth. It must not enslave or intimidate and it must not make men either subservient or arrogant, for this would weaken the love of freedom. It must not preach cruelty and hatred, for this would dry up the springs of humane feeling. It must not debase men or inspire contempt for them, for this would hurt their dignity and destroy the respect which such dignity inspires. Finally, it must not submerge the individual by an appeal to mass emotion or suggestion, by an exaggerated emphasis on discipline, or by enforced uniformity of belief.

Antidemocratic Morale

Those methods of building morale which offend the conscience of democracies and make the educational methods of totalitarian countries intolerable are precisely the antidemocratic methods named in the preceding section. Totalitarian countries have developed an effective morale because they have openly employed the methods of indoctrination and emotional appeal. For so doing they merit no reproach. They have a definite conception of their creed and begin systematically to implant it in the early and impressionable years. They know how to stir and direct emotion and how to form the will. They utilize for implanting their national and military creeds the technics which democracies have reserved for the comparatively trivial purposes of sport and advertising. Totalitarian nations have hitherto enjoyed a great advantage over democracies because they have not been deterred from using such technics by any false scruples. If democracies are to develop an equivalent fervor and loyalty, they must be similarly free from the fear of indoctrination and emotional appeal.

But in totalitarian countries these technics are used in a manner which is suited to their own antidemocratic creed. They use totalitarian means to serve totalitarian ends. They deceive and mislead their own people, appeal to the love of power or to fear, arouse the combative emotions and harden men's hearts, excite and justify the selfish appetites, and by mass appeal and rigid discipline develop to the extreme those elements of human nature which dispose men to lose their individuality.[3] These methods are forbidden to democracies because they would defeat the purpose of democracy and kill its spirit. Democracies must learn how to be equally or more effective in their own democratic way, which is, point for point, the opposite way to that of totalitarianism.

The art of morale is more difficult in a democracy than in a totalitarian country because of the restraints which the democratic creed imposes. It is difficult to arouse enthusiasm without confusion of mind and concealment of the facts. The way of the demagogs is easier than the way of enlightened political leadership, in which the people are taken into the leaders' confidence and encouraged to use their own minds for themselves. It is easier to win men's allegiance by promises of selfish gain than by appeal to the sentiments of justice and humanity. It is easier to unify the masses of the people by passion or hypnotic suggestion than by thoughtful agreement in the service of a common purpose. It is easier to stir men to fight by exciting hatred than by persuading them that it is sometimes necessary to kill in order to save.

But the democratic way, tho hard, is not impossible. It is possible to feel, and to feel intensely, without loss of the capacity to think.

---

[3] See: Ziemer, Gregor A. *Education for Death.* New York: Oxford University Press, 1941. 208 p.

It is possible to persuade without bribery or threats. It is possible to participate, obey, and unite and still retain the sense of an ultimate and inviolable personality. There is a difference between the hatred of persons or groups and the hatred of the evil that is in them, of which they are unhappily the instruments. There is such a thing as "just anger," or "righteous indignation," in which the use of force is subordinated to the service of mankind or the dictates of conscience. The common opinion that men must hate in order to fight is based on a gross oversimplification of the springs of human action. The aggressive behavior which is required for war may derive its ultimate motivation from the sentiment of love, as well as from the motive of hate.[4] The higher spiritual development of man consists in precisely this mixture and balance of elements, and tho the totalitarian way is easier its victories are hollow because they neglect the distinctive prerogatives and complex developments of human nature, by which men's greatest powers are released and short of which they will feel a sense of frustration.

Morale in a Democratic World Order

The changed conditions of human life, in which all parts of the world are brought into close communication with one another and human interdependence is extended to all mankind and to all the fields of human activity, create the necessity for a new level of morale. If a democracy such as the United States is to play a role of leadership in this new postwar world, its principles must be given a new and widened application.

If there is to be a world order there must be a world morale. This will have its physical conditions in public health, nutrition, housing, improved standards of living, and other forms of material welfare. It will have its psychological conditions. There must be a world *esprit de corps,* a sense of participation in the total life of mankind, and a regard for the honor of humanity. There must be an ideational morale, based on a worldwide creed. Every community, large or small, global as well as local, international as well as national, must possess a set of common beliefs and sentiments. If all men are to live *under* the same institutions, whether political, eco-

---

[4] Alexander F. Shand, in his *The Foundations of Character* (New York: Macmillan Co., 1914), distinguishes the four emotional dispositions of fear, anger, joy, and sorrow for the systematic "sentiments" into which they are built. See Book I, Chapters 4 and 5, p. 35-63.

nomic, or social, there must be something that all men live *for* which draws their lives together toward a common goal.

If the world order is to be democratic in principle, the common creed must be broad enough to allow to religious, national, party, local, and personal creeds the maximum of latitude that is consistent with peace and fruitful intercourse. That the world should be democratic in this fundamental sense does not imply that any one type of political mechanism, or economic system, or social custom, such as that of the United States, should be generally adopted. The ideas and ideals of this worldwide creed will be of the sort that deliver men from the fear of war or from the jealousies and suspicions of unfriendly rivalry and enable them to enjoy with security the fullest possible opportunity of self-expression, where "possible" means consistent with a like opportunity enjoyed by others. The worldwide creed will dispose men to multiply, enjoy, and profit by their differences. The ideas of the worldwide creed will be the same as those which characterize a democratic nation, but they must now by indoctrination and emotional appeal be implanted in all mankind. This means that individuals must add a new loyalty to those which they already have, and this new loyalty must constitute a prior obligation to which all narrower loyalties must be subordinated.

Worldwide morale, like national morale, must begin with instruction and elucidation. This involves an extension of knowledge to embrace nations and peoples in all parts of the world and an understanding of the changed conditions of communication and transport which have brought all parts of the earth's surface into contact with one another. It must be understood that "isolation" is now contrary to fact and that *all* human relations must now be organized if there is not to be recurrent and global conflict. It must be understood that with the modern development of industry, agriculture, and the technical arts, the maximum benefits to mankind are possible only in a worldwide economy, by which the resources of the earth and the productive capacity of its inhabitants are used to raise the standard of living of all men everywhere. It must be understood that human prosperity and development, like peace, are indivisible. But here, too, instruction must culminate in will and feeling. The underlying sentiments or attitudes which distinguish democracy must be extended to embrace all men.

LOVE OF TRUTH

There must be a worldwide confidence in the beneficence of knowledge and an extension to mankind at large of the benefits of knowledge. Ideas must circulate freely in order that all men may profit by a universal science and by its technological applications, and in order that there may be created a public opinion of the world as a support for international institutions. This implies that civil liberties shall be enjoyed by all men, so that all men may contribute from their own thought and invention to the good of all men and so that the light may spread from any place of origin to all parts of the earth's surface.

FREEDOM UNDER LAW

There must be a love of the freedom of all men everywhere—an unwillingness that there should be any master race or imperialistic nation that reserves freedom for itself and imposes servitude on the remainder of mankind. The frustration or exploitation of individuals or minority groups within any society must be intolerable to their fellow men in any other society. Men must learn to live and to prefer to live under a system of international law by which their several personal, group, and national freedoms are secured and reconciled.

FELLOW FEELING

Sympathy must be widened so that all human beings, however different in their racial attributes or national traditions, may be valued in terms of their own needs and aspirations. The primitive sense of kinship which prompts every man to feel for every other man and come to his aid must be freed from the narrowing influence of the group loyalties by which men learn to think of other men as rivals and enemies. As individual self-interest has been broadened into national self-interest, so this in turn must be broadened into a self-interest of the totality of mankind. The individual must, in other words, identify himself with the interest of mankind as a whole in its struggle against the forces of nature and in its effort to attain a fuller and more perfected life for all. The words "man," "humanity," and "mankind" must by the use of images and symbols be invested with the same vividness of meaning and the same power to allegiance as the word "American."

RESPECT FOR HUMAN DIGNITY

All men must be felt by all men to possess the high potentialities of human nature. As in universal religions all men alike are conceived as souls worthy of God's grace and providence, so all men must be thought of as having the capacity for truth, for artistic creation or enjoyment, and for moral goodness. They must be considered as ends in themselves and as educable. All men must be encouraged to take a pride in the creative achievements of all other men as achievements of the race of man for which they may claim a vicarious credit. The sense of human dignity is not a description of the actual condition of mankind but a *faith* in man which sees the best in every man and gives every man the benefit of the doubt. This faith will tend to confirm itself, since men will try to live up to what is expected of them—and often will succeed.

PERSONAL RESPONSIBILITY

The broadening of the sphere of human relations does not diminish the importance of the individual but, on the contrary, enhances it. The solidarities which tend to submerge and to obliterate the individual are the narrower solidarities of the family, the crowd, the class, or the nation. Those ages, such as the Hellenistic Age and the Age of the Enlightenment, which have been most individualistic have also been most cosmopolitan and universalistic. In proportion as the individual is freed from his immediate social surroundings he readily establishes relations with all other individuals. He tends to think of himself as a *man among men* rather than as this or that particular kind of man.

The individual person is not reduced by a consciousness of his worldwide human relations but assumes new functions and obligations. The individual is the unit or member, whatever the size of the group. When he becomes a parent, a neighbor, and a citizen of the state he does not cease to be the same person but adds new roles. So in a world order the same individual becomes a citizen of the world with added responsibilities and burdens. He must as a person integrate this new role with the old.

Democratic Morale a Challenge to the Schools

In the national field democracy is both a going concern and an unfinished task. It is both an occasion for pride and a challenge to courage. International democracy is as yet only an aspiration. But it is an extension of principles and experiences already familiar to members of a democratic nation such as the United States. The fact that it involves a bold advance into new ways of thought and feeling can be so presented as to elevate rather than depress morale. It is the latest and perhaps the greatest adventure in the ascending journey of mankind and can be made to draw out those spiritual reserves with which men respond to obstacles and resistances which stand in the way of a cause to which they have given their allegiance.

In the creation of a democratic morale, whether national or world-wide, the school plays a unique role. Its influence is exercised during the relatively plastic years when the fundamental attitudes are fashioned and fixed. It is a major channel of tradition by which the common creed is perpetuated. Thru its relative freedom from po-litical control it can escape the suspicion which attaches to all in-fluences emanating directly from official agencies—the suspicion that influence is being exerted to serve the government in power or to exalt authority and uniformity above the liberties of individuals and groups. Above all, the school is itself a social microcosm in which the universal principles of democracy can be exemplified and not merely taught; and in which the individual, associating with elders, contemporaries, and juniors, can learn by practice how to live in a free world. It provides a compact but representative community in which the spirit and not merely the letter of democracy can be spread by contagion and by the admiring love and emulation of its personal embodiments.

—*Newark, New Jersey, Public Schools, photograph by Pat Liveright*

★ *As the individual shares the satisfaction and the credit of a combined per-formance, there is a feeling of identification with all individuals who have contributed to it. This type of satisfaction is summed up in the seal of approval which America puts on teamwork.*

CHAPTER III
Getting Together

MORALE can be described and evaluated in terms of what it has meant in war and peace to nations and peoples. It can be seen as an element in individual life, with the morale of the individual dependent on physical, psychological, and ideational factors. It can be seen as an element in social organization, with every society—democratic or otherwise—demanding a high morale among its members in order that its ideals may be realized. The question then arises of how morale, so much desired, may be developed within groups that are working toward democratic ideals. This chapter attempts to describe basic ways of living in organized groups and to show how morale is developed and how it functions within these groups.

Individual and Group Morale

It seems desirable to comment first on the interrelations of individual and group morale. Quite obviously individual morale helps to create group morale and is created by it. Persons whose individual morale is good, will tend, when acting in harmony in a group, to keep high the morale of the group and inspire better morale among other members. Dependent as it may be on the morale of its members, the morale of a group would not appear to be, however, merely the sum total of individual morales. The group seems to have an identity and morale of its own. Nor is the morale of an individual the same in all times and places. An individual may have high morale in one group and low morale in another.[1] But clearly to distinguish individual from group morale is difficult indeed, because morale operates primarily in a social context, and, with the exception of Robinson Crusoe, perhaps, has meaning principally as it has social, or group, significance.

Men are born into group living. As children they are dependent on others not only for food and shelter but for affection and approval. To gain these things they must conform reasonably to the group. The group in order to maintain itself must have the alle-

---

[1] Bateson, Gregory, and Mead, Margaret. "Principles of Morale Building." *Journal of Educational Sociology* 15: 206-20; December 1941.

giance of its members and must, therefore, find means to keep them in line. This is true not only of the family but of larger groups. The kind of appeal which the group employs depends on its purpose and nature as well as on how imperative it may be to hold individuals in line. Force or the threat of force may be applied to young children to keep them out of danger (or to satisfy the power drive of parents). Force or threat of force exists in military bodies because of the critical nature of its duties. It is a condition of military life not because it is necessary so far as the vast majority of the members is concerned but because of the extreme danger to the group from any individual dereliction of duty. Civil authorities invoke military law in times of great emergency, but in civil life the sanctions of force are ordinarily applied only as a last resort. In adult life the use of force by a group against its own members indicates that no true morale exists in those members. This is true in dealing with criminals and irresponsible persons. The appeal of the group to the individual, however, is generally based on his own needs and desires, the factors physical, psychological, and ideational which are fundamental to his personal morale.

Conversely these same factors underlie group morale. What is true of the individual in his quest for the satisfactions which sustain his morale is measurably true of the group quest. The incentives, the sacrifices, and the rewards are parallel. They are also intertwined. That is why in the following discussion of the essentials of group morale, particularly with relation to goals and a sense of progress toward them, the individual aspect is first considered.

Essentials of Group Morale

Various writers and groups have enumerated in some detail what they regard as the essentials of high morale in a democracy. There seems to be sufficient agreement in their findings to justify for the present discussion the adoption of the following list.

A POSITIVE AND CLEAR-CUT GOAL

The more important the goal is to the individual or group, the more positive it will be; for example, to the individual, earning a living; and to the nation, winning the war. If there is uncertainty or confusion, if individuals or groups do not know what they want, integrative force for both the individual and the group is lacking. Youth especially rightly asks, "What are we headed for?"

Once he knows his goal, the strongest factor in a man's morale is confidence in his ability to attain it. A man must feel that he is getting somewhere. If for any reason he does not tackle his problems, feelings of guilt press upon him and his morale drops to the bottom of the psychic barometer. His natural powers, the training which gives him skill and competence, and his feeling of "can do" are all important. The greater his powers and the wider his skills, the greater his confidence that he can meet the unknown problems of the future. The means must be adequate to the objective. The guidance services of the school and community are extremely valuable in helping the individual to select attainable objectives as well as the means by which they may be reached.

Whether he can achieve it all by himself or not, the individual may at least set up his personal goal. But in establishing a group goal, at least in a democracy, all members of the group should have a voice.

A SENSE OF TOGETHERNESS IN THE GROUP

A sense of togetherness in the group may depend on several related factors:

Common purpose and standards—One's own beliefs and purposes are reinforced, one's own doubts and vacillations lessened, by joining with persons of similar goals, tastes, and interests. It takes more than one rail to make a railroad.

Mutual appreciation of personal worth and contribution—In a group each one looks for others who can supply toward the common purpose skills which he as an individual does not possess. Thus the baritone not only accepts but welcomes the first tenor as an equally essential part of a male quartet. As the individual shares the satisfaction and the credit of the combined performance, there is even a feeling of identification with all individuals who have contributed to it. This type of satisfaction is summed up in the seal of approval which America puts on *teamwork*. As a synonym for cooperation it is packed with emotional affects. Teamwork implies not only an effective means toward accomplishment but also the spirit of cooperation regarded as a valuable and thrilling end in itself. To be a member of a *team* is the ambition of all normal small boys in this country.

Status of the group—This feeling of identification is not merely with the other individuals in it but with the group as a group, the embodiment of certain ideals and standards. Its past as well as its present group achievements become an asset to the individual. He acquires a sense of pride and even of ownership in the group. It belongs to him. This means that the individual goal either must coincide with or be modified to meet the needs and purposes of the group. If the individual cannot make the required modifications, the group is not for him. Nor can the group succeed if many of the individuals who comprise it are "members with reservations."

A SENSE OF PROGRESS TOWARD THE GOAL

There must be conviction that progress is possible and that means of achieving it are available. If desirable and reasonable goals are always out of reach, a sense of futility and deterioration of morale may be expected. If there is no sensible progress toward the goal, interest wanes; hence, the need for subgoals, progress charts, and even report cards. Frequent failure and frustration of effort undermine individual morale and cause the prompt disintegration of groups. This is as true of adults as of children and youth. The apathy of many adults to social and political issues which affect their very lives is merely a reflection of their feeling that nothing they do will prove effective. They substitute "What's the use?" for "Let's go!" But with sensible progress of individual or of group comes a sense of power. Out of his experience in the group the individual realizes that "in union there is strength" is not just something somebody said.

On the other side of the ledger it must be recorded that if the goal is too easily or quickly won, the achievement fails to bring satisfaction. The goal must be high enough and far enough ahead to justify firing up the boiler—something "worth fighting for."

It should be noted also that, while the morale of the group is maintained best by progress in advancing its purposes, opinion outside the group may vary as to whether the purpose is praiseworthy and the internal morale desirable. Thus the morale of hell might be thought to slip were virtue to creep in. The morale of the Ku

Klux Klan and of *Fascismo* was highest when their deviltries were deepest.

If the group itself, say of Negroes or "foreigners," is rejected or held in low regard by other and more dominant groups and if the means of bettering its status are not at hand, the result is low morale and even in some cases antisocial or regressive behavior. All people want to feel that they are sufficiently like others in all essential respects to merit acceptance and regard with small and large groups of their society, including the nation.

Reaction to danger from without—Normally the feeling of membership is intensified by threat to the group and the things for which it stands. The individual realizes that he is safer when he has with him the benefit of numbers and organized strength. But outside threat to the group also stimulates a protective attitude toward those of the in-group. If, however, the cause for which the group stands is not truly his cause or if his individual morale is low, he may decamp rather than rally. Because danger from without is more readily recognized and resisted than danger from within, a cause may more easily suffer from divisive internal forces than from outward attack.

Good lines of intercommunication—In order that the members of a group may be reinforced in adherence to its principles and constantly stimulated to assist in its purposes, they must be kept aware of its problems and progress. The channels of communication between individuals, units, and leaders must be kept open for two-way traffic; hence, meetings, conferences, conventions, bulletins, house organs, and, most potently for large public groups, radio addresses and propaganda films. Without such contacts, cross-purposes develop. cohesion loosens, groups become demagnetized, and the particles fall away from the core.

A SENSE OF STATUS FOR MEMBERS OF THE GROUP

The recognition which comes to the individual from other members of the group, the fact of acceptance, social approval, and the sense of belonging are extremely important because his own sense of importance thereby is enhanced. He is wanted. He has a contribution to make. There is sad irony in the contrast youth now draws between its economic and social rejection in the depression years and the eagerness with which industry, Army, and society woo him in the war years. Thousands of older people, too, have come out of futility into war usefulness, determined to help end that greatest of futilities.

LEADERSHIP

No group can thrive as a group unless it possesses leadership which keeps purpose and means clear and recognizes the need of the membership for participation and recognition. All the instruments of an orchestra may be present but the music will be off beat and tune unless there is a competent conductor, someone who not only knows the various musicians but knows what they are there for and how to get them to see it and do it. The successful leader is able to express the purposes of the group better than can the group itself. His superior articulateness becomes a source of authority. Stephenson has shown in clear detail how the comparatively unknown Lincoln, a man without executive experience, became President almost entirely thru his ability to state the issues so clearly that he epitomized in himself the purposes of a large part of the nation.[2] It has been pointed out often that great leaders are generally great phrase-makers. They can sum up situations and make battle cries to fit them.

The true leader never loses touch with the group. His followers know that thru the leader's initiative and direction as well as thru his statement of their cause they are helped to fulfil their own purposes. Thus he builds a prestige by which he may strengthen and even enlarge those purposes. However great his authority may become he does not lose but improves his standing as a *member* of the group. He combines the power of command with companionship. He is *our* Washington, *our* Nelson, *our* Teddy.

The approval which the leader gives is greatly prized. One of the greatest functions of the leader is to praise and one of his greatest assets the ability to do it wisely. Identification with the leader becomes easy as he sums up each man's dream of himself. Tendencies toward hero worship and identification are particularly strong in adolescents.

While the leader does not lose touch with his group, not all leaders find their following among their contemporaries. Great spiritual

---

[2] Stephenson, Nathaniel Wright. *Lincoln.* New York: Grosset and Dunlap, 1930. 528 p.

leaders may be rejected in their own time but recognized in God's time. So with Jesus; so with the saints; so with Galileo. The characteristic of their leadership was that they did not strike the common mind. Their concepts ran counter to the thought of their time and to its vested interest. Their real leadership was the greater as they had the vision and the courage to proclaim even to martyrdom the truth which the multitude would not accept. Not out of the crowd or temporal realities but out of solitude and communion with the Unseen they drew eternal values for mankind. Abjuring physical and social comforts, they found their morale in the spiritual realm. The same willingness to rest their case with posterity and the same inner compulsion to sacrifice have marked many of the greatest masters in the creative arts, the great inventors, and benefactors of mankind. Some day perhaps we shall know enough to honor the prophets in their own countries and their own time.

In a democracy and all democratic organizations, the success of the group depends on the ability of the membership to recognize the need for leaders and to select as leaders those who are most capable. William James said that the best thing a college education can aspire to accomplish is to "help you to know a good man when you see him."[3] Either a majority of the group or an effective minority must be competent enough to recognize competence. It is safer to have a majority.

Competent leadership in a democratic group will lead the group in ways that are suited to the democratic ideal. Good leadership will meet Allport's requirements for a program to promote morale among civilians in a democracy: The program is good (a) if it arouses in Americans a sense of personal responsibility for sharing in the task of protecting democracy; (b) if it stresses the basic tenet of democracy that all have equal rights to life, liberty, and pursuit of happiness and if it previsions a better world; (c) if its aims and practices are intended to further the well-being, growth, and integrity of every individual; (d) if it provides for reasonable security, fair treatment, and honorable status for all individuals; (e) if it expresses the majority will of the people and enhances the acceptance of the principle of majority rule; (f) if it raises the confidence of the people in their chosen leaders; (g) if it recognizes

---

[3] James, William. "The Social Value of the College-Bred." *Memories and Studies.* New York: Longmans, Green and Co., 1917.

the creative role played by minorities and diminishes hostility among various in-groups of the nation; (h) if it respects the principles of freedom of thought and uncensored communication; (i) if it utilizes the full intellectual equipment of each individual so that the "whole man" is involved and not only an emotional segment of his personality; (j) if it recognizes that democracy is not a violent process but a matter of "piecemeal and retail" progress; and (k) if it aids in achieving a coordinated and voluntary division of labor for the solution of common problems.[4]

Humor and Good Humor

Perhaps not essential but certainly helpful to morale is a sense of humor. The same statement may be made about good humor. Whether these qualities are causes or effects or only signs is hard to say. At any rate, they are frequently associated with high morale. The gaiety of a mind, said Ninon de L'Enclos, is an indication of its strength.

Good humor may have its roots in good health and hormones or in good friends and good wages. It seems to proceed not so much from conscious benevolence as from a surplus of vitality, a natural zest for living. It is not just absence of acid indigestion. Its fortunate possessor finds life interesting and worthwhile. The elements are so mixed in him that euphoria is easy.

What is called a sense of humor is a sort of plus quality, too, but it is basically intellectual. It has been described as a sense of proportion, an ability to perceive likeness and unlikeness, with a special delight in the incongruous. It has been explained as an escape mechanism. But as displayed by the shrewd Yankee farmer and cowboy, as well as by the shrewd Yankee doughboy, wise-cracking about the crops or the critters or the Japs, it seems more like sheer mental resilience. It is a playfulness of the mind proceeding, as physical play proceeds, from abundance of energy. Those who have more than one idea to bless themselves with can rub them together and generate others. They can even be fascinated by the process, and they can fascinate others. Young people say they like teachers who have a sense of humor, but they want it to be good

4 Allport, Gordon W. "The Nature of Democratic Morale." *Civilian Morale.* Second Yearbook, Society for the Psychological Study of Social Issues. Boston: Houghton Mifflin Co., 1942. Chapter 1, p. 3-18.

humor, too. They abhor nothing so much as the twisted forms which they call sarcasm.

It is not strange that these plus qualities are so often found in great leaders. Whether humor is an escape or not, it is surely a tonic to the leader as well as to those he leads. His ability to perceive the incongruous saves him from absurdities. He may at times be an ass, but he will not be a pompous ass.

Morale-Forming Groups

In approximate order of appearance the morale-forming groups include the family, the neighborhood play group, the church, the school, the economic identification group, and "organizations." The contribution, real and potential, of each of these and of certain others is discussed in a later chapter. Here they are considered as background to a discussion of (a) the extent to which the five essentials of good morale are employed in various types of youth and adult organizations, and (b) the morale-building devices and technics which such groups employ.

THE FAMILY

The family has the first opportunity to establish morale. It is the parents who contribute the genes which set the basic biological pattern of the individual. To that extent a man's morale is determined by the precession of his forebears. Let us, however, dismiss the old question of whether heredity or environment is more important with the old retort, "heredity before you're born, environment afterwards," and go on from there.

Except for Romulus and Remus, Mowgli, Tarzan, and a few others, children are born into groups living in human families. Now the family is not a democratic institution so far as the baby is concerned. His helplessness and inexperience put him at the mercy of the group, tho out of his very helplessness he may set up tyrannies of his own. The first pattern he learns, therefore, is an authoritarian one. It is only as his parents and others in a parent relationship realize that full adulthood in a democracy involves a sort of statehood for the individual that he is put in the way of achieving the personal controls which equip him to share in handling the social controls of adult society. Only as parents accord to children opportunity and responsibility in proportion to their increasing capacity do young people develop competence for life in a social order in which government depends not only on the consent but on the active participation of the governed. A sense of responsibility comes from experiencing responsibility. Democracy is a form of government for civic adults. Fascism and other authoritarian forms treat adults as civic children who are expected to do as they are told and ask no questions. For that reason training for membership in a totalitarian state is infinitely simpler than training for membership in a democracy.

In the family setting comes the first pattern of living, learning, and striving. In the family comes the first experience of affection and companionship, of dependence and independence, of anger and fear. In the family comes the first means of communication, the first language experience. Thru precept and example the family is the first channel by which the child enters into his social inheritance and learns the racial mores, the traditions, and the taboos.

As the first and perhaps the only natural group is the family, it has the greatest influence for weal or woe. Broken families and those which are badly bent can hardly be called natural groups. There can be no question that unsatisfactory family experiences in early childhood offer the greatest damage to personality. Court and delinquency records are eloquent on this point. For the sake of the next generation high schools need more, and especially better, courses in family life. For young parents communities need adult courses in family life with an unobtrusive counseling service.

THE NEIGHBORHOOD PLAY GROUP

The neighborhood play group brings the next extension of group living, if grandparents, uncles, and aunts are considered as part of the family group. Status with the neighbors' children is of great importance to the child, whether or not he has brothers and sisters of his own. Association with children outside the family is not so inevitable as with those inside. It is also less monitored. In neighborhood contacts the ability of the child to adjust to others meets its first real test. His aggressions and withdrawals at this early level are extremely significant.

No matter how unsatisfying to the parent these outside contacts may be, they are generally better than none at all. Too much child frustration and snobbishness is generated by parents who think, often mutually, that their children are too good to play with the neighbors' children. And the irony of it is that this parent attitude is most often dominant in the one-child family. The nursery school is frequently the only remedy for this obsession, as well as for parental failures in other forms of training.

THE CHURCH OR RELIGIOUS GROUP

The church or religious group is one of the earliest with which children (some children) find themselves affiliated. For the small child the sanctions in general duplicate and intensify those of home and school. Church, however, has an aura of mystery and authority —an authority of unique quality not only because it derives from the Unknown but because it is accepted also by adults and because it is generally accompanied by ritual and music and invested with esthetic and emotional appeal. Church and Sunday school at their best are like day school, too, in providing child companionships and inspiring adult leadership.

In addition to contacts with the church as an institution, the child receives religious influences in the home that from his earliest years help to shape his character and his system of values. By the pattern of family living one child learns to be truthful only when personally convenient; another is taught that honesty is the best policy; another is taught to reverence truth as a religious principle of conduct. Many homes that have lost contact with the organized church still are transmitting a partial religious heritage that adds a strengthening element to character. In other homes where the child is taken at an early age to church the religious teachings in the home are amplified and enriched by the services of the church itself, and the child develops loyalties and attitudes of service of lasting import.

THE SCHOOL

After the family, the school is the one practically universal and inevitable experience. Fortunate is the child for whom school entrance has not been made a matter of dread by the teasings of older children. It is an adventure to be sought eagerly and with confidence. But while it should be accomplished with kindness, it should not be cushioned to the point where the adjustment process is hindered. There is little danger of this at the outset of school life, but there is a real question whether there is not too much concern on the part of parents and educators alike about some later transitions in school life—elementary to high school, high school to college. Every new experience should bring its excitements and, in moderation, its anxieties and difficulties. That is the way of growth. No youngster should have the changes in his life so modified as to blur their significance. We learn to change by changing. Young people have to learn to take the difficulties with the advantages. Some day they will get married or drafted or go to work. They will have to meet top sergeants and straw bosses. That fact, however, does not justify household Napoleons or classroom Hitlers.

The school opens to the child not only the world of books but the widest range of personalities and experiences he has yet known. Here group loyalty and group morale are consciously as well as unconsciously developed. Here they shift and grow with grade and school changes, with cliques and clubs, and with new friends and new teachers.

MEMBERSHIP IN ECONOMIC GROUPS

Morale is related to membership in economic groups. Children early become identified in their own minds with some economic interest group. The distinctions between rich and poor come quickly, too quickly, to children. There are comparisons of clothing and houses, of toys and treats available, and of parental occupation and status. This is true even in relatively homogeneous neighborhoods and schools. For many people, perhaps for most, morale is a sense of money in the bank or of getting it there. Numerous studies, as summarized by Child, show that high morale is definitely associated with higher occupational levels and higher income.[5] Wise parents and teachers strive to keep economic and social distinctions subordinate to other values. But what one assumes to be his own and his family's "place in life," even if he is resolved to change it, has a distinct bearing on morale. It helps determine with what groups and, therefore, with what group morales the individual will remain or become identified—with the labor, professional, management, or capital group; with pub or club. And yet in America social and economic life is the most fluid in all the world.

With the beginning of employment, economic identification is either strengthened or weakened, according to the individual's own

---

[5] Child, Irvin L. "Morale: A Bibliographical Review." *Psychological Bulletin* 38: 393-420; June 1941.

material progress. The American way seems to demand upgrading, if only by marrying the boss's daughter. Even with the growth of the chain store and the relative shortage of bosses and, therefore, of bosses' daughters, material progress is still sufficiently common and expectable as to be a strong factor in individual and national morale.

In fact, economic class distinctions in America may be said to exist only to be broken. Parents desire and expect their children to move on, up, and out—to get more education, to follow a different calling, to achieve a new and higher socio-economic status.[6] The Horatio Alger tradition—rags to riches, office boy to general manager, log cabin to the Capitol—survives all depressions and all middle-aged disillusion.

Here is the romantic aspect in American morale—the belief that the impossible is possible, at least for one's children. One man is as good as another. Given hard work, faith, and reasonable breaks, anyone can get anywhere. Not only the facts but success magazines and movies prove it.

Out of this morale factor so characteristic of the American way comes a relative instability in group allegiances. The employee of today is the owner or at least the manager of tomorrow. Proletarian consciousness is not native to America. When it appears, it appears locally and briefly as an importation from other cultures. It is true that there are fears that with the disappearance of physical frontiers the pioneering spirit of America will pass, too. And yet Americans in general are still reared not to keep down with, not to keep up with, but to beat the Joneses. And new Americans are even keener to prove their Americanism in this respect. To most of them "getting ahead" is America.

However unlovely our economic rivalry may be at times, it does put primary stress on personal effort and achievement rather than on inherited status. It recognizes individual worth. It makes America dynamic rather than static, progressive rather than volcanic, adolescent rather than senile. This spirit has gone along with the physical mobility of American life, the opening up of new land, farm boy turned industrial leader, necessity producing inventions, and inventions producing necessities.

Yet with all the rivalry of American life there has gone a cama-

<hr>

[6] For a full discussion of the American success pattern from an anthropologist's standpoint, see: Mead, Margaret. *And Keep Your Powder Dry.* New York: William Morrow and Co., 1942. 274 p.

raderie, as if the competition were not quite serious after all—a game rather than a battle. The prosperity of the individual has been linked with group prosperity. Individual initiative coupled with mass production has raised the standard of group living and group morale. Consider the sense of power and status which a youngster gets from the possession, or even the mere use, of the most ancient of jalopies.

Organized Groups

Organizations influence morale. The family is a natural or organic group. The church and the school are consciously organized groups, but as embodiments of great forces they rank as institutions. The neighborhood is relatively unorganized; so are such spontaneous groups as "our gang" and "our set." These latter, however, can have even more compulsive power and rigidity than groups with written constitutions and bylaws. On the whole, the "gang" is more liberalizing than the "set." The latter is apt to be mere ego extension, with or without annual dues. It may be even narrower in its social outlook than pure family selfishness of the "me and my wife and my son John and his wife" kind. What such groups lack in vision they make up in intensity.

Other groups are consciously organized—manufacturers' associations, boards of trade, labor unions, fraternities, clubs, lodges, leagues, consumer cooperatives, societies for this and that, and societies for the prevention of this and the promotion of that. Few of these are all-purpose groups, tho many try to be and for single-track minds frequently are. The all-purpose organization, Brook Farm, for example, generally assumes the proportions of a religious or social cult. But there are clubs organized primarily for political or business purposes which have added recreational, educational, and charitable programs in quantity and scope sufficient to absorb completely the free time of enthusiastic members.

Most organizations, however, have a single definite purpose or at least a single set of logically associated purposes. Most of them, in addition to a well-defined goal, strive to cultivate those other essentials of good morale: a sense of progress, of togetherness, of status for the members of the group, and strong leadership.

No nation has so high a percentage of "joiners" as has the United States. This may be all to the good. It generally means a wide experience in the technics of morale building. But much depends on the group and much on the individual. A man may seek merely to enhance his individual status by multiplying his group affiliations. He is your true "joiner." He may even carry his group identification so far as to have little identity of his own left.

Whether he seeks groups which tend to obscure his individuality and identity depends on his character, his training, and accident. He may derive his chief psychological satisfaction from submergence in the group, especially if he is weak and seeks freedom from individual responsibility, or he may seek submergence to compensate for a recognized tendency to exaggerated self-reliance. In any case, there is a seeking for a complementary relationship between his own needs and powers and those which can be supplied by the group. Strong individualists either shun groups or select them to supplement, not to complement, their egos—or to help them accomplish purposes in which they genuinely believe which are beyond their individual powers.

It is to be noted, however, that of those who shun membership in all organizations many are individualists not out of strength but out of weakness, thru inability to accept the responsibilities of group membership or thru selfishness, which is itself weakness. That is why schools should be alert to help the withdrawn child from his earliest days to make group contacts. To assist parents and teachers to recognize the social isolate as well as to help cope wisely with the many other personality problems, the trained psychiatric case worker, generally called visiting teacher, is an indispensable part of the personnel of the elementary school. Without the aid of specialists we are too apt to forget that what is on a child's mind may be more important than what is in it, and that nothing much will get in until something has been done to resolve the child's emotional conflicts. As incipient behavior problems, such cases are generally far more serious than those involving overt mischief or group misbehavior. From the social point of view "bad" companions may be better than no companions at all.

The strong personality may either get along with few group contacts or make them only as and when his intelligence shows his need for them. America and the world owe much to the souls whose strength flourished in solitude as well as to those who mingled with the crowd—to the Henry Thoreaus as well as to the Walt Whitmans.

Just as the extrovert may sometimes be helped by looking inward occasionally, the introvert can and with help may turn outward. Most people, however, are neither introverts nor extroverts but are somewhere in between and need alternate periods of seclusion and social contacts. For leaders both the years in the wilderness and the public ministry are essential.

The size, purpose, and type, as well as the number of the groups with which individuals affiliate, are significant. For most persons the breadth of group contacts in relation to opportunity is especially significant. The capacity for social living grows in importance as the world gets smaller and the range of possible contacts greater. The urban dwellers of today meet fifty times as many people in the course of a year as their rural grandfathers did. Altho these contacts may be less satisfying, the mere fact that they are a condition of modern life imposes a burden of adjustment not always easily carried. War is an upheaval in even the single fact that it brings together in close quarters thousands of men of all sorts of family, racial, and geographical backgrounds. For this experience as well as for the complex life of a modern metropolis, the large cosmopolitan high school is probably the best preparation. If we are to learn to live competently in crowds, we must learn to live competently in organized groups. Part of our problem, of course, is to find ways to escape the crowd for a time that we may preserve our individual souls and renew their strength for group living.

Youth Organizations

Juvenile clubs flourish easily in the American scene, where there is much point to the jest that wherever there are three Americans one is president, one secretary, and one treasurer. A club badge and if possible a club house are at an early stage the normal desire of every American boy and girl. The American advertiser clearly recognizes this urge and capitalizes on it for his product. Box tops will bring badges and engraved constitutions. Initiation rites, oaths of fealty, secret signs, and formulas copied from or imagined after those of high-school fraternities or older fraternal groups provide exciting paraphernalia, tho the activities may be only on the play level of cops and robbers or G-men and saboteurs. At a somewhat later stage these juvenile organizations may be metamorphosed into such anti-social bands as "gangs" and snob groups.

Boys' and girls' clubs with adult guidance tend to replace and counteract incipient antisocial groupings and to add conscious character-forming features. Schools and private foundations have worked out excellent programs for preadolescents. Notable among these is the Scout organization, with its junior and feeder group, the Cubs. The moral and stabilizing influence of such organizations is incalculable long after active association has ceased. Codes of conduct accepted by one's fellows, even tho frequently transgressed, tend to preserve standards. The code of the Scouts, for example, is in the Anglo-Saxon and Puritan tradition, recognizing that it is good to be good, that strength should be socially useful, and that compassion is a proper element in life. For many boys the concept of knight errantry, of *noblesse oblige,* is first met in such groups, and met pleasantly along with appeals to physical prowess, outdoor life, and craft ways. The Scouts are specially mentioned only as typical. Many parallel organizations both for boys and girls are doing splendid work.

Running all thru such groups is the idea of fair play, the very basis of the democratic ideal. What it may do for youngsters even at the slum level of environment is shown in the following rules evolved without adult assistance by the membership of a totally underprivileged group of boys. It could teach directness of expression as well as ethics to most privileged adults:

1. Don't talk during the meeting unless you are called upon.
2. Don't put feet on table (be polite).
3. Don't talk or act dirty.
4. Don't shoot paper wads.
5. Don't pick pockets.
6. Don't act funny.
7. Obey Arnold when out on the floor.
8. Don't hog the ball.
9. Don't get mad when you're put out.
10. Form an orderly line when leaving the meeting.
11. Don't hog coat hangers.
12. Don't insult the president.
13. Don't step on other people's feet.
14. Sit back in your seats.

Developments like this point their own contrast with such state-inspired and controlled youth organizations as the *Hitlerjugend.*

Adolescence brings a more conscious drive for adult forms of association and organization. Before the high school had an extracurriculum there were clubs. Generally they took the form of fraternities and sororities, with much aping of the least salutary features of their models. Frequently these groups missed entirely the high purposes on which the college fraternity, an outgrowth of the Romantic Movement, was founded. The members wanted their particular groups to be the best, but often they gave only lip service to their professed ideals or their sense of relative values was weak. As they generally exist the "fraternities" are utterly hostile to the purpose and needs of American schools. Effort, moderately successful, has been made to supplant the socially exclusive fraternity with the high-school honor society based entirely on acceptable purposes and methods. The Y.M.C.A. in its Hi-Y Clubs has taken the same course.

With the advent of the junior high school, educators sought deliberately to harness the associational urge in the service of character building and school morale. Most high schools today have a bewildering but valuable series of special clubs: athletic, debating, science, chess, photographic, philatelic, journalistic, language, and many more. They flourish and die and are reborn, the life cycle depending on the strength of the leadership, faculty or student, and on current interest. It is well that they die for in renascence they give practice in the creation as well as the maintenance of leadership.

The humanitarian and service ideal, rather than self-improvement per se, consciously dominates the Junior Red Cross and its activities in both elementary and high school. The High-School Victory Corps seeks to direct the interests and energies of youth, in every activity appropriate to their years, toward maximum contribution to the war effort.

One of the most practical means toward developing civic consciousness is the school safety patrol. The American Association of School Administrators yearbook on safety education says:

Twenty-five years ago there was nowhere to be seen in this country so splendid an example of positive regard for law as is today manifested by young people in their service on and obedience to school traffic patrols. It is estimated by the National Safety Council that there are nearly 300,000 school safety patrol members in the United States. One may travel on any school day thru hundreds of miles of country and at countless traffic points see boys and girls accepting without question the direction of persons of approximately their own age. They understand the motive behind the regulations and they comply. At the same time, those who serve on patrols are rendering a community service of a high order and developing in themselves patterns of civic responsibility and active concern for the welfare of others. With all the emphasis which schools have placed on character training, it is to be questioned whether they have ever found a better means for its development than safety education provides.[7]

The school itself is an organization. "School spirit" may be related to student government and faculty management, to winning football games and serving the community, but it transcends them all. It would seem to depend chiefly on the leadership of the principal and the extent to which he can evoke community, faculty, and student leadership. Can he and his associate leaders keep the goals clear? Can they create out of progress a sense of progress? Can they promote a sense of togetherness and a feeling of belonging? Can they make the old school tie something metaphysical rather than physical, something truly spiritual as well as sentimental? If they would do this for all as well as for the few perpetual alumni which every school has, they would give emphasis at every turn to sharing, to the concept that the school is inclusive in its exclusiveness. The race-conscious visitor beamed with approval as he remarked to the principal, "I see that you have several colored children in your orchestra." "You surprise me," said the principal. "I thought we had only Madison High School children in our orchestra."

The school is interested in developing patterns of loyalty to the school but chiefly as patterns for other and larger loyalties in adult life. For the same reason it is interested in youthful organizations. Whether it should be interested in "youth movements" is another matter—in youth as a youth bloc with a separate role to play rather than with youth as adult-becoming. Youth's needs should be served, but it is questionable whether this can best be done by setting youth entirely apart from adult groups, when the greatest need of "poor old youth" (the phrase is from *Time*) is to be absorbed into the adult community. There would seem to be little need for a youth movement or a youth bloc, except when young people are neglected and denied admission to older groups. The corrective is for established adult groups—churches, industry, business, political parties, and lodges—to welcome them to full membership. Surely, the interest of young people cannot long be a *youth interest* solely. Time takes care of that. An economic career and marriage soon rob youth

---

[7] American Association of School Administrators. *Safety Education.* Eighteenth Yearbook. Washington, D. C.: the Association, a department of the National Education Association, 1940. p. 46.

groups of their own best leadership, and that is as it should be. Besides, the young are needed to keep the old from growing senile.

Of particular interest to educators are two fairly recent developments in the realm of youth as youth groups. One is the hosteling movement, common in Europe before the war.[8] It recognizes the urge of young people to go places and provides wholesomely simple conditions under which boys and girls together may go on expeditions, exploring the countryside and coming to know themselves and the real America.

The other, an even more recent development, is the founding in the public schools of New York City of Youthbuilders' Clubs, convincingly described by Sabra Holbrook in *Children Object*.[9] In these clubs children begin not with a program evolved and handed out by adults but with a forum in which they first inquire what they want to find out about real problems of community living, then after interviews with civic leaders seek and accept their own practical part in bringing things to pass—good civic things.

Morale-Building Devices Employed by Organizations

A group singlehearted in its purpose may rely on that singleness of purpose alone to unite its members and to renew or increase its numbers. But just as organizations run the gamut in variety, so their organizational and morale-fostering devices traverse the whole chromatic scale. So numerous are they and so appealing in themselves that as sideshows they sometimes threaten to keep their members out of the main tent. Symbolism, pageantry, parades, crusades, and conventions all are designed not as ends in themselves but to attract, retain, and encourage, and to give the organization greater status with both the in-group and the out-group.

EXCLUSIVENESS AND SECRECY

Among the commonest devices is the cult of exclusiveness. "We don't take every Tom, Dick, and Harry. You have to rate to belong to our crowd." This attitude at the same time enhances the value of the neophyte in his own eyes. It is reflected in the alleged remark of

[8] Smith, Monroe, and Smith, Isabel, editors. *AYH Handbook, 1940*. Northfield, Mass.: American Youth Hostels, 1940. Vol. 5, 123 p.

[9] Holbrook, Sabra. *Children Object*. New York: Viking Press, 1943. 197 p.

the draftee to the volunteer soldier, "Huh, *you* had to *ask* to get in; they *sent* for *me*."

Where standards for the selection of members are based on the achievement or sincerity of purpose of candidates, much may be said for the limitations imposed. Certainly the Marine Corps has made good use of its rigid standards in promoting the spirit of the Corps. The highly selected individual feels an especially high obligation. He is not as other men are; he is consecrated by his preferment. Matthew Arnold's doctrine of the Remnant has point even in a democratic society. Certainly we want our doctors to be a highly selected group. Where, however, selection is based on considerations other than those of individual worth and common useful function, the organization is out of place in a democratic society.

Membership recruiting as providing continuity is of paramount interest to every group. Gains in numbers, being ancillary to most other purposes, generally both reflect and stimulate morale, especially if the gains may be considered qualitative as well as quantitative. This would not be altogether true, of course, in organizations which set exclusiveness as a primary goal. For certain purposes there is an optimum size.

Exclusiveness is heightened by secrecy. Much of the paraphernalia of secrecy in fraternal organizations is a carry-over from times or conditions in which concealment had true survival value. Tho the original need may have passed, the purposes and power of an organization are still presumed to be greater if its operations and rites are cloaked in mystery. While "secret symbols," signals, grips, and phrases are not themselves revealed to outsiders, the fact that there are such mystic means of communication, as well as more fundamental mysteries, is well advertised. A secret organization which is so secret that its existence is unknown is no fun.

Along with the Eleusinian urge, we find that antiquity, real or spurious, has a particular charm for members who in other areas of their lives are completely devoted to modernity. The ancient and honorable somehow lay hold on occult powers of the past. Some of this is genuine, developing perspective and a real sense of history; most of it is innocent; and a lot of it, childish—but childish only to those of such assured position that they fail to realize the need of other men and women for special sources of strength and status. Truly adult minds slough it off.

CODES, RITUALS, AND SONGS

The ideals of an organization are expressed in its pledge of fealty, its constitution, its rituals, and its songs. Except for the constitution, which is generally a legal or business document, these are most effective when touched with emotion. They become more than hooks for the memory. The familiar words have an attraction, a sensory and emotional appeal of their own, which tends to grow with the years, to help interpret experience, and to steady the possessor in emotional and moral crises. "To bear true faith and allegiance" is a phrase to conjure a man back to his duty. The circumstances and the sanctions which first surrounded it "come back" to him.

Codes and ritual are particularly useful to young people, seeking standards, wanting to be lifted out of themselves, and romantically moved by idealism and its symbols. Many adults in their sophistication find pageantry, particularly the more fanciful kind, hard to take. Or perhaps they are shying away from it because Hitler used it basely, tho effectively. At any rate, schools too infrequently make use, as they properly might, of symbols and ritual.[10]

"Let me write the songs of a nation and I care not who writes its laws." Music has a power to create and to evoke memories, as well as passions. We should say not "words and music" but "words times music," for the effect is one of geometric proportion. The hymns hallowed by memory are the best hymns. The songs associated with group gatherings in which aspiration and unity of understanding were high have become part of the group soul. Alma Mater ranks second only to Mother herself. The halls of Montezuma have led many a new Marine to the shores of Tripoli. The spirit of the Corps is in the song of the Corps. The caissons go rolling along, but they do not go alone; they stir the heart like a trumpet. When the Campbells are coming, everyone wants to be a Campbell, just as at times everyone wants to be carried back to Ole Virginny. In our striving for musical perfection our schools too often have neglected the folk songs and the songs of patriotism. We have not used as we properly might this great means to psychological unity. Few of us take the great masses of our students beyond "The Star-Spangled Banner," "America," and "America the Beautiful." We have neglected, too, the folklore of our country. We need to give our children more common memories to pass on to their children than we do.

---

[10] See descriptions of use of pageantry, p. 188-89, 217-18, 229-31.

THE BADGE AND THE UNIFORM

Among the devices most cultivated by organizations is that of the badge, which if sufficiently enlarged becomes the uniform. Badges (and how children love them!) promote solidarity by enabling members to recognize each other. They also have a symbolic value. In fact, they are generally compounded of a series of symbols associated with the organization, its purposes and origins. They may indicate not only membership but status within the organization—a double exclusiveness. They are reminders of duty. One must not disgrace the uniform. "Before committing any dishonorable act, I was always careful to remove the insignia of the order, that I might not become a reproach to my brethren."

In the uniform itself organizations build on pride in personal appearance, which is a strong factor in both individual and group morale. The soldier's chin, as well as his uniform, must be immaculate whenever conditions permit. The new Army has given added recognition to this factor in its special care for the fit of the G.I. uniform. The army tradition of "spit and polish," of looking one's best even under the most adverse conditions, has a sound basis in human nature. It has its sponsors in civilian life among parents, teachers, and employers. Children may resist but most of them ultimately develop personal pride from being kept clean behind the ears. Slum missions begin with a hot bath and a clean shirt. Clothing stores advertise "executive type suits." The lack of a party dress can spoil a party. People tend to live up to their clothes. Said Mother, "I don't need a doctor and I don't need a preacher; I need a new hat." Dressing for dinner in the jungle is absurdly sound.

TITLES AND PROMOTIONS

Organizations which go in for mystery, badges, and ancientry generally run also to hierarchial titles and degrees, tho it is amusing to note how often in the democratic climate of these United States the Topmost Exalted Grand Panjandrum, Ruler of the Stars and the Subway, has achieved his office by way of the Australian ballot.

Page, squire, knight; tenderfoot, scout, eagle scout; private first class, corporal, sergeant; second lieutenant, first lieutenant, captain; freshman, sophomore, junior, senior; apprentice, journeyman, master; A.B., A.M., Ph.D.; and hash marks, wound stripes, medals—in such distinctions organizations of all sorts recognize degrees of skill, of worth, and of service. Within the group additional status is possible. Step up, young man, and sense your progress. Prove yourself. The top is at the top. Here are tangible evidences of growth, looking ahead, realization of achievement, and responsibility to lead others over the same path. The onward and upward idea implies teaching. It is found in the rites of puberty as practiced by primitive peoples, in the bird pushing the young from the nest into flight.

If the road is open, one does not envy; he emulates. So by degrees we learn; by titles and offices we mark our progress, repeating, adapting, and marking with artificial steps and cachets the drama of natural growth.

In the realm of organized effort we find no inconsistency between our ideal concept of equality and distinctions of rank based on function or achievement. We say that we salute the office and the uniform, not the man in it. We have a party discipline, a group discipline, a democratic discipline. We elect presidents and vicepresidents, and we acknowledge the authority of the chairmen they appoint. We voluntarily place ourselves under orders. In a money-raising campaign we adopt military titles and organization forms, subordinating our individual wills to the command of others, and operate as teams, thrilled to be team members. Our individual morale is not impaired but strengthened.

MEETINGS AND CONVENTIONS

Meetings and conventions have been mentioned as a necessary part of a system of intercommunication. In their handling of these means organizations have developed special technics—the ritual, "the experience" period, the pep talk, the refreshments, community singing, the social hour, and the business meeting—something for everyone. In the division of labor, the planning and the executing, participation is secured and leadership developed. Three cheers for the committee! In the full flowering of a convention, including regalia, talent and discipline have an even greater testing.

Let no one underrate the importance of the social hour. Communal breadbreaking as a builder of morale among the members of a group goes far back to the mores of the human race. Mealtime rites are associated with ancient sacrifice, with the Last Supper, and with feudal life, as well as with the annual banquet and fellowship party of Merriwell's Retail Suitings, Inc., or free coffee with Jack and Heintz.

When you share food you share the substance; you are family and you are guest.

Many clubs not only capitalize on the fact that we all eat and enjoy it but also on that other fact that physical activity of the play type is natural to man and that companionship can frequently be best realized on this level. So we will bowl once a week, those of us who want to, or we will have a monthly golf tournament during the season. Some will find their chief opportunity for leadership here; others will take on the new role of followers; but we will have a fine time kidding each other about our handicaps and scores. In pseudo-rivalry we will find real friendship. Or, changing gender, we will just bring our mending and have a good time. It will be teamwork of a sort.

All this exposition of "joining" and its trappings may not represent morale building at its highest, but as a description of ordinary forces and customs operating among ordinary Americans it has its point. And even from an idealistic standpoint such Babbitry is not altogether to be reprobated. Most of it is shot thru with sheer friendliness and, in spite of the contradictions and absurdities, with the spirit of democracy. It develops a respect for the other fellow. It gives experience in "committee work"—and what is more American than a committee? It provides at least a rudimentary knowledge of parliamentary law. It may lead the way to wider associations and larger loyalties. The patterns and capacities which Americans develop in these humble ways may yet be found of great value in the development of democratic ways in the global age of the after-war. It is true, of course, that only some can or will make the jump to the larger loyalties. Many will have to go by easy stages. But most will reach at least the second stage. Certainly a great many who discover in themselves a talent for organization work or for group discussion seek, or are sought for, service in civic betterment groups.

Discipline and Human Values

Apart from government itself, the two greatest fields in which organizational talent operates are the armed forces and business and industry. The military services employ many of the morale-building devices just discussed. Rank and uniform, of course, are closely associated in our minds with the Army and Navy. But it is well in any survey of the subject of morale to stress the basic elements of leadership and discipline which rank and uniform symbolize. Nowhere more than in military organization is effort directed toward building up the health and the psychology of the individual. Nowhere is there more emphasis on teamwork for the common purpose. Pride in the unit is fostered at every turn. Every soldier is encouraged to believe and, believing, to make his squad the best in the platoon, his platoon the best in the company, his company the best in the regiment, his regiment the best in the division, and his division the best and the "fightin'est" in the Army. With a 24-hour-a-day program, with a stupendous training and retraining task, and with the necessity of operating under the most grueling and terrifying conditions, constantly meeting the final test of all, the armed forces should be concerned to know all there is to know about what makes men tick.

The Army must develop discipline without destroying desirable initiative. It must establish a sort of built-in courage. Colonel Hans Christian Adamson is responsible for the statement that "discipline carries you through long after courage is gone."

Special morale officers are assigned to military units, officers concerned with the personal, financial, and family problems of the men as well as with their attitudes toward military life as such. The army and navy manuals show constant regard for the development and maintenance of morale.[11] And yet it may be questioned whether our armed forces have gone as far as ideally they intend in setting up the morale units designed to make and keep clear America's role in the war and in history.

With the pressures of war production, industrial and business firms are devoting increased attention to employee morale. The federal government early in the defense program established a "Training Within Industry Service" which was operated as a part of the War Production Board and later under direction of the War Manpower Commission. The Service has established twenty-three districts for advisory and field service and has issued many bulletins compact with practical suggestions. These war agencies are encouraging management to follow the practices tested and proved over a long period by farsighted companies. Marked advances have been made in factory sanitation, cafeterias, rest periods, and recreation provisions; in training programs and job adjustment; and in group insurance

---

[11] For excellent chapters on "soldier" morale, see: National Research Council and Science Service. *Psychology for the Fighting Man.* Washington, D. C.: Infantry Journal (1115 Seventeenth St., N. W.), 1943. 456 p.

and wage dividends. Industry has found it profitable to set up joint committees of management and labor, to assist in establishing credit unions, and to take account of home conditions in dealing with employees. Home-front developments in the matters of transportation and rationing, Red Cross and blood bank, and bond drives have brought new calls for group morale, for which management-labor cooperation has been necessary. Especially helpful have been clear statements of policy and endeavors to create pride of employees in plant and product, a sense of belonging.

While the famous Jack and Heintz developments have been the most spectacular, many firms had discovered long before the war boom that human beings are human.[12] They discovered that wage rates are not the most potent factor in employee morale. The five essentials discussed early in this chapter are of transcendent importance, tho, of course, money reward has a distinct place under *sense of progress* and *sense of status*. Industry with all its facilities for research has been making a scientific and valuable approach to the problem of how to deal decently with our fellow men.

The findings of the experiments conducted at Western Electric's Hawthorne plant, beginning in 1927, are of considerable moment. They are summarized thus by Watson:

Morale improved when the group participated in planning their conditions of work.

Morale rose when the atmosphere was friendly rather than autocratic.

Variety in work helped morale.

Morale was better when the group developed a team-consciousness.

Group incentives did more for morale than did individual rewards.

Morale was built more easily in groups which enjoyed being together socially than in groups too disparate in age.

Problems in morale were found to arise sometimes from personal emotional experiences quite outside the group being observed.

Other problems arose from clashes of group mores. Groups formed themselves and took on distinctive characters which needed to be understood and respected.[13]

The Morale of Citizenship

Many organizations are based frankly on mutual interest, meaning mutual self-interest. This was true of many early insurance

---

[12] Public Opinion Quarterly. "Labor and Management in a Democracy." *Public Opinion Quarterly* 7: 353-456; Fall 1943. Includes: Jack, William S. "Jack & Heintz: Blueprint for Labor Relations." p. 413-30.

[13] Watson, Goodwin. "The Surprising Discovery of Morale." *Progressive Education* 19: 33-41; January 1942. Same condensed: *Education Digest* 7: 33-36; February 1942.

companies, burial societies, and library associations. But even the cemetery sodalities frequently took on social features and truly benevolent aspects. People just naturally wanted to do good; it made them feel good. Private educational ventures—kindergarten associations, for example—were really home missionary societies. Individuals found their power to accomplish their benevolent purposes multiplied by membership in such organizations. Fine group projects of today, represented, for example, by the endeavors of Community Chests and Red Cross chapters, are more than glorified barn raisings. We not only serve each other but we also help those who can render no service in return. This spirit is manifest in the so-called service clubs whose appeal to membership is based on something more than psychological compensation.

As boys and girls reach the age of social consciousness or are helped to reach it, they should be encouraged to seek membership in adult organizations with social and civic purposes. Unless the school has overlooked its own opportunities, this will be merely a transition from youthful to more adult service clubs. The debt-to-society and the *noblesse oblige* idea as a normal urge to be practically expressed in betterment projects should be a concern of every school. Unless the loyalties of the smaller group lead to loyalties to the larger groups—community, nation, and world groups—mankind will always lead a small-time, bush-league existence socially and morally.

Teachers will not be so bold as to imagine that they can blueprint world peace and an international order in the classroom, but they can help build men and women who will know how important the problem is to them and that their business is to study it. One of the first things to be done is to move away from indifference to local problems and local politics. Politics is a high calling. If the wrong people are the only ones interested in local government, the right people are wrong to be disinterested. When youth are shown the concentric rings of the citizen's responsibilities, not only should the complete set be shown, including that of world citizenship, but adequate stress should be laid on local citizenship with its immediate relation to town, ward, and city affairs. Participation of the new voter in political organization as well as in the franchise should be stressed as a civic must. We should teach that no person has a right to accept civic benefits without contributing to them or civic wrongs without protesting against them, so long as we teach also that a reasonable degree of civic patience is not the same thing as civic complaisance. If our young people have a high conception of civic virtue and the will to help, which is the highest virtue, we can trust that they will learn to make the right decisions.

While the citizenship of the ballot box needs fortifying, so does the citizenship that has to do with racial, social, educational, and business problems and progress, with schools, churches, and social agencies. It begins with interest, continues with study, and results in speech and action. Schools must remind themselves that they are preparing young people not simply for ornamental and intellectual but for useful citizenship. Straight thinking and unselfish purpose have their best chance before vested interest develops. But in the course of civic instruction the complexities of human problems in other ages should be sufficiently recognized so that the practical compromises of history will not appear so inglorious as they might seem in the oversimplification which retrospect makes so easy. Otherwise, the confusions of the present will appear twice as confounded and the tremendous difficulties and contradictions of the contemporary scene even more baffling than they are. Let us say, "*Those* problems we have conquered; *these,* too, can be made to yield." The atmosphere must be one of faith and resolution. Faith is characteristic of great men and great enterprise. Frank despair is better than cynicism, for despair is more often temporary. The morale of citizenship must be built on faith, and faith is catching.

As a major contribution to the morale of citizenship, high-school graduates should know not only what are the channels of government but what are the betterment agencies in their own communities and in the world and should be oriented toward membership in them. The school itself has been a more powerful betterment agency than the public generally realizes. It is tragic to let young people go out from it without at least the beginnings of affiliation with adult groups or institutions which also provide temptations upward.

There are unfortunately groups which provide temptations in the other direction. The distinguishing mark of the so-called "pressure groups" is that they use their strength to intimidate. For selfish purposes they employ class interest to obstruct the national interest. They employ ruthlessly all their vast organizational paraphernalia of shady propaganda to misinform the public mind and coerce the votes of legislators. High-school pupils of the eleventh and twelfth years, from their study of the problems of American democracy, should draw warning of the operations of selfish blocs.

Subversive groups operate less openly and even more diabolically. Their activities are harder to trace but their sinister purposes are more easily recognized. And yet so extensively and cunningly do they use the freedom of speech and press which our country permits, and in which it glories, that they frequently draw into their treacherous orbits those who otherwise would be sincere and patriotic citizens. Against such forces young people should also be warned.

The Impact of the War

The world is always at the crossroads, but sometimes we know it. This is one of those times, perhaps the greatest of them all. To the extent that we remain polarized toward the winning of the war *and* the winning of the peace we can rout the divisive forces in others and in ourselves. Pearl Harbor wrought or revealed an essential unity we were not sure we had.

If we can remember that unity to keep it intact, humanity may indeed go forward into a bright new day. It is relatively easy to be united *against* something which promises no good to any of us. It is hard to be united *for* something, there being so many somethings which we should like and so many of us to like them in varying degrees. But the very intensity of our common effort may give us a sufficient feeling for common needs to carry us thru together to the building of a new world structure. That is where morale for the long pull will come in. The question is whether we shall hang on now or go down for the third time. The question is whether we know that we must go forward to a new "normalcy" or again will think we can go back to an old one. How many freedoms do we want? How many for ourselves? For others? With what price are we willing to purchase these freedoms?

The war and the after-war we know will affect profoundly every one of our institutions. Whether we *can* do it or not, we shall at least be conscious that we *ought* to think in global terms. Certainly we must think or have someone to think for us in technological and aerological terms. Can we also think geopolitically and geosocially?

After the war children still will be born into families. Presumably they will go to school. Those families and those schools must be prepared to rear children able to live in a world so compact and closely organized that a defective gear anywhere will threaten to stop the whole machine—a smaller world for which bigger ideas will be necessary. In the past hundred years we have learned to live, competently or crudely, in a country which has doubled in size and population, whose parts have been brought a hundred times closer together in time, and in which sound has been made to travel at the speed of light. Socially and politically we have not kept up with ourselves. Can we be socially adult enough for a civilization in which Main Street is a sky path running clear around the world? Somebody has to be. Americans should have the skill and the will to reach this level if it is attainable by any people, anywhere.

—*New York City Public Schools, photograph by David Rosenfeld*

★ *An opportunity for occupational education leading to constructive employ-*
ment is an obvious necessity for wholesome individual and group development.
Our educational doctrines and practices should be concerned with the whole
man rather than with his intellect alone. Every person needs the satisfaction
of being able to do something well—a skill commensurate with his abilities and
goals.

CHAPTER IV

Background for Morale: The American Scene

FOR HIGH INDIVIDUAL OR GROUP MORALE, whether democratic or antidemocratic, the biochemical and physical needs, the social and psychological needs, and the ideational needs must be satisfied to a significant degree. The levels of motivation and need which are basic to morale are discussed in preceding chapters.

We have said that the specific undertakings of democratic groups and individuals must be based on the ideals of truth, freedom, humanity, dignity of man, and individualism, and that the individual in such a group will be best able to give all that he has in behalf of group undertakings if the following conditions are present: (a) a positive and clear-cut goal of value to the group, (b) a sense of progress and the means of progress toward the goal, (c) a sense of belonging in the group, (d) a sense of status for the members of the group, and (e) democratic leadership for the group.

As educators in the United States face the duty of educating for morale in relation to the long-time goals of democracy in America and in the world at large, they must consider the setting in which the schools have been working and are to work. In view of the fact that zest and devotion to the democratic cause are dependent upon the manner in which human needs are met, it is pertinent to view briefly the strengths and weaknesses of our present society in satisfying human needs and to consider the elements of a program to meet those needs better.

Advances under American Democracy

We readily recognize the many advances that have been made in all aspects of life under American democracy. In fact, social, economic, and political developments in the United States during the last 150 years would be matters of great surprise and disappointment to the monarchists, aristocrats, and antidemocrats of the Revolutionary and post-Revolutionary period, who believed the experiment in democracy would fail and wanted it to fail.

We have, to begin with, the constitutional guarantee of freedom of worship. This guarantee practically always is defended by government officials and other citizens alike, altho side by side with this guarantee and its observance there exists appreciable occupational and social discrimination on religious grounds. The complete separation of church from all aspects of government is, of course, a corollary to the guarantee of freedom of worship. The state and the church have been separated, as have the public school and the church school. We have a secular government, from top to bottom. There are no legal religious qualifications for voting or holding office.

One of the great achievements of American democracy is the development of its secular public-school system. Public education in the United States removed the stamp of class rigidity, sect, and charity from the training of the masses.[1] Ours are schools for the children of all the people. In spite of marked local and state inequalities, the United States offers its people more public education than does almost any other nation, with the result that there is widespread diffusion of knowledge and a high degree of literacy. The extension of public education is noteworthy, not only for the enormously increased school enrolments but also for differentiated courses of study designed to meet the requirements of a complex society and the capacities and interests of children and adolescents. Furthermore, our system of state universities offers opportunities for higher and professional education to thousands of boys and girls who without them would have no means of continuing their education. In fact, among the graduates of every American college and university, privately endowed or publicly supported, will be found men and women who completed their higher education in spite of poverty. We have witnessed an American epic of education for freedom, self-respect, and accomplishment.

Our provisions for adult education thru evening schools and university extension work have enabled men and women of all ages, degrees of capacity, and national origin to acquire knowledge and skills which otherwise they would not have obtained. Our educational doctrines and practices have been concerned with the "whole man" rather than with his intellect alone, for we recognize that

---

[1] Becker, Carl L. *The United States: An Experiment in Democracy.* New York: Harper and Brothers, 1920. p. 277.

the latter cannot be divorced from the rest of the person. Altho not ideal, American public schools and universities do, to a significant extent, help to eliminate inequalities, and they do in some measure enable men and women to enter occupations and professions on more nearly equal terms. At the same time the schools and universities in a measure tend to develop in American men and women attitudes, values, and behavior of a more nearly common, basic, democratic kind.

In the United States the social class systems are less rigid than in most other nations; mobility from one class to another is marked. Many men and women of humble origins have achieved "success" and status thru political, financial, or professional position. Mobility, however, was easier in the nineteenth century than it is now; for then we had an abundance of land and fewer people than we needed, natural resources were being exploited increasingly, and industrial organization was in its early stages. Becker has summarized the situation thus:

> Until recent years the successful transformation of the foreign-born population into "typical" Americans within a single generation has been one of the notable achievements of the United States . . . due . . . to the opportunity of the immigrant to live the life and enjoy the rewards of the ordinary American. Generally speaking, these favorable conditions prevailed up to . . . the decade from 1880 to 1890. . . .
>
> The conditions which so long existed in the United States not only brought about a fair degree of equality among individuals, but they prevented the formation of any defined or persistent class inequalities. Any individual could consent with some cheerfulness to be poor to-day, since there was always an even chance that to-morrow he would be "well fixed." . . . In a country where changes in fortune and social status were so rapid and so common the people inevitably acquired a spirit of buoyant optimism which discounted such inequalities as existed; if they had not equality they projected it into the immediate future, and in that future, rather than in the present, they lived their lives.[2]

The economic and psychological prospects indicated in these quotations were in part dependent upon the westward movement in this country and upon the undeveloped resources and opportunities for the entrepreneur thruout the nation. But this movement, which certainly inspired the common man, came to an end about

---

[2] Becker, Carl L., *op. cit.*, p. 235-36, 308-309.

forty years ago. Something promising and dramatic has been removed from American life. As a nation we do not have the same sense of opportunity as that which prevailed when the western movement was in progress, when resources and land were undeveloped, and when opportunities for "success" seemed open to all. We need now some other motivating conceptions in terms of human development and welfare, higher standards of economic, physical, intellectual, and esthetic living for all—now possible because of the vast economic and technological developments of the last century. Our "new frontiers" will have to be human, social, and political on a worldwide scale rather than only the physical and geographical boundaries of our nation.

Social legislation and awareness of social responsibilities on the part of government have increased in the United States. For example, recent developments are unemployment insurance, old-age pensions, workmen's compensation (for injury), progress in the elimination of child labor and in the abuses of women's labor, the Fair Labor and Standards Act, the NYA, the CCC, the WPA, the Federal Housing Administration, and the Farm Security Administration—all of which were designed to increase the people's security and thus to raise the level of their general welfare. In addition, for some years we have witnessed the growth of the more usual government services which, unlike "social legislation," have not been the subject of bitter controversy and attack. These more usual activities include public libraries, public health services and food inspection, public health nurses, hospitals for the tubercular and for the mentally ill, development of agricultural science under the patronage of federal and state governments, a federal department of commerce to provide service to business and industry at home and abroad, local welfare agencies, and others which we now take for granted. From the point of view of human welfare, and hence devotion to one's form of government and society, the significant aspect of the growth of these public enterprises and services, and those that will come later, is that they or similar enterprises are necessary in a nation that has developed with striking rapidity into a concentrated and complex industrial society.

It has been repeatedly stated in many quarters, and with essential justification, that in the United States we enjoy a higher average standard of living than do the inhabitants of most other countries. On the average, we are better fed, better housed, and better clothed than people in most other nations. We have benefited from epoch-making machines developed for lightening toil and multiplying production of goods; hours of labor have been reduced by one-third or more; fatigue has been reduced; and the "common man" has achieved a new leisure which awaits optimal utilization.

On the whole, we live a much more highly mechanized, labor-saving life, with our automobiles, radios, telephones, mechanical refrigerators, and modern plumbing. Associated, no doubt, with our improved living standards, educational opportunities, and health services are the facts that the average life span has increased and that the mortality rates, especially of infants and young children, have been markedly lowered. It is hardly necessary, however, to point out that we are far from having abolished poverty, slums, and unnecessary illness. Nor, we are constrained to add, is our superiority in mechanized labor-saving devices a test or criterion of democratic living and values, tho admittedly they release human energies for progress in this direction.

The United States has been populated by immigrants from all parts of the world. They have remained here; their children, grand-children, and subsequent generations have stayed on. Resettlement in ancestral native lands has occurred only infrequently; migration to other countries has been negligible. In general, then, it must be true that immigrants and their descendants have found life in the United States more satisfying and more promising than it would have been elsewhere. For this satisfaction and promise rested on a base of religious freedom and political and economic democracy; on the prospect of ready vertical mobility, not in terms of birth but of mentality, personal value, and demonstrated accomplishment. Especially noteworthy in the entire democratic scene and prospect was the public educational system which would facilitate the achievement of democratic equality of opportunity for social and individual development.

The nineteenth century in the United States was an era of promise, an era of the rising man, of the self-made man. It therefore contributed greatly to the growth of democratic convictions in this country and abroad; for the New World was a land of opportunity and freedom, a land where the bonds of social caste could be thrown off, a land where a larger life could be earned and enjoyed.

Deficiencies in the Present Situation

The close of the nineteenth century marked the end of an era. For nearly half a century economic and political changes and complexities have increased until they now can be ignored no longer by a laissez-faire doctrine. And now the whole picture is complicated by the "global" character of life in every country in the international sense, bringing with it an increased emphasis not alone upon economic and political problems but upon national and international problems and upon the eradication of widespread superstition, misinformation, and prejudice as well. "The time has come when the people of the United States must bring all their intelligence and all their idealism to the consideration of the subtler realities of human relations, as they have formerly to the much simpler realities of material existence: this at least they must do if America is to be in the future what it has been in the past—a fruitful experiment in democracy."[3] These words were written nearly twenty-five years ago. There has been some progress in this period, but what are the deficiencies? What remains to be done to improve not only the political and economic life of the nation but "the subtler realities of human relations" as well?

Human needs and behavior, upon which morale is based, do not operate in a vacuum. To evaluate the possibilities, therefore, of developing a higher degree of devotion to our democratic society, it is essential that we know the present state of affairs regarding the most important conditions that are necessary to implement high morale.

ECONOMIC SECURITY

The first and most elemental requirement is a steady and adequate job. The consequent economic security should provide the individual with more than the means of satisfying his biochemical needs. It should give him also a feeling of performing a task that is worthwhile, that is valued in the community, and that provides a basis for group and social status. Yet the unhappy economic and

---

[3] Becker, Carl L., op. cit., p. 333.

unemployment history of American youth during the 1930's is too well known to require detailed repetition.[4]

Since about 1910 the proportion of youth in gainful employment has been declining, and employers were becoming reluctant to hire young workers even before the onset of the depression in 1929. With the depression under way during the 1930's, workers by the hundreds of thousands were dropped, so that many younger employees without experience or seniority rights were excluded from employment.

By 1935 it is probable that of the 21,000,000 youth between sixteen and twenty-four years of age, over 4,000,000 of those out of school were unemployed. In 1937 a federal census showed that of those in the "labor market" between the ages of fifteen and nineteen, 41 percent were unemployed while of those between twenty and twenty-four years of age 24 percent were unemployed.[5] There were in 1940 and 1941 many American youth who, outside of school, knew little other than economic depression, until war jobs or enlistment in the armed forces brought about a change for them.[6]

Another youth employment problem is presented by the fact that the number of farm boys reaching maturity each year is more than twice the number of farms that annually become vacant and thus might be available to them. It is estimated that between 300,-000 and 400,000 farm youth are available annually for nonagrarian employment. The situation is made the more difficult by the fact that many of these surplus farm youth are Negroes from the cotton belt who are confronted with additional and often insuperable barriers in attempting to achieve economic security and status thru occupational and geographic migration.

While it is probably true that after the war large numbers of American soldiers and sailors will be necessary for policing and other services over the world, it may be expected that a large

---

[4] We are concerned here primarily with the problems of youth, since they and children are educators' major responsibility.

[5] American Council on Education, American Youth Commission. *Youth and the Future.* General Report. Washington, D. C.: the Council, 1942. p. 11-12.

[6] As late as January 1941, 2.8 million young people aged fourteen to twenty-four years were unemployed. This was about 24 percent of the total labor force of that age. See: Federal Works Agency, Work Projects Administration. *Monthly Report of Employment and Unemployment.* Special Memorandum No. 13. Washington, D. C.: Work Projects Administration, July 31, 1942. 5 p. (Mimeo.)

portion of our wartime Army and Navy will be demobilized. Simultaneously will come the release of hundreds of thousands, more probably several millions, of men and women from war industries. A large percentage of these industrial workers will be under twenty-five years of age. They will be seeking a peacetime adjustment; they will need jobs. They will constitute a youth problem. If economic and educational laissez faire is adopted as the policy, there will be a piling up of millions of unemployed young workers. To prevent this, the nation requires political and economic statesmanship and planning, on the one hand, and educational statesmanship and planning, on the other. It will be hardly sufficient to repeat the inspirational but statistically dubious slogans that any boy can "rise to the top" if he is willing to work or that "any boy may become President of the United States." Nor will discussions of abstract and antedated notions of "rugged individualism" solve the problem or satisfy the needs of youth. A survey of youth in the fall of 1942 showed that a large majority of them held the belief that everyone would be assured of work after the war.[7] If they prove to be wrong in their belief, the effect will be worse than mere disappointment; it will be a shocking disillusionment, with a prospect of violent reaction. The American Youth Commission has stated:

> Throughout the world for the last generation, there has been a general loss of confidence among the masses of the people in the economic system which we have inherited and adapted from nineteenth-century capitalism. It seems obvious that the loss of confidence is directly related to the failure of the present system to provide continuously a sufficient number of opportunities for employment. Young people especially are critical. Their own experience in many cases has included periods of unemployment, and has often been marked by a process of occupational frustration even when they were employed.[8]

Adults have the responsibility of providing occupational education and employment opportunity so that essential human needs may be satisfied and responsibilities assumed at the appropriate stages in the development of youth. The relative importance of agriculture has been declining, the importance of industry and commerce has been increasing, and large corporations are the most conspicuous

---

[7] Griffin, Alan. "Fortune Surveys Youth." *Progressive Education* 20: 16-19; January 1943. ¶ Also: School and Society. "The Second *Fortune* Survey." *School and Society* 56: 573-74; December 12, 1942.
[8] American Council on Education, American Youth Commission, *op. cit.*, p. 81.

factors in our economic life. In the last hundred years we have seen rapid industrialization, concentration of wealth and industrial power, concentrated control of natural resources, concentrated control of avenues of transportation and communication, and the disappearance of free land. The net result of these trends is a drastic decline in opportunities for self-employment and greatly increased individual dependence upon the prevailing economic system, principally upon the more powerful elements in that system.

Even the self-employed adult is often subject to the operations of the more powerful economic elements, as, for example, the small farmer, the grocery store owner, the small shopkeeper in general, the small manufacturer, and often the professional person. Thus most individual adults are hardly in a position to give their sons and daughters occupational security and status. Such security and status, then, become matters of social responsibility. In the postwar period, economic reconstruction to achieve sustained full employment under conditions of peace will be a most difficult yet a most urgent objective of American economic and educational planning. Effective planning and execution of plans will be especially necessary for those in our population who are skeptical regarding democratic organization of a state. The Educational Policies Commission states:

It has been estimated on the basis of indirect evidence that 10 to 15 percent of the population doubts the ability of democracy to deal satisfactorily with its economic problems. For at least this portion of the total population and probably for others as well, a most important contribution to morale would be a feeling of assurance that this democracy can and will cope with its economic problems.[9]

To achieve under our changed conditions and by new methods the necessary economic freedom and security is one of the urgent tasks of the coming years. Educational and economic planning by and in cooperation with the government (at whatever level) for the purpose of the greatest good is not, as some fear, a loss of freedom.

. . . if the democratic way of life is to survive we must give to the traditional concept of freedom a more positive content. The traditional concept

---

[9] National Education Association and American Association of School Administrators, Educational Policies Commission. *Education and the Morale of a Free People.* Washington, D. C.: the Commission, November 1941. p. 10.

of individual liberty is essentially negative. The freedom it emphasizes is free-dom from constraint, . . that is to say, governmental constraint. In the economic realm the result of freeing the individual from governmental constraint is that today far too many people are always in danger of losing those positive goods without which freedom from governmental constraint is of no value. What the average man now needs is the opportunity to acquire by his own effort, in an occupation for which he is fitted, the economic security which is essential to decent and independent living. This opportunity has now disappeared for something like a quarter of the working population. . . . it can only be restored, if at all, by such governmental regulations of our economy as may be neces-sary to enable private economic enterprise to function effectively and for the common good.[10]

MORALE DURING UNEMPLOYMENT

Unemployment has plagued this country periodically and will continue to do so unless there is economic and educational planning in place of a policy of laissez faire. A number of suggestive studies have already been made on the problem of morale during unem-ployment; and, tho the findings are not entirely consistent, dif-ferences appear to be in the matter of the degree to which morale is depressed. For example, Bakke [11] found progressive, serious deteri-oration of personality among unemployed men as their periods of joblessness were extended. Watson [12] found some positive cor-relation between deterioration of morale and length of unemploy-ment, but by no means as much as did Bakke. The difference in findings seems, however, to be a matter of analysis rather than of essential fact. Watson reports that morale problems due to unem-ployment are more serious among "working class people" than among those in the "higher occupations" (writers, salesmen, teach-ers, bankers, and social workers). Lowest morale was indicated by the unemployed labor groups: unskilled, semiskilled, skilled, and white-collar. He found also that high competence in almost any area is associated with better maintenance of morale.

Watson's findings are readily understandable, for those in the higher occupations are economically better able to withstand loss

10 Becker, Carl L. *Modern Democracy*. New Haven, Conn.: Yale University Press, 1941. p. 62-63.
11 Bakke, E. Wight. *The Unemployed Man*. New York: E. P. Dutton and Co., 1934. 308 p.
¶ Also: Bakke, E. Wight. *Citizens Without Work*. New Haven, Conn.: Yale University Press, 1940. 311 p.
12 Watson, Goodwin. "Morale During Unemployment." *Civilian Morale*. Second Yearbook, Society for the Psychological Study of Social Issues. Boston: Houghton Mifflin Co., 1942. Chapter 16, p. 273-348. ¶ Further evidence on low morale among the unemployed is given by: Rundquist, Edward A., and Sletto, Raymond F. *Personality in the Depression*. Minneapolis, Minn.: University of Min-nesota Press, 1936. p. 337.

or decrease of income. They have had the status which gives them confidence in their ability and security; they have the occupational and educational resources which place them in a preferred occupational status; and some regard themselves, perhaps subconsciously, as members of the preferred classes. Furthermore, those in the "higher occupations" enjoy better housing and physical conditions, under which occupational frustration can be the better tolerated. There is, then, a clearly demonstrable relationship between socio-economic levels and degree of morale.

The unemployed youth faces special psychological hardships. His family, to obtain direct relief, must pauperize itself thru the sale of its assets. It must continue pauperized and move its residence to an inferior environment if possible. This whole process is humiliating and at times dangerous to the development of children in the family. In periods of unemployment, youth's period of self-support is deferred while the period of dependence and "economic childhood" is prolonged. Feelings of futility and insecurity increase, accompanied at times by apathy and at other times by bitterness or anger. The many thousands of unemployed, defeated, and angered young members of the professions and university graduates formed a substantial segment of the Nazi-Fascist groups which flourished in Europe during the latter 1920's and the 1930's.[13]

An opportunity for occupational education and constructive employment is an obvious necessity for wholesome individual and group development. At the same time, occupational guidance and training must be realistic, in the sense that youth's wishful and at times dramatic thinking and aspirations have to be directed into activities within their range of abilities and within the range of the social and economic requirements. Otherwise the realities of employment, as well as of unemployment, may prove to be disappointing and disillusioning.

PERSONAL RECOGNITION ON THE JOB

Altho a job and a steady income will furnish the means whereby certain human needs may be satisfied, the job in itself is not enough to satisfy *all* human needs. A study of factory workers indicated

[13] Ulich, Robert. "Germany." *Educational Yearbook, 1936.* International Institute, Teachers College, Columbia University. New York: Teachers College, Columbia University, 1936. p. 339-61. ¶ Also: Kotschnig, Walter M. *Unemployment in the Learned Professions.* London: Oxford University Press, 1937. 347 p.

that, aside from security, personal attention given to individual workers plays a part in raising the level of productivity. This may be due to the enhanced feeling of status as a member of a group that results from individual attention.[14]

In those industrial plants where labor-management committees have been organized and permitted to function genuinely, production has increased and the morale of the workers has improved. Union-management cooperation has been effective not only in matters of wage structure but in job evaluation, wage incentive systems, and merchandising and selling:

> The worker . . . has a highly specific knowledge, drawn from his intimate daily contact with the process on which he is working and the machine he operates. As a result, he can often assist management materially in discovering ways of improving the process, of reducing waste, of increasing the efficiency of a machine.
> . . . he is frequently able to view the process on which he is working with a perspective which would be impossible for management. . . . The literature of union-management cooperation contains example after example of suggestions submitted by workers that have proved practical after management has overcome its initial skepticism sufficiently to experiment with them.[15]

Industrial plants and commercial organizations—in fact, all organizations—are on a sound psychological basis when they respect the dignity of each worker, promote friendly democratic relations, and give the workers a significant share in determining policies. The worker—whether in factory, office, or schoolroom—then is more than a mechanical cog in a machine, to be removed, inserted, or altered at the will of someone else. He then has a personal relationship to the situation beyond the mere performance of a monotonous assigned task which in itself offers no personal scope and few if any psychological satisfactions.

Under unsatisfying working conditions, all increases in pay, paid vacations, shorter hours, and better physical provisions for employees are significant, and indeed essential, in promoting morale,

---

[14] Roethlisberger, F. J. *Management and Morale.* Cambridge, Mass.: Harvard University Press, 1941. 194 p.

[15] Knickerbocker, Irving, and McGregor, Douglas. *Union-Management Cooperation: A Psychological Analysis.* Cambridge, Mass.: Department of Economics and Social Science, Massachusetts Institute of Technology, 1943. p. 13-14. Reprinted from *Personnel,* Vol. 19, No. 3, by American Management Association, New York, N. Y. ¶ See also: Golden, Clinton S., and Ruttenberg, Harold J. *The Dynamics of Industrial Democracy.* New York: Harper and Brothers, 1942. 358 p. ¶ Hartmann, George W., and Newcomb, Theodore, editors, *Industrial Conflict: A Psychological Interpretation.* First Yearbook, Society for the Psychological Study of Social Issues. New York: Dryden Press, 1939. 583 p.

because they provide the means whereby the individual may obtain the satisfactions he does not get in the work itself. In addition to these provisions, however, the attitudes of management must be such as to provide the psychological satisfactions that come with recognition of and respect for every worker, for every individual, as a person.

Labor organizations have contributed heavily to the morale of working men and women because they feel that, with the help of these organizations, they are getting somewhere in their efforts to acquire the means of a larger life. A few labor organizations, furthermore, have been successfully concerned with the educational, esthetic, social, and political development of their members, as well as with their economic welfare. These organizations thereby contribute to the satisfaction of their members' human needs, beyond those found on the job or brought within reach thru higher wages.[16] On the other hand, there are labor organizations which have concentrated solely on wage increases and improved working conditions—justified and necessary tho they are—to the exclusion of other aspects of their members' lives and facets of their personalities. Furthermore, on the negative side is the fact that some labor leaders, just as some employers, emphasize the cleavage between worker and employer. This tendency on the part of both labor and management must be reversed; for as the cleavage is reduced by a sense of respect and partnership on both sides, so will the workers' various and essential satisfactions be enhanced.

POSSESSION OF A SKILL

In spite of the modern industrial assembly line and routine machine types of occupation, there are still many forms of employment in which a high level of skill is required. Furthermore, even for those men and women whose regular jobs are of the extremely routine kind, the possession of a skill is a desideratum for their more wholesome development. If a person's occupation does not require the practice of a skill, then it is desirable that one be developed as a leisure-time activity. To be able to exercise a skill in one's leisure time requires, of course, a working day short enough

---

[16] John Dewey Society. *Workers' Education in the United States.* Fifth Yearbook. New York: Harper and Brothers, 1941. 338 p.

and an income large enough to permit the pursuit of an extra-vocational activity. In other words, what our modern industriali-zation fails to provide in psychological satisfactions on the job must be provided for in other ways.

Every person needs the satisfaction of being able to do some-thing well—a skill commensurate with his capacities. Practically everyone can learn some skill reasonably well. Educational theory has long recognized and insisted upon the essential principle that education and training at all levels should be consonant with the individual's abilities and goals. It is, therefore, the business of educational agencies to find out what those might be in every indi-vidual and to help in their development. Yet an appreciable number of Americans do not, for one reason or another, get enough school-ing to enable them to develop any particular competence or skills in and with the help of the schools.

It is known that the average education of the American adult is today about nine grades. Studies made by the American Youth Commission and other agencies show that of those pupils whose schooling ended before they completed high school, at least 50 percent left for sheer lack of financial resources. It is also a well-known fact among educators that many pupils who leave before completing high school do so because of the irrelevancy of their studies to their lives and because these studies fail to provide them with information and skills that will be significant for them.

The amount of educational unpreparedness and the frequency of illiteracy among men called by the selective service reveal dra-matically that "equal educational opportunity for all" is as yet an unattained ideal. While it is difficult to break down selective service and induction board statistics (because of broad and over-lapping categories), it is possible to observe several important items in these data. The 17,356,495 men who had registered by September 15, 1941, included 347,038, or 2.0 percent, who were so entirely illiterate that they signed their registration cards with a mark.[17] By April 30, 1943, selective service boards and armed forces induction authorities had examined about 8,328,000 regis-trants, of whom 287,000, or about 3.4 percent, had been rejected

---

[17] Director of Selective Service. *Selective Service in Peacetime.* First Report, 1940-41. Washing-ton, D. C.: Government Printing Office, 1942. p. 175.

because of educational deficiencies.[18] The U. S. Census Bureau has estimated that 1,458,000 men of draft age (eighteen thru forty-four years) in 1940 had not reached the military acceptance standard of fourth-grade schooling.[19]

It is noteworthy to observe that whereas for the eighteen- thru forty-four-year group of registrants examined 3.4 percent were rejected because of educational deficiencies, only 2.0 percent of the men in the eighteen- and nineteen-year-old group were disqualified for that reason.[20] This is gratifying and consonant with the educational trend of the last twenty years. Another striking fact is revealed, however, when the eighteen- and nineteen-year white group is compared with the same Negro age group. Of the former, 1.2 percent were rejected because of educational deficiencies, whereas of the latter, 12.2 percent were rejected for that reason.

Some of the men rejected because of educational deficiencies may be suffering from mental deficiency rather than lack of school opportunity. However, the total rejections thru April 30, 1943, covered not only the 287,000 educationally deficient but also 100,-500 who were rejected because of mental deficiency.[21] In any event, the number of men who, under favorable conditions, do not have the capacity to "achieve" the fourth-grade level in reading and writing, by the time they are adolescents, would constitute about 1 percent of our population. Yet in 1940 there were about 2,800,000 persons in the United States twenty-five years of age or over who had not completed even one year of schoolwork, that is, 3.7 percent of the entire population in those age limits. There were 10,105,000 persons who had not finished the fifth grade in schoolwork, or 13.5 percent of the total population of this age group.[22] It cannot be maintained that more than one-eighth of our population are not educable thru or beyond five grades.

[18] U. S. 78th Congress, 1st Session, House Committee on Appropriations. *Hearings on Labor-Federal Security Agency Appropriation Bill for 1944.* Washington, D. C.: Government Printing Office, 1943. Part III, "War Manpower Commission," p. 226.

[19] U. S. Department of Commerce, Bureau of the Census. *The Educational Level of Men of Military Age in the United States.* Sixteenth Census of the United States: 1940. Series P-9, No. 15. Washington, D. C.: the Department, 1942. p. 3. (For the eighteen thru thirty-four age group, 790,320 had not completed four years of school.)

[20] Rowntree, Leonard G.; McGill, Kenneth H.; and Edwards, Thomas I. "Causes of Rejection and the Incidence of Defects Among 18 and 19 Year Old Selective Service Registrants." *Journal of the American Medical Association* 123: 183; September 1943.

[21] U. S. 78th Congress, 1st Session, House Committee on Appropriations, *op. cit.*, p. 226.

[22] U. S. Department of Commerce, Bureau of the Census. *Educational Attainment of the Population 25 Years Old and Over in the United States: 1940.* Sixteenth Census of the United States: 1940. Series P-10, No. 8. Washington, D. C.: the Department, 1942. p. 4.

The educational status of our population is, however, considerably improved over what it was in 1917-18. At that time the average adult educational level was about six grades, as compared with nine at present. At that time, also, only about 9 percent of the drafted soldiers were graduates of high schools, as compared with 41 percent at present.[23] Today, therefore, skills, information, and general competence are more widespread and, in the general population, at a higher level than twenty-five years ago. This encouraging condition has also another aspect, for with more widespread and increasing skill and competence in our population the discrepancy between training and unemployment is increased, as is the likelihood of dissatisfaction that comes with unemployment.

The federal government made good progress with its CCC and NYA training projects, as emergency training and employment organizations. These two organizations gave thousands of young men and women necessary experience of work and achievement and even adventure, an opportunity to develop skills, to become equipped for jobs in our economic order, and thereby to find their places as accepted members of their communities. It is true that there were valid objections to the organization and control of the CCC and NYA. And while it is true that these two organizations are not needed during the war, nevertheless an improved substitute will be necessary after the war.

Without here attempting to specify the particular form federal educational support should take, it can be maintained that it is an obligation of educators to plan and work for federal financial assistance to educational organizations and facilities which will include provisions for work experience appropriate to youth of both sexes similar in type to that formerly offered by the CCC and NYA. But in formulating plans for the future, it is necessary to remember that these agencies began as part of a relief program. They met an essential educational need only in part. Any new plans must rest on the principle that this type of education is a legitimate and essential part of educational planning and operation *in a functioning educational system*. The new educational plans and organization should be such as will enable educators to surpass

---

[23] U. S. Department of Commerce, Bureau of the Census. *The Educational Level of Men of Military Age in the United States.* Sixteenth Census of the United States: 1940. Series P-9, No. 15. Washington, D. C.: the Department, 1942. p. 1.

the achievements of the CCC and NYA, thru the availability of funds provided by the federal government and handled by existing state and local educational bodies. If this goal is to be attained, state and local educators will have to be ready with plans based upon a broadened conception of the role of public schools in contributing to the development of human resources in a democratic society.[24] To neglect a form of education and training which will develop abilities, skills, and economic competence in our youth and give them the experience and feeling of self-respect, and a sense of achievement and progress, as well as a feeling of social-economic value, is to inflict a defeat upon several of the most important aspects of democratic living.

Our efforts to advance the educational level of the American people are being weakened, during the war emergency, by widespread attempts to set aside child labor restrictions, by frequent violations of these laws, and by attempts to suspend school attendance laws.

Child labor has increased at an unprecedented rate. Demands that young people be released from school to work on farms, in stores, in service industries, and in factories have become alarming to those who put the education and welfare of children before the commercial value of their services. Thousands have left school for work and other thousands are working outside school hours, often at jobs too strenuous to be carried in addition to schoolwork. The 1940 Census reported more than 900,000 minors of fourteen thru seventeen years of age employed.[25] Of this number about one-fourth were fourteen and fifteen years old. In April 1943 nearly 2,500,000 boys and girls fourteen thru seventeen years of age were at work; more than 500,000 of them, fourteen or fifteen years of age.

The number of work permits or age certificates for full-time or part-time work issued for minors fourteen thru seventeen years of age in 1941 was more than double the 1940 total. Another increase of nearly 100 percent occurred in September 1942 as

[24] See: National Education Association and American Association of School Administrators, Educational Policies Commission. *Education for All American Youth.* Washington, D. C.: the Commission. (In preparation.)

[25] U. S. Department of Commerce, Bureau of the Census. *Preliminary Figures on Employment Status of Persons 14 Years Old and Over . . . March 24-30, 1940.* Sixteenth Census of the United States: 1940. Series P-4, No. 9. Washington, D. C.: the Department, 1941. p. 4.

compared with September 1941. In the whole year 1942 more than 150,000 permits and certificates were reported to the U. S. Children's Bureau as issued for fourteen- and fifteen-year-old children and nearly 800,000 for boys and girls sixteen and seventeen years old. In the first six months of 1943—a period which includes the month of June, when much vacation work begins—there was an increase of more than 100 percent over the number issued in the first six months of 1942: 107 percent for the sixteen- and seventeen-year-olds and 173 percent for the fourteen- and fifteen-year-olds. Large numbers of these children, tho it is not known how many, had left school for work. Unfortunate as is the trek of fourteen- thru seventeen-year-olds from school to jobs, it is even more deplorable to find that employment of children under fourteen is mounting in agriculture, trades, stores, and miscellaneous jobs subject to little legal restriction.

Time and again during the last two years suggestions were made that child labor regulations be suspended or that school children be sent to work in violation of school attendance laws because of the war. During 1942 two states amended their attendance laws to permit school children to work in agriculture. During 1943, sixty-one legislative acts relating to the employment of young workers were passed in twenty-seven states; fifty-four of these acts contained some backward steps, such as lowering age limits and relaxing standards as to hours, night work, and other conditions of work. Several states authorized the employment of children under sixteen years of age in agricultural work and for night work in bowling alleys. Compulsory school attendance requirements have been affected also.[26]

With the proper use of manpower there should never be an occasion during this war when child labor would be necessary. While there can be no objection to youth fourteen years of age or older working before and after school and during vacation periods, under proper protection and working conditions, there should be general opposition to lowering of school attendance standards and to any breakdown in the enforcement of school attendance laws.

[26] U. S. Department of Labor, Children's Bureau, and Federal Security Agency, U. S. Office of Education. *Back to School!* Washington, D. C.: Children's Bureau, 1943. 12 p. ¶ U. S. Department of Labor, Children's Bureau, and Federal Security Agency, U. S. Office of Education. *Legislative Trends in Child Labor: 1943.* Washington, D. C.: Children's Bureau, 1943. 2 p.

Exploitation of child labor is a shortsighted social policy. It helps to defeat the aims of the American democratic educational principle and ideal that all children shall have an equal opportunity to foster and develop their capacities, to become well-qualified citizens, and to lead as broad a life as possible.

THE NEED TO BELONG

The desire for recognition and "belonging" in one's society is a universal one. It is the desire and need to be well thought of, to have the approbation of one's society, and to enhance one's standing in it. Individuals have a strong need to share in the life of their immediate communities and of their society in general.

In most complex societies like our own, there are unfortunately subgroups of *caste* and *class*, with special status and privileges accruing to some, whereas special restrictions are imposed upon others, among the latter being the "minority groups." This is best illustrated in the United States by the status of the Negro. There is the usual *caste* distinction as between white and Negro in general. The Negro's civil and economic opportunities, and in many areas his political rights, are severely restricted. If he follows the conventions of the system he is expected to accept a variety of discriminations. The Negro, regardless of individual capacity or achievement, is forced to adopt a role of personal and social inferiority. Such caste distinction cannot help but produce continued and cumulative frustrations and resentment in the Negro, adult and child alike, with consequent unwholesome effects upon individual personality.[27]

Similar frustrations, varying only in degree and based on *class* distinctions, are experienced by other minority or disadvantaged groups: Italians; Orientals; Mexicans; North American Indians; Jews; those from the Balkans, Near East, and the Middle East; "foreigners" in general; and day laborers and domestic servants. On the other side of the fence are the dominant groups who enjoy perquisites which are denied the "lower classes" or only grudgingly permitted them.

---

[27] Davis, Allison, and Dollard, John. *Children of Bondage*. Prepared for the American Youth Commission. Washington, D. C.: American Council on Education, 1940. 299 p. ¶ Also: Warner, W. Lloyd. "American Caste and Class." *American Journal of Sociology* 42: 234-37; September 1936. ¶ Also: Warner, W. Lloyd, and Lunt, Paul S. *The Social Life of a Modern Community*. New Haven, Conn.: Yale University Press, 1941. 460 p.

Individuals who are members of the minority and disadvantaged groups, treated as inferiors by reason of an undemocratic caste and class system, often develop feelings of anxiety and insecurity with regard to themselves and their children. Feelings of suspicious discontent, and at times resentment, grow out of their well-founded conviction that they will not get a square deal at the hands of those in the favored groups. Eventually they may and often do develop an attitude of apathy and inertia, consequent on feelings of inferiority; for they believe they do not have at stake anything of importance. The attitudes resulting from denial of political or economic opportunity to the youth of minority and disadvantaged groups will be a serious element of weakness in the peacetime morale of this country.

Some minority groups suffer from overcrowded housing and inadequate medical facilities, with consequent impairment of health. The crimes committed by their members are frequently magnified, with consequent unjust impairment of their reputations as citizens. They often are subjected to segregation in schools, recreation centers, theaters, clubs, transportation vehicles, and the United States Army and Navy. They are excluded from some skilled trades and professions and restricted in others; they are excluded from some labor unions.

These conditions, attended by attacks and outbreaks such as we witnessed in 1943 in various parts of the country, are surely destructive of democracy; for the segregated and restricted groups come to look with suspicion not only on the dominant groups but on the very government itself which sanctions or permits such a state of affairs. These conditions and practices are a denial of human needs and are wasteful of human potentialities and resources.

In this connection, the status of the Negro is most difficult and serious. The problem is not one that can be solved overnight; for it has a long and involved history, it is interwoven with cultural patterns, and it impinges upon strong attitudes. Yet the Negro's status and contributions could in a relatively short time be improved thru better housing, thru the removal of job barriers, thru increased opportunity for counseling, education, and training, thru much better and more extensive provisions for health education and

TABLE 1.—SCHOOL ATTENDANCE AMONG NEGRO CHILDREN, BY AGE GROUPS, 1910-40, UNITED STATES CENSUS

Year	Percent of children in school		
	7-13 years	14-15 years	16-17 years
1	2	3	4
1910............................	64.1	58.3	35.5
1920............................	76.5	68.7	39.2
1930............................	87.3	78.1	46.3
1940 [a]............................	91.3	82.2	52.9

Source: U. S. Department of Commerce, Bureau of the Census. Population, Volume II. Fifteenth Census of the United States: 1930. Washington, D. C.: Government Printing Office, 1933. p. 1096. ¶ U. S. Department of Commerce, Bureau of the Census. School Attendance for Persons 5 to 24 Years of Age in the United States. Sixteenth Census of the United States: 1940. Series P-10, No. 17. Washington, D. C.; the Department, 1942. p. 6.

[a] The increase between 1930 and 1940 is greater than the table indicates, for school attendance in the 1940 Census was determined on a more restricted basis than in earlier years. Until 1940 any child who had attended school at any time between September 1 and the census date was counted as an attendant. In 1940 only those who had attended school during the month of March were included.

medical care, and thru joint Negro-white commissions and conferences made up of men and women of goodwill representing both groups.

Some progress certainly has been made. School attendance among Negro children has risen markedly, as shown in Table 1. In 1941, 4800 Negroes received degrees in chemistry, engineering, other sciences, and the liberal arts. In the same year 56,000 Negroes finished industrial, clerical, trades, and professional courses.[28] Many Negroes are now preparing to be nurses, stenographers, and clerks, while a number have already become employees in some departments of the federal government. Some of the federal housing projects have been designed primarily for the Negro population. The federal government and certain states have made provisions or passed legislation against discriminatory employment practices.[29]

[28] United States News. "Negroes and the War: New Racial Conflicts." United States News 13: 20-21; December 4, 1942.

[29] For constructive suggestions see: Davis, John A. How Management Can Integrate Negroes in War Industries. Committee on Discrimination in Employment. Albany, N. Y.: New York State War Council, 1942. 43 p.

In a number of cities where salaries of Negro teachers were inferior to those of white teachers, the rates have been equalized or the differences have been appreciably reduced. In other cities, plans for gradual equalization have been put into effect, while in still others programs of adjustment are under consideration.[30] In the conferences and planning leading to these adjustments, both groups of educators and laymen concerned—white and Negro—have demonstrated a high degree of cooperation and mutual understanding. A federal court decision has given legal sanction to the Negro's claim of salary equality in teaching by requiring that equal salaries be paid both white and Negro teachers. Salary equalization does more than simply improve the economic status of Negro teachers. It redounds to the benefit of their pupils, for these teachers are now able to advance their professional education. All the foregoing are moves in the right direction.

The problem of discriminatory employment practices is not, however, an aspect solely of racial discrimination. Among groups of white workers there is fear of serious economic competition if Negroes should get equal work opportunity. This is understandable in view of our unemployment history of the 1930's and our previous cycles of employment and unemployment. If there were economic security for white workers, they would not fear Negro competition. The problem, then, of Negro employment is intimately associated with the general economic welfare and security of our entire population.

Frustration and bitterness can be detrimental in war also. In times of war, however, these minority groups in the United States are found loyal and eager to participate in the defense of their country, not only because they rightly fear something worse at the hands of a victorious Nazi-Fascist enemy but because with the help of their leaders they have come to see the slow progress of political and economic democracy and to envision continued progress, and also because some political leaders hold out the prospect of a better world for them. Moreover, war activity gives them a feeling of participation and importance lacking in their peacetime lives.

---

[30] National Education Association, Research Division. *Recent Adjustments in Salaries of Negro Teachers.* Washington, D. C.: the Association, April 1, 1942. 8 p. (Mimeo.) ¶ National Education Association, Committee on Equal Opportunity. *Progress and Problems in Equal Pay for Equal Work.* Washington, D. C.: the Association, June 1939. 30 p.

Prejudice of any kind against a minority group constitutes a threat to the unity and common democratic purposes of the total American society. In implementing one of the basic principles of our Declaration of Independence and of our Constitution—namely, that all men are equal before the law and in their rights to educational, economic, and social opportunity—the American schools, public and private, have a major role to fill. The schools must teach what science teaches, that is, that domestic and foreign policies and practices based upon alleged racial superiority are without basis in scientific fact. The problem of racial attitudes and prejudices, as they relate to both domestic and international relationships, is essentially one of education in the broadest sense. Since each individual has learned his attitudes and prejudices in his environment, it becomes a problem of education as to whether they shall be perpetuated or whether antidemocratic attitudes may not be unlearned. The Nazi-Fascist ideology would perpetuate the myth of the "master race"; the democratic ideal demands that the brotherhood of man and the value of all mankind be taught.

Some educators, in fact, are now contributing to the learning of desirable attitudes and to the unlearning of unsound and damaging ones in respect to race and cultural differences. They are seeking to understand in their own and other communities the cultural forces as found in family, church, school, social, and occupational groups, which consequently determine the development of the distinctive patterns of community and individual life. The task is to recognize the diversity of racial, religious, ethnic, and socio-economic subgroups within our population and to integrate them in the interest of national unity and welfare.[31] Our racial differences and diversity of national origin need not unfit us for participation and leadership in a free world; they might, rather, be used as a school for international brotherhood.

A person living in the United States will feel he is part of America and will believe in and defend its institutions if the same occupations

<hr />

[31] On planning a program of intercultural education, selecting and organizing materials, and methods and technics to be used from Grade I thru Grade XII, see: Vickery, William E., and Cole, Stewart G. *Intercultural Education in American Schools.* New York: Harper and Brothers, 1943. 214 p. ¶ Teaching materials at the secondary-school level may be found in: Benedict, Ruth, and Ellis, Mildred. *Race and Cultural Relations: America's Answer to the Myth of a Master Race.* Problems in American Life, Unit No. 5. Washington, D. C.: National Association of Secondary-School Principals and National Council for the Social Studies, departments of the National Education Association, 1942. 60 p.

are open to him as to anyone else, if he enjoys the same rights and privileges as others, and if he is able to lead much the same sort of life. If minority or disadvantaged groups get their human and constitutional rights in twentieth century United States only thru having to fight for them and if those rights are grudgingly granted by the dominant groups, there will be continued intergroup friction, encouraged by seductive and inflammatory leaders who promise a favorable solution of all problems if they are followed. If, however, those rights are achieved by all groups thru mutual understanding and cooperation, we may expect not only improvement in the status of the disadvantaged groups but a rise in the general welfare of the entire nation. Conversely, the denial of human, constitutional, and economic rights to any portion of our population lowers the general welfare and the spiritual level of the nation as a whole.

HEALTH AND INCOME

Good health and optimal physical development are not only a physical necessity for satisfactory living; they are symptomatic also of adequate provisions for this essential aspect of human development. Conversely, the prevalence of physical defects and preventable illnesses is symptomatic of social indifference and neglect.

The Director of Selective Service has reported that of the first 2,000,000 men examined 45 percent (900,000) were disqualified because of physical and mental defects (not including those rejected for educational deficiencies).[32] Among the most common causes were dental defects, defective eyes, cardiovascular diseases, musculoskeletal defects, venereal diseases, mental and nervous defects, and hernia. These figures represent the period prior to May 31, 1941. The high percentage of rejection is no doubt due in part to the high standards of physical fitness applied in selective service before the United States entered the war. Actually, of course, it may be that many of the causes of these early rejections do not seriously impair the individual for ordinary civilian occupations, and some of the defects may not seriously affect his health or longevity.

After December 7, 1941, physical standards for military service were appreciably relaxed. However, by April 30, 1943, the number

---

[32] Selective Service System. *Analysis of Reports of Physical Examination.* Medical Statistics Bulletin No. 1. Washington, D. C.: Selective Service System, National Headquarters, November 10, 1941. 31 p.

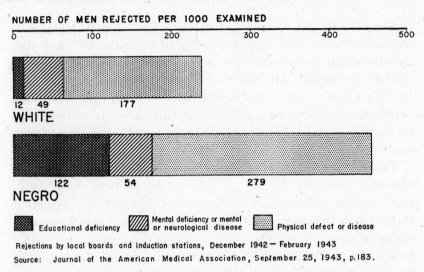

NUMBER OF MEN REJECTED PER 1000 EXAMINED

WHITE
12   49   177

NEGRO
122   54   279

▓ Educational deficiency   ▨ Mental deficiency or mental or neurological disease   ▒ Physical defect or disease

Rejections by local boards and induction stations, December 1942 — February 1943

Source: Journal of the American Medical Association, September 25, 1943, p.183.

FIGURE I.—REJECTIONS OF SELECTIVE SERVICE REGISTRANTS
AGED 18 AND 19 YEARS

of men rejected because of physical and mental defects (not including education) had reached 2,583,000, which was about 31 percent of those examined. The principal decreases (or relaxations of standards) were in defects of eyes and teeth.[33] Wartime conditions apparently led to stricter standards with respect to mental disease and venereal disease, as the rates of rejections for these causes were much higher for the entire period than for the period ending in May 1941.[34]

The highest rate of induction is in the eighteen- and nineteen-year-old group, but even in this young group the rate of rejection has been just about 25 percent because of physical defects, mental diseases, and educational deficiencies, taking white and Negro registrants as a whole.[35] When the two groups are separately considered, however, we have a different story. In the white group of eighteen to nineteen years, 22.6 percent were rejected for reasons of physical defects and mental diseases, whereas in the Negro group of eighteen- and nineteen-year-olds 33.3 percent were rejected for the same reasons. In the white youth of this age, syphilis was a cause of re-

[33] U. S. 78th Congress, 1st Session, House Committee on Appropriations, *op. cit.*, p. 226.
[34] For the entire period up to April 30, 1943, the two leading causes for rejection on physical or mental grounds were "mental disease," the principal cause for rejection of 13.9 percent of those rejected; and syphilis, the cause for 10.5 percent.
[35] Rowntree, Leonard G.; McGill, Kenneth H.; and Edwards, Thomas I., *op. cit.*, p. 182-83.

jection for only 0.2 percent, but in the Negro youth of eighteen to nineteen years syphilis caused rejection of 11.2 percent. These data and the conditions they represent are a challenge to educators, health officials, the medical profession, government officials, and the country as a whole. Medical and dental examinations in the schools are perfunctory; most of the smaller cities and towns are without clinical facilities; and in larger cities clinical facilities are sadly inadequate.

This country from a purely selfish group viewpoint, regardless of individual morale, is paying the price of the physical neglect of its men; for the military services are being deprived of hundreds of thousands of fighting men because of many preventable or remediable defects. If communities, schools, physicians, and public health officers will utilize the selective service findings by instituting necessary health education and medical services, the selective service will have contributed substantially to national health.

Altho there still remains much to be done in research on nutrition and deficiency diseases, there is at present on these subjects a large and valuable body of knowledge which can be made available to pupils and adults. The spreading of information on health and nutrition will, however, not solve the problem. Information must be implemented to be effective. Implementation is basically an economic problem.

In 1941 a family of four required about $2100 a year to live in an urban community in modest comfort and with an adequate diet.[36] Yet in 1941, as Table 2 shows, more than half of America's families were living on annual incomes of less than $2000.[37] Millions of children were growing up in families having incomes of $1000 or less annually. Thus, even under conditions of increased employment and higher wages in defense production in 1941, a large proportion of

---

[36] The Bureau of Human Nutrition and Home Economics has estimated that in June 1943 a moderate-cost wartime diet for an urban family of four could be purchased for about $18.50 a week, or $962 for a year. (U. S. Department of Agriculture, Bureau of Human Nutrition and Home Economics. *Wartime Diets for Good Nutrition.* Washington, D. C.: the Department, September 1943. 3 p. Mimeo.) At June *1941* prices this would have been about $715 for a year for food. Data of the Bureau of Labor Statistics show that urban families of four in the income range of $1500 to $2500 spend about one-third of their income on food; three times $715 equals $2145 for a total living cost that would include diet at moderate cost. (Williams, Faith M., and Hanson, Alice C. *Money Disbursements of Wage Earners and Clerical Workers, 1934-36, Summary Volume.* U. S. Dept. of Labor, Bureau of Labor Statistics, Bulletin No. 638. Washington, D. C.: Government Printing Office, 1941. p. 44.)

[37] U. S. Department of Labor, Bureau of Labor Statistics. *Spending and Saving of the Nation's Families in Wartime.* Bulletin No. 723. Washington, D. C.: Government Printing Office, 1942. p. 2. ¶ See also: *Monthly Labor Review* 55: 700-13; October 1942.

TABLE 2.—PERCENT DISTRIBUTION OF AMERICAN FAMILIES, BY MONEY INCOME, 1941

Income class, based on net income in money	Percent of families in each income class		
	Nonfarm (Urban and rural nonfarm)	Farm	All families
1	2	3	4
Negative income (net losses)........	{ 8%	2%	{ 16%
$0 to $500........................		32	
$500 to $1,000....................	14	25	19
$1,000 to $1,500..................	16	15	16
$1,500 to $2,000..................	16	11	14
$2,000 to $3,000..................	27	9	20
$3,000 to $5,000..................	13	{ 6	10
$5,000 and over...................	6		5
Total......................	100	100	100
Average money income..........	$1,641	$ 750	$1,481
Average income in kind.........	157	530	211
Average total income..........	1,798	1,280	1,692

Source: U. S. Department of Labor, Bureau of Labor Statistics. *Spending and Saving of the Nation's Families in Wartime.* Bulletin No. 723. Washington, D. C.: Government Printing Office, 1942. p. 2, 5, 16.

The term "family" is used by the Bureau of Labor Statistics to include families of two or more persons and also single consumers who do not pool expenses with anyone else. The estimated 32.9 million nonfarm families included 27.6 million families of two or more persons and 5.3 single consumers. The 6.3 million farm families included 6.1 million families of two or more persons and 6.4 million single consumers. Estimates cover the civilian noninstitutional population.

American families and their children were living at subminimal levels and were medically indigent. For them, learning about nutrition and essential medical care is at present an abstract exercise.

Families living on low incomes will hardly be moved to a level of morale that connotes enthusiastic support of our institutions by the forecast and materialization of increased corporate war profits [38]

[38] The U. S. Department of Commerce reported in September 1943 that estimated profits of corporations after provision for taxes for the first six months of 1943 were 14 percent above the first half of 1942. There has been a continuing upward trend since 1939. ("The Business Situation." *Survey of Current Business* 23: 5-6; September 1943.) ¶ Figures for industrial corporations only, issued by the National Industrial Conference Board, showed the still higher rate of 22.4 percent increase in net income after taxes, for the first half of 1943 as compared with the first half of 1942. (Frazer, Frances H. "Half-year Corporate Earnings." *Conference Board Economic Record* 5: 221-24; August 1943.)

while, prior to the rise in employment and wages due to the war, most of these families, as the American Youth Commission points out, did not:

> . . . get enough food; those with three or four children or more are often not far above the starvation level in actual fact. Yet they are compelled by sheer hunger to spend so much of their incomes for food that they are forced into the lowest grades of slum housing for shelter, and have virtually nothing left for clothing and the other essentials.[39]

All children must be supplied with proper and sufficient food, clothing, housing, and medical care. It is by far better that our social and economic system be such as to enable parents themselves to provide these rather than have them doled out as charity. But for those children whose families cannot meet the requirements of optimal conditions for child development, the school and community have a social obligation to provide these essentials.

High morale, all agree, requires that there be a desired goal to work for and defend, that there be something the individual cherishes. To these frustrated low-income groups and to the medically indigent, teachings and precepts on economic democracy must appear, as they view the whole scene, to lack a realistic basis.

LEISURE AND RECREATION

Leisure and wholesome recreation are necessary to both mental and physical health. That there is a significant relationship between lack of desirable recreational facilities and juvenile delinquency is well known by psychologists and sociologists. Yet in relatively few instances are the needs of youth being met by existing community programs and facilities. Furthermore, it is a well-known fact that following our entrance into the war juvenile delinquency increased in many parts of the country as a result of neglect of children, absence of wholesome recreational opportunities, and absence of guidance in free-time activities.

The need for recreational facilities and child supervision has become the more acute since the outbreak of the war, due to the many families in which both parents are employed outside the home. Families where both parents are employed are numerous thruout the country in centers of war industry. The youngsters of these

---

[39] American Council on Education, American Youth Commission, *op. cit.*, p. 170.

families are the "latchkey children" who come to school with house keys tied around their necks, let themselves into their homes in the evening, get their own suppers, and shift for themselves as best they can. This neglect of these children by the community is not the way to promote optimal child development or to convince the parents of these children that the community is concerned with the welfare of all children alike.

Very appreciable increases in public expenditures are necessary for the care, recreation, and supervision of children, not only for the duration of the war but in times of peace as well. Even in terms simply of the market place—not to speak of human values—such increases would be justified, for they would be an "investment" in the future of the United States.

Desirable use of leisure time and wholesome recreational activities are essential for the utilization of youthful energies and interests, to encourage development of extraoccupational skills, to provide opportunities for youthful creative interests, and to furnish a chance for desirable social participation in programs of community planning. The extremely inadequate leisure and recreational facilities that now exist are intended principally for children under about sixteen years of age and for more mature adults. In ordinary peacetimes the great body of youth, in process of adjusting itself and finding its place in society, is the group most neglected.

Need of a Unifying Purpose

This chapter thus far deals with the most important elements essential to satisfy the human's needs as a biological and social organism. Satisfaction of another category of human needs, the ideational, presupposes at least a minimum satisfaction of the first two which are necessary for physical and social survival.

To satisfy the ideational need, man requires a purpose and direction for his activities, that is, the coordination and unification of desires, activities, and concepts until they are fused into unity. The social purposes and directions of one's activities are learned; they are culturally determined. This signifies that man has certain loyalties which are the directive and cohesive forces in his behavior: loyalties to persons, groups, church, vocation, institutions, political party, ideals (such as the "Golden Rule," or "liberty, equality, fraternity," or "rugged individualism"), nation, and the world. These loyalties and their values are the integrating forces which give life its unity and significance beyond the satisfaction of immediate bio-chemical needs and the desire for membership in a group.

We in the United States have chosen the democratic goal with its faith in human values and intelligence; its goal of individual emo-tional, intellectual, and moral integrity; its doctrine of personal satisfaction and self-expression thru socially useful conduct; and its reliance upon forms of social organization that widen, even to the inclusion of all mankind, the area of common interests voluntarily shared. Mutual understanding and participation in the democratic way of life can become the basis for a common loyalty and faith. Accordingly, every person who seeks genuinely to promote demo-cratic living in his community, nation, and in the world at large thereby takes an attitude that can integrate his emotional forces with his intelligent choice of means and ends.

There cannot be loyalty to democratic institutions and doctrine if there is no feeling of hope and purpose under its institutions and organization. Youth and adults alike will ask what significant place there is for them. One problem of education, therefore, is to give to young people and adults such experiences as will reveal possible significant roles for them, and the larger purposes toward which they might direct their activities. It will be a duty of the community —large or small—to provide opportunities for the living of those roles.

Elements of a Program

It is not our function here to outline a program of educational and social planning that will implement democratic principles and teach-ings, but we are obligated at least to suggest some of the more im-portant elements that should go into such a program. There must be courageous educational as well as economic planning if the trends which have resulted in unemployment and deterioration of individuals in the past are not to assert themselves again.

Basically, in the educative process individuals should get a re-vitalized program in the values and practices of democratic living, the clearest possible understanding of the nature of the democracy which we foster and defend—its origins, its problems, and the ways and means of implementing democratic ideals both at home and abroad. In this matter, private schools have as great a responsibility and obligation as do public schools. Other matters of urgent concern are all aspects of health and physical education for children and youth; developing and fostering abilities, wherever found; the expansion of vocational education to supply training and understandings necessary for industrial, agricultural, and homemaking occupations; and the education of our people for esthetic living.[40]

The implications of these educational activities are far-reaching. They include extended public nursery schools and kindergartens, staffed by well-prepared professional personnel; reduction in size of overcrowded classes; adequate educational, vocational, and psychological guidance by competent professional personnel; broader undertakings in vocational education and work experience; adequate health services as well as health education; development of junior colleges and technical institutes, perhaps as part of local school systems; extended federal aid to education to improve and equalize educational facilities thruout the nation; adequate provision for adult education to meet the requirements of all adult groups, thru the variety of channels available, such as class study, forums, radio broadcasting, libraries, museums, and correspondence courses; the selection everywhere of competent educational officials on a professional basis; the selection of more representative school-boards and university boards of trustees; provisions for children who have the intellectual resources but lack the financial; greatly expanded educational provisions for those who need the various special types of instruction; extended and improved educational facilities for minority groups; improvement of teacher education and elevation of the social and economic status of the teaching profession; and courageous and vigorous educational leadership from teachers, educational administrators, and educational philosophers. In general, the educational plan and structure will have to be remodeled and enlarged to meet the needs of all children and youth and to provide for returning service men and women and for displaced industrial war workers, many of whom will have to go thru a process of educational and occupational readjustment and many of whom, after their war or industrial experiences, will no longer be content to return to their former educational routine.

---

[40] See also: National Resources Planning Board. *National Resources Development Report for 1943. Part I. Post-War Plan and Program.* Washington, D. C.: Government Printing Office, 1943. 81 p.

A program of democratic morale building involves other agencies and groups as well as schools and educators. First, socially conscious local, state, and federal governments are basic. The appropriate governmental and private agencies should formulate measures to effect a rapid expansion of employment in the postwar period. This will include, among other things, restoration and improvement under local educational sponsorship of educational opportunities and work experiences; public works and housing programs; and the extension of personal and public services (teaching; psychological and psychiatric clinical service; social service; law; medicine; dentistry; recreation; nursing; government services; research in physical, biological, and social sciences; librarianship; public health; public engineering; architecture; household arts; and agricultural science, to mention some of the more important).

If programs of private and governmental economic planning are to be effective in achieving the goals of full employment and the promotion of human values, several things at least will be essential.

Private industry and commerce will have to show a much greater awareness of their social functions and obligations and of human values. Labor organizations will have to abolish undemocratic practices. These organizations, furthermore, can enhance their value to workers by directing more of their efforts to the enrichment of the lives of their members, in addition to their basic concern with adequate wages to make an enriched life possible and with better working conditions which make the job itself more satisfying.

The unwarranted stigma that now attaches to those working on public projects will have to be removed. It should be just as honorable to be engaged in public works as in private enterprise. The company that gets the government contract is not stigmatized or ridiculed; nor is the industry that provides the government with its supplies, from paper clips to battleships. Yet they too are living "off the government." A change in public attitude is essential if workers on public projects, like all others, are to have the economic security and social status they need. After all, *everyone* lives off the public purse: the storekeeper, the distributor, the manufacturer, public utilities, the advertiser, the physician, and others in personal and professional services. The difference is only in the *manner* in which the public pays for its services and the voice it has in their control.

The prevailing attitudes and feelings about stratification along occupational lines must be minimized and eventually eliminated. In a democracy, driving a truck, doing domestic service, tailoring, laying a pipeline, installing a plumbing system or electrical wiring, or tending a lathe need not and should not be an unworthy occupation or a sign of menial status. In fact, it is not hard to realize that occupations such as these are more essential than some others, professions included, which are higher on the social scale. There has to be a change of attitude on the part of boys and girls with respect to these and similar occupations.[41] But much more important, this change on their part will not be achieved unless there is a radical change on the part of those who employ waiters, household workers, mechanics, and laborers of varying skill. The problem of developing well-being, occupational competence, and economic independence is not merely a matter of "the right job for the right individual." Developing a society which is consonant with *all* human needs is essential.

In the development of a democratic society, the men and women who make up the professions, in addition to educators, will have to evidence a greater degree of social awareness and be guided by democratic values far more than they have in the past. Physical scientists, biological scientists, lawyers, engineers, psychologists, psychiatrists, physicians, economists, and newspaper and magazine editors must have a democratic social viewpoint and an adequate conception of the social implications of their respective professions. But in this respect they have, as groups, remained surprisingly backward. To remedy this deficiency, educational institutions preparing men and women in the professions should feel obligated to provide their students with knowledge of the nature and operations of a democratic political-social-economic system, and of their roles in fostering such a system. Such education is increasingly essential for all groups, especially for those who enjoy a preferred social status in their communities by virtue of their occupations.[42]

[41] Teachers can help by presenting the realities of vocational opportunity to their pupils. Large majorities of high-school pupils consistently report their intention to enter professional occupations. But the U. S. Census shows that only one adult in sixteen is in a professional occupation. The high school is no longer a highly selective institution; high-school graduates may expect to follow approximately the general vocational distribution of the entire population, in which only about 30 percent at present are white-collar workers. (National Education Association, Research Division. "Schools and the 1940 Census." *Research Bulletin* 19; 201-32; November 1941. p. 223-24.)

[42] See: Freeman, Ellis. *Social Psychology.* New York: Henry Holt and Co., 1936. Chapters 12 and 13, p. 193-234. ¶ Also: MacLeish, Archibald. *The Irresponsibles.* New York: Duell, Sloan and Pearce, 1940. 34 p.

Proof of democracy as the most desirable way of life will depend upon the physical and mental health of the people, upon the human satisfactions they experience as members of a democratic society, and upon the values they cherish, as contrasted with those of other types of society. Children and youth will have to be nurtured under conditions necessary for healthy development and behavior; strife and misunderstandings between groups will have to be eliminated thru educational and other life experiences (for example, strife between urban-rural, labor-farmer, management-labor, consumer-distributor, religious, and racial groups); and mutual trust and willing cooperation of disadvantaged groups must be engendered thru more actual implementation of the democratic pattern of living.

Men in high stations have put into words what most people felt and wanted to feel if they were to exert all their energies toward waging and winning the war. It is equally necessary to put into words and *actions* the principles that will be necessary for peaceful living under democratic conditions. For this purpose we need more than men in high stations. We need the statesmanship of educators who will understand human behavior as motivated by human needs, goals, and satisfactions, and who will promote democratic doctrine thru democratic living. Teachers need a hope and a program for human welfare, such as was stated by the National Resources Planning Board in its "New Bill of Rights," as follows:

1. The right to work, usefully and creatively through the productive years.

2. The right to fair pay, adequate to command the necessities and amenities of life in exchange for work, ideas, thrift, and other socially valuable service.

3. The right to adequate food, clothing, shelter, and medical care.

4. The right to security, with freedom from fear of old age, want, dependency, sickness, unemployment, and accident.

5. The right to live in a system of free enterprise, free from compulsory labor, irresponsible private power, arbitrary public authority, and unregulated monopolies.

6. The right to come and go, to speak or to be silent, free from the spyings of secret political police.

7. The right to equality before the law, with equal access to justice in fact.

8. The right to education for work, for citizenship, and for personal growth and happiness.

9. The right to rest, recreation, and adventure; the opportunity to enjoy life and take part in an advancing civilization.[43]

---

[43] National Resources Planning Board. *National Resources Development: Report for 1942.* Washington, D. C.: Government Printing Office, 1942. p. 3.

If all these rights which would implement the Four Freedoms are put into operation, they will signify a social consciousness in all who claim these rights for themselves and acknowledge and defend them for others, in whatever land they may dwell.

One task of education today is to reflect and confirm those aspects of American life which are democratic in character and to work against those that are not. Schools, both public and private, have an essential obligation to lead in developing the best thought and action of an era.

★ *The attitudes of the group surround the child and furnish the background of his behavior. In an atmosphere in which the group has a clearly defined purpose, with all members contributing their share and manifesting similar attitudes, the problem of morale is simplified.*

CHAPTER V

Every Child a Citizen

HUMAN BEINGS ARE LEARNING to live together in larger and larger groups. Out of group living has come the democratic society in which each member participates and to which each contributes. Preparation for democratic living begins early. In a favorable environment that gives opportunities for responsibility and participation, democracy builds a morale among its members that is based upon willingness to respond rather than fear of not responding. Methods of developing such morale in children are the concern of this chapter.

Morale has been defined as the degree to which the individual gives all he has to the task at hand. Accomplishment is determined by what one has, that is, ability and skill, and by what one feels, that is, morale. Our concern is with the feelings transformed into action. Good morale shows itself in the capacity to carry thru for a long time without being broken or bowed down by untoward circumstances. Even tho morale, as a feeling, and accomplishment, as an act, can be distinguished at any one time, in the long run they are closely related, because morale is itself a significant factor in the effects one produces in the world of objects and persons. Morale has a double antonym. The first is that apathy, indifference, indecision, defeatism, and unwillingness which prevents striving, and the second that hesitancy, fear, and insecurity which leads to withdrawal from the struggle.

The problem of morale in children has some features in common and some that differ from the problem of morale in adults. On the one hand, the child participates in and responds to the social contexts of the moment, as do older people; on the other hand, he is being prepared for an adult world that will come into being years later. For adults morale is the maintenance of positive attitudes for situations as they arise; for the child the problem of morale is not so much tied in with the immediate situation. It is concerned also with the development of capacities and feelings that will enable the child in later years to live with high purpose in the world of his fellows. While the factors which build morale for the immediate occasion in the main contribute to future morale, they need not and often do not do so. Morale in children may be destroyed quickly by overemphasizing the demands of the present and by insisting that children meet them fully and completely. For example, by the skilful use of morale-building devices the children in a junior high school could be brought to such strenuous efforts and such a high emotional pitch for a school contest that they would actually do themselves harm from which they would suffer later. Here is morale for the moment at a heavy cost. While we may ask the adult to give all he has in a great emergency, to ask the child to give all he has, in the same sense, may do great damage to him and to society.

Those responsible for children are concerned primarily with helping them build the capacities, feelings, and skills that will enable them to meet situations in the future with high purpose and effectiveness. The clear recognition of this principle is of great practical importance. Because we are interested in the child's future, we must preserve some measure of balance and of wholeness in his present environment. We must not exploit him physically or emotionally; we must not overstimulate him; yet we should not understimulate him. Because we want him to be responsive to social demands, we encourage his participation in defense and war-related activities and thereby give him outlets for his desire to be of service. Yet at the same time, we encourage him to go on with his education and refuse to divert too much of his energy to the immediate moment, because we realize that the future is in his hands.

The Responsiveness of Children to Group Contexts

The attitudes of the group surround the child and furnish the background of his behavior. In an atmosphere in which the group has a clearly defined purpose, with all members contributing their share and manifesting similar attitudes, the problem of morale is much simplified. Where there is conflict, disharmony, and confusion, the child is presented with a difficult problem. Pressures are always arising that push or pull in opposite directions and make choice necessary. A mother says to an older child, "If you do not wash the dishes, I will punish you." The child wishes neither to wash the dishes nor to be punished. He first recalls the arithmetic lesson assigned as homework. But his mother, by telling him that he can do his arithmetic after the dishes are washed, refuses to let him go out of the field of forces. Thus, a choice is forced upon the child which grows out of the nature of the pressures about him—dislike of washing dishes, fear of punishment, and love of the mother. Conflict arises and the child becomes excited and perhaps loses his temper. He moves restlessly about. Soon his perturbation becomes intolerable, a choice is made, and behavior becomes structured. Once the decision is made, some children will wash the dishes with great fury, thus converting the energy created by the conflict into action, others will dillydally, and still others will wash the dishes while protesting or being sullen.

This instance mirrors the conflicting pressures out of which the child must work his way of life. The ability to withstand social pressure and to maintain an independent attitude is an achievement that accompanies maturing in a favorable environment. To a greater degree than adults, children respond to the attitudes and pressures about them. In case histories much evidence is found of the harmful effects upon children of an environment of indecision, conflicting attitudes, and open disagreement among the adults with children. The influences of divorce and separation, and particularly of the controversies that precede divorce, in producing maladjustment have long been stressed in the literature. Recent studies on marital adjustment indicate that happiness in childhood is an important factor in creating later an effective and happy adult married life. College students have been shown to be highly sensitive to the quarrels of parents. In the backgrounds of maladjusted students are many instances of parents who quarrel frequently among themselves or with in-laws and relatives. Students of family life stress the harmful influence of inconsistent and erratic discipline upon the personality of the child.

The social climate to which children respond may have a pattern that is simple and uniform or one that is complex and contains many discordant elements. The totalitarian states create a social climate in which a superman is the symbol of the state and in which all individuals and all activities are identified with his wishes. Children and young people are to serve the leader, to do what he says, and to think as he directs, without question. In our democratic society we have created a very different social climate in that the child is exposed to many conflicting attitudes and contexts. In some instances, we produce persons who are thwarted, ineffective, and unwilling to put forth much effort. But in others we produce positive attitudes, since one who matures in an atmosphere of some conflict develops internal strengths which later contribute to the social group. From the standpoint of society as a whole, a complex climate gives freedom for exploration and selection with the result that varying capacities and skills appear that over a time contribute to the effectiveness of the whole.

The central problem in rearing children is to expose the child to enough homogeneity to give him stability and orientation and at the same time enough diversity to enable him by breaking free from emotional dependence upon his parents and other adults to move toward control of his own impulses and the creation of an independent life pattern. The balancing of these two factors, *stability* and *diversity,* in the background of the child requires high skill on the part of both parents and teachers. Altho scientific studies which indicate the importance of the problem of discipline and control of attitudes have not as yet laid out an adequate program of practice, much more is known and is available than the naive observer or the critic of modern methods will admit. The extreme freedom of a former period in letting the child do exactly as he wishes is clearly not a solution from the standpoint of either immediate or remote morale.

Morale the Product of Many Factors

For adults it has been shown that morale results from many factors working together, any one of which if absent to a marked degree may destroy it but all of which must be present in some degree to insure it. While no detailed study has been made of the factors underlying morale in children, some of the most likely factors may be enumerated.

Health and vigor—The child who is ill, in poor physical health, or lacking the vigor of a sound body tends to have poor morale. In exceptional instances there is great accomplishment and high morale among the physically handicapped. Sometimes children in good physical health may have poor morale because of mental illness or serious difficulties. But, in general, and despite exceptions, morale is related to physical well-being, good nutritive condition, and that resiliency and capacity for quick repair that characterizes a physiologically good young organism.

Equipment—Where there is poor equipment and a lack of materials, children feel handicapped in comparison with their better equipped associates. Altho those with poor materials sometimes outdo all expectation, good equipment, adequate facilities, and readily available materials generally increase morale on the playground and in the home and school.

Knowledge of one's own competence and skill—Children enjoy doing. If facilities and opportunities are provided they are both active and interested. With growth come special interests and skills from which they secure much satisfaction. As more skill is acquired their pleasure is increased. A good environment, by affording an opportunity for the development of interests and skills, contributes directly to adjustment. Morale, in particular, is related to the individual's feeling that he can meet situations, that is, to pride in his own skill.

Pride and loyalty—As one moves from childhood to maturity he builds loyalties to his family, his vocation, his community, his state, and his nation. These not only reinforce similar feelings in others but are constantly reinforced in their turn. Morale grows with the organization of teams and the appearance of competitions and tests of loyalty. If the child becomes vitally interested in an organization, his morale is raised and his activity level increased. Able leaders of children's groups encourage these developments. Pride in an organization indicates the presence of morale, while apathy, indifference, and cynicism indicate its absence.

A goal or purpose—The human being neither lives for the moment nor is satisfied with the satisfaction of vegetative impulses. He works for remote goals, for the attainment of which he will endure pain and discomfort, overcome physical handicaps, compensate by extra effort for deficiencies in materials, acquire skills, and develop loyalties and cooperative relations with others. In early life, goals are immediate and close at hand; as children grow, goals move out and away from the immediate and present in both time and space and become determiners that often outweigh in importance objects and stimuli that are near at hand in either physical or psychological space. This steady enlargement of the life space is a striking feature of development. The child's progress toward his goals and purposes becomes an indicator of his morale to both him and others.

Level of Aspiration and Morale

Modern studies show that children enter situations with conceptions of what they should or can do and that they regulate their performance and, in turn, secure feelings of satisfaction in accordance with these conceptions. If the level of aspiration is high and performance low, feelings of frustration and inadequacy develop; if the level of aspiration is lower than performance, feelings of satisfaction and accomplishment appear. Levels of aspiration vary widely. Some children of much ability aspire so high that even substantial attainment results in frustration. Others, in whom the aspiration level is so low that attainment far below capacity is satisfying, seldom accomplish that of which they are capable.

Levels of aspiration arise out of the individual's personality make-up, his past experience, and the social influences about him at the moment. In some instances they are compensatory and are set off by frustrations; in others they are the outcome of parental ambitions; and in still others they result from group expectancy. Ideally the level of aspiration should be high enough to lead the child to full use of his resources, but not so high that he is certain to be disappointed whatever his effort.

The direction and content of the drives is also important. If the child's aspirations center about significant activities that enable him to arrive at some assessment of his own abilities and possibilities, he moves forward. If he fails continuously in all areas, he may become either "hard boiled," that is, well insulated against life, or extraordinarily sensitive and desirous of protection. If the child finds success in some areas, he can meet substantial amounts of failure in others without harm. Thus an area in which the child can be successful furnishes an integrating center for his subsequent personality development. Continuous and pervasive frustration destroys the child, while openings in the walls of frustration furnish opportunities for growth and development. For instance, successful children who win some social acclaim, whether it be in scholarship, athletics, art, music, or any other activity, are much less likely to have difficulties than are those whose efforts are blocked in every direction. With problem children, in general, the guidance worker is often appalled at the absence of any way out for one who seems so circumscribed in every respect. In successful treatment much time is spent in finding a way out.

If children enter situations with rather clear levels of aspiration, two problems arise. The first grows out of our tendency to emphasize what is not, rather than what is, to be done. Parents and teachers often tell the child what not to do rather than help find what he can do. Often adults in order to preserve their own comfort block children's positive approaches to their complex environment. By thus training the child to avoid difficulties, we produce indecision and hesitancy—nothing greatly wrong but nothing greatly right.

But to meet the strenuous demands of life tough and able children and adults are needed. The problems of society are not solved in a short time by luck but over a long time by initiative, energy, persistence, good work habits, and awareness of goals. These positive traits bring both the basic satisfactions and the rewards of life. To build them children must try themselves out, must succeed in some efforts and fail in others, in order to arrive at a fair evaluation of their own assets and liabilities.

The second problem concerns the nature of the environment. If strong and able children and adults are to appear, the environment itself must be broad and contain such possibilities in the way of materials, equipment, stimulation, and relationships as will permit the individual to achieve as a result of his aspiration and ability levels. Thus a boy with poor physical equipment should not aspire to an activity such as flying, in which a good physique is essential. Stimulation to a high aspiration level in an inappropriate area usually foredooms one to difficulty and failure. Good training seeks to find another area in which such a person can achieve skill and satisfaction. But if a boy has a good physique and a strong interest in flying and there are no airplanes about, he is also foredoomed to difficulty. Education for morale involves recognition of the reciprocal relation between the individual and his environment.

Depth of Experience and Level of Function

Not only should the environment be broad in opportunity, but it should provide for depth of experience. In recent years it has been said that our children and youth are soft, that we need more toughness. For the purposes of war, training has been speeded up and strengthened. A program of physical fitness extends into our schools. How can we produce strong adults, persons who physiologically and psychologically possess the quality of toughness?

Recent work on the relation between diet and activity throws light on this problem. Children and adults on a low dietary intake compensate by decreasing their activities. As a result of this low energy expenditure, the deficiency diseases that might be anticipated do not appear or are much delayed in their appearance. If food is increased, the activity level is increased; if the activity level is raised by outside stimulation, the need for food is increased and more food-seeking behavior may be expected. If little food is available and the organism expends energy at a high rate, deficiency diseases appear. Thus, there is a relation between energy expenditure and deficiency, as well as one between nutritive intake and deficiency. If either is stepped up without corresponding changes in the other, marked inadequacies appear; if both are stepped up together, a high level of functioning appears; and if both are reduced together, a low level of functioning appears. As a result of these observations, radical departures in the treatment of children with deficiencies have been introduced. These consist in providing not only a high nutritive intake but also a high energy expenditure, with the result that the recuperative processes are speeded up substantially. Active exercise is now used as a remedial device in some types of heart cases, and passive exercise of joints and limbs is used in infantile paralysis. Similar practices which are gradually breaking their way thru in other areas are based on the sound principle that the human organism is primarily an energy-expending mechanism.

It should be noted that a state of health and functioning can be achieved at any level; that is, the child on a deficient diet who is also inactive seems reasonably healthy. Unless careful examination is made, little real deficiency appears. Despite this negative appearance of health, such a child lacks the stamina or staying power possessed by a child in whom both energy expenditure and the intake function are nearer the maximum. In the past health has been thought of and measured in terms of the absence of deficiencies rather than of the presence of a more positive characteristic—stamina. The absence of defects, however desirable, is not the equivalent of good health.

On the mental side no real approach has been made to this problem. In mental hygiene we have assumed that the primary problems were the avoidance of behavior problems and the correction of individual defects. In education we have assumed that we can give children a high scholastic intake and let energy expenditure take care of itself. How can we secure maximum use of the educational materials made available to the child in order that he may develop the skills that will enable him to perform and do? Society needs adults with substantial skill. If the school does not provide opportunities for such skills, society trains the persons it needs thru other agencies. Since neither the child nor the teacher can know what the child can do until he tries and tries hard for some time in a favorable environment, breadth of exposure is not the equivalent of depth of experience in the organization and development of capacity.

One of our modern tendencies has been the explanation of failures and inadequacies in terms of psychological mechanisms. If the child fails, he has an inferiority complex, he has a low IQ, or he is maladjusted. While such knowledge may be of great value to the expert in guiding the child, it does not, when known in the group or by the child, make for that positive motivation which leads individuals on to meet their life situations with whatever physical and mental equipment they have. If humans waited for the correction of their frailties and inadequacies before meeting the problems of living, the world would be a sorry place. It makes a substantial difference for morale whether we talk about the absence of fear or anger or whether we talk about the presence of courage or the control of impulse. It makes some difference whether we excuse inadequacies because of defects or demonstrate what one can do with his physical and mental make-up in spite of such defects. Nowhere is this more evident than with handicapped children, for whom coddling produces helplessness, and encouragement in living produces good adjustment. The attitudes and expectancies of the child's social group and the family are of great importance, as shown by the fact that children from one family constantly make excuses while children from another constantly perform. A current definition of *psychological maturing* states that maturity comes when one realizes that an excuse is not the equivalent of performance.

The Child's Sense of Values

The child is born with a highly sensitive nervous system that reacts to stimuli about him. Behavior is modified by changing the stream of stimulation. The behavior of the infant and very young child is neither moral nor immoral but rather amoral. He still has to build his system of values. He is not, however, a blank to be completely fashioned by the environment; the quality of his nervous system will determine what he will do with the stimulation received.

Whence come the child's values? They come first from the home, which has access to him for twenty-four hours a day in the early years and for shorter periods of time thereafter thruout the entire period of development. In the home there is not only direct instruction by his parents in many specific items and values but also direct observation of the manner in which parents and other adults react to situations. The child sees and hears his mother greet the neighbors, and hears the incidental remarks made by his father at the dinner table about politics, business, and society; he sees and hears the emotional outbursts of his parents and experiences their consequences.

As the child grows older he sees more of other children and comes under the influence of their values. He learns that some things are done by boys and not by girls, others by girls and not by boys; he learns not to squeal on a friend or associate. The boy learns to endure pain without crying, for fear he may be called a "chicken." The influence of the family lessens as the influence of associates increases. Children and adolescents respond to fashions in clothes, pet phrases, music, and games current among their contemporaries and are in some degree set off by them from their elders. Unsympathetic parents often struggle quite helplessly with the codes and practices of the younger generation. Important in this picture is the content of the child's reading and particularly the material brought to him by the radio, the newspaper, and the motion picture. Substantial evidence exists to show that the source of many values and attitudes that govern conduct lie in these devices of universal stimulation.

When the standards of the home are in line with those of the associates, the school, the radio, newspapers, and the motion pictures, the child becomes fashioned to a marked degree. But in our society there are wide discrepancies in the attitudes to which children are exposed. Because attitudes are highly characteristic of particular families, the family is a source of both strength and diversity. In the totalitarian countries attempts were made to break the influences of the home in order to give an open field for the deliberate control of the child's attitudes and values by filling his leisure time with activities supervised closely by the state. In addition, children were taken from their homes for long periods to receive intense propaganda. So recently have the effective mechanisms for the central, universal, and quick control of attitudes developed that we are only beginning to know their possibilities. But the evidence now available indicates that the radio and the motion picture, with their all-pervading reach, their continuity of stimulation, the immediateness and directness of their appeal, and their ready control at a central source, make possible a degree and completeness of control of attitude never before attained in any society. Whether we like it or not, problems centering in the control of children's attitudes from central sources will be with us for many years to come. How are we to balance the homogeneity of attitude needed to maintain our society against the diversity of attitude needed to give it strength and vigor?

Conditions Favoring Morale

The child is not a fixed being but a system of appetites, impulses, interests, and wants, some of which arise from his internal nature and some from the stimulation afforded by his environment. He is also a member of a society which makes demands upon him and constrains his impulses. At any moment a balance exists; over a period of time a direction appears which may be toward or away from more effective functioning as a whole. Envisaging the dynamic character of this relation between the child and his psychological space, we can ask, what conditions and principles in the upbringing of children favor the development of morale for democratic living?

SENSE OF BELONGING AND SECURITY

Modern studies indicate a relation between the child's feeling of belonging and security and his stability and effectiveness in meeting life's demands. Anxious, tense, and nervous children come from anxious, tense, and nervous family environments. They come also from families in which a marked discrepancy between the family and the community cultural pattern creates conflict and tension. In an insecure situation an outcome of such tension may be undesirable and antisocial behavior. The orienting principle for the training of children in early childhood is one of developing confidence in the environment thru regular schedules of eating and sleeping, demonstrations of affection, a consistent and fair system of discipline, and by emphasis upon the child's accomplishments rather than upon his failures. A poor environment stresses failure rather than success and subjects the child to irregular, inconsistent, and erratic schedules and discipline. The contribution of this confidence in the environment to morale is that of providing a base upon which the child can move into adolescence, where the primary task is the conversion of this confidence in the environment into confidence in himself.

SELF-CONFIDENCE AND RESPONSIBILITY

Adolescence has been described as a "psychological weaning" and as an "emancipation from the family." At some time the bonds with the home must be broken in order that the child may move into the world as an independent, self-propelling vehicle able to withstand and meet the strains of adult life. To attain this end, parental authority must be gradually lessened and many of the restrictions of childhood removed. To remove them suddenly is as serious as to continue them too long. The child is to be brought from the dependency of infancy to the independence of adult life by a gradual and continuous process. In modern times the importance of emotional and intellectual independence as a correlate of citizenship in a democratic society is clearly recognized. A democratic society creates high morale not so much by dependence upon a leader as by building an independence which grows out of inner resources and strengths. Hence the teacher may well ask in connection with each practical procedure, "Does what I am doing make this child (or this youth) more dependent upon me or more independent of me?"

But independence is not enough. Self-reliance is also necessary. By gradually increasing the responsibilities of the child, we develop his skill and judgment in meeting the larger problems of later life. When children are given responsibilities commensurate with or slightly above their capacities they show amazing ability to manage their own affairs and to develop qualities that will stand them in good stead later. It requires more skill to give children opportunities for responsibility than it does to supervise them closely. But the gain in both morale and skill is well worth the effort. The first comment made by a volunteer assistant in one school was that she knew as much as the teachers. But on observing her behavior, it was clear that *she* did the routine job, *she* laced the shoes, *she* washed the hands, and so forth, all of which gave an appearance of efficiency; in fact, she and her children were always ahead of schedule. But she was not a good teacher, because efficiency for the moment is not the end desired. What is desired is the development in the child of the capacity to think and do for himself. It is *his* lacing of his shoes, *his* washing of his hands, in which we are interested. With the ability to do for oneself there comes self-reliance— an important condition of democratic morale.

What is needed is the schoolroom or home climate in which in situation after situation the child is given responsibility commensurate with his capacity. Here he develops that fiber and stamina so important for meeting the demands of adult life. But a caution must be given. American history abounds with the stories of boys who early, thru running away from home, the death of the father, or the necessity of eking out the family income, were given much responsibility and developed positive character traits of great value to our society. It does not so clearly record the many children who were broken under too great responsibility because of unfortunate circumstances. A balance between protection and responsibility is sought, decreasing protection and increasing responsibility as the child or adolescent grows older and, what is even more important, as he shows he can take and carry responsibility.

OPPORTUNITIES TO EXPERIMENT

Contrary to popular belief error seems to be an intrinsic part of learning. The apparently superfluous and inadequate movements which appear when an organism meets a new situation are gradually eliminated, while smooth-running, automatic, well-coordinated behavior comes as a final result after much time and energy are expended. Whatever is worth doing is worth doing badly. Putting a learner in a strictly limited and restricted environment with no possibility of going wrong—a sort of hothouse—has been shown to be ineffective. To be given complete freedom to experiment is also ineffective, since the learner has to run the whole gamut of human experience in order to organize his behavior. Teachers guide and control the learning process in order to save children time and energy. At the same time children should have substantial areas in which they can experiment and try themselves out.

When the nature of the environment is considered, it is seen to consist of a pattern of stimulation composed of many elements. Since the individual is also a system composed of many parts, we can say that two systems are interacting upon one another. In this reciprocal process, there is a high selectivity, part of which grows out of the nature of the environment and part out of the nature of the individual. It is actually true that the individual cannot know what he can do until he tries. The growing child is exploring both his environment and his own possibilities in order to achieve a way of life which will in some degree meet both the demands of his own nature and those of the environment. The child literally does not know whether he has high capacity for musical performance until he is exposed to much musical stimulation. If the environment fails to give him opportunity, his capacity cannot develop. But if he is exposed and lacks high capacity, environmental stimulation will not produce it. One of the greatest functions of the school in a democracy is that of giving all children opportunities to discover their own abilities. A rigid framework set from above will not explore human resources and after a time will make both individuals and the state intellectually and culturally sterile.

In a society of many people life is so organized that the individual must meet various requirements of time and place; otherwise he is unhappy and ineffective both as an individual and as a member of the group. Of necessity, he must build regular work habits, such as those of promptness and of getting a job done. But society also puts a premium upon ingenuity, initiative, and versatility. Ideally, then, at the same time that parents and teachers are building an orderly system of habits they should also be concerned with the preservation of the child's natural spontaneity and ingenuity. At one extreme is the completely docile, highly structured person who meets the routine demands of his environment with clock-like regularity. At the other are those who are so erratic, unpredictable, and unresponsive to every type of social demand that they are continuous trials to their friends, find no stable place in society, are socially isolated, and in some instances must be segregated. In between lies the ideal behavior so difficult to achieve but so important to both the individual and society.

In every child's life there is a substantial amount of restriction and limitation, some of which is physical and imposed by his own inabilities and some of which is imposed by the adults or the situations he meets. As he grows older, supervision and controls are reduced in some areas and increased in others; we both expect less and expect more of him. If the child is too completely surrounded by restrictions, he moves into adult life as either a docile person or one who throws off all restraints. If given complete freedom in all areas he fails to learn how to react to the demands of community living and as a result is isolated by those groups with which he ought to associate. This problem is met by surrounding the child with limitations and restrictions in some areas in order that he may build an orderly life, while giving him opportunities for freedom and initiative in other areas. As a result the child will acquire the capacity to take on restrictions and to put them off when necessary for adapting to the environment. Many have been amazed at the ease with which millions of American boys, with their democratic upbringing, have taken on the restrictions and duties of military life.

CHOICE AND DISCRIMINATION

Life as it unrolls consists of one decision after another; the individual meets one point of choice after another. Some decisions are minor and concern only the present moment; others are major and may modify the whole subsequent course of life. The mother decides whether there shall be a new dining-room rug or summer camp for her son; the adolescent decides whether he will take this high-school course or that. These "either or" situations begin early and continue thru life. Everyone lives within a budget of time and money whether he knows it or not. Much of his happiness, much of his zest for life, much of his drive depends on the wisdom of his choices. In a democratic society the area of freedom and choice is large; in a totalitarian society it is so small as to be almost at the vanishing point. In wartime this area of choice is much smaller than in peacetime.

Why do some children choose good books and some poor ones; some good pictures, others poor ones; and some listen to trashy radio programs, others to good ones? These are questions of importance.

Evidence indicates several principles are at work. Some children are given no choices; they are in a completely controlled environment in which decisions are made by elders. Some are given free choice with no guidance; others are fortunate enough to be in an environment that gives the opportunity both to make choices and to develop standards. Such an environment involves exposure to both the good and the bad, plus some opportunity to discuss and criticize what the environment affords. If choice is restricted by emotional devices such as powerful prohibitions, children may develop strong motivation toward what is forbidden.

Evidence indicates that children choose the good if both good and poor are equally available and time is given for experience and discussion in the situation. The principle of equal availability needs especial emphasis; it implies both physical and psychological availability. Young children exposed to large and small blocks which are equally available choose the large blocks; older children exposed to pictures good and bad in design choose those of good design. Younger children prefer participation to spectator roles in play and active to passive games, if the environment permits both equally. In families and in schools in which good and bad motion pictures are seen and discussed freely, children develop taste in their choice of pictures. Judgment comes with experience in judging.

If we would have high morale in children, we must have more confidence in their wisdom. We must expose them early to choice situations of a simple type when wrong decisions will not destroy their happiness or personality, in order that they may develop the capacity to make wise decisions on major matters later when a wrong decision would mean irreparable harm. Strength and wisdom do not come out of the thin air, nor do they grow by fiat; they are the products of the experience of the individual in meeting the problems which life presents. Future morale in a democracy, even the success of democracy itself, depends on the capacity of people to make wise choices.

IDEALS AND PURPOSES

The world of the human is not of the moment but extends forward and backward in time and outward and away in space. Young people undertake professional training years before they achieve competence. Education in a society is set up for remote as well as immediate results. Morale is intimately related to these ideals and purposes. Goals are needed in order to achieve results in the personal and the external worlds. Ideals and purposes are the joint products of one's past experience and one's relations with others. For the

Japanese the goal is to die for the Emperor; for the German boy service to the Fuehrer is the highest goal to be achieved. In a democratic society, in some degree, we have replaced the identification of goals with a particular person with the idea of allegiance to a set of principles and a group method of solving the problems that grow out of living together. Democratic societies have been experimenting with ideals and goals that are more abstract and less readily formulated than those of a society organized about leaders as persons. Making the ideals of a democratic society tangible and real to six- or twelve-year-olds is a major educational problem, especially when we encounter difficulty in making them tangible and real to adults. It is much easier to dramatize devotion to an individual or to a state than to dramatize devotion to ideals and principles. Nevertheless, we must make the attempt in wholehearted fashion.

In approaching this problem we must see the results as the outcome of a social climate that covers a substantial part of the child's life, and not as a matter of a few incidental stimuli now and then. This climate will include all the things we have been discussing: giving the child a feeling of belonging, developing confidence and self-reliance thru responsibilities and opportunities to experiment, the building of orderly and systematic work habits, and giving of opportunities for decision and choice. But more is needed. In this climate there should be frank and straightforward discussion of the purposes of individual and group life, continuous examples of democratic practices on the part of adults who are with children, and clear emphasis upon social responsiveness as distinct from self-aggrandizement. At the same time we must preserve the motivation of the individual by giving him pride in the accomplishments of his family, school, group, and nation. The child needs a stimulating environment that will search out his capacities, encourage the development of skills, motivate him to high energy expenditure, and supply him with socially- rather than self-centered goals and ideals.

Enlarging Horizons

As children grow, their life space extends forward and backward in time and out and away in space. Normally, the older child is interested in more things, reacts to stimuli at a greater distance, and has a wider knowledge and perforce a much larger universe than the younger child. And the child of our generation, who knows about events as they happen all over the globe and who hears and reads about and sees pictures of them, lives in a far wider world than the world of his grandparents or great grandparents, whose awareness was in the main limited to the local community. When we say that the world is growing smaller, we mean that the world comprehended by the individual is growing larger. This is true of children at all age levels as well as of adults. The time is not far distant when for children, as for adults, there will be one world. It is our responsibility in instructing children not only to facilitate their learning about other races, other people, and other countries but also to build in them the attitudes of democracy which will permit them to share in such a world. In this lies our hope for future peace and the morale that goes with accomplishment rather than destruction.

The Role of Example and of Opportunities for Service

The great majority of British children have shown high morale in withstanding the situations created by war, including bombing and evacuation, with both courage and fortitude. These attitudes seem to come in part from the example set by their parents and in part from the parents' confidence in the capacity of their children to withstand. A small proportion of children show anxiety, nervousness, and serious emotional difficulties. Traced back, these are found to antedate the war and to grow out of an insecure and unsatisfactory home life in which the child had previously manifested anxiety states. High correlations between the fears of mothers and those of their young children have been reported in studies which indicate the extent to which the emotional states of the person in intimate contact with the child communicate fears by example and comment. In a West Coast city the day after Pearl Harbor, because the teachers were nervous and distraught, the children in one school quickly went beyond control. In other schools in the same city, the teachers by maintaining control over themselves carried the school program forward without interruption.

What concerns us, however, so far as morale is concerned, is not the immediate effect of these single instances so much as their long-time and lasting effects. If the child for many years has been with parents who are brave and courageous and who show high morale thru a succession of testing experiences, we can expect a cumulation of effect into a family pattern. From successive experiences with parents who have shown the opposite type of behavior we can expect a different family pattern. In one family, each child in succession facing similar difficulties at approximately the same age has reacted with courage. In another family, children in similar situations have reacted with fear.

But a context of high morale and courage is not enough. In addition, opportunities for service and activity which will relieve the emotional tension created by difficult situations must be provided. Of what value are feelings without channels thru which they can produce changes in the environment? Many younger children externalize their reactions to the war by becoming interested in the details of war implements, such as the make-up of the airplanes and the different types and character of bombs, and by incorporating war activities in their play. Older children give service in factories and on farms.

While people wish to serve their country, such service also makes them more comfortable and increases their morale. If direct service is not possible, informal and formal outlets can be developed in the community, school, and home. An energetic child with many opportunities for activity is much more likely to show positive attitudes than a child who is unoccupied and has nothing to do except to think about his own feelings. Under war conditions we mobilize great energy and outdo in accomplishment all our peacetime expectancies. The emotional tension and the morale engendered by the conflict find outlets that unlock tremendous resources within the people. If we would have continuing high morale in children and adults, we must learn how to mobilize human energy in similar high degree for the important tasks of peace.

★ *In home and church from his earliest years the child receives influences that help to shape the system of values that will be central in his life's effort.*

CHAPTER VI
Morale-Building Agencies

A NY EFFORT TO LIST AGENCIES affecting morale leads inevitably to one conclusion—that there can be no complete list. It becomes apparent that our degree of confidence in ourselves and our institutions, our faith in the face of hardship and even injustice in social, economic, and political life, is not determined by a few specific influences but by the interaction of all forces affecting our lives. While some of these influences are virtually invisible in the complex fabric of modern civilization, it is true that most of them stem from certain major institutions and that the functioning of these institutions is responsible in part for our strengths or weaknesses of the spirit.

Since the measure of morale is the quality of our reaction to problems encountered in group living, this chapter is concerned with those agencies which develop our responses to the phenomena of life in a democracy. This means that we must examine educative influences, wherever found, which affect the individual's ability to cope with personal difficulties and which determine society's success in attempting to solve major problems.

If the agencies exerting these influences were beyond reproach and their practices faultless, there would be small reason, if any, for this yearbook. Like other human institutions, however, they are merely groping toward the light of a brighter day for mankind. In their imperfect functioning are found both the cause of many of our troubles and the promise that unceasing struggle for improvement will be rewarded.

A glance at the principal educational agencies reveals the vastness of the areas in which correction of faulty functioning of social mechanisms would strengthen democratic morale. The forces of home and neighborhood, subjected in recent years to the strains of technological advancement, depression, and war, present problems which demand solution. The church is far from having achieved its goal of bringing to everyone the benefits of personal religion. Government, enlarging its administrative bureaus in order to solve serious economic problems, has seemed to grow further away from the personal responsibility of the individual citizen. Occupational groups have made notable advances in technology but have sometimes withheld benefits from society and have engaged in wasteful internal strife. Social service organizations and other character-forming groups have extended their benefits to many but have been unable to meet the needs of countless others. The press, radio, and motion picture are by no means highly successful in their interpretation of the social scene. Literature and the arts serve too small an audience. While schools and colleges have improved their offerings and practices, they are still confronted with the need for greater improvement and with new responsibility for leadership.

What do these agencies do—good and bad—that affects morale? What kinds of attitudes are they developing? What can they do that they are not now doing? As we consider what each of these groups can do in helping to build morale, we must see how the school can help each of them while making its own direct contribution.

Home and Neighborhood

Since the home is one of the greatest single agencies of education and character building, its influence on morale is basic. Chapter V, in discussing the responsiveness of the child to group contexts and the development of his sense of values, points out how the highly sensitive nervous system of the child reacts to the stimuli about him. While other factors may compensate for adverse conditions in the home, it is difficult for the best kind of morale to come out of a quarrelsome home or one characterized by a background of limited education, by antidemocratic prejudice, or by lack of encouragement for worthwhile youthful activity. Much the same may be said of the influence of the neighborhood.

It has been said that a majority of the young men who were first to volunteer for army and navy service when war was declared against the Axis came from disadvantaged homes. This, however, does not disprove the value of good home conditions, for there are two distinct types of morale—one for war and one for peace—and the latter is the more difficult to build. Whether these same young men would maintain in peacetime the stamina shown in war is open to question. In many cases they would be found poorly prepared. This does not suggest that high morale cannot come from the poverty-stricken home. It can and does. However, the influence of bad home conditions is tremendous and poverty is a great breeder of these conditions. The homes of the economically secure also may be highly unfavorable to the fostering of democratic spirit, faith, and courage.

The parent who is poor in spirit and rich in prejudice often can be depended upon to transmit his own social heritage to his offspring. If he feels no pride in home, church, city, state, or nation, his child is thereby handicapped. If he places personal gain above common honesty, if he feels abused by the world, and if he does not share in guiding his child toward intelligent citizenship, other educative influences must indeed be strong if they are to overcome the fact that during many significant hours the child is in an environment detrimental to the development of desirable social attitudes.

Of basic importance is the matter of family income. So long as we have existing side by side great wealth and dire poverty, we are going to have attendant problems that are indeed difficult to solve. Obviously one of the greatest constructive influences we could have would be more perceptible progress toward the solution of our economic ills. Even the bravest spirits are cast down when unemployment, malnutrition, and ill health without adequate medical care have descended on a family. Our marked economic discrepancies give rise to resentment, conflict, and a justifiable feeling that the principles of equality of opportunity and treatment are not being implemented.[1]

Industrial changes, with increasing mobility of population, have greatly changed the neighborhood, both rural and urban, with consequent effect upon community spirit engendered by common problems and common interests. The once relatively stable population of the urban neighborhood has in many cities, and especially in war and boom times, become a constantly changing element. The man who lives for a short time in a neighborhood from temporary necessity rather than from choice, whose chief interest in the community is his job and the income from it, usually does not take the pride or interest in community affairs that one does whose family has been reared in the neighborhood. Multiply this transient citizen by thousands and you have a sizable element in the population of many cities.

[1] For further discussion of the effects of economic insecurity on parents' morale and for case studies of effects on children, see: Murphy, Lois B. "Children Are Important to Morale." *Civilian Morale.* Second Yearbook, Society for the Psychological Study of Social Issues. Boston: Houghton Mifflin Co., 1942. Chapter 6, p. 95-118.

The rural neighborhood likewise has changed. Paved highways have brought the people nearer town, and there they go for shopping, entertainment, and even education. While it is not suggested that this change or many others that have come about as aspects of modern civilization are necessarily bad, the fact remains that the rural citizen has less need for reliance on his neighbors and has not the vital interest in community affairs that he once had.

As home and neighborhood have changed with the rise of our industrial civilization, members of both have increasingly less in common. Once there were common tasks and common interests. Now the members of a family may have so little in common that the home loses much of its influence and becomes in effect a boardinghouse from which the members busily pursue their work and their pleasures and neglect the important aspects of family life. This is not so true of rural as of urban life, but farm homes, too, have suffered as well as profited from social and industrial changes.

The increasing diversity of callings open to members of the family is well illustrated in a recent study which showed that in 30 percent of the homes of public-school children in Washington, D. C., both parents were working.[2] The added fact of the instability of many American homes, shown in repeated studies, gives ample ground for anxiety as to attendant effects upon children. A study reported lately from England indicates what may be expected under such conditions. There prewar investigation of boys brought before the juvenile courts showed that 32 percent of the delinquents came from homes in which father and mother were not living together and that of the unbroken families of these young delinquents only 43.1 percent were giving "a normal home atmosphere" to the children. When home life was most severely dislocated during the sustained aerial attack on London in 1940-41, causes of delinquency were so aggravated that for a time children ran wild. Figures on delinquency for September 1940 thru August 1941 showed a 52 percent increase over the period from September 1938 thru August 1939. Fifty-eight percent of the delinquents were children under fourteen. The year following August 1941, with home conditions less abnormal, showed only a 30 percent increase over 1938-39.[3]

---

[2] District of Columbia Public Schools. *Curriculum Progress.* Washington, D. C.: Board of Education, June 1943. p. 9. (Mimeo.)

[3] British Information Services. *Juvenile Delinquency in Britain During the War.* New York: British Information Services (30 Rockefeller Plaza), April 1943.

The Washington study, except for absence of conditions caused by actual aerial attack, showed somewhat the same background factors. In the case of many children with both parents working it could hardly be said that they really had homes. Most of these children looked after themselves, many of them staying alone or with neighbors—or on the streets—after school. Others were left with maids, and the rapid turnover of these employees left the children with no feeling of security. There was less supervision by parents, for they were tired when they came home from work. Homes were crowded because extra rooms were rented out, and moving days were more frequent. While few fathers were unemployed, many worked away from home or were in the armed forces, as were older brothers. Inconvenient hours of work often meant irregular family life with parents and children eating their meals at different times.

It should be pointed out that some beneficial aspects of the situation were found. Children were walking more; they were better fed and clothed because of increased family income. They were being encouraged in thrift for the purchase of war bonds and stamps and for the conservation of commodities formerly taken for granted, and many were gaining useful work experience after school hours. Other benefits might be mentioned. The picture is not all dark; nevertheless, it is one which discloses alarming possibilities of harmful effects on American youth. Education will have the job of ridding the postwar world of unwholesome conditions caused by the war and encouraging worthwhile changes.

Bad home environment, however, is not characteristic only of a war period. In peacetime, also, many a child comes to the school suffering from neglect. His parents doubtless would deny this neglect, but its effects are there. It may be insufficient care in regard to clothing, manners, or health, or it may be neglect of the mind and spirit. School life may show the child to be low in morale and hampered by undesirable attitudes. The school may do much for him, but he is entering a new relationship and there is no assurance that the new attitudes developed in school will remedy basic weaknesses, the origins of which are in the home. Certain phases of lasting morale are more likely to result from a healthful situation in the home than from any remedial methods of the school.

The home has in recent years been seriously affected by two major social upheavals—the depression and the war. A third one—demobilization in the armed forces and industry—lies ahead. It cannot be foreseen just what that period will bring. Certainly it will be a time of serious economic dislocation, as millions of men are released from military service and war jobs to find places for themselves in an economic world which will be struggling to readjust itself to the changed needs of peacetime. Many of these men never have had a peacetime job or occupation. Millions of women now regarded as essential workers will be released from jobs and will have to make readjustment. Thousands of war widows will be trying to make a living and to rear children and many of them will have had no adequate training for either job.

We need an informed and intelligent citizenry whose interests and understanding extend beyond the immediate local community—or beyond even their own nation. We need leaders of integrity and followers of sound judgment. Adult education centers may help in meeting these needs, but many organizations of the community also may make a distinct contribution. More calls on individuals for help in community affairs would satisfy status needs of many a person and put him on the path of service, arousing in him an interest which in time would expand to include wider fields. An important contribution to morale will be made when means are devised to make the "forgotten man" in the community realize that he is needed. Organizations of many kinds can help in this by carefully cultivating increased participation in group affairs on the part of persons who otherwise would be apparently content to leave such activities to others.

Perhaps the greatest hope lies with tomorrow's adults. Here is the greatest opportunity for the school and other agencies. It is a common experience for the teacher to see a boy or girl who comes to school low in spirit emerge from his shell and become a new individual on finding that he can do something that is appreciated, that there is a place for him. It is relevant also to suggest here that more high schools include the study of child care and family life as a part of the curriculum. This is not only sound education but also a constructive way in which we can serve tomorrow's adults.[4]

It is important that every child be guided to good character, sound education, and wise vocational choice. If this is done, his future will be sounder and safer and *his* children will be more certain of good home morale.

---

[4] American Association of School Administrators. *Education for Family Life*. Nineteenth Yearbook. Washington, D. C.: the Association, a department of the National Education Association, 1941. 368 p.

Religion and the Church

Religion has a far greater influence on human lives than can be discerned by examination of facts pertaining to church attendance or to the number of persons directly affected by church activity programs. One of the bases of morale is integration of the personality thru belief in an ideal. This in itself is evidence of the contribution of religion to morale—the compelling power of an ideal that has emotional values so great that for many people the problem of morale is solved by religious faith.

The teachings of religion have become so pervasive that faith in whatever man normally considers right, whatever its immediate source, stems indirectly from fundamental religious concepts. Immediate sources of ideals may be the home, the school, the club, the political party, the professional code, or the playing field, but the ultimate source is likely to be basically religious. The church's direct advocacy of high standards of moral conduct is thus supplemented by man's religious impulses finding expression thru other channels. This is fortunate, since the direct influence of the church has been limited by declining church attendance. The church's position has been changed from one of authority to one of persuasion by development of a strong material civilization and the reconstruction of certain intellectual foundations of religious belief. While a full half of the 110,000,000 persons in the United States over ten years of age are church members, the influence of the church has not the weight it might have if more people looked to it for guidance.

Perhaps one reason why many people stay away from church is that they want something they do not get from it. These persons are not necessarily irreligious. It may be suggested that the church examine itself critically with the idea in mind that perhaps in some respects it has failed to keep step with the needs of society. It might, for example, ponder the question as to whether the ministry itself always understands and adheres to democratic doctrine. Has the church always been open-minded toward needed social, economic, and psychological remedies deemed necessary by society? And has it arrived at any democratic integration of the findings of science and the phenomena of modern civilization with the doctrines of religious leaders?

The foregoing are questions of the sort that any organization anxious to strengthen itself might well consider. Any emphasis given here to possible needed adjustment in the church is meant in no way to detract from the constructive work it is doing in giving strength, endurance, and faith to millions; it is meant rather as a possible answer to a question with which the church, to its credit, is eternally concerned—that of extending its service in the promotion of democracy and human rights.

The church has not been idle in this matter. Altho attendance at worship has declined, the church's influence has been widened by such organizations as the Young Men's Christian Association, Young Women's Christian Association, Young Men's Hebrew Association, and the Catholic Youth Association. In addition to sponsoring such youth groups, churches also provide for their congregations religious education and numerous other means of instruction, guidance, and inspiration. These activities give opportunity for development of leadership and of group and individual morale thru work in a common cause and thru satisfaction of social or status needs. The work these groups do in peacetime is highly worthwhile. In wartime they have risen to the demand for increased service. Their work has provided sound bases for good citizenship and enduring faith in human brotherhood. The church activity program in promoting democracy is highly worthwhile and deserving of even greater emphasis.

The church has meant much in the development of the educational program. For centuries it was the principal agent of education and moral teaching. The church in the eighteenth century helped bring about much needed reforms in the treatment of prisoners and the insane. Many services we now think of as ordinary governmental functions were begun by religious groups. Today the church has not abandoned this tradition but sponsors genuine forward-looking social work which is a vital factor in building up morale.

While separation of church and state in the United States is the foundation of cherished individual liberties of faith and worship, the principles upon which our nation is based are essentially religious. Civic morale and religion are closely related. The citizen's devotion to his political institutions and traditions will encourage him to respect other men's religious faith and to be loyal to his own. Religion, on the other hand, will strengthen citizenship because it recognizes the necessity of organizing political and economic relations so as to apportion their benefits justly and raise individuals to the maximum of development which their capacities permit.

The time has passed when religion can focus all attention on supernatural goods to be enjoyed in a future life and can persuade men to accept their present lot with passive resignation. Religion will always be looked to for consolation and perhaps for the crowning and more durable satisfactions of life, but only when at the same time every instrument of science, education, and organization is used to provide man with health, skill, material goods, recreation, and culture. There is, in the modern world, no conflict between the secular ideal of democracy and a progressively higher standard of living, on the one hand, and the religious ideal of spiritual regeneration or of hope that extends beyond death, on the other.

The quality of religion in the civic conscience extends to the world scene. The failure of the victors in the first World War to create a durable peace carries a lesson that must not be forgotten. It had been too readily assumed that free institutions would live on of their own momentum if only external threats were removed. The disastrous period between 1918 and 1939 proved beyond doubt that if the cause of justice and humanity is to prevail at home and abroad the adherents of that cause must serve it with zeal and consecration. They must subordinate their selfishness, whether of personal ambition or of class or national interest, to the good of mankind at large. Between such an aroused and intensified civic consciousness and the spirit of religion there is a profound agreement of quality and direction, so that as members of the state and of their chosen church men will feel no divided allegiance. The two great commandments, loving God with all one's heart and loving one's fellow man as oneself, are parts of the same love, having no boundaries of race or nation.

Government

Thru their governmental institutions, people have their greatest opportunity for developing group morale, as the very principles of democracy are affirmed or denied thru the working of the agencies of government. It is of utmost importance that we guard jealously the efficiency of these agencies. We must realize that if they are to function honestly and well we are the ones who must make them do so. Too many of us think of "the government" as something remote and separate from the people. Government cannot keep itself clean; all of us who are lazy citizens have helped to make some aspects of government dirty, and we are the only ones who can remedy matters.

Certain trends during the war have brought home a new consciousness of the personal responsibility of citizens. The Office of Civilian Defense, for example, has given millions of persons something definite to do to help in the war program. Activities of the organization have tended to revive and strengthen community and neighborhood spirit which in peacetime has lagged. How strong this spirit may become was shown in England as it withstood Nazi bombing attacks. In this country an interesting illustration of a wartime organization's meeting a peacetime need was seen in May 1943, when over eight hundred women block leaders of the OCD in Fort Smith, Arkansas, were called upon during a flood to set up overnight a system of water rationing. The pipelines from the city's water supply had been swept away and water reserves within the city were dangerously low. These women acted with speed and precision, notifying families as 8500 home water connections were cut off, setting up a rationing center for homes in each block, and superintending the citywide distribution of water for more than a week. Efficient and friendly handling of this situation bolstered the spirit of the citizens and gave them renewed faith in the ability of government-sponsored civilian service groups.

The war rationing programs have brought forth a tremendous amount of faithful service from private citizens, as has the sale of war bonds. Such activities as these, along with vastly increased taxation, are bound to create in the people a greater awareness of the need for government efficiency and of their personal stake in making certain that efficiency is forthcoming.

Probably the greatest single contribution any government agency makes to morale is that of effective operation. We have no such thing as a government morale agency, yet every significant government service efficiently operated helps build morale. Ordinary government services usually are instituted only because people consider them essential, and in many cases they are not undertaken until the need is so urgent that it can be ignored no longer. Thus we have such federal services as the Children's Bureau, the Social Security Board, the crop and marketing division of the Department of Agriculture, and during the war such agencies as the Office of Price Administration and the War Production Board. Not one is a morale agency as such, but how essential their effective service is to morale becomes immediately apparent when they fail to function properly:

Let any one of these or a score of other services falter, and almost overnight hundreds of thousands of families will develop the feeling that their Government is slipping and the war effort is bogging down. . . .

Go down to the local level. Is the local waterworks a "morale agency"? . . . Or your local power company? Paralyze any one of them for forty-eight hours, or even four, and you will see a town on the brink of hysteria, unless it has been well organized for the shock.[5]

Other government agencies which illustrate the importance of effective service are public libraries and health departments. Public libraries provide one of the more unobtrusive government services, yet it would be difficult to find an agency which renders more thoughtfully planned and far-reaching service. Library workers are a professionally trained and socially conscious group. An endless variety of calls for assistance comes to them. Loss of efficient library service would be a serious blow to any city. The scope of the library program for the armed forces was a recognition by military authorities of the morale-building value of books and other printed materials. Health departments perform constant service in all parts of the country, taking emergency measures to protect public health in times of disaster and waging an unrelenting fight in their day-by-day activities against the spread of disease. Like the public library and other government agencies not mentioned, much of the health department's work is not spectacular but its essential character underlines the importance to morale of effective operation of government.

Increasingly, social and economic affairs have been considered proper spheres for action of the people thru their government agencies. The great mass of people want and need intelligent and honest democratic leadership. The work of our schools and that of all our other agencies contributing to education for citizenship is our provision for developing leadership. Whether that provision is sufficient may be judged best by the fact that some individuals of dubious quality attain public office and by the common assumption that "politics is dirty." We should make more definite provision in our educational system for the training and selection of public servants.

Both the Army and the Navy have specific provision for training leaders in their academies. Government officials also need special training. The usual condemnation of politics will lose force only when a political career is regarded as an honorable one requiring definite preparation.

---

[5] Broughton, Philip S. "Government Agencies and Civilian Morale." *Annals of the American Academy of Political and Social Science* 220: 168-77; March 1942.

Some of our universities have taken steps in this direction. They should be encouraged to develop even stronger programs for the postwar demobilization period. Specialized training in government affairs should be given in addition to stressing the usual phases of liberal education. The work of these institutions should interest more of our best youth in careers of public service and drive home forcibly in the public mind the value of such preparation on the part of those who offer themselves as candidates. More thoughtful and intelligent voting should result. Existing units of government might cooperate in training programs.

Another guarantee of improved functioning of government agencies would be extension of the practice of selecting civil servants on the basis of merit and competitive examinations. The civil service movement is based on the principle that we must have efficient government agencies. England has gone far in developing the civil service as an honored calling so that today there are few government positions in that country that are not filled on the basis of competitive examination and merit. We have made substantial progress in this country with the idea but much is yet to be desired.

Further development of a system of training to produce qualified public servants and assurance of employment on a basis of merit would pay dividends not only in more honest and effective service but also in increased confidence in our leaders. These steps would eliminate many of the situations which have tended to lower morale and weaken interest in performance of the duties of citizenship.

Occupational Groups

Inextricably involved in the morale of any country are its occupational groups, whether in business, industry, or the professions. Their influence on the economic status of the people thru wages and salaries paid and amounts charged for goods or services is a potent factor in determining standards of living, public health, education, recreation, and spiritual development. In addition, their group activities in the field of legislation affecting social and economic affairs make their role a doubly important one, fraught with possibilities for good or for evil. If the success and policies of enterprises of these groups are such as to redound to public good, then democratic institutions are strengthened because the individual is helped to a fuller and happier life. If they are not, then their own long-range success is endangered and national strength is perilously weakened. Obviously, occupational groups in this country have rendered great service and have made much of our progress possible; just as obviously, they have demonstrated weaknesses, the correction of which would greatly strengthen our institutions.

Movements which help increase opportunities for making a living and facilities for public health and recreation owe much to business. Notable advances in technology may be traced in large part to industry. Labor unions have supported public education and other types of social progress and have improved working conditions for the great segment of our population who labor. Significant legislation for social advancement has had the help of lawyers; physicians have contributed to great advances in the field of medicine; outstanding ministers have fostered increased social consciousness on the part of the church; and teachers have pointed new directions in education.

But there is another view of the situation, one in which the accomplishments of these groups seem small in comparison with what they yet may do. Business and industry, for example, have not solved satisfactorily the problem of paying wages permitting development of strong social morale in all individuals. Nor have business and industry, in creating new enterprises, always helped solve attendant problems endangering health, education, and social welfare. To mention only a few of the problems in which business and industry have responsibilities, one might list monopoly, fraudulent advertising, opposition to pure food and drug laws and to reforms concerning patent rights, the high mortality rate of small business in conflict with large enterprise, opposition to quality standard labeling for the information of consumers, the wide price gap between producer and consumer, and the lack of employment security.

Largest among the occupational groups is the great body of laborers brought together under the banner of unionism—the giant weapon forged by workers in business and industry. Created to give the individual strength thru collective bargaining on points at issue between labor and employers, unions have helped bring about notable social developments. Wage standards have been raised so that in many fields of employment workers have been given some degree of economic security. Lessening of care and anxiety, improved standards of health, more opportunity for education, greater leisure for recreation, and cultivation of mind and spirit have resulted. In addition to achieving economic gains which have made these things possible, the unions themselves have in many cases directly provided health service, educational opportunities, and recreational facilities for both children and adults. The garment workers' union, for example, is a vast educational organization providing opportunities for cultivation in the fine arts, as witnessed by its "Pins and Needles" production, as well as in the more practical fields of self-improvement. These developments give the individual courage and faith.

The battle of unionism, however, has not been wholly won; nor is it likely that it ever will be, for there will always be points of difference. One objective won, another is set up and the battle resumed. Without denying the benefits of unionism, it must be pointed out that, like any other great movement, it has its weaknesses and dangers. The principles of unionism may be abused, and unscrupulous, self-seeking men may achieve positions of power which they may use more for personal advantage than for the workers they are supposed to represent. The strike, having demonstrated its effectiveness, may be used too often and not too wisely. We have the spectacle of individuals submerged in mass enterprises; of lack of democratic relations within and between unions; of union officials accountable to no one but themselves; of resistance to technological change; and, above all, the resort to violence on the part of employers and employees, comparable to the settlement of international questions by bloody war. A part of these evils is due to stubborn resistance by some employers to reasonable demands by unions; a part is due to irresponsible and unwise leadership within unions themselves. But the ugly facts exist, in a form that can only weaken morale and even shake faith in our institutions, the government included.

It is not implied here that these serious conditions are solely the fault of labor. Employers share the responsibility. Both groups must realize that they are not fighting a private battle but are endangering the society which makes their respective activities possible when they neglect common interests and cultivate differences, when labor and employers reach agreements advantageous to both groups but harmful to the consumer, when employers fail in reasonable adjustment of wages and working conditions, and when unions fail to keep a clean house and in the heat of the fight demand concessions which can only bring ultimate harm. Labor and the employers have a joint interest in America:

. . . the true battle-line of American industry . . . is not between Labor and Management; it is between the constructive forces of both Labor and Management together on the one side, and the unpatriotic forces of selfishness on the other. United in such a fight Labor and Management can launch a mighty counter attack against the organized forces of division and subversion.[6]

Management and labor would do well to seek the things they have in common rather than to cultivate differences. It should be clear that they both desire economic gain, prestige, increased job security, and the interest found in successful accomplishment. To secure these things in greater proportion than would be possible otherwise, they should aim at union-management cooperation. This, however, usually is feasible only after management and the union have passed thru an initial "fighting stage" and a later relatively neutral period in which successful collective bargaining takes place. In most cases a process of psychological growth is necessary before it becomes possible for both sides to realize that much more is to be gained thru friendly cooperation than thru fighting.[7] This growth usually is slow, but intelligent leaders will recognize it as a goal and strive for it, knowing that their constituents must be educated toward the ideal of union-management cooperation. Both labor and management have done much to make America's greatness possible. By intelligent cooperation they can accomplish much more.

Members of the various professions also have problems the solution of which would build morale thru a happier, healthier citizenry. Lawyers, physicians, architects, and other professional men and women are by education, wealth, and personal qualities in a position to take leading places in each community's efforts for human betterment. Greater emphasis on social responsibility in the professional education of groups such as these would strengthen the contributions they make to promoting the common ideals of democracy.

What are the answers? No panaceas are offered here. The object is simply to point out that the problem of morale is closely associated with solution of the problems of adequate income, properly safeguarded rights, and sound professional service within the reach of all citizens. Education may be cited as the best long-time way of

---

[6] Taylor, H. Birchard. *Industrial Statesmanship*. Address given at a meeting on "War Production for Victory," April 18, 1943. Philadelphia: George W. Elliott (General Secretary, Chamber of Commerce and Board of Trade of Philadelphia), 1943. p. 11.

[7] Knickerbocker, Irving, and McGregor, Douglas. *Union-Management Cooperation: A Psychological Analysis*. Cambridge, Mass.: Department of Economics and Social Science, Massachusetts Institute of Technology, 1943. Reprinted from *Personnel*, Vol. 19, No. 3, by American Management Association, New York, N. Y.

bringing these things about. Education does have an opportunity to help young people prepare for economic life thru work experience and other specific training. It has a chance to help them see the opportunities and responsibilities for community service in business, industry, the labor movement, and the professions. But solution of these problems need not wait on education in the formal sense. Answers can be found. Mere knowledge that they are being honestly and persistently sought by the groups who can accomplish most—business, industry, labor, and the professions—would bring a tremendous lift in morale.

Social Services and Character-Forming Groups

In keeping with the increasing social consciousness of our time are such institutions as the family welfare bureau, visiting nurse associations, juvenile protective agencies, settlement houses, public assistance departments, and similar agencies for giving help to those who need it. That they do much to strengthen morale by their help and by convincing people that the community *does* care is not to be doubted. The agencies at work in this field are well aware of many added services they could render had they the necessary resources. Some of these agencies are tax-supported while others depend on gifts. Increased public support should be given them so they can do greater work in taking medical help and other essential services to the many who get it in no other way.

While it is overoptimistic to hope that society can be so developed that such agencies will no longer be necessary, it should be borne in mind that to some extent these are crutches for a society which has not learned how to insure a minimum level of human welfare to all its members. While social service groups should receive greater support and more provision should be made for training social workers, it is imperative that we work to eliminate factors which create clients for these agencies. This is not a job for social workers alone but for all citizens. The nature of some of the problems involved is indicated in the preceding section. The occupational groups are not unaware of their obligation. Employers and unions have aided thru provisions for raising the common economic level and thru making available educational, cultural, and recreational activities. Thru the efforts of various groups some progress has been made in the matter of bringing the cost of medical care within the reach of those who need it. Governmental and other agencies have sought with some success to equalize educational opportunity and to provide that type of training best calculated to help society cast aside its crutches. Despite these and other hopeful signs, we have made but a beginning. The degree of success thus far encountered should inspire all these groups to greater and more sustained effort to prove the efficacy of democratic institutions.

Notable contributions have been made to the building of character and democratic attitudes by Boy Scouts, Girl Scouts, 4-H Clubs, Girl Reserves, Hi-Y Clubs, and similar groups. The honorable history of such organizations bears witness to their contribution. The record of the Scouts, for example, in war and in peace, is one of achievement which could be possible only thru the building of high individual and group morale. The long, patient hours of work required to advance in Scout work and the untiring service rendered in community and national projects bespeak the devotion of the Scouts to their cause. The outstanding factor in connection with Scout work is the degree in which the traits developed carry over into adult life. Like statements would be true of the influence of other bodies.

These groups, unlike the social service organizations, are not primarily remedial. They are positive agencies for the development of character and morale in the best manner—by placing youth in the presence of constructive influences before the need for redirection arises or becomes too great. While recognizing that the need for social service work will always exist, we should keep in mind that it will become less necessary as we extend the influence of the character-forming groups by increasing their number and bringing a greater proportion of youth into contact with the right one at the right time. Social participation is a major factor in maintaining good morale. It has been reliably estimated, however, that of our youth one in five is a social isolate, seldom chosen as a companion for work or play.[8]

It is obvious, of course, that many organizations other than the ones mentioned help to mold character, develop interests, and influence morale. Societies, lodges, and clubs of many types help or hinder. While these groups may give members a feeling of unity, afford opportunity for the development of latent abilities and qualities of character, and help achieve community benefits, it should be kept in mind that not all their influence is for good. In the social

[8] Murphy, Lois B., *op. cit.*, p. 113.

fraternity, for example, there exists the danger of cultivating too expensive tastes and fostering snobbishness and other antidemocratic attitudes and activities. Harm may result from the depressive and repressive effect on those excluded from the fraternity. Such an organization may damage the morale of members and nonmembers alike. Undesirable attitudes created by one organization may, thru individuals, be transmitted to other groups and cause harm far from their source.

Not a formally organized group, such as others that are mentioned here, but nevertheless definitely a character-forming group of major importance is the "gang" of the type which provides much work for the social agencies mentioned earlier. For youth not brought sufficiently under the influence of the more desirable character-building groups, the gang takes the place of the club or fraternity. Gangs often have been recognized as a cause of delinquency and of the development of attitudes which have serious social effects. The United States has continued to neglect the needs of youth, conserving everything else before getting around to human resources.

The social service agencies which seek to improve home conditions and to lessen the impact of economic inequality are of assistance in this connection and deserve greater support. Boys' and girls' clubs and other directed groups into which neglected youth may be guided render great service and should receive all possible aid from community, religious, and industrial groups. Improved guidance and recreational programs in schools may do much to combat the influence of the gang. Wise education for home and family life has also its place in the school curriculum. Services rendered after the juvenile court has been called upon may come too late.

Adult education offers one of the greatest hopes for correction of the problem of neglected youth. Conversion of schools into adult education centers will do much to eliminate some of the basic causes of juvenile delinquency by permitting development of greater job efficiency and the cultivation of interests and attitudes in the parents which will be reflected in greater capacity for the guidance of children. Most important of all, adult education may arouse parents to awareness of the need of children for intelligent direction and help them thru special courses to meet that need.

The problem of youth left to its own devices without proper guidance finds its roots in all the situations basically affecting morale. All the things which may cause ill health, dissension, anxiety, and distrust may contribute to juvenile delinquency. Strengthening of religious, educational, and economic factors affecting morale will contribute to solution of the problem of undirected youth.

Press, Radio, and Motion Pictures

Any agency of public communication obviously has tremendous possibilities of affecting morale, since it is largely thru such means that the public gets its picture of what is going on in the world and forms its opinions as to the efficiency and sincerity of its servants and institutions. It is on the basis of reports and impressions received that laws are made, officials are elected, reforms are achieved or defeated, war is waged, and peace is established. Economic, social, and political progress depends in considerable measure upon the nature of reports reaching the people, since it is upon public support that reforms must ultimately rely for success.

The press, radio, and motion picture, the three major forces of communication, are like many other institutions in that they have their fields of high achievement and their areas of weakness. Each can point to noteworthy wartime achievements. All three, considering the handicaps under which they have labored, for the most part have given much honest and courageous reporting and have sincerely supported the war program. Consistently preaching Americanism, they have made themselves highly useful in salvage drives, war stamp and bond sales, and other wartime activities.

Following the Second War Loan drive in the spring of 1943, the Secretary of the Treasury was reported in the May 29 issue of *The Publishers' Auxiliary,* trade paper of the Western Newspaper Union, as crediting the nation's newspapers, radio, and other mediums with "the greatest advertising operation in the history of the world." A total of 1758 daily and 7735 weekly newspapers had carried 79,939 Second War Loan advertisements with a value of $4,564,271. Radio, in the same period, was credited with 118,000 announcements and 8000 programs of fifteen minutes or more devoted to the Second War Loan drive.

The motion picture industry, likewise, has lent valuable assistance in many campaigns. In 1942, collections in moving picture theaters for the Greek War Relief, United Service Organizations, the Army-Navy Emergency Relief, and the fight against infantile paralysis totaled $5,316,250. In response to campaigns thru theaters there were turned in 326,000,000 pounds of scrap and several million pounds of fats. In one month the combined efforts of executives, stars, distributors, and exhibitors sold $353,701,058 in war stamps and bonds.[9] The motion picture industry, along with radio, has made a significant contribution to morale with programs for men in the armed forces and with inspirational work on the home front.

Similarly, these industries may point to peacetime work in the cause of social progress that must be marked on the credit side of the ledger. Information, interpretation, criticism, entertainment, and inspiration provided by these groups in no small measure help to smooth the path of progress and to make life pleasant. On the other side of the record, however, may be found areas in which these agencies need to improve in order to increase their services.

It cannot be denied that some aspects of the activity of the press, radio, and motion picture industries damage morale. All three sometimes engender public cynicism as to their sincerity by aspects of their work growing out of the fact that they are operated for profit. This is not meant to suggest that they should be transferred to government operation. We do not need a continuous flood of government-directed propaganda to build morale, as in Germany. One of our strengths is that while no one has forced them to do so our magazine writers, newspapermen, and radio commentators, along with radio and screen stars, with few exceptions, have spoken for Americanism at every opportunity.

It should be recognized that these agencies did not set themselves up primarily as educational agencies. The motion pictures and the radio were built into big business by people who were trying to make a living by providing entertainment and selling advertising. They have found themselves in a position of great influence which they did not seek in the first place. Because of the social implications of their work, however, they cannot escape this unasked-for responsibility. These agencies need only to purge themselves of their irresponsible elements and to adhere to higher standards to remove most causes of the suspicion which hampers them as educational, cultural, and democracy-building forces.

Press and radio's connection with questionable advertising, which any intelligent person recognizes as dishonest, is a major handicap. The publication and broadcasting of doubtful material on the

---

[9] War Activities Committee of the Motion Picture Industry. *Movies at War.* New York: the Committee (1501 Broadway), 1942. p. 19.

ground that it is what the public wants does not help build confidence in either agency of communication. Recourse to the freedom-of-the-press plea as justification for certain abuses promotes cynicism for it is frequently apparent that the real motive is more and greater profit, political self-seeking, or suppression of the truth. Similarly, it is worthy of thought that "freedom of the air" is a "freedom" available to those who can afford to pay for it and that the economically powerful can propagandize while others cannot.

These agencies have a special duty in connection with their presentation of labor news. Without denying the accuracy of some unfavorable reports on union demands and activities, it must be pointed out that there is a strongly antilabor bias in many news sources. Working people consequently feel that they are being misrepresented and their morale suffers. One of the biggest problems of the agencies of communication in the effort to build unity is that of fairer, more impartial reports on the activities of labor. The achievements of labor should be given such recognition that its faults will not be made to loom out of proportion.

During the war the press has generally realized and respected the fact that military and diplomatic plans cannot always be reported promptly. But on occasion it has hampered the work of leaders by adverse criticism which, as events developed, proved to be groundless. It is possible to place too much emphasis on shortages, handicaps due to strikes, wasteful expenditures, and bad planning.

The defects in our program should not be covered up—that would have a particularly poisonous effect upon morale—but they should be seen in the perspective of the whole. What America needs is not detailed knowledge of the plans for victory, but a certainty that the plans have been drawn, and a general understanding of the progress being made.[10]

The motion picture industry, in creating a new art, has done much that is good. Its wartime contribution already has been recognized. What will be its course in peace? If it has profited from experience, it will continue in some of its recent trends with documentary, historical, and patriotic films. Pictures giving honest portrayals of small-town life and rural scenes are also desirable. The industry must veer away from the course which has caused public absorption in meretricious treatment of sex and the more sensational aspects of

[10] Watson, Goodwin. "Five Factors in Morale." *Civilian Morale.* Second Yearbook, Society for the Psychological Study of Social Issues. Boston: Houghton Mifflin Co., 1942. p. 42.

life. Hollywood can continue best to demonstrate its value, in war and in peace, by greater devotion to truth. By so doing it can make its greatest contribution to education and to democracy. Any contention that it gives to the public what it wants when it produces cheap and sensational pictures is not valid except in that Hollywood gives the public what it has taught the public to want. It can teach the people to appreciate the values of American life and to understand its problems as they are instead of offering a large dosage of fantastic "super-colossal" productions. This does not mean that we should have no romantic and imaginative drama; some unreality should be encouraged, but the quality and direction are important.

All agencies of communication should accept more definitely their cultural mission and realize that if the average of public taste, information, and attitudes is low it can never be elevated by catering to their lower levels. The weaknesses of these agencies are understandable in the light of their history and the nature of their economic bases. It is not the nature, however, of American enterprise to recognize its weak points as beyond remedy.

Literature and the Arts

Books and magazines, the stage. music, sculpture, and the graphic arts must be recognized as builders of morale. They are carriers of fact and emotion that are of prime importance in building understanding. sympathy, and desire for service. They both reflect and help to shape trends of public opinion.

The hard-bitten realism in much modern literature and art is a protest against the failure of our society to make it possible for human beings to live in dignity and freedom. To some critics it has seemed that writers and artists were so fascinated by the sorrow and sordidness they pictured that they forgot the values for which they were crusading. Perhaps the time has come for the literati and the artists to make more explicit the message they are trying so urgently to give. The war seemed to release this spirit in many writers. In clarity of thought they spoke the faith that was in them. They were not self-conscious or afraid to discuss such subjects as the compatibility of democracy with human dignity or the nobility of free institutions. It is to be hoped that the writers who have helped to clarify American ideals in the face of a common danger can help America to keep those ideals alive in the face of a common hope. It is never really smart to be cynical; our writers can serve the country well if, having emerged from their intellectual no man's land, they can stay out of it. They can help us to deal sensibly with the mistakes and contradictions of the war and the after-war adjustment and can show us that "to fail to look past these dark by-products into the larger needs and the larger ideals is to pass up the greatest opportunity for constructive thinking in history."[11]

The great books, music, and art of the past and the present have values both as ends in themselves and as a means of building personal attitudes and understandings of importance in morale. *Julius Caesar* and *The Patriots* both can stir us with the love of country. *Oliver Twist* and *The Grapes of Wrath* alike challenge the civic conscience. Goya and Gropper tell the same story of the tragedy of war. Michelangelo's marble and Bufano's stainless steel both can portray the dignity of leadership.

As highways across barriers of race and language the arts have a place of their own. Tolstoy's books must be read in translation, but thousands of Americans have heard Russia's own voice of today in the music of Shostakovich. Chinese carvings, embroideries, and other exquisite works of skill give us insight into the quality of a people we should know better. Americans at war continue to sing German songs and to enjoy Italian opera.

Literature and the arts do not accomplish their full possibilities for usefulness partly because of their lack of an audience and partly because some writers and artists do not really understand and respect their fellow Americans. For example, those who think of all small-town people as hicks and all farmers as hayseeds are not qualified to interpret America to itself. Recent trends toward regionalism in writing may help to overcome the blind spots. The lack of an audience is being overcome in part thru the newspapers, the radio, and moving pictures; thru expanding services of libraries, museums, and art galleries; thru "popular" concert series; and thru education in schools and colleges.

Schools and Colleges in Relation to Other Agencies

Like all other forces affecting morale, schools and colleges have no clear field but must take into consideration and cooperate with the work of other agencies. The school can, however, be more

---

[11] Cousins, Norman. "Crisis Thinking." (Editorial.) *Saturday Review of Literature* 26: 14; August 28, 1943.

consciously directed by society toward the building of desirable attitudes than can any other agency. While it cannot separate students from the influence of other agencies, even if that were desirable, it does present a unit of society in which, more than in any other group, conditions and activities are subject to some degree of regulation with the desired objective in mind.

One of the principal ways in which the school can help other groups is by taking the initiative in securing coordinated activity by community organizations. When we consider the various agencies affecting youth it becomes evident that if a community has a youth problem it often is not due to lack of interest and effort but lack of coordination. Numerous civic organizations, service clubs, women's clubs, veterans' organizations, parent-teacher associations, and other groups are interested in the welfare of youth and in improving community conditions. The older institutions—the school, the church, and the local government—have shown widened conceptions of their responsibility for the welfare of children and adults. While leaders of these groups understand that no one organization is sufficiently strong to cope with problems facing youth in modern communities, they realize that thru coordination of all constructive forces there is a good chance of solving almost any problem facing a single community.[12] The device which in the past few years has been adopted increasingly as a means of coordinating constructive forces in the community is the council in which all groups seeking to promote the common welfare are represented. Schools, churches, service clubs, scout councils, commercial, labor, and farm organizations, and other groups should all be represented. This community council makes surveys, determines needs, and secures action thru the agencies represented. It avoids duplication of effort, prevents waste of funds, and creates a unity of spirit which permits of more effective community welfare work.[13]

Councils—coordinating, neighborhood, and rural—may provide an effective and democratic means of achieving community solidarity in serving youth. . . . The major responsibility for effecting such a coordination rests with school administrators.[14]

[12] Coordinating Councils, Inc. *A Guide to Community Coordination.* Los Angeles, Calif.: the Councils, 1941. p. 1.
[13] American Council on Education, American Youth Commission. *Community Responsibility for Youth.* Washington, D. C.: the Council, 1940. p. 6.
[14] American Association of School Administrators. *Schools and Manpower.* Twenty-First Yearbook. Washington, D. C.: the Association, a department of the National Education Association, 1943. p. 224.

Beyond its role of encouraging joint endeavors on behalf of building desirable youthful attitudes, the school thru its own program can strengthen the work of other morale-building agencies.

HOME AND NEIGHBORHOOD

In seeking to help improve home and neighborhood conditions the school should recognize more clearly that education is a continuing process thruout life. Adults are improvable. Given sufficient stimulus, they can make definite progress toward becoming more intelligent parents, more efficient workers, and more worthwhile citizens. The adult education movement, already strong, should be given greater impetus.

In addition, the school may help strengthen home and family life thru its extended services. Such workers as the home visitor, the school nurse, the physician, the dentist, the psychologist, and all those engaged in the counseling and guidance program may give important service in detecting, analyzing, and helping correct handicaps under which the children labor. Since most of these handicaps have their origins, at least in part, in the home, the school's social agencies division is greatly concerned with home and family life. Such services as nursery schools and after-school care of the children of working mothers have been extended greatly during the war. These programs have laid the foundation for similar services equally needed in peacetime. Set up as emergency measures, they have had as their major purpose the release of adult workers for the sake of boosting war production, a purpose which has been achieved in many cases at the sacrifice of the best type of family life and child care. Nevertheless it has been demonstrated that the scope of childhood education and family guidance can be extended. After the war there should be a continuation and expansion of such services with the avowed purpose of nurturing children and families as a national and world resource.

RELIGION AND THE CHURCH

The school can foster greater interest in religion and the church by giving increased emphasis in historical and literary studies to spiritual values and by emphasizing the principles of fair play, human brotherhood, and democracy, which are fundamentals of religion. In social studies there is a place for nonsectarian discussion of religion and its function in the individual life. Students should be made aware of the fact that everyone has a need for a core of belief that makes life worth living and that historically this has been provided by the church. They should be encouraged to find that type of meaning for their own lives.

GOVERNMENT

The school can give clearer understanding of the functions and mechanism of government and provide more adequate training for government service. It can educate future voters to choose their representatives wisely. Mere instruction in the forms and duties of governmental branches is not sufficient here. There should be careful study also of the qualities essential in public servants, and students should be led to see that they as citizens will be responsible for their government. The aim should be a more desirable attitude toward the responsibilities of citizenship, an attitude free from the taint of cynicism. More schools would do well to follow the lead of those institutions which give their students practical experience in the art of self-government as a phase of everyday school experience. A definite aim of the school in this training for citizenship should be to produce in the minds of students an emotional attachment to democratic institutions. Education has failed in an important matter if a student leaves school without having had endeared to him the institutions under which he lives.

OCCUPATIONAL GROUPS

Another need the school can meet is that of more adequate training for occupational life by more effective general training and by equipping students for jobs. While there is division of opinion as to the degree of emphasis on vocational training in the public schools, the consensus seems unmistakably to favor more rather than less attention to this problem. It is reasonable to believe that training which will help assure economic competence will help us progress toward goals which we failed to reach while clinging to traditional concepts of education. An encouraging sign of the times is the "Dutch Uncle" plan, under which adults of a community help provide vocational guidance for boys and girls. The guidance services within the schools are expanding. Schools have increased greatly their offerings in the field of commercial work, and, largely thru the aid of federal funds, they are steadily providing more opportunities for training in agriculture, home economics, and industrial fields.

While the various existing provisions for vocational education, along with some other school courses and activities, provide work experience for many students, provision should be made for every high-school student to be given training in how to work. "Young people as part of their equipment for the world in which they live have to learn how to work. Provision of work experience for students is a responsibility of society in which the school has an important role."[15] This obligation was recognized by many superintendents who saw values in the National Youth Administration in spite of its costly training and other objectionable features, because it did provide work experience which public schools had not been able to afford. Many devices for providing supervised work experience are within the reach of the school, especially if it makes full use of the resources which may be made available by securing the cooperation of community groups.

Advocacy of vocational training and work experience does not mean that intellectual and cultural aspects of education are to be neglected. It does mean that the more traditional objectives of education must be supplemented in recognition of the fact that there is increasing necessity for more specific equipment of youth for earning a living. The recent trend toward vocational guidance and counseling, given special wartime encouragement by the national government, is one acknowledgment of the need for economic training suited to the needs of the individual—a need which doubtless will become more pressing in the postwar period.

SOCIAL SERVICES AND CHARACTER-FORMING GROUPS

The school can cooperate more effectively with social service and character-forming groups by working in closer connection with them and by strengthening those aspects of its program which will do most to eliminate conditions creating clients for service agencies. This includes occupational training, encouragement of religious life, and study of social agencies and family relationships, as well as provision of various activities of educational, cultural, and social nature. Thru its own social services as represented by

---

[15] American Association of School Administrators, *op. cit.*, p. 32.

the home visitor, the school nurse, the psychologist, and the guidance worker, it can help community agencies in effective welfare work. Much good may be gained thru extracurriculum activities. Properly conducted, their effectiveness will carry over to after-school life. While providing additional knowledge and skills and guiding energy into desirable channels, they provide one of the best methods of training for citizenship. They give the individual a feeling that he is needed, show him that he has a part to play, and build thru his participation desirable attitudes which do not stop with school life but affect his attitude toward other activities in which he may engage. Unfortunately, in most schools only a small proportion of the students reap such benefit. Many of them do not take part, while many others merely "belong" and leave active work to the few. We have much to learn about effective use of organizations and activities.

PRESS, RADIO, AND MOTION PICTURES

It is within the power of the school to help students toward a more critical and evaluative attitude toward the newspaper, the radio program, and the motion picture. These means of communication are of such importance that any well-rounded school program must recognize in them not only a source of information but also the literature of the great body of our people. Social science and literature courses which ignore them can lay no claim to completeness. Some schools have set a good example by offering courses in how to read a newspaper. Courses or units which thus consider the newspaper as a social instrument might well be expanded to include attention also to radio and motion picture. All subjects, however, should be taught in the light of current developments as reported thru these avenues of communication. The importance of providing more effective guidance for children in the areas covered by agencies of communication has been emphasized in studies which suggested that in the course of a year the time spent by students in reading comic strips, listening to the radio, and going to movies approximates the time these students spend in school.[16] Educational procedure which makes no provision for meeting this situation clearly fails to meet a vital need.

---

[16] Ohio State University, Bureau of Educational Research. *News Letter.* Vol. 3, No. 1, November 1937, and Vol. 3, No. 3, January 1938.

LITERATURE AND THE ARTS

The school curriculum has long emphasized languages and literature, and recently more attention has been given to the arts. This instruction can be strengthened by continued emphasis on developing linguistic and artistic skills, by developing appreciation of literature and the arts in the general population, and in addition by a new emphasis on the function of writers and artists in a democratic society and on the place of languages as instruments of world cooperation. The music program in the schools, especially its emphasis on bands, orchestras, and glee clubs, makes a contribution to both morale and the increased enjoyment of good music. Students in school orchestras see the value of the discipline imposed in producing an artistic performance; each person has his part to play in the group effort, and each must do his best for the success of the whole. High-school students often give up their Saturday mornings thruout the year for special practice. Many of the music-making groups in school result in the formation later of neighborhood choral societies and instrumental ensembles, on an amateur basis. For other students school music is the first step into a lifetime vocation. The great majority of students are helped by school music to become an appreciative audience for the music of others.

The recent wartime activities of the schools of America demonstrate the degree to which the school may serve as an agency for morale. Hardly had the report of Pearl Harbor reached the nation before administrators and teachers began shaping their plans to meet the emergency. Precedent was scrapped. Traditional academic courses were recast to achieve wartime effectiveness; preinduction courses were set up to train boys and girls to take their places in industry or in the armed forces; patriotic programs were planned; scrap drives were conducted; school stamp and war bond sales brought in millions; and students became active in many phases of civilian defense work. Out of all this wartime activity may come much which will carry over its effectiveness to years of peace.

★ *The school that wishes to develop morale will so conduct its affairs as to encourage its children to grow, by sharing in its affairs, into the practice of democracy.*

CHAPTER VII

The Individual School Builds Morale

NOWHERE DOES THE RESPONSIBILITY for building the kind of democratic morale needed for a world of free men rest more heavily than upon teachers and the schools. This is true because they deal directly with the fabric from which the American future is to be woven and for a long enough time to be at least fairly effective. No other agency has an equal opportunity, for no other group of trained leaders has nearly so much contact with all the children of all the people—the millions of potential citizens of tomorrow. Both public and private schools share in this responsibility. What may be done in the individual school is the task to which this chapter addresses itself. No matter what may be the conditions without the walls of any school, those who work within may, if they have vision and courage, together build morale of the highest order.

The School Situation

The school has its setting within a community of parents and other adults whose interests and activities help to determine the work that the school must do. The principal and his administrative assistants provide leadership and services which set the stage for the processes of learning. Teachers and pupils together carry on the vital activities of teaching and learning thru which the school gives its young citizens the equipment they need to meet their individual and group responsibilities, both present and future.

CHILDREN AND YOUTH

Children are living in a world not of their own making or choosing—at all times a world full of wonders, but also a strange world full of stresses, strains, and fears, greatly augmented in times of crisis such as war or calamity. They too often see their elders disturbed by events of many kinds. They need and deserve every possible help that will give them a sense of calmness and certainty that is the rightful heritage of youth; that will give them a vital sense of being a factor in whatever situation faces the family, the school, and the community; and that will give them, each at his own level of understanding, the beginnings of a strong faith, based on reasonable expectation for the future, in the kind of world this generation must build. They must have confidence in a world into which they can enter with high hopes for their share in it. Only such sharing of the present and sure faith in the future can build the morale that is needed.

Youth ask for a place in the sun usually not heretofore accorded them. Their warm and valiant response to the challenges of the war situation leaves no doubt that one problem of education is to give to children and youth such experiences as will reveal possible significant roles for them. The increase in juvenile delinquency during the war is a sad commentary upon our lack of vision in failing to provide vitalizing and challenging opportunities for youth to share in the real work of the world, in sufficient and adequate leisure-time activities, and in cooperative school programs.

TEACHERS

The teacher is by far the most important factor in building morale in an individual school. It is he alone who is in daily intimate contact with child life; he who, probably next to the parents in the home, profoundly affects the thinking and habits of a child. In spite of the shortness of time at his command, in spite of the poor school facilities often afforded, and in spite of the barren leadership sometimes existing, the teacher can and often does rise to heights of statesmanship in his dealings with children. No teacher need let any of the barriers to complete success prevent him from giving his best to help children develop morale. It is after all largely a matter of the spirit and the spirit of master teachers everywhere rises above barriers and is beyond price.

Teachers must always be conscious of their own need for growth if they are to remain worthy of the confidence of children. The teacher in a large city system who boasted that she walked into the building with her children in the morning and out at the head of the line at night, that she had taught in one school for twenty-four years and had never taken a professional course since she started, and that she considered teachers' meetings a bore was certainly not showing much evidence that she was remaining, if indeed she had ever been, a valuable companion for children.

The master teacher, who is wanted and needed everywhere, is well educated professionally and believes in his profession as one of the noblest, with intangible rewards far beyond the financial. This teacher believes that it takes work and extra hours to do the job well but balances his living so that he has many other interests as well. His own morale is so high, calm, and steady that he can and does impart to his associates the feeling of certainty that he will stand calmly whatever comes and help others to do the same. He is careful to be well groomed, as rested as possible, and in the best possible state of health. He thinks about and does something about the effect the quality of his voice has on children. He is the kind of teacher who sees children as individuals, who knows no two of them are alike, who shares planning and responsibilities with them, and who knows it is no kindness to a child to let him be or do less than his best in behavior, work, and play. In short, he is the kind of person whom children trust, in whose presence they feel that all is right with their world. Given this kind of teacher, of whom fortunately there are many, the task of building morale in the individual school is more than half done, for important as is *what* they do, the *spirit* of the doing is more important.

Teachers who catch this vision of their role as one of the steadying influences in the lives of children and also a vision of the kind of world to which their pupils will some day fall heir can do much for the morale of youth, especially in troubled times. The educator who is prepared best to do this informs himself on the best thought available on the current situation and on the possibilities for worldwide peace for the future. He will thus contribute most to the morale of the generation that will shortly find itself face to face with problems undreamed of in earlier days. Those who taught us belonged to the horse-and-buggy era; we belong to the era of the automobile; these children of ours will point their vehicles straight toward the stars and their silver wings will carry them so far that we cannot follow them even in thought and can only be thankful if we helped them to find their wings.

THE PRINCIPAL AND THE NONTEACHING STAFF

The same atmosphere can be created in the school as a whole, depending upon the viewpoint of the principal or supervisor. To be sure, if higher authority has decreed a set procedure, there is little the principal can do but administer that procedure or move to a new field offering more scope for imagination. But having either the permission or active cooperation of the higher-ups to develop procedures for growth of morale throws the challenge straight into the lap of the principal. From this point he can take his choice of at least two kinds of procedure. If he is ill prepared professionally, too fond of ease and comfort to study, or lacking in vision or courage, it is likely that permission to develop his school as he sees fit will not result in much good to his staff or children. However, only those should be allowed to be principals or supervisors who are not afraid to work, who do not watch the clock, who study constantly, and who like to work for and plan for great opportunities for child growth and morale. It is the kind of job that is never-ending, all-absorbing, and vastly satisfying to the right kind of person.

The greatest service a principal or supervisor can perform probably is in helping to create a climate of opportunity for teachers and children, in removing as many as possible of the barriers to their greatest happiness and efficiency, in standing helpfully shoulder to shoulder with them when difficulties arise, in encouraging initiative and giving praise for its results, and in giving credit where credit is due. National and state associations of elementary- and secondary-school principals and many training institutions are doing valiant work to develop this concept of the principalship, and morale in thousands of schools is higher because of sincere, informed, cooperative, and inspiring leadership.

The democratic school will show in every phase of its existence the superior spirit and compulsions that motivate it. Whether one examines the climate of its instructional groups, the curriculum, the methods, the quality of the in-service growth of school personnel, the integration with the life of the community, the way children and all workers in the school greet and work with each other, or the way parents speak and act about their school including the way they support it, in each the cooperative school reveals itself for what it is. Here the custodial staff, the clerks, the teachers, the parents, the children, the nurses, and the supervisors are co-workers, each attacking the same problem from a different angle. It is in this kind of school that American democracy finds its best opportunity, on whatever level of child life, to build the kind of morale that is needed.

THE COMMUNITY

The school takes its tone quite largely from community expectations. If enough people are interested, they get just about what they want from their schools. In some schools the principal and teachers are deeply sympathetic with any good parent movement, welcome parents to the school, and cooperate with them in every way. In others professional people have no one but themselves to blame when the community contacts are poor. The democratic school that develops the best morale for free men will have back of it the support of the community in providing such health services, buildings, supplies, trained teachers, and leaders with sufficient vision as will make this possible.

The Place of the School in the Life of the Child

As is clearly pointed out elsewhere in this volume, school life is only one of the many factors that influence morale and a comparatively limited one at that. Indeed it is surprising that schools accomplish as much as they do since time spent at school is confined to so small a fraction of a child's life. It is high tribute to the efficiency and strength of school programs that in spite of time limitations they still seem to influence morale so tremendously.

Let us show the place of the school in the life of a child by a time graph. Suppose we take as an example the time during a year spent at various phases of life activity by an average ten-year-old who attends a rather good suburban school, where 189 days of instruction are provided annually, far more than the average for the country. Suppose he attends a school of religious instruction for one hour weekly, which is more organized religious instruction than is received by the average child; that he sits down at the table three times daily for one-half hour each time, to eat his meals in a leisurely, well-mannered fashion, which is more time and attention than is usually given by a ten-year-old to this important activity; that he spends about fifteen minutes a day each in preparing for the day, in preparing for bed, and in walking to and from school twice a day (this might be considered somewhat typical of such activities in which every child *must* daily engage); and that he sleeps ten hours each night, which is more time than is often given to this necessary habit by many ten-year-olds. Suppose the required school time is about five hours a day, extracurriculum time, if any, being somewhat at the option of child and parent. Then his personal time graph would look like Figure II.

Notice the small fraction of the total year in which schools are expected to do the enormous number of things already entrusted to their care, and in such a way that the desired morale results. It is not surprising, in view of this too little recognized fact, that leaders with vision plead for more time, better facilities, better and better trained teachers, and more cooperation with the home and the many other agencies whose influence helps build or break morale.

Attention is called to the enormous amount of so-called "leftover" time shown by this graph. There will be a variety of reac-

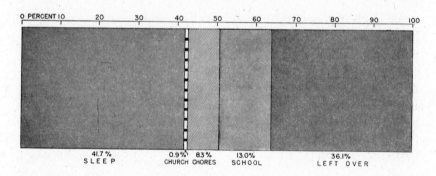

Sleep—Allowing ten hours per day for sleep—total 3650 hours, or 41.7 percent of year.

Religious instruction—Allowing one hour per week plus average time of fifteen minutes each way to come and go—total 78 hours, or 0.9 percent of year.

Necessary "chores"—Allowing thirty minutes per meal, plus average time of fifteen minutes each to dress and undress—total 730 hours, or 8.3 percent of year.

School—Allowing five required hours per day for 189 days, plus average time of fifteen minutes each way to come and go twice daily—total 1134 hours, or 13.0 percent of year.

"Left-over" time—Time left to be allotted to other pursuits after eating, dressing, sleeping, and school requirements are allowed—total 3168 hours, or 36.1 percent of year.

FIGURE II.—HOW AN AVERAGE TEN-YEAR-OLD SPENDS HIS

YEAR OF 8760 HOURS

tion to this claim. Studies have shown that in at least certain areas all manner of school and community activities have so completely absorbed this time that parents say they meet their children only coming and going. This would seem to argue for more and better parent-teacher planning so far as a wise regulation of extracurriculum school activities is concerned. Some families are not satisfied unless the children take part in everything offered by the school. It would also seem to argue for something that has been tried in several communities—an interactivity or interservice community council which attempts to plan wisely and to coordinate the activities offered the children and youth of the area so that the Scouts, the church, the school, the home, the music and dancing teachers, the Y.M.C.A. or Y.W.C.A., and others too numerous to mention are not all competing for use of the same hours.

On the other hand, in some areas these same "left-over" hours are the hours that produce the juvenile delinquency so alarmingly deterrent to good morale at all times and especially in times of crisis such as a depression or a war. This is the other side of the picture, and even in areas that provide a wide variety of valuable activities, surveys have shown a surprising number of children and youth who, for one reason or another, do not avail themselves of any of these. Perhaps a better guidance program is indicated here— more attention to what children think and want and to the reasons why they hesitate to join their fellows in the available resources of their community. In communities that provide little or no facilities for wise use of these "left-over" hours, the picture is black indeed, for children without guidance find their own activities, which are often anything but conducive to the kind of American democracy we want to build.

In this connection it should be noted, however, that there should be *some* "left-over" time in the life of every child and adult as well. There should be opportunity to dream, to think, to learn to organize one's own interests, and occasionally to do just nothing if one so wishes. Perhaps so many Americans would not arrive at middle life tied up in emotional knots if this were part of our practice. A wise balance between too little and too much planning and supervision in the affairs of a child is a delicate one to strike and varies greatly with the child—another argument for intelligent attention to individual differences.

Another comment that should be made regarding this analysis of time allotment is that parents have children alone or in small groups and during their most impressionable years, especially before they start to school at all, while teachers always have them in larger and often too large groups at a time when many habits are so fixed that changing them is often quite impossible. This seems to point out further the great importance of those early years with the parents and later time in the small, intimate, family group—so great that wise parents seek every available help to make these contacts as valuable as possible and schools with vision offer help in this area. It also highlights the need that teachers have for close cooperation with these parents who should and often do know the most about a child, to enable them to understand the child better and to supplement intelligently the training the parents are giving him.

The American school as a whole may not hope for complete success in building morale even in its somewhat limited sphere of time unless a far larger majority than at present of the children of school age are in school enough of the year and in schools of the right kind. Demand should be increased, particularly in times of crisis when so much pressure is always brought to bear in curtailing educational offerings, for a greatly extended educational program to meet better the needs of all children, for more effort to retain good teachers in schools, and for increasing rather than lessening school support.

Climate and procedure in instructional groups and the variety of school offerings vary so much that we do not deserve the reputation of "equal opportunity for all." The complete lack of any school facilities for some children; the short terms for others; the miserable excuses for school buildings with meager, old-fashioned equipment, almost no supplies, and low standards of cleanliness found in some rural communities and in some sections of our cities also; and the incompetent teachers sometimes found— all these conditions contrast strangely in democratic America with the lot of the fortunate children whose communities provide beautiful buildings, spacious play space, splendidly trained teachers, ample programs, and time enough to do a good job. It is time for America to wake up to these inequalities and to equalize opportunity more nearly for all the children of all the people.

Good School Practices in Building Morale

The guiding philosophy for the practices that build morale and lay foundations for morale in the long future is stated in preceding chapters. To repeat in terms of school practice, we may say:

1. The school must recognize and strive to meet for each child his human needs for physical health and well-being.

2. The school must recognize and strive to meet for each child his psychological needs for social status and the sense of security and *esprit de corps* that comes thru being a needed and valuable member of his society.

3. The school must recognize and strive to meet for each child his need for a unifying element in life that will integrate his activities toward a *common cause* that he can share with others. For our society and for the better future we hope to build, that common cause will be the *ideals of democracy*. Our children should understand and earnestly desire for themselves and for all other people the opportunity to live lives guided by truth, freedom, fellow feeling, human dignity, and personal responsibility.

In any single hour of a school's living, the contribution which the school is making to these three foundations of democratic morale can scarcely be pulled apart and identified as separate activities. They constantly supplement and interact upon each other. But for purposes of discussion and emphasis they are considered separately in the following pages.

MEETING THE NEED FOR HEALTH AND PHYSICAL WELL-BEING

The basic service of the school to the health and physical well-being of pupils and thus to future citizenship is mentioned here only briefly. The responsibilities of the school in this area are six-fold:

1. A healthful environment must be provided.
2. A health guidance program is essential.
3. Emergency health conditions demand immediate care.
4. Accurate health information should be taught.
5. Sound health habits and attitudes need to be established.
6. The exceptional child requires a modified school program.[1]

The war situation has greatly accentuated the need for more and better health and physical fitness programs. This is something children and youth can and do understand and, if rightly presented, is a need in which it is easy to arouse their intense interest and

[1] American Association of School Administrators. *Health in Schools*. Twentieth Yearbook, Washington, D. C.: the Association, a department of the National Education Association, 1942. p. 12-13.

fairly complete cooperation. Certainly schools building a demo-cratic morale for the long future will find this fundamental service worthy of more intelligent planning, more financial aid, and more widespread cultivation than ever before. It would seem that a rather universal tendency to do corrective work at high-school and college levels might give way to more preventive and devel-opmental work at earlier ages. One important point here lies in teaching a child to know how much he can take and when he ought to stop. Children must be taught the elements of play if they are to play happily together. Some children need more time to play by themselves without too close supervision and direction. On the other hand, many children have far too little supervised play or far too few of the elements of constructive play available if they do play by themselves. Families that play together and have fun are those with excellent morale.

On the point of providing a healthful environment, the matter of cleanliness needs stressing in many situations. Soap, water, and elbow grease produce such magical results! There are preparations for finishing and refinishing hardwood floors which keep them per-manently fresh and new looking. These are little if any more expensive than others which allow floors to become blacker year by year. Desks and other furnishings can easily be refinished, not only to prolong their usefulness but to enhance cleanliness and beauty, and perhaps most of all to give each new generation of users pride in ownership and good care. Paint of lovely and varying colors costs no more than the drab, monotonous colors too often found in school buildings. One school in its twenty-eighth year of use looks like a new building. Each teacher was allowed to choose the color for her room which best expressed her own personality (within the range of the colors and shades permissible for light conservation). The halls are in a different color scheme for each floor and opposite walls are different in the same hall, for instance, pale yellow and sea green. The effect is pleasing, with light and color everywhere that give a great lift to the morale and pride of everyone in the school. Buildings are usually so expensive that, comparatively speaking, maintenance is a minor item but a most important one from many points of view. A well-built school build-ing should be and can be in excellent and beautiful condition several generations later if properly maintained, thus spreading the cost to taxpayers besides improving morale of children, teachers, and patrons thru the years because of greater cleanliness, better health conditions, and pride in appearance. It may, however, be argued with considerable justice that, since school programs and needs change rather rapidly, perhaps school buildings should *not* be too permanent, but they should in any case be adequately maintained, clean, and beautiful while they are in use.

Morale is influenced by pleasant surroundings for children and teachers, especially if everyone is responsible to some extent for obtaining or at least maintaining these surroundings. Many children who will wreck further a dilapidated old shack will glow with pride and react with great care to new, gay, or otherwise improved buildings or equipment. Certainly they will be proud and take excellent care of a room or a building for which their efforts have resulted in betterment. Probably most children who are old enough to understand would profit by a situation in which they might have opportunity to help build, remodel, or improve their own school buildings, schoolyards, or school gardens, rather than to have all these provided for them at great expense by adults. Color, artistic arrangement, beauty in design, cleanliness, light, and restful spaces all have their quiet influence in the lives of everyone and children are especially susceptible. Pleasant places to eat, to rest, and to play, with responsibility for their care, are a good investment for any school.

Building morale in an individual school is influenced, too, by the number and quality of special services available to children and teachers. One teacher *can* attempt to do everything needed for every type of child but that this is often a difficult and discouraging task, and inefficient as well, for both teacher and child is obvious. As examples let us mention the child whose hearing is not good, the child with low mentality, the child affected by tuberculosis, the child with serious psychological maladjustments, the child having serious reading difficulties, the child with speech disorders, the child whose sight is badly impaired, and the crippled or spastic case. How fortunate is the school with specially trained teachers in these fields, either within the building or school system itself or available nearby, to take over the actual teaching of such children or actively to supervise their training. Imagine the improved morale of such children, of their parents, of the teacher who is a good classroom teacher but not trained for these special cases, and of the children of her room who thus receive the time formerly spent on an impossible task.

An important aspect of fitness and well-being has to do with fear and strain. Strains, thought of largely in terms of fear, worry, rush, and tenseness, of all types, are destined to become the world's next great killers. Science is well on the way to the conquest of infectious disease but strain takes its place as even more deadly.

An Arab folk tale relates that Pestilence once met a caravan upon the desert way to Bagdad. "Why," asked the Arab chief, "must you hasten to Bagdad?" "To take 5000 lives," Pestilence replied. Upon the way back from the City of the Caliphs, Pestilence and the caravan met again. "You deceived me," the chief said angrily. "Instead of 5000 lives you took 50,000!" "Nay," said Pestilence. "Five thousand and not one more. It was Fear who killed the rest."

Our children are exposed to complex situations far beyond the capacity of their nervous systems. Often the school itself, badly lighted and ventilated, with seats none too comfortable at best, adds to this tension. Ambitious parents press music and dancing lessons upon the children outside of school hours and expose them to social affairs beyond their capacity to enjoy or appreciate. In some instances, homework is required which puts tension on the too young child. Too often the school sponsors night meetings and athletic contests which not only step up the tension but cut down the hours of sleep. City life adds to this complexity. During a crisis, people are stirred by broadcasts, headlines, and news films. All these accumulate to the point of real danger.

What are some of the antidotes to these strains? We need *some* drama, even some of the drama of insecurity; we need the ups and downs of struggle, but the irony is that while a little is good too much is destructive, especially for little children.

Sleep, rest, adequate nutrition, and wholesome exercise form an excellent resistant to the strains of the day. As complicated situations increase, definite periods of rest and sleep should increase also. Topping all the antidotes for strain, however, is that range of activities with pleasurable emotional states accompanying them, which might be classified under the abused word "joy." Happiness is a condition in which development is proceeding unhindered.[2]

_____
[2] Nash, Jay B. *Building Morale*. New York: A. S. Barnes and Co., 1942. p. 89-91.

Other foundations of physical fitness and well-being are work for work's sake and recreation that recreates. For the latter there must be provision. The town that is a "monument to monotony" will scarcely raise the morale of its children by this means.

MEETING THE NEED FOR SOCIAL STATUS

The American school that wishes to develop morale will so conduct its affairs as to encourage its children to grow, by sharing in its affairs, into the practice of democracy, the greatest morale-building political concept yet developed among men. Not that democracy is completely realized. As Allport says, "Democracy is not a fixed and absolute array of moral scruples to which unswerving obedience is demanded. It is an unrealized ideal, a light from beyond the horizon."[3] Therefore, we need the school where every person under its roof feels himself a necessary, appreciated, and significant member and fills his role with pride. Here each learns to accept his share of responsibility for his own and the common good, learns that no rights come to anyone without accompanying responsibilities, shares the common heritage of the fortunate citizens of the best of democracies, and learns to evaluate himself in terms of the rights of others.

What are the most necessary elements in building for social status and *esprit de corps?* We may expect that the group morale of a school will be high when all the people, children and adults, in the school (a) have a clear understanding of what they are trying to do thru their school organization—their goals; (b) are making observable progress toward those individual and group objectives; (c) have a sense of "togetherness" within the school organization; (d) have a self-respecting status as members of the school organization; and (e) are having the stimulus of democratic leadership.

Worthy objectives and progress toward them—What could have kept Ghiberti at work for fifty years on the bronze doors of the Florence Cathedral but his vision of the goal he wanted—perfect artistic workmanship? What else could have made him prepare model after model, one better in this way, another better in that

---

[3] Allport, Gordon W. "The Nature of Democratic Morale." *Civilian Morale.* Second Yearbook, Society for the Psychological Study of Social Issues. Boston: Houghton Mifflin Co., 1942. p. 8.

way, than the realization with each attempt that progress was being made, that the perfection acceptable to his artistic soul was ahead and attainable? The doors "fit to be the gates of Paradise" would long ago have fallen into the oblivion of other works of the past had not this sense of goal, of progress toward it, been present in their creator.

In schools with the best morale, teachers, administrators, parents, and children are the most conscious of what the school and each schoolroom are trying to do. Knowing that one is making progress, moving toward the goal in such steps as the climber needs to take, and receiving approval on each hardly won step— all these have to do with morale.

A sense of "togetherness"—Another factor in building morale in children lies in their consciousness of being a part of the larger community of effort—parents, teachers, and children in common enterprise. It lies partly in their consciousness of the degree of cooperative feeling between the school and the home. There are many ways of bringing this about, some of which are briefly discussed here.

One school system has a plan for teacher-parent conferences, asked for by the parent-teacher association and approved by the board of education, in which some school time is used every month for carefully prepared, personal interviews with parents of one child at a time. School closes at 2:30 on that day and the next two hours are used by each teacher for at least four interviews for which the teacher has prepared carefully. He has before him all the latest information available about each child; the interview is private and nothing is allowed to interrupt it. The teacher attempts to assure the parent on the child's strong points, to seek information that will help him correct the child's weaknesses, and to enlist the help and cooperation of the parent (or parents) where it is needed. Not only this but he definitely seeks to learn all he can from the parent that will help him better to understand the child. The teacher becomes better acquainted with all the parents of the children in his room and often is able to discuss helpfully their questions or suggestions about the school in general. Since there are ten such conference periods annually and four parents are seen each time, teachers are thus able to give every family in the school from one to several conferences annually of this prepared kind, besides many of the usual more casual kind. Children grow to enjoy having parents come to school. Everyone comes and the coming is no evidence that anything is wrong. Indeed, one of the best ways to build cooperative attitudes is to talk to a parent when everything is right.

Another school system has active parent-teacher associations which promote potluck suppers, open-house meetings in which parents follow the programs of their children to sense as fully as possible the atmosphere and quality of the school, and midwinter festivals or parent-child play nights in which children, parents, and teachers all take part and have fun. Parents come into the school to show their movies and to help in taking children on trips; mothers help in the office, in the lunchroom, and at all sorts of affairs; the parents entirely manage the Scout, Brownie, and Cub activities of the children at school. Mothers in great numbers come to the school for all sorts of study groups, not only for child study but for music, book reviews, home decorations, physical fitness; the building is made available to mothers for Red Cross work, home nursing, and first-aid classes. In these and many more ways the community and the school can and do work together in a spirit which is reflected in the morale of its children.

Another evidence of good cooperation between home and school is found in the plan of some parent-teacher associations of having many of their meetings by grade groups instead of general groups. What interests a parent most is, "What is happening and should happen to my child this year since he never will live thru this particular year again?" Thus the parents of any one age group come to know each other rather well, and over the twelve to fourteen years that their children associate with each other at school the parents continue to find common problems that only cooperative effort will solve. These problems are legion and meetings of these interested groups are dynamic and helpful. The resulting agreement on procedure does much for morale. Typical subjects discussed at various age levels are:

1. Child study in early years particularly, when parents learn that problems seeming peculiar to their own child are quite common at his age.
2. How to manage home study effectively.
3. What about children listening to the radio while they study?

4. What kind of clothing girls of junior high age ought to wear in cold weather.
5. The movie question, especially when "dating" begins.
6. Class parties and proms.

One of the best means for raising the level of morale that one school has experienced is its program of adult education. The movement has been rapidly gaining ground for several years and is surely indicative of future trends. The school briefly described here has been actively growing for two decades and each year sees undreamed-of development. For some time there have been more adults in the "Opportunity School," which meets largely in the evenings, than children in the day school. It is in a fortunate residential suburb where one would scarcely expect enthusiasm for night classes. Every kind of course is offered—more than one hundred of them constantly. Any kind of class asked for by as many as a dozen people is begun. The best available teacher for that class is chosen from the metropolitan area. If the class grows and interest is shown, it will be continued indefinitely. If not, it is dropped at the end of the semester. If an instructor's class attendance falls off, his pay decreases accordingly, so it is to his interest to help the class succeed by making it as vital as possible. The cost of the Opportunity School is borne in three ways: first, by a student fee of one dollar a semester; second, by state and federal aid under the vocational school law; and third, by a small tax levied on the residents of the village by the Opportunity School board. This board consists of two employers, two employees, and the superintendent of schools ex officio. Classes are held from the first of October until about the end of April. Certain pleasure classes, such as golf, badminton, bridge, and ballroom dancing, are required to be self-supporting, but nearly all come under the general ruling as to fees. The school runs a huge summer play program as well as dozens of exercise classes in winter, a most successful winter lecture course on Sundays, an almost professional players' group that puts on a series of fine plays annually, and a wood and metal shop where people from the finest homes build furniture for those homes. All these classes are held in the day-school buildings. Four nights a week these completely lighted buildings are a shining testimony to the increased understanding, shared pleasures, pride in community, and high morale engendered.

A school system develops morale by many interrelated plans. The community is a real part of the school and the school of the community. One system has recently published a description of its methods of organization and procedure called *Together We Learn,* written largely by parents and teachers, partly by the superintendent, and illustrated entirely by children—all of it the result of many discussions and of actual procedure. In this school system nearly all planning is done by teacher committees with a friendly attitude toward the community and passed on to the children in "dealing with them as the teachers are dealt with." This planning means many meetings but no one resents it because they are always "our" meetings. This contributes to a sense of responsibility and accomplishment—intimate relationships between patrons, board of education, and the school. Teachers, supervisors, superintendent, and board members call each other by their first names. Board members as well as parents constantly attend all sorts of social, educational planning, and child-performance affairs at the school. There are no "bored members" in this school. One unusual feature was a series of lectures on religion at the school by different religious leaders. Out of all this, plus much more of which space forbids description, has come and is coming an increasingly high degree of morale for all.

A young man teacher describes a most unusual experience with fathers' clubs, carried on over a three-year period and in two quite different communities separated not only geographically but culturally. In each the fathers' club was equally successful.

In one community he organized the club and carried it on for two years when he was teaching a nonreading first grade. Here parents lived in a government housing project community, where incomes ranged from $1000 to $2200. Many of the fathers were skilled laborers in a nearby city, some of them teachers, and some young professional men beginning their careers. Most of them were comparatively young. The average size of family was "two and two-thirds" children. They lived in small but well-designed homes in a carefully planned community. The low rents made it possible to house adequately even the largest families on the salaries mentioned.

The other fathers' club was organized in a small town in another state. Housing was much poorer, average family size much larger ("five and a fraction" children), and *range* of salaries much greater tho none larger than in the first situation. In most homes there was no inside plumbing, bathtubs were the exception, and eight to ten people lived in two or three small rooms. Few of the men had attended high school; the average number of years these fathers had spent in school was about five. Because of the large families even the largest salaries were inadequate.

Yet the teacher makes the following significant statements about these two clubs:

"I have long felt the need for more fathering in this world. When a child is thirteen or fourteen years old he does not want a stranger, even if he is his father, suddenly interfering in his business. It is so very easy for a father to become a stranger to his own child. Time, too, plays havoc in the family. The father does not grow any younger as his children grow older. As a teacher of young children I feel it only fair that I help fathers avoid becoming bogeymen in place of boon companions.

"Although each community was of distinctly different economic and social level, the techniques and attitudes which seemed essential to bring about a successful relationship were about the same. In each group I used an informal, frank, personal approach. I tried to make sincerity and friendliness our watchwords. In neither group did we have formal organization with officers or stabilized leadership. This helped to avoid any jealousies which may have developed from aspirations to that type of leadership. The work of each group was shared by voluntary committees who served as the need for committees arose. We have always dealt with each other as men who have a mutual problem and a mutual responsibility. That responsibility has been to do what we sincerely felt to be best for the children of these men and the children whom I have been trained and employed to guide to the best of my ability.

"I challenged the fathers at almost every meeting to take walks with their children, to play with their children, to read with their children and to them, to share with them as many experiences as they possibly could. I am seeing evidences that this is being done.

"From the trend of our discussion on sex problems I suggested that I would like to introduce to them Frances Bruce Strain's book called *New Patterns in Sex Teaching*, which they could, if they wished, use as a basis for future study. They decided in favor of undertaking this study and made a plan for buying some of the books, and circulating them in the group.

"At the end of the year the fathers suggested and voted to continue meeting the next year with the fathers of the incoming group. We had an average attendance of somewhat over twenty fathers per meeting and a top at one meeting of forty men.

"At the end of each year we had a party in the home of one of the men. A fine attitude grew out of our meetings. In both situations we had open nights when the mothers were invited—difficult however for both parents to leave home at the same time. In the first situation there was also a more formal club for mothers which met in the afternoon once a month.

"In the second situation the men at first were somewhat embarrassed and apologized for open shirt fronts and rolled sleeves. I took off my coat and tie and rolled my sleeves as I talked to them and introduced them to one another. At first the men responded slowly but, by *directly addressing each one* and *asking his opinion,* I soon had most of them actively taking part.

"In the course of our discussion, some of the fathers felt that the Parent-Teacher Association meetings which the school was having were not the kind they would like. I made the suggestion that we take over a Parent-Teacher Association meeting and see if we could do any better. Which they did—and how!

"The men have brought their friends into the club whether they had children in my room or not. We have let this group function as a social as well as a study club and it meets the needs of this community." [4]

The experience here reported emphasizes once more the need of the schools for more men to share in the teaching of young children. There is need also for more women, as well as men, who are interested in a community because of ties that marriage and a home bring and who would thus lose themselves in the life and enterprises of that community.

A sense of status in the group, of worthy membership—In terms of morale building we recognize that the concept of meeting individual differences is one of the bases for a sense of status within the group. We have long sought to establish in the mind of every teacher this concept of individual differences. Certainly no truer concept was ever urged upon schools and even more should be done to recognize the diversified needs of pupils. When classrooms contain few enough children so that attention to individuals is possible, when every teacher has the urge and the technics which are most helpful in accomplishing this, and when organization of schools is such as to permit more of it, a great and significant advance will have been made.

We need people who can and will speak out for themselves and for others when justice demands it, who develop fine qualities of leadership in many and varied areas. Democracy needs leaders more than other forms of organization; the difference is that they are freely chosen by their fellows and can be changed. But there is another equally important consideration and that is the need for educating for cooperative effort. We need people capable of living with their fellow men in the finest spirit of cooperative endeavor. There is a fine line of balance between these two ideals, worthy of much thought and needing more study and experimentation in practice than has so far been given it. We need the ability to lead here but follow there if it is best for the total

---

[4] Reported by Kenneth Bateman, Milwaukee, Wisconsin.

enterprise of the group. Individual differences need to be recognized
and leadership encouraged, but for what? Not solely for the sake
of the individual, altho a well-adjusted individual is society's best
asset, but for the betterment of society because of that individual.
Gambs has expressed this idea well, challenging the notion that the
world would be better off if each individual followed the line of
thrifty self-interest.

> The underlying principle—the false principle—is that each man can realize
> himself through his own efforts alone, that self-realization is primarily an in-
> dividual achievement, and only secondarily a social process.
> Emphasis should be placed in exactly the opposite direction. The truth is
> that man is weak and pitiable unless he receives strength from his fellowman.
> Even this is only part of the truth. The really great truth is that men and
> women become strong by giving their strength to others. Who gives most gets
> most. . . .
> To be socially aware means to know ·in every fibre of our being . . . the
> profound psychological principle that men and women have importance only
> as members of a group, that they can realize themselves only by giving them-
> selves freely and generously to their group.[5]

Schools *can* change attitudes; they *can* and *should* combat prejudice.[6] Some of the most insidious forms of attack on morale lie in
this realm, including attitudes toward certain races and creeds,
toward some types of work, and toward incompetent people. Ways
and means of improving morale thru a broadening of sympathies,
thru intelligent understanding of the contributions of various
groups, and thru recognition of the values of honest work of different kinds are much needed.

One excellent source of help in overcoming racial and nationalistic prejudices is a pamphlet on intercultural education called
Unity through Understanding, intended as a guide for the use of
the publication *Americans All.*[7]

An area in which prejudice has been destructive of the sense
of status essential to good morale is in regard to the kinds of
work people do. The war situation, with its call for all kinds of
manual as well as other labor, has increased considerably the
respect accorded various occupational groups. Fuller treatment in

[5] Gambs, John S. "What Does It Mean to Be Socially Aware?" (Editorial.) *Childhood Education*
19: 51; October 1942.
[6] See page 312 for references on changing attitudes thru education.
[7] Edman, Marion. *Unity through Understanding.* A manual for use with *Americans All.* Washington, D. C.: Department of Supervisors and Directors of Instruction, National Education Association,
1942. 50 p. ¶ National Education Association, Department of Supervisors and Directors of Instruction.
Americans All. Fourteenth Yearbook. Washington, D. C.: the Department, 1942. 385 p.

another chapter emphasizes the need for a new evaluation of employment on public works and emphasizes the responsibility of teachers in presenting the realities of job opportunities to their pupils.[8]

How easy is it to change attitudes, to overcome prejudice, and to give a child a changed sense of his status, of his worth to his group? It is not easy at all. Usually real changes occur only as the agonizingly slow results of an ongoing program, even where every known avenue of help in this program has been explored and used. Results are often, if not usually, so far in the future and compounded of so many factors that it is very hard to say, "I helped build this" or "I am to blame for that." But given the best ongoing high-level program which it is possible to provide, results do unquestionably come, and out of such a program occasionally spring such "teachable moments" as may seem to be a turning point in a child's life. The teacher who is sensitive to these "teachable moments" uses many an occasion to turn the tide of prejudice, to give some individual just the lift he needs, to give a child the opportunity to do something he can do competently that establishes him in the eyes of his fellows. "Nothing succeeds like success" and playing up strengths is much better than showing up weaknesses. The shy little sixth-grade girl, rather mediocre in all her work, will never again be the same child since an understanding music teacher discovered the true pitch and quality of her soft voice and encouraged her to try so that last year she sang a lovely solo with all her mates humming the accompaniment in the midst of a musical Christmas presentation. Since then she has been "somebody" in that school and even her parents came out from their shell of anonymity to become acquainted with the school.

The boy who to his own great surprise had his modeled "Sleeping Boy" chosen as a gift to the school was a different student thereafter. Another boy's face shone when he was looked up to by his schoolmates as the marbles champion. In such unexpected ways are status and worthy membership established in the minds of children. They are not small to a child and if they seem so to adults it exposes a lack of the sensitivity needed by those who deal with children.

---

[8] See Chapter IV, p. 108-109.

The schoolroom group with high morale will plan together, will undertake projects after joint decision, will have good order of the kind that is socially useful and imposed by the group, will give attention to individual differences in many ways, will give opportunity for and appreciation of the varied talents of each, will often have fun among its members, will be gay and full of life interests, and will have evidences of those interests all about the room. The word "we" will be heard often, "I" rather infrequently. Such a classroom will have lines of communication extending beyond its walls into the community. Wherever possible its problems will be life problems that actually exist. There will be committees for all sorts of purposes, giving every child his chance to feel needed and useful. There will be group discipline for those who persistently neglect their duties. In this classroom parents will not only feel welcome but will feel they are needed and have much to contribute.[9]

Democratic leadership—That morale is much influenced by the type of leadership found in the group is shown in many ways all thru this volume. To be sure, the individual soldier or company of soldiers sometimes develops a high group spirit in spite of inadequate leadership. The individual school or the individual teacher or pupil can and sometimes does develop a morale to be envied regardless of the leadership afforded. But given persons of this type, they could accomplish much more and with much more ease if the right kind of leader were helping them on.

The kind of school which *best* develops fine morale among its children will first have developed it among its faculty, of course. One way to do this is thru what McClure calls the cooperative study of the total processes of pupil growth, as opposed to what was formerly thought of as "supervision." [10]

The American Council on Education reported recently on "the vitalizing effect of purposeful group activity and responsible participation" in the schools of a county in Georgia. Emphasis in these schools, during the last three years, has been on doing things together in ways and on a scale that had not been followed before.

---

[9] See descriptions of parent-teacher cooperation in *Childhood Education* 19: 177-81; December 1942.
[10] McClure, Worth. "Fundamentals of In-Service Improvement; Part A: The Problem of In-Service Growth." *In-Service Growth of School Personnel.* Twenty-First Yearbook. Washington, D. C.: Department of Elementary School Principals, National Education Association, 1942. p. 235-41.

Such things are reported as planning conferences each fall before school opened; grade-by-grade meetings of the county teachers; committees to study child growth, sanitation, recreation, and city beautification; notable increase in significant contact with parents thru visiting in homes; children increasingly bringing in things from home or community to be used in class; less nervous tension among children; evidence that children like school better and take livelier interest in classroom activities; much more give and take among teachers; changes in content and procedure of classroom teaching; and emphasis increasingly placed on studying the immediate environment. This program has resulted in greatly improved morale for the entire community. Attitudes of teachers in this situation are suggested by this incident:

One Friday afternoon after school was out . . . a certain teacher decided to go around his building and see if anything was going on. He found several small groups of teachers in the home-economics room where they had just finished tea. Three of them who worked at the same grade level were in one corner discussing some of their pupils; they remained over an hour pooling their impressions, information, and plans for each boy or girl in question. In another corner two apprentice teachers were describing their experiences and problems to each other. Two other teachers were in the kitchen talking about the junior play to be put on some three weeks later. Half a dozen teachers of freshmen and sophomores were sitting around a table discussing the immunization work of their health program. A home-economics teacher was collecting materials for an evening class for adults. A chemistry teacher was cleaning her laboratory with some of her students. Two other teachers were in another room discussing ways and means of improving writing skills. All this on a Friday afternoon when no meetings had been scheduled![11]

MEETING THE NEED FOR A COMMON CAUSE

The practices in building *esprit de corps* already described, and others which might equally well have been mentioned, give living experience in the ways of democracy and in maintaining morale as members of a democratic group.[12] We need also, thru organized class studies, dramatics, and other regular school activities, as well as school organizations, to give conscious attention to an intellectual

---

[11] American Council on Education, Commission on Teacher Education. "Growing by Sharing." *Newsletter* 3: 1-3; November 1942.

[12] No school searching for help in this field can afford to ignore the volume *Learning the Ways of Democracy* published by the Educational Policies Commission. Many ways of developing morale thru increased understanding of the democratic process are suggested in considerable detail. Another "must" is the Commission's 1941 pamphlet, *Education and the Morale of a Free People.* ¶ Every teacher and principal will be helped in this quest by the Twenty-First Yearbook of the Department of Elementary School Principals, *In-Service Growth of School Personnel.* It contains so many practical ideas for the growth of school people and hence for the liberation of the minds and habits of children that all thinking leaders will welcome it.

understanding of and an emotional attachment to the ideals of democracy.

For several years our deepest emotions and fears have been stirred by the demonstration that has been abroad in the world that democracy *could* be taken away from us—that the chance to go on learning how to practice it successfully has been in great danger. This has made us more conscious than ever of the need to reexamine our faith, to search for ways to strengthen our own democracy, and to give the oncoming generation an understanding and love of democracy that will arouse a flaming determination to support its principles so that America may take a place of leadership in the international organization that must come if we are not to enter another dark age. If this new generation is to become acutely conscious of the ways of democracy when their turn comes to carry its burden, they must learn it now by living it now. As is said earlier:

> A democratic society is distinguished by its *attachment* to democracy—by its being in favor of democracy, as distinguished from taking a neutral or hostile attitude. Democracy must be an "ideal" and not merely an "idea"; the letter "l" makes all the difference.[13]

The curriculum of the schools of America is as varied as its kinds of schoolrooms. Fortunate the school where an expert in the enormously developed field of the curriculum works constantly with teachers and children to study and experiment with the best materials and methods of developing the kind of citizen we want. Decisions are difficult as to how the few precious hours of school time shall be spent. We are hearing much of the need for more and better background in all the skills, in science, in health, in physical training, and in other fields. In the building of long-time democratic morale the social studies fill a strategic role.

The outlook for the future demands on the part of all citizens an understanding of tremendous social problems. Without doubt there is a large core of skills, knowledges, attitudes, and appreciations which should be the heritage of every American child. These are part of our basis for unity and common understanding. But the future beckons us, too, and time is so pressing. What has been is not good just because it has been. What beckons is not good just because it is different. The continuous development of the curriculum is worthy of the most serious consideration that school people can give it.

---

[13] Chapter II, p. 32.

State leadership, not state prescription, is desired. The individual school needs wise guidance in the selection of knowledge to be taught and in methods of adapting it to the needs of individual children in the schools.

Joint efforts of school and community—Several ways, large and small in scope, of uniting all in a common cause should be mentioned. Thousands of similar ideas are actively at work in all our best schools.

A project undertaken by an entire community, led by the school, was tree conservation in a midwestern town where for some reason trees were dying. The town has become tree conscious thru the children's efforts.

One school issued a questionnaire asking parents to list their hobbies concerned with nature, photography, and other fields of activity; to report skills such as cooking, carpentry, music, and handicraft; to indicate the possibilities of loaning pictures, museum pieces, and other articles; and to state the kinds of personal service persons were willing to give, such as talks on various subjects (for instance, one's own work), musical numbers, and home movies. One group of parents opened and maintained a library for the school. Teachers and parent-teacher association officers constantly made use of these personal resources thus offered for public service.

Another school system features a weekly forum in all elementary schools where parents can come and receive information concerning school plans and programs, can raise questions, and can help in finding solutions to problems.

The Young Citizens League in a western state has made a reputation for itself in the field of community service. Now twenty-five years old, it is represented in more than 4000 schools of the state and in the course of a year it included about 50,000 children in its activities. In fact, this organization is so important that it is partly supported by legislative appropriation. "Most important are these local school units, these miniature democracies in which children actually get work done." [14]

Dramatics and pageantry—The modern curriculum will, among many other matters, include opportunity for participation in

[14] Federal Security Agency, U. S. Office of Education. *What Democracy Means in the Elementary School.* Education and National Defense Series, Pamphlet No. 6. Washington, D. C.: Government Printing Office, 1942. p. 20.

pageantry and drama. The modern type of training that is available for teachers in the field of speech has revolutionized practice in this area in the best schools. Teachers without special preparation, however, do the best they can. There is no doubt that many of the things we want children to learn can be taught best thru the visual, kinesthetic, muscular, and auditory processes of the drama, pageantry, and symbol.

Much time is doubtless wasted in some schools on rather silly, time-consuming "programs" which are unrelated to the work of the school. Many neighborhoods, especially in days of reduced travel, need the community contact that school "programs" can give them, but they ought to be composed of worthy material. Just entertaining is worthy and the more fun the better if it serves to bring together neighbors who will thus become more of a unit, but the quality of the program should be such as to elevate morale when it emanates from a school.

The war brought home to us in no uncertain terms the fact that we have taken our country, with its blessings and privileges, very much for granted. We have not dramatized sufficiently the history that brought us where we are; we have not been proud enough nor have we made enough of our great heroes of democracy nor of the music that stirs us emotionally as patriots; and we have not used our flag with all the veneration and dramatic possibilities it deserves for what it means to Americans. Every school should greatly increase its offerings in this respect, not to insist that our country is always right, nor to teach a narrow nationalistic patriotism and mere flag waving, but to instil real understanding and emotional appreciation of the blessings of democracy that our country has given us and that we wish for all people everywhere.

One school found an element of unity in bringing dramatically before children's understanding the matter of school costs and the need for all together to preserve what they have and to unite for the purpose of getting more and better facilities.

A common cause was surely deeply felt by the children and teachers who worked to produce and the parents who enjoyed the two projects mentioned in the following paragraphs:

One was a beautiful dramatic and musical production, called "Ring, Freedom, Ring!—A Living History of the American Dream." It was first presented in June 1941. With the passage of time it has become even more timely. There has been insistent request for its repetition and a meeting of a Music Educators Institute furnished the appropriate occasion in March 1943. The program, following the National Anthem, an overture by the interhigh-school orchestras and combined choirs, and a prologue, dealt dramatically, thru individual speaking voices, choirs, characters in pantomimes, and dancers, with the following episodes:

> "The Mayflower Compact"—1620
> "The Flight of Roger Williams"—1636
> "The Peter Zenger Trial"—1735
> "Patrick Henry's Speech on the Stamp Act"—1765
> "The Declaration of Independence"—1776
> "Westward Migration"—1845
> "Free Public Schools"—1850
> "Slavery"—1862
> "Public Utilities"—1870
> "Child Welfare"—1890
> "Pure Food Laws"—1906
> "Woman Suffrage"—1920
> "Rights of Labor"—1943
> "The People's War"—1943
> "Ballad for Americans."

The other was the publication of a booklet, *Thank God I Am an American*, in December 1942, in which the pupils had opportunity to express their sentiments on this topic in short, simple essays. The results were both surprising and gratifying. Such opportunities to express unashamed the sense of gratitude we Americans feel especially in times of crisis is an encouraging sign.[15]

Students Sharing in School Management and Program

We say that we want the next generation to emerge as dependable leaders and intelligent cooperators in the new, free world of tomorrow. We believe that the democratic form of government is the nearest approach to the teachings of the Golden Rule yet devised in the political world. We want the ideals of this form of government so ingrained in the thinking and acting of the next generation that no other ideals seem tolerable. If we want this to come about, it must be learned by living that way, and the place to start it in school is in the earliest grades. This is not the easy way to run a school for it implies the right to make mistakes, to be helped to learn from those mistakes, and to try again.

Democracy is a vast and complex cultural achievement in the sphere of human relations and values. Like all of man's finest achievements, it is ex-

---

[15] Rochester, New York, Public Schools.

tremely delicate and fragile, difficult to maintain at the highest level of
excellence and easy to let follow a course of gradual degradation. Democracy
exists only in the patterns of behavior, feeling, and thought of a people.
Let these patterns be destroyed and democracy itself is destroyed. And they
will be destroyed if they are not acquired anew by each generation, acquired
by the complicated process of teaching and learning. Much attention is devoted
in the schools to insure the mastery by the young of reading, writing, and
arithmetic, of technical skills and processes, of the arts and the sciences.
This is all very good and necessary. But the mastery of the ways of democracy
is a far more difficult task of teaching and learning, and certainly quite as
important to free men. The doctrine that children will learn these ways, if
left to themselves, is as unsound as the thought that they would master geometry without the help of their elders.[16]

Many attempts to live the way of democracy in school have been
and are being made. For purposes of illustration, this section describes two programs, one at the elementary level and one at the
secondary level, in which pupils have a leading part in planning and
executing certain school activities. It is hopefully believed these
have led and will further lead to a better understanding of the
democratic process—the essence of morale building.

IN THE ELEMENTARY SCHOOL

About four years ago it was felt by the principal and teachers of a suburban elementary school of 550 children, from kindergarten thru Grade VI,
that more should be done than was being done (a) to help children who had
many privileges see that responsibility goes with rights and privileges; (b) to
help children learn more about the democratic way of life and about cooperative
endeavor by giving them more share in the life of the school; and (c) to help
children learn more self-control by a larger share in determining what is right
and what is not so good in the life of a group and then taking the consequences. These teachers had come to feel that there is no evidence in history
to support the thesis that democracy is "natural" and believed it had to be
learned like other high ideals.

Much faculty discussion ensued, with time freely given on the part of
teachers since they felt the need for it so much themselves. In fact nearly
everything that was discussed came from the group. A steering committee
was chosen which studied thoughtfully at several meetings. Each time the
committee took its deliberations back to the entire group for further clarification and direction. Having thus cleared their own minds as to what *kind of
thing* was needed, the whole matter was taken to the students for discussion,
not with a set plan, but with a suggestion of the needs. Since these children
were from four- or five-year-old kindergartners to sixth grade only, naturally

[16] National Education Association and American Association of School Administrators, Educational
Policies Commission. *The Education of Free Men in American Democracy*. Washington, D. C.: the
Commission, 1941. p. 48-49.

the discussion had to be fitted to their level of understanding. It was finally decided that the plan would include kindergarten teachers but not kindergarten children excepting as their teachers interpreted the plan to them. But all the rest of the school voted unanimously to go into the modified plan together.

It was decided that a school organization was to be built, beginning with four elected officers from the student body. These were to be selected by the fourth, fifth, and sixth grades (those old-enough to vote) exactly as their parents vote in the suburb, using their form of ballot, their voting machines, their plan of registration, even the same time for election (one day later so as to be out of the way), and using the same names and kinds of jobs so far as possible for these four officers as those used in the suburb—president, manager, clerk, and treasurer. Capable sixth-grade children were nominated by their peers, passed upon by their teachers, and this number reduced to four by the election board (consisting of current officers and all Grade VI teachers), so that on election day each would receive *some* office (to avoid too much tension and danger of hurting some child). A campaign manager for each candidate was then chosen by him, campaign speeches prepared by each manager and a "political" speech by each candidate for presentation in assembly, campaign posters scattered about the school, and campaign talks given before various rooms. Finally came election day to see which office each of the four would hold. Every adult in the school voted—custodial staff, principal, health advisors, clerks, and teachers—and all Grade IV, V, and VI pupils. A celebration and introduction assembly was arranged.

The second step was to turn attention to ways of functioning, and it was decided that every possible kind of work about the school, involving all decisions in which it was possible for children and teachers to share, should be entrusted to committees, the chairmen of which should be older children, the sponsors of which should be teachers, and the membership of which should be as many children as needed from any grade level in the school. At first seven such committees were formed, but this gradually grew until twenty-five are now in existence, caring for many of the most important aspects of the school life. These committees are:

1. *Noon Leaders' Club*—Supervises play of children who stay for lunch, after they leave the dining room.

2. *Kitchen Kadet Korps*—Helps serve those who stay for lunch; helps the cook and the person who supervises the dining room.

3. *Primary Assistants*—This group cares for primary-grade children at a school movie on committee meeting days, while all teachers meet the committees of which they are sponsors.

4. *Assembly*—Provides ushers, collects entrance fees or tickets, arranges seats for assemblies, etc.

5. *Grounds*—Supervises the plan voted by the school of having each class care for its assigned section of the spacious grounds—seven acres in all.

6. *Bicycle*—In charge of bicycle racks and regulations about bicycle riding on the grounds, made by vote of entire school in conformity with the village bicycle ordinance.

7. *Stage Crew*—In charge of all stage work, properties, curtain, etc., for plays or other programs.

8. *Light Crew*—In charge of the light-board, spotlights, house lights, etc., for any kind of assembly.

9. *Visual Education Machine Crew*—Learns to operate the silent or sound movie machine, the projector, the slide machine, and does so for any group requesting its services.

10. *Monitors*—Group has charge of the five outer doors; sees that all children stay out of doors and play when weather is nice but are admitted promptly if not, that little children are given consideration as groups come in, etc.

11. *Traffic Squad*—Each room is responsible for its own "traffic in the hall and washroom" problem. A representative from each room forms the "Traffic Squad," and general agreements on such matters are made by vote of entire school finally.

12. *Historians*—A yearbook of the doings of the entire organization and of each committee is compiled by this group.

13. *Fire Drill and Air Raid Drill*—Four representatives from each room form this committee who with their sponsors handle these two events completely.

14. *Milk Service*—A group sees that milk ordered by parents is made available to primary rooms.

15. *Health Card*—A record of attendance goes from each room to the nurse and principal daily. This group cares for the collection and delivery of these cards.

16. *Lost and Found*—Lists all such articles in the weekly news sheet that goes home with every child, holds weekly displays, urges names on all articles so they can be returned, finally disposes of the left-overs.

17. *Conservation*—Manages paper drives, rubber drives, silk stocking collections, or any like project undertaken by the school. It also urges conservation of school supplies.

18. *War Stamp Sales*—Has charge of such sales on Victory Day, once a week, and makes an arithmetic project of it for all sixth-grade children—a very responsible job.

19. *Bookstore*—Has charge of all sales of school supplies—also a very responsible and important task.

20. *Patriotic Observance*—Arranges for patriotic songs, salutes, and other such observances at all assemblies; helps lower grades in such observances; studies the correct form of salute and instructs the school.

21. *Junior Red Cross*—Attends the county meetings, reports on them, coordinates the work of the local group with that of the county.

22. *Publicity*—Takes care of advertising school events both inside and outside of school.

23. *Finance*—Composed of elected officers and a special chairman. Handles any money earned by the association, submits its recommendations to the school for a vote. (They have earned many hundreds of dollars.)

24. *Election*—Studies the village election procedure and arranges details of school election thru the social studies classes.

25. *Victory Day and Music Hour*—Arranges a music program in school lobby, with all doors open, anyone who wishes sitting in lobby, once a week at a twenty-minute homeroom period, and for the playing of the National Anthem and the flag salute by entire school on Victory Day once a week. Provides piano, chairs for guests and players, and for other details.

The third phase was the decision to have two representatives from each room, in Grades I thru VI, and two special rooms as part of the plan. These are elected by each room and while "in office" are the responsible student heads of that room as well as its representatives at the assembly that shortly developed.

The next step was the formation of a "Representative Assembly" as a clearing-house for all these types of helpers. It was decided that this "Assembly" should consist of (a) the four elected officers; (b) the principal sometimes and two faculty sponsors (these are elected by the teaching group for one year of service each, one "new" one and one "old" one serving each semester; more often than not the principal takes care of some group or groups of children to let other teachers visit this interesting assembly); (c) the two representatives from each room; and (d) the chairmen of the standing committees.

This makes a large assembly—about sixty persons—but to belong is considered a real honor. Even the little first graders seem to get so much out of it, contribute so intelligently to the discussions, and take so much back to their rooms that their teachers voted against a suggestion to have a junior and a senior assembly. Even tho the assembly meetings begin fifteen minutes before the opening of the afternoon session not one child will ever be tardy if he can help it; they seldom forget, and there has seldom been the slightest need for discipline because of disorder. The discussions on all sorts of problems would do credit to many an adult group. Visitors (other children, other teachers, parents, and friends) are occasionally encouraged to come and they do. They may take part in discussion but have no vote. However, the Assembly as a "show place" is distinctly frowned upon.

This Representative Assembly meets once a week for a thirty-five-minute period for three weeks and in the fourth week the twenty-five committees meet, each in the room of the teacher sponsor and presided over by the child chairman, to transact the business necessary to carrying on its work. At this time all children not on one of these committees attend a movie program in the auditorium in charge of the special committee for this purpose. This year every fifth- and sixth-grade child is on some committee, as well as many lower grade children.

In order to give the entire school a voice in the deliberations of the Representative Assembly, a discussion period is set aside on the day following the Assembly, at which the representatives report what took place the day before, ask for discussion on issues on which the Assembly wants a decision by each room, or receive instructions to take to the next Assembly on matters initiated by the class.

The president, secretary, and sponsors, following a meeting of the Representative Assembly, try to summarize briefly the points made at the meeting, which are distributed to all homerooms for use in their discussion period next day. This is done because it is felt that so much has been discussed that many of these young children would not remember accurately all the information that homerooms should have brought to them. Following are a few sample items from one of these discussion sheets, which reflect the type of discussion that is held:

1. The Fire Drill Committee reports that there was too much congestion at all doors as we came in from the fire drill. How can we improve this?

2. Keep buying stamps—we improved our sales this week. Discuss with your room how we can try to get the 90% flag. Shall we all get together on this and—push?

3. How can each room plan to keep its part of the lawn clear? Please discuss this and report your plan to A.S.T.A. next week. We would like to hear about plans that really work successfully.

4. It has been reported that children tip the bicycle racks over in order to play games. Is this a good practice? Discuss this.

5. Would you like to knit squares for the Red Cross in your home room? If you are interested in seeing what the 6B class has done, invite Gaar Lund to show you.

6. The A.S.T.A. Rule Books were passed out. Discuss these with your home room.

7. It has been suggested by the Conservation Committee that we begin a drive for collecting fur for the Navy. Discuss this and send your answers to the A.S.T.A. meeting.

At the Representative Assembly the chairmen of standing committees also make their reports or make recommendations to the Assembly on which they want the discussion and decision of the entire school. Thus no important decision is reached on which children and teachers have a right to vote that is not decided by a majority vote of the entire school.

Outcomes are of course usually on children's levels but they do get things done, and most of them are really necessary things. The insistence of the children on getting mirrors installed in boys' and girls' lavatories so as to help children keep cleaner and neater, wastebaskets with hinged covers all around the halls to improve conditions there, the location of the bicycle racks (three times changed until it was satisfactory), and the closing of one end of a driveway to the building from the street so that cars would not go dashing thru endangering lives—all of them finally were carried thru. Other outcomes include such matters as the organization of the Noon Leaders' Club to supervise the play of children who stay for lunch, of handling all war stamp sales, of completely manning the bookstore, of being responsible for themselves wherever they are, of a Patriotic Observance Committee, and of a Conservation Committee. All reflect the type of thing largely initiated by these young citizens.

The name was finally chosen after much deliberation and a final vote by all. It is called the Allschool Student-Teacher Association, of course shortened to its initials in accord with the fashion of the times. The stress always is that it is student-teacher, a *cooperative* venture; the opinion of students on various matters is constantly sought but always weighed *with* that of the teachers; and the right and honor of being chosen or elected to these many jobs carries with it in *every* case responsibilities, work to do, work that either would not otherwise get done or would have to be done by someone else. Teachers are unanimous in their belief that it has raised the morale of the school to a higher level and no one mentions giving up the plan. Parents have had nothing but commendation for the plan so far as is known.

Elections are always held in May so that it is known early who the next year's officers will be, and plans are made before school closes for the choosing of committee chairmen and election of room representatives at once when school opens in the fall—in fact during the first two or three days. This is done because no one feels that the school can run even for a week without the functioning of the Allschool Student-Teacher Association.

Children are increasingly free but courteous in the discussion. They are not "fresh" but they recognize that they have the same rights of opinion and inquiry as older people. Typical of child comment is this: A sponsor of last year who was no longer with the school asked a sixth-grade boy how the new president was getting along. "Well, to tell the truth, he's not holding us together so well in meetings yet, but he's getting better—and we're all helping him get better!" And indeed long before the end of the year he was felt to be thoroly efficient.

The fact that the organization has lived and grown thru several changes of adult leadership is further proof of its vitality. Too often a student-government association is the baby of one or a few individuals. But it cannot succeed unless it is the business of *every* individual in the school.

IN A SECONDARY SCHOOL

In the secondary school the need is equally urgent to afford opportunity for these young people who are so soon to be taking great responsibilities in life to learn by doing that democracy can and does work. Two examples of student sharing in one secondary school may be offered in some detail, since without this detail the essence of the plan is lost:

Pupil-parent-teacher discussion of mutual problems—In this secondary school many teachers, youth, parents, and the principal became concerned about the variety of social practices indulged in by its student body and cooperatively attempted to think thru the problem. The principal sends a message in printed form to each home and teacher several times a year, called *Planning It To-*

gether. The introduction to the message sent on October 30, 1942, explains in the principal's own words the procedure adopted in this cooperative venture:

Conflicts between youth and their parents over what constitutes desirable personal and social practice are nothing new; but they have become more acute in the quickened tempo of complex city life.

If these conflicts could be decreased, by that much would the pains of "growing up" and of "rearing children" be lessened and the happiness of living together increased.

In the hope of some progress toward this state, Shorewood High School undertook early last Fall a joint study of the problem with its pupils and their parents. Committees of parents were elected from the seventh, eighth, ninth, and eleventh grades. Likewise, committees of students were elected from these grades. Meetings of each grade group, both of parents and of pupils, were held separately with counselors, dean and principal. Twenty such meetings were held.

The conflicts experienced by each group subsumed themselves under three headings:

1. After-dinner practices during the school week.
2. Week-end social practices.
3. Use of the period between the close of school and the dinner hour.

This issue of *Planning It Together* will summarize the conflicts and the consensus of parental and student reactions on the first problem, "After-dinner Practices During the School Week." This summary has its basis in the minutes of the twenty committee meetings which faculty members held with parents and with students. It then received the thoughtful study of a thousand parents gathered in small groups at Open House on September 17. Thereafter, it challenged the consideration of our 1275 pupils under their respective counselors. Thus, with quite general agreement, it emerges in printed form from the interaction of many minds.

The summaries of committee efforts on the other two problems—"Week-End Social Practices" and "Use of the Period Between the Close of School and the Dinner Hour"—will receive parental scrutiny at Open House on November 20. Then they will pass through the crucible of student judgment. The outcomes will constitute the next two issues of *Planning It Together.*

Neither this summary nor those to follow are to be regarded as a code that must be followed. Instead, they are simply guide-lines for the evolution of mature, socially effective personalities. They should be kept for reference when there is difference of opinion between parent and youth. That these guidelines may be helpful both to parents and students is the hope of the committees which worked so earnestly to prepare them.

They should have value to him who recognizes that in human development nothing just happens, but that behavior patterns result from a chain of attitudes and actions. From behavior patterns, character emerges weak or strong.

If one desires that behavior patterns should produce a personality well equipped for useful service, as the chief source of satisfaction, and for wholesome recreation as a second source of happiness, then these guide-lines should have value; for they are the composite judgments of just such thoughtful, life-loving youth and adults. If, on the other hand, one is actuated by a Spartan philosophy at the one extreme, or an "eat, drink, and be merry" philosophy on the other, these guide-lines do not lead in those directions.

Because elimination of conflict between youth and adults is a cooperative process, these summaries present not only some desirable practices in each area, but also what youth, the parent, and the teacher can contribute toward making these practices habitual.

Parent and child can make progress toward understanding one another by discussing these practices and arriving at common decision as to which, in their family, are desirable and which are not. They might best do this, not when conflict arises, but *now*, before sharp issues appear.

That such discussions at home should prove fruitful would seem evident from the school's experience in the twenty conferences held with parents and pupils; for every group approached the problems in a spirit of inquiry as to what practices are best. No one felt himself in possession of the answers. Each contributed his own thinking and then, listening thoughtfully to the ideas of others, modified his own viewpoints as further insight suggested.

Both parent and student committees did splendid jobs of co-operative thinking, but especially worthy of commendation were the attitudes of the student committees; for since their own practices were under discussion, "heat" rather than "light" might have characterized their reactions. The spirit which prevailed is well illustrated by what one junior said, "I have differed with faculty and students in this part of the discussion. Now I am convinced I was wrong. Since I see I was wrong, I want to say that I think there are few schools where a student would have been privileged to speak as freely as I did." [17]

The detailed suggestions on "After-dinner Practices During the School Week" covered eight printed pages, dealing chiefly with homework, the amount to be done, activities that interfere with it, and how best to do it.

The pamphlet from which the foregoing quotation was taken and the two later ones on "Graduated Opportunities in Week-end Social Activities" and "Use of the Period Between the Close of School and the Dinner Hour" were sent to each home and teacher. These pamphlets have been used as the basis for many a classroom and home discussion.

Cooperative thinking on postwar citizenship—Another problem which faced the planning and program committees of this school arose early in the war. Feeling deeply the obligation for preparing its students to face realistically the war situation and to plan for the world of tomorrow, these committees, composed of principal, teachers, and pupils, studied together for some time.

[17] Shorewood High School, Shorewood, Milwaukee, Wisconsin. *Planning It Together*. October 1942. 12 p. Introduction quoted, with slight abridgments.

Out of their deliberations grew convictions such as these: We who have seen how a *victory without peace* was the outcome of a former *peace without victory* want this war fought thru to a peace that will not be a mere training period for another war. Whether we are optimistic or skeptical about the part education can play in the molding of politics, the fact remains that this war and this peace will be made *for* and *with* our present students. Our students must learn that this is a war not between *people* but between fundamentally different concepts of man and life. Students must acquire the necessary tools for world reconstruction—must learn how to think clearly and profoundly and how to use imagination in the discussion of human relationships and social groups. In addition to gearing all subjectmatter toward this desired end, it will be necessary to discuss plans for the shaping of the postwar world. These discussions are necessary if we do not want to sacrifice lives in this war for a peace treaty imposed and enforced by reactionary and resentful diplomats. One objection will inevitably be heard—that there is no time to think of reconstruction now, that we have to win the war, everything else can be done after the armistice. This is impossible. People of all countries will be exhausted after the war and not able to plan much or well unless they have come to certain conclusions beforehand.

Having thought themselves to some such conclusion these committees recommended and carried out a far-reaching plan for such understanding and consequent raising of student morale. After discussion with entire faculty and student council it was decided that a series of five lecture-discussion assemblies would be arranged on the general theme, "What Kind of World Do I Want after the War?" These assemblies were attended by the entire student body of the high school, Grades VII thru XII, and by all of the teachers in the school system. Each assembly was conducted entirely by students with a panel of students discussing the subject by themselves for the first meeting, thereafter having an address by an authority in political science and international relations, followed by discussion. These lecture-discussions were followed each time by study and discussion on the same theme in all English and social studies classes, so that every student had ample opportunity to understand the matter at hand. At about the close of the series the staff had decided to encourage writing on the subject when a fortunate offer appeared. Usually the school frowns upon essay contests of any sort, but when the local Co-operative Club, a group of businessmen, hearing of the interest aroused in the school, offered a prize for the best piece of writing done on this topic, the offer was seriously considered.

The teachers suggested that instead of a prize to one student, the Club entertain at dinner the five students from each of the six classrooms who would do the best piece of writing. This idea was enthusiastically accepted and further study ensued. Entrance into the contest was voluntary but more than 1200 of the 1250 students tried it. The writing was to be of any type desired by the student: poetry, essay, a letter, or other literary form. Finally, with great labor the thirty "best" ones were chosen and their authors were entertained. At this dinner, which attracted wide attention among club members and their friends, one paper from each class was read by its author, chosen not altogether for its excellence over others but for variety. All of the other twenty-four were subsequently printed in the local newspaper. The Club was much pleased and continued the same plan the next year on the topic, "What Can I Do To Help Bring About the Kind of World I Want?"

No one can estimate the degree of morale developed by this one project but it was great. Certainly a great improvement resulted in the level of understanding not only among students, teachers, and members of the Co-operative Club but in every home where material for these papers was sought and discussed. Surely hundreds of these young people will be a long step nearer the level of acceptance of some rational kind of peace plan and world reorganization than they could have been without it. Surely they caught a vision of the "light over the hill," the chance for a better day, that would have been denied them had not this faculty and these friends given them such an opportunity.

These detailed descriptions are merely typical of what may be done and what has been done. There is no one best type of student participation in school management. The activities should recognize the needs of the students and the community. They should go as far as the student body and the faculty are able to go, in view of their previous experience and skill in democratic procedures, in placing ever greater responsibility on the students themselves for making decisions about their own school policies. Changes in practice should spring from examination of purposes, not from imitation; current practices should be appraised in terms of their success in producing the kind of school citizens needed in a democratic country.[18]

At this level it would not be difficult to cite many such excellent examples of student participation and yet a word of caution is offered in a recent report as to the functioning of student government in high schools. It was found that of 1801 schools reporting only 252 reported no form of student government; but in those schools having student governments the importance of the duties assigned to the organizations differed widely:

. . . not many of the functions concern government. Such items as planning, managing elections, and improving student-faculty relations are low on the list. . . . It is important that all students have significant and useful things to do. The question as to why and how they do it is more important. If these tasks are part of a cooperative enterprise, each contributing toward making the school a better place in which to live and work, then the tasks may well be significant.

---

[18] National Education Association and American Association of School Administrators, Educational Policies Commission. *Learning the Ways of Democracy.* Washington, D. C.: the Commission, 1940. Chapters 4 and 5, p. 191-328. ¶ Carr, William G. "Learning Citizenship thru Student Activities." *Journal of the National Education Association* 31: 55-56; February 1942.

Monitor duty is often mentioned. It is probable that much monitor service could best be dispensed with. Students do not learn self-control while being watched."[19]

This report also stated that in 40 percent of the schools reporting the students do nothing but vote and that in 86 percent of the schools everything that the student councils do is subject to the veto of the principal. The report offers the following suggestions for improvement in student governments:

1. A more democratic choice of student officers with fewer ineligibility rules
2. Government a daily working affair with the classroom as the unit
3. More effort to teach government and to make students government conscious thru the student government method
4. Improvement in the tasks and responsibilities given to students
5. Careful thinking out of areas in which students can operate without being subject to veto
6. Selection of teacher sponsors sensitive to youth's needs
7. Time for the sponsor to be an effective guide
8. A place of meeting that carries dignity and a sense of importance to the school.

The Look Ahead

There seems little reason to doubt that the events of the past few years, the needs, the demands on the high schools and colleges during the war period, and the consequent improvement of vision as to the needs of the postwar situation will bring many changes into the curriculum. To face the postwar world this generation will need to grasp such social concepts as planned social control, the postwar employment problems, the war debt, the world economic order, rehabilitation of devastated areas, the cooperative movement, the race problem, the illiteracy that handicaps three-fifths of the world's people, the "migrant minority" in our population, adult education, equalization of educational opportunity, the education of statesmen, and conservation of natural resources. These and a hundred other problems which this generation will be called upon to solve will be forced into the schools increasingly. How shall we share the time that is already far too limited between these important social problems and the skills and knowledges demanded by the new air age?

Have we a right to expect a generation which will be freer from suspicion, hatred, and greed than those that have gone before? That

[19] Kelley, Earl C. *Student Cooperation: A Report of Student Government in High Schools.* New York: National Self Government Committee (80 Broadway), 1941. p. 12.

will know how to work cooperatively on big issues because they have practiced working on smaller ones? That will think of the world as the new air maps show it, with no isolating boundaries, no barriers to trade, communication, and friendship? That believes deeply in the democratic process for itself but can work side by side with groups having differing views? That will have racial questions and problems of creed, labor, and minority groups thought thru and on the way to solution? That believes in the orderly processes of cooperation instead of the way of ruthless competition? With such goals the effort to build morale in every school in America should be a challenge to the best minds in the profession and increasingly should attract to the profession the best minds America has to offer.

★　*Day after day, upon my classroom walls*
I spread my maps and pictures; with these tools,
With books and globes, striving to build a world
Within the understanding of a child.

Oh, while I teach them may I have the power
To clear away the mists that still arise,
Born of old ignorance and prejudice,
Around these children! May my soul and mind
Become so broad, so all-encompassing,
That, building on the old foundation-stones,
Location, surface, crops, cities, and trade,
I rear, firm, steadfast, clear, in each child-mind,
A world of other people like himself,
Swayed by the self-same longings, high and low,
Loving their homelands as we love our own!

Oh, may I feel that I have failed unless
I teach each child to seek in every race
The common traits of brotherhood; to feel
Within his breast the heartbeats of the world!

—AUTHOR UNKNOWN

CHAPTER VIII

The Individual Classroom Builds Morale

EDUCATION FOR MORALE covers a wide battle front. It is fought daily, hourly, on many different fields. The schools cover a definite sector of that front, and the skirmishes that go on in the classrooms of every schoolhouse in the country will in the last analysis determine whether the line as a whole moves forward or back, in ultimate victory or defeat.

In every classroom every teacher is a general, every pupil a soldier. How often we have been told that "the classroom is but the lengthened shadow of the teacher," or "where McGregor sits, there is the head of the table," or "every teacher is a statesman." Here is the opportunity for the development of a profession in the front ranks of service to free men. Here lies the challenge to every teacher in every classroom in the United States of America. For in the words of President Roosevelt, "What the schools do may prove in the long run to be more decisive than any other factor in preserving the form of Government we cherish." [1]

Individual and Group Citizenship

On the death of Charles W. Eliot a leading newspaper began its editorial comment with these words, "He was Boston's most useful citizen." To everyone who read that editorial the meaning was clear. Thruout his long life President Eliot had given services of high order to his community—city, state, nation, and the world at large. Somewhere in his education there had been instilled in him the sense of responsibility to all the groups of which he was a member.

Every individual finds himself a member of several highly important groups. These groups help him meet his needs in life and help him to attain his goals. Somewhere in the years he is in school he should have training so that he may become a worthy member of each of these groups. There is first, of course, the family group

[1] A letter "To the Patrons, Students, and Teachers of American Schools." *Journal of the National Education Association* 29: 226; November 1940.

where he hopes to play a worthy role. He would like, also, to be a good neighbor; an upright member of a church group; an intelligent member of a political party; a contributing citizen in his sense of personal responsibility to his town, city, and nation; and a co-operating member of social and cultural organizations. As he has a living to make for himself and family, he hopes to achieve material success and economic security in his profession or business. All these relationships are of great significance; each and every one of them is a facet of his total personality. These relationships of life are his basic human needs.[2] These gratify his need for belonging. High morale thus involves the intelligent and purposeful pooling of intellectual, physical, social, vocational, and civic assets of the community.

These individual and group needs lead us directly to the issue as far as our schools are concerned. *What are you as a teacher doing in your classroom to help young citizens meet their essential needs? What are you as a teacher doing in your classroom to prepare them for their civic responsibilities?*

We, as teachers, cannot escape the challenge of these issues. It is definite and specific and must have definite and specific answers. Let us survey the classrooms of America with the hope that we may find some answer to this imperative problem, and then let us examine our own classroom procedures, holding fast to that which is good but pressing forward to meet the demands of a new age.

It is axiomatic to say that every teacher in every classroom can help build morale. Every subject and every classroom activity has its own peculiar and important contribution to make in training each and every individual citizen. In this chapter, however, many of the illustrations come from the field of the social studies, due in large measure to its direct relationship to the vital problem of education for citizenship.

Teaching in the Home Classroom

"Children's attitudes are more directly influenced by their homes than by any other institution. . . . The beginning of education for freedom is in the hearts of those who would teach it."[3]

---

[2] Chapter II, p. 29-31.
[3] Kingdon, Frank. "Cultivating The Four Freedoms." *Parents' Magazine* 17: 17, 58; January 1942.

The first circle of the social order that the child knows is, of course, the home. In fact the *raison d'être* of the home is the child—or, far better for the purpose of training in citizenship, children. All that is best in our national character rallies around the hearthstone; the very word "family" implies joint responsibility. The family is a unit, each contributing, each cooperating, and each performing useful home tasks for "ye generall Goode," to use the fine old phrase of the Mayflower Compact.

Those of us of an older generation recall the useful, cooperative tasks of our childhood. We called them "chores." What a far cry from those old days! Many of us have moved cityward since then; the wood shed is a garage; and the wood box, a steam radiator. We love to talk about "the disciplinary value" of those old chores and deplore their absence today for the many children who are now living in cities. Could we not better spend our time in a frank recognition that times have changed and that we are confronted today with the task of finding those "new occasions" that in their turn "teach new duties"? And they must be found. In each home the problem is a different one because the three factors of heredity, environment, and guidance are different.

There are many helpful and cooperative tasks for young citizens in their own homes. Such a list may seem trivial, possibly, yet these little things which compose so much of life may be made greatly worthwhile in character training; for example, dressing and undressing, caring for toys, putting things away, playing without quarreling, being a good sport, having a place in the house or yard that is one's own, running errands, delivering messages, answering the telephone, and helping mother with the housework and father in the garden or around the car. Does all this sound commonplace? It is "commonplace." Yet life is made up in great measure of common tasks. They contain the essential elements out of which one carves a character.

Young citizens, like young athletes, must have adequate training grounds for the proper exercise and development of their "citizenship muscles." One father and mother who live in a suburban community devised the following plan of action:

We have three children. The boys always have a "gang" around the house. We do not put up a sign "Keep off the Grass," for we are raising children and not grass. But there is little available land about us, and footballs and baseballs sometimes roll onto our neighbors' lawns, thru windows, and into gardens with unfortunate results. We must have play space for our children. Some of the best civic principles are learned on the playground. Playgrounds are as essential for young folks as mother's kitchen is to her, or father's office to him.

For winter days we conceived the idea of fitting up the basement for a boys' club. Old furniture now found a use. The walls were whitewashed and the woodwork painted. We added banners and pictures, a shelf for boys' books and another for games, an old rug, and a table with electric light extension in the center. One of the boys with his carpenter's tools made benches and a bookcase. There the "gang" assembles.

Here they organized their football and baseball teams with equal assessments for gloves, balls, and bats. A cooperative enterprise developed this Thanksgiving, when they got together to contribute to a destitute family. Sometimes they hold parties in their cellar clubroom, with pantomimes, stereopticons, and charades. "What a lot of confusion and noise they must make!" some of you are saying. Yes, they do, but it is wholesome noise, and rather that than "Keep off my lawn!" "Go somewhere else!" "Stop that confounded racket!" It is often that type of attitude that makes our children "go somewhere else," and that may be where bad habits are begun.

Every parent, of course, desires good things for his children. We all would like to have them well trained in the fundamental civic virtues, for example, honesty, obedience, courtesy, and cooperation. But it is of the utmost importance, particularly in their earlier years, that we adopt a method of procedure, in both the home and the school, that will start these young citizens aright. Well begun is half done. As the twig is bent so does the tree of citizenship incline.

Teaching Civic Attitudes in the Schoolroom

The school no less than the home seeks to influence children's attitudes. The capstone of the teacher's service to his pupils is the building of attitudes that typify love of truth, love of freedom, fellow feeling, respect for the dignity of man, and a sense of personal responsibility for the general welfare.

The pyramid in Figure III shows the three levels of the learning process. Facts are basic. Yet facts are important not so much in and of themselves as for what we do with them. On the second or thought level we use facts in thinking situations. With all our fact getting we try to get understanding, for surely we cannot think straight unless we have straight facts with which to think. But to develop right attitudes is the ultimate purpose of using facts in thought situations. Information, interpretation, and attitudes—all three of these are essential in the learning process. In the last analysis we are our attitudes and the attitudes we hold motivate all our activities, all our conduct. Action is the ultimate goal of civic teaching. Ideas must become ideals. There is a natural relationship between subjectmatter on the one hand and attitude teaching on the

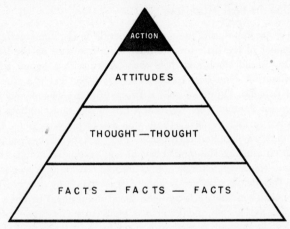

FIGURE III.—THE LEARNER'S PYRAMID

other. We can never be sure, of course, that the pupil's behavior will be in line with his expressed attitude. We may be getting only lip service. However, the three great goals of the teacher are still information, inspiration, and participation, and like faith, hope, and love the greatest of these is participation—action—*doing the thing.* "By their fruits ye shall know them."

BUILDING CIVIC ATTITUDES IN THE EARLY GRADES

Thorndike has said, in regard to the civic virtues and the method of training to be used in building them:

Self-reliance, initiative, and originality are not little deities of the mind which act according to caprice. They are as truly determined by natural law as the fall of a stone or the rise of the tides.

They are not intelligent slaves which hasten to act when bidden. No child becomes independent merely by being told to think for himself, or original merely by being ordered not to be a copy-cat. . . .

Nor will indiscriminate practice make them perfect. Self-reliance, initiative, and originality (which we may call the active virtues of citizenship in contrast to obedience, docility, and conformity) are specialized in their development. . . .

What shall be done to cultivate these active virtues? The general answer is, "Provide those situations which . . . call the active virtues into play; and make their exercise satisfying to the individual. Induce these tendencies to act; and reward their action." [4]

Sometimes as teachers we seem to forget the importance of developing character in the many contacts and reactions that come in just living together. The following cases are illustrative of citizenship training in real situations: [5]

Case one—One day during the free play period in the kindergarten at Horace Mann, a number of the little tots were having a fine time on the long slide. Up the steps they would climb and then swoop down with a happy, gasping shout of pure exhilaration. Now here comes Peter, Only Son Peter, a sturdy little lad, a miniature dynamo. Down he goes with an exultant whoop and then hurries back at once for another ride. But others are in line and climbing up ahead of him. He rushes in, brushes aside those who are in his way, pulls down a little girl who is part way up, and then "O.S." Peter gets a little training right then and there in citizenship. His mother would not have liked it. His teacher, however, was not "too much a teacher" and did not see it. Peter, you see, was only one unit in this democratic group and he was struck by the cruelest weapon society has ever been able to forge—the social disapproval of one's own group. His action was anti-social, and Peter was given to understand in no uncertain manner that if he wanted to play with them he must learn to "take his turn." Isn't that good American doctrine? And wasn't it just the civic training "O.S." Peter needed?

Case two—The following series of incidents took place in a fourth grade. The teacher came to the supervisor somewhat downcast over a situation that had developed in her room. It seems she had desired the class to cooperate in a certain activity and had suggested that they choose a leader to direct their efforts. Here was a real situation and something in which they were vitally interested. Candidates were nominated and the election proved a tie, John and Elizabeth receiving the same number of votes. This divided the class. They would not pull together in anything and as the deadlock continued the morale of the group grew poorer and poorer. In fact, one morning the teacher discovered John offering a top to Billy and an apple to Mary if they would change their votes and cast them for him. John was beginning his political career early.

The next day the supervisor came into the room, went to the blackboard, and wrote, "A government *of, by,* and *for* the people." They knew the author and discussed ably indeed the meaning of those little but important words "of, by, and for." The supervisor then told them they could have such a government in their room and that there was a way in which they could elect their own officers so that they would be sure of its being "of, by, and for" the class. He then drew up a preferential ballot, and altho they did not talk about "preferential," "majority," or "minority," they actually cast such a ballot, saw its fundamental

[4] Thorndike, Edward L. "Education for Initiative and Originality." *Teachers College Record* 29: 89-100; November 1927.
[5] Hatch, Roy W. *Training in Citizenship.* New York: Charles Scribner's Sons, 1926. 338 p.

justice, and elected Elizabeth as their leader. John had lost something he wanted, something he wanted very much. There was a tear in his eye, in fact, but he got to his feet and, altho his voice faltered a bit, said, "I move that we make it unanimous." He was a good loser and from that day supported the duly elected leader, and, the teacher reported, the spirit of the class changed immediately. All got behind Elizabeth and cooperated in the undertaking in hand.

Case three—Another illustration of citizenship training in a real social situation occurred in a sixth grade recently. The pupils were unduly eager, so eager that they constantly interrupted the one who had the floor. The customary methods of repression were tried but this lack of proper courteous behavior persisted. Earlier in the year the grade had organized itself into a Civic League with officers and constitution. At one of their League meetings arrangements had been made to hold an old-fashioned New England town meeting. The warrant was drawn up and posted in due form. The various articles dealt with real situations in their school community, and one of them read as follows: "To see what action the League will take in regard to courteous attitude in class." When the moderator called up this article there was considerable open discussion; the worthwhileness of it was generally recognized; and a resolution was passed to the effect that henceforth the League should be more courteous and mindful of the rights of others.

But the matter was not allowed to rest here. A wrong habit must be made over into a right one. There was need of an ideal of courtesy which could be realized only by everyday activity in checking this particular fault, namely, interrupting others. An acrostic was drawn up which read as follows:

C — consideration
and
O — obedience
U — you
R — resolved
T — today
E — every day
S — satisfactory
to
Y — yourself

This was placed on the board in colored chalk. It was to serve as a guidepost to individual and class conduct. It was their ideal; they felt a responsibility in seeing that it was lived up to. Whenever any member of the group broke over after this it was nearly always sufficient merely to point to the acrostic. This was done either by the teacher or by some member or members of the class. The social disapproval of the group soon made itself manifest. The teacher was after a right attitude in a specific case, and it was her hope that the tendency to act produced by the ideal would develop into an almost automatic action in accordance with the ideal.[6] There were several especially difficult cases. Old

---

[6] Bagley, William C. *The Educative Process.* New York: Macmillan Co., 1920. Chapter 14, "The Development of Ideals the Chief Work of Education," p. 218-24.

habits are not easily changed and made over into new. One hundred percent perfect was never realized, but the method employed was justified by its results.

However, a word of caution is needed at this point. Building civic attitudes is not a routine process. No single case is just like any other. No teacher should follow blindly the outlined procedure of another in this type of training in citizenship. These cases are illustrative only. It should always be remembered that "the spirit giveth life."

BUILDING CIVIC ATTITUDES IN JUNIOR AND SENIOR HIGH SCHOOLS

In the junior and senior high schools the problem changes with the pupils and with the available materials. We are now more in the field of subjectmatter, fact, content. While we are greatly concerned with the building of right attitudes and with offering rich and varied fields of activity, we should never forget as teachers the fundamental importance of well-taught and well-learned subjectmatter. There is no good substitute for facts. Good study habits and good subjectmatter are still worthy elements in building individual pupil morale. This is not to be interpreted as an argument for a return to the Three R's, single subjects, or the theory that "what was good enough for father is good enough for me." We should evaluate carefully all subjectmatter to see that it has value and meaning for growing adolescents and that it will be of service to adults in meeting the challenge of the new world in which they will live.

Teaching the good neighbor policy: junior high school—The following project was the combined work of a teacher of English and a teacher of the social studies in a ninth-grade class. While one of the teachers used the basic materials of geography and history, the other developed the fine arts and culture of our neighbors to the South.

Each teacher had the class for one period a day four days a week. Each of the pupils made himself or herself a responsible authority on one of the Latin American countries. A large frieze, extending across the whole front of the room, was made depicting "The Twenty-Two Links of Pan-American Friendship." The flags of all these countries were strung across the room from corner to corner. A *Who's Who* of the great Latin American leaders was assembled by a special committee, and portraits of these men were posted about the room. The committee in charge of the bulletin board kept it well organized with news items of importance regarding Latin America. These were carefully arranged, frequently discussed, and constantly changed. A special shelf in the school library was reserved for books on Latin America, and a reading list by each student was posted and checked. Large colored maps of individual countries appeared frequently. These were sometimes physical outline maps, often in relief, and sometimes political or product maps. Thru the instrumentality of films and records the pupils were introduced to examples of the best in music, in literature, and in the arts, particularly architecture and the domestic arts.

Each pupil selected and made a handiwork project that especially appealed to him, for example:

1. The Christ of the Andes
2. A Relief of the Harbor and City of Rio de Janiero
3. The Andean Railroad with Bridge and Tunnel
4. The Costumes of the People of Nicaragua
5. A Mayan Temple to the Sun.

These, when completed, were put on exhibition. Not only was the entire school invited but also teachers from other schools as well as parents and friends. Each pupil stood by to explain his own project. They evidently were proud of their handiwork and happy to talk about it to others.[7]

This ninth grade was in and of itself a small committee for better cultural relations with Latin America. If the understandings and attitudes they gained in this classroom could be experienced by "all the children of all the people" of the New World, the Pan American Union and other efforts at coordination in inter-American affairs would have a splendid base for a sound and lasting good neighbor policy.

Living with others: an eighth-grade demonstration lesson—A better understanding and appreciation of the interdependence of mankind is a worthy objective in a citizenship course for eighth-grade students, who are beginning to accept the responsibilities of adolescents in group life. A class session on this theme is here described:

To introduce this lesson a blackboard outline map of the world was prepared with colored crayon so as to show a house located within the respective boundaries of the local community, the state, and the nation in which the students lived. The students were led to realize that by living within the house pictured, they were automatically members of a number of groups of people, each contained within the other.

---

[7] "Latin-America and the Good Neighbor Policy," as taught by E. S. Fulcomer and W. H. Snyder in the demonstration school of Montclair State Teachers College, Montclair, New Jersey. ¶ Many school systems have prepared curriculum materials which are proving helpful in giving a new emphasis to inter-American friendship. For example: Kansas Commission on Education and the Civilian War Effort. *Inter-American Understanding: A War and Peace Program for Kansas Schools.* Defense Bulletin No. 3. Topeka: State of Kansas, 1942. 36 p. ¶ Dallas Public Schools. *Our World Neighbors.* Dallas, Texas: the Schools, 1942. 47 p.

One member of the class was asked to tell of his family, a group of seven people, and describe his relationships to his mother, father, brothers, and sisters. As other students volunteered descriptions of the ways of life in their homes, many interdependencies became apparent. Every day their lives were influenced by the others of the family group, as they rendered services or were served. The basic principles of interdependence of peoples living together satisfactorily as a group were thus suggested and codified by the students easily and naturally. They accepted the family as their basic social institution. They tabulated the demands that it makes upon each of its members, stressing loyalty, services, sacrifices, and defenses. One student climaxed this part of the lesson by remarking, "I never realized until now how much it means to be born into a cooperating family."

With this analysis of one's family relationships as a start, the class followed the course, as outlined by the map, to a consideration of the larger groups of which they were members. As if passing from one concentric circle to the next, they moved from the consideration of their home circle to that of the local community, the state, the nation, and the world. In the case of each, the boundaries of the smaller and more intimate group dissolved into those of the larger and more formal. This may be graphically indicated on the map by erasing in turn the boundary lines of the various units or by pointing out that today "no spot on this once-wide globe is farther than 60 hours' flying time from your local airport." [8] The students thus come to realize the responsibilities as well as opportunities that are theirs by virtue of living with others.

Before the lesson came to a close, the students were led to discover that the job of living with others is both a science and an art. That is, they came to realize that obeying laws, conforming with conventions, and submitting to the points of view of others will do little more than insure them an easy, carefree life. To enjoy the art of living and thus "paint" a masterpiece of interdependence will require initiative in both thought and action. They will want to become not members only but contributors to all their groups. Thus the world community will come to have point, purpose, and opportunity for junior high-school students. They will grasp the significance of the remark of the old Greek philosopher Diogenes: "I am a citizen of the world." With this background of understanding they should envision the more closely knit and interdependent world in which they hold membership today, and will continue to be a part of tomorrow. This is the long look ahead.

The teacher closed on the note with which the lesson began by writing a challenging Shakespearian quotation across the map of the world, terminating the last word at the doorway of the little house representative of the home of every student: "I hold the world but as the world, . . a stage where every man must play a part." [9]

---

[8] Consolidated Vultee Aircraft Corporation. *Maps and How To Understand Them.* New York: the Corporation (P. O. Box 157), 1943. 32 p.

[9] This demonstration lesson was taught by W. H. Snyder before a teachers' convention at Fairfield, Connecticut, in 1942.

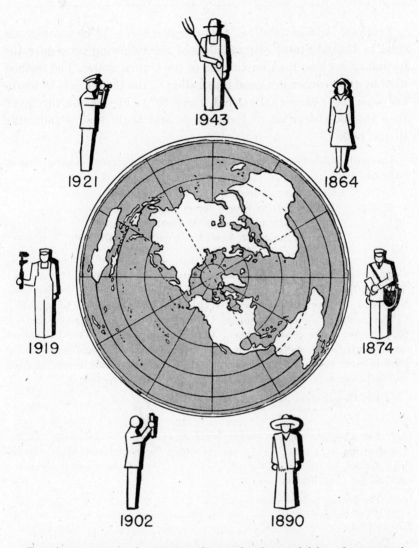

For three-quarters of a century international organizations have served mankind. Typical of those now active with which the United States cooperates are these: *International Red Cross Committee,* organized 1864; *Universal Postal Union,* 1874; *Pan American Union,* 1890; *Pan American Sanitary Bureau,* 1902; *International Labor Organization,* 1919; *International Hydrographic Bureau,* 1921; *United Nations Interim Commission on Food and Agriculture,* 1943.

FIGURE IV.—INTERDEPENDENT NATIONS ARE SERVED BY
COOPERATIVE AGENCIES

Teaching the Constitution: senior high school—An eleventh-grade
class in United States history adopted the following procedure for
its unit of work on the Constitution of the United States. The method
used by this teacher is a good illustration of the three levels of learning (see the Learner's Pyramid, page 207). First came the facts,
then the interpretation of these facts, and lastly their significance
to the pupils.

The goal or ideal was set the first day by reading from Kipling's poem,
"The Old Issue":

> All we have of freedom; all we use or know—
> This our fathers bought for us long and long ago.
> Ancient right unnoticed as the breath we draw—
> Leave to live by no man's leave, underneath the law.

Each member of the class during the first week selected a member of the
Constitutional Convention and became the recognized authority on that member.
The class then built up a picture of the Convention in action: the leading mem-
bers, the three great compromises, and the outstanding differences of opinion.

Then followed a close study of the Constitution itself. Each student read and
gave thought to the entire document, from "We the People" to the last amendment. During their study and the class discussion that followed, each student
filled in a mimeographed outline in completion form, consisting of several sheets
and including over two hundred factual completions; for example:

1. The Constitution has certain unwritten features:

    1 . . . . , 2 . . . . , 3 . . . .

2. The Constitution has always been amended in the following manner:
Congress has by a . . . . vote proposed the amendment. When this has
been ratified by the legislatures of . . . . of the states it becomes a
part of the Constitution.

3. The present federal ratio is . . . .

4. What the Senate may do that the House cannot do:

    1 . . . . , 2 . . . . , 3 . . . .

5. Complete the preamble to the Constitution:

    "We the People of the United States, in order to . . . .
    . . . ."

When this aspect of the work was completed, the teacher on a day appointed
gave out new sheets and the class took its test on the two hundred factual items.
Those who got below 90 percent repeated the test.

Naturally many discussions arose in class as this study proceeded; for example, the third term issue; the great power of the Supreme Court; the veto
power of the President; the Senate, its organization and its treaty powers; and
the various amendments and their historical backgrounds.

This phase of the work was checked by a carefully prepared true-false (or judgment) test of fifty statements on the Constitution; for example:

1. The essential defect of the Articles of Confederation was that they failed to give Congress sufficient authority to run the government.
2. The Constitution may be amended by a two-thirds vote of Congress.
3. Thomas Jefferson was a member of the Constitutional Convention.
4. The Supreme Court was given the power to declare acts of Congress "null and void."

The many differences of opinion during the study of this unit and the free discussion of these issues in class led naturally to the observation that the same must have been true at the original Convention. It was suggested that the class stage a session of the Constitutional Convention, each student representing the man for whom he had been responsible.

So it was that the eleventh grade put together and staged before the entire school at an assembly "The Constitutional Convention at Philadelphia in 1787." They dressed for their parts, and on the desk in front of each student was printed in large letters the name of the delegate he or she represented. The first of the great compromises, dealing with the question of how the several states, large and small, should be represented in the new Congress, was the issue debated by the Convention. Delegates from the small states ranged themselves against the delegates from the large states. There were strong differences of opinion, strongly expressed, and more than one delegate flung himself out of the room crying that he would have no more to do with the Constitution or the men who made it. At this juncture there arose the venerable delegate from Pennsylvania, Benjamin Franklin. His role was played with true dramatic power, and the entire audience, like the Convention itself at the time, was quieted and moved by his famous plea for harmony. Here are his words:

"Mr. Chairman, the longer I have lived the more I have come to respect other men's opinions. I have often noticed that when the joiner wishes to make a perfect joint, he planes a little from both boards. Let us emulate his prudence. Let each and every one of us be willing to give up some of his own cherished views for the good of the whole. For what we need, Gentlemen, in these debates is *light* not *heat*."

This attitude prevailed and the delegates compromised their differences. Recalling the earlier challenge of their chairman, George Washington—"Let us raise a standard to which the wise and honest can repair. The event is in the hands of God"—they came forward and wrote their names below the final draft of the Constitution of the United States.

Attitude building in every classroom—Every subject of instruction has its own special materials for morale building. These are the times when we are demanding that every teacher in every subject re-examine his special content so that new emphases may be given to those elements most worthwhile in building better civic attitudes.

And they can be found in every field. The brief statements that follow are intended to be illustrative of some of these possibilities.
Every wide-awake teacher will be able to expand these suggestions
to meet the needs of his own pupils:

English

Here is a subject of special significance, for the teachers of English meet
every pupil in every grade every day of the week. One school, realizing the
importance of this factor, has recently reorganized its offerings in both literature and composition as follows:

In the literature sections much time is spent on material that has a patriotic
motif. Some of this material has been committed to memory, with emphasis upon
appreciation. Such materials as Arch Oboler's radio play, "This Precious Freedom," and Benet's "Nightmare at Noon" have been used.

In the composition classes, subjects for themes were frequently chosen in these
important fields. Some of the resulting compositions reflected genuine feeling
and appreciation of democratic institutions.

Selections of a patriotic nature have been read, studied, and committed to
memory. These included such material as "The Call to Arms," by Patrick Henry;
"The Recessional," by Rudyard Kipling; "The Building of the Ship," by Longfellow; and Lincoln's "Gettysburg Address." Topics for speeches to be written
were "What Is Meant by the American Way of Life?" "National Defense,"
"Youth and Defense," "Builders of Democracy," "The Trojan Horse," and
many others. Some students broadcasted for the city teachers' series on the
topic, "Citizens of Tomorrow." The Debating Club discussed many topics in this
general field; for example, "The League of Nations" and "Our Relations to
Russia."

Mathematics

In these classrooms may be shown the contribution of mathematics in the
winning of a war, in the successful prosecution of a business career, in the building of an airship, in the compilation of graphs and statistics. There should be a
uniform effort thru classes in mathematics to develop correct habits of logical
thinking, to distinguish between what is true and what is false. Here, also, are
splendid possibilities for the developing of intellectual integrity. Take the case
of geometry, for instance. Ability to work out originals is a test of individual
power. However, altho acceptance of a solution would hardly be honest, acceptance of a hint or "a lift" is permissible, if acknowledged. The obvious evidence of this in one class is the variety of statements appended to the solutions
of originals; for example, "I did this independently," or "Jane suggested step 3,"
or "Father drew the construction lines but I did the proof."

Science

The scientific method encourages an honest search for truth, which is indispensable to all scientific progress. This is particularly true in all laboratory work.

Not only is the question raised of personal honesty in reporting in one's note-book the actual conclusions of one's observations in experiments, but there must be a consideration of the honor of the instructor who must vouch for the book as a piece of independent work to the school or college to which it is presented. The very nature of science in its many relations to life offers endless opportunities for presenting high ideals of intellectual honesty. The scientist often has to make investigations and interpret results, and in reporting findings intellectual integrity is imperative.

The Modern Languages

Perhaps never before in our history has there been so strong a motivation for the study of the modern languages as today. It is a good sign that we are not following the pattern set during the first World War when the study of German, for instance, fell off so greatly in our high schools and colleges. Today we realize the necessity of knowing the languages of our enemies as well as our friends. The government has introduced courses in what are termed the "War Languages," and young men are being trained in Russian, Japanese, Chinese, Portuguese, Czechoslovakian, Spanish, French, and Italian. Here the government is showing the way to the educators. Perhaps the chief gainer in our schools is Spanish, due in large measure to our new interest in our recently discovered Latin American neighbors. In all these modern language groups there are in-numerable opportunities to understand and interpret the culture and civilization of other nations, with all of whom we must deal if we are to establish a sound basis for the peace of the world.

Physical Education

In physical education opportunities are legion for developing the "citizenship muscles" of teamwork, fair play, courtesy, and, to use an all-embracing term, good sportsmanship. Good public health can be built only on good private health. The responsibility of the individual to maintain a high standard of personal health is one of his major civic obligations. This is the basis, also, for the study of the factors of public health; for example, pure water, food inspection, ade-quate recreation facilities. Here he examines his own personal hygiene as it relates to the community. He should come to see this close interrelationship and his own individual responsibility. There are many avenues that lead out from the all-important field of physical education; for example, better housing, recrea-tion programs for young and old, family diet, sanitation in the home and com-munity, and correct health habits for all. In both the first World War and the second World War we have been astounded and ashamed at the number of young men who were unable, because of physical disabilities, to meet the obligation of military service.

Assemblies

In every school the assembly is the master tuning fork. Every member of the school—principal, supervisor, teacher, and pupil—should come to feel his personal responsibility in making the assembly period a success. Here the school traditions are nourished and maintained; here inspirational ideals are set forth; here the cooperative spirit of the whole school is strengthened. The pupils themselves should participate freely and naturally. One of the best types of assembly periods occurs when some matter of great interest in a classroom walks out of that room and on to the stage in order that all the school may see and hear; for example, the dramatization of a session of the Constitutional Convention at Philadelphia in 1787, mentioned on pages 214-15.

Other types of worthwhile assemblies are the open meetings of the General Government Association; debates on current issues of real importance; science talks concerning everyday facts about which the layman might well know but does not; travelogues, a period in which those members of the school who have gone to interesting spots give travel talks, often illustrated by slides; a "Let Us All Sing" period where the whole school joins in and sings old and new favorite songs; the presentation by a special committee of the life story of some outstanding man or woman; a safety-first drive; a nominating convention of the school candidates for office at a coming election; an Armistice Day assembly; a Thanksgiving pageant where various phases of American life, such as government, education, and labor, are portrayed symbolically; a Four Freedoms day presenting the ideas and ideals behind the four paintings of Rockwell Kent prominently exhibited on the stage; a Bill of Rights day; a Constitution day; the Flag Day; and readings and dramatic portrayals of Stephen Vincent Benet's "Western Star." Assemblies of this type are eagerly awaited, thoroly enjoyed, and their instructive and inspirational content and spirit are often the basis for the finest civic attitudes in the life of the school and in the attitudes of the student long after school days are over.[10]

"Watch This Spot!"—an attitude builder—"Watch This Spot!" is a specially reserved bulletin board, prominently placed in the classroom. Its purpose is to serve the pupils by bringing to their attention an idea or an ideal, preferably arising out of the content of the unit of work being studied. Sometimes it comes naturally right out of classroom procedure, for example, "Light not Heat" in the unit on the teaching of the Constitution. It should be open to the students as well as the teacher, and it should change frequently. Students often of their own accord reserve a special place in their notebooks for these quotations:

1. Now, God be thanked, who has matched us with his hour.—Rupert Brooke.
2. I have sworn upon the altar of God eternal hostility against every form of tyranny over the mind of man.—Thomas Jefferson.

[10] Several illustrations from the foregoing series of paragraphs were taken from the following report: Wichita, Kansas, Public Schools. *The American Way in Wichita.* Wichita, Kans.: the Schools, 1942. p. 10-13.

3. Morale is:
> The spine in your back,
> The lift of your chin,
> The grit in your craw,
> The width of your grin,
> The song on your lips,
> And the faith deep within.

4. The whale gets into trouble only when he starts to blow.—A Pupil.
5. It is not the size of the dog in the fight that counts, but the size of the fight in the dog.—A Pupil.
6. Napoleon's axiom that "The moral is to the physical as three to one" has been upset. The ratio now stands as six to one.—General George C. Marshall.
7. It is rather for us to be here dedicated to the great task remaining before us—that from these honored dead we take increased devotion to that cause for which they gave the last full measure of devotion; that we here highly resolve that these dead shall not have died in vain; that this nation, under God, shall have a new birth of freedom; and that government of the people, by the people, for the people, shall not perish from the earth.—Abraham Lincoln.

Morale and the Social Studies

There is no field of study where the possibilities for education for morale are more significant than in the field of the social studies. The social studies have their own particular purpose to serve, and that purpose is of primary importance. First, the social studies should serve as a means of awakening the children to our common stake in this world of ours. They must come to see the world as an interdependent whole. This was Woodrow Wilson's vision: "The interests of all nations are ours, also. We are partners with the rest. Whatever affects mankind is inevitably our affair as well as the affair of the nations of Europe or Asia." Here instruction in the social studies sets the goals. Leaders in the social studies should attempt to analyze the total situation. They must study causes, evaluate programs of procedure, analyze the needs of their pupils, and point the way along the road we are going to the ultimate goals for a free people in a free world.

That the social studies teachers of the United States are awake to this challenge is evidenced in a statement by the National Council for the Social Studies. Abstracts from this statement, entitled *The Social Studies Mobilize for Victory*, are given here:[11]

---
[11] The numbering and sequence of these items vary from the original.

1. Heavy responsibility for developing informed and purposeful citizenship, whether in war or peace, rests on the social studies.

2. War and coming reconstruction emphasize as never before the importance of education for democratic citizenship.

3. American citizens must give increased study to such topics as:

> The meaning of democracy
> American traditions and institutions
> World geography
> The peoples and cultures of Latin America, Asia, and the nations with which we are at war
> The problems of the reconstruction period
> The establishing anew of essential institutions of human government.

4. School administrators and social studies teachers must plan a three-year sequence in history and contemporary problems.

5. In the study of United States history, at every school level, special emphasis should be given to the study of dramatic, key episodes in the development of our democracy, such as: the signing of the Mayflower Compact; the adoption of the Virginia Bill of Rights; the announcement of the Monroe Doctrine; the Emancipation Proclamation; the adoption of the Open Door policy; the establishment of free public schools; and the passage of the Social Security Act.

6. In the elementary and secondary schools pupils should study the great documents of our national democratic tradition and present crisis, such as the Declaration of Independence, the Constitution, the Gettysburg Address, Wilson's Fourteen Points, the Atlantic Charter, and the Four Freedoms.

7. Schools and adult education agencies should utilize dramatic incidents and impressive ceremonials for the purpose of building the emotional drives of loyalty to democracy.

8. In the study of United States history special attention should be given the world relations—economic, social, and political—of the United States.

9. The study of geography must be increased in order that pupils can interpret maps, globes, the significance of polar projections, the effects of aviation, etc.

10. Racial and national hatreds and intolerances must be attacked if we hope ever to be able to build desirable racial attitudes.

11. War duties for young citizens should be recognized as stirring opportunities for apprenticeship in citizenship.

12. The social studies teacher has a very important role in strengthening community morale. As active citizens, teachers should participate in the widest possible range of opinion-forming public services.

13. Social studies teachers and school administrators must shape together the relation of social studies to all other phases of school work and to community enterprises.[12]

---

[12] National Council for the Social Studies. *The Social Studies Mobilize for Victory.* A statement of wartime policy. Washington, D. C.: the Council, a department of the National Education Association, 1942. 16 p. Also in: *Social Education* 7: 3-10; January 1943.

This particular statement of the National Council for the Social Studies has value for every school administrator, every teacher of the social studies, and every member of a schoolboard. It is brief, directly worded, and forward looking as a statement not alone of wartime policy but as a help in determining future policies and programs for the schools of the United States.

THE NEW GEOGRAPHY

"The study of geography must be increased." This is the urgent recommendation of the National Council for the Social Studies:

> As the map of the world is unfolded for us by the far-flung action of American troops; as the lines of strategy in global war become clearer; as the extent, control, and distribution of the earth's natural and human resources are seen in better perspective; as aviation marks out new trails, establishes new foci of distribution, and creates new relationships, the basic importance of geography as a social study becomes more evident.[13]

Our young citizens are at the threshold of a new world. The sign and symbol of this new world is the airplane. This is the age of the air. As we look down upon our world from the cabin of an airplane, we find beneath us a new earth. Land spaces, water areas, mountain barriers, island steppingstones, and trade routes all have changed in significance. Our world is growing smaller; we are nearer our neighbors in our new "One World."

The modern Magellan winging aloft thru cloud and space has discovered new routes as he follows the beam of the Great Circles. The new world our children will live in demands a basic knowledge and understanding of the far-reaching significance of global strategy, human ecology, and the distribution of the world's natural resources:

> Global warfare has made global geography a functioning experience for each of us. . . . Teachers of children in the elementary grades have long realized that any functioning geography program must be a part of the actual living experiences and interests of their pupils. The traditional organization of subject matter as it was outlined in the older courses of study has been discarded in many places because this organization seemed didactic, and frequently was far removed from interests and living experiences of elementary-grade children. How fortunate are teachers today in planning their geography programs with girls and boys vitally interested in the whole world![14]

---

[13] National Council for the Social Studies, *op. cit.*, p. 10.
[14] Garrels, Agnes F. "Global Geography in the Elementary Grades." *Social Education* 7: 221-23; May 1943.

Yes, change is in the air. Stoddard challenged every teacher of geography in the nation when he said recently, "Are we of this generation, the last generation of the earth-bound, able to teach this new generation, the first generation with wings?" [15]

This background understanding of the world in which we now live is basic if we wish a correct interpretation of the history and present situation of other people. Many of the important economic and political problems which confront the world today find their roots in the soil. Semple said years ago: "Civilization is at bottom an economic fact, at top an ethical fact. Beneath the economic lie the geographical conditions, and these in the last analysis are factors in the formation of ethical standards." [16] As an illustration of this principle, she submits the issue of slavery in the United States:

> The question of slavery in the United States was primarily a question of climate and soil, a question of rich alluvial valley and fertile coast-land plain, with a warm, moist, enervating climate, versus rough mountain upland and glaciated prairie or coast, with a colder, harsher, but more bracing climate. The morale of the institution, like the right of secession, was long a mooted question, until New England, having discovered the economic unfitness of slave industry for her boulder-strewn soil, took the lead in the crusade against it. The South, by the same token of geographical conditions, but conditions favorable to the plantation system which alone made slave labor profitable, upheld the institution both on economic and moral grounds.[17]

If in our study of the history of our own and other lands we could first get over to young people the geographic significance of issues like these, would we not as we view the picture in total perspective be able to create a clearer understanding and therefore a better attitude on our gravest conflicts?

The hope of the world today lies in just such international understandings. Children are never too young to start toward this goal. Building on this foundation with a sympathetic understanding of the peoples of all countries and their problems, may we not have the right to hope for those more friendly relationships upon which must ultimately rest the peace and happiness of the world? [18]

[15] Stoddard, Alexander J. "The Role of the Schools in the Present Emergency." *Official Report, 1942.* Washington, D. C.: American Association of School Administrators, a department of the National Education Association. 1942. p. 38-45.
[16] Semple, Ellen Churchill. *American History and Its Geographic Conditions.* Boston: Houghton Mifflin and Co., 1903. p. 280.
[17] Semple, Ellen Churchill, *op. cit.,* p. 280.
[18] Hildebrand, Pauline. "Applying the Lessons of This War: II. The Teaching of Geography." *Proceedings of the Middle States Council for the Social Studies, 1942-1943.* Philadelphia: the Council (Girard College), 1943. p. 42-46.

THE TEACHING OF HISTORY

All history that is worth teaching is alive, vitally significant in the present. History is not a tale that is told; it should not be a picture of the dead past burying its dead; and it never does repeat itself, despite that oft-repeated statement.

In the words of America's great philosopher Emerson, in his essay on "History": "All that Shakespeare says of the king, yonder slip of a boy that reads in the corner feels to be true of himself. . . . The student is to read history actively and not passively; to esteem his own life the text, and books the commentary." Herein lies the significance of history. The tale is vital to the student reading it and he visualizes himself as an active participant. History, therefore, should give our children a better understanding of the world they live in today because they have seen how other people have lived in other times and other places. History should bring out the fact that we and all generations are linked to a long past. Most significant of all, history should teach our children that they in their turn have a distinct role to play in this ever unfolding drama of life and that the day is not far distant when they in their turn will become active participants in what someone has called "the unfinished business of our fathers."

One of the most thoughtful statements in the recent discussion of the teaching of American history in our schools is Hunt's article, which concludes with this paragraph:

We need effective teaching of American history. As already indicated, that involves decisions as to what knowledge is basic to an understanding and appreciation of America. It involves articulation of the three cycles of American history now generally taught in the schools, so that learning is effective, and so that the second and third cycles are fresh and vital rather than repetitious and deadening. We need teaching materials for groups, like poor readers, that present special problems. We need social studies teachers with the means and the leisure to buy books and magazines, to read, to travel, to keep professionally alert. And we need the sympathy and support of the public—including the press —as we try to achieve what everybody wants: a body of young citizens informed about our past, conscious and informed about problems and issues in the present, devoted to our democratic traditions and ideals, and capable of participating in the advancement of those traditions and ideals now and in the future.[19]

---

[19] Hunt, Erling M. "The *New York Times* 'Test' on American History." *Social Education* 7: 195-200, 240; May 1943.

PROBLEMS OF AMERICAN DEMOCRACY

The study of problems of American democracy should be the crowning year of work in the social studies. Here, in the senior year of high school, we have the right to expect of the students a more intelligent grasp of subjectmatter, the capacity to evaluate evidence, the power to interpret and generalize, and the ability to express themselves clearly, soundly, and forcefully. It would be well if this work could be preceded by a full year's course in American history and government. This would give the factual background and setting out of which many of our social, economic, and political problems arise.

At no other time in our history has it been so important to study and evaluate our democracy. The teachers who have the responsibility for presenting a course in Problems in American Democracy are confronted with an unusual opportunity to make real the meaning and practice of American democracy. It is needless to say that these teachers are obligated to help every young person to achieve an understanding, an acceptance and a participation in democracy. It is our belief that pupils in our secondary schools when given adequate opportunity to learn about and to live in our American democracy make effective contributions to its development.[20]

The foregoing statement is quoted from a bulletin recently published by the New Jersey State Department of Public Instruction, which outlines for the use of teachers twenty carefully organized units of instruction dealing with outstanding political, economic, and social problems. Each of these units is organized as a lesson plan with bibliography at the end of each unit for both students and teacher. In addition there is a section (pages 20-64) on "Suggestions for Teaching," which discusses such vital issues as:

1. The discussion of controversial questions
2. The unit method of teaching
3. The place of the textbook
4. Panel discussions
5. Individual and committee reports
6. Field studies: the community as a problem laboratory
7. The use of case studies based on current news stories
8. The teaching of current events
9. Visual and auditory aids
10. The evaluation of outcomes.

---

[20] New Jersey State Department of Public Instruction. *A Guide for Teaching Problems of American Democracy.* Trenton, N. J.: the Department, 1941. p. 5.

The great need for a full year's work in the study of our major social problems was well brought out in a recent poll by *Fortune* magazine.[21] This poll took samplings on the issue of union labor. It ascertained that many of those who had positive opinions did not know the meaning of certain significant terms, such as "closed shop," about which, however, they had positive and bitter opinions. These opinions, no matter how inadequately based, are of course the ones they register at the polls. Do not the schools have an obligation to send out people who know something, who know *how* to learn, and who will make use of objective facts in solving problems?

Somehow we need to get over to our pupils a respect for facts, a knowledge of where to go to get them, and the courage to follow their findings when they believe them soundly established.

> First find the facts,
> Next filter the facts,
> Now fuse the facts,
> Then follow the facts.

One of the surest procedures to inculcate a respect for facts is for the student to recognize it in his teachers. Scholarship and balanced judgment in the teacher beget a like respect in the pupil. If the teacher "knows his stuff" and holds his pupils to the same high standard he has gained respect not only for himself but for the subject he teaches.

The Discussion of Controversial Issues

Perhaps no question comes to the fore more frequently than this: What shall be the attitude of the teacher in handling controversial issues in the classroom? Controversial issues are those about which people have conflicting beliefs and emotions. And these are many. To avoid them is to avoid that part of the program which is most powerful in determining citizenship behavior.[22]

The chief function of the teacher in this process is to teach. He is there to encourage and guide, to help his students to gather facts, to help them to the best sources of informational and inspirational content, and, in the give and take of the class discussion, to condemn the superficial and commend the well-considered. That is

[21] Fortune. "The Fortune Survey." *Fortune* 25: 97-100; February 1942.
[22] See: New Jersey State Department of Public Instruction, *op. cit.*, p. 25-28.

why, as a teacher, he believes in a great deal of real discussion. He is after the sober expression of sound opinions as against the oratorical display of ignorant opinions, and these in the classroom, as in life, must meet often and fight out their age-old conflict. Above all, he tries to get students to do their own thinking, to evaluate their own ideas, and to formulate and express them well. This is teaching, and he is to remember that above all he is a teacher and not a pleader of special causes.

The most unfortunate aspect of the insertion of the teacher's point of view, if it comes either too early or too often, is that he thereby retards the intellectual development of his students. One of the gravest charges to be laid at the door of overindoctrination is that it is poor teaching. The teacher has a right to his own point of view and to the expression of it. It should come, however, at the close of the work or unit under discussion and never at the beginning. The students will come to respect the teacher's judgment in the direct proportion that he, in the handling of the class discussion, has respected theirs. Emerson told us this years ago: "I believe that our own experience instructs us that the secret of Education lies in respecting the pupil. It is not for you to choose what he shall know, what he shall do." Respect the child. Be not too much his teacher.

As President Roosevelt has said:

A true education depends upon freedom in the pursuit of truth. No group and no government can properly prescribe precisely what should constitute the body of knowledge with which true education is concerned. The truth is found when men are free to pursue it. . . . It is this belief in the freedom of the mind, written into our fundamental law and observed in our everyday dealings with the problems of life, that distinguishes us as a nation.[23]

The following is an abridged portion of a stenographic report of a lesson where a controversial issue was under discussion. The issue was "Does the New Deal deserve a re-deal?" After a rather full and free discussion of the Agricultural Adjustment Act the class was turned into a Supreme Court of twenty-nine judges who voted as follows: eleven students favored the majority decision in that case; eighteen agreed with the minority judges.

At this juncture one of the students rose and challenged the teacher, "And how, sir, would you have voted?"

---

[23] Address at Temple University, February 22, 1936.

The Teacher: I am ready to tell you how I feel about the AAA case, but before I do I would like to know if you think I should stand before you and give you my opinion? I wonder how you would feel about my doing this.

Dorothy Phillips: I think first the facts should be taken into consideration both for and against the question and discussed. Then after we have had the discussion and the students have formed their opinions, I believe that the teacher should tell the way that he would have stood on the question, and in that way sometimes teachers will bring out points that perhaps have been omitted.

The Teacher: I know, but suppose I do that and I do not agree with you? How are you going to feel about that? You have stated an opinion and I say that I do not agree—what about that?

Dorothy Phillips: I think that the students should listen to your point of view. Then, if you have a good argument on your side, they should be willing to take it into consideration.

The Teacher: And when you took the examination, which one would you put down on your paper, I wonder?

Dorothy Phillips: I would put down the one which I thought best in my own opinion, and believe you would respect it.

The Teacher: I appreciate that compliment. I hope to be willing to respect your points of view as I should want you to respect mine. Walter?

Walter Rohlfing: I think you have a right to your opinions if you do not try to swing us your way. I think some teachers do that but I do not think that you will do that.

The Teacher: Wait a minute, Walter—you brought out a serious charge. You say it is all right "if you do not try to swing us." When I ask you your opinion, I ask you to state it as well as you can. When you ask me to state mine, I shall do the same and in that statement I may be "swinging" you my way, and you do not think I ought to do that.

Walter Rohlfing: I do not see where you would be swinging us. I know you could not swing me. My opinion would be just the same.

The Teacher: Now, Walter, I want to make a confession. One of you got up the other day and said something so well that it made me modify a position I had taken. But, "I cannot swing you" and "you cannot swing me." I wonder if that is the attitude we should take, both of us? Go ahead, Walter.

Walter Rohlfing: Maybe it is not the attitude we should have but I think you have your ideas and I should listen to them. Whether we want to adopt them or not, I do not know.

The Teacher: You said I could not swing you but I confess that you made me shift and change. Does this not work both ways?

Walter Rohlfing: I will admit that I will consider your ideas.

The Teacher: Then I want to ask you, what is the good of all this thing if you come in and take a "cannot-change-me" attitude and I come in and say, "I know so much more than you that you cannot change me"?

Walter Rohlfing: We get the attitude of the other person into our consideration. This will tend to make us think and maybe give us better ideas.

The Teacher: Dorothea is anxious to talk on that.

Dorothea Collins: The teacher is going to influence us on everything studied or discussed, but we would much prefer to have him take a definite stand so we can form our own ideas. We would much rather have it openly than to have him attempt to make us think one way or another by more subtle means.

And the lesson closed on this note:

The Teacher: Yesterday in one of the St. Louis newspapers, there was a splendid editorial called "The Great Adventure." In this there was a quotation which came from the large stone panel of this very building, a quotation from one of Missouri's own statesmen known as "the ideal Senator"—Carl Schurz. I have asked Frank to read it.

Frank Fenenga: "Democratic government will be the more successful the more the public opinion ruling it is enlightened and inspired by full and thorough discussion. The greatest danger threatening democratic institutions comes from influences tending to stifle or demoralize discussion." [24]

The Emotional Appeal

Nor is there anything in the democratic creed which forbids emotional appeal. . . . a creed does not consist merely in beliefs concerning matters of fact or in an intellectual grasp of meanings or proofs but involves an alignment of will and feeling.[25]

Many school systems have prepared material along the lines of education for morale during this wartime period. Some of these have excellent permanent value in training for citizenship in a democracy.[26] Special bulletins have been prepared dealing with various phases and activities for every grade in the school system.

---

[24] "Teaching Controversial Subjects in the Classroom." *Official Report, 1936.* Washington, D. C.: Department of Superintendence, National Education Association, 1936. p. 175-90. ¶ See also discussion of the teaching of controversial issues in: Portland Public Schools. *Building American Loyalties: A Teacher's Guide.* Portland, Oreg.: Board of Directors, 1941. p. 41-47.

[25] See Chapter II, p. 37.

[26] For example, see: Baltimore, Maryland, Department of Education. *Educational Priorities for the Baltimore Public Schools during the War Period.* Baltimore: the Department, 1942. p. 15-19. ¶ Boston Public Schools. *A Handbook for Teachers on the Principles of American Democracy.* School Document No. 4, 1941. Boston: the School Committee, 1941. 90 p. ¶ Cincinnati, Ohio, Public Schools. "War-Time Role of Schools Studied." *Better Teaching* 4: 1-12; January 1942. ¶ Detroit Public Schools. *The Detroit Schools and the War.* Detroit, Mich.: the Schools. ¶ Indianapolis Public Schools. *A Primer for Unity of Emphasis in Interpreting Our American Way.* Indianapolis, Ind.: the Schools, 1942. 6 p. ¶ Long Beach Public Schools. *The Democratic Way of Life in America; Educational Philosophy for the Long Beach Public Schools.* Long Beach, Calif.: the Schools, 1941. 14 p. ¶ Los Angeles City School District. *Teaching the Ways of Democracy: Our National Heroes.* Special Bulletin No. 92. Los Angeles: the District, 1941. 49 p. ¶ Maryland State Department of Education. *Redirection of the School Program in Wartime.* Maryland School Bulletin, Vol. 24, No. 2. Baltimore: the Department, December 1942. 149 p. Chapter 17, "Opportunities for the Practice of Democracy in the School," p. 111-14. ¶ Missouri State Department of Education. *A Wartime Program for Missouri Schools.* Jefferson City: the Department, 1942. "Stress the teaching and practice of democracy and the essentialness of its survival," p. 24-27. ¶ Perry, H. Arnold, and others. *Teaching Democracy in the North Carolina Public Schools.* Publication No. 229. Raleigh, N. C.: State Superintendent of Public Instruction, 1941. 56 p. ¶ Portland, Oregon, Public Schools. *Building American Loyalties: A Teacher's Guide.* Portland: Board of Directors, 1941. 64 p. ¶ Providence Public Schools. *Readings in American Life: A Reading and Discussion Core to Correlate Eleventh Grade Literature with the Eleventh Grade Course in American History.* Providence, R. I.: the Schools. 16 p. ¶ Toledo Public Schools. *A Plan of Procedure for Emphasizing the Values of Democracy Through Education.* Toledo, Ohio: the Schools, 1941. 41 p. (Mimeo.)

Many of these programs and activities extend into ever widening circles of community action—local, state, national, and international.

"The Flag Speaks"—As an illustration of the use of pageantry to carry the message of democracy, a program prepared by the Iowa State Teachers Association was given at a convention on the theme "The Flag Speaks":[27]

A dozen different episodes were prepared and presented by pupils representing practically every grade of the school system. These episodes were woven around the central theme taken from Franklin K. Lane's famous speech, "The Making of Our Country's Flag." A great flag was full-spread across the entire rear of the stage, and when the curtains were parted a boy in Scout uniform stepped forward and said:

"This morning, as I passed into school, the flag dropped me a most cordial salutation, and from its rippling folds I heard it say: 'Good morning, Mr. Flag-maker.' 'I beg your pardon, Old Glory,' I said. 'You are mistaken. I am not the President of the United States, nor a member of Congress, nor even a General in the Army. I am only an ordinary citizen.' "

Then a large school band, concealed behind the flag, played "The Stars and Stripes Forever," followed by a fanfare of trumpets, as the curtain swung open wide and revealed the flag, lighted by localized lighting. A loud speaker behind the flag carried the voice of the flag:

"I am not the flag at all, I am but its shadow. I am whatever you make me, nothing more. I am your belief in yourself, your dream of what a people may become. Sometimes I am strong with pride. Sometimes I droop and lose courage. Sometimes I am loud and boastful. But always I am all that you hope to be and have the courage to try for. I am no more than what you believe me to be, and I am all that you believe I can be. I am what you make me, nothing more. I swing before your eyes as a bright gleam of color. My stars and my stripes are your dreams and your labors. They are bright with cheer, brilliant with courage, firm with faith, because you have made them so, *for you are the makers of the flag.*"

After this introduction the episodes followed. They represented incidents in the lives of these young people both in and out of school:

1. A girl who had not been absent or tardy from school for a year. (This was an actual case.)

2. Safety-first episode, involving first-aid treatment.

3. Three girls who sold war stamps and did Red Cross work.

4. A scene where the issue of cruelty to animals was involved.

5. A basketball game where fair play and good sportsmanship were revealed.

6. An episode involving boys of recent immigrant groups and boys of older "American" stock. Theme—"Immigrants All: Americans All."

---

[27] The text of this pageant is available, at 25 cents a copy, from the Iowa State Teachers Association, Des Moines, Iowa.

7. "I Pledge Allegiance." Where did the phrases of this pledge come from? Busts of Jefferson, Washington, and Lincoln on stage.

8. An episode bringing out the significance of William Tyler Page's "American Creed."

9. Final tableau: All the participants march on stage. They break in the center, revealing a high-school girl dressed in flowing white and flanked by a Girl Scout and a Boy Scout carrying large flags. As the girl and her guards slowly come forward she sings this verse from "The Battle Hymn of the Republic":

> In the beauty of the lilies
> Christ was born across the sea,
> With a glory in His bosom
> That transfigures you and me;
> As he died to make men holy,
> Let us die to make men free;
> While God is marching on.

All on stage and in the audience rise and sing the chorus:

> Glory, glory, Hallelujah!
> His truth is marching on.

"We Cannot Escape History"—Another illustration of the effective use of the emotional appeal in driving home the meaning of democratic ideals is found in the following account of an assembly. The Lincoln Day observance was turned over to the senior social studies class. The program was carefully planned and was given respectful and appreciative attention by the entire school body. After it was over there were requests that some of the finest portions of the program be recorded as a permanent record for the school. The following is a direct transcription of one of the records. The speaker is the teacher; the singer, a senior girl with a rich contralto voice.

The Speaker: And now we come to the closing number of our Lincoln program on this momentous February 12, 1943. We of *this* generation cannot escape history. This is as true today as when Lincoln said it. And it is our hope that you have caught here today not only his sure faith in our democratic ideals but his confident hope in their ultimate victory. That is the note on which we close. A new dawn will break all over the world when the lights go on again, as surely they will, so that his ideals "shall not perish from the earth."

The Singer: When the lights go on again all over the world,
　　　　　　And the boys are home again all over the world,
　　　　　　Then we'll have time for things like wedding rings,
　　　　　　And free hearts will sing
　　　　　　When the lights go on again all over the world.

The Speaker: And the lights will go on again all over the world if we maintain the principles underlying the Four Freedoms—Freedom of Speech, Freedom of Religion, Freedom from Want, and Freedom from Fear itself.

These freedoms undergird our great democratic hope, as set forth in the immortal Declaration, as established in our Constitutional Bill of Rights, as given deathless utterance at Gettysburg, and as reaffirmed in the Atlantic Charter.

The Singer: Repeats "When the Lights Go on Again."

The Speaker: Every year since this school was founded we have held a Lincoln assembly. This has come to be one of our most cherished traditions. And each and every year we have rededicated succeeding generations of young citizens of this school to this belief, embodied in these significant lines from Drinkwater's dramatic poem on Abraham Lincoln:

> When the High Heart we magnify,
> And the clear vision celebrate,
> And worship greatness passing by,
> Ourselves are great!

★ *Education has a tremendous challenge in the great movement which must take place toward conservation and development of human values and the rebuilding of human life according to those values. Exciting, colorful, even spectacular lies the road ahead. It is not easy but it is something big enough to give one's life for.*

CHAPTER IX

Morale of Teachers

I F A GREAT PURPOSE IS NECESSARY for stimulating morale, the teaching profession has the needed challenge at the present time. Never was there greater clamor for enlightenment and the improvement of living conditions than that which is now apparent. Never was there a time of greater need for care and protection of children and youth, nor a time when the next generation was more precious, so important is it for the preservation and advancement of those values for which men have laid down their lives. Teachers, whose responsibility it is to work closely with children, youth, and adults, have the opportunity to engage in those activities which foster in masses of people the ideals which promote democratic living: the search for truth, the selfless struggle for freedom against frustration and exploitation of individuals and minority groups, the establishment of kinship among all people, the pride in the dignity of man, and the recognition of individual worth. There is opportunity for great intellectual prowess in the work and responsibility of teaching. There is challenge for people with great enthusiasm who, giving of their own best effort, can inspire others with their ideals and stimulate them to work for the welfare of mankind with a sense of joyous satisfaction in so doing. Every teacher should be a statesman.

Building Morale thru Improving Teacher Education

One of the first problems to be met in building teacher morale is in the improvement of teacher education. That, in turn, depends on making the profession of teaching so challenging and attractive that young people will be eager to choose teaching as a lifework and be energetic in preparing for it. If we are correct in our belief that the example of strong, able teachers, the records of excellent school systems, and the public recognition of education in the front ranks of world influences would capture the imagination and effort of these new recruits best fitted for teaching, then it is time that our effort should be extended toward achieving this state of affairs and publicizing it.

ADMISSION OF ABLE STUDENTS

In the United States of America teaching has been more attractive to women than to men. To many women it has seemed that work with children was not so much a challenge to exert an influence in public affairs as a preparation for domestic life and that teaching offered a chance for a short period of employment in the interlude between college graduation and marriage. Such motives are by no means unworthy, but with the increase of social and political status of women since suffrage was granted them there has been a marked increase in statesmanship among members of that sex. Now with the loss of men in war and the tremendous upheaval we are experiencing, there is more than ever a challenge to women to decide what kind of a world they want and to take steps to achieve it. Women teachers should be in the front ranks of this movement; and, considering their function in world affairs, they should be recruited with the same care and acclaim as such avowedly patriotic workers as the WACS and the WAVES, but naturally by different standards.

The biological function of childbearing, which gives women their unique opportunity for service to mankind, despite its tremendous importance, is a deterrent to continuity in professional life. A family, altho it may limit professional activity in certain respects, is a stabilizer, normally increasing human satisfactions and broadening the outlook of the person. It gives incentive, adding morale for the job. Many able women enriched by the experiences of family life find that they participate in public affairs more intelligently because of its influences. As a profession we should gain much strength and prestige by encouraging continuity in the service of married women. During the war many schoolboards have suspended the rules that barred married women from teaching. The schools and the teaching profession will be stronger if those old rules are not put into effect again.

A profession with power and high morale would attract more men—men of competence and leadership. A better balance of the sexes is needed. This balance should not be achieved by having men on one side of the scale and women on the other. There is ample opportunity for working together, the masculine and feminine contributions blending in a richer effort. A profession with such fusion would engage the imagination of young recruits who often consider teaching a feminine and cloistered job.

LENGTH OF COURSE

In the United States of America there is a marked trend toward raising the requirements for the preparation of teachers, and in consequence courses of study have been lengthened in the teachers colleges. This action raises several problems with regard to morale of young teachers and teachers in preparation. The longer course insures greater maturity from the standpoint of mere age alone and, if properly executed, gives greater insight and skill before the exacting demands of a teaching post are met. Keen insight is necessary for the kind of morale we are talking about, demanding comprehensive vision of the goals of education in society. Skills give stability in marking progress toward the goals. Because it takes time and maturity to achieve these things, teachers colleges were reluctant to adopt accelerated courses during the early days of the war when many institutions of other types were bending every effort to put young people thru as rapidly as possible so that they might sooner engage in productive work.

A thorogoing course of preparation tends to strengthen the profession, but there is every need for caution that the zest for the chosen calling be kept alive during the requisite period of time. Bursting with youthful enthusiasm for service, prospective teachers have to wait longer now than formerly before coming in contact with children, before having a job and earning their own money and hence before attaining independence, and before getting married. They have to endure longer suspense before satisfactions come.

Learning a time perspective in relation to morale is in itself a maturing process and a good thing. But those in teacher education cannot afford to overlook the fact that it has to be learned or the new crop of teachers in whom we have so much hope will go stale in the process of becoming. The problem is that of finding intermediate goals relating to the larger outcome until the young person is mature enough to realize the full meaning of his professional choice.

INSIGHT INTO GOALS

We can never safely lose sight of the fact that young people preparing to be teachers are still immature, needing the appeals normal to later adolescent development. They are, most of them, leaving home for the first time; they are concerned about breaking the restrictions of home ties, about finding a mate, and about becoming independent citizens able to earn a living by successful pursuit of their chosen vocation.

These important, self-centered interests need to be taken into consideration in developing thru college years a strong personal fiber in the young teaching group. But the adolescent is not entirely self-centered. Characteristically, young people are deeply concerned with finding and testing a philosophy of life. They want to know by what principles and for what ends to live. This normal youthful desire can and very likely will go stale if they are taught primarily the methods of course presentation, class management, and school keeping. But if young people can be helped to see that education can be one of the major forces for the advancement of truth, freedom, fellow feeling, human dignity, and personal responsibility in the evolution of a democratic world order, the vision of their place in the teaching profession in the future will be one to capture their enthusiasm and inspire their best effort.

Those who have charge of the preparation of teachers need to have this broad vision of the function and possibilities of education in the modern world. Nor is intellectual acceptance of the importance of the teaching profession enough. They should have a love for their work and an energetic enthusiasm for it which will kindle a similar fire in the younger group. There is no intent here to applaud the professor who, taking advantage of adolescent desire for a perspective on ultimate values of life, sways them to unreasoned conclusions and rouses them to ill-considered campaigns. But the emotional appeal which encourages youth to achieve thoughtfully a better education for all people is legitimate and essential in the faculty of teachers colleges.

Fortunately in the United States of America a general movement toward the improvement of teacher education made some advancement during the latter years of the depression. Following the period in our history when teachers were educated rapidly to fill positions in the schools with a minimum of preparation, the declining birth-rate and the apparent surplus of teachers enabled cities and states to raise their requirements for certification and appointment of teachers. Correlatively certain leading institutions for the preparation of teachers cut thru barriers of tradition, demanded higher standards for admission of students, and offered educational programs of greater vitality than had been, or is now, the general rule.

Extensive surveys of teacher education [1] attested loudly to needed reforms in professional preparation, and there followed the establishment of the Commission on Teacher Education of the American Council on Education,[2] which for several years has worked with selected institutions and organizations on a program demonstrating means of improving the qualifications of teachers.

It is not our function to recount the findings of these pioneer movements toward the advancement of teacher education, but they indicate that thousands of schools which employ teachers should demand that positions be filled by persons with sound education, citizens with vision and insight, and teachers with skill, enthusiasm, and artistry. They are signs of the times for hundreds of institutions which by state, municipal, or private endowment are responsible for developing the stamina of teachers for fulfilling the obligations of their profession in the advancement of order and peace in the world.

COLLEGE ACTIVITIES

Teacher preparation usually, and wisely, includes active laboratory experience with children. It is a matter of common observation that the morale of students increases as soon as they engage in student teaching. Even tho the work may be difficult and the success limited, there is seldom a student who does not put forth unflinchingly an unlimited effort during this practical experience. Here is the immediate challenge, the concrete thing to be done, which youth demands. As the scope of teacher preparation has increased, many colleges have been able to provide different types of experiences which extend the usual areas covered by student teaching and carry the same qualities of vigor and vitality. Among these are activities which bring students into contact with family, community, and world problems: community organization, travel, participation in progressive social movements such as housing developments, and work camps. There are evidences, too, of increased participation of students in college life itself thru college councils and planning committees. There is the danger that such activities, which are of course

---

[1] U. S. Department of the Interior, Office of Education, National Survey of the Education of Teachers. Evenden, E. S., associate director; Frazier, B. W., coordinator. *National Survey of the Education of Teachers, Vols. I-VI.* Bulletin 1933, No. 10. Washington, D. C.: Government Printing Office. Vol. I, 118 p.; Vol. II, 258 p.; Vol. III, 547 p.; Vol. IV, 123 p.; Vol. V, 484 p.; Vol. VI, 253 p.

[2] See publications of the Commission on Teacher Education of the American Council on Education, 744 Jackson Place, N. W., Washington, D. C.

time-consuming, may become divorced from thoughtful, scholarly work. They should rather enhance the student's understanding of problems of life which education should help to solve. If the morale which is generated by active experiences can be a challenge to study for greater understanding and appreciation and for greater facility in solving personal, professional, and world problems, then we shall have developed in our prospective teachers the greatest forces possible for the advancement of our profession.

Factors Which Break Morale

There are many teachers in the United States of America who have a vision of the importance of their profession to social progress and who attack their work with intellectual prowess and contagious enthusiasm. Certain conditions in the lives of teachers, however, tend to blur the purpose they serve in society and to cause some of them to feel drab and others to assume a saintly instead of statesmanlike role. In consequence of the force of these conditions some teachers carry the burden of their profession like a clubfoot. They adjust to it as a necessity and with varying degrees of grace, hoping that the public will not notice the stigma which it casts upon them as individuals different from the general population. Others of the teaching profession imagine it a halo which signifies to the world in symbol if not in words, "Respect and protect me; see, I have a child in my arms."

When the lives of teachers are considered in the light of the concepts of morale developed in preceding chapters, the factors which cause them to take such attitudes toward themselves and their work are revealed. The thwartings of basic human motives which are peculiar to this profession must be recognized and dealt with before the morale necessary for adequate public service of teachers can be built up in this group.

VICTIMS OF TRADITIONAL PUBLIC REGARD

There is a definite tradition as to the status of teachers in various civilized societies which inevitably influences members of the group. In the United States of America, for instance, the "schoolmarm" is, or perhaps we should say has been, in the minds of the public a caricature endowed with maidenly virtue and kindly but unsatiated sentimentality toward children and the regenerative processes of

life. This attitude makes it difficult for vigorous, well-informed
women teachers to take a prominent place in society and gives ven-
turesome men who enter the profession a hard row to hoe. Teachers
are thought to be victims of perfectionism and exactitude but lacking in shrewd insight into business and politics, devoid of the graces
and minor vices (not to mention the major ones) which are found in
other citizens, and incapable of appraising or functioning in practical affairs. There is both a stigma and a halo in such a conception,
placed there by people who carry impressions of their early teachers
into their adult years without troubling to revise them in the light
of mature observation and judgment. The caricature is perpetuated
by thoughtless people, cartoonists, and "smart" writers. Often there
is no considered intent to be malicious, but these influences become
important when they circumscribe the vigorous activities of a professional group and break down the self-respect of individual teachers. The alarming thing is that some teachers become frustrated and,
instead of changing the public sentiment, tend to perpetuate it when
they allow their frustrations to impair their effectiveness as teachers
and citizens. The public mind can be changed by vigorous contributions of statesmanlike teachers to the field of education in national
life.

Already some teachers are making such contributions and lack
only the acclaim and recognition which if given might enable us to
write the preceding paragraph in the past rather than the present
tense. Many teachers are courageously and constructively working
with children and families in the midst of such problems as acute
mobility of population, deportation and detention of alien groups,
and the instability of family life brought about by war. The threats
to civilization which have challenged an all-out effort to win the
war and the peace have tended only to increase the morale of such
teachers.

PUBLIC EMPLOYEES

Teachers in public schools constitute the majority of the profession. As public employees, paid by funds derived from their fellow
citizens and dealing with the lives of all classes and types of society,
teachers have a tacit if not an actual mixed allegiance to the great
variety of purposes and philosophies of the people whose children
they teach. This fact tends to deny them freedom of speech and

enterprise which some other professions enjoy. For this reason they are excluded often from the conference tables and forums where public policies are determined and social conditions are created. They may choose whether they will accept a teaching post where certain policies and conditions exist; but, once having chosen, their chief method of effecting change is that of educating the next generation. And then often they are hampered either by tact or by statutory prescription from any adequate approach to controversial issues and practical affairs.

The only justification for such restrictions lies in the fact that school attendance is compulsory. Hence it is often the case that a child and his family may not choose whether he will enter one class or another in charge of this teacher or that. But rather than curtail the citizenship rights of a professional group it would seem that those teachers should be selected who have vision and leadership in dealing with problems of political, economic, and social democracy and whose search for truth and human decency, if liberated, will become a telling force in world reconstruction. Perhaps such teachers are too rare to be found in every location. Then steps should be taken—and indeed they are under way—to increase their number.

RESTRICTIONS ON NONTEACHING ACTIVITIES

It appears that many teachers get personal stimulation, courage, and satisfactions outside of their professional life. The testimony of such individuals as to the most potent factors promoting adequacy in personal-professional life indicates that they value the security of home life and the affection which good family life brings. They desire pleasant living conditions offering wide horizons and close friendships outside the profession, and social life in the community.

Yet it is interesting to note in the face of our demand for effective citizenship in the teaching group that in many places women teachers lose their jobs when they marry and many other restrictions are placed on the personal lives of teachers. Teachers who testify that social and family life are not satisfying say that these lacks are devastating influences, cutting deep into their personal development. In many places teachers lack opportunity to meet other people on a social basis, lack friends of the opposite sex, fail to marry at the proper time, and lack freedom and naturalness in social life due to rigid standards of conduct expected of teachers.

WORK WITH IMMATURE MINDS

The fact that members of this profession work with immature minds is at once a challenge and a caution. For teachers working under favorable circumstances there is all the challenge, hope, and satisfaction of guiding a new generation to right wrongs and improve conditions of living, and there is always a chance that because of this guidance the job may be done gloriously. There is also the caution that efforts to spur on the courage of the young may, because of their limited experience and mental immaturity, give those pupils visionary, half-baked notions which may never grow beyond stunted prejudice. Teachers who are too cautious or who lack intellectual vigor and emotional tone are often hampered in their own growth because they do not have the challenge which comes from dealing with other adults. It is easy, in the midst of clanging class bells, wriggling bodies, passing classes, and correcting papers, for minds to become fixed on details and to lose sight of the great educational goal which is a vital challenge to adult minds.

INTANGIBLE OUTCOMES

Just as it is difficult to keep up courageous morale without a mature insight into the nature of the objectives of education, it is also difficult to do so without specific assurances of progress. The outcomes of teaching are less tangible than those of some other professions or of industry. Teachers cannot say at the end of the day that they have filled so many orders and taken in so many dollars, netting so much profit. Schools cannot say at the end of the year that they have built so many ships or constructed so many bridges. Those which have adopted objective measures to the exclusion of all other forms of appraisal have overlooked some of the greatest human values. Young human beings are slow in their growing up and many of the outcomes of the teacher's work are delayed. Teachers scarcely know when their efforts blight or bear fruit, and by the time they do many other forces have contributed to the result. A teacher carries on with faith and hope, learning to recognize and appreciate many small signs and symptoms of greater things.

SCHOOL ORGANIZATION AND ADMINISTRATION

Perhaps it is because of the intangible nature of educational outcomes and the flexibility of teaching technics that many teachers testify to discouraging influences within the schools themselves. Among the most frequently cited conflicts are those between teachers and the administration of the school. Teachers engrossed in work with children feel themselves hampered by the dictates of supervisors, principals, and superintendents. They believe themselves to be at variance with the ideals and philosophy set up tacitly or otherwise in the school or school system by those in administrative positions. Administrators, on the other hand, find themselves embroiled in a complication of restrictions placed upon them by schoolboard members, legislators, and taxpayer groups. Instability of working relationships and often shifts of policy and of regulations are outcomes of a system having such a network of strains at its base. Teachers fall into the habit of keeping an attractive external front supposed to please administrators, and administrators spend their time devising ways of getting on with the groups representing their clientele instead of uniting all forces to study and provide for the educational needs of children and the crying hungers of a world starving for the bread of life which the next generation must provide. Beneath this external effort to please there is often a negative form of morale which may take the form of active resistance but is more likely to descend to the level of whispering discontent, which is destructive to progress.

Several bases for such unwholesome thwartings are apparent. One is the remnant of a caste system which gives recognition and acclaim to administrative positions and relegates teaching to a subordinate status. Money talks, too. It is usual for administrators to have a higher salary status than teachers. Teachers are dependent upon the goodwill of administrators, and they in turn on their boards of education in many places for salary increases and indeed for the very security of their jobs. The effects of these conditions of caste and status are to make both teachers and administrators timid about effecting a constructive program of mutual understanding and united effort. In such instances administrators are thought of as vested with authority rather than entrusted with leadership.

Teachers should be growing constantly. Some administrators attempt to insure this growth by requiring teachers to pursue given amounts of advanced study, often making such study a necessary condition for salary increases or promotion. Such requirements are

merely objective devices intended to bring good professional results. The noticeable decline in morale of some teachers while they
are fulfilling the requirements, however, gives cause for question.
Sometimes the process is contradictory to its purpose, as teachers
strain themselves to take evening and Saturday courses which will
"count." Growth will come when teachers have a personal drive
toward self-improvement and improvement of service demanding
reflective study both in and out of courses, according to their need.

The leadership of teachers in winning the war and winning the
peace and the morale which they have as persons and citizens are
inevitably tied up or released by the kind of leadership they have
from the administrative group in schools. This fact is not only a
personal challenge to administrators but one which should be the
concern of everyone in the profession. There is much chaff which
should be sifted out of our school organization, such as inequalities
in school support, pressures from vested interests, unintelligent
statutory provisions for schools, undemocratic lines of authority,
and hampering methods of grading, grouping, and examining of
children. It is for all of us to clear the way for growth and enlightenment of teachers on social, political, and economic affairs which will
give depth to their thinking and will remove the shackles which keep
teachers from developing the positive leadership which the world
needs from this profession.

Where leadership in a school system is good, there is probably no
more potent factor in developing the courage and endurance of a
group of teachers to persist in the face of danger, fatigue, and discouragements. In some schools and school systems there is a spirit of
unity and determination to improve education that can be explained
only by knowing the leaders of the group. Some one man or woman
may be chiefly responsible. Or there may be a group of men and
women whose combined abilities in places of leadership release the
latent abilities of the entire teaching group.

Teachers who testify to positive influences of school administration on themselves and on their work maintain that the most potent
factors are good professional leadership, cooperation and understanding between principal and faculty, sympathetic and intelligent
schoolboards, friendly teaching associates, and committee work in
the school. These relationships lead to a human understanding of

each other, a belief in common philosophy and purposes, and an open and frank defense of differences.

That there are great inequalities in teacher compensation is a well-known fact. Salaries paid teachers may depend more on their sex, the type of school they are in, its geographical location, and the age level of the children taught than on the amount of responsibility they assume or the expertness of their leadership. The important thing in relation to this discussion is not to elaborate on these conditions but to note their effect upon teacher morale.

There is always a lively interest on the part of the public in teachers' salaries in tax-supported schools. Often the worth to society of the services of teachers receives little or no consideration in the feverish effort to keep the budget of public expenditures in bounds. When this happens teachers feel a lack of recognition of the value of their work and build up antagonisms toward legislative and taxpaying groups. Not only do they feel a lack of recognition but they often feel an actual pinch for money. Because of the nature of their education, aspirations, and desires, teachers' demands for books, travel, and the arts are beyond the income which most of them receive. Furthermore there is in the tradition of American life a prestige factor in financial adequacy which has caused teachers to take a back seat among some other occupations, say, the law, medicine, banking, and acting.

Teachers who have campaigned for better pay and more security have had varied results. On the side of the teachers it is said that they are the people best informed about standards of efficiency in their important profession and the remuneration that is essential for maintaining them. On the other side it is maintained that the work of teaching is so important that teachers should not neglect it by spending their time and energy on campaigns for more money. Let them prove their contentions in deeds and not words, say the adversaries. It must be conceded that some teachers have not done so. Some of them, however, have proved their cause in both deeds and words, the most successful being those who have so convinced the public of the worth of the school's services that citizen groups are moved to give testimony to the need for greater expenditures on the schools even tho such action will cost them more in tax money.

The effect of controversies about salaries and other school expenditures is twofold and somewhat contradictory. On the one hand there is a dissipation of energy and morale when groups line up against each other; on the other hand issues come out in the open which have an educational value to both sides. Teachers learn things they would not otherwise know about the relationship of the schools to other public affairs. The public learns about its schools. If the issue is fairly considered there are strong morale-building factors involved. It is when political trickery dominates the situation that the morale of teachers is broken.

A controversy about salaries which may arise within the educational system is that of equal pay for equal work and equal preparation. This grows out of the traditional regulations that teachers of little children should be paid less than teachers of high school or college and again that women teachers should be paid less than men. The development of a new body of knowledge about young children and a conviction that the early years are among the most important in the life span has created a demand for better prepared teachers at preschool and elementary levels and is tending to bring about equality in monetary recognition for service of teachers of younger children. The case for equality of men and women teachers is more difficult to reconcile. There are no sex differences in efficiency in the teaching profession, but there are demands of society upon men as bread winners and supporters of families. A young man eager to assume the responsibilities of family life finds himself thwarted when his salary is fixed at a level to attract young women who will work for just enough to keep themselves in a boardinghouse for a year or so until they can marry and leave the profession. The solution often has been to promote young men to administrative positions altho they are needed in classrooms and would prefer to stay there if pay were adequate. This practice tends to widen the cleavage between teachers and administrators by adding the factor of sex to that of caste and between men and women by adding the factor of caste to that of sex. It seems that the solution should be found in more adequate pay for all classroom teachers, so that women too might care for the dependents who often fall to their lot, so that more men might be attracted to teaching, and that teachers might marry without encountering financial crises.

That money can be raised for purposes which people care enough about has been demonstrated during the war. Patrons of the school and citizens of the commonwealth would do well to consider the many morale factors involved in an adequate system of monetary compensation for teachers.

Building Morale thru Improving Conditions for Teachers in Service

The conditions facing teachers in service, discussed in the previous section, may seem to be a drab backdrop against which to develop a statesmanlike profession, but strong colors will emerge when the one who is apologetic for being "only a classroom teacher" and the other who beholds himself exalted because of the idealistic character of his work lose themselves in the march toward better human living, side by side with statesmen who are engaged in solving the problems created by war. True we shall get further when we have enlarged our concept of our role in society and have revised the attitude of the general public toward the teaching profession. But by merely taking thought we cannot add one inch to our stature. It is rather by conceiving our goals as worth the effort and by working steadfastly to attain them in the face of obstacles both within and outside of the profession itself that we shall change the structure of the group and the function of its individuals.

MUTUAL SUPPORT

The best school systems are those in which administrators, teachers, and patrons are working together on their problems. Working together does not mean that the administrator or supervisor sets out what is to be done and teachers, after producing a project with the children, call in the superior officer to see how well his idea has been carried out. If, thru education, we are to move mankind one peg toward better living, there must be in our profession a unity and cohesiveness which allow for individual imagination, for give and take, pooling and consensus of ideas, experimentation, and further conference. The spirit of morale which is demanded in our time implies unified effort in which compromises and even personal sacrifices are made because of the worth of the goal to which all members of the group are committed. School systems where there is search for personal favor, internal dissension, external appeasement, or strife for the protection of vested interests may have strong negative morale existing in small groups and individuals; but it is impossible to see how under such conditions, by act or precept, these teachers can be a constructive force with children or communities.

Many schools make provision for the induction of teachers into the system and the direction of their teaching activities so as to insure unity among teachers, progress in the work, and growth in individuals. For example, new teachers are assigned to older ones for guidance and help. They are given visiting days in their own building so that they may see and know what is going on and the sooner become an integral part of the group. Building committees of teachers are formed to make plans and solve problems. Workshops and institutes are organized for improving the work of the schools, sometimes under the leadership of the school supervisors, sometimes with the help of colleges or universities whose offerings are arranged to meet the needs of the teachers. The best of these efforts, naturally, are those which engage individual and group effort for improvement of service.

The centralization of schools and the rapid shifts in status of community life make it difficult for school workers to keep a close relationship with patrons. Some few nursery schools have been loaded on trucks and moved bodily from place to place with itinerant groups. Teachers have been transported with alien groups in detention camps. Schools deserted by their constituents have been closed and others as quickly opened. Children have been transported long distances from their homes where they are inevitably the only vital link between their own community and the school. In some sections where close ties were quite possible geographically, parents have organized and operated private schools because they wanted the cooperative relationships with their children's schools which seemed impossible in the public system. How else than by studious observation of how and where children live can teachers and administrators determine specifically what needs to be done for them? And where else do they have a better laboratory of life and its problems and processes? How else can educators unify the learning experiences of children than by enlisting the efforts and talents of those with whom they live? The morale which we seek for ourselves as teachers must be contagious in the communities in which we work.

TEACHERS ORGANIZATIONS

Effective organization of teachers is essential for united action and prestige in the advancement of education as well as for personal inspiration and growth. Thru organization teachers should come to feel a kinship for all members of the same profession, and laymen should learn to recognize the pronouncements of this united group as representing the best judgment and authority of specialized workers in this field of service. Altho teachers organizations abound in the United States of America, there is still need for nationwide unity in the teaching group for the advancement of education.

This is not to say that an over-all affiliation of teachers should preclude the organization of small groups. Probably the most effective morale builder is the local organization which has national or even world affiliation. In the local group there is opportunity for stimulating personal contacts and for attack on immediate vital problems. There are opportunities in local groups for each one to function and by a system of rotation to be a committee member or officer. The larger affiliations add strength and help to avoid provincialism.

In the larger affiliation teachers of different fields of specialization come to find their common purposes and broaden and intensify these purposes. College teachers who give much time and professional effort to the discovery of knowledge as well as to its dissemination will find that teachers of childhood and youth are adding to our knowledge of how to conserve human resources thru new ways of dealing with boys and girls in schools and with families in varied walks of life. Teachers of younger levels will become aware of the contributions of higher education.

Working together on the process of education is not easy when large and complex groups are involved, since each must have his part to do and not hinder the effort of others. Democratic methods are not easy to use. When men are desperate enough it is far easier to secure a united front by rallying them around a dynamic leader who will dictate to each one his share in the work. But that is not the morale of free men, and it is not the morale by which teachers in a society of free men will gain the benefits which we crave for them and for society.

There are great opportunities for statesmanship open to members of a united profession. Teachers have been laggard in their recognition of this relationship and in perfecting their knowledge of the political, statutory, and administrative factors which set the conditions under which they work. They have been prone to leave such matters to legislators, boards of education, and superintendents of schools. But if teachers are wise they will, for the sake of the protection and efficiency of their work with children, inform themselves about these conditions so that they may strengthen the hands of those who are working for the best welfare of teachers, and, if need be, protest action which stands in the way of effective progress in education. Legislators, schoolboards, and administrators will do well if they get the advice and counsel of teacher experts. When teachers are asked what are the conditions which should be obtained for the best progress in the education of children and youth in the next decade or two decades, let them be sure that they have the understanding and vision to say what it is. Let them be sure, too, that they know how to use, for the best benefit of their pupils, those facilities which they have or which can be provided. That is their part and it is no meager or inferior one. With united effort the time may come sooner than we think for the participation of educational leaders in organizing a program of education for world reconstruction which will rank in importance with such considerations as disarmament, national boundaries, and self-determination of nations in the negotiations for peace. It is expertness of this sort which constitutes the true statesmanship of the teacher in his own field of human relations and human development.

The organized profession of education, thru the Educational Policies Commission of the National Education Association and the American Association of School Administrators, has outlined recently in broad strokes the need for a larger place for education in world affairs and has shown how the lack of a common charter of education among the free and peaceful peoples of the world is perhaps the supreme cause of the failure of their past efforts to teach the young the information and attitudes necessary for the prevention of war.[3] Teachers should understand how effectively education has been used to shape national policies that led to international ill will, aggression, and war. That trend should be and

---

[3] National Education Association and American Association of School Administrators, Educational Policies Commission. *Education and the People's Peace.* Washington, D. C.: the Commission, 1943. 59 p.

can be reversed when education is a force for safeguarding peace and extending democracy.

Teachers who have pioneered for political action have met with varying success. Comments have been made to the effect that they have worked for their own self-advancement, demanding undeserved salary increases without regard for other and greater social needs, that they have sought to protect inefficient individuals with supposed grievances, and that they have bickered among themselves for the group support of certain political parties. There may be proof for these accusations in some places, altho they would not be applicable to teachers as a general rule. Sometimes teachers are awkward and inept in the ways of functioning in public affairs. Because of the peculiar status they hold in society they have been assigned a role which is difficult to break thru without arousing suspicion and condemnation. Awkwardness and lack of shrewd insight are difficult to forgive in an intelligent group, but so are indifference and neglect toward this group on the part of society. For the sake of the work which this profession must do if it is to achieve the challenging objective which lies before it, teachers must improve their physical vigor and mental well-being, their social status, their self-respect, and the respect of other citizens by taking an active and intelligent part in the world of affairs.

COMMUNITY LEADERSHIP

For many teachers the way to service lies not in spectacular campaigns but in the support and leadership of projects for human betterment within local communities. These are the projects in which teachers are, or should be, adept: helping people to see how they can secure better sanitation, better housing, better care of children, better breeds of stock, improvement of soil, better crops, more adequate preservation of foods, and more adequate diets. Work on such projects, altho lacking spectacular effects, is not sheltered. It must be done in conjunction with and often in opposition to existing agencies, statutory regulations, political parties, and ward bosses. Working alone teachers will not get far, but they can be effective forces if they help people to see the way of helping themselves. Furthermore, when one works for the advancement of people there follows a unity of group support of a common cause. It is the wise teacher who will raise his own status and the status of the profession by getting citizens to support the schools because they have been convinced by enterprising teachers that the schools are doing something important which should enlist their support.

This is one of the best ways for teachers in service to learn what is involved in their new role of statesmanship. Most of those now at work in the schools had little or no preservice preparation for activities other than those involved in classroom teaching. The most important thing for them to add thru experience and with the help of administrative leadership is this matter of helping people to solve better their problems of living. This generation of teachers must learn this type of service by experimentation on the job. The next generation should have some preparation for it in institutions which educate teachers.

WORTHY OBJECTIVES

The basic necessity in raising the morale of teachers, as of any group, is that of making clear the objectives worth working for. The crisis brought about by the war and reconstruction sheds a new light and increased significance upon the need for conservation and development of human resources. This has always been the major concern of teachers. Yet sometimes, with undue concern over subjectmatter, standard tests, behavior problems, and other details of school keeping, and with discouragements peculiar to their profession, teachers have lost sight of the woods for the trees and have forgotten the challenging purposes they were working for. If we needed an awakening to the significance of education, we have had it in the past few years as we have seen its effectiveness in Nazi and Fascist countries in producing a way of life directly opposed to our own. As a result of this kind of education we have seen human life and human values rolled under the treads of tanks and blasted and burned by explosives dropped from the skies. The young people who are the products of those schools have used their mathematics to determine the operation of guns, their chemistry for producing bombs, and their study of anatomy not for building strong bodies but for mending broken ones. The population of the world after years of prevalent unemployment found its jobs on the march from industry to industry as war production sprang up overnight. Efforts to produce more services that man might work and live well were nipped in the bud. Civilians found themselves rationed in commodities and curtailed in activities.

Of what good is the teaming of science and invention, which in the present generation have excelled the progress in all earlier periods, if man is not to use the machines he has created but be crushed by them? Was there ever greater challenge for those who are experts in human values and human relationships? The teaching profession stands in the ranks of these experts. Education has a tremendous challenge in the great movement which must take place toward conservation and development of human values and the rebuilding of human life according to those values. Exciting, colorful, even spectacular lies the road ahead. It is not easy but it is something big enough to give one's life for.

The search for specific goals in itself does not appear to be spectacular. It involves the rediscovery of the truths by which men should be able to live together: the Four Freedoms, the Bill of Rights, and the Sermon on the Mount. The translation of these into the ways of life of men and women, boys and girls, in our modern labyrinth of economic, social, and geographic structure is a glorious task.

It is a glorious task because of challenging new conditions which affect our work. In a democratic nation we have always accepted the ideal of freedom as a truth. But we have somehow believed that we could maintain our freedoms and rights untouched by downtrodden people in other lands and often with disregard for the underprivileged immigrant groups who came to our shores seeking the American way of life. The war has taught us that we are citizens not of a nation alone but of the world. What happens in other countries and in islands of the sea which we never heard of before the world conflict has touched our lives intimately. This new concept of world citizenship colors our whole idea of what we should teach about responsibilities and human rights.

There is need for clearer concepts of cultural and physical geography so that we may know conditions under which all men live. There is greater need for learning the truth about how people in varying conditions have solved their problems. After the severe test of war the tradition of superiority of races is being revised. There is an acute need to prepare our children and youth for the responsibility of dealing with others who now are being reared to ideals and beliefs opposed to our own. This involves not only the understanding of their philosophies and ways of life but training in technics of dealing with them outside of war. There is no time for superficialities such as we have indulged in previously in our study of people of other lands. The need is direct and urgent for coming to grips with truth, if the children we teach, when grown, are to be able to deal with the postwar world problems.

Not only should children learn with their teachers to search for truth but they should also learn the ways of freedom, which demand courage, self-confidence, clear thinking, and responsibility. Children in this generation must be taught a perspective on the world situation; they must be helped to find themselves in relationship to immediate and world affairs; and they must learn the dignity of work, the joy and security of affection and service—all this as well as the intelligent use of the three R's. The artistic, literary, and musical experiences of children should not only be safeguarded; they should be expanded and made joyous and meaningful.

The urgent needs of the world and the hope reposed in the next generation for meeting these needs constitute the challenge to teachers of the present. In the response to this challenge lies the direction of their work and the key to their morale.

★ *The primary human problem of group morale in any school system is how to secure the cooperation of every member of the staff in realizing the aim of the organization. This aim is to reach every educable person in the community and present to each individual the maximum educational opportunity.*

CHAPTER X

Human Relations in School Administration

PRIDE IN GROUP ACHIEVEMENT has always strengthened loyalty. With this pride there must go the conviction that the whole enterprise is dedicated to a common objective which is worth the effort. Kipling expresses the thought in the poem "A Song in Storm," written during the dark days of the first World War:

> No matter though our decks be swept
> And mast and timber crack—
> We can make good all loss except
> The loss of turning back. . . .

> Then welcome Fate's discourtesy
> Whereby it is made clear,
> How in all time of our distress,
> As in our triumph too,
> The game is more than the player of the game,
> And the ship is more than the crew!

This concept of morale which submerges the individual in a great cause exalts the word and gives it the dignity and importance which justify its use in measuring the tenacity and effectiveness of any organization in war and peace.

However, morale is more than tenacity; it is a state of mind which maintains each individual as an effective working member of a group. Since democracy depends upon the capacity of each citizen to share experiences with others and to pull his share of the load, it seems that morale is definitely a part of the design for democratic living.

Among the enemies of morale are fear, frustration, discouragement, disillusionment, selfishness, and boredom. To meet these enemies the United States Armed Forces are striving to develop in officers and men, as the basis for a high state of morale, the following qualities: loyalty, self-respect, cheerfulness, enthusiasm, initiative, resourcefulness, aggressiveness, discipline, and tenacity. These qualities are as important in peace as in war. Here is a challenge for education which extends beyond the classroom and becomes vitally important in the field of administrative relationships, involving the whole personnel which is engaged in the educational program.

Evolving Concepts in School Administration

Public education as a function of government has been established by the American people in harmony with the structure and development of the American way of life. The school system thruout the years has been closer to the people than other governmental enterprises and should be more responsive to social changes than many other institutions and governmental agencies. In the early days of our country's history, school organization was a simple, local problem and in many communities was controlled by methods similar to the New England town meeting. However, as local and state school organization and administration have developed in size and complexity, many new problems in human relations have emerged. A standard pattern of city-school organization has developed which is based upon the line and staff form as exemplified in the Army. This military influence has been combined with the lay board of education invested with legal authority to determine administrative policies and having a relationship to the professional school administrator which is somewhat analogous to that which the board of directors of an industrial or business enterprise has to the general superintendent. If school administration is to be efficient, the distinction between the function of the lay board and that of the professional leader must be clearly understood. Altho all American cities have not yet solved this problem in practice, nevertheless there is an unmistakable trend toward sound principles of administration which seek to center responsibility in a single executive officer. A federal committee stated these fundamental principles in 1937:

Fortunately the foundations of effective management in public affairs, no less than in private, are well known. They have emerged universally wherever men have worked together for some common purpose, whether through the state, the church, the private association, or the commercial enterprise. They have been written into constitutions, charters, and articles of incorporation, and exist as habits of work in the daily life of all organized peoples. Stated in simple terms these canons of efficiency require the establishment of a responsible and effective chief executive as the center of energy, direction, and administrative management; the systematic organization of all activities in the hands of a qualified personnel under the direction of the chief executive; and to aid him in this, the establishment of appropriate managerial and staff agencies. There must also be provision for planning, a complete fiscal system, and means for holding the Executive accountable for his program.[1]

[1] President's Committee on Administrative Management. *Administrative Management in the Government of the United States.* Washington, D. C.: Government Printing Office, 1937. p. 2.

During the past twenty years there has been a vast improvement in the efficiency of public-school administration in American communities. In many systems current practice has kept pace with theory. However, in too many places there is still a wide gap between theory and practice. Altho the plan is there for all to read, simple problems become complex because the maintenance of authority is substituted for genuine educational leadership.

Friction in the school machinery seldom can be remedied by charts reminding people of the ideal administrative setup or by rules designed to keep individuals in their proper places. Such difficulties are essentially problems in human relationships which can be solved only by considering the strength and the weaknesses of those who are involved. Altho there are in every organization a few grumblers who work for their own personal aggrandizement rather than for the good of the team, most people have an instinctive desire to cooperate if they are given an opportunity. In the interest of efficiency, school authority, which is nominally democratic, has tended in some cases to become autocratic, thus diminishing the capacity for spontaneous cooperation by personnel in the school system.

There is a need for a philosophy of school administration which provides for all persons in the organization, whose efficiency and happiness are affected by the establishment of a policy, an opportunity to have a voice in making the decision. It is possible to provide for participation without any weakening of the leadership of the superintendent of schools or the board of education. The time which is consumed in consultation is no more than the time used in straightening out the difficulties which arise after decisions are made without discussion. In the long run, there is a saving of time and an increase in efficiency if decisions affecting the welfare of children or teachers are discussed with those who execute the policies. Such a policy of participation develops possibilities of friendliness, comradeship, and teamwork which are the basis of proper human relations in a school system.

From the standpoint of effective group morale the primary human problem of any school system is how to secure the cooperation of every employee *in realizing the aim of the organization.* This aim, in the case of a school system, is to reach every educable person in the community and present to each individual the maximum educational opportunity. All phases of personnel administration in the school system are to some extent related to this objective. Significant human problems related to morale and to understanding the primary aim of the schools may be partially solved or they may be further confused as a result of the type of policy pursued in the selection and placement of teachers, the promotion and the improvement of teachers, and the handling of problems involving personnel.

BASIC PRINCIPLES

Since the solution of these human problems depends upon the recognition and acceptance of certain underlying principles which are the foundations of high morale, teachers and all other members of the school organization must:

1. Have faith in the intrinsic importance of the work which they are doing and its contribution to the aims of the organization.

2. Have the right and opportunity to contribute their ideas to the improvement of the system as far as they are able and willing to do so.

3. Know what their responsibilities are. (The channels of communication should be open at all times for questions and directions in regard to duties and responsibilities.)

4. Have sufficient confidence in the integrity and loyalty of co-workers and superior officers to contribute to effective teamwork in the prosecution of the common task.

5. Feel that their best work will bring its just reward, thus challenging them to give their best efforts to their daily tasks.

6. Be dealt with as human beings eager to find opportunities for self-realization.

7. Be given the opportunity to grow and to achieve promotion by recognition of achievement.

8. Be given assignments of work in which they have an opportunity to succeed.

9. Be consulted before decisions are made which affect the conditions under which they work.

10. Be conscious of professional leadership which assists them in meeting new problems dealing with individual children or with community situations.

The professional enthusiasm of teachers may be increased by democratic attitudes and patterns of administration which are mindful of these canons.

PROBLEMS OF COMMUNICATION

The size and complexity of the school organization in cities and large rural-school systems have brought to the conscientious school administrator problems of communication which are growing in importance. How can the superintendent of schools, who is legally responsible to the board of education for making many final decisions and initiating action in line with far-reaching policies, be kept informed of what is going on in the classrooms? In the larger school systems this is one of the major problems. It is difficult for the superintendent of schools to have intimate, firsthand acquaintance with all principals, teachers, clerks, custodians, and other co-workers. How can they be kept informed, thru the supervisory organization, of aims, policies, and plans? Likewise, and just as important, how can the way be kept open for information going to the superintendent's office? It is this two-way flow of information, questions, suggestions, and achievement reports which encourages individual initiative in the organization and strengthens morale.

PROBLEMS OF TEAMWORK

How can the executive of a school system maintain an effective working equilibrium among the various social groups within the system? Principals, supervisory officers, teachers, custodians, and clerks must have sufficient confidence in the integrity and loyalty of co-workers and superior officers to contribute to effective teamwork in the prosecution of the common task. Can we be sure that no one group in the organization will line up in opposition to some other group or to the organization as a whole? How can people be transferred, promoted, or demoted without impairing the morale of the group in which these changes occur? These constitute another group of human problems which are vital to the morale of any school organization. The superintendent must be the leader of a cooperative group. He must be able to weave into the whole fabric of education the best efforts of every individual in the group by directing each individual into the type of work in which he can make the greatest contributions.

The line officers in the organization are the school principals. It is they who keep the machine running. No success can be possible without harmonious relations between superintendent and principals. His contact with principals involves three different aspects:

1. The administrative, involving the division of authority and the relationships encountered in promoting the everyday work of the schools

2. The professional, which includes the consideration of the ethical niceties which should govern the conduct of both

3. The social, which deals with contacts not specifically related to everyday duties.

The trend at the present time is to accord to the principal of the school an increasing amount of power and responsibility in the educational program of his school. The principal should have a voice in the selection and assignment of teachers. The principal should have responsibility for making the daily program and should have authority to make rules and regulations governing routine matters. A strange anomaly has developed in many large school systems at the present time. The superintendent of schools in his zeal for democratic administration has allowed the school principal more and more power. In the mind of the superintendent, the school system is characterized by a desire for democratic procedure, while in some individual schools, where the principal makes all the decisions without consulting the staff, there is the essence of autocratic control.

Much strife may be stirred up in school systems by the wrong relationship between the principal and the superintendent. The principals may practice a sort of unconscious disloyalty by constantly grumbling and groaning about the work which is imposed upon them by the central office. In most cases the criticism is more or less impersonal, but it does not contribute to effective morale. A feeling of mutual confidence and responsibility is necessary between the superintendent and the principals. The principal must be worthy of the understanding and trust which he receives from the superintendent and should be willing to subordinate his own personal views to the welfare of the system when necessary.

PROBLEMS OF INDIVIDUAL EFFECTIVENESS

How can administrators, teachers, and other employees secure the maximum of satisfaction from their jobs? Of course, adequate monetary compensation is one incentive to willing and competent service. Nevertheless, the effective leader is concerned with the stimulation of interest in the work as an incentive to service. This inner zeal is largely a question of wholesome conditions of employment. How can the superintendent help to create an environment in which the worker loses himself in the objective which is broader than his individual interest? In American democracy that environment must respect the personality of every individual. There must be satisfaction which comes from recognition of achievement, merited praise, and expressed appreciation of human values.

Administrative Relationships—Autocratic versus Democratic

School administrative policies and practices vary in every section of the country and differ from one community to another. Personnel administration which emphasizes human values and relationships has received special attention in a few cities, but in most school systems it has been assumed that these problems will take care of themselves or will be taken care of by the intuition of the superintendent and administrative officers. Even in a system which claims to be democratic it cannot be assumed that these problems of communication, of maintaining teamwork, and of developing maximum personal effectiveness are being adequately solved. For example, a teacher may be well paid in relation to the standards of the community in which he works, but he may feel that his salary does not express his rightful position in the social group of which he is a member. A custodian may be given an opportunity to express himself but may feel that what he says is misunderstood. A secretary may study and work to improve her efficiency and find that no one recognizes the higher quality of the service she is rendering. Opportunity for advancement may be knocking at the door of school employees, but there may be no one in a supervisory capacity who can give enough time and attention to their personal problems to enable them to hear the knock.

Altho democratic administration does not necessarily solve these problems, it is a step toward their solution. By democratic administrative procedures we mean plans which depend on cooperative action by all members of the school group, not only in forming policies but in building programs for the school:

In a small school system the superintendent works to a great extent directly with the teachers. He knows all of them by name, visits their classrooms, and holds conferences with them on numerous problems, such as methods of teaching, the selection of textbooks, and the promotion of pupils. In a large city the superintendent's contact with the teachers is largely through assistant superintendents, supervisors, and principals. The superintendent, however, counsels not only with supervisors and principals but also with teachers as a group or with teachers' committees in regard to various questions of policy. The teachers are consulted regarding changes in the course of study, change of textbooks, teacher-rating schemes, school building plans especially as they relate to classroom arrangements and equipment, plans for the promotion of pupils, and numerous other matters. Such procedure helps in bringing up questions in which the teachers are especially interested. The final decision on all such matters, however, rests with the superintendent; but with the advice of teachers he should be able to make much wiser decisions than by merely relying upon his own knowledge and experience.[2]

Autocratic, procedures are administrative patterns or devices which do not permit cooperation by members of the group in the settlement of problems pertaining to school programs or policies. The administration of an autocratically controlled *school-system* is usually highly centralized with the office of the chief administrator passing on all questions of policy and making all important decisions for the schools; similarly, in an autocratically controlled *school* the principal or chief administrative officer of the school makes all decisions pertaining to general administration.[3]

An extreme example of autocratic procedure is that of a former superintendent of a large city-school system who so autocratically ruled his staff that, it was literally true, he boasted with pride that he could tell what everyone was doing in his school system at a certain hour. He would pull out his watch and say, "It is now 9:45; all the fifth-grade boys and girls are studying fractions." Some of the critics of progressive education may declare that this assurance is better than to have the superintendent wondering if the boys and girls are studying arithmetic at all that day or that week. Nevertheless, few school administrators today would attempt to justify the kind of efficiency which was exemplified by this superintendent, who ruled a large city-school system in this manner for nearly twenty years.

Autocratic procedures are still to be found in many school systems of democratic America. Too many teachers find their initiative hampered by administrative prescription of methods but hesitate to assert themselves because they fear reprisals thru undesirable assignments, delayed promotions, or even dismissal.

We believe, however, that better morale is developed and maintained by cooperative democratic procedure than by autocratic

---

[2] Deffenbaugh, W. S. *Know Your Superintendent.* U. S. Dept. of the Interior, Office of Education, Leaflet No. 48. Washington, D. C.: Government Printing Office, 1939. p. 6.

[3] Mackey, George M. *A Survey of the Literature on Cooperation and Democratic Practices in School Administration.* Master's thesis. Washington, D. C.: George Washington University, 1939. p. 2.

methods. A successful administrator who believes in democracy as a way of life must believe in democratic school practices. We believe that the successful school administrator of the future will depend more and more on cooperative procedures.[4]

Historically, administrative attitudes were largely autocratic. The curriculum and methods were handed down to teachers in a despotic fashion. It seemed the easier way to develop efficiency, especially in schools staffed with young, immature, and poorly trained teachers. Results of this type of military "lock step" in administration were impressive from without, but such a philosophy developed neither spontaneous cooperation nor genuine skill and effectiveness in teaching, nor did it regard the help which the administration may get from resourceful, cooperative teachers.

Autocratic practices lead to disappointments and personal maladjustments which block initiative and freedom to use professional insight. Supervision of an unsympathetic type may cause a breakdown in the mental and emotional health of the teacher. The teacher's work is difficult to measure. There may be a great disparity between the apparent performance in the classroom at a given hour and the ideals and actual results of the teacher's continuing program.

The growing complexity of teaching duties in a large school system is another source of strain. Today the school has taken over many responsibilities which formerly were assumed by the home. Health programs, free lunch service, sale of penny milk, and cumulative record cards all add to the burden of the teacher. Many of these new duties are administrative and constitute opportunities for teachers to make unique contributions to the school.

Since democratic school administration is a matter of wholesome personal relations, there should be recognition of the contributions which each different teacher makes to the school. Today's school program should utilize the special talents of each and every one. There should be voluntary participation by each individual according to capacity and interests. Opportunities should be offered for the utilization of special talents in social service activities, health and nutrition, curriculum committees, discussion groups, assemblies,

[4] Misner, Paul J. "Cooperation in Administration and Supervision." *Cooperation: Principles and Practices.* Eleventh Yearbook. Washington, D. C.: Department of Supervisors and Directors of Instruction, National Education Association, 1938. Chapter 7, p. 81-94.

and extracurriculum activities. In this kind of environment the only frustrations which develop are in those individuals who thru lack of ability or lack of enthusiasm have nothing to contribute to the program, and such cases should be few indeed if the personnel of the school system has been carefully selected. In such a situation there is no need of grievance committees. Teacher criticism of existing policies and practices should be welcomed. If the prime function of a school is service to society and if the critical human problems within the school organization are to be met, antiquated autocratic methods must be abandoned. Only in this way can we develop school programs which can be adjusted to meet presentday emergencies.

Retention of Teachers

Today the social and economic equilibrium of the world is disturbed by war for the second time in this generation. In spite of the efforts of the government to correct economic maladjustments, prices are rising and the value of the dollar is decreasing. The depreciation of the dollar affects the teaching profession more directly than many other groups of workers. For them there are no swollen war incomes or profits. Most teachers have no income except their salary. The funds from which they are paid are raised from taxes levied many months before the salary contracts are drawn. Under these conditions there is much delay in needed salary raises for teachers, no matter what the justification might be for such raises.

Today teachers are leaving the profession for which they have prepared themselves by years of study. They are going into industrial employment in order to make a living. Forty percent of the teachers in the United States were receiving in 1943 a salary of less than $1200 a year. They are expected to buy war bonds, contribute to the Community Chest, the Red Cross, their church, and other good causes. Until 1940 most public-school teachers paid no federal income taxes; now they are carrying their full share of the heavy wartime financial burden.

At the time that the teacher is undergoing this financial struggle, boys and girls just out of high school are securing jobs at a higher salary than their teachers are receiving. As a result of these conditions there is today a general exodus from the teaching profession, which is resulting in the loss of many promising young teachers.

Teacher-training institutions are losing their students and failing to attract new ones because the future seems to hold little prospect for a living wage for teachers. The nation is facing a shortage of 75,000 teachers in 1943-44.

Under these conditions it is necessary for the united profession to continue its nationwide campaign to secure adequate financial support for education, both locally and nationally; and while this campaign is going on school administrators are called upon to improve the quality of the teaching service and to conserve the interest and welfare of children by preventing, as far as possible, the fears and maladjustments which are typical in a period of emergency.

SELECTION, APPOINTMENT, AND PLACEMENT OF TEACHERS

The way teachers are selected, appointed, and placed in their particular jobs within the system may help to build or destroy good morale. Teachers should be selected with the greatest of care to be sure that high professional standards are at all times maintained. Since the educational needs of the children in the schools are making increasingly broader demands upon the intelligence, the general culture, the social insight, the professional preparation, and the personality characteristics of the teachers, it is increasingly true that the most important task which confronts the superintendent of schools is the selection of teachers for his school system.

The selection and appointment of teachers by professional methods requires intelligent cooperation between the superintendent of schools and the schoolboard. New teachers should be nominated by the superintendent after a careful consideration of the best talent available and should be appointed by the board only on nomination of the superintendent. The facts concerning the qualifications of all candidates should be part of the official records of the superintendent's office, open to inspection by schoolboard members. The basis of the superintendent's recommendation should be clearly defined and open to investigation.

The minimum eligibility requirements for every teaching position should be clearly defined. Such requirements should include academic education, a high degree of culture, professional training, and supervised teaching experience or practice teaching. These standards should be published by the board and should be known to all. Also, the details of the appointment procedure are important and should be clearly stated in writing and understood by all.

The appraisal of merit and fitness should be made by the superintendent or by those officials to whom this duty is delegated. The selecting officials should be trained in the specialized professional procedure necessary to appraise merit and fitness. Experienced school administrators know that photographs of applicants, specimens of their handwriting, and letters of recommendation presented by applicants are usually of little value in determining fitness, and that college degrees and rating must be evaluated in terms of the known standards of the reporting college.

Reliable evidence of general intelligence and broad scholarship should be a factor in selecting teachers. There has been some evidence to the effect that there is a great variability of standards among colleges and universities and within the same college so that a mere record of time spent in studying certain subjects is not always evidence of cultural achievement. There is a tendency in large cities to require examinations to test the candidate's knowledge of the subject which he wishes to teach. Carefully prepared and standardized written tests may be desirable as one objective factor. The question as to whether candidates should be required to take an examination in certain prescribed subjects as evidence of specific skills which may be required in the position sought is answered in various cities according to the relative value placed upon the records of school achievement and the standards of various schools. In most small school systems eligibility is based on certification by the state, which is of varying validity in different states thruout the nation. Whether candidates are certified on the basis of school records or as a result of examinations, there will certainly be differences in qualifications.

Whatever plan is followed to evaluate intelligence and scholarship, the process of selection should include a personal interview which should be conducted in accordance with approved procedures. If possible, there should be observations of the actual teaching of the candidate, evaluated by the best professional assistance available.

In large school systems there should be eligible lists from which applicants should be appointed in order of their merit. This method of selection is fair to the children and to the teaching profession. Whatever standards of eligibility are established must be consistently observed in order to inspire the confidence of citizens and teachers. There is always the danger, since schools are controlled by a lay board of education representing the people, that an indifferent community may allow that control to pass temporarily into the hands of self-seekers and petty politicians who are anxious to serve relatives, friends, and acquaintances, and who lose sight of the interests and needs of the children. With such shortened vision, the school system may become primarily a relief department, resulting in a defeatist attitude among the worthwhile teachers.

The suspicion that teaching positions may be obtained in a school system by personal friendship, by the wish of a prominent citizen, by membership in a certain political party or a certain church, or by any factor not related to the teaching ability of the candidate will help to destroy the confidence of teachers in their superior officers and in their colleagues.

If teachers are appointed as a result of personal influence rather than merit, they may keep their positions and obtain advancement by that means. Thus the whole ideal of efficiency and fairness is subverted. Obviously the person best qualified by merit is the one least in need of personal influence in securing a position in a school system which follows professional ideals in making appointments. A school system in which appointments are made upon any other basis than that of the highest professional ethics does not attract or hold personnel possessing the best qualifications. Such incorrect procedure also sows the seeds of distrust and disloyalty in the organization.

During periods of industrial unemployment, the superintendent is faced with an increasing demand on the part of his community for the employment of the local teacher. The argument that the taxpayer's daughter deserves first consideration is fortified by the equally emphatic but somewhat less philanthropic consideration that local candidates can be secured for a much lower salary than the imported ones, whatever the relative merits of either. The relief idea and the home-talent idea develop rapidly and flourish luxuriantly in the mind of the local politician and create just one more problem for the administrator.

After teachers are chosen they should be assigned to specific positions for which they are especially qualified. If superintendents are forced to reduce the number of teachers in the system, and such reductions necessitate reassigning of work, a most difficult personnel problem results. Such a problem cannot be solved on the basis of seniority rights alone but must take into consideration the rights of children and the professional standards which are involved. Hasty or autocratic decisions in such situations may wreck the morale of the organization and result in lower standards of teaching efficiency.

In some school systems there is a strange dualism which maintains professional standards for teacher selection but permits patronage and pull to operate in filling the nonteaching jobs. Such a condition destroys the integrity of the school system, belittles the value of the nonteaching services, and is a threat to the maintenance of proper standards for the professional personnel. The *esprit de corps* of both the teachers and the nonteaching staff suffers when unsound methods of selection exist in any part of the school system.

EQUITABLE ADMINISTRATION AND DISTRIBUTION OF TEACHING LOAD

In most communities, especially during wartime and depression periods, every teacher necessarily has a heavy teaching load. Most teachers do not rebel when their burdens have to become greater if they feel there is an equitable distribution of duties. By teaching load is meant more than just teaching; it includes:

> Number of preparations
> Average size of classes
> Section periods per week
> Teaching periods per week
> Assigned special periods per week
> Committee assignments
> Time for lesson preparation weekly
> Activities after school hours
> Reports of all types
> Conferences with individual students.

For the welfare of both the teachers and their pupils, administrators must see that the classes are equitably distributed, that extracurriculum activities do not fall on the shoulders of a few willing teachers, and that committee work does not always go to teachers who are the most industrious. The total teaching load should be such as to permit sufficient time for thoro preparation for the teaching job and for continued professional growth.

In many school systems class size is too large to permit teachers to render effective service to the individual pupils in their classes. Continued efforts by school administrators to reduce the average pupil load, as well as to equalize loads among teachers, are necessary. Many teachers ask for help in assisting individual students who are in difficulty. Success in this area contributes much to satisfaction in teaching.

A factor in teacher load often not recognized by administrators is the nervous strain of constant interruptions to classwork. A large group of teachers who reported to the Research Division of the National Education Association mentioned class interruptions, such as bulletins, announcements, errands, and special events, as one of the sources of heavy or extreme pressure in their assignments. No other factor in teacher load was reported as a point of heavy pressure as frequently as interruptions, which were felt to be a burden by 28 percent of the elementary teachers and 31 percent of the high-school teachers.[5] Many interruptions could be avoided by better planning on the part of principals and other administrators, to the definite benefit of teacher morale and to the improvement of the service rendered to pupils.

Still another factor in teacher load which might be eased by administrative planning is that of clerical work. Twenty-three percent of the elementary teachers in the Research Division study reported that clerical work, such as mimeographing class materials and transcribing records and test results, was a source of unduly heavy or extreme pressure; 26 percent of the high-school teachers emphasized the daily load of correcting and grading papers, notebooks, tests, and homework.[6] In this connection school administrators may give thought to Houser's studies of morale among industrial employees. A survey of one large organization showed that the most striking difference found between employees with low morale and those with high morale was that those with low morale felt that they were not "receiving help necessary to get results expected by management."[7] As the increased demands of the modern school pile up upon teachers, the school administrator

[5] National Education Association, Research Division. "The Teacher Looks at Teacher Load." *Research Bulletin* 17: 223-74; November 1939. p. 242.

[6] National Education Association, Research Division, *op. cit.*, p. 242.

[7] Houser, J. David. *What People Want from Business.* New York: McGraw-Hill Book Co., 1938. p. 29.

has an obligation to recognize the weight of these added duties and convince the board of education and the public of the need for added personnel. Every elementary school needs clerical service, and most high schools need far more clerical help than is now provided. A full-time clerk for every five hundred pupils could make an inestimable contribution to teacher morale and public welfare.

NEED FOR SECURITY IN EMPLOYMENT

Certification requirements which demand longer training and more specialization make it less easy to use the teaching profession as a "stopgap" in preparing for some other occupation. Because of this longer period of preparation the teacher needs more than ever to be protected in the job:

> Stabilization or permanence of personnel may be considered a basic prerequisite of a profession. Adjustment to a community, acquaintance with its traditions, and knowledge of its social needs can come only through continued residence.[8]

There can be little morale among teachers who are not sure of their jobs. This does not mean that teachers should never be dismissed, but it does mean that there should be definite professional reasons for dismissing teachers. This field needs a great deal of careful study in large cities where the administration of tenure sometimes protects the weak rather than safeguarding the strong.

The National Education Association for more than twenty years has been active in improving the tenure status of teachers. Since 1920 there have been annual reports and many special studies by tenure committees which outline the progress made.

The reasons for tenure as set forth by the National Education Association Committee on Tenure in 1941 are as follows:

1. To protect classroom teachers and other members of the teaching profession against unjust dismissal of any kind—political, religious, or personal.

2. To prevent the management or domination of the schools by political or noneducational groups for improper or selfish purposes.

3. To secure, for the teacher, employment conditions which will encourage him to grow in the full practice of his profession, unharried by constant pressure and fear.

---

[8] Evenden, Edward S.; Gamble, Guy C.; and Blue, Harold G. *National Survey of the Education of Teachers: Teacher Personnel in the United States.* U. S. Dept. of the Interior, Office of Education, Bulletin 1933, No. 10, Vol. II. Washington, D. C.: Government Printing Office, 1935. p. 32.

4. To encourage competent, independent thinkers to enter and to remain in the teaching profession.

5. To encourage school management, which might have to sacrifice the welfare of the schools to fear and favor, to devote itself to the cause of education.

6. To set up honest, definite procedures by which undesirable people may be excluded from the teaching profession.

7. To protect educators in their efforts to promote the financial and educational interests of public school children.

8. To protect teachers in the exercise of their rights and duties of American citizenship.

9. To enable teachers, in spite of reactionary minorities, to prepare children for life in a democracy under changed conditions.[9]

From the standpoint of a superintendent of schools, it might be well to add two more aims to this list:

1. To make tenure of office absolutely secure for good teachers, and for poor teachers just as insecure.

2. To protect professional teachers from competition with the unprofessional.

As a result of the activity of the National Education Association and other teachers organizations, there has been much progress made in tenure legislation during the past twenty years. However, it is still true in many communities that teachers have less security than firemen, policemen, government clerks, and railroad employees. Few workers in these categories have to run the chance of an annual election but may keep their jobs as long as their work is reasonably satisfactory. In contrast to these workers, the teachers in many towns and cities are legally out of a job at the end of each school year. Where there is no tenure law, it is still not uncommon for a board of education to drop a score of teachers, with little regard to professional fitness, and then later under pressure from relatives, friends, and newspapers to reinstate those who have been able to muster the best defense before the board. It is true that city teachers have tenure protection in thirty-seven states, but rural teachers have some protection in only twenty-four states.

Under these conditions of insecurity there may be no high standards of morale. On the other hand, there are serious problems connected with the permanent tenure systems which exist in some cities. In most of these situations, there is a provision that teachers

[9] National Education Association, Committee on Tenure. *Report of the Committee on Tenure.* Washington, D. C.: the Association, 1941. p. 3-4.

may be dismissed, after a hearing, for immorality, incompetency, insubordination, neglect of duty, or unprofessional conduct. In some cities teachers who have been dismissed after hearings have been reinstated by the courts with such regularity that boards and superintendents have practically given up all attempts to bring charges of inefficiency against teachers. While nominally these court proceedings constitute a trial of the teachers against whom the charges have been filed, in reality they become a trial of the superintendent of schools, principals, and other officers who have preferred charges. The airing of grievances engendered by such public trials does a good deal of damage to the public relations of the school systems. Parents who may have great sympathy for a teacher, but no accurate information concerning the teacher's work in the classroom, are ready to testify for the defense. Legal technicalities often may seem to be more important than the professional opinion of the school principals, supervisors, and superintendent.

While the principle of tenure is sound in the large cities as elsewhere, the *procedure for hearings* is unsatisfactory at the present time. If it is necessary for the teacher to have an attorney to present his case, the board of education should also be represented by an attorney.

A basic principle of tenure is the right of a teacher to a public hearing on the charges against him, if he so desires. In 718 recent dismissals of teachers by city boards of education, 16 percent of the dismissals followed a hearing, and in 45 percent a hearing would have been held but was waived at the wish of the teacher concerned.[10]

All school administrators will hail the day when there is permanent tenure for all efficient teachers, but there should be a clear understanding of the right of the board of education to terminate employment when the reasons are good and sufficient. To deny this right is to subordinate the educational rights of children to the teachers' rights. No teacher should be liable to dismissal without being told of his weaknesses and being given an opportunity to remedy them and to present his own case to the school authorities. If after a reasonable amount of help the teacher's work does not come up

---

[10] National Education Association, Research Division. "Teacher Personnel Procedures: Employment Conditions in Service." *Research Bulletin* 20: 83-116; May 1942. p. 105.

to standard, then there should be a clear understanding of the right of the board to dismiss the inefficient teacher without itself having to go on trial.

The dismissal of married women in communities where they are not protected by tenure has been destructive to teacher morale in many ways:

To abolish the celibacy rule . . . would do much over a period of years to remove the "old-maid school teacher" cliché which is so distasteful to many teachers and so injurious to the morale of many of the younger members of the profession. Also, it would save to the profession some excellent teachers who give up their work at time of their marriage only because they are forced to do so.

The effect of the current wartime demands for women workers in all fields probably will cause many boards of education to try to retain rather than to dismiss women teachers who marry.[11]

An important factor in morale is for a superintendent to remain consistent in his policy toward employment of married women as teachers. If he feels that they contribute to the school system and that they help to maintain high standards, then he should not shift his attitude when adverse criticism piles up during depression periods. One school executive, who had always believed that married women should be allowed to teach, found himself criticized for continuing to employ married women during the depression. When he made a study of the efficiency ratings given by the principals he found that the vast majority of the married women teachers were classified by their principals as essential to the system. But criticism continued, and the following year the superintendent had the married teachers fill out a blank as to their financial needs. If the teacher's ethics were low enough to enable her to misrepresent her financial condition or if she were penniless or in debt because she was thriftless, she was allowed to stay in the service, as were those whose husbands were disabled or unemployed. The superintendent in this case disregarded the issue of efficiency in service and employed one class of women on the basis of need for work. Welfare jobs are distributed on the basis of need, but in no other profession except teaching are jobs parcelled out in this way. The whole point is that a superintendent must maintain definite prin-

[11] National Education Association, Research Division. "Teacher Personnel Procedures: Employment Conditions in Service." *Research Bulletin* 20: 83-116; May 1942. p. 108-109.

ciples for dismissal based on efficient service and must not allow political pressure to change his opinions.

NEED FOR PAY ADEQUATE TO MAINTAIN ECONOMIC SELF-RESPECT

Morale and income go hand in hand:

If the teacher is to be a leader in our developing and complex society, his economic status must assure him further study, travel and other cultural advantages, and home ownership.[12]

One of the barriers to successful recruitment of teachers is the combined effect of low salaries and the fact that teachers in many places are regarded almost as a separate social class whose activities and enjoyments should be of a more ascetic tone than those of other people.[13]

A teacher who lacks money for clothes, living accommodations, books, and recreation is plainly at a disadvantage in most community activities. In some situations, however, the reverse is true. People refer to the fact that individual women teachers are able to wear fur coats and attend the opera while other women in the community cannot afford such luxuries. Their own financial problems and economic distress cause them to be jealous of anyone who has a steady income. They forget that teachers have spent years of time and many dollars in preparing for the profession and that they should be able to associate with other professional and business people.

Again, many persons believe that teachers do not need as much money as people in other professions because the majority of teachers are single women and therefore have no one to support but themselves. This is not universally true. Many unmarried teachers find themselves obliged to assist relatives or even to provide their entire support. In studies of teacher status made by committees of the National Education Association, it was found that 46.4 percent of the single women teachers reporting from large city-school systems were providing full support for one or more dependents. For the entire group of single women teachers, the average was nine-tenths of one dependency unit.[14] Among rural teachers, it was

[12] National Education Association and Department of Superintendence, Joint Commission on the Emergency in Education. *Report of National Conference on the Financing of Education.* Washington, D. C.: the Department, 1933. p. 19.

[13] National Education Association, Research Division. "City Teachers: Their Preparation, Salaries, and Experience." *Research Bulletin* 18: 3-47; January 1940. p. 36.

[14] National Education Association, Committee on the Economic Status of the Teacher. *The Teacher's Economic Position.* Washington, D. C.: the Association, 1935. p. 16. (Published also as: National Education Association, Research Division. "The Teacher's Economic Position." *Research Bulletin* 13: 165-267; September 1935. p. 180.)

found that 36.1 percent of the single women teachers were supporting one or more dependents, and that the average for the group was seven-tenths of one full dependency unit.[15] A teacher's salary is thus like the salary of other individuals; it may go to support many or few. If too low it causes financial distress in the home and it has an effect on the morale of the teacher in the classroom.

An adequate and just salary schedule is an important factor in maintaining morale in a school system. The construction of such a schedule is an approved method of bringing about the in-service growth of teachers.[16] Teachers who participate in such a project have an opportunity to gain a wider understanding of the problems of public education. Salary schedules which are constructed by the cooperative efforts of committees made up of representatives of the school personnel are likely to take into account the special problems of all employee groups and usually are better schedules than those prepared without the help of the personnel concerned.

NEED FOR WHOLESOME PHYSICAL CONDITIONS OF EMPLOYMENT

Environment includes both the physical equipment of the schoolroom in which the teacher works and the living conditions after the day's work is done. Neither teachers nor pupils can do their best work in poor environments. If teachers are expected to keep themselves at their best, the schools must not neglect the physical comforts that will make the work easier.

Physical surroundings can irritate teachers and other school employees and interfere with morale. Dingy walls and ceilings, dirty windows and floors tend to lower standards of teaching performance and to breed discontent and dissatisfaction. The financial problem cannot be solved by reducing necessary operating expenditures or by neglecting the repair and upkeep of school property.

In small towns many teachers become discontented with their jobs because they find rooming and eating places in the community undesirable. Several teachers in a town of 10,000 spent the first

---

[15] National Education Association, Committee on the Economic Status of the Rural Teacher. *Teachers in Rural Communities*. Washington, D. C.: the Association, 1939. p. 24.

[16] Lewis, A. B. "Teacher Participation in Salary Scheduling." *In-Service Growth of School Personnel*. Twenty-First Yearbook. Washington, D. C.: Department of Elementary School Principals, National Education Association, 1942. p. 473-77. ¶ National Education Association, Committee on Salaries. *Problems and Principles in the Scheduling of Teachers Salaries*. Washington, D. C.: the Association, 1940. 36 p.

two days in the community trying to find a room that was clean and well heated. They were willing to pay almost any price within reason, but few people in that rich community during prosperous years cared to share their homes with roomers. Such an introduction to a new teaching venture is not conducive to good morale. In this case a canvass of the situation should have been made before school started and help should have been given to all the new teachers. The friendly assistance that can be provided by the school system in helping the new teacher to make a good start may pay large returns in morale and efficiency. No school system can be indifferent toward the physical welfare of teachers.

LOYALTY, RECOGNITION, AND PROMOTION

Every problem of education has its administrative aspects. Altho the administrator is charged with the responsibility of getting things done, his powers are limited by special local conditions. He and his co-workers can be effective only if all understand the purposes which the organization is trying to achieve. Here is the place where the lines of communication must be open. Not only must the teachers and other employees understand these purposes, but the leader must know what is going on in the classrooms and to what extent the purposes are being realized.

In a democratic school environment there must be developed loyalty to professional ideals and to the principles and the purposes of the total school group. Personal loyalty is but one factor in the whole problem. When administrators and teachers believe in the integrity and honesty of each other, there will be loyalty to the common aims and ideals of democratic education. If the time comes when the majority of the teaching staff can no longer have faith in an administrator's justice and his knowledge of the effectiveness of his teachers, the staff should then ask for a new superintendent. When the superintendent and other teachers lose faith in the integrity and loyalty of a teacher, it is time to give careful consideration to his or her permanent value to the organization.

The superintendent must get groups together to discuss mutual problems. To quote David Josiah Brewer, Associate Justice of the U. S. Supreme Court:

The time is past in the history of the world when any living man or body of men can be set on a pedestal and decorated with a halo. True, many criticisms may be, like their authors, devoid of good taste, but better all sorts of criticisms than no criticism at all. The moving waters are full of life and health: only in the still waters is stagnation and death.[17]

The professional growth of teachers depends, to a large extent, upon recognition. To maintain high morale in a school system, the road to advancement must be kept open to all employees. Teachers must feel that the total job of school administration is being done in the most efficient way under intelligent leadership and that they can help by putting forth extra effort. However, these efforts must be recognized and appreciated. There are many ways in which this can be done. Superior teachers can be given assignments in keeping with their achievements. Such teachers can be given an opportunity to teach demonstration lessons, to train apprentice teachers, to serve on important committees, and to lead discussions. Teachers who achieve unusual results should be commended by conference or letter. Teachers may find it helpful to publish articles in professional magazines. Subsidies may be secured for superior teachers to attend conventions, workshops, and summer schools. Sabbatical leaves may be granted for study or travel. These devices and many others may be used to give proper recognition to those teachers whose work is outstanding. When vacancies occur which call for promotion from within the ranks, these professional achievements and recognitions should weigh heavily in favor of the candidates for promotion. It should be remembered, however, that some individuals who are extremely successful in the classroom do not enjoy the same success in administrative positions and that administrative promotion for such teachers may remove them from their best opportunity for effective service. It is also true that academic achievement does not always measure the ability of a person to organize, administer, or supervise. Nevertheless, in many cases the superior teacher has already given evidence of administrative ability and can give larger service in an administrative position.

UNDERSTANDING AND PARTICIPATION

During the last decade there has been a growing unrest in the teaching body of the nation, caused by the desire to be recognized in matters concerning the welfare of the school system which lie

[17] Molohon, Bernard, compiler. *Voices of Democracy*. Federal Security Agency, U. S. Office of Education, Bulletin 1941, No. 8. Washington, D. C.: Government Printing Office, 1941. p. 17.

outside the classroom. There has been a growing resentment against supervision which is merely instructional and against courses of study which allow little or no opportunity for initiative or individuality on the part of teachers. This movement is to be expected. It is a sign of the times. The same thing has been going on in industry and commercial organizations. It has been intensified by the recent professional awakening of teachers and by the demand for better educated people in the classrooms.

A superintendent who disregards this trend is like King Canute who placed his chair on the beach at the seashore and commanded the flood tide to stop its rush. It is inevitable that intelligent, well-trained teachers should have an interest in school policies. Teachers can be more effective when they come directly to the superintendent with their troubles, their criticisms, and their constructive suggestions than when they merely talk about these things to other teachers or to parents. If there is always an open door to the superintendent's office, the first step has been taken in democratic methods.

Altho there is a growing tendency to recognize the rights of teachers to express their opinions upon school policies and to propose ideas of their own for improving conditions under which they are working, there are certain obligations which condition the exercise of these rights. Teachers who participate in administrative councils should be competent to originate worthwhile ideas which will command the attention of serious-minded members of the group. They must be competent to criticize constructively, to think things thru, to anticipate fully the consequences of initiating and promoting an idea, and to accept those consequences. They must be willing to work vigorously and to cooperate fully in carrying out the will of the majority.

In order to provide for the participation of school employees, parents, and interested citizens in the formulation of school policies many cities have organized advisory councils to meet with the superintendent of schools for the discussion of school problems. Such councils furnish a representative agency by which the point of view of teachers, other employees, and citizens may be expressed in matters affecting the school program.

The members of these councils are sometimes appointed by the superintendent but more often are elected by the various organizations of school employees and parent groups. In one city, the superintendent's conference meets each Saturday morning for a cooperative study of school problems. The scope of the study includes the entire range of instructional and administrative planning. Thru the deliberation of the conference and by virtue of the research studies undertaken by the group, the superintendent has the benefit of the contributions made by work committees from every part of the school system. Such a conference is a clearinghouse for ideas and suggestions from many individuals. These proposals are thoroly discussed in committees before being presented to the conference.

Advisory councils such as this contribute decidedly to the morale of the school system by furnishing an opportunity for the participation of employees in planning and, at the same time, subjecting the plans and suggestions to a thoro analysis before presentation to the superintendent and board.

The most effective participation by teachers and other employees is achieved by the desire for cooperation, for personal growth, and for genuine improvement of administrative practices. Such participation should not be forced and should not be stimulated and controlled by pressure groups from within or without the school system. Such pressure groups seeking advantages for their own members tend to break down the confidence and understanding so essential to effective cooperation. The chief executive of a school system has unlimited opportunity to make effective for the school system the excellent training and superior intelligence of teachers, custodians, clerks, and other school employees in the solution of important administrative problems. The contribution of all employees should be encouraged by a plan which utilizes the enthusiasm and energy of those who are eager to help. Such cooperation not only results in better school administration but develops high morale in the spirit of democratic management.

★ *When schools evaluate and seek to improve their procedures in building for morale, pupils will have more opportunities to share in the evaluation, by better understanding of the goals being sought, by giving their own ideas as to possible improvements in practice, and by self-appraisals of their own progress. Counseling and guidance will be broadened in scope. The services of both the full-time counselor and the classroom teacher will be required to diagnose and meet the personal and civic needs of each pupil.*

CHAPTER XI

Checking Up on Progress

SUPPOSE THAT THE TEACHERS, the principals, and the other members of the school staff have studied the proposals in this book. Suppose that they are willing to adapt their present practices in the direction of building higher morale. Someone will ask: How shall we know whether we are getting results? How can we tell when an individual or a group has high morale? Which of our school experiences are most likely to build morale?

These questions are reasonable but they are not easy to answer. Educational returns will be coming in for decades after the school experiences are past, as pupils live out their lives. The school is only one of many agencies influencing morale. The methods of measurement are still imperfect; the concept of morale may have to be divided and subdivided in the process of learning how better to identify and measure the quality itself. But to say that it is hard to evaluate morale and still harder to evaluate education for morale is not to suggest that the effort should not be made.[1] Evaluation is itself a most important part of the basic undertaking. Aims of teaching are clarified when plans are made for studying students' reactions in the light of those aims. Interpreting the results of the evaluation will suggest ways in which the school program can be improved.

Altho the different stages of evaluation may be occurring at the same time, and also may follow one another in a continuing cycle, the steps seem essentially to be three: First, the general goals and

---

[1] To reduce the number of footnote references, general acknowledgment is made at this point for materials drawn from the following publications: Boyd, George Robert. *The Construction of an Instrument for Measuring Attitudes toward Desirable Food Practices.* University of Kentucky, College of Education, Bulletin of the Bureau of School Service, Vol. 16, No. 1, September 1943, Lexington, Ky.: the University, 1943. "Survey of Literature Concerning Attitudes," p. 10-18. ¶ Briggs, Thomas H., and others. *The Emotionalized Attitudes.* New York: Teachers College, Columbia University, 1940. 107 p. ¶ Chein, Isidor. "The Meaning of 'Morale' in Relation to Morale Building and Morale Research." *Psychological Review* 50: 311-29; May 1943. ¶ Cronbach, Lee J. *Exploring the Wartime Morale of High-School Youth.* American Association for Applied Psychology, Applied Psychology Monographs, No. 1. Stanford University, Calif.: Stanford University Press, 1943. 79 p. ¶ National Education Association and American Association of School Administrators, Educational Policies Commission. *Learning the Ways of Democracy.* Washington, D. C.: the Commission, 1940. Chapter 7, "Evaluation of Outcomes," p. 379-433. ¶ Smith, Eugene R., and others. *Appraising and Recording Student Progress.* Progressive Education Association, Commission on the Relation of School and College. Adventure in American Education, Vol. 3. New York: Harper and Brothers, 1942. 550 p. ¶ Watson, Goodwin, editor. *Civilian Morale.* Second Yearbook, Society for the Psychological Study of Social Issues. Boston: Houghton Mifflin Co., 1942. 463 p.

the specific subgoals in education for morale need to be defined. Second, the morale of pupils with respect to realizing those goals should be observed. Other related evidence on public opinion and public affairs may need to be studied. Third, the educational processes should be changed if the results of the testing and observation suggest that changes are needed. This chapter deals only briefly with the first and third stages of evaluation and gives more attention to the second.

What Are the Common Goals?

The morale of the individual in the group must be evaluated in terms of his devotion to the goals of the group. In building morale for democracy in a free world the schools have the double task of helping their pupils to know and to love the ideals of democracy and of helping those pupils to learn habits of thinking and acting that will advance those goals.

Any school faculty that goes to the roots of education for morale, as the preceding chapters in this yearbook outline its scope, probably will conclude that the ultimate aim of such a program is to develop a mature and well-rounded citizenry, prepared at all times to render service and share sacrifices for the common welfare. The schools have long emphasized civic education; what is distinctive is the emphasis on *emotional attachment* to the ideals of human welfare, as well as the *intellectual understanding* of those ideals. It is proposed here that educators can speed the advance of humanity in America and beyond America by developing in their pupils habits of thinking, feeling, and acting that form a sound foundation for continued high morale in service for the general good.

Intelligent, unselfish, persistent service for the common welfare of humanity must be based on deeply rooted values. The proposal that the school should help the individual to determine those values raises the old question as to whether the schools in the United States, the agents of localities and states, can take a position of leadership in forming opinions on national and world issues. The extent to which the teaching in the schools *can* be different from the thinking in the community and the question as to whether the teaching *should* be different from community thinking are problems that each school faculty or school system needs to explore for itself. Local citizens other than teachers can help in this analysis.

Some such exploration is necessary if teachers are in earnest about educating for active service in the long campaign for human freedom. Their pupils must use the great democratic ideals of truth, freedom, fellow feeling, human dignity, and personal responsibility in making concrete choices among ways of acting. Ethics and religion and all values underlying human behavior will make a contribution to defining and specifying the aims of the teaching.

Many of the issues are controversial. Faculty and students might agree that democratic ideals are expressed in the Atlantic Charter, the Four Freedoms, and the Nine Freedoms and Rights. But they will disagree as to the specific personal, local, national, and international actions needed to make those ideals effective. Perhaps all schools can teach pupils to know and to identify themselves with these basic principles and to understand some of their implications. Beyond these broad generalizations, teachers have the problem of drawing out the specific issues which in their particular school or community most need further study and can be emphasized most effectively in various subjects and activities of the school program.

Evaluation, then, will be related to adjustments in the course of study and to the planned experiences of pupils which have been designed to make those principles vital realities in their lives.

Measuring the Level of Morale

This section refers for the most part to ordered observations and records as a basis for judging the level of morale. There is also the impressionistic appraisal of morale: many teachers are sensitive to the emotional reactions and personal attitudes of their pupils. Systematic observation should not take the place of efforts to sense directly the attitudes of the members of a group. Organized efforts to study attitudes and other aspects of morale, however, are rich in suggestions for the more informal appraisal that may be made by the individual teacher as well as for the more systematic studies made by committees or research groups.

Morale is a complex quality.[2] Merely to make records on attitudes and behavior related to morale is not enough. The further

---

[2] See Chapters II, III, and V. ¶ A report from the Harvard University Seminar in Psychological Problems of Morale (headed by Gordon W. Allport and Henry A. Murray) listed twelve determinants of morale, for example, "economic health," "something to do"; and forty-seven subitems, for example, "enough income to sustain life and health," "feeling that one's job is useful." (Sanford, Fillmore H., and Holt, Robert R. "Psychological Determinants of Morale." *Journal of Abnormal and Social Psychology* 38: 93-95; January 1943.)

effort should be made to interpret those records in terms of what
the pupil wants and knows. A pupil may appear to be doing nothing
on behalf of the program of the student-government council. But
he may have failed to receive a copy of the proposed outline of
activities; or he may be carrying so heavy a program of outside
work that added duties would be a hazard to health; or other
explanations may be found. Merely to observe the student's overt
behavior in relation to the student council would not be a fair indicator of his morale as a student citizen.

It appears that morale must be diagnosed and treated differently
in different persons and that every effort either to build or to measure morale should include a rigorous definition of scope. The attitudes and activities of pupils might be measured, for example, with
respect to observing the principle of freedom of speech, to their
responsibilities as members of their homes, to their course of study
at the Main Street High School, or to the current school scrap-col-
lection campaign. A pupil whose score was high in one activity might
be low in another, but the several studies would be more meaningful for future school practice than an effort to lay hold of the entire
concept of morale.

INDICATORS OF MORALE

Morale is judged by what people do in bodily action, what they
say thru the spoken word, and what they write. Clinical studies
might in addition include such things as blood pressure, resistance
to fatigue, and glandular secretions. For educational practice, however, laboratory studies of this type would not be as practicable as
studies of behavior, speech, and paper-and-pencil reactions, as clues
to pupils' feelings and attitudes toward action.

Several pages that follow discuss the use of these three indicators
of morale in various studies. Many of these studies do not refer
directly to "morale" at all. All of them, however, are believed to
have suggestive value for school faculties wishing to evaluate their
own school practices. The literatures of anthropology, education,
personnel administration, social psychology, and sociology all are
rich in discussions that help to clarify the meaning of morale and
its measurement. The studies mentioned in this chapter were selected to illustrate methods and to suggest ways in which these
methods might be applied to educational practice.

EXTERNAL BEHAVIOR

The Special Services officers of the Army have used behavior as an index of morale when they charted the rise and fall of such things as soldiers' arrests, courts-martial, absences without leave, and the number of prisoners in the guardhouse. The army morale officers also have used impressionistic methods to record the ups and downs of fighting between soldiers, listlessness of attitude, lack of initiative, complaints, lack of comradeship, military inefficiency, insubordination, gambling cliques, and night prowling.[3]

Civilian morale can be measured roughly, on a large scale, by trends in certain types of behavior on which records are kept. Many of these records deal with negative rather than positive behavior. Convictions for drunkenness or drunken driving, housebreaking, other crime statistics, strikes, voluntary quitting of jobs, mental illness, suicides, and accident rates all are possibilities.[4] The federal Department of Justice records certain "indices of tension," such as the violations of civil liberties, the frequency of certain kinds of violence, and the frequency of antidemocratic publications and organizational activities.[5]

Behavior as reflected in the amount of work done has been studied often in industrial research. Only recently have studies been made which recognize output as a form of social behavior and show the relationship between output and morale. The Hawthorne inquiries, for example, began as a coldly objective study of the effect of such things as lighting and rest periods on output, but they developed into studies of human relations.[6] In the later projects in this series the records were not limited to rates of production but included all sorts of person-to-person relationships of the workers, such as their actions in the presence of supervisors in different grades of authority, the frequency of helping one another, playing games together, joking and horseplay, friendships, antagonisms, and cliques.

[3] Shils, Edward A. "A Note on Governmental Research on Attitudes and Morale." *American Journal of Sociology* 47: 472-80; November 1941.
[4] Bateson, Gregory, and Mead, Margaret. "Principles of Morale Building." *Journal of Educational Sociology* 15: 206-20; December 1941. ¶ Durant, Henry. "Morale and Its Measurement." *American Journal of Sociology* 47: 406-14; November 1941.
[5] Shils, Edward A., *op. cit.*
[6] Roethlisberger, F. J.; Dickson, William J.; and Wright, Harold A. *Management and the Worker.* Cambridge, Mass.: Harvard University Press, 1943. 615 p. (An account of a research program conducted by the Western Electric Company, Hawthorne Works, Chicago.)

Direct observation of behavior as a method of research in education has received much attention in the past fifteen or twenty years. Jersild and Meigs made a general review of the whole field, discussing many technical problems of method.[7] They predicted that systematic classroom observation will be increasingly useful in planning and appraising the curriculum.

In the studies of social climates directed by Lewin, attention was focused on behavior of members of groups in atmospheres of democracy, autocracy, and laissez faire. These studies are outstanding in their effort to record as fully and insightfully as possible the total behavior of the group. Each group consisted of five children, matched for various personality factors, organized in a club to make theatrical masks. Four observers made simultaneous records, on separate sheets that could be matched for each minute of time, on (a) social interactions, (b) subgroup organization, (c) member activity analysis, and (d) member interest. The published report includes the detailed schedule of observation. The following outline for the rating of "Group Unity" is illustrative:

1. No interdependence of members as far as activity is concerned, no group seems to exist.

2. Very low interdependence of member functioning but not completely parallel activity. Change or cessation of activity of one member has very little effect on the other members of the group.

3. Co-operation to the extent of not duplicating function or conflicting in activity function. Some "we" feeling but no great loss if a member drops out.

4. Good co-operation, clearly a group moving together toward a goal, very hard for any member to leave without creating noticeable loss in the function of the group.

5. A very high degree of interdependence of member function, co-operation of all members. Activity of each member is very incomplete when considered by itself without relation to that of the other members.[8]

Reports on the Lewin studies mention differences among the groups in such items of behavior as the amount of hostility, the volume of social interaction, the stability of the group structure, the

[7] Jersild, Arthur T., and Meigs, Margaret F. "Direct Observation as a Research Method." *Review of Educational Research* 9: 472-82, 597-99; December 1939.

[8] Lewin, Kurt. "Experiments on Autocratic and Democratic Atmospheres." *Social Frontier* 4: 316-19; July 1938. ¶ Lewin, Kurt; Lippitt, Ronald; and White, Ralph K. "Patterns of Aggressive Behavior in Experimentally Created 'Social Climates.'" *Journal of Social Psychology, S.P.S.S.I. Bulletin* 10: 271-99; May 1939. (Also Vol. 10: 359-98; August.) ¶ Lippitt, Ronald. "An Experimental Study of the Effect of Democratic and Authoritarian Group Atmospheres." *Studies in Topological and Vector Psychology I.* (Kurt Lewin, Ronald Lippitt, and Sibylle Korsch Escalona.) University of Iowa Studies in Child Welfare, Vol. 16, No. 3. Iowa City, Iowa: University of Iowa Press, 1940. Part II, p. 45-195, 305-307.

extent to which children work by themselves rather than in groups, the amount of dominating behavior, the appearance of apathy or indifference, the constructiveness of the group in the absence of the leader, the treatment of group property, and the relationships of individuals after the groups were disbanded.

Anecdotal records have been used as a method of studying the actions of pupils.[9] These brief notes written almost on the spot describe the pupil's conduct in various situations. The following examples are quoted by Traxler:

Oct. 4. John came to my room and studied during the lunch hour today. When I asked him if he wasn't going to lunch, he said that he had to prepare his history lesson for the next hour, but I learned afterward that he has had no money for lunch for several days.

April 11. Although not a club officer, Ralph stayed away from the ball game this afternoon to mimeograph copies of the constitution for the new Hobby Club so that they would be ready for the meeting tomorrow.[10]

To write anecdotal records takes not only keen interest and observation but a great deal of time. The records must be cumulative as one or two anecdotes about a pupil may tell little about his real needs and attitudes. To be most useful they should be recorded by all teachers, should report both "desirable" and "undesirable" behavior, should include all pupils, and should be centralized and summarized. In the beginning the scope of the records might be limited to some one aspect of behavior, such as cooperation or dependability. Used in such fashion, these records may be useful in helping pupils to develop personal standards for democratic conduct.

Those who are teaching for democratic morale will find much of value in studies such as those of Anderson, both for the insight they throw on pupil behavior and for their analysis of the attitudes of teachers themselves. Anderson wanted to test the theory that dominating behavior has a tendency to produce the same kind of behavior in return and, likewise, that integrative behavior induces integrative behavior.[11] He defines dominative behavior as rigid behavior in

[9] Jarvie, L. L., and Ellingson, Mark. *A Handbook on the Anecdotal Behavior Journal.* Chicago: University of Chicago Press, 1940. 71 p. ¶ Traxler, Arthur E. *The Nature and Use of Anecdotal Records.* Educational Records Supplementary Bulletin D. New York: Educational Records Bureau, 1939. 31 p.

[10] Traxler, Arthur E., *op. cit.,* p. 25, 26.

[11] Anderson, Harold H. "Domination and Social Integration in the Behavior of Kindergarten Children and Teachers." *Genetic Psychology Monographs* 21: 287-385; August 1939.

which the dominating person knows what he wants, tries to preserve status, and resists change. Integrative behavior is flexible; the person shows no fear of change but yields spontaneously to differences and thus is free to become new and different himself. Little children by two's playing together with toys in a sandbox were observed. For each child a count was made of the frequency of activities that could be described as follows:

Dominating behavior
    Verbal demands to secure materials
    Forceful attempts to secure materials
    Succeeds in securing materials
    Defends, snatches back materials
    Verbal commands to direct companion's behavior
    Forceful attempts to direct behavior
    Succeeds in directing behavior
    Criticizes, reproves companion
Integrating behavior
    Verbal request or suggestion to direct companion's behavior
    Verbal request to secure material
    Setting of pattern, including gesture, which companion imitates.

When Anderson found that his original theory was verified so far as the children were concerned, he continued his studies into the field of teacher-child relationships. Three kindergarten teachers at work were observed intensively. He described one sample of dominating activity by a kindergarten teacher. The children were gathered around a circle painted on the floor:

"Who wants to suggest a game?" the teacher asked. "All right, John, what do you suggest?" (Democratic technique. Teacher encourages social participation, self-expression.)

John: "Let's play doggie with the bone." (Social participation; child working with the teacher.)

Teacher: "We played that this morning in the gym. Let's get another suggestion. Willie?" (Dictator. Decision based uniquely on teacher's judgment, teacher's desires.)

Willie: "Let's play doggie with the bone." (It was not clear to the observer whether or not Willie had heard John's suggestion or the teacher's reply.)

Teacher: "I just told John that we played that game this morning in the gym. Who has another suggestion? Mary?"

Mary: "Let's play hide the nutmeg."

Teacher: "That's a sitting down game. We'll play that another time. We are standing now." (Dictator. Decision based on teacher's desires and judgment.)

Within hearing of the observers but out of hearing of the teacher, Ann whispered to Jane who was standing beside her, "I wish we'd play doggie and the bone." (Fear of expressing oneself in opposition to "authority." Child conceals her real wishes from the teacher. . . .)

To which Jane whispered in reply, "So do I."

"Who has another suggestion?" asked the teacher. (By this time a request for suggestions has become a mockery.) And when no further suggestions were forthcoming the teacher announced what game they would play—and they played it.[12]

The observation form used by Anderson in studying teacher-child contacts in kindergarten classes included the following categories:

Dominating activity by the teacher
　　Determines a detail of activity or acts for the child in carrying out a detail
　　Gives direct refusal to some statement or request of child
　　Relocates, reseats, or places children in different relations to each other or to property from the relations which the children themselves have selected
　　Postpones or slows up action by the child
　　Disapproves, blames, or obstructs purpose of child
　　Warns, threatens, or makes conditional promises
　　Calls child to attention or to group activity
　　Makes decisions as to amounts of material to use
Hybrid dominating-integrating activity
　　Defines problem for the children, anticipates questions, and gives answers—the lecture method
　　Asks questions of the type which require a specific answer, only one is acceptable—the lecture method
Integrating activity by the teacher
　　Approves pupil activity
　　Accepts difference (child declines an invitation, or votes "no," or rejects an offer, and teacher accepts this difference without reproof or renewal of the request)
　　Extends invitation to activity
　　Asks question or makes statement regarding child's expressed interest or activity
　　Asks perfunctory questions or makes perfunctory answers or matter-of-fact statements
　　Helps child to define or solve problem without giving the final answer—the build-up
　　Participates in joint activity with children
　　Shows sympathy
　　Grants permission in response to a child's request.[13]

[12] Anderson, Harold H. "Measuring Democratic and Undemocratic Behavior." *Childhood Education* 17: 350-53; April 1941.

[13] Anderson, Harold H. "Domination and Social Integration in the Behavior of Kindergarten Children and Teachers." *Genetic Psychology Monographs* 21: 287-385; August 1939.

In all combinations of the results Anderson found that the dominative contacts by the teachers outnumbered the integrative contacts by at least two to one. He offers no theories as to the desirable balance between dominating and integrating activities.

Wrightstone's study of elementary-school children is likewise suggestive to teachers who are trying to interpret behavior of pupils in relation to morale. His problem (so far as behavior is concerned) was to find out whether pupils of "experimental" schools or of "traditional" schools in the New York City Curriculum Experiment were more likely to behave in ways that showed initiative, cooperation, leadership, and work spirit. He developed a plan of controlled observation to record both number and quality of acts of the following types:

A. Self-initiated activities
    1. Voluntarily bringing contributions (clippings, exhibits, books, charts, etc.) for school activities.
    2. Voluntarily and orally submitting data, or information, gained outside school (observation, trips to buildings, factories, places, etc.).
    3. Presenting a report on a self-directed investigation.
    4. Suggesting methods, materials, activities, etc., for developing a project or problem.

B. Co-operative activities
    1. Helping other pupils or teacher with problems or projects.
    2. Offering objects (book, chair, pencil, tool, etc.) to teacher, pupil, or visitor.
    3. Responding quickly to requests for quiet, materials, etc.

C. Critical activities
    1. Criticizing (praising or challenging) work of others by bringing out good points, suggesting improvements.
    2. Defending points of view.
    3. Asking pertinent questions of teacher or other pupils.

D. Experimental activities.
    1. Trying out new things, putting things into new combinations, as in manual, mechanical, and fine arts, or in social studies, natural sciences, mathematics, etc.
    2. Creating or constructing an original poem, art form or subject, a melody, story, chart, diagram, replica, miniature building, instrument, etc.

E. Leadership activities.
    1. Organizing, directing, or controlling new combinations of persons and things (e.g., setting up plan of procedure, acting as group chairman, etc.).

F. Work-spirit activities
   1. Using time wisely when completing work sooner than others.
   2. Requesting only necessary help while working.
   3. Concentrating deeply upon work which requires close attention.
   4. Working as efficiently whether the teacher leaves the room or is near by.
   5. Clearing materials or paper from the floor.
   6. Producing work neatly arranged, legible, free from blots and eraser marks.[14]

The behavior of school children during class excursions was studied in another evaluation of the New York City Curriculum Experiment. The observers kept a brief diary of each trip and in addition gave qualitative ratings on a nine-point scale to various features of behavior. The following are typical items rated:

Degree of control by adults necessary en route and while at the destination
Social acceptability of behavior
Quality of contacts with the public
Quality of interest and participation
Social spontaneity during lunch period
Responsibility for cleanup after lunch period.[15]

Another study only recently launched deserves mention here because of its potential contribution to research in the building of morale. The Board of Education of the City of New York, in cooperation with the New York Foundation, has started a two-year program in three schools in the Harlem area, in the hope of reducing the present high rate of juvenile delinquency and of serving more fully the educational needs of the entire community. Extensive after-school use of the school buildings, enlistment of parental interest and assistance, full cooperation with existing community agencies, and substantial adjustments in the school curriculum are in prospect. Plans are being made in cooperation with the Teachers College Institute of Educational Research for a continuing evaluation of the demonstration.[16]

---

[14] Wrightstone, J. Wayne. *Appraisal of Newer Elementary School Practices.* New York: Teachers College, Columbia University, 1938. p. 173-74.

[15] Morrison, J. Cayce, director. *The Activity Program.* New York City Curriculum Experiment. Albany, N. Y.: State Education Department, 1941. p. 98-100. ¶ Thorndike, Robert L.; Loftus, John J.; and Goldman, Bernard. "Observations of Excursions in Activity and Control Schools." *Journal of Experimental Education* 10: 146-49; December 1941.

[16] Information from J. Wayne Wrightstone, assistant director, Division of Tests and Measurements, Board of Education of the City of New York, October 1943.

A number of standardized rating scales of behavior are available. For example, several investigators have used the Haggerty-Olson-Wickman Behavior Rating Schedules.[17] The thirty-five items include questions such as these: "Can he compete with others on a physical basis?" "How does he accept authority?" "Does he worry or is he easygoing?" For each question five answers are suggested, in the form of a graphic. rating scale which forms the basis for a profile chart. This type of scale might be used by a teacher in evaluating the personality strengths and weaknesses of each member of his class.

A "Behavior Description" card for secondary pupils, providing space for six years' records, was devised by the Evaluation Staff of the Commission on the Relation of School and College.[18] The card includes eleven characteristics which are followed by five-point scales of description. The eleven are:

Responsibility-dependability
Creativeness and imagination
Influence
Inquiring mind
Open-mindedness
The power and habit of analysis; the habit of reaching conclusions on the basis of valid evidence
Social concern
Emotional responsiveness
Serious purpose
Social adjustability
Work habits.

Four items are listed about which the only judgment asked is whether they are present or absent to a marked degree. The four, which are defined on the blank, are physical energy, assurance, self-reliance, and emotional control. The form provides space for recording descriptions of behavior given by all the teachers of the pupil concerned. This card is believed to show a pupil's most common behavior and range of behavior, as judged by adults having a variety of associations with the pupil concerned.

[17] Haggerty, M. E.; Olson, W. C.; and Wickman, E. K. *Behavior Rating Schedules*. Yonkers-on-Hudson, N. Y.: World Book Co., 1930. 6 p. (*Manual of Directions*, 11 p.) ¶For reference to more recent scales of this general type, see: *Review of Educational Research* 9: 526, 617-19; December 1939. 11: 71-79; February 1941.

[18] Smith, Eugene R., and others, *op cit.*, Chapter 10, p. 470-87. Further information is available from the Progressive Education Association, 221 West 57th Street, New York, N. Y.

Several laboratory studies, using technics that scarcely could be adapted to the schoolroom, have dealt with behavior that revealed perseverance, level of aspiration, and time perspective. This type of study deserves at least brief mention because of the significance of the general findings for teachers. A successful individual typically sets his next goal somewhat, but not too far, above his last achievement. How high he sets his goal is affected by the standards of the group to which he belongs, as well as by the standards of groups below and above him. One of the teacher's great opportunities in the building of morale is in making it possible for each pupil to achieve success, in helping each pupil to raise his own realistic goals for himself, and in helping each pupil to enlarge the scope of his goals beyond his own personal interests.[19] Evaluation should include an effort to appraise the levels of aspiration at which pupils are working.

Teachers and others who try to observe and understand pupil behavior as a basis for helping those pupils to become good citizens in a democracy will have to make judgments about the value of that behavior. The educational philosophy of most teachers makes them shy away from labeling a given action as "good" or "bad," even when the total situation and the pupil's equipment to meet it are considered. Perhaps such labeling is not necessary. But certainly some choice must be made as between "more democratic" and "less democratic" if teachers are going to use the study of pupil behavior as a guide to improve their own work as teachers in influencing future behavior.

CONVERSATION AND INTERVIEW

The daily give and take of conversation in the classroom and elsewhere in school gives the teacher many opportunities to judge pupil morale and to appraise attitudes and knowledge that are basic to citizenship. Insights gained in this way help many teachers to give a good intuitive or impressionistic appraisal of student attitudes. What people say does not always give a true picture of how they feel or what they will do but there is considerable correspondence of word to action.

Casual conversation in public places has been recorded as a source of information on public opinion. The observers move about

[19] Hilgard, Ernest R. "Success in Relation to Level of Aspiration." *School and Society* 55: 423-28; April 11, 1942. ¶Lewin, Kurt. "Psychology of Success and Failure." *Occupations* 14: 926-30; June 1936. ¶Lewin, Kurt. "Time Perspective and Morale." *Civilian Morale*. Second Yearbook, Society for the Psychological Study of Social Issues. Boston: Houghton Mifflin Co., 1942. Chapter 4, p. 48-70.

with crowds or establish themselves at listening posts and make verbatim reports on the talk that is overheard. Records may be made of all conversations heard, thus finding out the types of subjects people are talking about, or the records may be limited to some one topic. There are obvious problems of sampling and this device usually is only a supplement to other methods, as in the Mass-Observation studies in England.[20] Overheard conversation plus "controlled" casual conversations were useful in Srole's study of the impact of the war on "Ameriton" in the days just after the Pearl Harbor attack:

> We had to sound the largest possible number of townspeople at once, and without formalities or preliminaries. This was accomplished by scattering the staff daily among the community's "talking-places," taverns, bars, restaurants, barber shops, beauty parlors, food stores, street corners, etc. They listened to talk, and where possible, they unobtrusively provoked talk. They looked for clues to the townspeople's temper and mood, watched their behavior, and caught their word-thinking (all described in detail in daily reports). To supplement these over-all data, each observer in the second week began the cultivation of a number of informants who could be informally interviewed at regular intervals.[21]

When Srole spoke of interviews, he called attention to the basic presentday method of studying public opinion on a large scale. The poll conducted by the American Institute of Public Opinion, Princeton, New Jersey, directed by George Gallup, is reported in many newspapers. A regular department in *Fortune* is "The Fortune Survey," based on research conducted by the firm of Elmo Roper. Crossley Incorporated, headed by Archibald M. Crossley, makes nationwide surveys of opinion, especially in marketing research. There are several others. One of the newer agencies is the National Opinion Research Center, University of Denver, directed by Harry H. Field. This differs from others in that it is privately endowed and operates on a nonprofit basis. Its services are available at cost to governmental and noncommercial groups.

The basic device employed by these agencies is a definite interview schedule, used thruout the country by trained interviewers who reach a small number of people—3500 to 5000 are typical numbers —carefully selected to sample in due proportions all representative

---

[20] Willcock, H. D. "Mass-Observation." *American Journal of Sociology* 48: 445-56; January 1943.
[21] Srole, Leo. *The Total Impact of the War upon Ameriton, U. S. A.* First Progress Report, Community-Research Program. Geneva, N. Y.: the Author (Hobart and William Smith Colleges), March 1942. p. 2.

groups in the nation. The Gallup poll, for example, tests every sample for proportional representation by states, sex, urban-rural distribution, age, size of income, and political partisanship. Religious and racial distributions are also considered. The *Public Opinion Quarterly,* published at Princeton University, reports the results of several national polls and includes many articles on polling technics. These articles give less attention to problems of sampling, which apparently have been fairly well met, than to discussions of the improvement of questions and the use of successive polls to study trends in opinion.

Several types of questions are used, including those requiring a "yes" or "no" answer, attitude scales, "open" questions which do not restrict the respondents' answers in any way, "filter" questions which seek out informed opinion, the cross-examination approach which offers an opportunity to dissect attitudes, and a secret ballot which may be handed to the person interviewed where prestige or personal factors may influence answers.[22]

Rugg and Cantril, in a general discussion of the technic of questioning, emphasized the relationship of questions to one another—the sequence of questions. They felt that it is dangerous to interpret an opinion on the basis of less than "a pattern of questions that places the opinion squarely in a number of contexts and surrounds it with varying contingencies just as it usually is in everyday life."[23] They call attention to the value of "filter" questions, in which the answer to the first question determines the following queries. They warn against deviations from objective wording and call attention to the warping influence of prestige names or stereotypes. For example, 97 percent of one sample believed in "freedom of speech" but 30 percent of the sample thought that people who oppose our present form of government should be forbidden to express their opinions in public. These authors also mention the fact that a personalized question may be answered differently from a general question; more people said "Yes" to the question, "Would you enlarge the Army even if it means more taxes?" than said "Yes" to "Would you enlarge the Army even if you have to pay a special tax?"

---

[22] Gallup, George. "Reporting Public Opinion in Five Nations." *Public Opinion Quarterly* 6: 429-36; Fall 1942. ¶Roper, Elmo. "Checks to Increase Polling Accuracy." *Public Opinion Quarterly* 5: 86-90; March 1941.

[23] Rugg, Donald, and Cantril, Hadley. "Wording of Questions in Public Opinion Polls." *Journal of Abnormal and Social Psychology* 37: 469-95; October 1942.

The fixed schedule of questions which is repeated in each interview until a representative sample is secured is a part of the *extensive* interview technic. An alternative device is the *intensive* interview, which is less formal and can explore more fully the intensity and qualifications with which people hold opinions and the reasons why they feel as they do. The intensive interview is characteristic of clinical and laboratory studies of personality. For example, Murray's extended explorations in personality included hours of interviewing of each subject.[24] "Frustration" experiences were included, obviously of interest to the student of morale. Such methods are not practicable for large-scale field studies, but there has been an effort to carry over into field methods some of the insights gained thru laboratory studies.

Outstanding among such efforts is the attitude research in the U. S. Department of Agriculture.[25] These studies began as an effort to go back to the grass roots for an appraisal of federal agricultural policies. For a time one sociologist traveled thru rural areas talking informally with farmers about the way the farm programs were working. From this beginning the Division of Program Surveys developed, with field interviewers in most of the major crop regions. Problems are studied on the basis of cross-section samples. The type of interview has changed to one in which selected problems are considered. The interview form is merely the skeleton of a discussion, in which all questions are of the "open-ended" form. The respondent is encouraged to reveal his experiences and attitudes freely and naturally. Technics of the nondirective interview, developed by Rogers, have been used in training the interviewers to confine their contribution to presenting the specific questions on the interview form.[26] Beyond that, all ideas, topics, and suggestions come spontaneously from the respondent. The report on each interview quotes or condenses the respondent's actual words.

The data are classified by the Division of Program Surveys in several ways. A simple rating of the individual on a pro-con scale

[24] Murray, Henry A., and others. *Explorations in Personality.* New York: Oxford University Press, 1938. 761 p.

[25] Skott, Hans E. "Attitude Research in the Department of Agriculture." *Public Opinion Quarterly* 7: 280-92; Summer 1943.

[26] Rogers, Carl R. *Counseling and Psychotherapy.* Boston: Houghton Mifflin Co., 1942. 450 p. ¶Rogers, Carl R. "The Use of Electrically Recorded Interviews in Improving Psychotherapeutic Techniques." *American Journal of Orthopsychiatry* 12: 429-34; July 1942.

relating to the particular topic usually is made. Reasons given for the attitude are also tabulated. Further analysis reveals interrelations the respondent sees between the different aspects of the problem. The terms in which he discusses it, for example, personal terms or social terms, are noted. Likewise the values he invokes in expressing preferences are recorded.

The Committee on Food Habits of the National Research Council made use of intensive interviews as one device in appraising attitudes toward various food problems related to the war. These studies were made under the direction of an anthropologist, Margaret Mead. Emphasis was laid on the importance of recording the answers verbatim, on the theory that insight into the emotional background of an attitude is dependent upon knowledge of the words chosen to make a reply to a given question and upon the actual position of a particular response within the total answer.[27]

Both intensive and extensive interviews were used in the studies of opinions about the war, made in 1942 and 1943 by the Office of War Information. The agency staff defined the range of the issues to be covered in a series of intensive interviews, then prepared a schedule of questions which was used in interviews conducted by the National Opinion Research Center. The questions were selected from preliminary tests which thru the use of multiple-factor analysis had revealed four clusters of opinion which seemed to reflect basic attitudes on the war effort. These four attitudes were (a) satisfaction—the United States is doing all it can to win the war; the people are taking the war seriously enough; (b) overconfidence—the war will not last long; the way we are working now we cannot possibly lose; (c) identification with the war effort—there should be a limit on how high wages may go during the war; yes, I am helping out with a civilian defense job; and (d) social awareness—the United Nations idea is sound; the government must participate in the solution of economic problems. Successive samplings thru extensive interviews were used to identify trends in these four attitudes toward the war effort.[28]

[27] Metraux, Rhoda.. *Qualitative Study of Current Attitudes on Food Problems.* Unpublished memorandum in files of the Committee on Food Habits, National Research Council, Washington, D. C. ¶See also: Mead, Margaret. "The Committee on Food Habits." *Psychological Research Bulletin* 40: 290-93; April 1943.

[28] Based on information received in July 1943 from the Surveys Division of the Office of War Information. ¶See also: Barth, Alan. "The Office of War Information: The Bureau of Intelligence." *Public Opinion Quarterly* 7: 66-76; Spring 1943.

There is need for more research and reporting on the use of interviews in educational practice.[29] Much that has been reported deals with the interviewing of seriously maladjusted children. For example, the Detroit Behavior Scale is a standardized interview schedule which outlines questions on sixty-six items related to health and physical condition, personal habits and recreation, personality and social factors, parental and physical factors of the home, and home atmosphere and school factors.[30]

Information is not available as yet on the method of interviewing developed by the armed forces in the placement of enlisted men and in the selection of officer candidates. Counselors, classroom teachers, and all others engaged in personnel work will await with interest the extensive reports on the use of such technics which may be expected following the war.

One trend that seems likely to continue is a greater use of the nondirective interview, in which the counselor talks little and the pupil is given opportunity to release and express his own feelings. Rogers quotes with apparent approval the following suggestions for interviewing which were developed in the Hawthorne studies with industrial workers:

1. The interviewer should listen to the speaker in a patient and friendly, but intelligently critical, manner.
2. The interviewer should not display any kind of authority.
3. The interviewer should not give advice or moral admonition.
4. The interviewer should not argue with the speaker.
5. The interviewer should talk or ask questions only under certain conditions.
   a. To help the person talk.
   b. To relieve any fears or anxieties on the part of the speaker which may be affecting his relation to the interviewer.
   c. To praise the interviewee for reporting his thoughts and feelings accurately.
   d. To veer the discussion to some topic which has been omitted or neglected.
   e. To discuss implicit assumptions, if this is advisable.[31]

[29] For summaries of research, see: Wrenn, C. Gilbert. "Technics of Guidance and Counseling: The Interview." *Review of Educational Research* 9: 201-204, 242-43; April 1939. ¶Strang, Ruth. "The Interview." *Review of Educational Research* 9: 498-501, 607-608; December 1939. ¶Hubbard, Frank W. "Questionnaires, Interviews, Personality Schedules." *Review of Educational Research* 12: 534-41; December 1942. ¶See also the references by Rogers, cited in footnote 26.
[30] Baker, Harry J., and Traphagen, Virginia. *The Diagnosis and Treatment of Behavior-Problem Children.* New York: Macmillan Co., 1937. 393 p.
[31] Roethlisberger, F. J.; Dickson, William J.; and Wright, Harold A., *op. cit.,* p. 287.

The Hawthorne interviewers were "outsiders," who by assuring the employees that the conversations would not be reported to supervisors secured frank reports on the attitudes of employees toward their jobs. In school practice such impersonal relations will scarcely be possible, but the Hawthorne methods should be of some help, within the limits of the school situation, in releasing free expression by pupils.

PAPER AND PENCIL

Objections have been made to the overuse of paper-and-pencil tests in studying personal adjustment, attitudes, and other factors basic to morale because what is written does not always correlate with what is done. The space given in this chapter to the evaluation of behavior and speech should make it clear that this yearbook recognizes the need for a well-rounded evaluation program which is not limited to traditional devices. There is, however, an important place for the use of written materials in the evaluation of education for morale. This section does not discuss the familiar essay examinations and objective tests for measuring the extent to which pupils have mastered the intellectual concepts underlying democratic living. Attention will be given to the use of other types of written materials in measuring morale, with special emphasis on tests and scales for the measurement of attitudes.

Letters to the editor, letters to the President and other government officials, and the whole range of published material can be studied as indicators of civilian morale. Even before the United States entered the war, federal agencies were surveying attitudes on selective service, defense production, foreign policy, and numerous other topics. Analysis of press content was one important part of most of these studies. News items, columns, editorials, photos and photo captions, and cartoons were analyzed separately and scored on a five-point scale of favorability-unfavorability. Letters of complaint to government offices were also analyzed to locate points of tension. Correspondence panels which include editors, clergymen, social workers, businessmen, and farm leaders have been enlisted by the Office of War Information to send in letters on national problems. These letters have been found helpful in clarifying the motivations which lie behind popular sentiment. Weekly reports by the Office of War Information, based largely on published material but including also the opinion reflected in radio and moving pictures, have been sent to key personnel in all agencies of the federal government.

Cronbach called attention to the value of free writing by students as a clue to morale. He analyzed essays by high-school pupils in November 1941 on the subject: "If the United States enters the war, how will your life be affected, both during the war and permanently?" These essays showed that pupils were intensely emotional about the war and that serious conflicts were present which might be helped thru education.[32] Altho the major outcome of Cronbach's study was a test on the effects of war, he offers the following suggestion:

> It may be advisable for the schools, as a standard and frequently used technique, to appraise the morale of the pupils. Perhaps a standard instrument can be found, but it is doubtful if one can be made flexible enough to apply from year to year. A simpler and in many ways better device is to ask the pupil, without formality or fanfare, how he expects to get along in life. This question, disguised in various ways, can keep the school abreast of its pupils. . . . If the schools study the trends in the minds of their own pupils, they can revise their plans more rapidly and more adequately than if they must wait for a "research worker" to discover pupil needs.[33]

The value of student writing as a measure of social sensitivity and personal attitudes was emphasized also by the Commission on the Relation of School and College. Materials that students write on topics of their own choosing provide some clues, but only sporadically. To secure more systematic evidence, controlled assignments were used in which all students responded to the same general problem, issue, or experience. By this method the individual is not asked directly to reveal his social values but he is provided an object of attention to which he can respond freely and personally. The object is chosen so as to draw out revelations of the student's pattern of social sensitivity. Examples were given of differing responses from pupils when asked to react to a paragraph that began, "Nothing can be done about poverty." Another type of assignment asked the pupils to list their thoughts which might be of social importance, about selected quotations from current newspapers.[34] Obviously,

---

[32] Sherman reported similar findings by analyzing English themes on the subject, "How the War Affects Me." (Sherman, Mandel. "The Attitudes of Youths of High School Age Toward the War." *Psychological Bulletin* 40: 294-99; April 1943.)

[33] Cronbach, Lee J., *op. cit.*, p. 72.

[34] Smith, Eugene R., and others, *op. cit.*, p. 165-68.

the teacher who uses this method of studying attitudes will need practice before he becomes skilful in interpreting the reports submitted.

At the college level, the Cooperative Study in General Education summarized essays on "What difficulties or concerns have you experienced, or do you expect to face, as a result of the war?" The replies clustered around these topics: morale and life values, present social problems, postwar reconstruction, problems of educational planning, problems of vocational planning, and other personal problems.[35]

Tests and questionnaires, rather than free writing, are used in many of the studies based on reading and writing materials that are of greatest meaning for morale. Those who study the evidence find that tests of attitudes measure whatever they do measure with considerable reliability. Some investigators have used both paper-and-pencil tests and personal interviews and have found that people tend to express the same opinions in both speech and writing. Several studies have shown agreement between social attitudes in practice and social attitudes as expressed thru tests.[36]

Tests have been devised for measuring attitudes toward various public issues, such as internationalism, capital punishment, and public ownership of utilities, and toward various practices, such as birth control, lynching, drinking, and Sunday observance. The persistence of the testers in probing into people's feelings about topics that are wrapped in prejudice and emotion has added to the difficulties of an already difficult undertaking. Many efforts have been made to measure liberalism versus conservatism. Tests of social distance have revealed interpersonal attitudes toward classmates and toward members of various racial groups. Attitudes of pupils toward school teachers, and parents have been studied. It is chiefly in the study of job satisfaction and attitudes toward employment that the word "morale" has appeared.

The kinds of attitude tests are almost as varied as the subjects covered. Many of them call for some kind of *comparison* or ranking of two or more objects toward which an attitude might be ex-

[35] American Council on Education, Cooperative Study in General Education. "Students' Essays on Their Wartime Problems." *Staff News Letter* 4: 2-6; May 20, 1943.
[36] For appraisal and bibliography see: Briggs, Thomas H., and others, *op. cit.* ¶Stagner, Ross. "Attitudes." *Encyclopedia of Educational Research.* (Edited by Walter S. Monroe.) New York: Macmillan Co., 1941. p. 69-75. ¶Watson, Goodwin. "Social Attitudes." *Review of Educational Research* 5: 259-72, 320-25; June 1935.

pressed. For example, the person taking the test may be asked to express by numbers the relative merit of a group of occupations. One of the early tests was the "social-distance" measure used by Bogardus. He listed forty groups (for example, Jews, Chinese, and Negroes) and asked those who filled out the blank to indicate the degree of acceptance they would accord to members of each group, using the following scale:

1. Would admit them to close kinship by marriage
2. Would admit them to my club as personal chums
3. Would admit them to my street as neighbors
4. Would admit them to employment in my occupation
5. Would admit them to citizenship in my country
6. Would admit them as visitors only to my country
7. Would exclude them from my country.[37]

Similar tests have been used for asking students how they would feel about working with each of their classmates and for other studies of personal relations in social groups. The use of such devices is one of the basic technics in what Moreno calls "sociometry." [38]

Attitudes and opinions are tested *indirectly* by various inquiry blanks which avoid mention of the particular issue or stereotype which the investigator is trying to study. For example, Stagner collected statements from Hitler's and Mussolini's speeches and submitted them for approval or disapproval without identifying their Fascist origin.[39] He used this approach in an effort to measure people's attitudes toward the ideas and practices of Fascism rather than toward the word "Fascism." Values have been tested by asking the individual to select from a brief narrative the most *interesting* or the most *important* phase of the incident described. "What would you do?" situations may be presented, with a choice of possible lines of action. Or the subject is given a list of words or phrases and is asked to cross out those which he does not like or to rate them as liked, disliked, or neutral. Scoring the results of such tests is sometimes challenged; judges may disagree as to the inter-

[37] Bogardus, Emory S. *Immigration and Race Attitudes.* Boston: D. C. Heath and Co., 1928. 268 p. (Among more recent studies of this type is the report based on opinions of 1000 fifth- to eighth-grade school children in: Meltzer, H. "The Development of Children's Nationality Preferences, Concepts, and Attitudes." *Journal of Psychology* 11: 343-58; April 1941.)

[38] Chapin, F. Stuart. "Trends in Sociometrics and Critique." *Sociometry* 3: 245-62; July 1940. ¶Moreno, Jacob L. *Who Shall Survive?* Nervous and Mental Disease Monograph Series, No. 58. New York: Nervous and Mental Disease Publishing Co., 1934. 440 p.

[39] Stagner, Ross. "Fascist Attitudes: Their Determining Conditions." *Journal of Social Psychology* 7: 309-19, 438-54; August, November 1936.

ests that show a religious attitude, the lines of action that indicate fairmindedness, or the combination of preferences that identify a radical. Procedures have been developed, however, for getting an agreement of judges as a basis for the scoring.

The *specific* approach is also used, in which some one institution, group, or practice is named and is made the object of the questions or statements in the test. Thurstone's work in developing scales for the measurement of attitudes is used as a starting point for most of the research of this type.[40]

Thurstone was not satisfied to know merely that Jones was more favorable to a given idea than was Smith; he wanted to know how much more favorable Jones was. To do this he needed a scale with a constant unit so that the difference between 3.0 and 4.0 on the scale is the same as the difference between 6.0 and 7.0. To do this he developed his method of "equal-appearing intervals," enlisting the help of judges to scale the items used in his tests.

Remmers and his students have produced a series of tests based on the Thurstone method except that many of them are *generalized* scales.[41] Instead of separate scales for attitude toward, for example, the Negro or the Chinese, Remmers has a generalized scale for measuring attitude toward any racial or national group.

Likert worked out a short method that several other investigators have used. He obtained results apparently as reliable as Thurstone's by selecting items without benefit of scaling by judges, and by having the subjects indicate their agreement or disagreement with each item on a five-point scale. He gave values from one to five to each item and summed the values to get the score for a given individual. Low scores indicated a favorable attitude toward the subject being appraised. The following items from the scale on "Imperialism" illustrate the form and scoring of the statements:[42]

---

[40] Thurstone, L. L., and Chave, E. J. *The Measurement of Attitude.* Chicago: University of Chicago Press, 1929. 96 p.

[41] Remmers, Hermann H., editor. *Studies in Attitudes, Series I.* Purdue University Bulletin, Vol. 35, No. 4, December 1934. Studies in Higher Education, 26. Lafayette, Ind.: Purdue University, 1934. 112 p.

[42] In quoting sample items from this and other tests the purpose is to illustrate the type of wording and method of scoring rather than to emphasize the worth of the particular item as a measure of the quality under discussion. Investigators who prepare standardized tests of attitudes (as in any other field) include in the final form of their tests only those items which are selected thru preliminary trials. It is a mistake to judge the value of an item on *a priori* grounds; sometimes an item which seems barely worth including in a preliminary list for trial proves to have a high discriminative value. The total score does not rest on the response to any one item but on the responses to a number of items.

AN AMERICAN COMMITTING A CRIME IN SHANGHAI SHOULD BE TRIED BY A CHINESE
JUDGE.

Strongly approve	Approve	Undecided	Disapprove	Strongly disapprove
(5)	(4)	(3)	(2)	(1)

OUR ARMY AND NAVY SHOULD BE USED WHEN NECESSARY TO DEFEND AMERICAN
PROPERTY RIGHTS IN MEXICO.

Strongly approve	Approve	Undecided	Disapprove	Strongly disapprove
(1)	(2)	(3)	(4)	(5)

A preliminary trial was used to select items that discriminated most sharply between those whose attitude was favorable and those whose attitude was unfavorable. The scores on such a test make comparisons possible but they do not represent "equal-appearing intervals" as Thurstone's method aims to do.[43]

Likert's often quoted suggestions for wording statements for an attitude scale have been helpful in various types of inquiries dealing with opinions. They are given here in abbreviated form:

1. Item should refer to desired behavior and not to fact. Refer to *present* attitude; deal with value judgments, as shown by the verb *should*.

2. Use straightforward, clear, concise statements. Avoid double-negative elements and every kind of ambiguity.

3. Try to word the items so that the typical response is in the middle of the possible responses.

4. Vary the statements so that a person will alternate from side to side in the checking in about an equal number of cases.

5. Multiple-choice items should involve only a single attitude variable.

The work of Thurstone, Remmers, and Likert has been given special attention because several of the studies aimed directly at the measurement of morale have used their methods.[44] For example, Rundquist and Sletto undertook to measure the individual morale of several groups of persons, including unemployed adults.[45] They devised a "Survey of Opinions" which included twenty-two items

---

[43] Likert, Rensis. *A Technique for the Measurement of Attitudes.* Archives of Psychology, No. 140. New York: Columbia University, 1932. 55 p.

[44] The war rendered obsolete many of the actual testing instruments devised by these pioneer investigators. Regardless of current events, however, several writers were challenging Thurstone's theory that an attitude could be measured as a single continuum, claiming that the attitude toward war, for example, was a complex of many attitudes. (See: Dudycha, George J. "Attitudes Toward War." *Psychological Bulletin* 39: 846-60; December 1942.)

[45] Rundquist, Edward A., and Sletto, Raymond F. *Personality in the Depression.* Minneapolis: University of Minnesota Press, 1936. 398 p. ¶ See also: Hall, O. Milton. *Attitudes and Unemployment.* Archives of Psychology, No. 165. New York: Columbia University, 1934. 65 p.

each for the measurement of morale, feelings of inferiority, economic conservatism, and attitudes toward family, the law, and education. In the following sample items from "The Morale Scale" the small numbers show the scores assigned to each response. In this scale a low score indicates high morale:

THE FUTURE LOOKS VERY BLACK

5	4	3	2	1
Strongly agree	*Agree*	*Undecided*	*Disagree*	*Strongly disagree*

IT DOES NOT TAKE LONG TO GET OVER FEELING GLOOMY

1	2	3	4	5
Strongly agree	*Agree*	*Undecided*	*Disagree*	*Strongly disagree*

The Houser Associates have used questions such as the following as a test of employee morale (each question has a series of five answers not shown here, covering a range of feeling from favor to disfavor):

Are there other companies in which you would rather work at the same earnings if you could get a job for which you feel equally qualified?

To what extent are you made to feel that you are really a part of the organization?

How fair do you feel the top management of the company is with people in jobs such as yours?

How fair do you feel that the people immediately above you are in their treatment of you?

Are you reasonably sure of being able to keep your job as long as you do good work? [46]

Several studies of industrial morale have used such questions on general morale, along with questions on more specific details such as, "Are employees ever bawled out or criticized when they do not deserve it?" Employees making the highest and the lowest morale scores can be compared to observe differences in their answers to the specific question.[47]

Since the defense program began in 1940 various investigators have used scales or questionnaires for measuring individual morale

[46] Hull, Richard L., and Kolstad, Arthur. "Morale on the Job." *Civilian Morale*. Second Yearbook, Society for the Psychological Study of Social Issues. Boston: Houghton Mifflin Co., 1942. Chapter 17, p. 349-64. ¶ See also: Houser, J. David. *What People Want from Business*. New York: McGraw-Hill Book Co., 1938. 250 p.

[47] Hoppock, Robert. *Job Satisfaction*. New York: Harper and Brothers, 1935. p. 175.

in relation to the current war effort.[48] Several of these studies have reported several different clusters of answers and have suggested that scores on these components of morale were more meaningful than a general score that blurred the variables. Miller listed five basic factors in national morale and devised test questions related to each of the factors:

1. Belief in the superiority of the social structure in the ingroup
2. Identification of personal goals with national goals
3. Confidence in the competence of national leadership
4. Belief that resources are available to hurl back any threats to the ingroup
5. Confidence in the permanence of the national goals.

Harding used intercorrelations to locate four clusters of questions, centered around attitudes, which he labeled as:

1. *Confidence* in the broad framework of capitalist democracy in the U. S.—as opposed to cynicism
2. *Tolerance* for various groups, a liberal attitude—as opposed to factionalism and setting up of scapegoats
3. *Realism*—as opposed to wishful thinking
4. Assertive *idealism* in international affairs.

Harding used Likert's method for obtaining replies and scoring on a five-point scale. The following items are typical:

(Confidence) Would you favor changing to a different form of government in this country if it would promise you more in the way of a job?
(Tolerance) Labor unions should be suppressed during the present national emergency
(Realism) Within the next six months the United States will be completely safe from attack by any foreign power.

Cronbach suggested the use of a "Test on the Effects of War" as an aid to schools in adapting their practices to the aspects of the war situation which appeared to be most damaging to morale. His test was aimed to measure the tendency of high-school pupils to predict

---

[48] American Council on Education, Cooperative Study in General Education. *Checklist of Wartime Problems.* Chicago: University of Chicago, 1942. 7 p. ¶ Gilliland, A. R. "A Brief Review of Recent Morale Studies." *Journal of Social Psychology,* S.P.S.S.I. *Bulletin* 17: 355-58; May 1943. ¶ Gilliland, A. R., and Katzoff, E. T. "A Scale for the Measurement of Attitudes toward American Participation in the Present European Conflict." *Journal of Psychology* 11: 173-76; January 1941. ¶ Harding, John. "A Scale for Measuring National Morale." *Journal of Psychology* 12: 101-10; July 1941. ¶ Miller, Delbert C. "The Measurement of National Morale." *American Sociological Review* 6: 147-98; August 1941. ¶ Sanford, R. Nevitt, and Conrad, Herbert S. "Some Personality Correlates of Morale." *Journal of Abnormal and Social Psychology* 38: 3-20; January 1943. ¶ Young, Florene M. "The Psychological Effects of War upon College Students." *Journal of Psychology* 15: 75-97; January 1943.

realistically the hardships or lack of hardships they would face in the future. Predictions that are either overoptimistic or overpessimistic are signs of poor morale, according to this concept. Cronbach's test took the form of a series of statements about the future, for example, "Women will be drafted for non-military service," to which students could respond on a five-point scale of acceptance or rejection. A group of judges classified the statements as being either optimistic or pessimistic. The low intercorrelations discovered, even among similar items, and the fact that background factors of social and economic status seemed not to be related to the optimism scores led Cronbach to conclude that the score on the test was really a composite rather than the measure of a single trait.[49]

Interesting results were obtained by the use of the Cronbach test with secondary-school pupils and teachers in the schools of Washington, D. C., in March 1943. Scores from 1000 pupils and 424 teachers revealed the following relationships: The pupils of lower intelligence ratings showed greater variation in optimism scores than the brighter group, and at the junior high-school level the duller group had lower optimism scores. The relation of socio-economic background to optimism was too slight and inconsistent to be significant. In both the total optimism score and the subsections of the test, the scores for junior high-school pupils were more optimistic than for senior high-school pupils, and for senior high-school pupils the scores were more optimistic than those for faculty members. It was noted that in general the scores of this group of pupils in the District of Columbia in 1943 were higher than the average scores of high-school pupils tested in three other states during November and December 1942. Sex differences were negligible.[50]

Personal and civic morale in respect to postwar adjustments will be a major educational problem for the next few years. One of the early steps toward meeting this need was taken by the Cooperative Study in General Education. A test was designed to answer these questions: "What types of social knowledge are required in order that we may meet the problems of the postwar world?" "How can social science instruction best be carried on so as to make this knowledge available?" As a way of finding out the actual needs of students

49 Cronbach, Lee J., *op. cit.*, 79 p.
50 District of Columbia Public Schools, Department of Educational Research, Divisions I-IX. *Annual Report, 1942-43*. Washington, D. C.: the Schools, 1943. Part IV, Section 4, "Report of the Survey of Youth and Morale in Wartime," p. 54-74.

in this field, an "Inventory of Beliefs about Post-war Reconstruction" was prepared. Three hypotheses or assumptions were basic in constructing the test: (a) People are prone to make broad, general statements without at the same time recognizing the specific beliefs or courses of action to which these logically lead; thus broad generalizations and related specific policies were included in the test. (b) The general issues of social policy remain substantially the same in peacetime and in time of crisis. The test included items on government versus business, race relations, and democratic principles. (c) There is a significant distinction between domestic problems and international problems; both were included in the test. The 150 items of the inventory consist of statements of opinion of which the following are typical:

> Full employment is the key to national prosperity
> After the war large population movements should be subject to international regulation.

Those who take the test are asked to express agreement, disagreement, or uncertainty regarding each item.[51]

Of particular interest for the evaluation of morale as defined by this yearbook are some of the recent developments in testing the social and civic attitudes of pupils in school. As examples may be mentioned the New York Regents' Inquiry,[52] the New York City Curriculum Experiment,[53] and the Progressive Education Association's Eight-Year Study of the Relation of School and College.[54] Evidences of civic competence included what children knew about their own community's affairs, how well they understood the meaning of social terms, and their reactions to tests of civic beliefs.

The studies that dealt with the current attitudes of pupils as citizens in a school have a direct bearing on morale. If children learn their citizenship by living their citizenship, teachers should know as much as possible about the attitudes of pupils toward their current civic responsibilities. The "What Would You Do?" test in the Regents' Inquiry included situations such as this one, on which students were asked to choose among several proposed courses of action:

[51] American Council on Education, Cooperative Study in General Education. "An Inventory of Beliefs about Post-war Reconstruction." *Staff News Letter* 4: 1-12; May 17, 1943.
[52] Wilson, Howard E. *Education for Citizenship*. Regents' Inquiry into the Character and Cost of Public Education in the State of New York. New York: McGraw-Hill Book Co., 1938. 272 p.
[53] Morrison, J. Cayce, director, *op. cit.*, 182 p.
[54] Smith, Eugene R., and others, *op. cit.*, 550 p.

A very popular senior student is carrying a heavy study schedule, and takes part in many school activities. The president of the Student Council is forced to resign because of illness, and this boy, as the best qualified student, is asked to accept nomination of the office. If he does so, he will have to give up most of his other interests.[55]

The "What Do You Believe?" test used with elementary-school children in the New York City experiment was designed to learn whether the child tends to accept passively the current ideas, prejudices, and slogans or is tending to take a questioning attitude toward such statements. In a broad sense this was a test of civic beliefs or civic attitudes. It consisted of fifty items on which children were asked to report agreement or disagreement. Sample items are these:

> Most people who talk against the government should be put in jail.
> Most people who go on strike are just too lazy to work.[56]

In the Eight-Year Study the emphasis was as much on clarity of thought, consistency, and logical discrimination as on the actual attitudes held by the students, altho the latter were studied also. In studying the ability of students to apply social values the following structure for the test was adopted:

1. *A problem situation* describing an important issue was presented. The problems were new to the students. Significant contemporary problems were chosen whenever possible; actual problems reported in newspapers or magazines were used.

2. Three *courses of action* representing three different positions toward the issue were formulated. The students were to choose the one or ones which they thought most desirable. The courses of action represented different points of view and were not to be marked as "right" or "wrong."

3. A list of *"reasons"* consisting of value principles was given from which students could choose the ones they would use to support the course of action chosen. In order to discover dominant value patterns, it seemed that statements of contrasting beliefs and values were needed. These statements included reasons which logically supported each suggested course of action as well as reasons which were contradictory, irrelevant, or untenable.[57]

Both the courses of action and the supporting reasons were keyed for values representing "democratic," "undemocratic," or "compro-

[55] Eckert, Ruth E., and Wilson, Howard E. "What Would You Do? A Survey of Student Opinion, Parts I and II." See: Wilson, Howard E., *op. cit.*, p. 255-66.
[56] Wrightstone, J. Wayne. *What Do You Believe?* Elementary School Series. New York: Board of Education of the City of New York, 1941. ¶ See also: Wrightstone, J. Wayne. *Scale of Civic Beliefs.* Yonkers, N. Y.: World Book Co., 1938. 4 p.
[57] Smith, Eugene R., and others, *op. cit.*, p. 176-77.

mise" positions. The test included problems on conservation of national resources, free speech, unemployment, protection of health, distribution of wealth, collective bargaining, socialized medicine, and working conditions.[58]

The tests entitled "Beliefs on Social Issues" and "Beliefs about School Life" each consisted of brief statements of opinion, to be marked for agreement, disagreement, or uncertainty. The first consisted of two hundred items which included in random order statements which sampled opinions on democracy, economic relations, labor and unemployment, race, nationalism, and militarism. The replies were keyed to represent "liberalism" and "conservatism" and were scored for liberalism, conservatism, uncertainty, and consistency. It was believed that this test was helpful in finding out:

1. Whether increased understanding of social problems brought about an ability and willingness to take personal positions on an increasing range of social issues.

2. What direction, whether liberal or conservative, was suggested by the positions taken by students.

3. How consistent the students' beliefs were. Consistency was regarded as a desirable characteristic of social beliefs, no matter which position was taken.[59]

The test on "Beliefs about School Life" sampled six areas: school government, curriculum, grades and awards, school spirit, pupil-teacher relations, and group life. The following items are typical:

The teachers and principal should have pupils help in deciding what books to buy for the school library.

Trips outside of the school building should not be taken at a time when they interfere with the regular class schedule.

If grades were done away with, pupils would have no way of knowing whether they were making progress in their studies.

One of the best ways for a pupil to show that he is a good school citizen is always to defend his school when others criticize it.[60]

The report suggests that these tests of social sensitivity may be useful for such purposes as these:

---

[58] *Test on the Ability to Apply Social Values: Application on Social Facts and Generalizations. Form 1.5.* For information on this and other tests in the Eight-Year Study, write to: Evaluation in the Eight-Year Study of the Progressive Education Association, 5835 Kimbark Avenue, Chicago 37, Ill.

[59] Smith, Eugene R., and others, *op. cit.*, p. 212-14.

[60] Smith, Eugene R., and others, *op. cit.*, p. 229-34.

Teacher may want to diagnose the strengths and weaknesses of the individuals in his class.

Teacher may want to check the effectiveness of his curriculum.

Teacher may want to see whether his students are achieving an increasingly consistent social viewpoint.

Teacher may be interested in changes occurring over a period of time but should not expect a striking change. Changes in fundamental value patterns, in methods applying values, and in using information to gain deeper insight into complex problems do not take place overnight. Results may not show up until a good time later.[61]

The foregoing pages give a limited sampling to suggest the wide range of uses that may be made of written materials in appraising both individual and group morale. The use of scientifically prepared tests and questionnaires already available should be continued. They will be especially effective when used under the guidance of skilled research workers. Workers in both university centers and school research bureaus should continue to develop instruments for testing attitudes, beliefs, and probable courses of action.

Individual teachers should not hesitate to use such formal tests and scales where they will be useful in studying the needs of a particular group of pupils. Teachers of course should be on guard against reading too much significance into their findings, as compared with group norms. Fully as useful as the actual tests themselves, however, should be the suggestions they offer to teachers in preparing and interpreting evaluation materials of their own, based directly on the school experiences of their own pupils. Teachers will find that attention to emotional, civic, and social attitudes expressed in all written work by pupils will be helpful in assessing the morale needs of each pupil.

Changing Practices To Achieve the Goals

There are some things that every teacher can do to change his own practices to meet the morale problems of his pupils as they are revealed by evaluation. He can constantly improve the quality of his own relationships with pupils so that the atmosphere of the classroom is one of mutual respect among all the members, with individual responsibilities clearly understood and willingly met. He can enrich the experience of pupils by multiplying situations which lay the foundation for enduring morale in the future.

---

[61] Smith, Eugene R., and others, *op. cit.*, p. 238-44.

But just as the school is only one of the many agencies of the community that build character and establish values, so the teacher in his classroom is only one of the influences of the school on the personality of the pupil. Basic features of school organization, reaching back to the policies established by the board of education, may be of significance in laying the groundwork for civic and social attitudes. An evaluation of the attitudes basic to morale may reveal the need for fundamental changes in the curriculum, in the administration of the school personnel, in methods of grading, in the organization of student activities, or in the extent to which parents and the public generally share and understand the purposes of the schools. If the process of evaluation is based squarely on a clear statement of valid purposes and if tests and observation show that those purposes are not being attained but are actually being denied attainment by existing school practices, then there should be a change.

Changes of such depth as to make a difference in education for morale cannot come from some one teacher's wish nor by administrative fiat. They can come only when all persons connected with the process of evaluation, including the students themselves, understand the purposes to be achieved and are willing to support them. There must be understanding of the kinds of changes that school experience should make in pupils. For high morale as a citizen, the individual needs a proud, possessive sense of responsibility for realizing the goals of America and he needs to be secure in his own role as a citizen in working for these goals. The role of the good citizen must be understood and lived by the teachers, and increasingly by their pupils.

There is ample evidence that pupils' attitudes on basic social and civic issues *can be changed* by their school experiences. Apparently, however, there is little probability of a change of attitudes unless the instructor makes a special effort to effect a change. If he deliberately sets out to change an attitude, there is strong possibility that he will succeed.[62] The fact that teachers are in a position to wield

---

[62] Briggs, Thomas H., and others. *op. cit.*, "The Modification of Emotionalized Attitudes," p. 69-93. ¶ Bugelski, Richard, and Lester, Olive P. "Changes in Attitudes in a Group of College Students During Their College Course and After Graduation." *Journal of Social Psychology* 12: 319-32; November 1940. ¶ Remmers, H. H. "Propaganda in the Schools—Do the Effects Last?" *Public Opinion Quarterly* 2: 197-210; April 1938. (See also: Studies in Higher Education, 31; Bulletin of Purdue University, Vol. 37, No. 4, 1936.) ¶ Watson, Goodwin. "Social Attitudes." *Review of Educational Research* 5: 259-72, 320-25; June 1935.

so great an influence on the character of their pupils' basic attitudes underlines the strategic position of the teacher himself in every aspect of education for morale. The real change in school practice may have to be in the basic attitudes and beliefs of the faculty.

These are some of the procedures that may accompany a progressive improvement in the service of schools in building for morale:

Cumulative records of pupils will include more information on personal and civic achievements of pupils, and these records will be used more widely by teachers and counselors.

Counseling and guidance services will be broadened in scope. More time by teachers and full-time counselors and consequently more personnel will be required to diagnose and meet the personal and civic needs of each pupil.

Reports to pupils and parents on school achievement will reflect the fact that evaluation of the teaching and learning process includes conduct and attitudes as of central rather than secondary importance.

Pupils will have more opportunities to share in evaluation, by better understanding of the goals being sought in the field of conduct and attitudes, by giving their own ideas as to possible improvements in school practice, and by self-appraisals of their own progress toward maturity.

Schools will extend their program of evaluation to include information on the civic achievements of their graduates, both as a means of checking on the success of the school's program and as a means of keeping the school close to the community and to the needs of its present pupils.

Extracurriculum activities will provide for broader participation by all students.

Opportunities for education will be more nearly equalized to reduce the educational handicaps now carried by children and youth in low-income areas and in low-income families.

Human relationships thruout the school and the school system will be marked by greater respect for the dignity of each individual.

Curriculum content and personal example will give increasing weight to the concept of personal obligation and responsibility to the home, the school, the community, and to all society.

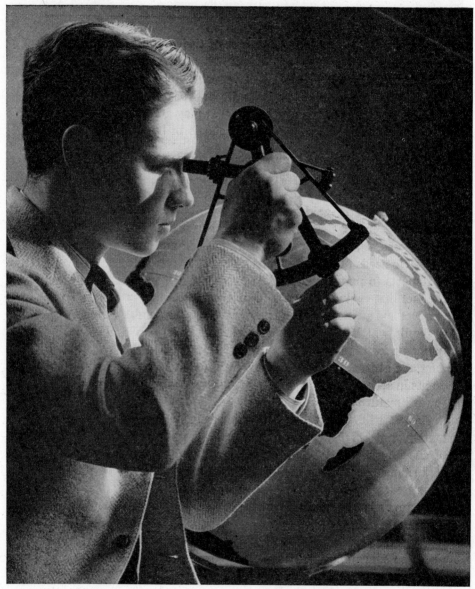

★ *Schools and colleges should help their students to realize the distance yet to be covered before the ideals of democracy are to be attained in America and in all the world and should try to create within those students a sense of responsibility for doing their part in making those ideals come true.*

CHAPTER XII

"Years of the Unperformed"

THE SCHOOLS AND TEACHERS this year can take little either of credit or of blame for the efficiency of this year's government, for the quality of our present national leadership, for the general economic and political welfare of our people today, or for the wisdom of our dealings with other nations. Whatever of praise or blame attaches to schools or teachers for present conditions attaches to the schools and the teachers of earlier years. But the schools and teachers of today do have a responsibility for what improves or degrades America next year and in each year thereafter for many years to come.

This yearbook was planned to help educators understand better their opportunities to build a national morale that will be high in peace or in war, in times of calm and prosperity as well as in times of crisis and disaster—a morale that will fit America for its responsibilities in a free world.

The book does not speak of morale as a general glow of optimism or well-being; it speaks of morale as the quality of giving fully of one's best efforts to carry out a purpose. But the book does not talk about any or all purposes; it talks about the purposes of the United States—the goals of America. It raises questions and suggests answers about what education can do to help the citizens of the United States to give their best efforts toward reaching great goals for America and the world.

People have high morale when certain conditions are met: when they have individual physical and mental security; when their social relations with other people are carried on in an atmosphere of mutual respect and understanding; and when they are aware of values and high purposes with which they are able to identify their own lives. To the extent that life in the United States guarantees these conditions to every individual and every group of individuals, to that extent the possibility of the highest level of national morale is assured.

The fact that barriers now exist to the highest national morale

calls for courage and determination. Conditions that need changing can be changed when enough people want to change them.

The processes by which individuals work together to reach
group goals under democratic leadership are being learned. But
only a start has been made. Of the many centuries of human history,
only the last two have seen any large-scale efforts at government of
the people, by the people, and for the people. Some things have been
learned; for example, that people will work together more effectively
when each one is treated with respect as a worthy member of the
group and when each one is able to share in setting the policies that
govern the group. There must be leadership that inspires and
merits confidence. We know, too, that when there is a deeply seated
system of values defining the aim of the group, people will work
their hardest, in spite of hazards and handicaps. Our forefathers
risked their lives, their fortunes, and their sacred honor in the cause
of freedom because in the depths of their beings they *believed* in
freedom. That same belief is needed today, and tomorrow.

Teachers in schools and colleges can help their students understand and think thru for themselves what the goals of America are.
What are the values and high purposes for which this nation should
ever strive? These values and purposes are not stated in the same
way from year to year, but as they are progressively reclarified—
and the schools can help to clarify them—they should be built into
the foundations of thought and belief of every young person in
school and college.

It is not enough merely to memorize and understand the Mayflower Compact, the Bill of Rights, or the Four Freedoms, or whatever the latest and best formulation of these principles may be.
Schools and colleges—public and private—should strive to build
these ideals into the very fiber of thought and belief of their students. At the same time they should help their students to realize
the distance yet to be covered before those ideals are to be attained
in America and in all the world, should try to create within those
students a sense of responsibility for doing their part in making
those ideals come true, and should give them a rich and varied
experience in working together for the common good.

Schools and colleges in which this kind of teaching is done will
upset traditional privileges and taboos. But some teachers already

are teaching democratic ideals and are teaching them well. Some schools are practicing the ways of democracy and are graduating young citizens who are ready to give their best efforts thruout their lives to making the ideals of democracy come true in the United States and in the world. This book is an effort to speed the time when all schools, in all communities, will be serving thus the nation and the world.

In the stress and strain of war, the American people have renewed their faith in the democratic process. They have searched the ancient roots of that faith. They have gained new confidence in their future. They have achieved new understanding of their responsibilities. In the trial of war they have learned that the United States can work with other nations. They have learned that the peoples of the world look to us for more than tanks and guns, for more than food and shelter. They know now that their children and their children's children for uncounted generations have a great role to play in the world's affairs. To the teachers of the children of free men in America and "not America only" this book is offered.

SELECTED REFERENCES

Chapter I. For a Thousand Years

1. FARAGO, LADISLAS, and GITTLER, L. FREDERICK, editors. *German Psychological Warfare*. New York: Committee for National Morale (51 East 42d St.), 1941. 155 p. $2.50.
2. GODDARD, HAROLD. *Morale*. New York: George H. Doran Co., 1918. 118 p.
3. GULICK, LUTHER H. *Morals and Morale*. New York: Association Press, 1919. 192 p.
4. HALL, G. STANLEY. *Morale, the Supreme Standard of Life and Conduct*. New York: D. Appleton and Co., 1920. 378 p.
5. HOCKING, WILLIAM ERNEST. *Morale and Its Enemies*. New Haven, Conn.: Yale University Press, 1918. 200 p.
6. HOLMES, HENRY W. *The Road to Courage; Sources of Morale in Men and Nations*. New York: Alfred A. Knopf, 1943. 249 p. $2.50.
7. JAMES, WILLIAM. *Memories and Studies*. New York: Longmans, Green and Co., 1917. Chapter 11, "The Moral Equivalent of War," p. 267-96.
8. MANN, THOMAS. *The Coming Victory of Democracy*. New York: Alfred A. Knopf, 1938. 70 p. $1.
9. PERRY, RALPH BARTON. "The Meaning of Morale." *Educational Record 22*: 446-60; July 1941.
10. POPE, ARTHUR UPHAM. "The Importance of Morale." *Journal of Educational Sociology 15*: 195-205; December 1941.
11. WATSON, GOODWIN, editor. *Civilian Morale*. Second Yearbook, Society for the Psychological Study of Social Issues. Boston: Houghton Mifflin Co., 1942. 463 p. $3.50.

Chapter II. Democratic Morale in a Free World

12. ALLPORT, GORDON W. "The Nature of Democratic Morale." *Civilian Morale*. Second Yearbook, Society for the Psychological Study of Social Issues. Boston: Houghton Mifflin Co., 1942. Chapter 1, p. 3-18.
13. AMERICAN JOURNAL OF SOCIOLOGY. "National Morale." (Symposium.) *American Journal of Sociology 47*: 277-480; November 1941.
14. CHILD, IRVIN L. "Morale: A Bibliographical Review." *Psychological Review 38*: 393-420; June 1941.
15. KOESTLER, ARTHUR. *Darkness at Noon*. (Translated by Daphne Hardy.) New York: Macmillan Co., 1941. 267 p. $2.
16. MANN, ERIKA. *School for Barbarians*. New York: Modern Age Books, 1938. 159 p. 50¢.
17. NATIONAL EDUCATION ASSOCIATION and AMERICAN ASSOCIATION OF SCHOOL ADMINISTRATORS, EDUCATIONAL POLICIES COMMISSION. *The Education of Free Men in American Democracy*. Washington, D. C.: the Commission, 1941. 115 p. 50¢.
18. PERRY, RALPH BARTON. *On All Fronts*. New York: Vanguard Press, 1941. 189 p. $1.75.

19. Perry, Ralph Barton. *Our Side Is Right*. Cambridge, Mass.: Harvard University Press, 1942. 153 p. $1.75.

20. Shand, Alexander F. *The Foundations of Character*. New York: Macmillan Co., 1914. 532 p.

21. Ziemer, Gregor A. *Education for Death*. New York: Oxford University Press, 1941. 208 p. $2.

See also items 4, 5, 6, and 7.

Chapter III. Getting Together

22. Bateson, Gregory, and Mead, Margaret. "Principles of Morale Building." *Journal of Educational Sociology* 15: 206-20; December 1941.

23. Chein, Isidor. "The Meaning of 'Morale' in Relation to Morale Building and Morale Research." *Psychological Review* 50: 311-29; May 1943.

24. Hilgard, Ernest R. "Success in Relation to Level of Aspiration." *School and Society* 55: 423-28; April 11, 1942.

25. Merrifield, Charles, special editor. "Civilian Morale Agencies in War and Peace." *Journal of Educational Sociology* 15: 381-429; March 1942.

26. Nash, Jay B. *Building Morale*. New York: A. S. Barnes and Co., 1942. 154 p. $1.

27. Pardue, Austin. *Your Morale and How To Build It*. New York: Charles Scribner's Sons, 1942. 132 p. $1.50.

28. Prescott, Daniel A. *Emotion and the Educative Process*. Report of the Committee on the Relation of Emotion to the Educative Process. Washington, D. C.: American Council on Education, 1938. 323 p. $2.

29. Saturday Review of Literature. "Special Issue on Morale." *Saturday Review of Literature* 25: 1-32; July 4, 1942.

See also items 9, 13, and 14.

Chapter IV. Background for Morale: The American Scene

30. American Council on Education, American Youth Commission. *Youth and the Future*. General Report. Washington, D. C.: the Council, 1942. 296 p. $2.50.

31. Bakke, E. Wight. *Citizens Without Work*. New Haven, Conn.: Yale University Press, 1940. 311 p. $3.

32. Becker, Carl L. *The United States: An Experiment in Democracy*. New York: Harper and Brothers, 1920. 333 p.

33. Benedict, Agnes E. *Progress to Freedom: The Story of American Education*. New York: G. P. Putnam's Sons, 1942. 309 p. $3.

34. Commission on Post-War Training and Adjustment. *Report of the Commission on Post-War Training and Adjustment*. New York: Institute of Adult Education, Teachers College, Columbia University, 1942. 54 p. Free.

35. Davis, Allison, and Dollard, John. *Children of Bondage*. Prepared for the American Youth Commission. Washington, D. C.: American Council on Education, 1940. 299 p. $2.25.

36. Freeman, Ellis. *Social Psychology*. New York: Henry Holt and Co., 1936. 491 p. $2.50.

37. JOHN DEWEY SOCIETY. *Workers' Education in the United States.* Fifth Yearbook. New York: Harper and Brothers, 1941. 338 p. $2.50.

38. NATIONAL EDUCATION ASSOCIATION, DEPARTMENT OF SUPERVISORS AND DIRECTORS OF INSTRUCTION. *Americans All: Studies in Intercultural Education.* Fourteenth Yearbook. Washington, D. C.: the Department, 1942. 385 p. $2.

39. PRATTIS, PERCIVAL L. "The Morale of the Negro in the Armed Services of the United States." *Journal of Negro Education* 12: 355-63; Summer 1943.

40. ROETHLISBERGER, F. J. *Management and Morale.* Cambridge, Mass.: Harvard University Press, 1941. 194 p. $2.

41. RUGG, HAROLD O. *Now Is the Moment.* New York: Duell, Sloan and Pearce, 1943. 269 p. $2.50.

42. VICKERY, WILLIAM E., and COLE, STEWART G. *Intercultural Education in American Schools.* New York: Harper and Brothers, 1943. 214 p. $2.

CHAPTER V. EVERY CHILD A CITIZEN

43. ANDERSON, JOHN E. "The Development of Social Behavior." *American Journal of Sociology* 44: 839-57; May 1939.

44. ANDERSON, JOHN E. *Happy Childhood.* New York: D. Appleton-Century Co., 1933. 321 p. $2.50.

45. BARKER, ROGER G.; KOUNIN, JACOB S.; and WRIGHT, HERBERT F., editors. *Child Behavior and Development.* New York: McGraw-Hill Book Co., 1943. 652 p. $4.

46. BINGHAM, FLORENCE C., editor. *Community Life in a Democracy.* Chicago: National Congress of Parents and Teachers, 1942. 246 p. $1.

47. BURGESS, ERNEST W., and OTHERS. *Environment and Education.* Supplementary Educational Monographs, No. 54. Human Development Series, Vol. 1. Chicago: University of Chicago Press, 1942. 66 p. $1.

48. FOLSOM, JOSEPH K. *Youth, Family, and Education.* Prepared for the American Youth Commission. Washington, D. C.: American Council on Education, 1941. 299 p. $1.75.

49. JERSILD, ARTHUR T. *Child Psychology.* Revised and enlarged edition. New York: Prentice-Hall, 1940. 592 p. $3.

50. JERSILD, ARTHUR T., and MEIGS, MARGARET F. "Children and War." *Psychological Bulletin* 40: 541-73; October 1943.

51. JERSILD, ARTHUR T., chairman. "Growth and Development." *Review of Educational Research* 11: 475-618; December 1941.

52. MURPHY, LOIS B. *Social Behavior and Child Personality.* New York: Columbia University Press, 1937. 344 p. $3.50.

53. NATIONAL SOCIETY FOR THE STUDY OF EDUCATION. *Child Development and the Curriculum.* Thirty-Eighth Yearbook, Part I. Bloomington, Ill.: Public School Publishing Co., 1939. 442 p. $3.25.

54. NATIONAL SOCIETY FOR THE STUDY OF EDUCATION. *The Psychology of Learning.* Forty-First Yearbook, Part II. Bloomington, Ill.: Public School Publishing Co., 1942. 502 p. $3.25.

55. REMMERS, H. H., and GAGE, N. L. "The Family, Education, and Child Adjustment." *Review of Educational Research* 13: 21-28; February 1943.

56. U. S. DEPARTMENT OF LABOR, CHILDREN'S BUREAU. *Conference on Children in a Democracy; Papers and Discussions at the Initial Session, Held in Washington, D. C., April 26, 1939.* Bureau Publication No. 265. Washington, D. C.: Government Printing Office, 1939. 149 p. 20¢.

57. U. S. DEPARTMENT OF LABOR, CHILDREN'S BUREAU. *Proceedings of the White House Conference on Children in a Democracy, Washington, D. C., January 18-20, 1940, Including the General Report Adopted by the Conference.* Bureau Publication No. 266. Washington, D. C.: Government Printing Office, 1940. 221 p. 25¢.

58. U. S. DEPARTMENT OF LABOR, CHILDREN'S BUREAU. *White House Conference on Children in a Democracy, Washington, D. C., January 18-20, 1940: Final Report.* Bureau Publication No. 272. Washington, D. C.: Government Printing Office, 1942. 392 p. 65¢.

59. WASHBURN, RUTH W. *Children Have Their Reasons.* New York: D. Appleton-Century Co., 1942. 257 p. $2.

See also item 28.

CHAPTER VI. MORALE-BUILDING AGENCIES

60. AMERICAN ASSOCIATION OF SCHOOL ADMINISTRATORS. *Education for Family Life.* Nineteenth Yearbook. Washington, D. C.: the Association, a department of the National Education Association, 1941. 368 p. $2.

61. AMERICAN ASSOCIATION OF SCHOOL ADMINISTRATORS. *Schools and Manpower.* Twenty-First Yearbook. Washington, D. C.: the Association, a department of the National Education Association, 1943. 448 p. $2.

62. AMERICAN COUNCIL ON EDUCATION, AMERICAN YOUTH COMMISSION. *Community Responsibility for Youth.* Washington, D. C.: the Council, 1940. 12 p. (Out of print.)

63. AMERICAN LIBRARY ASSOCIATION. "Libraries and the War." *ALA Bulletin* 36: 3-10; January 1942.

64. BROUGHTON, PHILIP S. "Government Agencies and Civilian Morale." *Annals of the American Academy of Political and Social Science* 220: 168-77; March 1942.

65. KNICKERBOCKER, IRVING, and McGREGOR, DOUGLAS. *Union-Management Cooperation: A Psychological Analysis.* Cambridge, Mass.: Department of Economics and Social Science, Massachusetts Institute of Technology, 1943. 20 p. Reprinted from *Personnel*, Vol. 19, No. 3, by American Management Association, New York, N. Y.

66. NATIONAL EDUCATION ASSOCIATION and AMERICAN ASSOCIATION OF SCHOOL ADMINISTRATORS, EDUCATIONAL POLICIES COMMISSION. *Education and the Morale of a Free People.* Washington, D. C.: the Commission, 1941. 29 p. 10¢.

67. NATIONAL EDUCATION ASSOCIATION and AMERICAN ASSOCIATION OF SCHOOL ADMINISTRATORS, EDUCATIONAL POLICIES COMMISSION. *A War Policy for American Schools.* Washington, D. C.: the Commission, 1941. 47 p. 10¢.

68. National Education Association, Department of Superintendence. *Character Education.* Tenth Yearbook. Washington, D. C.: the Department, 1932. 536 p. (Out of print.)
See also item 11.

Chapter VII. The Individual School Builds Morale

69. Federal Security Agency, U. S. Office of Education. *Living Democracy in Secondary Schools.* Education and National Defense Series, Pamphlet No. 7. Washington, D. C.: Government Printing Office, 1941. 32 p. 15¢.

70. Federal Security Agency, U. S. Office of Education. *Practicing Democracy in the College.* Education and National Defense Series, Pamphlet No. 8. Washington, D. C.: Government Printing Office, 1942. 31 p. 20¢.

71. Federal Security Agency, U. S. Office of Education. *What Democracy Means in the Elementary School.* Education and National Defense Series, Pamphlet No. 6. Washington, D. C.: Government Printing Office, 1942. 35 p. 15¢.

72. Gambs, John S. "What Does It Mean to Be Socially Aware?" (Editorial.) *Childhood Education* 19: 51; October 1942.

73. Holbrook, Sabra. *Children Object.* New York: Viking Press, 1943. 197 p. $2.

74. Melby, Ernest O. "The Responsibility of Education in Wartime." *Frontiers of Democracy* 8: 176-77; March 15, 1942.

75. National Education Association and American Association of School Administrators, Educational Policies Commission. *Learning the Ways of Democracy.* Washington, D. C.: the Commission, 1940. 486 p. $1.

76. National Education Association, Department of Elementary School Principals. *Elementary Schools: the Frontline of Democracy.* Twenty-Second Yearbook. Washington, D. C.: the Department, 1943. 591 p. $2.

77. National Education Association, Department of Elementary School Principals. *In-Service Growth of School Personnel.* Twenty-First Yearbook. Washington, D. C.: the Department, 1942. 576 p. $2.

78. Peters, Charles C. *The Curriculum of Democratic Education.* New York: McGraw-Hill Book Co., 1942. 367 p. $2.75.

79. Russell, John D., and Jackson, T. Eldon. *America's Schools: Education in Democratic Citizenship.* Problems in American Life, Unit No. 16. Washington, D. C.: National Association of Secondary-School Principals and National Council for the Social Studies, departments of the National Education Association, 1943. 62 p. 30¢.

80. Studebaker, John W. "Morale Building in Our Schools." *Journal of the National Education Association* 31: 105-106; April 1942.
See also items 26 and 66.

Chapter VIII. The Individual Classroom Builds Morale

81. Bagley, William C. *The Educative Process.* New York: Macmillan Co., 1920. Part V, "The Selection of Experiences for Educational Purposes: Educational Values," p. 203-38.

82. BAGLEY, WILLIAM C., and HATCH, ROY W. "History and Citizenship." *The Classroom Teacher.* Chicago: Classroom Teacher, 1927. Vol. 5, p. 495-554.

83. BURKE, AGNES, and OTHERS. *A Conduct Curriculum for the Kindergarten and First Grade.* Series on Childhood Education. (Edited by Patty Smith Hill.) New York: Charles Scribner's Sons, 1923. 123 p.

84. CHASE, W. LINWOOD. *Wartime Social Studies in the Elementary School.* Curriculum Series, No. 3. Washington, D. C.: National Council for the Social Studies, a department of the National Education Association, 1943. 51 p. $1.

85. HATCH, ROY W. "Teaching Controversial Subjects in the Classroom." *Official Report, 1936.* Washington, D. C.: Department of Superintendence, National Education Association, 1936. p. 175-90.

86. HATCH, ROY W. *Training in Citizenship.* New York: Charles Scribner's Sons, 1926. 338 p. $1.60.

87. HUNT, ERLING M. *Wartime Social Studies in the Secondary School.* Curriculum Series, No. 4. Washington, D. C.: National Council for the Social Studies, a department of the National Education Association. (In press.) $1.

88. MOLOHON, BERNARD, compiler. *Voices of Democracy.* Federal Security Agency, U. S. Office of Education, Bulletin 1941, No. 8. Washington, D. C.: Government Printing Office, 1941. 84 p. 15¢.

89. NATIONAL COUNCIL FOR THE SOCIAL STUDIES. *The Social Studies Mobilize for Victory.* A Statement of Wartime Policy. Washington, D. C.: the Council, a department of the National Education Association, 1942. 16 p. 10¢.

90. NATIONAL EDUCATION ASSOCIATION. *The American Citizens Handbook.* Washington, D. C.: the Association, 1941. 366 p. $1.

91. NEW JERSEY STATE DEPARTMENT OF PUBLIC INSTRUCTION. *A Guide for Teaching Problems of American Democracy.* Trenton, N. J.: the Department, 1941. 342 p.

92. THORNDIKE, EDWARD L. "Education for Initiative and Originality." *Teachers College Record* 29: 89-100; November 1927.

93. U. S. DEPARTMENT OF THE INTERIOR, OFFICE OF EDUCATION. *Let Freedom Ring!* (Thirteen radio scripts.) Bulletin 1937, No. 32. Washington, D. C.: Government Printing Office, 1938. 379 p. 60¢. *Manual,* Bulletin 1937, No. 33. 83 p. 20¢.

See also item 75.

CHAPTER IX. MORALE OF TEACHERS

94. BEALE, HOWARD K. *A History of Freedom of Teaching in American Schools.* Report of the Commission on the Social Studies in the Schools, American Historical Association. New York: Charles Scribner's Sons, 1941. 343 p. $2.

95. BIGELOW, KARL W. "The Education of Teachers in a Democracy." *Educational Record* 19: 292-303; July 1938.

96. BURTON, WILLIAM H. "The Teacher's Morale as an Important Factor in Teaching Success." *California Journal of Elementary Education* 6: 218-26; May 1938.

97. CRALLE, ROBERT E., and BURTON, WILLIAM H. "An Examination of Factors Stimulating or Depressing Teacher Morale." *California Journal of Elementary Education* 7: 7-14; August 1938. (Companion to article by Burton published in same magazine in May 1938.)

98. ELSBREE, WILLARD S. *The American Teacher.* New York: American Book Co., 1939. 566 p. $2.75.

99. EVENDEN, E. S. *Teacher Education in a Democracy at War.* Prepared for the Commission on Teacher Education. Washington, D. C.: American Council on Education, 1942. 118 p. 75¢.

100. GIVENS, WILLARD E. "Our Profession Faces the Future." *Journal of the National Education Association* 32: 157-58; September 1943.

101. JOHN DEWEY SOCIETY. *Teachers for Democracy.* Fourth Yearbook. New York: D. Appleton-Century Co., 1940. 412 p. $2.50.

102. NATIONAL EDUCATION ASSOCIATION, DEPARTMENT OF CLASSROOM TEACHERS. *Teacher and Public.* Eighth Yearbook. Washington, D. C.: the Association, 1934. 240 p. $1.

103. NATIONAL EDUCATION ASSOCIATION, DEPARTMENT OF SUPERVISORS AND DIRECTORS OF INSTRUCTION. *Mental Health in the Classroom.* Thirteenth Yearbook. Washington, D. C.: the Department, 1940. 304 p. $2.

104. NATIONAL EDUCATION ASSOCIATION, RESEARCH DIVISION. "The Teacher Looks at Teacher Load." *Research Bulletin* 17: 223-74; November 1939.
See also item 77.

CHAPTER X. HUMAN RELATIONS IN SCHOOL ADMINISTRATION

105. BIMSON, OLIVER H. *Participation of School Personnel in Administration.* Lincoln, Nebr.: the Author (University of Nebraska), 1939. 118 p. $1.75.

106. JONES, WILLARD T. "Administrative Relationships to the Personnel." *Review of Educational Research* 10: 335-39, 386-87; October 1940.

107. KOOPMAN, GEORGE ROBERT; MIEL, ALICE; and MISNER, PAUL J. *Democracy in School Administration.* New York: D. Appleton-Century Co., 1943. 330 p. $2.25.

108. NATIONAL EDUCATION ASSOCIATION and AMERICAN ASSOCIATION OF SCHOOL ADMINISTRATORS, EDUCATIONAL POLICIES COMMISSION. *Learning the Ways of Democracy.* Washington, D. C.: the Commission, 1940. Chapter 6, "Administration," p. 331-77. ¶ See also: Carr, William G. "Efficiency thru Democratic Administration." *Journal of the National Education Association* 31: 83-84; March 1942.

109. NATIONAL EDUCATION ASSOCIATION, DEPARTMENT OF SUPERINTENDENCE. *Critical Problems in School Administration.* Twelfth Yearbook. Washington, D. C.: the Department, 1934. Chapter 7, "The Teaching Staff and the Formulation and Execution of Administrative Policies," p. 154-85.

110. NATIONAL EDUCATION ASSOCIATION, DEPARTMENT OF SUPERVISORS AND DIRECTORS OF INSTRUCTION. *Cooperation: Principles and Practices.* Eleventh Yearbook. Washington, D. C.: the Department, 1938. 244 p. $2.

111. NATIONAL EDUCATION ASSOCIATION, DEPARTMENT OF SUPERVISORS AND DIRECTORS OF INSTRUCTION. *Leadership at Work.* Fifteenth Yearbook. Washington, D. C.: the Department, 1943. 248 p. $2.
112. NATIONAL EDUCATION ASSOCIATION, RESEARCH DIVISION. "Teacher Personnel Procedures: Employment Conditions in Service." *Research Bulletin* 20: 83-116; May 1942.
113. NATIONAL EDUCATION ASSOCIATION, RESEARCH DIVISION. "Teacher Personnel Procedures: Selection and Appointment." *Research Bulletin* 20: 51-79; March 1942.
See also item 77.

CHAPTER XI. CHECKING UP ON PROGRESS

114. BOYD, GEORGE ROBERT. *The Construction of an Instrument for Measuring Attitudes toward Desirable Food Practices.* University of Kentucky, College of Education, Bulletin of the Bureau of School Service, Vol. 16, No. 1, September 1943. Lexington, Ky.: the University, 1943. "Survey of Literature Concerning Attitudes," p. 10-18.
115. BRIGGS, THOMAS H., and OTHERS. *The Emotionalized Attitudes.* New York: Teachers College, Columbia University, 1940. 107 p. $1.35.
116. CRONBACH, LEE J. *Exploring the Wartime Morale of High-School Youth.* American Association for Applied Psychology, Applied Psychology Monographs, No. 1. Stanford University, Calif.: Stanford University Press, 1943. 79 p. $1.25.
117. DURANT, HENRY. "Morale and Its Measurement." *American Journal of Sociology* 47: 406-14; November 1941.
118. JERSILD, ARTHUR T., and MEIGS, MARGARET F. "Direct Observation as a Research Method." *Review of Educational Research* 9: 472-82, 597-99; December 1939.
119. NATIONAL EDUCATION ASSOCIATION and AMERICAN ASSOCIATION OF SCHOOL ADMINISTRATORS, EDUCATIONAL POLICIES COMMISSION. *Learning the Ways of Democracy.* Washington, D. C.: the Commission, 1940. Chapter 7. "Evaluation of Outcomes," p. 379-433.
120. ROGERS, CARL R. *Counseling and Psychotherapy.* Boston: Houghton Mifflin Co., 1942. 450 p. $3.60.
121. SMITH, EUGENE R., and OTHERS. *Appraising and Recording Student Progress.* Progressive Education Association, Commission on the Relation of School and College. Adventure in American Education, Vol. 3. New York: Harper and Brothers, 1942. 550 p. $3.
See also items 11 and 23.

CHAPTER XII. "YEARS OF THE UNPERFORMED"

122. BROWN, J. F. "Morale for the American Dream." *New Republic* 106: 598-600; May 4, 1942.
123. CARR, WILLIAM G. *Education for World-Citizenship.* Stanford University, Calif.: Stanford University Press, 1928. 225 p. $1.

124. GALLOWAY, GEORGE B. *Postwar Planning in the United States.* New York: Twentieth Century Fund, 1942. 158 p. 60¢.

125. HUNTER, FREDERICK M. "Education for a Free People—The Essentials of a Permanent Morale." *Official Report, 1942.* Washington, D. C.: American Association of School Administrators, a department of the National Education Association, 1942. p. 22-29. Same condensed: *Nation's Schools* 29: 31-32; March 1942.

126. JOINT COMMISSION OF THE COUNCIL FOR EDUCATION IN WORLD CITIZENSHIP AND THE LONDON INTERNATIONAL ASSEMBLY. *Education and the United Nations.* Washington, D. C.: American Council on Public Affairs, 1943. 112 p. $1.

127. KALLEN, HORACE. "Toward the Four Freedoms." *Saturday Review of Literature* 25: 3-4, 14-15; May 23, 1942.

128. NATIONAL EDUCATION ASSOCIATION and AMERICAN ASSOCIATION OF SCHOOL ADMINISTRATORS, EDUCATIONAL POLICIES COMMISSION. *Education and the People's Peace.* Washington, D. C.: the Commission, 1943. 59 p. 10¢.

129. NATIONAL EDUCATION ASSOCIATION, RESEARCH DIVISION. "Organizations Interested in International Relations." *Research Bulletin* 17: 163-217; September 1939.

130. STANFORD UNIVERSITY, SCHOOL OF EDUCATION. *Education in Wartime and After.* New York: D. Appleton-Century Co., 1943. 465 p. $3.

131. STUDEBAKER, JOHN W. "As Beacon Lights." *School Life* 27: 97, 104; January 1942.

See also item 34.

OFFICIAL RECORDS

AMERICAN ASSOCIATION OF SCHOOL ADMINISTRATORS

A Department of the National Education Association
of the United States

Officers 1943-44

President

WORTH McCLURE, Superintendent of Schools, Seattle, Washington

First Vicepresident

HOMER W. ANDERSON, Acting Superintendent of Schools, Newton, Massachusetts

Second Vicepresident

W. FRANK WARREN, Superintendent of Schools, Durham, North Carolina

Executive Secretary

SHERWOOD D. SHANKLAND, 1201 Sixteenth Street, N. W., Washington 6, D. C.

Executive Committee

HENRY H. HILL, Superintendent of Schools, Pittsburgh, Pennsylvania

CHARLES H. LAKE, Superintendent of Schools, Cleveland, Ohio

W. HOWARD PILLSBURY, Superintendent of Schools, Schenectady, New York

JOHN L. BRACKEN, Superintendent of Schools, Clayton, Missouri

The President, First and Second Vicepresidents, ex officio

ANNUAL REPORT OF THE EXECUTIVE SECRETARY

To the President, Executive Committee, and Members:

IN ACCORDANCE with the provisions of the constitution adopted at the New Orleans convention in 1937, the annual report of the activities of the American Association of School Administrators is presented herewith. It covers the period from January 1, 1943 to December 31, 1943.

THE CONVENTION NEVER HELD

"The Role of the Nation's Schools in Winning the War and Earning the Peace" was the theme selected by President Homer W. Anderson for the seventy-third annual convention, scheduled for St. Louis, February 26-March 2, 1943. In planning the convention every effort was made to cooperate with national war agencies. Early in the fall, acting under advice from the Office of Defense Transportation, the Executive Committee adjusted the convention dates to avoid weekend travel and materially shortened the meeting period. An official statement was issued urging that attendance be confined to those whose presence and participation would be helpful to the war effort.

Shortly before Christmas, the Office of Defense Transportation began an energetic campaign to reduce passenger traffic on American railroads. H. F. McCarthy, director of the Division of Traffic Movement, called a series of conferences with the officers of our Association. The gist of these conferences was summarized in a letter in which the Office of Defense Transportation officially requested the cancellation of the St. Louis convention.

Upon receipt of this letter, a special meeting of the Executive Committee was called for Saturday, January 16, at which time the Committee prepared a letter to the Office of Defense Transportation, stating that in the opinion of the Executive Committee the St. Louis convention should be held and setting forth the reasons why those responsible for the conduct of the schools should meet for deliberation and counsel.

"The American Association of School Administrators," wrote the Executive Committee, "represents all the public schools of the United States and many institutions of higher learning, both private and

[329]

public, in which over 25,000,000 boys and girls are enrolled, who in turn are taught by nearly 1,000,000 teachers. It is the unique function of our convention to stimulate the planning, leadership, and united effort without which these vast human resources cannot be used to best advantage." Further the Executive Committee said, "It is our judgment—reached after hours of deliberation together and consultation with many other school leaders—that this meeting will advance the war effort."

All arguments were in vain. The Office of Defense Transportation advised that it could not concur in the decision of the Executive Committee to go forward with convention plans. Meanwhile the situation was further complicated by the announcement that the dates when the schools were to distribute War Ration Book No. 2 had been set to overlap the opening days of the convention, thus making it necessary for many school administrators to remain at home.

The cancellation of the St. Louis convention became inevitable. With extreme reluctance, announcement to this effect was made in a letter to members dated January 26, 1943.

The St. Louis convention had been designed to meet actual wartime needs. At the time when the convention was cancelled, plans for the general sessions, as well as for the discussion meetings, were practically complete. Nine ranking government officials and several representatives of the various United Nations had accepted speaking assignments. Altogether, it was an unusually significant and timely program, one of the best ever outlined for a winter meeting.

The exhibit at St. Louis had been fully organized and gave promise of even greater usefulness to convention attendants than in normal years. The participating exhibitors had planned to make their displays and organize their activities in such ways as to provide the maximum values under wartime conditions to their patrons and to themselves. On the day when cancellation was announced, space had been assigned to 186 firms and organizations. Some companies whose products no longer were manufactured, or thru scarcity were not readily marketable, had planned representation for the purpose of serving the administrators thru advice as to maintenance or substitution.

A special feature that promised valuable help to our members was an exhibit of federal government activities in which some eighteen different government units were to participate. This exhibit was planned in cooperation with the Office of War Information. In addition to displays showing the activities of these units, federal government representatives of the war effort agencies were to have been present, prepared to discuss specific problems with school officers.

To offset the loss of the convention, which for over seventy years has been an educational clearing-house toward which school administrators have looked forward with eagerness, two methods were adopted. First, a "Convention of the Air," featuring seventeen radio programs, was presented over the four major networks. Second, an *Official Report of the Convention Never Held* was printed. It included addresses prepared for delivery at the convention, official data, and significant wartime information gathered from many sources. And so, over the airways and in print, the convention message came at last to those who normally would have assembled in a convention hall to hear it.

THE EXECUTIVE COMMITTEE

Article IV of the constitution provides that the Executive Committee shall consist of seven members. The president and first and second vicepresidents are members ex officio and are elected annually. Four members chosen by election hold office for terms of four years.

In view of the transportation problem of the country due to the war emergency, a special meeting of the Executive Committee was held to determine whether or not to proceed with plans for the seventy-third annual convention of the American Association of School Administrators, scheduled for St. Louis, Missouri, February 26-March 2, 1943. The Committee met in Washington, D. C., on January 16, 1943, in the Board of Directors Room of the National Education Association. Members present were Homer W. Anderson, Washington, D. C., president; W. Howard Pillsbury, Schenectady, New York, first vicepresident; Charles H. Lake, Cleveland, Ohio, second vicepresident; William J. Hamilton, Oak Park, Illinois; and Henry H. Hill, Pittsburgh, Pennsylvania. Others in attendance were Executive Secretary Sherwood D. Shankland; Executive Secretary Willard E. Givens of the National Education Association; and Business Manager H. A. Allan.

There was presented and read to the meeting a letter from the Office of Defense Transportation requesting the cancellation of the

The Board of Tellers assisted by the headquarters staff count the primary ballots, November 13, 1943

—Photograph by National Education Association

St. Louis convention. After weighing the matter carefully, it was the conviction of the Executive Committee that the convention had been so planned as to contribute materially to the war effort and, on motion of Mr. Pillsbury, seconded by Mr. Hill, it was voted to draft a letter advising the Office of Defense Transportation to this effect. Four days later a reply was received from the ODT insisting upon the cancellation of the convention.

The executive secretary reported that the annual election had been held according to the constitution and bylaws and that the tellers had certified to the election of Worth McClure, superintendent of schools, Seattle, Washington, as president of the American Association of School Administrators for the year beginning March 15, 1943.

Attention was called to the vacancy on the Executive Committee occasioned by the election of Mr. McClure as president. On motion of Mr. Hamilton, seconded by Mr. Hill, it was voted to appoint W. Howard Pillsbury to fill the vacancy, his term of office to expire March 15, 1946.

The annual meeting of the Executive Committee was held at Hotel Cleveland, Cleveland, Ohio, April 18 and 19, 1943. Members present were Worth McClure, Seattle, Washington, president; Homer W. Anderson, Washington, D. C., first vicepresident; Charles H. Lake, Cleveland, Ohio, second vicepresident; William J. Hamilton, Oak Park, Illinois; Henry H. Hill, Pittsburgh, Pennsylvania; and W. Howard Pillsbury, Schenectady, New York. Executive Secretary Sherwood D. Shankland also was present.

The minutes of the meetings of the Executive Committee on September 19-20, 1942, and January 16, 1943, were read and approved.

In a letter dated February 13, Superintendent Stanley H. Rolfe, a member of the Executive Committee, stated that his doctor had ordered him to give up work. Accordingly, he had filed his application with the Board of Education of Newark, New Jersey, for disability retirement, effective March 1. The letter continued, "This will mean my resignation from the Executive Committee of the American Association of School Administrators, and you will construe this letter as my resignation." On motion of Mr. Anderson, seconded by Mr. Hamilton, Mr. Rolfe's resignation was accepted with keen regret.

Article IV of the bylaws of the Association provides, "All vacancies occurring in any office other than that of President shall be filled by the Executive Committee."

On motion of Mr. Hamilton, seconded by Mr. Hill, it was voted to appoint Superintendent Charles H. Lake of Cleveland, Ohio, to fill Mr. Rolfe's unexpired term of office, ending March 15, 1945.

Attention was called to the fact that, due to the cancellation of the St. Louis convention, no elections had been held to fill the offices of second vicepresident and member of the Executive Committee for the four-year term ending March 15, 1947. On motion of Mr. Anderson, seconded by Mr. Hamilton, Superintendent W. Frank Warren of Durham, North Carolina, was elected second vicepresident. His term of office will expire March 15, 1944. On motion of Mr. Hamilton, seconded by Mr. Anderson, Superintendent John L. Bracken of Clayton, Missouri, was elected a member of the Executive Committee for the four-year term.

The annual report of the executive secretary was presented in writing. It included the budget for the calendar year 1943. On motion of Mr. Lake, seconded by Mr. Hamilton, the report was received and the budget, as proposed, was adopted. The budget was summarized as follows:

Balance January 1, 1943	$17,710.47
Estimated receipts for 1943	37,300.00
Total to account for 1943	$55,010.47
Less estimated expenditures for 1943	46,151.84
Probable balance December 31, 1943	$ 8,858.63

A four-day meeting sponsored by the Council on Cooperation in Teacher Education was held in Chicago, Illinois, March 27-30. About a dozen national organizations were represented. The delegates of the American Association of School Administrators were Superintendents Henry H. Hill and William J. Hamilton. They reported that the conference afforded school administrators an excellent opportunity to see the problems of teacher education in the large, thus leading away from the handicaps which are frequently found in provincial thinking. It was reported that the next undertaking of the Council on Cooperation in Teacher Education would be a work conference on the campus of the University of Wisconsin, August 17-28. Each cooperating organization would be entitled to three representatives. On motion of Mr. Lake, seconded by Mr. Pillsbury, it was voted that the American Association of School Administrators should participate in this summer conference.

The executive secretary reported that Anna Haddow, chief of the Educational Research Service, had been granted leave of absence to accept a commission in the WAVES. He recommended the appointment of Mrs. Maxine Lindemood as acting chief of the Educational Research Service, with classification 3AA and a double increment. On motion of Mr. Hill, seconded by Mr. Hamilton, the recommendation was approved, the appointment to become effective June 1, 1943.

Past-President Homer W. Anderson announced that he had appointed four members of the Association to serve as a core committee to explore proposals for the 1945 yearbook. Those appointed were Superintendent William J. Hamilton, Oak Park, Illinois, *chairman;* Superintendent Willard E. Goslin, Webster Groves, Missouri; Dean Paul C. Packer, College of Education, State University of Iowa— on leave with the U. S. Army; and Professor Alfred D. Simpson, Graduate School of Education, Harvard University.

Superintendent Pillsbury gave a report of a recent meeting held in Washington of the Conference Committee of the American Association of School Administrators and the Committee on Education of the Chamber of Commerce of the United States. He mentioned four recommendations which were included in a report adopted at the meeting and later distributed in printed form to members of both organizations. They were:

1. The National Youth Administration should be discontinued. The use of its equipment should be transferred to local and state authorities, and operated under U. S. Office of Education direction.
2. Local public schools, chambers of commerce, employers, labor organizations, and civilian war service organizations should cooperate in providing employment or other practical application of special wartime training given in the high schools.
3. Support should be given to public school authorities by business organizations in bringing to the attention of the War Production Board the necessity of allocating sufficient materials for training war production workers, and for the regular day-school programs.
4. In the interest of economy and efficiency, it is considered advisable to establish area vocational schools in lieu of the development of many small, less effective units.

President McClure stated that the prospects of holding a national convention in February 1944 seemed to be remote. He proposed that serious consideration be given to a plan of regional conferences to be held during the coming fall and winter. On motion of Mr. Hill, seconded by Mr. Anderson, the proposed plan of holding regional conferences was approved in principle, and the president and executive secretary were given power to act.

The fall meeting of the Executive Committee was held at Hotel Cleveland, Cleveland, Ohio, October 17 and 18, 1943. Members present were W. Frank Warren, Durham, North Carolina, second vicepresident; Henry H. Hill, Pittsburgh, Pennsylvania; Charles H. Lake, Cleveland, Ohio; W. Howard Pillsbury, Schenectady, New York; and John L. Bracken, Clayton, Missouri. Executive Secretary Sherwood D. Shankland also was present.

It was reported that President Worth McClure was in Great Britain at the invitation of the U. S. Office of War Information, the British Board of Education, and the British Ministry of Information; and that First Vicepresident Homer W. Anderson was unavoidably detained on account of duties in his new position at Newton, Massachusetts.

The minutes of the meeting of the Executive Committee on April 18-19, 1943, were read and approved.

Attention was called to the fact that a vacancy existed in the membership of the 1945 Yearbook Commission. On motion of Mr. Hill, seconded by Mr. Bracken, it was voted to appoint Newton Edwards of the University of Chicago to fill this vacancy. Superintendent Willard E. Goslin of Webster Groves, Missouri, a member of the Commission, was elected chairman to succeed Superintendent William J. Hamilton, who resigned because of ill health.

It was reported that arrangements had been completed for holding five regional conferences. After extended discussion of plans for the conferences, it was agreed to delegate responsibility for the programs. The places, dates, and program chairmen are as follows:

SEATTLE, WASHINGTON—January 10-12, 1944—Worth McClure
ATLANTA, GEORGIA—February 15-17—Willis A. Sutton
NEW YORK, NEW YORK—February 22-24—W. Howard Pillsbury
CHICAGO, ILLINOIS—February 28-March 1—Charles H. Lake
KANSAS CITY, MISSOURI—March 8-10—Herold C. Hunt.

It has been customary to hold a meeting of the Executive Committee in connection with the winter convention. Such a meeting is impossible in February 1944 since the officers and members of the Committee will attend various conferences and a quorum will not be available at any one of them. Attention was called to the fact that on March 15, 1944, vacancies will occur in the offices of second vicepresident and member of the Executive Committee for the term ending March 15, 1948. On motion, Superintendent W. Frank Warren was reelected second vicepresident for the year ending March 15, 1945, and Superintendent Henry H. Hill was elected a member of the Executive Committee for the four-year term.

Past-President Milton C. Potter of Milwaukee, Wisconsin, and Superintendent William F. Shirley of Marshalltown, Iowa, represented the American Association of School Administrators at the conference held under the auspices of the Council on Cooperation in Teacher Education at the University of Wisconsin during the last two weeks in August. Their report to the Executive Committee was presented in writing. In brief, it suggested ways in which the Association can most helpfully carry on and implement the work of the Commission on Teacher Education. On motion of Mr. Hill, it was voted to continue cooperation with this project in such ways as may be feasible.

It was voted to present an honorary life membership in the American Association of School Administrators to Milton C. Potter at the Chicago regional conference. He retired as superintendent of the Milwaukee public schools on July 1, 1943, after twenty-nine years of service in that city. He was president of the Department of Superintendence in 1932-33.

A special joint meeting of the Executive Committees of the National Education Association and the American Association of School Administrators was held at the Hotel Statler, Cleveland, on Monday, October 18. All officers and members of the Executive Committee of the American Association of School Administrators were present, except President Worth McClure and First Vicepresident Homer W. Anderson. Members of the Executive Committee of the National Education Association who attended were Mrs. Edith B. Joynes, president; Leonard L. Bowman; A. C. Flora; Glenn E. Snow; B. F. Stanton; Emily A. Tarbell; and John W. Thalman. Executive Secretary Willard E. Givens also attended.

TABLE 1.—MEMBERSHIP BY STATES FOR THE YEARS 1938-1943
AMERICAN ASSOCIATION OF SCHOOL ADMINISTRATORS

formerly the Department of Superintendence

State	1938 Atlantic City	1939 Cleveland	1940 St. Louis	1941 Atlantic City	1942 San Francisco	1943 No convention
Alabama	52	55	66	61	50	48
Arizona	23	25	24	23	28	34
Arkansas	32	31	45	36	29	27
California	144	144	150	153	1,214	254
Colorado	51	48	59	60	62	57
Connecticut	81	76	71	92	67	57
Delaware	23	20	19	25	18	17
District of Columbia	64	69	71	66	67	65
Florida	22	22	17	21	20	24
Georgia	63	63	63	63	49	45
Idaho	12	9	8	10	12	13
Illinois	300	328	352	331	273	270
Indiana	103	106	114	101	96	95
Iowa	74	93	107	82	86	79
Kansas	86	98	115	95	82	76
Kentucky	51	58	56	49	39	35
Louisiana	51	52	47	43	37	36
Maine	27	27	22	23	20	17
Maryland	64	63	69	76	60	55
Massachusetts	190	169	161	174	138	150
Michigan	200	219	223	231	175	175
Minnesota	87	110	110	99	93	88
Mississippi	38	41	44	40	37	34
Missouri	146	139	184	140	128	119
Montana	16	15	13	15	20	22
Nebraska	43	46	57	48	45	41
Nevada	4	4	3	4	4	4
New Hampshire	32	28	30	37	25	25
New Jersey	277	249	234	287	212	206
New Mexico	20	22	29	18	23	19
New York	448	424	379	417	319	319
North Carolina	65	56	60	63	55	50
North Dakota	17	15	15	16	18	15
Ohio	230	266	261	251	187	175
Oklahoma	61	60	60	55	45	41
Oregon	15	21	25	29	38	27
Pennsylvania	345	353	334	401	279	274
Rhode Island	42	37	38	42	32	29
South Carolina	39	37	36	37	30	29
South Dakota	20	21	24	15	18	14
Tennessee	39	40	43	44	28	30
Texas	240	227	244	227	229	191
Utah	26	24	25	24	31	23
Vermont	28	27	26	24	22	21
Virginia	61	62	61	75	56	51
Washington	23	26	27	28	35	34
West Virginia	51	53	47	46	40	36
Wisconsin	128	136	131	129	106	102
Wyoming	12	13	14	13	13	11
Alaska	2	2	3	1		1
Argentina						1
Bahamas			1	1	1	
Canada	13	13	11	11	11	11
Canal Zone	2	1	1	2		
China	1	1				
Guam					1	
Hawaii	3	2	2	1	3	3
India		1	1			
Iraq	1	1		1		
Mexico	1		1		1	1
Philippine Islands	3	4	2	6	2	
Puerto Rico	6	6	4	8	5	4
Scotland		1				
Virgin Islands	1					
Total	4,299	4,359	4,439	4,470	4,814	3,680

NOTE: The count includes 3,498 members who paid dues for the year 1943, 11 honorary members, 169 life or twenty-five-year members, and 2 six-year members.

This joint meeting was held for the purpose of electing three new members of the Educational Policies Commission to fill the vacancies occurring on December 31, 1943, due to the expiration of the terms of the following members: Frederick M. Hunter, Chancellor, Oregon State System of Higher Education; John K. Norton, Teachers College, Columbia University; and Emily A. Tarbell, Syracuse, New York.

After discussing at length the problems facing the Educational Policies Commission, the areas of education not now adequately represented in the personnel of the Commission, and the qualifications desirable for membership on the Commission, the joint committees considered a carefully prepared list of 242 well-qualified individuals.

In order to secure representation from fields of education not at present represented in the membership of the Educational Policies Commission, it was agreed to elect one member only on each of three ballots. The ballots were cast as agreed upon and the following persons were elected to membership on the Educational Policies Commission for a period of one year beginning January 1, 1944: Prudence Cutright, acting superintendent of schools, Minneapolis, Minnesota; Paul T. Rankin, assistant superintendent of schools, Detroit, Michigan; and Maycie Southall, professor of elementary education, George Peabody College for Teachers, Nashville, Tennessee.

THE FINANCES

The Department closed the year 1943 with a balance in the regular fund of $9,011.04. The balance one year ago was $17,710.47. Two years ago it was $18,551.84. The principal source of revenue is the annual membership fee of five dollars. The Department enrolled 1,263 members in 1922; 4,013 in 1931; 3,110 in 1933, which was a depression year; and 4,814 in 1942, which was the year of the San Francisco convention. Due to the cancellation of the St. Louis convention, the membership dropped to 3,680 in 1943. The membership distribution by states for the last six years is shown in Table 1.

The income from the exhibits at the winter meeting has been another considerable source of revenue, which has been used in large part to pay convention expenses. At San Francisco in 1942, the net exhibit profit was $13,349.96. This item was entirely eliminated in

1943 due to the cancellation of the convention, but on the other hand there were no convention bills to pay.

The statement of receipts and expenditures on the opposite page covers the calendar year 1943. Receipts for 1942 amounted to $59,328.98 and in 1943 to only $37,883.03. In spite of rigid economy, the operating balance is now $8,699.43 less than it was a year ago.

THE AUDIT COMMITTEE

The books and accounts of the American Association of School Administrators are audited twice each year. In June, certified public accountants make a complete examination of the finances of the National Education Association, including all its departments. The constitution of the American Association of School Administrators also requires that a committee of three members of the Department shall audit the accounts at the close of each fiscal year. The constitution further provides that its fiscal year shall correspond with the calendar year.

The report of the Audit Committee for the year ended December 31, 1943, will be printed in full in the 1944 *Official Report*. The members of the Committee are Superintendent Jesse H. Binford, Richmond, Virginia, *chairman;* Superintendent Ray E. Cheney, Elizabeth, New Jersey; and Superintendent Evan E. Jones, Port Chester, New York.

PERMANENT EDUCATIONAL RESEARCH FUND

At the Boston convention in 1928, it was voted to appoint a committee to make plans for creating a permanent fund that should yield an annual income sufficient to finance important studies in education on a nationwide basis. Money was plentiful in those days and the committee set its goal at $1,000,000. Just as the campaign was getting under way, the depression caused its postponement. Conditions since then have not warranted resumption of a money-raising campaign.

For a time the Fund was gradually built up thru the generosity of a number of interested members. Some of them took out ten-year endowment insurance policies in the amount of $250 each; others took out $100 life memberships or raised substantial sums as direct contributions. The last of the insurance policies matured in 1941. At present, the only increments come from life memberships. During the calendar year 1943, receipts from this source amounted to $280. The total is now $31,919.55.

RECEIPTS AND EXPENDITURES, 1943

REGULAR RECEIPTS DURING CALENDAR YEAR 1943

Annual dues, 3,078 members, 1943	$15,390.00	
Annual dues, 430 members, 1944	2,150.00	
Interest—Permanent Research Fund	1,180.79	
Yearbooks sold	5,816.95	
Educational Research Service	13,145.93	
Other income	199.36	
Total receipts		$37,883.03
Balance, January 1, 1943		17,710.47
Grand total		**$55,593.50**

REGULAR EXPENDITURES DURING CALENDAR YEAR 1943

Salaries, administrative unit	$9,990.16	
Printing 9½M Twenty-First Yearbooks	7,281.10	
Printing 5M Official Reports	2,035.55	
Printing Research Bulletins, 4 issues	531.74	
Other printing	1,509.27	
Postage, express, and stationery	4,998.29	
Mimeographing, multigraphing, typing, etc.	1,115.00	
Telephone and telegraph	183.34	
President's expense	197.60	
Secretary's expense	572.83	
Executive Committee expense	1,588.97	
Audit Committee	61.84	
Board of Tellers	177.84	
1944 Yearbook Commission	2,135.34	
1945 Yearbook Commission	1,064.90	
Bad debts and worthless checks	90.20	
Educational Research Service, salaries	6,341.90	
Educational Research Service, miscellaneous	3,633.34	
Retirement fund	816.03	
Supplies and equipment	137.22	
Surety bonds	20.00	
Educational Policies Commission	2,000.00	
American Council on Education	100.00	
Total general expense		$46,582.46
Balance, December 31, 1943		9,011.04
Grand total		**$55,593.50**

The Board of Trustees of the National Education Association reports assets in the investment account to the credit of the Permanent Educational Research Fund on December 31, 1943, as follows:

	Par Value	Book Value
U. S. Treasury Savings Bonds due 1946	$3,000.00	$2,250.00
U. S. Treasury 3¼% Bonds due 1944-46	150.00	150.00
U. 'S. Treasury 2⅞% Bonds due 1955-60	150.00	150.00
U. S. Treasury 2¾% Bonds due 1956-59	3,000.00	3,092.28
South Carolina Highway Certificate of Indebtedness 4¾% due 1946	2,000.00	2,077.28
Newport News City Street Improvement and Sewerage Construction Bonds 5½% due 1950	11,000.00	11,285.00
Portsmouth, Virginia, Waterworks Bonds 5% due 1948	3,000.00	3,160.51
Port of New York Authority 3% Bonds due 1976	2,000.00	2,017.50
City of New York Corporate Stock 3% due 1980	500.00	498.75
U. S. Treasury Defense Bonds, Series G, due December 1953	6,000.00	6,000.00
U. S. Treasury Defense Bond, Series G, due November 1954	500.00	500.00
U. S. War Savings Bonds, Series G, due September 1955	400.00	400.00
Cash on hand		338.23
Total		$31,919.55

THE EDUCATIONAL RESEARCH SERVICE

Since its inception twenty years ago the Educational Research Service has shown a gradual and steady growth. In the past year, however, the valuable services rendered by this organization have become even more apparent as indicated in Table 2. The number of subscribers has increased from 489 members in 1942 to 558 members in 1943.

This clearing-house of research on school administration, which the American Association of School Administrators and the Research Division of the National Education Association maintain cooperatively, is supported on a subscription basis, with an annual fee of $25. Altho intended more directly to meet the needs of city-school systems, the Service includes in its list of 558 members state departments of education, colleges and universities, and other agencies.

One of the most important functions of the Educational Research Service is to furnish up-to-the-minute information on request from

TABLE 2.—EDUCATIONAL RESEARCH SERVICE SUBSCRIBERS AND INCOME FROM SUBSCRIPTIONS

Year	Number of subscribers	Cash receipts from subscribers
1	2	3
1924.	40	$ 525.00
1925.	131	2,555.00
1926.	177	3,325.00
1927.	213	5,790.00
1928.	245	6,225.00
1929.	271	6,362.00
1930.	323	8,112.50
1931.	338	8,100.00
1932.	324	7,443.75
1933.	319	7,514.58
1934.	346	8,496.75
1935.	359	8,714.56
1936.	369	9,254.17
1937.	408	9,887.82
1938.	445	10,800.44
1939.	445	10,460.42
1940.	468	11,662.50
1941.	483	11,888.75
1942.	489	11,968.75
1943.	558	13,145.93

its subscribers. Bibliographies, memorandums, and tabulations are prepared as occasion requires. Representatives of the Educational Research Service are constantly alert to activities of various governmental agencies. The staff has access to facilities of the many splendid libraries in the nation's capital.

During the past year many questions on salaries of school employees have been answered in the special reports sent to subscribers to the Educational Research Service. These reports present the detailed findings from the biennial salary study made by the Research Division of the National Education Association. The school official who has at hand the 1942-43 *Special Salary Tabulations* can compare the median salaries paid to various groups of employees in his system with those paid in cities of comparable size. Three of the Educational Research Service *Circulars,* prepared especially for subscribers, give an analysis of the basic salary schedule provisions for classroom teachers in cities above 30,000 in population and for principals in regular day schools and special schools in the large cities.

Other *Circulars* of particular significance issued during 1943 include a report on activities of public schools in the war effort and a bibliography of questionnaire studies. A review of articles on education in noneducational magazines has been issued every three months in an abstract entitled "Education in Lay Magazines."

The Service, in addition to making studies of its own, sends subscribers selected publications of the various departments of the National Education Association and of outside agencies. The materials furnished during 1943 cover such pertinent topics as schools and current economic trends; federal legislative events; education and manpower; social security and teachers; tenure policies; expenditures per pupil; education and the people's peace; wartime vocational training; gearing secondary schools for victory; and plans, proposals, and discussions of issues in education and their effect on the world of today and tomorrow.

PUBLICATIONS

In my report a year ago, it was pointed out that two major ways in which a national association such as ours can serve its members are by the spoken word at conventions and by the printed word prepared to meet the current needs of its members. The cancellation of the St. Louis convention deprived school administrators of the "spoken word" during 1943. We have had to depend on the "printed word"—form letters and publications.

Schools and Manpower, the 1943 yearbook, was completed and distributed in February. This volume emphasizes the necessity of finding the real abilities of youth, developing them fully, and then putting young people in the place of greatest usefulness. It has proved valuable to school administrators, counselors, and teachers.

The *Official Report of the Convention Never Held* came from the press at the time when the official convention report usually is issued. Four issues of the *Research Bulletin* were sent to members during the year. Their titles were "Salaries of City School Employees, 1942-43"; "The Nation's Schools after a Year of War"; "High-School Methods with Slow Learners"; and "Teachers' Salaries and the Public Welfare."

Members also received the *Classified List of Educational Periodicals,* two editions of the Radio Calendar, and the *Wartime Handbook for Education* which was prepared cooperatively by seventeen departments and divisions of the National Education Association.

We have learned from our own personal reactions that mimeographed form letters, no matter how well written, are too often deposited in the wastebasket before they are read. Late in 1943, we printed the first edition of a little two-page newspaper-style bulletin which we named *The School Administrator.* Comments have been favorable and we plan to continue this bulletin at irregular intervals as long as the WPB will allot us the paper on which to print it.

Morale was a popular word during the first World War. When peace came, it was put away and forgotten like a used army uniform. At the San Francisco convention in February 1942, with Pearl Harbor still fresh in mind, President W. Howard Pillsbury built much of his convention program around ways of morale building. This 1944 yearbook was a direct outcome of the San Francisco convention. The commission to conduct the study was appointed by President Pillsbury immediately after the convention. In its membership a variety of educational experience was represented. Manuscripts were subjected to critical examination by the entire commission at four meetings, each covering a period of three days.

Lessons of the war will be considered in the 1945 yearbook which is in course of preparation by a commission consisting of Willard E. Goslin, superintendent of schools, Webster Groves, Missouri, *chairman;* L. Frazer Banks, superintendent of schools, Birmingham, Alabama; Newton Edwards, University of Chicago; Philip H. Falk, superintendent of schools, Madison, Wisconsin; Alonzo G. Grace, state commissioner of education, Hartford, Connecticut; Emerson H. Landis, superintendent of schools, Dayton, Ohio; Edward Landy, director of research and guidance, Public Schools, Montclair, New Jersey; Jay B. Nash, New York University; E. T. Peterson, State University of Iowa; and Alfred D. Simpson, Harvard University.

TABLE 3.—YEARBOOKS OF THE DEPARTMENT

Year	Title	Number copies printed	Cash sales of all yearbooks for the year
1923	The Status of the Superintendent	3,200	$ 142.45
1924	The Elementary School Curriculum	4,500	1,364.13
1925	Research in Constructing the Elementary School Curriculum	11,000	4,707.65
1926	The Nation at Work on the Public School Curriculum	12,000	8,467.94
1927	The Junior High School Curriculum	11,000	8,844.57
1928	The Development of the High School Curriculum	10,000	9,830.58
1929	The Articulation of the Units of American Education	11,000	7,842.51
1929	Reprint of 1926 Yearbook	4,000	
1930	The Superintendent Surveys Supervision	11,348	10,603.43
1931	Five Unifying Factors in American Education	11,572	8,375.87
1932	Character Education	12,000	10,053.94
1933	Educational Leadership	8,000	4,922.85
1934	Critical Problems in School Administration	7,000	5,021.13
1935	Social Change and Education	9,000	7,844.99
1936	The Social Studies Curriculum	14,000	9,128.17
1937	Improvement of Education: Its Interpretation for Democracy	9,000	6,965.99
1938	Youth Education Today	11,000	6,789.56
1939	Schools in Small Communities	9,000	5,483.96
1940	Safety Education	11,000	8,894.92
1941	Education for Family Life	9,000	7,411.29
1942	Health in Schools	12,000	9,563.43
1943	Schools and Manpower	9,500	5,816.95

EDUCATIONAL POLICIES COMMISSION

EDUCATIONAL POLICIES COMMISSION

The Educational Policies Commission is composed of twenty members selected solely on the basis of ability to contribute significantly to the solution of problems confronting education in the United States. Aided by a special grant from the NEA War and Peace Fund, the Educational Policies Commission plans to make the year 1944 outstanding in its entire history. A seven-point program has been adopted to include:

1. Efforts to secure a voice for education in the peace.
2. Publication of a substantial volume describing in concrete terms two postwar secondary schools—one in a rural area and one in a large city.
3. A report on modern teaching and curriculum.
4. Meeting the problem of juvenile delinquency.
5. Educational services for children below the first grade.
6. State and federal relations in education.
7. A proposed constitution for American education.

PROFESSIONAL WARTIME ACTIVITIES

In a seven-story, debt-free, brick building on Sixteenth Street, five blocks from the White House lawn, the National Education Association has its headquarters. Life memberships paid the mortgage. Here, at 8:15 o'clock every weekday morning, over two hundred workers report for duty. In peacetimes there were fifty more, who now are in the armed forces, the WAVES, the WACS, the Red Cross, and the government services. Replacements are well-nigh impossible.

In addition to the parent Association, nine departments maintain permanent staffs at 1201 Sixteenth Street. Relationships are cordial. Cooperation and mutual understanding do much toward increasing the efficiency of individual units. The NEA War and Peace Fund campaign was an inspiring example of what can be accomplished by united effort.

In February 1943, it became apparent that there would not be sufficient income from memberships to enable the National Education Association to meet the demands made upon it for assistance and leadership. Accordingly, it was voted to conduct an intensive campaign to help raise funds to carry on the Association's war and peace program. Plans were vigorously prosecuted by a special committee headed by George D. Strayer. In a series of ten regional conferences, to which educational leaders from every state in the Union were invited, the profession was awakened to the crisis in education. The response was prompt and generous. Quotas were exceeded by twenty-one states before December 1. One-third of the money goes to the state associations and two-thirds to the national Association. Department staffs materially aided the campaign, which may well mark a turning point in the advancement of education in the United States.

In the field of federal relations and legislation, there has been unusual activity. Among the agencies with which the NEA headquarters staff maintains contact are Selective Service, Bureau of Internal Revenue, War Production Board, State Department, Navy Department, War Department, Children's Bureau, War Manpower Commission, Pan American Union, Federal Works Agency, National War Labor Board, Office of Defense Transportation, Office of Price Administration, and the Coordinator of International Affairs. Close relations exist with the Office of Education.

As the year draws to a close, President Worth McClure is in Great Britain, working on problems which are common to the schools of the United Kingdom and of the United States. He was selected for this important mission by the U. S. Office of War Information, upon invitation of the British Board of Education and the British Ministry of Information. After his arrival in England, warm greetings were exchanged on behalf of British and American educators. Because of their permanent historical value, they are here reproduced in full. President McClure's message to the teachers and school administrators of the United Kingdom, delivered on November 15, was as follows:

> "American teachers have been thrilled by the magnificent devotion of British teachers to childhood and youth and the steadfastness with which your profession has held the front line trenches of democratic education during its darkest hours. To express this thought on behalf of the National Education Association of the United States, the Educational Policies Commission, and the American Association of School Administrators is the very first assignment with which I am charged as I begin my visit for the purpose of studying with you those problems which are common to the schools of the United Kingdom and of the United States of America.

"I hope to carry back to the teachers of America an account of your educational adjustments to the war conditions. We have been engaged in developing a great program of universal education. We believe in it firmly but we have met many problems upon which we should like to compare notes with you. We feel we have much to learn from your war-sharpened thinking and much to gain from your experience. I hope to visit many types of British schools and to engage in discussions in which an exchange of information and ideas will be mutually helpful and effective in winning the war and the peace.

"After victory, the normal stream of cultural progress, released from the strictures of war, must be made to flow again. Educational opportunity must be restored among the devastated nations. Somehow in enemy countries a new generation, emancipated from false doctrines, must learn to recognize those principles of justice and tolerance and respect for individual human beings which constitute a common denominator for all liberty-loving people. Let us hope that our working together in accomplishing these tasks will lay the foundations for an exchange of mutual understanding, beginning among the English speaking peoples, which will extend as a mighty bulwark for permanent peace among all the peoples of the world."

In a special broadcast to America two days later, Sir Frederick Mander, the general secretary of the National Union of Teachers, replied in the following terms:

"A few days ago I had a long and interesting talk with Dr. Worth McClure, who is representing you over here on a special mission. He handed me a message of goodwill from the NEA to the teachers of the United Kingdom. I can assure you they will deeply appreciate your greeting and your generous tribute to the steadfastness with which they have held the front line trenches of democratic education during its darkest hours. It's a real joy to send you a message in return from the teachers on this side.

"Certainly, we have been through thrilling times. Our children with their teachers have been scattered to the four corners of the land, and a thousand new problems have been thrown up to us. But difficulty has been turned into opportunity. Ingenuity and good humour have pulled us through. The children are in good health and high spirits, and we are all looking hopefully to the future. Never for a single moment has belief in our destiny faltered. May I give you just one little picture?

"On May 11, 1941, London received its worst and most cruel battering from the skies. On the evening of the 12th I stood on the roof of one of London's great hotels. In the gathering dusk I could see fires still smouldering in the City, sad witness to last night's barbarity. The Rest Centres were crowded with homeless people. In them the teachers of London had been working for twenty-four hours, and the time had come for some of them to stand off. But they didn't go home to bed—not they! A thousand of them made their way to Westminster to hear the Education Minister and myself lay out a programme for a better educational future for the children. It was, indeed, a grand demonstration of faith in survival. But it was just typical of the teachers of this country, even when we stood alone against the might of Germany.

"And that faith has been justified. To-day we are no longer alone. We are proud to hail you as comrades in arms. Russia and China are also with us, and in a score of countries teachers are awaiting the hour of liberation, when they can be with us too.

"We send you our warmest greetings. We shall look forward to an early and happy reunion, when together we can dedicate ourselves anew to those great tasks which assuredly will be ours in the rebuilding of a peaceful world."

THE OUTLOOK IN SCHOOL ADMINISTRATION

Twenty-one years ago the Department of Superintendence issued its first yearbook. It was entitled *The Status of the Superintendent*, and was the outcome of a three-year study by a committee of which Dean Charles E. Chadsey of the University of Illinois was chairman.

At that time the typical city superintendent of schools was a married man between 38 and 49 years of age, with three children in his family. The middle 50 percent had from 7.8 to 9.4 years of education beyond the eighth grade. Educational experience ranged from fourteen to twenty-six years. Most of them had about five years' experience as classroom teachers and from four to ten years as principal of elementary, secondary, or normal schools.

In 1923 the salaries of city superintendents ranged from $1000 to $12,000. The middle 50 percent received from $2876 to $4050. Their living expenses varied from $1890 to $3046. It was stated that forty-eight percent of the superintendents owned automobiles. Most of them took two daily papers, four professional magazines, and three other periodicals. The superintendent of 1923 was usually a member of seven professional, civic, and fraternal organizations, and was an officer in three of them.

The functions in which superintendents most frequently participated were the appointment, transfer, and dismissal of teachers and principals; selection of textbooks and instructional supplies; determination of curriculum content; supervision of classroom instruction; preparation of the budget; and inauguration of new policies.

In the light of the facts revealed by the study, the committee recommended a larger amount of professional training on the part of the superintendent of schools, including from one to three years of specialized graduate work; an increase in the general level of salaries in order to attract capable men to the profession, as well as to justify the requirement of additional professional preparation; longer periods of tenure; selection based on personal character, administrative skill, and superior training. The report made plain that if the superintendent of schools is to be held responsible for results, he must be recognized as the chief executive officer of the board of education.

Ten years later, progress in school administration was reported in another yearbook prepared by a commission of which Alexander J. Stoddard was chairman. The 1933 yearbook was more voluminous than its predecessor and was well authenticated by painstaking research. It contained 132 tables with statistics on a wide range of topics covering everything from salaries to foreign places visited by superintendents of schools.

Again the typical city-school superintendent is described. The median age ranged downward gradually from 55 years in the larger cities to 37 years in communities of less than 2500 population. Significant advances in the amount of graduate study were reported.

Sixty percent of the superintendents in 1933 had the master's degree or higher, as against 35 percent in 1923. There was a marked increase in attendance at summer schools.

In the decade the median salary had advanced $798, or 24 percent, while living expenses had increased $577. The typical superintendent spent $386 per year for recreation and personal improvement and saved $838. He supported a wife and two children; owned a home; read three newspapers, five professional magazines, and four popular magazines—with *The Literary Digest,* which is no longer published, leading the list. He belonged to a service club and to at least one other civic group. Nine out of ten superintendents attended the convention of the state teachers association, and five out of ten went to the winter meeting of the Department of Superintendence.

The study disclosed that the city superintendent in 1933 gave much of his time to initiating action, delegating the actual execution to others, and then "following thru." In large cities his functions were largely concerned with personnel, and in small communities with classroom supervision. Routine administrative duties had a relatively smaller place. Nevertheless, the commission issued a sharp warning that business matters may easily absorb most of the superintendent's time and that his services are worth more to the schools as an educator than as a bookkeeper. The solution is to employ a competent secretary to whom clerical details can be delegated. The board of education cannot afford to pay the salary of an educator for the service of a clerk.

Handicaps to successful school administration were carefully tabulated and discussed in this yearbook. Some superintendents had too much authority and some too little. In many places relationships with the board of education were unsettled. The superintendent should have adequate authority and bear adequate responsibility. No superintendent should usurp the function of his board of education, nor should the board of education usurp the professional function of the superintendent. The commission's own attitude is summed up in a quotation from Henry Suzzallo: "Every democratic citizen's life is a chain of moments in some of which he initiates and leads and in some of which he appreciates and follows."

In a series of tributes, the 1933 yearbook presented interesting glimpses of the lives and work of ten men and women of the past who helped to make our nation great thru leadership in education. The list represented the consensus of fifty experts in various fields of education. Those chosen were William T. Harris, Thomas H. Gallaudet, Horace Mann, Emma Hart Willard, Henry Barnard, Francis W. Parker, James M. Greenwood, Booker T. Washington, William H. Maxwell, and Charles W. Eliot.

We are being told that more attention should be given to history. Test your knowledge of the history of education by writing a five-line summary of the major contribution made by each of these great leaders. Now take the 1933 yearbook off the shelf and check your answers.

It was the original plan to survey again the progress and possibilities of educational leadership at the end of another ten-year period, but war compelled consideration of more pressing problems. There are, however, certain definite trends which are worth noting. They have been gleaned thru participation in many conferences, attendance at educational meetings, and perusal of current lay and professional periodicals. They are submitted for consideration, not as facts gathered by painstaking research, but only as the observations of one individual.

First, the school administrator must learn what is essential and what is nonessential. His sense of values must be reappraised in the light of present conditions. Many agencies seek to use the schools. Faced with a multiplicity of well-meaning demands from many governmental agencies, as well as from welfare and patriotic organizations, school authorities must so coordinate these activities as to safeguard the essential interests of children and youth. To ill-advised requests, however well meant, the answer must be, "No."

Whenever practicable, the wartime activities of the schools should be used to advance the educational process. Wise teachers can turn to advantage the opportunities provided by salvage campaigns, Red Cross drives, sales of war savings stamps and bonds, air-raid precautions, rationing demands, first-aid courses, victory gardens, making of model aircraft, and canning of food products. Thus, the schools may be enrolled among the citadels of democracy without unduly sacrificing regular work in the classrooms.

The nation needs a reawakening in the field of character education. Education without character is dangerous. In wartime it is easy to neglect life-time values which must be built up by painstaking effort from early childhood. Character development is an around-the-clock process. The school has the child for about thirty hours a week from September to June. Out-of-school hours and days, altho a matter of deep concern, are beyond its jurisdiction. It is, however, in a position to coordinate and encourage programs designed to promote character development and good citizenship centered in homes, churches, and lay organizations concerned with the spiritual, moral, and recreational life of children. At least one objective should be to develop in youth a great purpose in life, worthy of free men and women in American democracy.

To meet the needs of our times, revision of the curriculum is necessary. New conditions make new demands. Some things which were once considered of importance must give place to instructional materials keyed to current needs. Specifically, the presentday curriculum is expected to provide, among other things, for improved health teaching, more emphasis on physical fitness, plans for work experience, consideration of the impact of new discoveries and inventions such as the airplane and the radio, study of world civilizations, provision for terminal vocational courses, expansion of guidance services, occupational adjustments, consumer education, preparation for family life, renewed emphasis on the teaching of geography and American history; all these, without abandoning any time-honored essential services. Perhaps the time is at hand for another national commission on the curriculum.

Many of our best teachers and younger school administrators are now serving in the armed forces or working in war industries. Retired teachers, married women, and persons with substandard qualifications have been recruited to staff the schools. Thousands of schools in rural communities are closed. Meanwhile, juvenile delinquency, exploitation of child labor, the breakdown of homes due to the absence of working mothers, and the plight of "latch-key children" are renewed challenges to educational leadership, even tho the causes for such conditions lie for the most part outside the schools. Solutions are not easy, but the best efforts of all concerned must be enlisted to alleviate conditions.

The services which the public is now demanding of the schools will cost money. The test of the sincerity of those who make demands is the ability and willingness to pay the bills. A report of the Educational Policies Commission, entitled *Education and Economic Well-Being,* offers abundant evidence that education contributes materially to our economic well-being and that with a hugely expanded national income, it is fiscally practical to pay for it. Investment in education is one means of preventing inflation.

Danger lies in the tendency of the federal government to filter funds thru noneducational federal agencies, such as the Federal Works Agency. More than a score of federal agencies have active and well-financed programs of education for which the cooperation of state and local school officers is urged and sometimes demanded, regardless of the relative importance of the proposed programs. In place of this haphazard system, it should be the policy of the federal government to provide that all requests which are made on the schools should be routed thru the Office of Education. Thus, much conflict and misunderstanding will be eliminated. Another phase of the same issue is concisely summed up in a statement by the Educational Policies Commission: "When educational needs arise which affect the national welfare, cut across the bounds of states, and are beyond the unaided powers of states to meet, the federal government should move to meet these needs. It should not, however, itself operate and control educational programs. Rather it should work through the state and local educational systems and strengthen these established agencies by supplying leadership and financial aid without control." [1]

Finally, school administrators are charged with the responsibility of building and maintaining morale. Morale for an individual has been defined as a state of mind characterized by confidence and courage. It is deeply rooted in a healthy body, a sound mentality, and a dauntless spirit.

Morale for a group exists wherever people have confidence in leadership, faith in each other, and loyalty to a common cause. In the creation of such morale, the school has a unique opportunity. Its influence extends beyond the millions of children, youth, and adults whom it touches directly, to other millions of parents and their neighbors with whom it has indirect contacts. In the plastic

---

[1] National Education Association and American Association of School Administrators, Educational Policies Commission. *The Civilian Conservation Corps, the National Youth Administration, and the Public Schools.* Washington, D. C.: the Commission, 1941. p. 78.

years of childhood are formed the habits and attitudes for future years. Every classroom is a compact unit where, by example as well as by precept, the essentials of morale suitable for group living among a free people can be put into daily practice. The classroom teacher cannot do his part without the sympathetic cooperation of the principal. Above all, there must be clear-cut, courageous leadership at the central office. The influence of a capable superintendent will make itself felt in a helpful way thruout the school system. Only the ablest and best should be called to high posts in school administration.

Respectfully submitted,

Sherwood D. Shankland

Executive Secretary

December 31, 1943

Acknowledgments

The Yearbook Commission is indebted to a number of publishers for permission to quote copyrighted materials from books and periodicals. Footnote citations in each case identify the source of these quotations.

Assistance was received from various federal agencies in Washington in assembling source materials for the preparation of Chapter XI. Several members of the Society for the Psychological Study of Social Issues also gave helpful suggestions in connection with this chapter.

Curriculum materials and photographs were made available for examination and use by a number of local school systems. Grateful acknowledgment is given for this help and particularly for the use of photographs from the public schools of Denver, Colorado; Detroit, Michigan; Fordson School District, Dearborn, Michigan; Long Beach, California; Newark, New Jersey; New York, New York (thru the courtesy of David Rosenfeld); Rochester, New York; St. Louis, Missouri; and San Bernardino, California.

LIST OF MEMBERS

The American Association of School Administrators

A Department of the

National Education Association of the United States

Corrected to December 11, 1943

(*) indicates the Life Members of the Department

A

Aaker, S. O., B.A.'24, St. Olaf Col.; Supt. of Sch., Rushford, Minn.

Aaron, Sadie, B.A.'25, Stanford Univ.; M.A.'29, Tchrs. Col., Columbia Univ.; Psychologist, Pub. Sch., Houston, Texas, since 1929.

Abbett, Merle J., A.B.'07, Franklin Col.; A.M.'18, Tchrs. Col., Columbia Univ.; Supt. of Sch., Admin. Bldg., Ft. Wayne, Ind., since 1932.

Abbott, A. D., Supt. of Sch., Littleton, Colo., since 1943.

Abbott, Pansy Jewett, M.A.'31, Stanford Univ.; Co. Supt. of Sch., Redwood City, Calif., since 1925.

Abbott, Warren W., Supt. of Sch., Keego Harbor, Mich.

Abell, J. A., A.B.'10, A.M.'14, Ind. Univ.; Supt. of Sch., Nappanee, Ind., since 1923.

Abernethy, Robert R., Diploma '15, Keystone State Normal Sch., Kutztown, Pa.; B.S.'23, Muhlenberg Col.; M.A.'25, Univ. of Pa.; Supt., Haverford Twp. H. S., Llanerck, Upper Darby, Pa.

Abraham, Harry G., B.A.'20, North Central Col.; M.A.'29, Univ. of Chicago; Supt. of Sch., Woodstock, Ill., since 1943.

Ackley, E. L., A.B. and A.M.'05, Pd.B.'08, Syracuse Univ.; Supt. of Sch., Johnstown, N. Y., since 1910.

Adams, Edwin W., B.S.'14, Temple Univ.; M.A.'22, Univ. of Pa.; Ed.D.'28, Temple Univ.; Assoc. Supt. of Sch., Philadelphia, Pa., since 1930.

Adams, Henry L., B.S.'20, Colgate Univ.; M.A.'26, Pa. State Col.; Supt. of Sch., Seymour, Conn., since 1937.

Adams, Karl Langdon, Diploma in C.E.'08, B.S.'09, Ohio Univ.; M.A.'29, Tchrs. Col., Columbia Univ.; Pres., Northern Ill. State Tchrs. Col., De Kalb, Ill., since 1929.

Adams, Mary A., B.S.'25, M.A.'30, Johns Hopkins Univ.; Asst. Supt. of Sch., 3 E. 25th St., Baltimore 18, Md., since 1942.

Adams, Ray H., A.B.'27, M.A.'28, Univ. of Mich.; Supt. of Sch., Dearborn, Mich., since 1916.

Adams, Ruby M., B.S.'25, M.A.'29, Tchrs. Col., Columbia Univ.; Dir. of Elem. Educ., Pub. Sch., Schenectady, N. Y., since 1935.

Adcock, E. L., Bus. Mgr., Pub. Sch., 624 Lamar St., Knoxville, Tenn., since 1924.

Addicott, Irwin O., A.B.'22, Univ. of Calif.; M.A.'24, B.D.'25, Pacific Sch. of Religion; Ed.D.'39, Stanford Univ.; Prof. of Educ. and Prin. of Tr. Sch., Univ. of Denver, Denver, Colo., since 1939.

*Ade, Lester K., B.A.'21, M.A.'24, Bucknell Univ.; Ph.D.'31, New York Univ.; M.A.'32, Yale Univ.; LL.D.'35, Bucknell Univ.; Litt.D.'36, Temple Univ.; L.H.D.'38, Beaver Col.; Consultant, War Relocation Authority, Barr Bldg., Washington, D.C., since 1942.

Aden, Fred, Dir., Colegio Ward, Ramos Mejia F C O., Buenos Aires, Argentina.

Adkins, Stanley, A.B.'10, Ohio State Univ.; M.A.'35, Tchrs. Col., Columbia Univ.; Supt. of Sch., Ely, Minn., since 1935.

Ahern, T. James, B. A. '23, Alfred Univ.; A.M.'35, New York Univ.; Supt. of Sch., Mamaroneck, N. Y., since 1942.

Aikins, Frederick, H., B.S.'17, Univ. of Maine; M.Ed.'37, Bates Col.; Supt. of Sch., South Windham, Maine, since 1926.

Aikins, Lincoln J., A.M.'35, Bates Col.; Supt. of Sch., Glendive, Mont., since 1942.

Akerly, Harold E., B.S.'08, Univ. of Rochester; S.B.'10, Mass. Inst. of Tech.; M.A.'33, Univ. of Rochester; Asst. Supt. of Sch., 13 Fitzhugh St., S., Rochester 4, N. Y., since 1929.

Akridge, Garth H., B.S. in Ed.'31, Ark. State Tchrs. Col., Conway, Ark.; M.A.'32, Ph.D.'37, Tchrs. Col., Columbia Univ. Address: 1501 S. W. 20th Ave., Miami 35, Fla.

Albers, Martin Z., A.B.'15, Hope Col.; A.M.'19, Des Moines Col.; Co. Supt. of Sch., Eldora, Iowa, since 1936.

Albright, Denton M., A.B.'15, Albright Col.; A.M.'22, Columbia Univ.; Supt. of Sch., Crafton, Pa., since 1938.

Alexander, E. L., A.B.'35, Shurtleff Col.; M.A.'37, Wash. Univ.; Supt. of Sch., Edwardsville, Ill., since 1937.

Alexander, Gerald, Supt. of Sch., Washington, Ind., since 1943.

Allan, Harold A., A.B.'06, Bates Col.; Dir., Business Div., Natl. Educ. Assn., 1201 16th St., N. W., Washington 6, D. C., since 1923.

Allbaugh, Edgar B., Diploma '01, State Tchrs. Col., Emporia, Kansas; Supt. of Sch., Concordia, Kansas, since 1929.

Alleman, Sam A., A.B.'98, La. State Univ.; Parish Supt. of Sch, Napoleonville, La., since 1905.

Allen, C. J., Diploma '30, State Tchrs. Col., Jacksonville, Ala.; B.S.'31, M.A.'33, Univ. of Ala.; Co. Supt. of Sch., Anniston, Ala., since 1932.

Allen, David G., M.Ed.'38, St. Lawrence Univ.; Supvg. Prin. of Sch., Lake Placid, N. Y., since 1934.

Allen, Frank E., A.B.'16, A.M.'23, Ind. Univ.; Supt. of Sch., South Bend, Ind., since 1931.

Allen, Howard A., B.A.'16, Morningside Col.; Prin., W. H. Adamson H. S., Dallas, Texas, since 1935.

Allen, J. O., M.A.'20, Univ. of S. C.; Supt. of Sch., Albany, Ga., since 1937.

Allen, Lyman Richards, B.S.'98, Harvard Univ.; A.M.'20, Columbia Univ.; Union Supt. of Sch., Framingham, Mass., since 1929.

Allen, Richard D., A.B.'10, A.M.'12, Ph.D.'21, Brown Univ.; Asst. Supt. of Sch., 20 Summer St., Providence, R. I., since 1918.

Allison, Eugene F., B.S.'26, Northwest Mo. State Tchrs. Col., Maryville, Mo.; A.M. '32, Univ. of Mo.; Supt. of Sch., Chillicothe, Mo., since 1941.

Allman, H. B., B.S.'10, Tri-State Col.; M.A.'31, Ind. Univ.; Supt. of Sch., Muncie, Ind., since 1936.

Allman, John I., B.S. in Ed.'29, Mercer Univ.; M.A.'34, Tchrs. Col., Columbia Univ.; Asst. State Supt. of Sch., State Capitol, Atlanta, Ga., since 1941.

Alltucker, John R., Supt. of Sch., Vallejo, Calif.

Aloysia, Mother M., Ph.D.'26, Fordham Univ.; Pres., Good Counsel Col., White Plains, N. Y., since 1923.

Altstetter, M. L., A.B.'09, M.A.'27, Ohio State Univ.; Ph.D.'29, George Peabody Col. for Tchrs.; Prof. of Educ., Univ. of Tenn., Knoxville, Tenn., since 1939.

Alverson, G. Carl, A.B.'06, D.Ped.'29, St. Lawrence Univ.; Supt. of Sch., Syracuse, N. Y., since 1927.

Alvey, Edward, Jr., B.A.'23, M.A.'28, Ph.D.'31, Univ. of Va.; Dean, Mary Washington Col., Fredericksburg, Va., since 1934.

Ambrose, Rell A., M.A.'33, Univ. of Mich.; Supt. of Sch., Oxford, Mich., since 1942.

Ambruster, John Rea, B.S.'17, M.S.'28, Univ. of Ill.; Prin., The Greendale Sch., Greendale, Wis., since 1938.

Ames, Verson S., A.B.'04, Colby Col.; Supt. of Sch., Wilton, N. H., since 1923.

Amidon, Edna P., B.S.'19, M.S.'27, Univ. of Minn.; Chief, Home Economics Educ. Serv., U. S. Office of Educ., Washington 25, D. C., since 1938.

Amidon, Paul S., B.S.'24, M.A.'34, Univ. of Minn.; Supt. of Sch., St. Paul 2, Minn., since 1936.

Andersen, C. T., A.B. and M.A.'26, Univ. of Mich.; Asst. Secy., Bd. of Educ., 1354 Broadway, Detroit 26, Mich., since 1940.

Anderson, A. B., B.S. in Ed.'27, N. Dak. State Col.; Supt. of Sch., Salmon, Idaho, since 1936.

Anderson, A. Helen, A.B.'14, A.M.'31, Univ. of Denver; Supvr. of Publications, Pub. Sch., 414 14th St., Denver, Colo., since 1929.

Anderson, Charles A., B.A.'12, Williams Col.; M.A.'26, Univ. of Pa.; D.D.'31, Tusculum Col.; D.D.'34, Williams Col.; Pres., Coe Col., Cedar Rapids, Iowa, since 1942.

*Anderson, Earl William, A.B.'18, Univ. of Ill.; A.M.'25, Ph.D.'26, Tchrs. Col., Columbia Univ.; Prof. of Educ., Dept. of Educ., Ohio State Univ., Columbus, Ohio.

Anderson, Ernest B., B.A.'09, Gustavus Adolphus Col.; M.A.'32, Univ. of Minn.; Supt. of Sch., Cloquet, Minn., since 1923.

Anderson, Esther L., B.S.'33, State Tchrs. Col., Pittsburg, Kansas; State Supt. of Pub. Instr., Cheyenne, Wyo., since 1939.

Anderson, Harry D., LL.B.'22, Univ. of Ill.; B.Ed.'25, Western Ill. State Tchrs. Col.; M.A.'32, Univ. of Ill.; Supt., Twp. H.S., Ottawa, Ill., since 1932.

Anderson, Homer W., B.A.'10, Highland Park Col.; M.A.'15, Ph.D.'25, State Univ. of Iowa; Pres., American Assn. of Sch. Admin., 1942-43; Acting Supt. of Sch., Newton, Mass., since 1943.

Anderson, Howard R., B.A.'22, Augustana Col.; M.A.'28, Univ. of Chicago; Ph.D.'30, State Univ. of Iowa; Prof. of Educ., Cornell Univ. and Dir., Social Studies, Pub. Sch., Ithaca, N. Y., since 1937.

Anderson, Hulon N., A.B.'18, M.A.'38, Sam Houston State Tchrs. Col., Huntsville, Texas; Dist. Supt. of Sch., Conroe, Texas, since 1905.

Anderson, J. E., B.A. in Ed.'11, Univ. of Minn.; Supt. of Sch., Mankato, Minn., since 1931.

Anderson, J. L., A.B.'21, Mich. State Normal Col., Ypsilanti, Mich.; Supt. of Sch., Trenton, Mich., since 1914.

Anderson, James T., A.B.'16, Nebr. Wesleyan Univ.; A.M.'27, Univ. of Nebr.; Ed.D.'33, Univ. of Southern Calif.; Pres., Nebr. State Tchrs. Col., Wayne, Nebr., since 1935.

Anderson, Leland Erastus, B.S.'28, M.A.'29, Univ. of Utah; Dist. Supt. of Sch., Manti, Utah, since 1937.

Anderson, Marion, B.A.'24, M.A.'26, Ph.D.'35, State Univ. of Iowa; Ginn and Co., Statler Bldg., Park Square, Boston, Mass.

Anderson, Milburn P., Supt., Sch. Dist. No. 7, Berkley, Mich.

Anderson, Raymond, A.M.'37, Ed.D.'43, New York Univ.; Dist. Supt. of Sch., Swanton, Vt., since 1940.

Anderson, Robert R., Diploma '08, State Normal Sch., Millersville, Pa.; Supvg. Prin. of Sch., Brackenridge, Pa., since 1918.

Anderson, William Cato, A.B.'19, Syracuse Univ.; A.M.'35, Univ. of Pa.; Vice-Prin., Wash. Jr. H. S., Baltimore 17, Md., since 1941.

Andresen, Dorothea H., Prin., Earle Sch., 8210 Kimbark Ave., Chicago, Ill.

Andrews, Sterling M., B.S.'04, Valparaiso Univ.; Supt. of Sch., Walsenburg, Colo., since 1908.

Andrews, Walter A., M.A.'31, Univ. of Minn.; Supt. of Sch., New Ulm, Minn., since 1939.

Anibal, Earle W., Ph.B.'08, Hamilton Col.; A.M.'23, Tchrs. Col., Columbia Univ.; Supvg. Prin. of Sch., Mountain Lakes, N. J., since 1932.

Aniceta, Sister M., Ph.D.'38, Univ. of Ill.; Pres., Col. of St. Francis, Joliet, Ill., since 1938.

Ankenbrand, William W., A.B.'20, Marietta Col.; A.M.'24, Ohio State Univ.; Ph.D.'32, New York Univ.; Supt. of Sch., Yonkers, N. Y., since 1937.

Anketell, Richard N., A.B.'26, Bates Col.; M.Ed.'38, Boston Univ.; Supt. of Sch.. North Adams, Mass., since 1943.

Annear, Mrs. Margaret L., Co. Supt. of Sch., Modesto, Calif., since 1939.

Antholz, H. J., Ph.B.'26, Univ. of Chicago; Supt. of Sch., Spooner, Wis., since 1922.

Antrim, G. Harold, A.B.'25, Wash. and Jefferson Col.; M.A.'29, Tchrs. Col., Columbia Univ.; Supvg. Prin. of Sch., Point Pleasant Beach, N. J., since 1930.

App, Isaac D., B.S.'05, M.S.'10, Susquehanna Univ.; Co. Supt. of Sch., Harrisburg, Pa., since 1922.

Appenzellar, J. L., A.B.'08, Lebanon Valley Col.; A.M.'16, Columbia Univ.; Supvg. Prin. of Sch., Wyomissing, Pa., since 1923.

Appleton, William B., A.B.'13, Harvard Col.; Supt. of Sch., Leominster, Mass., since 1937.

Aquinas, Mother Thomas, Ph.D.'25, Fordham Univ.; Dean, Col. of New Rochelle, New Rochelle, N. Y., since 1939.

Ardis, Evart W., Supt. of Sch., Inkster, Mich.

Argo, A. C., B.S.'12, Univ. of Wash.; M.A.'21, Stanford Univ.; Dist. Supt., Sequoia Union H. S., Redwood City, Calif., since 1937.

Armour, Pliny Lawrence, M.A.'39, Texas Col. of Arts and Indus.; Asst. Supt. of Sch., El Paso, Texas, since 1943.

Armstrong, J. Harding, A.B.'07, A.M.'08, Harvard Univ.; Supt. of Sch., Westboro, Mass., since 1924.

Armstrong, Louis W., Supt. of Sch., Villisca, Iowa.

Armstrong, T. H., Interstate Tchrs. Agency, Genesee Valley Trust Bldg., Rochester, N. Y.

Armstrong, Vernon B., B.S.'14, State Col. of Wash.; Supt. of Sch., Toppenish, Wash., since 1943.

Arnesen, Arthur E., A.B.'29, Univ. of Utah; M.A.'32, Univ. of Chicago; Supvr. of Curriculum and Research, 440 E. First South St., Salt Lake City, Utah, since 1934.

Arnold, Dorothy Livingston, Diploma, New York Sch. of Fine and Applied Art; Dir. of Educ. Relations and Head, Dept. of Tchr. Tr., New York Sch. of Fine and Applied Art, New York, N. Y., since 1934.

Arnold, Lena M., Supvr. of Elem. Sch., 20 Summer St., Providence, R. I., since 1918.

Arnold, William E., A.B.'21, Ky. Wesleyan Col.; M.A.'27, Columbia Univ.; Ph.D. '32, Ohio State Univ.; Prof. of Educ., Univ. of Pa., Philadelphia, Pa., since 1935.

Arnspiger, V. C., Ph.D.'33, Columbia Univ.; Erpi Classroom Films, Inc., 1841 Broadway, New York, N. Y.

Arrants, John H., A.B.'16, M.S.'32, Univ. of Tenn.; Supt. of Sch., Bristol, Tenn., since 1936.

Arthur, Sister Marie, B.S.'25, Mich. State Col.; Dean and Registrar, Nazareth Col., Nazareth, Mich., since 1939.

Asfahl, W. D., A.B.'27, Univ. of Okla.; M.A.'30, Univ. of Colo.; Supt. of Sch., Delta, Colo., since 1935.

Ash, Mrs. Sadie V., Life Diploma '35, San Jose State Col., San Jose, Calif.; Co. Supt. of Sch., Colusa, Calif., since 1935.

Ashbaugh, E. J., A.B.'12, A.M.'13, Ind. Univ.; Ph.D.'19, State Univ. of Iowa; Dean, Sch. of Educ., Miami Univ., Oxford, Ohio, since 1929.

Ashburn, G. L., Prin., Woodrow Wilson H. S., Dallas, Texas.

Ashland, Homer Butler, Ph.B.'24, M.Ed.'39, Univ. of Vt.; Dist. Supt. of Sch., Bellows Falls, Vt., since 1940.

Ashley, Frederick A., B.B.A.'21, Boston Univ.; Supt. of Sch., Everett, Mass., since 1932.

Ashley, Lawrence Floyd, B.Sc.'21, The Stout Inst.; A.M.'34, Ph.D.'36, Ohio State Univ.; Chief, Div. of Voc. Educ., Pub. Sch., Yonkers, N. Y., since 1938.

Atkinson, Carroll, A.B.'20, Lawrence Col.; A.M.'29, Univ. of Southern Calif.; Ph.D.'38, George Peabody Col. for Tchrs,; Dir., Nelson Memorial Library, 651 Henry St., Detroit, Mich., since 1941.

Atwood, Clinton H., B.S.'19, Colgate Univ.; A.M.'23, Syracuse Univ.; Supt. of Sch., Solvay, N. Y., since 1938.

Atwood, Wallace W., B.S.'97, Ph.D.'03, Univ. of Chicago; Prof. of Physical and Regional Geography and Pres., Clark Univ., Worcester 3, Mass., since 1920.

Atwood, Will G., Litt.B.'10, Rutgers Univ.; Co. Supt. of Sch., Court House, Belvidere, N. J., since 1928.

Aurand, E. D., B.E.'33, Northern Ill. State Tchrs. Col., De Kalb, Ill.; M.S.'36, Northwestern Univ.; Supt. of Sch., Lyons, Ill., since 1940.

Aurand, O. H., B.S.'21, Susquehanna Univ.; M.A.'32, Tchrs. Col., Columbia Univ.; Supt. of Sch., Steelton, Pa., since 1935.

Austin, Everett L., A.B.'17, Moores Hill Col.; B.S.'18, B.S. in Agr.'23, Purdue Univ.; Ph.D.'28, Cornell Univ.; State Supvr. of Sec. Educ., State Office Bldg., Providence, R. I., since 1939.

Austin, George R., A.B.'33, Bates Col.; Ed.M.'41, Harvard Univ.; Union Supt. of Sch., Middleborough, Mass., since 1941.

Averill, Forrest G., A.B.'24, M.A.'28, Univ. of Mich.; Supt. of Sch., East Grand Rapids, Mich., since 1935.

Avery, Andrew, Diploma '27, Young Harris Col.; A.B. in Ed.'29, Univ. of Ga.; Co. Supt. of Sch., Court House, Bainbridge, Ga., since 1933.

Ayer, Fred C., B.S.'02, Upper Iowa Univ.; M.S.'05, Georgetown Univ.; Ph.D.'15, Univ. of Chicago; Prof. of Educ. Admin., Univ. of Texas, Austin, Texas, since 1927.

Ayres, Frank M., A.B.'24, M.A.'26, Univ. of Mich.; Supt. of Sch., Dundee, Mich., since 1924.

B

Babcock, Earl H., Diploma '09, Mich. State Normal Col., Ypsilanti, Mich.; B.A.'22, M.A.'29, Univ. of Mich.; Supt. of Sch., Grand Haven, Mich., since 1923.

Babcock, S. H., Co. Supt. of Sch., Medina, Ohio, since 1921.

Bachman, Walter E., B.S.'14, Drake Univ.; M.R.E.'20, D.R.E.'23, Boston Univ.; Dean and Prof. of Philosophy and Religious Educ., York Col., York, Nebr., since 1936.

Bachmann, Sophie C., Diploma '96, Detroit Normal Tr. Sch.; Prin., Majeske Sch., Detroit, Mich., since 1925.

Bachrodt, Walter L., A.B.'20, A.M.'21, Stanford Univ.; Supt. of Sch., San Jose, Calif., since 1921.

Bacon, Allen E., Ph.B.'11, Lafayette Col.; Supt. of Sch., Wilkes-Barre, Pa., since 1934.

Bacon, Charles Edward, A.B.'96, Harvard Univ.; Publisher, Allyn & Bacon, 50 Beacon St., Boston 8, Mass., since 1917.

Bacon, Francis Leonard, A.B.'12, Southwestern Col.; A.M.'16, Columbia Univ.; LL.D.'32, Southwestern Col.; L.H.D.'37, Williams Col.; Supt., Evanston Twp. H. S., Evanston, Ill., since 1928.

Bacon, Paul Valentine, A.B.'98, Harvard Univ.; Editor-in-Chief, Allyn & Bacon, 50 Beacon St., Boston 8, Mass., since 1921.

Bacon, Willard H., A.B.'00, Brown Univ.; Ed.D.'34, R. I. Col. of Educ.; Supt. of Sch., Westerly, R. I., since 1913.

Baer, D. C., B.S.'12, Heidelberg Col.; Supt. of Sch., Bucyrus, Ohio, since 1935.

Bagnall, J. R., Supt. of Sch., Mt. Pleasant, Utah.

Bahner, W. G., A.B.'15, M.A.'17, Wittenberg Col.; M.A.'24, Columbia Univ.; Supt. of Sch., Cuyahoga Hgts., Ohio, since 1943.

Bail, Phillip M., B.A.'20, Mo. Valley Col.; M.A.'28, Ph.D.'31, State Univ. of Iowa; Dean, Col. of Educ., Butler Univ., Indianapolis 8, Ind., since 1940.

Bailey, C. L., B.S.'11, Otterbein Col.; M.A.'32, Miami Univ.; Supt. of Sch., Greenville, Ohio, since 1929.

Bailey, Edna W., B.S.'06, M.S.'07, Ph.D.'10, Univ. of Calif.; Prof. of Educ., Univ. of Calif., Berkeley 4, Calif., since 1927.

Bailey, Floyd P., M.S.'29, Univ. of Calif.; Pres., Santa Rosa Jr. Col., Santa Rosa, Calif., since 1935.

Bailey, Francis L., A.B.'21, A.M.'24, Univ. of Mich.; Ph.D.'39, Columbia Univ.; Prin., Western State Normal Sch., Gorham, Maine, since 1940.

Bailey, John F., A.B.'23, Baylor Univ.; M.A.'31, Univ. of Colo.; Supt. of Sch., Breckenridge, Texas, since 1939.

Bailey, Thomas D., A.B.'19, Wofford Col.; M.A.'38, Univ. of Fla.; Supvg. Prin. of Sch., Tampa 3, Fla., since 1943.

Bailie, Lorraine M., Prin., Columbus Sch., Glendale, Calif.

Baily, Carl S., A.B.'19, Wash. and Jefferson Col.; Supt. of Sch., Swissvale, Pa., since 1933.

Bain, Winifred E., Ph.B.'24, Univ. of Chicago; M.A.'26, Ph.D.'29, Columbia Univ.; Pres., Wheelock Col., Boston, Mass., since 1940.

Bair, Carl M., Ph.B.'09, Grinnell Col.; M.A.'30, Columbia Univ.; Supvg. Prin. of Sch., Lakewood, N. J., since 1930.

Bair, Frederick H., A.B.'12, Grinnell Col.; M.A.'17, Ph.D.'33, Tchrs. Col., Columbia Univ.; Supt. of Sch., Bronxville, N. Y., since 1936.

Bair, Medill, B.S.'35, State Tchrs. Col., Trenton, N. J.; M.A.'39, Tchrs. Col., Columbia Univ.; Supt. of Sch., East Greenwich, R. I., since 1942.

Baird, Paul R., A.B.'12, A.M.'15, Hamilton Col.; M.Ed.'42, Springfield Col.; Supt. of Sch., Ludlow, Mass., since 1931.

Baird, William J., A.B.'18, Univ. of Ala.; A.M.'21, Tchrs. Col., Columbia Univ.; Prin., Jefferson Co. H. S., Tarrant, Ala., since 1921.

Baker, B. B., A.M.'08, Ohio Northern Univ.; Supt. of Sch., Fairfield, Ala., since 1923.

Baker, Clara Belle, A.B.'09, A.M.'11, Northwestern Univ.; Dir., Children's Sch., Natl. Col. of Educ., Evanston, Ill., since 1926.

Baker, Edna Dean, B.E.'13, Natl. Col. of Educ.; B.A.'20, M.A.'21, Northwestern Univ.; Pres., Natl. Col. of Educ., Evanston, Ill., since 1920.

Baker, Frank E., A.B.'05, Allegheny Col.; A.M.'09, Harvard Univ.; L.H.D.'28, Allegheny Col.; Pres., State Tchrs. Col., Milwaukee, Wis., since 1923.

Baker G. Derwood, A.B.'22, Pomona Col.; A.M.'26, Ed.D.'39, Tchrs. Col., Columbia Univ.; Supt. of Sch., Boulder, Colo., since 1940.

Baker, George C., Ph.B.'10, Lafayette Col.; A.M.'13, Univ. of Pa.; Supt. of Sch., Moorestown, N. J., since 1913.

Baker, Harold V., A.B.'18, Baker Univ.; M.A.'26, Univ. of Colo.; Prin., Daniel Webster Sch., New Rochelle, N. Y., since 1932.

Baker, Ira William, A.B. in Ed.'14, Kansas State Tchrs. Col., Emporia, Kansas; B.S.'15, Kansas State Agrl. Col.; A.M. in Ed.'20, Univ. of Chicago; Prin., Classen H. S., Oklahoma City, Okla., since 1933.

Baker, L. D., M.A.'29, State Col. of Wash. Address: 253 S. 152nd St., Seattle 88, Wash.

Baker, Stuart K., Supt., Big Beaver H.S., Birmingham 4, Mich.

Baker, William Wallace, A.M.'31, Tchrs. Col., Columbia Univ.; Supt. of Sch., Marion, Ark., since 1928.

Baldwin, Robert Dodge, A.B.'13, Princeton Univ.; A.M.'16, Columbia Univ.; Ph.D.'26, Cornell Univ.; Prof. of Educ., W. Va. Univ., Morgantown, W. Va., since 1931.

Ball, James J., Asst. Supt. of Sch. in charge of Bus. Management, 414 14th St., Denver, Colo., since 1927.

Ballentine, Will G., Supt. of Sch., Menomonie, Wis., since 1920.

Balliette, Ralph Ernest, Ph.B.'23, Ph.M.'27, Univ. of Wis.; Supt. of Sch., Platteville, Wis., since 1933.

Ballou, Frank Washington, B.S.'04, Tchrs. Col., Columbia Univ.; M.A.'08, Univ. of Cincinnati; Ph.D.'14, Harvard Univ.; Pres., Dept. of Superintendence, 1925-26; Supt. of Sch., Washington, D. C., 1920-1943. Address: 3117 45th St., N. W., Washington, D. C.

Balyeat, Orley E., Diploma '01, Mich. State Normal Col., Ypsilanti, Mich.; Supt. of Sch., Sparta, Mich., since 1908.

Bangs, Cecil W., B.A.'26, Iowa State Tchrs. Col., Cedar Falls, Iowa; M.A.'29, State Univ. of Iowa; Supt. of Sch., Manchester, Iowa, since 1922.

Banks, Charles, A.B.'10, Northeast Mo. State Tchrs. Col., Kirksville, Mo.; M.A.'25, Columbia Univ.; Supt. of Sch., 6701 Delmar Blvd., University City, Mo., since 1925.

Banks, L. Frazer, A.B.'21, Univ. of Colo.; M.A.'28, George Peabody Col. for Tchrs.; LL.D.'34, Birmingham-Southern Col.; Supt. of Sch., Birmingham 1, Ala., since 1942.

Banks, Ralph H., A.B.'27, Ind. State Tchrs. Col.; M.S.'33, Ind. Univ.; Supt. of Sch., Vincennes, Ind., since 1943.

Bankston, J. H., B.A.'28, North Texas State Tchrs. Col., Denton, Texas; M.A.'36, Colo. Col. of Educ., Greeley, Colo.; Supt. of Sch. and Pres., Jr. Col., Victoria, Texas, since 1939.

Barber, Joseph E., B.S.'26, M.S. in Ed.'33, Syracuse Univ.; Prin., H. S., East Aurora, N. Y., since 1934.

Barclay, Robert W., B.S.'23, Norwich Univ.; M.A.'29, Boston Univ.; Supt. of Sch., Grafton, Mass., since 1939.

Barden, Earle K., M.A.'31, Univ. of Texas; B.S.'27, Sam Houston State Tchrs. Col., Huntsville, Texas; Supt. of Sch., Sugar Land, Texas, since 1933.

Bardwell, Richard W., A.B.'10, Univ. of Ill.; M.A.'22, Univ. of Chicago; Ph.D.'39, Univ. of Wis.; Supt. of Sch., La Crosse, Wis., since 1942.

Bare, Thurman H., B.S.'26, Univ. of Mo.; M.A.'36, Columbia Univ.; Supt. of Sch., Montpelier, Vt., since 1941.

Bargen, William J., Pres., Welfare Engineering Co., 42 Madison St., Waukegan, Ill.

Barker, Howard L., A.M.'37, Northwestern Univ.; Supt. of Sch., Bangor, Mich., since 1922.

Barlow, Nathan J., B.S.'24, Univ. of Utah; Co. Supt. of Sch., Cedar City, Utah, since 1924.

Barner, Raymond T., Diploma '16, Keystone State Normal Sch., Kutztown, Pa.; Ph.B.'26, Muhlenberg Col.; A.M.'34, Univ. of Pittsburgh; Supvg. Prin. of Sch., Brownsville, Pa., since 1940.

Barnes, B. H., Deputy Supt. of Sch., Burbank, Calif., since 1941.

Barnes, B. N., A.B.'26, Wake Forest Col.; A.M.'31, Univ. of N. C.; Supt. of Sch., Kings Mountain, N. C., since 1934.

Barnes, George F., Rand McNally & Co., 538 S. Clark St., Chicago, Ill.

Barnum, Walter Lawrence, A.B.'07, Middlebury Col.; A.M.'36, Northwestern Univ.; Asst. Prin., Evanston Twp. H. S., Evanston, Ill., since 1927.

Barrett, John Ignatius, J.C.L.'12, Catholic Univ. of America; Ph.D.'23, Loyola Col.; LL.D.'23, Gonzaga Col.; Supt. of Parish Sch., Archdiocese of Baltimore, 415 Cathedral St., Baltimore, Md., since 1922.

Barrett, Lawrence Adams, B.S.'25, Kansas State Tchrs. Col.; M.S.'29, Univ. of Colo.; Ph.D.'41, McKinley Roosevelt Foundation; Supt. of Sch., Salida, Colo., since 1941.

Bartels, L. W., B.S. in Ed.'32, Southeast Mo. State Tchrs. Col., Cape Girardeau, Mo.; M.A.'33, Univ. of Mo.; Supt. of Sch., Vanduser, Mo., since 1939.

Barthel, Oscar P., B.S.'31, Eureka Col.; M.S.'37, Univ. of Wyo.; Prin., Com. H. S., Marengo, Ill., since 1943.

Bartky, John A., Ph.D.'40, Northwestern Univ.; Pres., Chicago Tchrs. Col., 6800 S. Stewart Ave., Chicago, Ill., since 1938.

Bartrug, C. M., B.S.'23, M.S.'27, Iowa State Col.; Supt. of Sch., Iowa Falls, Iowa, since 1928.

Baruch, Dorothy W., E.B.'30, M.E.'31, Whittier Col.; Ph.D.'37, Claremont Col. Address: Whittier Col., Pasadena, Calif.

Bass, M. Reed, B.S.'24, Colo. State Col. of Agr. and Mech. Arts; Dir., The David Ranken, Jr. Sch. of Mech. Trades, 4431 Finney Ave., St. Louis, Mo., since 1937.

Bass, W. A., M.A.'28, Univ. of Chicago; Supt. of Sch., Nashville 3, Tenn., since 1938.

Batchelder, Carl J., A.B.'18, Eastern Col.; A.B.'18, Valparaiso Univ.; Deputy State Commr. of Educ., Montpelier, Vt., since 1923.

Batchelder, Mildred L., A.B.'22, Mt. Holyoke Col.; B.L.S.'24, N. Y. State Library Sch.; Sch. Library Specialist, The School and Children's Library Div., American Library Assn., 520 N. Michigan Ave., Chicago, Ill., since 1936.

Bateman, E. Allen, B.A.'17, Univ. of Utah; M.A.'29, Univ. of Chicago; Supt. of Sch., Logan, Utah, since 1933.

Bates, Harold S., B.S.'21, Knox Col.; A.M. '34, Columbia Univ.; D.Ed.'42, Univ. of Cincinnati; Supt. of Sch., Norwood, Ohio, since 1936.

Bates, Horace Freeman, A.B.'98, Ed.M.'28, Harvard Univ.; Supt. of Sch., Somerset, Mass., since 1922.

Bates, Ralph F., A.B.'11, Colgate Univ.; A.M.'14, Columbia Univ.; Supt. of Sch., Chatham, N. J., since 1920.

Batho, Marshall G., B.S.'31, State Univ. of Iowa; M.Ph.'34, Univ. of Wis.; Supt. of Sch., West Bend, Wis., since 1942.

Battle, Elizabeth G., Supt. of Sch., Pittston, Pa.

Battles, E. E., B.A.'26, M.Ed.'39, Univ. of Okla.; Supt. of Sch., Henryetta, Okla., since 1934.

*Bauer, Nicholas, B.S.'97, M.A.'99, Tulane Univ.; Supt. of Sch., New Orleans, La., 1923-1942. Address: 3425 Canal St., New Orleans, La.

Baugher, Jacob I., A.B.'23, Elizabethtown Col.; A.M.'25, Ph.D.'30, Columbia Univ. Address: 9202 Sligo Pkwy., Silver Spring, Md.

Baum, Paul B., A.B.'19, Aurora Col.; A.M.'21, Univ. of Wis.; Dean, Colo. Woman's Col., Denver 7, Colo., since 1935.

Bawden, William T., A.B.'96, Denison Univ.; B.S.'10, Ph.D.'14, Tchrs. Col., Columbia Univ.; Head, Dept. of Indus. and Voc. Educ., Kansas State Tchrs. Col., Pittsburg, Kansas, since 1935.

Baxter, Bernice, Ph.D.'35, Yale Univ.; Admin. Asst. to Supt. of Sch., Oakland, Calif., since 1943.

Baxter, Solomon, Diploma '21, State Tchrs. Col., Troy, Ala.; B.S.'29, Univ. of Ala.; Co. Supt. of Sch., Dothan, Ala., since 1933.

Baylor, Carl W., B.S.'33, M.A.'37, Univ. of Ill.; Supt. of Sch., Libertyville, Ill., since 1938.

Bayne, Stephen F., B.S.'98, Col. of the City of N. Y.; A.M.'03, Columbia Univ.; Ph.D., Fordham Univ.; Assoc. Supt. of Sch., 110 Livingston St., Brooklyn 2, N. Y., since 1934.

Berger, Harry S., B.S. in Ed.'21, Northeast Mo. State Tchrs. Col., Kirksville, Mo.; M.A. in Ed.'29, Univ. of Mo.; Supt. of Sch., Deadwood, S. Dak., since 1928.

Berger, Lowe, B.A.'19, Columbia Univ.; M.A.'20, Univ. of Mich.; Vice-Pres., The Bobbs-Merrill Co., 730 N. Meridian St., Indianapolis, Ind., since 1935.

Bergman, Frank V., B.S.'17, Kansas State Tchrs. Col., Emporia, Kansas; M.A.'21, Univ. of Colo.; Supt. of Sch., Manhattan, Kansas, since 1942.

Bergquist, Ernest B., B.A.'02, Gustavus Adolphus Col.; M.A.'29, Univ. of Minn.; Supt. of Sch., Rapid City, S. Dak., since 1929.

Bergstrom, B. L., Prin., El Monte Union H. S., El Monte, Calif.

Berry, Frank A., A.B.'07, Wesleyan Univ.; Supt. of Sch., Bethel, Conn., since 1914.

Berry, Merrill M., A.B.'19, Baldwin-Wallace Col.; A.M.'22, Ohio State Univ.; Supt. of Sch., Chillicothe, Ohio, since 1935.

Bertram, Joseph Francis, B.Ed.'28, State Tchrs. Col., Milwaukee, Wis.; M.A.'35, Univ. of Wis.; Supvg. Prin. of Sch., Algoma, Wis., since 1935.

Bessire, M. Ethel, Dir., Mar-Ken Sch., 6107 Franklin Ave., Hollywood, Calif., since 1936.

Best, Howard R., B.A.'17, Yankton Col.; Certif.'19, Univ. of Montpelier, France; M.A.'29, Univ. of Nebr.; Ed.D.'39, Tchrs. Col., Columbia Univ.; Supvg. Prin. of Sch., Cranford, N. J., since 1935.

Bettinger, George Edward, A.B.'15, M.A.'28, Univ. of Southern Calif.; Supt. of Sch., Alhambra, Calif., since 1934.

*Betts, Emmett Albert, B.S.'25, Des Moines Univ.; M.A.'28, Ph.D.'31, State Univ. of Iowa; Research Prof. and Dir. of Reading Clinic, Pa. State Col., State College, Pa., since 1937.

Beumer, Edward H., A.B. and B.S.'14, Univ. of Mo.; A.M.'25, Univ. of Ill.; Asst. Supt. of Sch., 911 Locust St., St. Louis 1, Mo., since 1942.

Bevens, Bruce B., B.S.'31, Univ. of Okla.; M.Ed.'37, Univ. of Cincinnati; Supt. of Sch., Pottsville, Ark., since 1942.

Bicking, Ada, Diploma '06, Northwestern Univ.; B.Ped.'24, Cincinnati Conservatory of Music; Dir., Arthur Jordan Conservatory of Music, Indianapolis, Ind., since 1935.

Bickley, James M., M.A.'32, Univ. of N. Mex.; Supt. of Sch., Clovis, N. Mex., since 1921.

Biehn, A. L., A.B.'27, A.M.'34, Ph.D.'40, Univ. of Nebr.; Supt., Niles Twp. H. S., Skokie, Ill., since 1942.

Bierbaum, Milton Wesley, A.B.'28, Central Wesleyan Col.; A.M.'38, Wash. Univ.; Supt., West Walnut Manor Schs., 7053 Emma Ave., St. Louis County, Mo., since 1933.

Bierkoe, George O., A.B.'22, Muhlenberg Col.; B.D.'25, Lutheran Theol. Sem., Philadelphia, Pa.; A.M.'35, New York Univ.; Pres., Endicott Jr. Col., Pride's Crossing, Mass., since 1939.

Biernacki, Stanley R., Asst. Supt. of Sch., Hamtramck, Mich.

Biery, J. E., M.A.'36, Columbia Univ.; Supvg. Prin. of Sch., Brookville, Pa., since 1936.

Biester, Fred L., A.B.'14, North Central Col.; M.A.'38, Univ. of Chicago; Prin., Glenbard Twp. H. S., Glen Ellyn, Ill., since 1918.

Bigelow, Edwin Lawrence, A.B.'13, Middlebury Col.; A.M.'26, Columbia Univ.; Dist. Supt. of Sch., Manchester Center, Vt., since 1926.

Bigelow, Karl W., B.A.'20, Clark Univ.; Ph.D.'29, Harvard Univ.; L.H.D.'38, Clark Univ.; LL.D.'41, Parsons Col.; Dir. Commn. on Tchr. Educ., American Council on Educ., 744 Jackson Pl., N.W., Washington, D. C., since 1938.

Biggs, Alfred, Dir. of Sales, Sch. and Library Div., The Grolier Society, Inc., 2 West 45th St., New York, N. Y.

*Bigler, Frank William, A.B.'27, Southwestern Col.; M.A.'36, Univ. of Wichita; Supt. of Consol. Sch. Dist. No. 36, Oil Hill, Kansas, since 1928.

Billett, Roy O., B.Sc.'23, M.A.'27, Ph.D.'29, Ohio State Univ.; Prof. of Educ., since 1935 and Head, Dept. of Sec. Educ., Boston Univ., Boston, Mass., since 1942.

Billington, Lillian Emily, M.A.'34, Stanford Univ. Address: Natl. Arts Club, 15 Gramercy Park, New York 3, N. Y.

Billman, Dale C., A.B.'19, Wabash Col.; M.A.'27, Univ. of Wis.; Supt. of Sch., Sullivan, Ind., since 1928.

Bimson, Oliver H., A.B.'14, Nebr. Wesleyan Univ.; A.M.'25, Ph.D.'39, Univ. of Nebr.; Asst. Supt. of Sch., Lincoln, Nebr., since 1927.

Binford, H. E., A.B.'17, Ind. State Tchrs. Col., Terre Haute, Ind.; A.M.'23, Tchrs. Col., Columbia Univ.; Supt. of Sch., Bloomington, Ind., since 1935.

Binford, Jesse H., A.B.'96, Univ. of Richmond; A.M.'15, Univ. of Wis.; Supt. of Sch., Richmond, Va., since 1933.

Bingman, C. W., M.Pd.'11, Ohio Univ.; M.A.'26, Univ. of Texas; Dist. Supt. of Sch. and Pres., South Park Jr. Col., Beaumont, Texas, since 1923.

Birchard, C. C., Pres., C. C. Birchard and Co., 221 Columbus Ave., Boston, Mass.

Bird, E. S., Mgr., American Book Co., 88 Lexington Ave., New York, N. Y.

Bird, Robert L., A.B.'01, Mo. Valley Col.; Co. Supt. of Sch., San Luis Obispo, Calif., since 1919.

Birdwell, A. W., A.M.'16, George Peabody Col. for Tchrs.; Pres., Stephen F. Austin State Tchrs. Col., Nacogdoches, Texas, since 1922.

Bishop, Charles C., A.B.'06, M.A.'19, Univ. of Wis.; Supt. of Sch., Oshkosh, Wis., since 1921.

Bishop, Frank Edward, A.B.'16, Nebr. Wesleyan Univ.; M.A.'30, Leland Stanford Jr. Univ.; Supt. of Sch., Corona, Calif., since 1935.

Bishop, Fred G., Diploma '05, State Tchrs. Col., Oshkosh, Wis.; A.B.'15, Univ. of Wis.; M.A.'30, Tchrs. Col., Columbia Univ. Address: Pub. Sch., Two Rivers, Wis.

Bixler, Lorin E., A.B.'21, Mt. Union Col.; M.A.'23, Tchrs. Col., Columbia Univ.; Ph.D.'31, Ohio State Univ.; Prof. of Educ., Muskingum Col., New Concord, Ohio, since 1929.

Bjork, Ray, B.S.'27, State Tchrs. Col., Moorhead, Minn.; M.A.'36, Univ. of Minn.; Supt. of Sch., Helena, Mont., since 1943.

Black, George H., B.A.'98, Toronto Univ.; M.A.'32, Ph.D.'33, New York Univ.; Pres., Univ. of Newark, Newark, N. J., since 1939.

Black, H. B., M.A.'24, Univ. of Ill.; Supt. of Sch., Mattoon, Ill., since 1921.

Black, Lester, B.S.'14, Denison Univ.; A.M.'26, Columbia Univ.; Co. Supt. of Sch., Newark, Ohio, since 1923.

Blackburn, Elisha Phillips, A.B.'28, Oakland City Col.; M.S.'35, Ind. Univ.; Supt. of Sch., Union City, Ind., since 1940.

Blackford, J. D., B.S. in Ed.'26, M.A.'37, Miami Univ.; Supt. of Sch., Upper Sandusky, Ohio, since 1941.

Blackhurst, Stephen, M.A.'26, Univ. of Mo.; Supt. of Sch., 911 Kingshighway, St. Charles, Mo., since 1926.

Blackwelder, D. Lee, A.B.'17, Howard Col., Birmingham, Ala.; M.A.'30, Tchrs. Col., Columbia Univ.; Supt. of Sch., McComb, Miss., since 1936.

Blackwell, J. D., B.S.'14, Univ. of Mo.; M.A.'23, Columbia Univ.; Ph.D.'29, Johns Hopkins Univ.; Pres., State Tchrs. Col., Salisbury, Md., since 1935.

Blackwell, R. Henry, B.S.'27, Stephen F. Austin State Tchrs. Col., Nacogdoches, Texas; M.A.'32, George Peabody Col. for Tchrs.; Supt. of Sch., Pecos, Texas, since 1934.

Blair, Clarence D., B.Ed.'30, Ill. State Normal Univ., Normal, Ill.; Co. Supt. of Sch., Belleville, Ill., since 1939.

Blair, James Seaborn, A.B.'26, Univ. of N. C.; Co. Supt. of Sch., Elizabethtown, N. C., since 1936.

Blakley, William J., A.B.'29, Westminster Col.; M.Ed.'37, Univ. of Pittsburgh; Supvg. Prin. of Twp. Sch., Turtle Creek, Pa., since 1940.

Blankenship, A. H., Supt. of Sch., Oak Ridge, Tenn.

Bliss, Walton B., A.B.'15, Heidelberg Col.; M.A.'29, Ohio State Univ.; Exec. Secy., Ohio Educ. Assn., 213-15 E. Broad St., Columbus, Ohio, since 1935.

Blodgett, Darrell R., Ph.B.'24, Shurtleff Col.; M.A.'35, Wash. Univ.; Supt. of Sch., Jacksonville, Ill., since 1943.

*Blom, Edward Charles, A.B.'11, Southeast Mo. State Tchrs. Col., Cape Girardeau, Mo.; B.S. in Ed.'15, A.M.'17, Univ. of Mo.; Ph.D.'30, Columbia Univ.; Prin., Laboratory Sch. and Prof of Educ., State Tchrs. Col., Fredonia, N. Y., since 1937.

Bloom, Edward F., A.B.'27, M.A.'34, Univ. of Wash.; Supt. of Sch., Aberdeen, Wash., since 1938.

Bloser, Robert E., A.B.'18, Ohio State Univ.; Pres., The Zaner-Bloser Co., 612 N. Park St., Columbus, Ohio, since 1928.

Blossom, Virgil T., B.S.E.'30, Mo. Valley Col.; M.S.'39, Univ. of Ark.; Supt. of Sch., Fayetteville, Ark., since 1942.

Blue, J. W., A.B.'08, Ind. Univ.; The American Book Co., 300 Pike St., Cincinnati, Ohio.

Blunt, Katharine, A.B.'98, Vassar Col.; Ph.D.'07, Univ. of Chicago; LL.D.'36, Wesleyan Univ.; LL.D.'37, Mt. Holyoke Col. Address: 38 Glenwood Ave., New London, Conn.

Boak, Edward Kendrick, A.B.'07, Bates Col.; A.M.'26, Columbia Univ.; Supt., Windham Southwest Sch. Dist., Wilmington, Vt., since 1935.

Boardman, Walter S., Ed.D.'41, New York Univ.; Supt. of Sch., Oceanside, N. Y., since 1940.

Bock, Thomas Andrew, A.B.'10, Ursinus Col.; A.M.'28, Univ. of Pa.; Ed.D.'40, New York Univ.; Prof. of Educ., State Tchrs. Col., Kutztown, Pa., since 1930.

*Boehm, Charles H., A.B.'23, Franklin and Marshall Col.; A.M.'26, Tchrs. Col., Columbia Univ.; Co. Supt. of Sch., Doylestown, Pa., since 1940.

Bogardus, Glen F., B.S.'16, St. Lawrence Univ.; Supt. of Sch., Canastota, N. Y., since 1926.

Boggan, T. K., B.Ph.'03, LL.B.'13, Univ. of Miss.; M.A.'24, George Peabody Col. for Tchrs.; Supt. of Sch., Wiggins, Miss., since 1943.

Bohn, Julius Edward, A.B.'20, Heidelberg Col.; A.M.'26, Ohio State Univ.; Supt. of Sch., Ashland, Ohio, since 1935.

Boland, Michael P., A.B.'30, St. Joseph's Col.; M.S. in Ed.'36, Univ. of Pa.; Registrar, since 1930 and Head, Dept. of Educ., St. Joseph's Col., Philadelphia, Pa., since 1938.

Bole, Lyman W., B.S.'19, Cornell Univ.; M.E.'39, Univ. of Vt.; Supt. of Sch., Springfield, Vt., since 1940.

Bole, Rita L., A.B.'20, Middlebury Col.; M.A.'36, Tchrs. Col., Columbia Univ.; Prin., State Normal Sch., Lyndon Center, Vt., since 1927.

Boliver, Thomas Earl, A.B.'21, Geneva Col.; Ed.M.'35, Univ. of Pittsburgh; Major, U. S. Army Infantry Command and General Staff Sch., Ft. Leavenworth, Kansas, since 1942.

Boltz, I. K., B.S.'29, State Tchrs. Col., Pittsburg, Kansas; M.A.'36, Colo. Col. of Educ.; Supt. of Sch., Grand Junction, Colo., since 1943.

Bonar, Carl F., Dean of Instr., West Liberty State Tchrs. Col., West Liberty, W. Va.

Bonar, Hugh S., B. Accts.'16, B.A.'18, Mt. Morris Col.; M.A.'24, Univ. of Chicago; Mgr., Indus. Relations, Taylor Forge and Pipe Works, Cicero, Ill.

Bond, George W., B.S.'20, Univ. of Ark.; M.A.'23, Univ. of Chicago; Ed.D.'38, Columbia Univ.; Dean of Admin., Southeastern La. Col., Hammond, La., since 1938.

Bond, Mrs. Helen Judy, Diploma '14, Iowa State Tchrs. Col., Cedar Falls, Iowa; A.B.'23, State Univ. of Iowa; A.M. and Ph.D.'29, Tchrs. Col., Columbia Univ.; Head, Dept. of Home Economics, Tchrs. Col., Columbia Univ., New York 27, N. Y., since 1937.

Bond, Horace Mann, Pres., Ft. Valley State Col., Ft. Valley, Ga.

Bonner, John Joseph, S.T.D.'17, Univ. of Propaganda, Rome, Italy; LL.D.'29, Villanova Col.; Diocesan Supt. of Sch., 19th and Wood Sts., Philadelphia 3, Pa., since 1926.

Booker, W. R., A.B.'16, A.M.'26, Ind. Univ.; Supt. of Sch., Muskegon Hgts., Mich., since 1928.

Booth, Clarence L., A.B.'17, Otterbein Col.; M.A.'27, State Col. of Wash.; Supt. of Sch., Pasco, Wash., since 1929.

Booth, John Martin, M.S.'29, Univ. of Idaho; Supt. of Sch., Kellogg, Idaho, since 1935.

*Boothby, Arthur Z., Pd.B.'00, N. Y. State Col. for Tchrs., Albany, N. Y.; B.S.'16, A.M.'20, Tchrs. Col., Columbia Univ. Address: Weston, Vt.

Borst, Guernsey J., A.B.'03, Cornell Univ.; Pd.M.'09, Pd.D.'11, Ph.D.'12, New York Univ.; A.M.'21, Columbia Univ.; Prof. of Educ., Skidmore Col., Saratoga Springs, N. Y., since 1921.

Bos, Bert P., Diploma '24, N. J. State Normal Sch., Montclair, N. J.; B.S.'29, A.M.'31, Ed.D.'37, New York Univ.; Supvg. Prin. of Twp. Sch., Mountain View, N. J., since 1937.

Bosshart, John H., A.B.'02, Cornell Univ.; State Commr. of Educ., Trenton, N. J., since 1943.

Boston, Paul Frederick, A.M.'25, Tchrs. Col., Columbia Univ.; Supt. of Sch., Greencastle, Ind., since 1932.

Boston, W. Theodore, A.B.'30, Wash. Col.; Co. Supt. of Sch., Cambridge, Md., since 1938.

Boswell, G. C., B.A.'26, East Texas State Tchrs. Col., Commerce, Texas; M.A.'33, Simmons Univ.; LL.D.'39, Texas Wesleyan Col.; Pres., Ranger Jr. Col. and Supt. of Sch., Ranger, Texas, since 1941.

Boswell, George M., B.A.'32, North Texas State Tchrs. Col., Denton, Texas; Supt. of Sch., Coahoma, Texas, since 1934.

Bosworth, Clarence W., A.B.'09, A.M.'10, Brown Univ.; Supt. of Sch., Cranston, R. I., since 1935.

Botleman, L. J., Supt., Sch. Dist. No. 1, Trinidad, Colo.

Bouelle, Frank A., A.B.'12, Univ. of Southern Calif. Address: 845 S. Tremaine Ave., Los Angeles, Calif.

Bousfield, Mrs. Maudelle B., A.B.'06, Univ. of Ill.; A.M.'31, Univ. of Chicago; Prin., Wendell Phillips H. S., 244 E. Pershing Rd., Chicago, Ill., since 1939.

Boutwell, William Dow, B.S.'22, Univ. of Ill.; Chief, Div. of Radio, Publications, and Exhibits, U. S. Office of Educ., Washington 25, D. C., since 1939.

Bouvé, Marjorie, Diploma '03, Boston Normal Sch. of Gymnastics; B.S. in Ed., Boston Univ.; Dir., Bouvé-Boston Sch. of Physical Educ., 105 S. Huntington Ave., Boston, Mass., since 1930.

Bow, Warren Edward, B.S.'14, Univ. of Ill.; M.A.'23, Univ. of Mich.; LL.D.'31, Battle Creek Col.; Supt. of Sch. and Pres., Wayne Univ., 1354 Broadway, Detroit 26, Mich., since 1942.

Bowdle, C. P., A.B.'21, Ohio Wesleyan Univ.; M.A.'25, Akron Univ.; Supt. of Sch., Van Wert, Ohio, since 1942.

Bowers, Harold J., B.S. in Ed.'26, Ohio Northern Univ.; M.A.'37, Ohio State Univ.; Supvr. of Certification, State Office Bldg., Columbus, Ohio, since 1936.

Bowlby, Roswell S., B.S.'13, New York Univ.; Supt. of Sch., Dover, N. J., since 1920.

Bowley, Harold C., Ph.B.'20, Univ. of Vt.; Union Supt. of Sch., Milford, N. H., since 1939.

Bowlus, Edgar S., A.B.'11, St. John's Col.; A.B.'12, Univ. of Md.; A.M.'16, St. John's Col.; A.M.'32, Columbia Univ.; Supt. of Sch., Greenwood, Miss., since 1942.

Bowman, C. R., Co. Supt. of Sch., Medford, Oregon, since 1933.

Bowman, George A., A.B.'17, Western Reserve Univ.; M.A.'31, Columbia Univ.; Supt. of Sch., Youngstown, Ohio, since 1941.

Bowman, Grover Chester, B.A.'06, Williams Col.; M.A.'12, Yale Univ.; Ed.D.'41, R. I. Col. of Educ.; Pres., State Tchrs. Col., North Adams, Mass., since 1937.

Bowman, John F., 721 S. Elmwood Ave., Oak Park, Ill.

Bowsher, E. Leslie, A.B.'13, Defiance Col.; M.A.'26, Univ. of Mich.; LL.D.'27, Ashland Col.; LL.D.'42, Defiance Col.; D. Ped.'42, Bowling Green State Univ.; Supt. of Sch., Toledo 2, Ohio, since 1937.

Bowyer, Vernon, S.B.'21, A.M.'23, Univ. of Chicago; Sponsor's Director of WPA Educ., Bd. of Educ., 228 N. La Salle St., Chicago, Ill., since 1937.

Boyer, B. J., Ph.B.'18, Lafayette Col.; Supvg. Prin. of Sch., Middlesex, N. J., since 1941.

Boyer, Clarence Edwin, Supt. of Sch., Boonton, N. J.

Boyer, Fred A., Asst. Supt. of Sch., Coronado, Calif.

Boyer, John B., B.S.'08, A.M.'25, Bucknell Univ.; Asst. Co. Supt. of Sch., Herndon, Pa.

Boyer, Philip A., Ph.D.'20, Univ. of Pa.; Dir., Div. of Educ. Research and Results, Admin. Bldg., Parkway at 21st St., Philadelphia, Pa., since 1925.

Boyle, Joseph E., A.B.'25, Mt. St. Mary's Col.; M.Ed.'36, Pa. State Col.; Supt. of Sch., Mahanoy City, Pa., since 1942.

Boyne, Edwin M., A.B.'20, Alma Col.; A.M.'26, Univ. of Mich.; Supt. of Sch., Mason, Mich., since 1937.

Bracewell, Ray H., B.S.'15, Ill. Col.; M.A.'25, Univ. of Chicago; Supt. of Sch., Burlington, Iowa, since 1937.

Bracken, John L., A.M.'22, Univ. of Chicago; Supt. of Sch., Clayton, Mo., since 1923.

Bradley, Clifton E., B.S.'26, Colgate Univ.; M.Ed.'33, Boston Univ.; Union Supt. of Sch., Hanover, Mass., since 1943.

Bradner, J. W., B.S.'94, Tri-State Col.; A.B.'08, Ind. Univ.; A.M.'24, Tchrs. Col., Columbia Univ.; Supt. of Sch., Middlesboro, Ky., since 1922.

Bradshaw, G. V., Supt. of Sch., Valley Park, Mo.

Brady, Francis James, A.B.'16, A.M.'19, Brown Univ.; LL.B.'22, Harvard Law Sch.; Chmn., Sch. Com., Industrial Trust Bldg., Providence, R. I., since 1928.

Brady, John F., Chief Deputy Supt. of Sch., San Francisco 2, Calif.

Braham, W. J., Supt. of Sch., North Platte, Nebr., since 1922.

Brainard, Alanson D., B.Sc.'25, Midland Col.; M.A.'35, Univ. of Nebr.; Asst. Supt. of Sch., Muskegon, Mich., since 1940.

Brame, Scott Miller, A.B.'02, A.M.'32, La. State Univ.; Prin., Bolton H. S., Alexandria, La., since 1909.

Brammell, P. Roy, A.B.'23, McPherson Col.; A.M.'28, Univ. of Mich.; Ph.D.'30, Univ. of Wash.; Dean, Sch. of Educ., Univ. of Conn., Storrs, Conn., since 1940.

Branch, Mary E., Ph.B.'22, A.M.'25, Univ. of Chicago; LL.D.'35, Howard Univ.; D.Ped.'35, Va. State Col.; Pres., Tillotson Col., Austin 22, Texas, since 1930.

Brand, J. H., M.A.'38, Univ. of Mo.; Co. Supt. of Sch., Steelville, Mo., since 1923.

Branigan, John, B.Sc.'15, Univ. of Nebr.; A.M.'26, Stanford Univ.; Supt. of Sch., Redlands, Calif., since 1937.

Branom, Wayne T., B.Ed.'32, Ill. State Normal Univ., Normal, Ill.; M.S.'34, Northwestern Univ.; Ed.D.'41, New York Univ.; Supvg. Prin. of Sch., Carteret, N. J., since 1941.

Brant, Ralph E., B.A.'27, Olivet Col.; M.A.'32, Columbia Univ.; Supt. of Sch., Menominee, Mich., since 1943.

Brantley, G. D., A.B.'20, Talladega Col.; A.M.'26, Columbia Univ.; Prin., Sumner H. S., 4248 W. Cottage Ave., St. Louis, Mo., since 1929.

Bratcher, E. E., A.B.'19, M.A.'27, Univ. of Ky.; Ph.D.'36, Univ. of Chicago. Address: Pub. Sch., Hot Springs, Ark.

Braucher, Howard S., A.B.'03, Cornell Univ.; Secy., Natl. Recreation Assn., 315 Fourth Ave., New York 10, N. Y., since 1909.

Braulick, Edward J., A.B.'07, Wartburg Col.; M.A.'16, Capitol Univ.; S.T.D.'41, American Theol. Seminary; Pres., Wartburg Col., Waverly, Iowa, since 1935.

Brawner, R. B., Supt. of Sch., North Little Rock, Ark., since 1943.

Bray, Frank C., Ph.B.'03, M.A.'26, Univ. of Wis. Address: 336 S. Main St., Fort Atkinson, Wis.

Bray, Mildred N., B.S.'14, Mills Col.; State Supt. of Pub. Instr., Carson City, Nev., since 1937.

Breckenridge, J. L., A.B.'08, Oberlin Col.; Supt. of Sch., Hood River, Oregon, since 1927.

Breedlove, C. B., B.A.'29, Sul Ross State Tchrs. Col., Alpine, Texas; Supt. of Sch., Haskell, Texas, since 1928.

Breitwieser, Joseph Valentine, A.B.'07, A.M.'08, Ind. Univ.; Ph.D.'11, Columbia Univ.; Dean, Sch. of Educ. and Dir., Grad. Div., Univ. of N. Dak., Grand Forks, N. Dak., since 1928.

Brennan, Fred J., A.B.'17, A.M.'18, Clark Univ.; LL.B.'32, Northeastern Univ.; Asst. Supt. of Sch., Worcester 8, Mass., since 1943.

Brent, William S., B.S.'17, M.A.'38, Col. of William and Mary; Div. Supt. of Sch., Heathsville, Va., since 1928.

Bres, Joseph Hughes, A.B.'06, Tulane Univ.; Parish Supt. of Educ., Port Allen, La., since 1908.

Bresnehen, Ella L., A.B.'25, Radcliffe Col.; Ed.M.'27, Harvard Univ.; Ph.D.'31, Boston Col.; Dir., Investigation & Measurement, Pub. Sch., 45 Myrtle St., Boston, Mass., since 1932.

Brewer, Karl M., B.A.'33, M.Ed.'38, Pa. State Col.; Supt. of Sch., Du Bois, Pa., since 1942.

Brewington, Ann, S.B. in Ed.'20, Northeast Mo. State Tchrs. Col., Kirksville, Mo.; Ph.B.'21, M.A.'22, Univ. of Chicago; Assoc. Prof., Sch. of Business, Univ. of Chicago, Chicago, Ill., since 1942.

Brickey, L. H., 405 Third Ave., Fountain City, Tenn.

Briggs, Eugene S., B.S.'12, Central Col., Fayette, Mo.; M.A.'17, Univ. of Mo.; Ph.D.'34, Columbia Univ.; Pres., Phillips Univ., Enid, Okla., since 1938.

Bright, Ira J., B.S.'16, State Tchrs. Col., Emporia, Kansas; M.A.'18, Tchrs. Col., Columbia Univ.; Supt. of Sch., Times Bldg., Leavenworth, Kansas, since 1919.

Bright, Orville T., Jr., Ph.B.'35, M.A.'39, Univ. of Chicago; Supt. of Sch., Lake Bluff, Ill., since 1943.

Brillhart C. D., A.B.'16, Albright Col.; M.A.'32, Univ. of Mich.; Supt. of Sch., Napoleon, Ohio, since 1925.

Briner, Francis William, B.S.'23, State Tchrs. Col., Emporia, Kansas; M.A.'32, Tchrs. Col., Columbia Univ.; Supt. of Sch., Harper, Kansas, since 1941.

Brinton, Charles A., Supvg. Prin., Clifton Hgts. Schs., Upper Darby, Pa., since 1935.

Bristow, Mrs. Norma S., Supvr. of Elem. Sch., Montgomery 5, Ala.

Bristow, William H., B.S.'20, Central Mo. State Tchrs. Col., Warrensburg, Mo.; A.M.'22, Ed.D.'36, Tchrs. Col., Columbia Univ.; Asst. Dir., Bureau of Reference, Research, and Statistics, Bd. of Educ., 110 Livingston St., Brooklyn 2, N. Y., since 1940.

Britton, Lewis H., A.B.'05, Stanford Univ.; Co. Supt. of Sch., San Jose, Calif., since 1935.

Broad, Lambert E., A.B.'27, Lehigh Univ.; A.M.'31, Univ. of Pittsburgh; Prin., Mining and Mech. Inst., Freeland, Pa., since 1934.

Broady, Knute Oscar, B.S.'20, Washburn Col.; M.A.'27, Univ. of Chicago; Ph.D.'30, Columbia Univ.; Dir. of Univ. Extension Div., Univ. of Nebr., Lincoln, Nebr., since 1941.

Brock, Frank M., B.S.'41, Western Wash. Col. of Educ.; Asst. Supt. and Bus. Mgr., Pub. Sch., Seattle 9, Wash., since 1943.

Broening, Angela M., A.B., Goucher Col.; A.M., Ph.D., Johns Hopkins Univ.; Instr. in Educ., Johns Hopkins Univ., Baltimore, Md., since 1926 and Head English Dept., Forest Park H. S., Baltimore, Md.

Brooks, B. P., B.A.'08, Union Univ.; M.A.'32, George Peabody Col. for Tchrs.; Dean, Sch. of Educ., Miss. State Col., State College, Miss., since 1940.

Brooks, Elwood E., Supt. of Sch., Salem, Ind., since 1934.

Brooks, Ercell W., B.A.'30, West Texas State Tchrs. Col., Canyon, Texas; M.A.'39, Baylor Univ.; Supt. of Sch., Gatesville, Texas, since 1936.

Brooks, James Furman, A.B.'14, Univ. of S. C.; M.A.'16, Clark Univ.; Co. Supt. of Educ., Spartanburg, S. C., since 1937.

Brooks, Ralph G., A.B.'25, Nebr. Wesleyan Univ.; A.M.'32, Univ. of Nebr.; Supt. of Sch., Wymore, Nebr., since 1934.

Brooks, T. Latimer, B.A.'06, Dickinson Col.; M.A.'15, Columbia Univ.; Supvg. Prin. of Sch., Somerville, N. J., since 1921.

Brooks, Wiley G., A.B.'10, York Col.; B.E.'11, Nebr. State Tchrs. Col., Peru, Nebr.; A.M.'15, Columbia Univ.; Ph.D.'36, State Univ. of Iowa; Pres., State Tchrs. Col., Chadron, Nebr., since 1941.

Broome, Edwin C., Ph.B.'97, A.M.'98, Brown Univ.; Ph.D.'02, Columbia Univ.; LL.B. '07, St. Lawrence Univ.; LL.D.'25, Ursinus Col.; Ed.D.'27, Brown Univ.; Litt.D.'30, R.I. Col. of Educ.; LL.D.'34, Juniata Col.; L.H.D.'34, Univ. of Pa.; Sc.D.'37, Temple Univ.; Pres., Dept. of Superintendence, 1931-32; Honorary Life Member, American Assn. of Sch. Admin.; Attorney, 217 E. Sedgwick St., Mt. Airy, Philadelphia, Pa.

Broome, Edwin W., LL.B.'16, A.B.'20, George Washington Univ.; Co. Supt. of Sch., Rockville, Md., since 1916.

Brophy, Byron J., A.B. and B.Sc.'22, Tri-State Col.; A.M.'30, Univ. of Mich.; Prin. Tr. Specialist, War-Manpower, O.E.M. Address: 3516 S. Stafford St., Arlington, Va., since 1943.

Brothers, C. A., A.B.'11, Lake Forest Col.; A.M.'24, Tchrs. Col., Columbia Univ.; Supt. of Sch., Dwight, Ill., since 1911.

Brotherton, Ralph S., A.B.'26, Western State Tchrs. Col., Kalamazoo, Mich.; M.A.'33, Univ. of Mich.; Supt. of Sch., Harbor Beach, Mich., since 1931.

Brougher, John F., A.B.'26, Columbia Univ.; M.A.'29, Tchrs. Col., Columbia Univ.; Acting Prin., Calvin Coolidge H. S., Washington, D. C., since 1941.

Brourink, R. R., A.B.'11, Simpson Col.; Supt. of Sch., Ft. Morgan, Colo., since 1931.

Browe, Herman, A.B.'11, M.A.'22, Univ. of Mich.; LL.B. and J.D.'24, Detroit Col. of Law; LL.D.'37, Univ. of Detroit; Deputy Supt. of Sch., 1354 Broadway, Detroit 26, Mich., since 1942.

Brown, Arlo Ayres, A.B.'03, Northwestern Univ.; B.D.'07, Drew Theol. Seminary; D.D.'21, Cornell Col., Mt. Vernon, Iowa; LL.D.'27, Syracuse Univ.; Litt.D.'29, Univ. of Chattanooga; LL.D.'38, Northwestern Univ.; L.H.D.'39, Boston Univ.; Pres., Drew Univ., Madison, N. J., since 1929.

Brown, B. Frank, B.L. and B.A.'09, Georgetown Col.; Supt. of Sch., Gulfport, Miss., since 1922.

Brown, Clarence S., M.A.'37, Univ. of Southern Calif.; Supt. of Sch., Ajo, Ariz., since 1929.

Brown, Edward W., B.S.'23, Princeton Univ.; Headmaster, Calvert Sch., Tuscany Rd., Baltimore, Md., since 1940.

Brown, Emmett, B.A.'96, Univ. of Nashville; Supt. of Sch., Cleburne, Texas, since 1913.

Brown, Forrest Dumont, B.S. in Ed.'29, M.S.'30, Ft. Hays Kansas State Col.; Ph.D.'33, Univ. of Cincinnati; Dean, Simpson Col., Indianola, Iowa, since 1939.

Brown, Francis W., A.B.'21, Univ. of Mich.; A.M.'31, Western Reserve Univ.; Supt. of Ottawa Hills Schs, Toledo, Ohio, since 1936.

Brown, George Earl, Diploma '06, State Normal Sch., Emporia, Kansas; A.B.'13, State Tchrs. Col., Greeley, Colo.; A.M.'19, Univ. of Denver; A.M.'26, Columbia Univ.; Supt. of Sch., Ocean City, N. J., since 1931.

Brown, Harold S., Chas. E. Merrill Co., 373 Fourth Ave., New York, N. Y.

Brown, Herbert C., A.B.'17, Greenville Col.; A.M.'30. George Washington Univ.; Co. Supt. of Sch., Ellicott City, Md., since 1933.

Brown, James F., LL.B.'30, Lake Erie Sch. of Law; Dir. of Sch., Bd. of Educ., Cleveland, Ohio, since 1937.

Brown, Joseph C., B.S.'01, M.A.'13, Columbia Univ.; Supt. of Sch., Pelham, N. Y., since 1929.

Brown Leland P., A.B.'16, Univ. of Wash.; Supt. of Sch., Olympia, Wash., since 1931.

Brown, M. W., Supt. of Sch., Glen Ridge, N. J.

Brown, Minter E., A.B.'22, Southwestern Col.; M.A.'31, Univ. of Kansas; Supt. of Sch., Anthony, Kansas, since 1939.

Brown, Oliver, Dist. Supt. of Sch., Gilroy, Calif.

Brown, Paul V., A.M.'30, Univ. of Chicago; Supt. of Sch., Tiffin, Ohio, since 1931.

Brown, Raymond N., B.S.'09, Amherst Col.; M.A.'35, Yale Univ.; Supt. of Sch., Meriden, Conn., since 1938.

Brown, Samuel Mortimer, B.B.A.'25, Univ. of Texas; M.A.'31, Tchrs. Col., Columbia Univ.; Ph.D.'41, Univ. of Texas; Supt. of Sch., Nacogdoches, Texas, since 1941.

Brown, Winston D., A.B.'33, Univ. of Wis.; M.E.'41, Marquette Univ.; Co. Supt. of Sch., Waukesha, Wis., since 1941.

Brownell, Samuel M., A.B.'21, Univ. of Nebr.; A.M.'24, Ph.D.'26, Yale Univ.; Prof. of Educ. Admin., Grad. Sch., Yale Univ., New Haven, Conn., since 1938.

Bruce, David Harry, M.A.'38 Univ. of Pittsburgh; Supvg. Prin. of Twp. Sch., Terrace, Pa., since 1929.

*Bruce, Imon E., B.A.'32, Henderson State Tchrs. Col., Arkadelphia, Ark.; M.A.'37, La. State Univ.; Supt. of Sch., Fordyce, Ark., since 1937.

Bruce, M. E., Ph.M.'28, Univ. of Wis.; Supt. of Sch., East St. Louis, Ill., since 1942.

Bruce, William C. A.B.'01, A.M.'10, Marquette Univ.; Editor, *American School Board Journal*, Milwaukee, Wis.

Bruggeman, L. L., A.B.'36, Rutgers Univ.; Mgr., Eastern Div., American Book Co., 88 Lexington Ave., New York 16, N. Y., since 1943.

Brugler, V. C., Supvg. Prin. of Sch., Hackettstown, N. J., since 1922.

Brumbaugh, Louise, A.B.'26, A.M.'27, Univ. of Ill.; Dir., Bureau of Research and Measurement, Central H. S., Fort Wayne 2, Ind., since 1936.

Brunell, Horace P., Pd.B'16, Colo. Col. of Educ.; B.S. in Ed.'37, M.A.'40, Univ. of N. Mex.; Supt. of Sch., Estancia, N. Mex., since 1923.

Bruner, Charles, A.B.'10, A.M.'13, Ind. Univ.; Supt. of Sch., Kewanee, Ill., since 1920.

Bruner, Fred, B.S.'16, Northeast Mo. State Tchrs. Col., Kirksville, Mo.; A.M.'23, Univ. of Mo.; Supt. of Sch., Bonne Terre, Mo., since 1922.

Bruner, Herbert Bascom, A.B.'13, Central Col., Fayette, Mo.; A.M.'15, Univ. of Mo.; Ph.D.'25, Columbia Univ.; Supt. of Sch., Oklahoma City, Okla., since 1943.

Brunner, Howard B., A.B.'23, Swarthmore Col.; A.M.'28, Columbia Univ.; Supvg. Prin. of Sch., Scotch Plains, N. J., since 1936.

Brunswick, Frederick H., B.S.'23, M.A.'33, Tchrs. Col., Columbia Univ. Address: 54 Rock Rd., Glen Rock, N. J.

Bryan, James Edmund, A.B.'90, Johns Hopkins Univ.; Ph.D.'08, Univ. of Pa.; Supt. Emeritus, Pub. Sch., Camden, N. J., since 1931. Address: 124 S. Springfield Ave., Merchantville, N. J.

Bryan, John Edwards, A.B.'15, Hampden-Sydney Col.; LL.D.'37, Howard Col.; L.H.D.'37, Birmingham-Southern Col.; Co. Supt. of Sch., Birmingham, Ala., since 1936.

Bryan, Paul C., A.B.'24, M.A.'25, Leland Stanford Univ.; Supt. of Sch., Albany 6, Calif., since 1941.

Bryant, George E., A.B. and A.M., New York Univ.; Supt. of Sch., Roslyn, N. Y., since 1943.

Bryant, Hayden C., B.S.'25, Emory Univ.; A.M.'29, Univ. of Chicago; Supt., Druid Hills Schs., Emory University, Ga., since 1937.

Buchanan, David W., B.S.'24, N. Dak. State Col.; Supt. of Sch., Davenport, Wash., since 1941.

Buchanan, James H., A.B.'28, Univ. of Denver; A.M.'32, Univ. of Colo.; Supt. of Sch., Boulder, Colo., since 1943.

Buck, J. L. Blair, Ph.B.'06, Yale Univ.; Ed.M.'26, Harvard Univ.; Ph.D.'42, Univ. of Mich.; Dir. of Tchr. Educ., State Dept. of Educ., Richmond, Va., since 1940.

Buckingham, Burdette R., A.B.'99, A.M.'00, Wesleyan Univ.; Ph.D.'13, Columbia Univ.; Ginn and Co., Statler Bldg., Park Square, Boston, Mass.

Buckley, Horace Mann, A.B.'08, Northwestern Univ.; M.A.'12, Columbia Univ.; Fellow '13, Univ. of Chicago; Asst. Supt. of Sch., Bd. of Educ., Cleveland, Ohio, since 1925.

Buckmaster, Stella, M.A.'32, Tchrs. Col., Columbia Univ.; Supvg. Prin., James B. Bonham and Ben Milam Schs., Dallas, Texas, since 1920.

BuDahn, L. A., M.A.'22, Columbia Univ.; Supt. of Sch., Pottsville, Pa., since 1930.

Budd, Harrell, B.A.'16, Guilford Col.; M.A. '25, Univ. of Texas; Dist. Prin., Trinity Hgts. Sch., Dallas, Texas, since 1942.

Bufkin, William Ernest, A.B.'20, Millsaps Col.; M.A.'33, Columbia Univ.; Supt. of Sch., Leland, Miss., since 1933.

Bugbee, Lloyd Harrison, B.S.'12, Dartmouth Col.; M.A.'29, Columbia Univ.; Ed.D.'34, American Internatl. Col.; Supt. of Sch., 51 Memorial Rd., West Hartford, Conn., since 1922.

Buikema, Benjamin J., A.B.'26, Western State Tchrs. Col., Kalamazoo, Mich.; M.A.'36, Univ. of Mich.; Asst. Supt. of Sch., Grand Rapids, Mich., since 1936.

Buker, William H., A.B.'10, Bates Col.; M.A.'24, Columbia Univ.; Supt. of Sch., Shelburne Falls, Mass., since 1933.

Bulick, Samuel B., B.S.'17, Susquehanna Univ.; M.Ed.'33, Univ. of Pittsburgh; Supt. of Sch., Greensburg, Pa., since 1942.

Bullock, William J., A.B.'24, Duke Univ.; A.M.'27, Col. of William and Mary; Supt. of Sch., Kannapolis, N. C., since 1931.

Bumgardner, Walter L., B.S.'18, Pa. State Col.; Supt. of Sch., East Aurora, N. Y., since 1932.

Bunce, Edgar F., Ed.D.'39, New York Univ.; Pres., N. J. State Tchrs. Col., Glassboro, N. J., since 1937.

Bunderson, Hervin, B.S.'12, Utah State Agrl. Col.; Supt. of Sch., Brigham City, Utah, since 1933.

Bunge, A. Frederick, A.B.'30, Univ. of Redlands; M.S. in Ed.'37, Univ. of Southern Calif. Address: 4780 Bancroft Dr., La Mesa, Calif.

Bunn, B. D., B.A.'20, Wake Forest Col.; M.A.'28, Univ. of N. C.; Co. Supt. of Sch., Oxford, N. C., since 1935.

Bunn, P. C., Ph.B.'09, Col. of Wooster; M.A.'22, Columbia Univ.; Supt. of Sch., Lorain, Ohio, since 1935.

Burch, R. L., Supt. of Consol. Sch., Hudson, Iowa.

Burdick, Andrew J., A.B.'15, Colgate Univ.; M.A.'27, Columbia Univ.; Litt.D.'42, Colgate Univ.; Supt. of Sch., Utica, N. Y., since 1941.

Burdick, Raymond C., A.B.'14, Alfred Univ.; M.A.'25, Columbia Univ.; Supt. of Sch., 59 Dewey Ave., Huntington, L. I., N. Y., since 1933.

Burgener, Charles E., M.A.'40, Univ. of Colo.; Supt. of Sch., Louisville, Colo., since 1930.

Burkard, William E., B.S.'17, M.A.'25, Ph.D. '27, Univ. of Pa.; Dist. Supt. of Sch., Wm. F. Miller Sch., Philadelphia, Pa., since 1942.

Burke, Harry A., M.A.'28, Ed.D.'42, Stanford Univ.; Supt. of Sch., Great Falls, Mont., since 1942.

Burke, J. L., Jr., B.S.'29, West Texas State Tchrs. Col., Canyon, Texas; M.A.'33, Texas Technological Col.; Supt. of Sch., Jal, N. Mex., since 1935.

Burke, P. J., Diploma '13, State Tchrs. Col., East Stroudsburg, Pa.; Cert. '23, Wharton Sch. of Accts. and Finance, Univ. of Pa.; B.A.'26, St. Thomas Col., Scranton, Pa.; M.A.'36, Bucknell Univ.; Supt. of Twp. Sch., Locust Gap, Pa., since 1933.

Burke, Regina C. M., Assoc. Supt. of Sch., 780 Riverside Drive, New York, N. Y., since 1938.

Burkhard, William J., M.A.'30, Univ. of Calif.; Asst. Supt. of Sch., Admin. Bldg., Sacramento, Calif., since 1940.

Burkhart, Harvey J., D.D.S.'90, Baltimore Col. of Dental Surgery, Univ. of Md.; LL.D.'20, Univ. of Rochester; D.Sc.'40, Univ. of Md.; Dir., Eastman Dental Dispensary, Sch. for Dental Hygienists, Rochester, N. Y., since 1915.

Burkman, Joel A., A.B.'24, M.A.'25, Univ. of Wash.; Ed.D.'31, Univ. of Calif.; Asst. State Dir. of Educ., Sacramento, Calif., since 1938.

Burnham, Archer L., A.B.'16, Univ. of Nebr.; A.M.'27, Tchrs. Col., Univ. of Nebr.; Ph.D.'38, Colo. State Col. of Educ.; Exec. Secy., Nebr. State Educ. Assn., 605 S. 14th St., Lincoln, Nebr., since 1938.

Burns, Robert, B.S.'16, Tchrs. Col., Columbia Univ.; A.M.'19, Ph.D.'28, Columbia Univ.; Lecturer in Educ., Sch. of Educ., Fordham Univ., New York, N. Y., since 1932 and Prin., Cliffside Park H. S., Cliffside Park, N. J., since 1918.

Burr, Samuel Engle, Jr., Litt.B.'19, Rutgers Univ.; M.A.'25, Univ. of Wis.; A.M.'27, Tchrs. Col., Columbia Univ.; Ed.D.'36, Univ. of Cincinnati; Capt., U. S. Army AGD, Third and Delaware Sts., New Castle, Del.

Burrell, C., Prin., Union H. S., Arroyo Grande, Calif.

Burroughs, E. B., A.B.'31, McKendree Col.; M.A.'36, Wash. Univ.; Supt. of Sch., Collinsville, Ill., since 1937.

Burrows, Charles N., Acting Dean, Simpson Col., Indianola, Iowa, since 1942.

Bursch, Charles, Chief, Div. of Schoolhouse Planning, State Dept. of Educ., Sacramento, Calif.

Bursch, James F., Ph.D'27, Stanford Univ.; Deputy Supt. of Sch., Admin. Bldg., Sacramento, Calif., since 1928. Major, U. S. Army, 551 Pico Way, Sacramento, Calif.

Burson, Susan Marie, B.S.'20, Univ. of Ga.; M.A.'30, Columbia Univ.; Federal Agt., Home Economics Service, U. S. Office of Educ., Washington, D. C., since 1935.

Burt, C. Vinton, B.S.'28, Jamestown Col.; M.A.'31, Columbia Univ.; Supt. of Sch., Owatonna, Minn., since 1941.

Burton, R. H., B.S.'27, Central State Tchrs. Col., Edmond, Okla.; M.S.'32, Okla. Agrl. and Mech. Col.; Supt. of Sch., Idabel, Okla., since 1935.

Burtt, Jerome, Ph.B.'14, Yale Univ.; A.M. '20, Tchrs. Col., Columbia Univ.; Prin., Williams Memorial Inst., New London, Conn., since 1938.

Bush, Clinton V., Supt. of Sch., Jamestown, N. Y., since 1938.

Bush, Mrs. Louise P., Supt., Lockport City Sch., Lockport, Ill., since 1930.

Bush, Maybell G., Ph.M.'28, Univ. of Wis.; Supvr. of Elem. Sch., State Dept. of Pub. Instr., 522 N. Pinckney St., Madison, Wis., since 1917.

Bussewitz, Walter R., B.A.'14, M.A.'17, Univ. of Wis.; Supt. of Sch., Horicon, Wis., since 1917.

Bussey, E. D., B.S.'13, Agrl. and Mech. Col. of Texas; B.A.'23, East Texas State Tchrs. Col., Commerce, Texas; Supt. of Sch., Garland, Texas, since 1923.

Bustard, Joseph L., B.S.'30, Rutgers Univ.; M.A.'33, Tchrs. Col., Columbia Univ.; Supvg. Prin. of Sch., Roselle, N. J., since 1937.

Butler, John H. Manning, A.M.'96, Pd.D'24, Livingstone Col.; Dean, Col. of Educ. and Head, Graduate Dept., Union Col. of Manila, Manila, P. I., since 1940.

Butler, Leslie A., Ph.B.'13, Univ. of Chicago; M.A.'19, Columbia Univ.; M.Ed.'21, Mich. State Normal Col., Ypsilanti, Mich.; LL.D.'27, Alma Col.; Dir. of Laboratory Schs. and Placement, Mich. State Normal Col., Ypsilanti, Mich., since 1939.

Butler, Rock L., B.S.'23, Grove City Col.; M.S.'37, Bucknell Univ.; Supvg. Prin. of Sch., Wellsboro, Pa., since 1914.

Butterworth, Julian E., A.B.'07, M.A.'10, Ph.D.'12, State Univ. of Iowa; Prof. of Rural Educ., since 1919 and Dir., Sch. of Educ., Cornell Univ., Ithaca, N. Y., since 1931.

Butz, Franklin J., A.B.'21, Muhlenberg Col.; A.M.'26, Univ. of Pa.; Supt. of Sch., Waynesboro, Pa., since 1943.

Buzzard, Robert Guy, Diploma '14, Ill. State Normal Univ., Normal, Ill.; S.B.'16, S.M.'17, Univ. of Chicago; Ph.D.'25, Clark Univ.; A.M.'38, Univ. of Ill.; Pres., Eastern Ill. State Tchrs. Col., Charleston, Ill., since 1933.

Byerly, C. C., A.B.'18, Manchester Col.; M.A.'34, Univ. of Chicago; First Asst. State Supt. of Pub. Instr., Springfield, Ill., since 1943.

Byers, B. H., B.S.'20, B.A.'23, M.S.'29, Pa. State Col.; Supvg. Prin. of Sch., Elizabeth, Pa., since 1929.

Byers, Carl C., B.S.'32, Otterbein Col.; M.A.'37, Ohio Univ.; Supt. of Sch., Thoreau Park Sch., Parma, Ohio, since 1942.

Byrd, H. C., B.S. in C.E.'08, Univ. of Md.; LL.D.'36, Washington Col.; LL.D.'37, Dickinson Col.; D.Sc.'37, Western Md. Col.; Pres., Univ. of Md., College Park, Md., since 1935.

Byrd, Rawls, A.B.'18, Col. of William and Mary; M.A.'25, Columbia Univ.; Supt. of Sch., Williamsburg, Va., since 1928.

C

Cain, H. L., Diploma '22, La. State Normal Col.; B.S.'24, Centenary Col.; M.A.'27, Baylor Univ.; Supt., The American Sch. Foundation, San Luis Potosi 214, Mexico, D.F., since 1926.

Calavan, Wade, B.A.'28, Col. of Puget Sound; Supt. of Sch., Sumner, Wash., since 1930.

Caldwell, A. B., A.B.'16, Maryville Col.; M.A.'21, Ed.D.'36, Tchrs. Col., Columbia Univ. Address: 2247 N. Hi-Mount Blvd., Milwaukee, Wis.

Caldwell, Lee L., A.B., Simpson Col.; B.A., Iowa State Tchrs. Col., Cedar Falls, Iowa; Supt. of Sch., Hammond, Ind., since 1922.

Caldwell, Otis W., B.S.'94, Franklin Col.; Ph.D.'98, Univ. of Chicago; LL.D.'18, Franklin Col.; Genl. Secy., American Assn. for the Advancement of Science, Yonkers, N. Y. Address: New Milford, Conn.

Callahan, John, LL.D.'34, Carroll Col.; State Supt. of Pub. Instr., State Capitol, Madison, Wis., since 1921.

Calloway, Andrew H., B.A.'29, M.A.'41, Ohio State Univ.; Asst. Co. Supt. of Sch., Charleston, W. Va., since 1933.

Calvert, E. T., George Washington Elem. Sch., 1520 N. Raymond Ave., Pasadena, Calif.

Cameron, Christina B., Asst. Supt. of Sch., Richmond, Calif., since 1928.

Camp, Harold L., B.A.'14, Grinnell Col.; M.A.'17, Cornell Univ.; Ph.D.'21, State Univ. of Iowa; Prof. of Educ., State Tchrs. Col., Indiana, Pa., since 1930.

Campbell, A. B., B.S.'23, M.A.'33, Univ. of Calif.; Asst. Supt. of Sch., 1414 Walnut St., Berkeley, Calif., since 1938. On military leave since 1943.

Campbell, C. G., Pres., Kewaunee Mfg. Co., Adrian, Mich., since 1920.

Campbell, Doak S., B.A.'11, Ouachita Col.; M.A.'28, Ph.D.'30, George Peabody Col. for Tchrs.; Pres., Fla. State Col. for Women, Tallahassee, Fla., since 1941.

Campbell, Ernest W., A.B.'18, LL.B.'22, Univ. of Wash.; Asst. Supt. of Sch., 810 Dexter Ave., Seattle 9, Wash., since 1940.

Campbell, Harold L., B.A.'28, Univ. of British Columbia; M.Ed.'38, Univ. of Wash.; Municipal Inspector of Schs., City Hall, Victoria, B. C., Canada, since 1936.

Campbell, J. M., B.A.'10, Maryville Col.; Supt. of Consol. Sch., Selah, Wash., since 1912.

Campbell, John Lucas, B.S.'15, Southwest Mo. State Tchrs. Col., Springfield, Mo.; A.M.'30, Univ. of Mo.; Supt. of Sch., Carthage, Mo., since 1929.

Campbell, T. J., A.B.'25, Univ. of Ala.; Supt. of Sch., Attalla, Ala., since 1942.

Campbell, W. M., Ph.B.'16, Parsons Col.; Ed.M.'34, Univ. of Oregon; Supt. of Sch., Roseburg, Oregon, since 1927.

Campion, Joseph W., B.Ed.'36, State Tchrs. Col., Kutztown, Pa.; Supvg. Prin. of Twp. Sch., Heckscherville, Pa., since 1936.

Campton, Charles E., B.A. in Ed.'13, Univ. of Minn.; M.A.'28, Tchrs. Col., Columbia Univ.; Supt. of Sch., Two Harbors, Minn., since 1915.

Cantor, Robert Lloyd, 1475 Grand Concourse, New York, N. Y.

Cantrick, George T., A.B.'14, Adrian Col.; A.M.'28, Univ. of Mich.; Supt. of Sch., Monroe, Mich., since 1932.

Capen, Samuel Paul, A.B. and M.A.'98, Tufts Col.; A.M.'00, Harvard Univ.; Ph.D.'02, Univ. of Pa.; LL.D.'20, Lafayette Col.; L.H.D.'21, Tufts Col.; L.H.D. '25, Hobart Col.; Sc.D.'27, George Washington Univ.; LL.D.'32, Univ. of Chicago; LL.D.'33, Univ. of Pa.; Litt.D.'37, Clark Univ.; LL.D.'38, McMaster Univ.; Chancellor, Univ. of Buffalo, Buffalo, N. Y., since 1922.

Carder, W. H., M.S.'38, Univ. of Idaho; Supt. of Sch., Port Townsend, Wash., since 1926.

Carey, Katharine Lee, A.B.'05, Univ. of Wis.; M.A.'27, Univ. of Southern Calif.; Asst. Supt. of Sch., Chamber of Commerce Bldg., Los Angeles, Calif., since 1929.

Carey, Raymond B., B.A.'13, Nebr. Wesleyan Univ.; M.A.'30, Univ. of Nebr.; Supt. of Sch., Gering, Nebr., since 1936.

Carlson, C. Allen, B.Ped.'14, State Tchrs. Col., Mansfield, Pa.; B.S.'36, A.M.'38, Univ. of Md.; Co. Supt. of Sch., Princess Anne, Md., since 1940.

Carlson, J. E., Jr., A.B. and B.Ed.'20, Univ. of Wash.; Supt. of Sch., Douglas, Ariz., since 1920.

Carlson, L. L., B.S.'24, M.S.'32, Univ. of Idaho; Supt. of Sch., Lewiston, Idaho, since 1941.

Carlson, Paul A., Ph.B.'21, Ph.M.'31, Univ. of Wis.; Dir. of Comml. Educ., State Tchrs. Col., Whitewater, Wis., since 1917.

Carmichel, Omer, A.B.'14, Univ. of Ala.; A.M.'24, Columbia Univ.; Supt. of Sch., Lynchburg, Va., since 1932.

Carothers, Milton W., A.B.'19, Univ. of Ala.; A.M.'27, Tchrs. Col., Columbia Univ.; State Dir. of Instr., Tallahassee, Fla., since 1937.

Carpenter, Estelle, Fairmont Hotel, San Francisco, Calif.

Carpenter, W. W., Ph.D.'26, Columbia Univ.; Prof. of Educ., Univ. of Mo., 124 Edgewood Ave., Columbia, Mo., since 1928.

Carr, George Eldon, A.B.'20, Ohio Univ.; A.M.'27, Ohio State Univ.; Supt. of Sch., Logan, Ohio, since 1930.

Carr, John Wesley, A.B.'85, A.M.'90, Ind. Univ.; Ph.D.'13, New York Univ.; Pres., Dept. of Superintendence, 1905-06.; Honorary Life Member, American Assn. of Sch. Admin. Address: State Tchrs. Col., Murray, Ky.

Carroll, George C., Supt. of Sch., Terre Haute, Ind., since 1927.

Carroll, John S., B.A.'30, San Diego State Col.; M.A.'32, Univ. of Southern Calif.; Ph.D.'40, Yale Univ.; Co. Supt. of Sch., Civic Center, San Diego 1, Calif., since 1943.

Carroll, Raymond J., A.B.'27, Univ. of Dubuque; M.A.'34, State Univ. of Iowa; Supt. of Sch., Oskaloosa, Iowa, since 1937.

Carrothers, George E., B.A.'09, Ind. Univ.; M.A.'15, Tchrs. Col., Columbia Univ.; Ph.D.'24, Columbia Univ.; Dir., Bureau of Cooperation with Educ. Inst. and Prof. of Educ., Univ. of Mich., Ann Arbor, Mich., since 1928.

Carruth, Irby B., M.A.'32, Univ. of Chicago; Supt. of Sch., Bonham, Texas, since 1938.

* Carson, C. C., B.A.'16, Ind. State Tchrs. Col., Terre Haute, Ind.; M.A.'23, State Univ. of Iowa; Ed.D.'30, Universidad de la Habana, Havana, Cuba; Prof. of Educ., Extension Div., Univ. of Fla., Gainesville, Fla., since 1931. Address: 229 36th St., Miami Beach, Fla.

Carson, Charles A., A.B.'21, Univ. of Ariz.; M.A.'24, Stanford Univ.; Asst. Supt. of Sch. in charge of Sec. Educ., Tucson, Ariz., since 1934.

Carson, L. F., A.B.'21, Furman Univ.; Ed.M.'38, Duke Univ.; Supt. of Sch., Gaffney, S. C., since 1936.

Carter, C. D., Supt. of Educ., Heart Mountain War Relocation Center, Heart Mountain, Wyo., since 1942.

Carter, David V., A.B.'17, Univ. of N. C.; Co. Supt. of Sch., Clinton, N. C., since 1927.

Carter, E. Frank, B. S.'33, State Tchrs. Col., California, Pa.; M.A. in Ed.'37, Univ. of Pittsburgh; Supt. of Rostraver Twp. Sch., Belle Vernon, Pa., since 1938.

Carter, Gordon L., B.S. in Ed.'35, Univ. of Wash.; Co. Supt. of Sch., Bellingham, Wash., since 1941.

Carter, Guyon J., B.S.'10, Alfred Univ.; M.A.'24, Columbia Univ.; Dist. Supt. of Sch., Avoca, N. Y., since 1911.

Carter, William H., A.B.'10, Middlebury Col. Address: Princeton Ave., Berkeley Hgts., N. J.

Case, R. D., A.B.'22, M.A.'23, Univ. of Denver; Ed.D.'31, Stanford Univ.; Supt. of Sch., Salinas, Calif., since 1931.

Casey, Charles Clinton, A.B.'04, Ark. Conference Col.; A.M.'06, LL.D.'34, Univ. of Denver; Pres., Western State Col., Gunnison, Colo., since 1930.

Casey, John C., B.S.'08, Ark. Col.; M.A.'09, Univ. of Denver; Supt. of Sch., Eaton, Colo., since 1922.

Cash, Ernest F., B.A.'34, Eastern Wash. Col. of Educ.; M:A.'42, Univ. of Wash.; Supt. of Sch., Montesano, Wash., since 1942.

Cassel, Lloyd S., A.B.'13, Ursinus Col.; M.A.'28, Columbia Univ.; Supt. of Sch., Freehold, N. J., since 1929.

Cassell, George F., Asst. Supt. of Sch., 228 N. La Salle St., Chicago, Ill., since 1936.

Cassidy, Rosalind, B.A.'18, Mills Col.; M.A.'23, Ed.D.'37, Tchrs. Col., Columbia Univ.; Convenor, Sch. of Educ., Mills Col., Oakland 13, Calif., since 1939.

Cassler, George W., B.S.'20, Susquehanna Univ.; M.S. in Ed.'31, Pa. State Col.; Supvg. Prin. of Sch., Coraopolis, Pa., since 1938.

Caswell, Hollis L., Ph.D.'29, Columbia Univ.; Prof. of Educ. and Dir., Div. of Instr. and Sch. Experimentation, Tchrs. Col., Columbia Univ., New York 27, N. Y., since 1937.

Caudill, C. C., Asst. Co. Supt. of Sch., East Bank, W. Va.

Cavanaugh, James Franklin, Ph.B.'30, Ph.M. '32, Univ. of Wis.; Supt. of Sch., Kaukauna, Wis., since 1925.

Caverly, Ernest R., A.B.'15, Harvard Univ.; A.M.'27, Columbia Univ.; Supt. of Sch., Town Hall, Brookline 46, Mass., since 1931.

Cavness, Raymond M., B.A.'25, Southwest Texas State Tchrs. Col., San Marcos, Texas; M.A.'30, Univ. of Texas. Address: 712 Academy St., San Marcos, Texas.

Cayer, L. A., B.A.'25, La. Col.; Parish Supt. of Sch., Marksville, La., since 1937.

Center, Leslie R., M.A.'30, Tchrs. Col., Columbia Univ.; Prin., James S. Hogg Jr. H. S., Houston, Texas, since 1937.

Center, Stella Stewart, A.B.'01, George Peabody Col. for Tchrs.; Ph.B.'11, Univ. of Chicago; A.M.'13, Columbia Univ.; Litt.D.'29, Univ. of Ga.; Dir., Reading Clinic, New York Univ., New York, N. Y., since 1935.

Chadd, Archie R., B.S.'28, Butler Univ.; M.S.'31, Columbia Univ.; Supt. of Sch., Anderson, Ind., since 1942.

Chalk, J. D., Jr., B.A.'19, Baylor Univ.; Prin., Sunset H. S., Dallas, Texas, since 1942.

Chambers, M. M., B.A.'22, Ohio Wesleyan Univ.; M.A.'27, Ph.D.'31, Ohio State Univ.; Capt., U. S. Air Corps Hqtrs., 455 Lake Ave., St. Louis 8, Mo.

Chambers, Mary A., Prin., Pub. Sch. 71, Buffalo, N. Y., since 1912.

Chambers, W. Max, B.S.'15, Berea Col.; A.B.'21, M.S.'29, Univ. of Okla.; Supt. of Sch., Okmulgee, Okla., since 1931.

Champlin, Carroll D., A.B.'14, A.M.'15, Haverford Col.; Ph.D.'25, Univ. of Pittsburgh; Prof. of Educ., Pa. State Col., State College, Pa., since 1926.

Champlin, George R., M.A.'35, Ed.D.'38, Tchrs. Col., Columbia Univ.; Asst. Prin., H. S., New Rochelle, N. Y., since 1942.

Chandler, H. E., A.B.'11, Washburn Col.; A.M.'27, Tchrs. Col., Columbia Univ.; Assoc. Prof. of Educ. and Dir. of Tchrs. Appointment Bureau, Univ. of Kansas, Lawrence, Kansas, since 1934.

Chandler, Paul G., Ph.D.'30, Columbia Univ.; Pres., State Tchrs. Col., Clarion, Pa., since 1937.

Chapelle, Ernest H., A.M.'25, Univ. of Mich.; Supt. of Sch., Ypsilanti, Mich., since 1934.

Chapman, Ernest T., Diploma '11, Ashland Col.; B.S.'26, Univ. of Pittsburgh; Supt. of Sch., New Kensington, Pa., since 1924.

Chapman, Harold Benjamin, B.A.'11, Yale Univ.; M.A.'24, Tchrs. Col., Columbia Univ.; Ph.D.'26, Ohio State Univ.; Asst. Dir., Bureau of Research and Statistics, Sch. Admin. Bldg., 3 E. 25th St., Baltimore 18, Md., since 1926.

Chappell, S. G., A.B.'27, Univ. of N. C.; Supt. of Sch., Wilson, N. C., since 1938.

Charitas, Sister Mary, Head, Dept. of Educ., Mount Mary Col., Milwaukee 13, Wis., since 1931.

* Charters, W. W., A.B.'98, McMaster Univ.; B.Paed.'00, Univ. of Toronto; Ph.B.'03, Ph.D.'04, Univ. of Chicago; Dir. of Educ. Research, Stephens Col., Columbia, Mo.

Chase, Lawrence S., B.S.'09, Colgate Univ.; A.M.'16, Columbia Univ.; Co. Supt. of Sch., Hall of Records, Newark, N. J., since 1933.

Chemberlen, Frederick T., Supt., Jr. Col. and Union H. S., Fullerton, Calif.

Cheney, Ray E., A.B.'20, Central State Tchrs. Col., Mt. Pleasant, Mich.; M.A.'25, Univ. of Mich.; Ph.D.'33, Columbia Univ.; Supt. of Sch., Elizabeth, N. J., since 1940.

Cheney, Thomas M., Prin., H. S., Trona, Calif.

Chenoweth, Arthur S., B.A.'06, Univ. of Colo.; M.A. (Oxon.); Supt. of Sch., Atlantic City, N. J., since 1931.

Cherry, David, Asst. Supt. of Sch., San Diego 1, Calif.

Chesky, Edward J., A.B.'11, A.M.'15, Univ. of Kansas; Supt. of Sch., Herington, Kansas, since 1928.

Cheves, Charles Judson, A.B.'19, Mercer Univ.; A.M.'30, Columbia Univ.; Supt. of Sch., Gainesville, Ga., since 1934.

Chidester, Albert J., A.B.'05, Syracuse Univ.; A.M.'12, Harvard Univ.; Head, Dept. of Educ., Berea Col., Berea, Ky., since 1922.

Childs, James R., A.B.'03, Amherst Col.; Supt. of Sch., Holden, Mass., since 1916.

Chisholm, J. Wilber, Diploma '20, State Normal Sch., Oneonta, N. Y.; B.S.'29, New York Univ.; M.A.'40, Tchrs. Col., Columbia Univ.; Dist. Supt. of Sch., Mineola, N. Y., since 1936.

Chisholm, Leslie L., A.B.'29, Southern Ill. State Normal Univ., Carbondale, Ill.; A.M.'33, Univ. of Chicago; Ph.D.'36, Columbia Univ.; Assoc. Prof. of Educ., State Col. of Wash., Pullman, Wash., since 1935.

Chittenden, Harold E., A.B.'09, Yale; Supt. of Sch., Naugatuck, Conn., since 1918.

Chittick, Murray A., B.S.'16, Rutgers Univ.; Supvg. Prin. of Twp. Sch., Old Bridge, N. J., since 1929.

Chittim, Harold David, B.S. in Ed.'32, M.Ed.'35, Boston Univ.; Supt. of Sch., Billerica, Mass., since 1941.

Cholet, Bertram, Adv. Mgr., Higgins Ink Co., Inc., 271 Ninth St., Brooklyn, N. Y.

Christensen, W. W., B.S.'23, M.S.'33, Utah State Agrl. Col.; Supt. of Sch., Idaho Falls, Idaho, since 1934.

Christenson, Christine A., Diploma '26, B.E. '42, State Tchrs. Col., Oshkosh, Wis.; Co. Supt. of Sch., Marinette, Wis., since 1927.

Christman, Paul Snyder, B.S.'19, M.Sc.'21, Franklin and Marshall Col.; Supvg. Prin. of Sch., Schuylkill Haven, Pa., since 1931.

Christy, Robert H., B.S.'32, Bowling Green Univ.; M.A.'40, Ohio State Univ.; Supt. of Sch., Delphos, Ohio, since 1940.

Church, Ernest E., A.B.'18, Waynesburg Col.; M.A.'26, W. Va. Univ.; LL.D.'40, Waynesburg Col.; Pres., Potomac State Sch., Keyser, W. Va., since 1936.

Church, Harold H., A.B.'18, Albright Col.; A.M.'29, Columbia Univ.; Supt. of Sch., Elkhart, Ind., since 1939.

Church, W. H., A.B.'19, Waynesburg Col.; M.A.'26, Wash. and Jefferson Col.; D.Ed. '42, Univ. of Pittsburgh; Supt. of Sch., McKees Rocks, Pa., since 1936.

Clark, Emmett, B.A.'22, Pomona Col.; M.A. '32, Claremont Colleges; Supt. of Sch., Pomona, Calif., since 1927.

Clark, Eugene A., A.B.'08, Williams Col.; A.M.'24, Columbia Univ.; Ed.D.'40, Morgan State Col.; Pres., Miner Tchrs. Col., Washington, D. C., since 1930.

Clark, Felton G., A.B.'24, Beloit Col.; A.M.'25, Ph.D.'33, Columbia Univ.; Pres., Southern Univ., Baton Rouge, La., since 1938.

Clark, Harold F., Ph.D.'23, Tchrs. Col., Columbia Univ.; Prof. of Educ., Tchrs. Col., Columbia Univ., New York 27, N. Y., since 1928.

Clark, J. Leon, B.A.'24, La. Col.; M.A.'27, Ph.D.'31, Univ. of N. C.; Pres., Southeastern La. Col., Hammond, La., since 1937.

Clark, K. J., Asst. Supt. of Sch., Mobile 9, Ala.

Clark, Lois M., A.B.'28, Western State Tchrs. Col., Kalamazoo, Mich.; M.A.'31, Tchrs. Col., Columbia Univ.; Adviser, Early Childhood and Elem. Educ., State Dept. of Pub. Instr., Harrisburg, Pa., since 1938.

Clark, Max R., B.S.'31, Iowa State Tchrs. Col., Cedar Falls, Iowa; M.A.'36, State Univ. of Iowa; Supt. of Sch., Sac City, Iowa, since 1940.

Clarke, C. L., Ph.D.'28, Univ. of Chicago; LL.D.'41, Alfred Univ.; Dean and Prof. of Educ., Lewis Inst. of Arts and Sciences, Chicago, Ill., since 1928.

Clarke, L. Katherine, B.A.'31, M.A.'33, State Univ. of Iowa; Prin., Merames Elem. Sch., Clayton, Mo., since 1940.

Clarson, James Willis, Jr., B.S.'18, Iowa State Col. of Agrl. and Mech. Arts; A.M.'22, Ph.D.'28, Univ. of Chicago; Dean, Col. of Educ., Univ. of Ariz., Tucson, Ariz., since 1927.

Claypool, Vincent B., B.S.'24, Univ. of Calif.; M.A.'35, Claremont Col.; Prin. and Dist. Supt., Union H. S., Barstow, Calif., since 1936.

Cleland, H. L., A.B.'13, Westminster Col., New Wilmington, Pa.; M.A.'28, Tchrs. Col., Columbia Univ.; Dir. of Personnel, Bd. of Educ., Pittsburgh 13, Pa., since 1941.

Clement, Rufus E., A.B.'19, Livingstone Col.; B.D.'22, Garrett Biblical Inst.; A.M.'22, Ph.D.'30, Northwestern Univ.; Pres., Atlanta Univ., Atlanta, Ga., since 1937.

Clemons, Howard H., B.S. in Agronomy '18, Iowa State Col. of Agrl. and Mech. Arts; B.S. in Agrl. Ed.'26, Mont. State Col.; A.M. in Ed.'30, Univ. of Chicago; Supt. of Sch., Lake Geneva, Wis., since 1935.

Cleveland, Ernest D., B.A.'23, Baylor Univ.; M.A.'40, Southern Methodist Univ.; Supt. of Sch., Overton, Texas, since 1931.

Climenhaga, A. W., A.B.'19, Taylor Univ.; M.A. in Ed.'40, Wittenberg Col.; Dean, Registrar, and Tchr. of Educ., Messiah Bible Col., Grantham, Pa., since 1928.

Cline, Frank P., A.B.'26, Bridgewater Col.; M.A.'31, Univ. of Va.; Acting Co. Supt. of Sch., Monterey, Va., since 1942.

Clish, Herbert C., B.S.'26, M.A.'27, Ed.D.'40, Columbia Univ.; Supt. of Sch., New Rochelle, N. Y., since 1940.

Cloud, Archibald J., B.L.'00, Univ. of Calif.; LL.D., St. Mary's Col.; Pres., San Francisco Jr. Col., San Francisco, Calif., since 1935.

Cloud, Roy Walter, A.B.'05, Stanford Univ.; Exec. Secy., Calif. Tchrs. Assn., 155 Sansome St., San Francisco, Calif., since 1927.

Clove, James, A.B.'14, Brigham Young Univ.; M.A.'24, Univ. of Utah; Ph.D.'32, Univ. of Southern Calif.; Supt. of Sch., Murray, Utah, since 1933.

Coates, James Pierce, A.B.'11, M.A.'26, Univ. of S. C.; Secy., S. C. Educ. Assn., 1510 Gervais St., Columbia 5, S. C., since 1925.

Cobb, Bruce B., B.A.'10, M.A.'28, Univ. of Texas; Secy.-Treas., Texas State Tchrs. Assn., 410 E. Weatherford St., Ft. Worth, Texas, since 1935.

Cobb, Thomas Howell, M.A.'26, Univ. of Ill.; Bd. of Educ., Urbana, Ill.

Cobb, W. K., A.B.'17, Pomona Col.; M.A. '32, Univ. of Southern Calif.; Co. Supt. of Sch., Ventura, Calif., since 1935.

Cobbins, O. B., A.B.'28, Miss. Baptist Col.; M.A.'39, Fisk Univ.; Dir. of Colored Schools, 248 E. Ash St., Jackson, Miss., since 1929.

Coblentz, C. R., B.S. in Ed.'32, Miami Univ.; Co. Supt. of Sch., Eaton, Ohio, since 1923.

Cochran, J. Chester, B.S.'29, Sul Ross State Tchrs. Col., Alpine, Texas; M.A.'31, Univ. of Texas. Address: 2413 Albans Rd., Houston, Texas.

Cocking, Walter D., B.A.'13, Des Moines Col.; M.A.'22, State Univ. of Iowa; Ph.D. '28, Columbia Univ.; Mng. Editor, The School Executive, 470 Fourth Ave., New York 16, N. Y., since 1943.

Cocklin, Warren H., B.S.'23, Franklin and Marshall Col.; A.M.'31, Univ. of Pa.; Supvg. Prin. of Upper Merion Twp. Sch., Bridgeport, Pa., since 1938.

Codding, Donald W., A.B.'26, Ohio Northern Univ.; M.A.'32, Ohio State Univ.; Supt. of Sch., Nelsonville, Ohio, since 1942.

* Cody, Frank, M.Pd.'12, Mich. State Normal Col., Ypsilanti, Mich.; M.A.'24, Univ. of Mich.; LL.D.'33, Univ. of Detroit; Pres., Dept. of Superintendence, 1929-30; Pres. Emeritus, Wayne Univ., Supt. Emeritus of Sch., Detroit, Mich., since 1942. Address: 725 Burlingame, Detroit, Mich.

Coe, Milton E., B.Sc.'22, Linfield Col.; Supt. of Sch., Lebanon, Oregon, since 1937.

Coffeen, Carl, B.S.'14, Ohio Wesleyan Univ.; M.A.'33, Western Reserve Univ.; Co. Supt. of Sch., Akron, Ohio, since 1935.

Cohen, Rose N., B.A.'32, Hunter Col.; M.A.'40, Tchrs. Col., Columbia Univ. Address: 66 S. Ninth St., Brooklyn 11, N. Y.

Colahan, Wayne J., B.A.'16, Univ. of Minn.; M.A.'35, Univ. of Chicago. Address: 500 South St., Woodstock, Ill.

Cole, C. E., Diploma '06, State Tchrs. Col., Kutztown, Pa.; B.S.'18, Muhlenberg Col.; A.M.'21, Columbia Univ.; Supt. of Twp. Sch., Temple, Pa., since 1925.

Cole, David S., B.A.'21, Univ. of Chicago; M.A.'39, De Paul Univ.; Prin., Talcott Sch., 1840 W. Ohio St., Chicago, Ill., since 1934.

Cole, Page E., M.A.'30, St. Lawrence Univ.; Supt. of Sch., Whitehall, N. Y., since 1923.

Coleman, Maurice L., Ed.D.'38, Univ. of Mo.; Supt. of Sch., Asbury Park, N. J., since 1940.

Colgan, Edward J., A.M.'20, Harvard Univ.; Head, Dept. of Educ., Colby Col., Waterville, Maine, since 1924.

Collier, Clarence B., A.B.'09, Tusculum Col.; A.M.'22, Ph.D.'26, George Peabody Col. for Tchrs.; Dean, State Tchrs. Col., Florence, Ala., since 1918.

Collins, Eleanor Freeman, M.A.'32, Stanford Univ.; Dir. of Curriculum, Elem. Sch., Redwood City, Calif., since 1926.

Collins, M. D., A.B.'31, M.A.'32, Pd.D.'33, Oglethorpe Univ.; LL.D.'38, Mercer Univ.; State Supt. of Sch., Atlanta, Ga., since 1933.

Colson, Ephraim P., A.B.'07, Bates Col.; Supt. of Sch., North Scituate, R. I., since 1920.

Columkille, Sister M., A.B.'13, A.M.'14, Ph.D.'23, Catholic Univ. of America; Pres., Incarnate Word Col., San Antonio, Texas, since 1923.

Combs, A. B., B.A.'10, M.A.'11, Wake Forest Col.; Assoc., Div. of Instructional Serv., State Dept. of Pub. Instr., Raleigh, N. C., since 1929.

Combs, Morgan LaFayette, A.B.'17, Univ. of Richmond; A.M.'22, Univ. of Chicago; Ed.M.'26, Ed.D.'27, Harvard Univ.; Pres., Mary Washington Col., Fredericksburg, Va., since 1928.

Compton, John L., A.B.'24, Whittier Col.; M.A.'29, Univ. of Southern Calif.; Supt. of Sch., Bakersfield, Calif., since 1940.

Comstock, Ernest Bernard, A.B.'05, Oberlin Col.; M.A.'26, Univ. of Chicago; Prin., North Dallas H. S., Dallas, Texas, since 1922.

Conant, James Bryant, A.B.'13, Ph.D.'16, Harvard Univ.; Pres., Harvard Univ., Cambridge, Mass., since 1933.

Conant, Lewis H., Ph.B.'03, Brown Univ.; Supt. of Sch., Methuen, Mass., since 1926.

Condrey, Ralph S., A.B.'13, McKendree Col.; A.M.'34, Northwestern Univ.; Supt. of Sch., Mt. Carmel, Ill., since 1920.

Cone, Charles E., B.S.'24, M.S.'30, Univ. of Idaho; Supt. of Sch., Chelan, Wash., since 1935.

Congdon, Randolph T., B.A.'00, Syracuse Univ.; M.A.'08, Harvard Univ.; Pd.D.'23, N. Y. State Col. for Tchrs., Albany, N. Y.; Exec. Secy., N. Y. State Tchrs. Retirement System, 152 Washington Ave., Albany 6, N. Y., since 1939.

Conger, Lester W., Ph.B.'23, Univ. of Wis.; Supvg. Prin. of Sch., Kohler, Wis., since 1922.

Conklin, Paul S., B.S.'17, Univ. of Ill.; M.S.'31, Univ. of Wis.; Co. Supt. of Sch., Rockford, Ill., since 1938.

Conley, William Henry, B.S.'30, Loyola Univ.; M.B.A.'32. Northwestern Univ.; M.A.'35, Loyola Univ.; Dean, Wright Jr. Col., 4261 Waveland Ave., Chicago, Ill., since 1935.

Conner, Forrest E., A.B.'23, Univ. of S. Dak.; M.A.'33, Ph.D.'37, State Univ. of Iowa; Sec. Sch. Supvr., Pub. Sch., Hibbing, Minn., since 1937.

Connor, William L., A.B.'14, Ind. State Normal Sch., Terre Haute, Ind.; M.A.'24, Columbia Univ. Address: 1839 Hamilton St., Allentown, Pa.

Conrad, B. W., A.B.'16, Union Col.; M.A.'38, New York State Tchrs. Col., Albany, N. Y.; Supt. of Sch., Scotia, N. Y., since 1927.

Conway, William F., A.M.'04, Seton Hall Col.; A.M.'17, Columbia Univ.; Supvg. Prin. of Sch., Edgewater, N. J., since 1909.

* Cook, Albert S., A.B.'95, A.M.'06, Princeton Univ.; Litt.D.'23, Western Md. Col.; Litt.D.'23, St. John's Col., Annapolis, Md.; Litt.D.'24, Univ. of Md.; LL.D.'37, Gettysburg Col. Address: Tuxedo Park, N. Y.

Cook, Charles E., A.B.'13, A.M.'17, Ind. Univ.; Supt. of Sch., North Manchester, Ind., since 1923.

Cook, Denton L., M.A.'40, Univ. of Fla.; Supvg. Prin. of Sch., Plant City, Fla., since 1942.

Cook, Frederic William, B.S.'14, New York Univ.; Supt. of Sch., Plainfield, N. J., since 1926.

Cook, Hugh Oliver, B.A.'99, M.A.'25, Cornell Univ.; Prin., Lincoln H. S., Kansas City, Mo., since 1923.

Cook, Mrs. Katherine M., A.M.'12, Columbia Univ.; Chief, Div. of Special Problems, U. S. Office of Educ., Washington 25, D. C., since 1921.

Cook, Paul M., A.B.'18, Central Wesleyan Col.; M.A.'27, Univ. of Chicago; Exec. Secy., Phi Delta Kappa, 2034 Ridge Road, Homewood, Ill., since 1928.

* Cook, Walter Wellman, B.A.'23, M.A.'26, Ph.D.'31, State Univ. of Iowa; Prof. of Educ., Univ. of Minn., Minneapolis, Minn., since 1938.

Cooke, Dennis H., A.B.'25, M.Ed.'28, Duke Univ.; Ph.D.'30, George Peabody Col. for Tchrs.; Head, Dept. of Educ. Admin. and Prof. of Sch. Admin., George Peabody Col. for Tchrs., Nashville 4, Tenn., since 1930.

Coon, Beulah I., B.S.'18, Univ. of Wis.; M.S.'26, Tchrs. Col., Columbia Univ.; Agt., U. S. Office of Educ., Washington 25, D. C., since 1930.

Cooper, Clarence G., B.S.'11, Tchrs. Col., Columbia Univ.; Co. Supt of Sch., Towson, Md., since 1920.

Coor, L. F., A.B.'36, Ariz. State Tchrs. Col., Tempe, Ariz.; Prin., Sch. Dist. No. 44, Avondale, Ariz., since 1936.

Copeland, S. D., A.B.'11, Mercer Univ.; Supt. of Sch., Augusta, Ga., since 1934.

Corey, Arthur F., Exec. Secy., Calif. Tchrs. Assn., Southern Section, 408 S. Spring St., Los Angeles 13, Calif., since 1942.

Corey, Stephen M., B.S.'26, Eureka Col.; M.A.'27, Ph.D.'30, Univ. of Ill.; Prof. of Educ. Psychology and Supt. of Laboratory Sch., Univ. of Chicago, Chicago, Ill., since 1940.

Corlett, Lewis T., Pres., Northwest Nazarene Col., Nampa, Idaho, since 1943.

Cornell, Ethel L., A.B.'14, Cornell Univ.; Ph.D.'19, Columbia Univ.; Educ. Research Div., State Educ. Dept., Albany, N. Y., since 1920.

Cornell, F. G., U. S. Office of Educ., Federal Security Agency, Washington 25, D. C.

Cornick, Homer H., A.B.'20, M.A.'22, Univ. of Calif.; Supt. of Sch., Santa Cruz, Calif., since 1940.

Corning, Hobart M., Ph.B.'11, A.M.'12, Dickinson Col.; A.M.'31, Tchrs. Col., Columbia Univ.; Supt. of Sch., Omaha, Nebr., since 1940.

Corona, Sister Maria, M.S.'22, Univ. of Notre Dame; Ph.D.'29, Fordham Univ.; Dean, Col. of Mt. St. Joseph, Mount St. Joseph, Ohio, since 1933.

Corrigan, Mrs. Grace J., State Dept. of Pub. Instr., Santa Fe, N. Mex.

Cory, Frank Mirl, A.B.'17, Ind. Univ.; A.M.'23, Tchrs. Col., Columbia Univ.; Supt. of Sch., Hagerstown, Ind., since 1926.

Cory, John J., E.M.'05, Colo. State Sch. of Mines; M.A.'25, Tchrs. Col., Columbia Univ.; Asst. Supt. of Sch., 414 14th St., Denver, Colo., since 1939.

Cosgrove, John K., M.S.'25, Univ. of Mich.; Supt., Everett Pub. Schs., 3426 S. Cedar St., Lansing, Mich., since 1936.

Costello, Maurice H., Ph.D.'27, St. Vincent Col.; Dean, St. Vincent Col., Latrobe, Pa., since 1938.

Cottingham, Claybrook, B.A.'99, M.A.'00, Univ. of Richmond; LL.D.'21, Baylor Univ.; Pres., La. Polytechnic Inst., Ruston, La., since 1941.

Cottrell, D. R., B.A.'29, Iowa State Tchrs. Col., Cedar Falls, Iowa; M.A.'33, State Univ. of Iowa; Supt. of Sch., Webster City, Iowa, since 1942.

Cottrell, Donald P., B.A.'23, Ohio State Univ.; M.A.'27, Ph.D.'29, Columbia Univ.; Prof. of Educ., Tchrs. Col., Columbia Univ., New York 27, N. Y., since 1941.

Coulbourn, John, LL.B.'10, Univ. of Md.; B.S.'24, Johns Hopkins Univ.; M.A.'31, Ph.D.'37, Tchrs. Col., Columbia Univ.; In charge of Jr. and Sr. H. S., Pub. Sch., Garden City, L. I., N. Y., since 1931.

Coulter, Kenneth C., A.B.'30, Ohio Univ.; M.A.'34, Columbia Univ.; Supvg. Prin. of Sch., Glen Rock, N. J., since 1941.

Coultrap, Harry M., A.B.'08, Univ. of Colo.; A.M.'14, Ohio Univ.; A.M.'37, Northwestern Univ.; Supt. of Sch., Geneva, Ill., since 1912.

Courter, Claude V., B.S.'11, Kalamazoo Col.; M.A.'25, Univ. of Chicago; D.Ed.'38, Kalamazoo Col.; Supt. of Sch., Cincinnati 2, Ohio, since 1937.

Courtis, Stuart A., B.S.'19, M.A.'21, Tchrs. Col., Columbia Univ.; Ph.D.'25, Univ. of Mich.; Prof. of Educ., Univ. of Mich., since 1924, and Wayne Univ., since 1932. Address: 9110 Dwight Ave., Detroit 14, Mich.

Covey, R. S., Diploma '16, North Texas State Tchrs. Col., Denton, Texas; B.S.'20, Texas Agrl. and Mech. Col.; M.A.'29, Univ. of Texas; Supt. of Sch., Sweetwater, Texas, since 1935.

Cowles, LeRoy E., Ph.B.'10, A.M.'13, Univ. of Chicago; Ph.D.'26, Univ. of Calif.; Pres., Univ. of Utah, Salt Lake City, Utah, since 1941.

Cox, Edwin A., Union Supt. of Sch., New Salem, Mass.

Cox, Floyd B., A.B.'18, M.A.'21, W. Va. Univ.; Co. Supt. of Sch., Morgantown, W. Va., since 1930.

Cox, Frank W., A.B.'24, Col. of William and Mary; M.A.'31, Univ. of Va.; Co. Supt. of Sch., Princess Anne, Va., since 1933.

Cox, Larue, B.A.'22, Howard Payne Col.; M.A.'26, Univ. of Texas; Supt. of Sch., Jacksonville, Texas, since 1927.

Cox, R. A., B.A.'25, State Tchrs. Col., Conway, Ark.; M.A.'29, George Peabody Col. for Tchrs. Address: Pub. Sch., North Little Rock, Ark.

Coxe, John E., B.A.'09, M.A.'28, La. State Univ.; State Supt. of Educ., Baton Rouge, La., since 1940.

*Coxe, Warren W., B.Sc.'11, Dakota Wesleyan Univ.; Ph.D.'23, Ohio State Univ.; Dir., Div. of Research, State Educ. Dept., Albany, N. Y., since 1923.

Coy, S. Clay, A.B.'31, State Tchrs Col., Peru, Nebr.; M.A.'39, Univ. of Colo.; Prin., Jr.-Sr. H. S., Grand Junction, Colo., since 1943.

Coy, William Stacy, A.B.'03, Ohio State Univ.; Secy., Ohio Tchrs. Reading Circle, 1454 N. High St., Columbus, Ohio, since 1920.

Crable, A. L., B.A.'17, Austin Col.; M.A. '27, Univ. of Okla.; Ph.D.'37, Austin Col.; State Supt. of Pub. Instr., Oklahoma City, Okla., since 1936.

Crackel, Verne E., B.A.'37, M.A.'40, Univ. of Chicago; Supt. of Sch., Crete, Ill., since 1927.

Craig, Mrs. Helen Baldock, A.B.'26, Iowa State Tchrs. Col., Cedar Falls, Iowa; Supt. of Sch., Superior, Ariz., since 1943.

Craig, John Alexander, A.B.'09, A.M.'10, Univ. of Mich.; Supt. of Sch., Muskegon, Mich., since 1929.

Crakes, C. R., B.A.'30, M.A.'41, Northwestern Univ. Address: 444 St. James Pl., Chicago, Ill.

Cralle, Robert E., M.A.'26, Univ. of Calif.; Supt. of Sch., Inglewood, Calif., since 1932.

Cram, Fred D., M.Di.'08, Iowa State Normal Sch.; B.A.'09, Iowa State Tchrs. Col., Cedar Falls, Iowa; M.A.'20, State Univ. of Iowa; Assoc. Prof. of Educ., Extension Div., Iowa State Tchrs. Col., Cedar Falls, Iowa, since 1920.

Cramblet, Wilbur H., A.B.'10, Bethany Col.; A.M.'11, Ph.D.'13, Yale Univ.; Pres., Bethany Col., Bethany, W. Va., since 1934.

Cramblitt, De Fore, A.B.'27, Linfield Col.; Supt. of Sch., Anacortes, Wash., since 1932.

Cramer, John Francis, A.B.'20, A.M.'21, Willamette Univ.; M.Ed.'32, D.Ed.'37, Univ. of Oregon; Supt. of Sch., Eugene, Oregon, since 1937.

Cramer, William Floyd, B.S.'17, Univ. of Mo.; M.S.'26, Univ. of Kansas; Dean, Sch. of Arts and Sciences, Central YMCA Col., 19 S. La Salle St., Chicago, Ill., since 1936.

Crandell, A. William, Dean of Faculties, Loyola Univ., New Orleans, La., since 1942.

Crane, Harold A., Ph.B.'17, M.A.'25, Lafayette Col.; Supt., Wilson Borough Sch., Easton, Pa., since 1941.

Crawford, Clarence L., A.B.'25, Cotner Col.; M.A.'28, Univ. of Nebr.; Ph.D.'36, Univ. of Mich.; Supt. of Sch., Council Bluffs, Iowa, since 1940.

Crawford, David, M.A.'36, Univ. of Chicago; Supt., Pub. Elem. Schs., Rochelle, Ill., since 1941.

Crawford, Floyd W., A.B.'08, LL.B.'09, M.A.'19, Univ. of Mich.; Supt. of Sch., Niles, Mich., since 1924. ♦

Crawford, Robert T., A.B.'27, M.A.'30, W. Va. Univ.; Dean, Glenville State Col., Glenville, W. Va.

Crawford, Will C., A.B.'13, Pomona Col.; A.M.'15, Columbia Univ.; Ed.D.'40, Univ. of Southern Calif.; Supt. of Sch., San Diego 1, Calif., since 1934.

Creel, John Paul, B.S.'21, Ala. Polytech. Inst.; M.A.'32, Tchrs. Col., Columbia Univ.; Prin., B. B. Comer Memorial Sch., Sylacauga, Ala., since 1925.

Cressman, Paul L., B.S.'25, Univ. of Pittsburgh; Ed.D.'34, Pa. State Col.; Dir., Bureau of Instr., State Dept. of Pub. Instr., Harrisburg, Pa., since 1936.

Croad, J. R., A.B.'28, Chico State Col.; M.A.'29, Stanford Univ.; Supt. of Sch., San Bernardino, Calif.

Crodian, J. P., B.S.'23, Ind. State Tchrs. Col., Terre Haute, Ind.; M.A.'28, Columbia Univ.; Supt. of Sch., Peru, Ind., since 1934.

Cromer, Sturgeon, A.B.'32, State Tchrs. Col., Flagstaff, Ariz.; M.A.'41, Univ. of Ariz.; Supt. of Sch., Globe, Ariz., since 1943.

Crooke, Charles R., A.B.'33, San Jose State Col., San Jose, Calif.; A.M.'35, Leland Stanford Jr. Univ.; Dist. Supt. of Sch., Union H. S., Mountain View, Calif., since 1936.

Cross, Albert L., A.B.'21, Baker Univ.; M.E.'39, Univ. of Kansas; Prin., Shawnee-Mission H. S., Merriam, Kansas, since 1933.

Cross, Arnett, A.B.'25, Okla. Baptist Univ.; Supt. of Sch., Clinton, Okla., since 1938.

Cross, C. Willard, B.A.'15, Carleton Col.; Diploma '21, Union Theological Seminary; M.A.'21, Tchrs. Col., Columbia Univ.; Supt. of Sch., Faribault, Minn., since 1935.

Crouse, J. Robert, Diploma '97, Univ. of Mich. Address: 1841 Wilton Rd., Cleveland, Ohio.

Crowley, Arthur J., Diploma '13, State Tchrs. Col., Potsdam, N. Y.; Dir., Educ. Staff, *The Reader's Digest*, 353 Fourth Ave., New York 10, N. Y., since 1940.

Cruikshank, Mrs. Ernest, B.S.'11, Tchrs. Col., Columbia Univ.; A.M.'37, Duke Univ.; Pres., St. Mary's Sch. and Jr. Col., Raleigh, N. C., since 1932.

Crull, Howard D., B.S.'31, Western State Tchrs. Col., Kalamazoo, Mich.; M.A.'37, Univ. of Mich.; Supt. of Sch., Port Huron, Mich., since 1941.

Crum, J. Wesley, B.S.'36, Seattle Pacific Col.; M.S.'38, Univ. of Wash.; Supt., King County Sch. Dist. No. 406, Seattle 88, Wash., since 1942.

Crumb, Herbert H., A.B.'05, A.M.'09, Hamilton Col.; Supt. of Sch., Endicott, N. Y., since 1913.

Crumpacker, H. C., A.B.'08, McPherson Col.; Ph.M.'10, Univ. of Chicago; Supt. of Sch., Hoquiam, Wash., since 1922.

Crutsinger, George M., B.A.,'08, Central Col., Fayette, Mo.; M.A.'10, Univ. of Mo.; Ph.D.'32, Columbia Univ.; Asst. Supt. of Sch., Westfield, Mass., since 1942.

Cryer, C. A., Supt. of Sch., Borger, Texas.

Cullimore, Allan Reginald, B.S. in C.E.'07, Mass. Inst. of Tech.; Sc.D.'41, Univ. of Newark; Pres., Newark Col. of Engineering, Newark 2, N. J., since 1927.

Culpepper, J. Broward, Supt. of Sch., Tallahassee, Fla.

Cummings, Adison Gilmore, B.S.'27, M.S.'35, Univ. of Va.; Div. Supt. of Sch., Bedford, Va., since 1932.

Cummins, Mrs. Grace M., Co. Supt. of Sch., Silver City, N. Mex.

Cunnard, Julia Helen, Ph.B.'32, M.A.'39, Univ. of Chicago; Prin., Elem. Sch., 4033 Waveland Ave., Chicago, Ill., since 1937.

Cunningham, Daniel F., A.B.'16, M.A.'18, Loyola Univ.; LL.D.'32, De Paul Univ.; Supt. of Catholic Sch., 755 N. State St., Chicago, Ill., since 1927.

Curry, Lawrence, A.B.'24, Wofford Col.; Dist. Supt. of Sch., Clover, S. C., since 1940.

Curtis, Charles La Rue, B.S. in Ped.'27, M.A.'42, New York Univ.; Supvg. Prin. of Sch., Rockaway, N. J., since 1919.

Curtis, George R., M.A.'34, Col. of Puget Sound; Prin., Univ. Place Sch., Tacoma, Wash., since 1926.

Curtis, Loren S., A.B.'32, M.A.'37, Univ. of Ariz.; Supt. of Sch., Marana, Ariz., since 1942.

Cusack, Alice M., A.B.'16, Univ. of Nebr.; A.M.'19, Columbia Univ.; Dir. of Kdgn.-Prim. Educ., Bd. of Educ., Kansas City, Mo., since 1921.

Cushing, Herbert L., A.B.'14, Grand Island Col.; M.A.'30, Univ. of Nebr.; D.Ed.'37, Nebr. Wesleyan Univ.; Pres., State Tchrs. Col., Kearney, Nebr., since 1936.

Cushing, J. Stearns, Supt. of Sch., Middleboro, Mass., since 1927.

Cushman, Charles Leslie, A.B.'21, Grinnell Col.; Ph.D.'27, State Univ. of Iowa; Assoc. Supt. of Sch., The Parkway at 21st St., Philadelphia, Pa., since 1943.

Cutts, Harvey C., A.B.'20, Mercer Univ.; M.S. in Ed.'41, Univ. of Ga.; Supt. of Sch., Greenville, Ga., since 1933.

Cylkowski, Angela Margaret, Ph.B.'26, M.A.'31, Loyola Univ.; Dist. Supt. of Sch., 641 E. 60th St., Chicago 129, Ill., since 1939.

Cyr, Frank W., B.Sc.'23, Univ. of Nebr.; Ph.D.'33, Columbia Univ.; Prof. of Educ., Tchrs. Col., Columbia Univ., New York 27, N. Y., since 1930.

D

Dailard, Ralph C., A.B.'28, Nebr. State Tchrs. Col.; A.M.'35, Univ. of Nebr.; Ph.D.'39, Columbia Univ.; Asst. Supt. of Sch., 825 Union St., San Diego, Calif., since 1939.

Dale, Tracy Earle, B.S.'25, Northwest Mo. State Tchrs. Col., Maryville, Mo.; M.A. '30, Univ. of Mo.; Supt. of Sch., St. Joseph 54, Mo., since 1939.

Daley, Mary Wood, B.A.'08, M.A.'11, Wellesley Col.; Dir. of Educ., Sleighton Farm Sch. for Girls, Darling, Pa., since 1919.

Dalthorp, Charles John, B.S.'20, S. Dak. State Col.; M.A.'32, Univ. of Minn.; Supt. of Sch., Aberdeen, S. Dak., since 1929.

Daniel B. Roy, Supvr. of Curriculum, Pub. Sch., Enid, Okla.

Daniel, J. McT., A.B.'17, Wofford Col.; A.M.'29, Univ. of S. C.; Ed.M.'31, Ed.D.'35, Harvard Univ.; Prof. of Educ., Univ. of S. C., Columbia, S. C., since 1932.

Daniel, W. P., B.S.'28, Miss. State Col.; M.A.'39, George Peabody Col. for Tchrs.; Supt. of Sch., New Albany, Miss., since 1932.

* Dann, George J., A.B.'96, Union Col.; Pd.D.'14, New York Univ.; Supt. of Sch., Oneonta, N. Y., since 1910.

Dannelly, Clarence Moore, B.Ped.'07, State Tchrs. Col., Troy, Ala.; A.B.'12, Birmingham-Southern Col.; M.A.'26, George Peabody Col. for Tchrs.; L.H.D.'31, Birmingham-Southern Col.; Litt.D.'31, Southwestern Univ.; LL.D.'32, Centenary Col.; Ph.D.'33, Yale Univ.; Supt. of Sch., Montgomery, Ala., since 1936.

Darling, William T., Ph.B.'26, Ph.M.'28, Univ. of Wis. Address: Hazelhurst, Wis.

Darnall, Maynard C., A.B.'16, A.M.'31, Ind. Univ.; Supt. of Sch., Crawfordsville, Ind., since 1930.

David, Bert B., Ph.B.'21, Muhlenberg Col.; M.A.'26, Columbia Univ.; Supt. of Sch., Lehighton, Pa., since 1928.

Davis, Albert M., M.A.'33, Stanford Univ.; Supt. of Sch., Monterey, Calif., since 1942.

Davis, Angus Charles, B.S.'01, Denison Univ.; Supt. of Sch., Yakima, Wash., since 1913.

Davis, B. Woodhull, B.S.'19, Wesleyan Univ.; M. S.'27, Columbia Univ.; Supvg. Prin. of Sch., Princeton, N. J., since 1929.

Davis, Bernard L., A.B. and B.S.'20, Tri-State Col.; M.A.'31, Univ. of Mich.; Supt. of Sch., Hillsdale, Mich., since 1929.

Davis, Blynn Edwin, B.S.'13, Bates Col.; Ed.M.'29, Harvard Univ.; Supt. of Sch., Littleton, Mass., since 1936.

Davis, Donald P., A.B.'20, A.M.'30, Ph.D.'35, Univ. of Pittsburgh. Address: 3004 N. Fifth St., Harrisburg, Pa.

Davis, E. C., B.S.'27, New York Univ.; M.Ed.'33, Univ. of Pittsburgh; Supt. of Sch., North East, Pa., since 1927.

Davis, Frank G., Ph.B.'11, Bucknell Univ.; M.A.'24, Tchrs. Col., Columbia Univ.; Ph.D.'30, New York Univ.; Prof. of Educ., since 1924 and Acting Dir. of Admissions, **Bucknell Univ., Lewisburg, Pa., since 1943.**

Davis, George W., B.S. in Ed.'20, Northeast Mo. State Tchrs. Col., Kirksville, Mo.; M.S.'39, Univ. of Mo.; Supt. of Sch., Keosauqua, Iowa, since 1939.

* Davis, Harvey H., A.M.'23, Ph.D.'28, State Univ. of Iowa; Prof. of Educ., since 1936, Chmn., Dept. of Educ., since 1937 and Vice-Pres., Ohio State Univ., Columbus, Ohio, since 1942.

Davis, Hazel, B.S.'32, Tchrs. Col., Columbia Univ.; M.A.'36, Univ. of Chicago; Ph.D. '40, Tchrs. Col., Columbia Univ.; Asst. Dir. of Research, Natl. Educ. Assn., 1201 16th St., N. W., Washington 6, D. C., since 1937.

Davis, J. Thomas, A.B.'18, Univ. of Texas; B.S.'20, Agrl. and Mech. Col. of Texas; M.A.'21, Univ. of Texas; LL.D.'26, Howard Payne Col.; Dean, John Tarleton Agrl. Col., Stephenville, Texas, since 1919.

Davis, Jackson, A.B.'02, Col. of William and Mary; A.M.'08, Columbia Univ.; LL.D.'30, Univ. of Richmond; LL.D.'31, Col. of William and Mary; Assoc. Dir., Genl. Educ. Bd., 49 W. 49th St., New York, N. Y., since 1933.

Davis, James Willard, A.B.'15, Washington Col.; M.A.'24, Tchrs. Col., Columbia Univ.; Co. Supt. of Sch., Easton, Md., since 1935.

Davis, John W., A.B.'11, A.M.'20, Morehouse Col.; Litt.D.'31, Univ. of S. C.; LL.D.'39, Wilberforce Univ.; LL.D.'40, Howard Univ.; Pres., W. Va. State Col., Institute, W. Va., since 1919.

Davis, M. G., A.B.'14, Ind. Univ.; A.M.'20, Univ of Wis.; Ph.D.'35, State Univ. of Iowa; Supt. of Sch., Lake Forest, Ill., since 1936.

Davis, Olin W., A.B.'26, Huntington Col.; M.A.'31, Univ. of Cincinnati; Supt. of Sch., Dayton, Ky., since 1930.

Davis, Percy R., Ph.B.'04, Northwestern Univ.; Ed.D.'30, Univ. of Calif.; Supt. of Sch., Santa Monica, Calif., since 1932.

Davis, Sheldon E., B.S.'07, A.B.'08, A.M.'09, Univ. of Mo.; Ph.D.'17, Columbia Univ.; Pres., Mont. State Normal Col., Dillon, Mont., since 1919.

Davis, Walter A., A.B.'07, A.M.'13, Ind. Univ.; Pres., Vincennes Univ., Vincennes, Ind., since 1924.

Davis Warren C., Ed.D.'36, Univ. of Buffalo; Member, Dept. of Liberal Educ., Rochester Athenaeum and Mech. Inst., Rochester, N. Y., since 1929.

Davison, J. H., B.S.'25, M.A.'38, Ohio State Univ.; Supt. of Sch., Shamokin, Pa., since 1941.

Davison, O. W., A.B.'32, Central State Tchrs. Col., Edmond, Okla.; M.A.'36, Okla. Agrl. and Mech. Col.; Supt. of Sch., Chandler, Okla., since 1935.

Daw, Seward E., M.A.'33, Univ. of Chicago; Ph.D.'40, Univ. of Pittsburgh; Supt. of Sch., Wellsville, Ohio, since 1922.

Dawald, Victor F., A.M.'34, Ind. State Tchrs. Col., Terre Haute, Ind.; Supt. of Sch., Beloit, Wis., since 1938.

Dawson, Howard A., B.S. and M.A.'24, Ph.D.'26, George Peabody Col. for Tchrs.; Dir. of Rural Service, Natl. Educ. Assn., 1201 16th St., N. W., Washington 6, D. C., since 1936.

Dawson, Walter W., Pres., Co. Bd. of Educ., Oakland, Md.

Day, Edmund E., S.B.'05, A.M.'06, Dartmouth Col.; Ph.D.'09, Harvard Univ.; LL.D.'31, Univ. of Vt.; LL.D.'37, Harvard Univ.; LL.D.'37, Univ. of Pa.; LL.D '37, Syracuse Univ.; LL.D.'37, Dartmouth Col.; LL.D.'42, New York Univ.; LL.D. '43, St. Lawrence Univ.; Pres., Cornell Univ., Ithaca, N. Y., since 1937.

Day, Elbert E., B.S.'05, Marion Col., Marion, Ind.; A.B.'10, M.A.'15, Ind. Univ. Address: 1524 S. Gallatin, Marion, Ind.

Day, Lorey Clifford, B.A.'13, M.A.'16, Clark Univ.; Prin., State Normal Sch., Farmington, Maine, since 1940.

Deamer, Arthur, A.B.'09, Ind. Univ.; A.M. '13, Columbia Univ.; D.Ped.'39, Cornell Col.; Supt. of Sch., Cedar Rapids, Iowa, since 1921.

Dean, Clifford D., B.S.'25, Kansas Wesleyan Univ.; A.M.'35, Univ. of Kansas; Supt. of Sch., Lawrence, Kansas, since 1939.

Dearborn, Ned H., Ph.D.'25, Columbia Univ.; Exec. Vice-Pres., Natl. Safety Council, 20 N. Wacker Dr., Chicago, Ill., since 1942.

De Fraga, Harold, A.B.'32, San Jose State Col.; Dist. Supt. of Sch., Pittsburg, Calif., since 1940.

Degan, Sister Mary Lorian, M.A.'33, Univ. of Kansas; Vice-Pres., St. Mary Col., Xavier, Kansas, since 1934.

Degnon, D. T., Curtis Pub. Co., Independence Square, Philadelphia, Pa.

DeGroat, Harry DeWitt, A.B.'94, Williams Col.; Pd.D.'18, State Col. for Tchrs., Albany, N. Y.; A.M.'24, Williams Col. Address: 44 Graham Ave., Cortland, N. Y.

Dehn, A. O., A.B.'25, Univ. of Toledo; M.A.'30, Ohio State Univ.; Co. Supt. of Sch., Port Clinton, Ohio, since 1914.

DeKock, H. C., B.A.'26, Central Col.; M.A. '34, State Univ. of Iowa; Supt. of Sch., Tipton, Iowa, since 1940.

De La Hunt, Walter Keyes, B.S. in Ed.'28, M.S. in Ed.'31, Univ. of N. Dak.; Supt. of Sch., Benson, Minn., since 1936.

DeLaurenti, John C., M.A.'39, New York Univ.; Supt. of Sch., Highland, Ill., since 1942.

DeLay, Glenn A., B.A.'14, State Tchrs. Col., Emporia, Kansas; A.M.'28, Tchrs. Col., Columbia Univ.; Supt. of Sch., Neodesha, Kansas, since 1924.

Del Manzo, Milton C., Ph.D.'24, State Univ. of Iowa; Provost, since 1929 and Prof. of Educ., Tchrs. Col., Columbia Univ., New York 27, N. Y., since 1928.

Demaree, Paul H., A.B.'17, Ky. Wesleyan Col.; M.A.'35, Univ. of Southern Calif.; Prin. and Dist. Supt., Anaheim Union H. S., Anaheim, Calif., since 1941.

Deming, Leon J., A.B.'22, Phillips Univ.; M.A.'25, Univ. of Okla.; Supt. of Sch., Oyster Bay, N. Y., since 1928.

DeMoranville, Aaron F., Diploma '25, R. I. Col. of Educ.; A.B.'30, A.M.'34, N. Y. State Col. for Tchrs., Albany, N. Y.; Supt. of Sch., Johnston 9, R. I., since 1938.

Dempsey, John A., Supt. of Sch., 306 S. Valley Ave., Olyphant, Pa.

Deneke, Wesley A., B.S.'26, Southeast Mo. State Tchrs. Col., Cape Girardeau, Mo.; A.M.'31, Ed.D.'43, Univ. of Mo.; Supt. of Sch., Flat River, Mo., since 1936.

Dengler, C. F., Diploma '14, Keystone State Normal Sch., Kutztown, Pa.; B.S.'25. Muhlenberg Col.; A.M.'30, Columbia Univ.; Supt. of Sch., Wharton, N. J., since 1942.

Denlay, R. E., Supt. of Sch., Santa Paula, Calif.

Denman, G. E., Ph.B.'27, Ripon Col.; M.A. '32, State Univ. of Iowa; Supt. of Sch., Green Bay, Wis., since 1935.

Denman, George E., B.S.'16, Kansas State Col.; M.A.'32, Univ. of Idaho; Supt. of Sch., Burley, Idaho, since 1930.

Denmark, Annie D., B.Mus.'08, Meredith Col.; A.B.'25, Anderson Col.; Litt.D.'41, Furman Univ.; Pres., Anderson Col., Anderson, S. C., since 1928.

Dennis, Lindley Hoag, B.S.'12, Pa. State Col.; M.A.'33, Columbia Univ.; Exec. Secy., American Vocational Assn., 1010 Vermont Ave., Washington 5, D. C., since 1934.

Dennis, Merrill L., B.S. in Ed.'19, Ohio Univ.; M.A.'37, Columbia Univ.; Supt. of Sch., Mingo Junction, Ohio, since 1937.

Denniston, A. Bruce, B.S.'25, M.A.'28, Ed.D. '42, Univ. of Pittsburgh; Supt. of Sch., Greenville, Pa., since 1938.

Densberger, Frank C., A.B.'08, Syracuse Univ.; A.M.'21, Tchrs. Col., Columbia Univ.; Supt. of Sch., Kenmore, N. Y., since 1915.

Densmore, David W., B.S. in Ed.'28, Univ. of Rochester; A.M.'35, Cornell Univ.; Asst. Supt. of Sch., 13 S. Fitzhugh St., Rochester, N. Y., since 1940.

Dent, Ellsworth C., B.S. in Ed.'23, Kansas State Tchrs. Col.; Society for Visual Instr., 100 E. Ohio St., Chicago, Ill.

Dent, Lettie Marshall, A.B.'15, Western Md. Col.; Co. Supt. of Sch., Leonardtown, Md., since 1928.

Derthick, L. G., M.A.'30, Univ. of Tenn.; Supt. of Sch., Chattanooga 2, Tenn., since 1942.

Devers, Nancy O., Diploma '19, State Tchrs. Col., Florence, Ala.; B.S. and M.A.'25, George Peabody Col. for Tchrs.; Instr. in Geography, Univ. of Ala., University, Ala., since 1943.

Dewey, John, A.B.'79, Univ. of Vt.; Ph.D. '84, Johns Hopkins Univ.; LL.D., Univ. of Wis., Univ. of Mich., Columbia Univ., Univ. of Vt., Harvard Univ., St. Andrews, Paris; Honorary Life Member, American Assn. of Sch. Admin.; Prof. Emeritus of Philosophy, Columbia Univ., 1 W. 89th St., New York, N. Y.

Dewey, Ralph S., M.S.'19, Allegheny Col.; M.A.'27, Tchrs. Col., Columbia Univ.; Supt. of Sch., Corry, Pa., since 1926.

De Wolf, George E., A.B.'12, Univ. of Nebr.; A.M.'20, Harvard Univ.; Supt. of Sch., Downers Grove, Ill., since 1931.

Dexter, Walter F., A.B.'16, Penn Col., Oskaloosa, Iowa; M.A.'19, Columbia Univ.; Ed.M. and Ed.D.'21, Harvard Univ.; State Supt. of Pub. Instr., Sacramento, Calif., since 1937.

Dexter, William A., A.B.'28, Clark Univ.; A.M.'36, Univ. of Mich.; Supt. of Sch., Stockbridge, Mass., since 1940.

DeYoung, Chris A., A.B.'20, Hope Col.; A.M.'29, Columbia Univ.; Ph.D.'32, Northwestern Univ.; Dean, Ill. State Normal Univ., Normal, Ill., since 1943.

Dice, Norvell R., A.B.'28, Santa Barbara State Col.; M.S.'33, Univ. of Southern Calif.; Dist. Supt. of Sch., La Canada, Calif., since 1939.

Dick, Margaret D., B.S.'33, M.A.'42, New York Univ.; State Helping Tchr., Phillipsburg, N. J., since 1930.

Dickason, Henry L., B.A.'13, M.A.'14, Ohio State Univ.; Pres., Bluefield State Col., Bluefield, W. Va., since 1936.

Dickerson, Douglas Francis, Diploma '10, Nebr. State Tchrs. Col.; B.Ac.'11, Southwestern, Knoxville; A.B.'30, Univ. of Nebr.; M.A.'34, Central Univ.; Sc.D.'40, Webster Univ.; Supt. of Twp. Sch., Nashwauk, Minn. since 1939.

Dickison, Mary Ellen, Pres., H. S. Tchrs. Assn. of Los Angeles, 847 S. Grand Ave., Los Angeles, Calif.

Dickson, Bryan, B.B.A.'23, Univ. of Texas; M.A.'35, Southern Methodist Univ.; Supt. of Sch., San Angelo, Texas, since 1940.

Dickson, Virgil E., Ph.D.'19, Stanford Univ.; Supt. of Sch., Berkeley 7, Calif., since 1936.

Diefenbach, Carl M., A.B.'19, Syracuse Univ.; M.A.'26, American Univ.; Supvg. Prin. of Sch., Collingswood, N. J., since 1939.

Diehl, Fred W., B.S.'22, M.S.'35, Bucknell Univ.; Co. Supt. of Sch., Danville, Pa., since 1918.

Diemer, George Willis, B.S.'17, Central Mo. State Tchrs. Col., Warrensburg, Mo.; A.M.'25, Tchrs. Col., Columbia Univ.; Pres., Central Mo. State Tchrs. Col., Warrensburg, Mo., since 1937.

Diener, U. E., B.S.'17, Miami Univ.; M.A. '30, Ohio State Univ.; Supt. of Sch., Fremont, Ohio, since 1938.

Dietrich, George C., Ph.B.'98, Ohio State Univ.; Supt. of Sch,. Piqua, Ohio, since 1909.

Dillehay, Claude H., A.B.'16, Baylor Univ.; M.A.'17, Brown Univ.; Supt. of Sch., Vernon, Texas, since 1938.

Dillon, Hubert, A.B.'28, Friends Univ., Wichita, Kansas; M.S.'36, Kansas State Tchrs. Col., Pittsburg, Kansas; Supt. of Sch., Fowler, Kansas, since 1936.

Dimmett, W. S., Ph.B.'31, M.A.'36, Univ. of Chicago; Supt. of Sch., Forest Park, Ill., since 1930.

Dimmick, Earl A., A.B.'16, Albright Col.; M.A.'25, Ed.D.'37, Univ. of Pittsburgh; Assoc. Supt. of Sch., 341 Bellefield Ave., Pittsburgh 13, Pa., since 1938.

Dinsmore, B. M., B.A.'27, North Texas State Tchrs. Col., Denton, Texas; M.A.'29, Southern Methodist Univ.; Supt. of Sch., Electra, Texas, since 1917.

Dispanet, Raymond S., A.B.'38, Shepherd Col.; M.A.'42, W. Va. Univ.; Co. Supt. of Sch., Moorefield, W. Va., since 1943.

Dittes, William H., B.S.'21, Univ. of Minn.; M.A.'27, Tchrs. Col., Columbia Univ.; Supt. of Sch., Sherburn, Minn., since 1932.

Ditto, George W., B.S.'22, Univ. of Ala.; M.A.'27, Columbia Univ.; Supt. of Sch., Biloxi, Miss., since 1934.

Dixon, Frank A., A.B.'29, Central State Tchrs. Col., Mount Pleasant, Mich.; M.A. '33, Univ. of Detroit; Supt. of Sch., St. Clair Shores, Mich., since 1933.

Dobbs, Ella Victoria, B.S.'09, Columbia Univ.; A.M.'13, Univ. of Mo.; Emeritus Prof. of Applied Arts, Univ. of Mo., Columbia, Mo. Address: Frederick Apt., Columbia, Mo.

Dodd, John W., B.S.'20, A.M.'22, Tchrs. Col., Columbia Univ.; Ph.D.'35, New York Univ.; Supt. of Sch., Freeport, N. Y., since 1925.

Dodd, Lawrence V., B.S.'30, Susquehanna Univ.; M.S.'37, Columbia Univ.; Supt. of Sch., Lawrence, N. Y., since 1935.

Dodd, Maurice R., B.A.'14, Ph.D.'35, W. Va. Univ.; Asst. Co. Supt. of Sch., Charleston, W. Va., since 1933.

* Dodge, Harrison S., B.S. and Pd.B.'15, Syracuse Univ.; M.A.'30, Columbia Univ.; Supt. of Sch., Hornell, N. Y., since 1919.

Dodson, Edwin C., A.B.'04, Ind. Univ.; A.M.'14, Columbia Univ.; Supt. of Sch., Connersville, Ind., since 1921.

Dodson, Walter Lawrence, M.A.'27, Univ. of Texas; Supt. of Sch., Kilgore, Texas, since 1932.

Doe, Chester W., A.B.'10, Harvard Univ.; B.D.'13, Auburn Theological Seminary; M.Ed.'32, Univ. of N. H.; Union Supt. of Sch., Northwood, N. H., since 1928.

Doerfler, Frank P., B.A.'35. Mont. State. Univ.; Supt. of Sch., Ashton, Idaho, since 1942.

Domian, O. E., B.A.'21, Hamline Univ.; M.A.'29, Univ. of Minn.; Supt. of Sch., Waseca, Minn., since 1940.

Dominick, Leo H., B.A.'20, M.S.'30, Univ. of N. Dak.; Supt. of Sch., Fergus Falls, Minn., since 1937.

Donahoe, G. L., A.M.'36, Univ. of Mo.; Supt. of Sch., El Dorado Springs, Mo., since 1942.

Dondineau, Arthur, A.B.'14, A.M.'15, Univ. of Mich.; First Asst. Supt. of Sch., 1354 Broadway, Detroit 26, Mich., since 1942.

Donehoo, C. A., Supt. of Sch., Gadsden, Ala.

Donnelly, Rev. Thomas J., A.B.'05, Xavier Univ.; M.A.'12, St. Louis Univ.; Pres., John Carroll Univ., Univ. Hgts., Cleveland 18, Ohio, since 1942.

Donohue, Francis J., A.B.'34, M.A.'36, Fordham Univ.; Asst. Prof. of Educ. in charge of Tchr. Certification, Univ. of Detroit, Detroit, Mich., since 1943.

Donovan, H. L., A.B.'14, Univ. of Ky.; M.A.'20, Tchrs. Col., Columbia Univ.; Ph.D.'25, George Peabody Col. for Tchrs.; LL.D.'33, Univ. of Ky.; Pres., Univ. of Ky., Lexington, Ky., since 1941.

Donovan, Rev. James J., J.C.D.'38, Catholic Univ. of America; Pres., Col. of Educ., Great Falls, Mont., since 1938.

* Dorsey, Julius, M.A.'19, George Peabody Col. for Tchrs.; Supt. of Sch., Admin. Bldg., Dallas, Texas, since 1941.

Dorsey, Mrs. Susan M., A.B.'77, Vassar Col.; LL.D.'20, Univ. of Southern Calif.; LL.D.'25, Pomona Col.; LL.D.'27, Occidental Col.; LL.D.'28, Univ. of Calif.; Honorary Pres., Natl. Educ. Assn.; Honorary Life Member, American Assn. of Sch. Admin.; Supt. Emeritus, Pub. Sch., Los Angeles, Calif., since 1929. Address: 1506 Arapahoe St., Los Angeles, Calif.

Dotter, Charles Garfield, A.B.'08, Lebanon Valley Col.; Supvg. Prin. of Sch., Annville, Pa., since 1902.

Doudna, Edgar G., Ph.B.'16, Univ. of Wis.; M.A.'26, Lawrence Col.; L.H.D.'41, Milton Col.; Secy. and Dir. of Tch. Tr., State Bd. of Regents of Normal Schools, Madison, Wis., since 1928.

Dougall, John Bernard, B.A.'08, Adelphi Col.; M.A.'24, Yale Univ.; Chief, Bureau of Certification and Academic Credentials, State Dept. of Pub. Instr., Trenton, N. J., since 1940.

Douglass, Aubrey A., Supt. of Sch., Modesto, Calif.

Douthett, Walter R., A.B.'12, Ursinus Col.; A.M.'21, Univ. of Pa.; Supt. of Sch., Darby, Pa., since 1922.

Down, Edgar F., Normal Life Cert.'03, State Normal Sch., Cortland, N. Y.; A.B.'17, Univ. of Mich.; J.D.'25, Detroit Col. of Law; Supt. of Sch., Ferndale, Mich., since 1925.

Downey, James E., A.B.'97, A.M.'05, Amherst Col.; A.M.'12, Harvard Univ.; A.M.'13, Ph.D.'30, Boston Col.; Headmaster, H. S. of Commerce, Boston, Mass., since 1910.

Downey, Michael J., A.B.'04, A.M.'14, Boston Col.; Asst. Supt. of Sch., 15 Beacon St., Boston, Mass., since 1924.

Downey, Walter F., A.B.'06, Amherst Col.; Ed.M.'21, Harvard Univ.; L.H.D.'41, Amherst Col.; Head Master, English H. S., Boston, Mass., since 1922.

Downing, Carlton B., B.S.'29, North Texas State Tchrs. Col., Denton, Texas; Supt. of Sch., Albany, Texas, since 1934.

Doyle, Florence A., B.S. in Ed.'25, M.S. in Ed.'27, Temple Univ.; Dist. Supt. of Sch., Philadelphia, Pa., since 1941.

Drag, Francis L., M.A.'42, Stanford Univ.; Curriculum Coordinator, Co. Schs., Civic Center, San Diego 1, Calif., since 1943.

Driscoll, W. A., A.B.'22, Wilmington Col.; M.A.'28, Ohio State Univ.; Co. Supt. of Sch., Dayton, Ohio, since 1935.

Drummond, Glenn, A.B.'09, Ohio Northern Univ.; A.B.'11, Antioch Col.; M.A.'26, Ohio State Univ.; Supt. of Sch., Wapakoneta, Ohio.

Duboc, Jessie L., M.A.'22, Univ. of Chicago; Asst. Prof. of Educ., Mont. State Normal Col., Dillon, Mont., since 1925.

Dubois, Frank A., M.A.'16, Tchrs. Col., Columbia Univ.; Dist. Supt. of Sch., Ardmore, Pa., since 1940.

Dudley, L. E., B.A.'00, Southwestern Univ.; M.A.'16, Univ. of Texas; LL.D.'41, Hardin-Simmons Univ.; Supt. of Sch., Abilene, Texas, since 1937.

Dudley, L. Leland, S.B.'21, Ed.M. and Ed.D.'27, Harvard Univ.; Supt. of Sch., Amherst, Mass., since 1935.

Duffy, John M., Supt. of Catholic Sch., Diocese of Rochester, 50 Chestnut St., Rochester, N. Y., since 1929.

Dugan, Howard F., Vice-Pres., Hotels Statler Co., Inc., Hotel Pennsylvania, New York, N. Y.

Dugdale, R. E., LL.B.'17, Hamilton Col. of Law, Chicago, Ill.; A.B.'19, Univ. of Toledo; M.A.'34, Univ. of Mich. Address: 1628 N. E. Knott, Portland, Oregon.

Dumas, Rev. Gustave, B.Litt.'23, Univ. of Montreal; B.A.'24, M.A.'25, Woodstock Col.; Ph.D.'36, Sorbonne, Paris; Dean, Grad. Sch., Fordham Univ., Bronx 58, N. Y., since 1938.

Duncan, Gilmore A., M.A.'30, Stanford Univ.; Prin., Shandon Union H. S., Shandon, Calif., since 1930.

Dungan, J. U., B.S.'19, Univ. of Ill.; A.M. '31, Univ. of Cincinnati; Supt. of Sch., Lockland, Ohio, since 1923.

Dunkle, John L., B.S.'12, W. Va. Univ.; M.A.'17, Tchrs. Col., Columbia Univ.; Pres., State Tchrs. Col., Frostburg, Md., since 1923.

Dunlavy, V. A., Dist. Supt., Union H. S., Sonora, Calif.

Dunn, Burton W., M.S.'33, Oregon State Col.; Supt. of Sch., Coquille, Oregon, since 1937.

Dunn, D. Y., B.S.'22, A.M.'32, Univ. of Ky.; Co. Supt. of Sch., Lexington, Ky., since 1929.

Dunwiddie, Walter Rockwood, B.S.'16, M.S. '27, Univ. of Wis.; Supt. of Sch., Port Washington, Wis., since 1926.

Dupre, Naasson K., M.A.'22, Univ. of Texas; Dean, Univ. of Houston, Houston, Texas, since 1934.

Duran, Troy R., B.S. '34, Sam Houston State Tchrs. Col., Huntsville, Texas; Supt. of Sch., New London, Texas, since 1939.

Durrell, Thomas J., A.B.'07, Princeton Univ.; A.M.'30, Columbia Univ.; Asst. State Commr. of Educ., Trenton, N. J., since 1940.

Durst, David M., B.S.'12, M.A.'15, Univ. of Calif.; Supt. of Sch., Petaluma, Calif., since 1931.

DuShane, Donald, B.S.'06, M.A.'13, Hanover Col.; M.S.'16, Univ. of Wis.; LL.D. '38, Wabash Col.; Pres., Natl. Educ. Assn., 1940-41; Secy., N.E.A. Commn. on the Defense of Democracy Through Educ., 1201 16th St., N. W., Washington 6, D. C., since 1941.

Dutter, Homer W., A.B.'11, Ind. Univ.; A.M.'16, Columbia Univ.; Supt. of Sch., Coleraine, Minn., since 1925.

Dwyer, W. K., Supt. of Sch., Anaconda, Mont.

Dyer, John H., Ph.D.'27, Univ. of Pa.; Supt. of Sch., Scranton, Pa., since 1929.

Dyer, W. P., M.A.'20, Univ. of Minn.; Ph.D.'27, Columbia Univ.; Supt. of Practice Schs., Tchrs. Col. of Conn., New Britain, Conn., since 1926.

E

Eades, Roscoe, B.S.'21, Eureka Col.; M.A '38, Columbia Univ.; Supt., Sterling Twp. H. S., Sterling, Ill., since 1931.

Early, J. J., A.B.'01, Ind. Univ.; A.M.'27, Tchrs. Col., Columbia Univ.; Supt. of Sch., Sheridan, Wyo., since 1908.

Easson, McGregor, D.Pd.'34, Univ. of Toronto; Pub. Sch. Insp., 330 Gilmour St., Ottawa, Canada, since 1928.

Eaton, Edwin M., B.S.'12, Univ. of Calif.; Member, Bd. of Educ., 915 Van Ness Ave., Fresno 1, Calif., since 1941.

Ebbert, Lida M., Ph.B.'08, Dickinson Col.; A.M.'21, Columbia Univ.; Prin., Linden H. S., Linden, N. J., since 1910.

Eber, Woodrow J., A.B.'37, Western Mich. Col. of Educ.; Supt. of Sch., Caledonia, Mich., since 1943.

Eccleston, Howard B., Supt. of Sch., Johnson City, N. Y.

Echols, Silas, Prin., Twp. H. S., Mt. Vernon, Ill., since 1905.

Eck, Lee, A.B.'26, Albright Col.; M.S.'31, Lebanon Valley Col.; Supvg. Prin. of Sch., Richland, Pa., since 1926.

Eckles, Port, A.B.'14, Hiram Col.; A.M.'24, Univ. of Pittsburgh; Supt. of Sch., Homestead, Pa., since 1922.

Eddy, Paul, B.S.'35, Fla. Southern Col.; M.A.'37, George Peabody Col. for Tchrs.; State Supvr. of Sch. Evaluation, 644 Ingleside Ave., Tallahassee, Fla., since 1937.

Eddy, Paul Dawson, A.B.'21, A.M.'24, Univ. of Pa.; B.D.'24, Crozer Theol. Seminary; Pres., Adelphi Col., Garden City, N. Y., since 1937.

Eddy, Rhoden B., B.S.'20, Colby Col.; Ed.M.'28, Harvard Univ.; Supt. of Sch., Laconia, N. H., since 1943.

Eddy, Theo V., A.B.'15, Hillsdale Col.; M.A.'28, Univ. of Mich.; Supt. of Sch., St. Clair, Mich., since 1930.

Edgar, James W., B.A.'28, Howard Payne Col.; M.A.'38, Univ. of Texas; Supt. of Sch., Orange, Texas, since 1939.

Edgren, W. T., A.B.'27, Ellsworth Col.; Supt. of Sch., Rake, Iowa, since 1935.

Edman, V. Raymond, A.B.'23, Boston Univ.; M.A.'30, Ph.D.'33, Clark Univ.; LL.D.'41, Houghton Col.; Pres., Wheaton Col., Wheaton, Ill., since 1941.

Edmands, Mrs. Ruth, Rural Sch. Supvr., Colusa Co. Free Library, Colusa, Calif.

Edminster, W. H., A.B.'16, Univ. of Maine; Supt. of Sch., Norway, Maine, since 1922.

Edmonson, James Bartlett, A.B.'06, M.A.'10, Univ. of Mich.; Ph.D.'25, Univ. of Chicago; Dean, Sch. of Educ., Univ. of Mich., Ann Arbor, Mich., since 1929.

Edmundson, William Dean, B.D.'39, Univ. of Wash.; Acting Supt. of Sch., Kent, Wash., since 1943.

Edwards, Harry O., M.S. in Ed.'41, Univ. of Idaho; Supt. of Sch., Sequim, Wash., since 1934.

Edwards, Paul B., B.Sc.'17, M.A.'36, Ohio State Univ.; Supt. of Sch., Newark, Ohio, since 1936.

Edwards, Violet, B.A.'29, Univ. of Ariz.; M.A.'36, Tchrs. Col., Columbia Univ.; Pub. Affairs Com., 30 Rockefeller Plaza, New York, N. Y.

Edwards, William B., B.A.'31, Ohio Univ.; M.A.'38, Kent State Univ.; Supt. of Sch., South Euclid, Ohio, since 1942.

Egan, Rev. Joseph M., A.B.'22, St. Louis Univ.; S.T.D.'32, Gregorian Univ., Rome; Pres., Loyola Univ., 6525 N. Sheridan Rd., Chicago 26, Ill., since 1942.

Egan, Thomas A., M.A.'11, St. Louis Univ.; Dean, Loyola Univ., 6525 Sheridan Rd., Chicago 26, Ill., since 1931.

Egbert, Sister St., A.B.'24, A.M.'28, Ph.D. '31, Fordham Univ.; Dean, Notre Dame Col. of Staten Island, Tompkinsville, S. I., N. Y., since 1931.

Eggert, Walter A., A.B.'28, State Tchrs. Col., Valley City, N. Dak.; M.S.'31, Northwestern Univ.; Ph.D.'39, Univ. of Chicago; Prof. of Educ., Grad. Sch., De Paul Univ., Chicago, Ill., since 1939.

Eichelberger, James W., A.B.'04, Livingstone Col.; A.M.'23, Northwestern Univ.; Secy. of Christian Educ., African Methodist Episcopal Zion Church, 128 E. 58th St., Chicago, Ill., since 1932.

Eichler, George A., A.B.'14, Muhlenberg Col.; M.A.'28, Ed.D.'34, Pa. State Col.; Supt. of Sch., Northampton, Pa., since 1930.

Eikenberry, D. H., A.B.'11, A.M.'15, Ind. Univ.; Ph.D.'26, Tchrs. Col., Columbia Univ.; Prof. of Educ., Ohio State Univ., Columbus, Ohio, since 1927.

Elbin, Paul N., Ph.D.'32, Columbia Univ.; Pres., State Col., West Liberty, W. Va., since 1935.

Elder, Rhodes, Dir., Div. of Adult Educ., Pub. Sch., Burbank, Calif.

Eldred, Arvie, A.B.'05, A.M.'21, Williams Col.; Pd.D.'25, N. Y. State Col. for Tchrs.; Exec. Secy., N. Y. State Tchrs. Assn., 152 Washington Ave., Albany 6, N. Y., since 1930.

Elkema, Charles E., A.M.'40, Tchrs. Col., Columbia Univ.; Supt. of Sch., Wallingford, Conn., since 1940.

Elkins, C. C., Supt. of Parish Sch., Jonesville, La.

Ell, Carl Stephens, A.B.'09, DePauw Univ.; S.B.'11, M.S.'12, Mass. Inst. of Tech.; Ed.M.'32, Harvard Univ.; Sc.D.'35, De Pauw Univ.; Pres., Northeastern Univ., Boston, Mass., since 1940.

Ellestad, Theo. A., B.S.'15, B.S.'16, Oregon State Col.; Supt. of Sch., Coalinga, Calif., since 1938.

Elliff, Miles A., B.S.'25, Kansas State Tchrs. Col., Pittsburg, Kansas; M.A.'27, Univ. of Mo.; Supt. of Sch., Lebanon, Mo., since 1932.

Ellingson, Mark, A.B.'26, Gooding Col.; M.A.'30, Univ. of Rochester; Ph.D.'36, Ohio State Univ.; Pres., Rochester Athenaeum and Mech. Inst., Rochester, N. Y., since 1936.

Elliott, E. A., A.B.'17, M.A.'28, Univ. of Kansas; Supt. of Sch., Joplin, Mo., since 1930.

Elliott, Edward C., B.S.'95, M.A.'97, Univ. of Nebr.; Ph.D.'05, Columbia Univ.; Pres., Purdue Univ., Lafayette, Ind., since 1922.

Elliott, Eugene B., B.S.'24, M.A.'26, Mich. State Col.; Ph.D.'33, Univ. of Mich.; LL.D.'36, Albion Col.; Ed.D.'37, Hillsdale Col.; State Supt. of Pub. Instr., State Capitol, Lansing, Mich., since 1935.

Elliott, John Wesley, B.A.'13, Univ. of Richmond; B.D.'16, Colgate Univ.; M.A. '17, Univ. of Chicago; D.D.'35, Kalamazoo Col.; D.D.'36, Univ. of Richmond; Pres., Alderson-Broaddus Col., Philippi, W. Va., since 1939.

Elliott, Loyd C., B.S.'13, Univ. of Ariz.; A.M.'29, Leland Stanford Jr. Univ.; Prin., North Phoenix H. S., Phoenix, Ariz., since 1939.

Ellis, Henry G., A.B.'10, Randolph-Macon Col. Address: Pub. Sch., Petersburg, Va.

Ellis, Homer C., B.S.'23, Mt. Union Col.; M.A.'39, Oberlin Col.; Supt. of Sch., Norwalk, Ohio, since 1933.

Ellis, Mabel R., Diploma '06, San Francisco State Col.; Prin., Pacific Hgts. Elem. Sch., San Francisco, Calif., since 1939.

Ellis, Stanley B., B.S.'30, Northeast Mo. State Tchrs. Col., Kirksville, Mo.; A.M. '40, Univ. of Mo.; Dist. Supt. of Sch., Livermore, Calif., since 1942.

Elmendorf, George M., Ph.B.'05, A.M '29 Union Col.; Supt. of Sch., Plattsburgh, N. Y., since 1920.

Elsbree, Willard S., Ph.D.'28, Columbia Univ.; Prof. of Educ., Tchrs. Col., Columbia Univ., New York 27, N. Y., since 1926.

Elsdon, Cyril Lorme, B.S.'28, Univ. of Pittsburgh; M.S.'30, Columbia Univ.; Sch. Accountant, Pub. Sch., Admin. Bldg., Pittsburgh, Pa., since 1936.

Elsea, Albert F., B.S.'17, Northeast Mo. State Tchrs. Col., Kirksville, Mo.; M.A. '22, George Peabody Col. for Tchrs.; Educ. Editor, The Edwards Press, Osceola, Mo.

Emens, John R., A.B.'26, Mich. State Normal Col., Ypsilanti, Mich.; A.M.'27, Ph.D. '38, Univ. of Mich.; Chmn., Personnel Com., Bd. of Educ., Detroit 26, Mich., since 1940.

Emerson, D. A., B.A.'23, Univ. of Wash.; M.A.'24, State Col. of Wash.; State Dir. of Sch. Admin. and Sec. Educ., Salem, Oregon, since 1934.

Emerson, Lynn Arthur, E.E.'11, Univ. of Minn.; Ph.D.'32, New York Univ.; Prof. of Indus. Educ., Sch. of Educ., Cornell Univ., Ithaca, N. Y., since 1938.

Emmons, Purley C., A.B.'00, Ind. Univ.; A.M.'14, Tchrs. Col.; Columbia Univ.; Supt. of Sch., Mishawaka, Ind., since 1921.

Enderis, Dorothy C., Diploma '01, State Tchrs. Col., Milwaukee, Wis.; M.A.'35, Lawrence Univ.; Asst. to Supt. of Sch. in charge of Dept. of Municipal Recreation and Adult Educ., 1914 W. Kilbourn Ave., Milwaukee, Wis., since 1920.

Enestvedt, Harold R., B.A.'28, St. Olaf Col.; M.A.'31, Univ. of Minn.; Supt. of Sch., Sleepy Eye, Minn., since 1939.

Engel, Anna M., Diploma '03, B.S.'24, Detroit Tchrs. Col.; M.A.'31, Univ. of Detroit; Asst. Dir., Special Educ. Pub. Sch., 453 Stimson Ave., Detroit, Mich., since 1937.

Engelhardt, Fred, Ph.B.'08, Yale Univ.; M.A.'15, Ph.D.'24, Columbia Univ.; LL.D. '40, Univ. of Maine; Pres., Univ. of N. H., Durham, N. H., since 1936.

*Engelhardt, N. L., A.B.'03, Yale Univ.; Ph.D.'18, Columbia Univ.; Assoc. Supt., New York City Pub. Sch., 110 Livingston St., Brooklyn 2, N. Y., since 1943.

Engelhardt, N. L., Jr., B.S.'29, Yale Univ.; M.A.'37, Ph.D.'39, Columbia Univ.; Dir., Air-Age Educ. Research, 100 E. 42nd St., New York 17, N. Y., since 1943.

England, Byron, B.A.'28, Hardin-Simmons Univ.; M.A.'36, Univ. of Texas; Asst. Supt. of Sch., El Paso, Texas, since 1943.

Engle, Gertrude, Vice-Prin., Roosevelt Jr. H. S., Richmond, Calif.

Englehart, George D., A.M.'29, Univ. of Mo.; Supt. of Sch., Leadwood, Mo., since 1935.

English, Colin, Ph.B.'17, Emory Univ.; M.A.'34, Columbia Univ.; State Supt. of Pub. Instr., Tallahassee, Fla., since 1937.

English, Mildred E., B.S.'21, M.A.'26, George Peabody Col. for Tchrs.; Ed.D.'40, Columbia Univ.; Supt., Peabody Tr. Sch., Ga. State Col. for Women, Milledgeville, Ga., since 1935.

English, O. H., B.S.'29, A.M.'32, D.Ed.'42, Univ. of Pittsburgh; Supt. of Borough Schs., Brentwood, Pittsburgh 10, Pa., since 1940.

English, William J., A.B.'13, Dartmouth Col.; Supt. of Sch., Lebanon, N. H., since 1925.

Enyeart, Buel F., B.A.'23, Northeast Mo. State Tchrs. Col., Kirksville, Mo.; M.A. '27, Ed.D.'40, Univ. of Southern Calif.; Supt. of Sch., 320 W. San Fernando Blvd., Burbank, Calif., since 1934.

Erb, Donald Milton, B.S.'22, M.S.'24, Univ. of Ill.; M.A.'26, Ph.D.'30, Harvard Univ.; Pres., Univ. of Oregon, Eugene, Oregon, since 1938.

Erdly, Calvin V., B.S.'20, Susquehanna Univ.; M.S.'33, Pa. State Col.; Supt. of Sch., Lewistown, Pa.

Erickson, A. C., M.A.'33, Stanford Univ.; Supt. of Sch., Poulsbo, Wash., since 1935.

Erickson, Arthur G., A.B.'11, A.M.'16, Univ. of Mich.; M.Ed.'22, Mich. State Normal Col.; Supt. of Sch., Ecorse, Mich., since 1939.

*Erickson, Everett Russell, A.B.'26, M.S. in Ed.'33, Univ. of Idaho. Address: c/o Bo Henry, 906 S. Lake, Colfax, Wash.

Erickson, John E., A.B.'09, A.M.'25, Univ. of Mich.; Supt. of Sch., Hazel Park, Mich., since 1929.

Ernest, Robert B., B.Ed.'29, Ill. State Normal Univ., Normal, Ill.; M.A.'32, Univ. of Ill.; Co. Supt. of Sch., Decatur, Ill., since 1939.

Erney, Fred G., A.B.'23, Univ. of Kansas; Prin., William Lipscomb Sch., Dallas, Texas, since 1940.

Erwin, Charles C., A.B.'27, Univ. of N. C.; M.A.'40, Tchrs. Col., Columbia Univ.; Supt. of Sch., Forest City, N. C., since 1926.

Erwine, Russell H., B.L.'07, Ohio Wesleyan Univ.; M.A.'22, Wittenberg Col.; Supt. of Sch., Euclid, Ohio, since 1939.

Eshelman, Walter W., A.B.'30, Elizabethtown Col.; LL.B.'31, Blackstone Inst.; A.M.'33, Columbia Univ.; Ed.D.'41, New York Univ.; Supvg. Prin. of Twp. Sch., Stowe, Pa., since 1936.

Essert, Paul L., B.A.'22, Univ. of Wyo.; M.A.'30, Colo. State Tchrs. Col.; Ed.D.'41, Tchrs. Col., Columbia Univ.; Supt. of Sch., Grosse Pointe 30, Mich., since 1941.

Essex, Don L., A.B.'17, A.M.'25, Ind. Univ.; Ph.D.'30, Columbia Univ.; Chief, Bureau of Instrl. Supvn., Elem. Educ. Div., State Educ. Dept., Albany, N. Y., since 1940.

Essig, J. Fred, B.S.'27, State Tchrs. Col., Emporia, Kansas; M.A.'31, State Univ. of Iowa; Supt. of Sch., Greeley, Colo., since 1943.

Eucharia, Sister Mary, B.A.'29, Immaculate Heart Col.; M.A.'93, Loyola Univ., Los Angeles, Calif.; Pres., Immaculate Heart Col., 2021 N. Western Ave., Los Angeles, Calif., since 1939.

Evangela, Sister Mary, A.B.'21, St. Lou's Univ.; M.A.'27, Fordham Univ.; Supvr., Sch. Sisters of Notre Dame, 320 E. Ripa Ave., St. Louis 23, Mo., since 1933.

Evans, Evan E., A.B.'20, Baker Univ.; A.M.'28, Univ. of Chicago; Supt. of Sch., Winfield, Kansas, since 1931.

Evans, James Carmichael, A.B.'21, Roger Williams Univ.; B.S.'25, M.S.'26, Mass. Inst. of Tech.; Admin. Asst. to the Pres., W. Va. State Col., Institute, W. Va., since 1928.

Evans, John W., A.B.'29, Rio Grande Col.; M.A.'33, Ohio State Univ.; Supt. of Sch., New Philadelphia, Ohio, since 1942.

Evans, R. O., B.Pd.'20, Northwest Mo. State Tchrs. Col., Maryville, Mo.; B.S. in Ed.'23, Univ. of Mo.; M.A.'24, Ed. D. '38, Tchrs. Col., Columbia Univ.; Supt. of Sch., Quincy, Ill., since 1938.

Evans, William C., A.B.'19, Lebanon Valley Col.; M.Ed.'34, Univ. of Pittsburgh; Supt. of Sch., Braddock, Pa., since 1936.

Evenden, Edward S., Diploma '03, Oregon Normal Sch., Monmouth, Oregon; A.B.'10, A.M.'11, Stanford Univ.; Ph.D.'19, Columbia Univ.; Prof. of Educ., Tchrs. Col., Columbia Univ., 525 W. 120th St., New York 27, N. Y., since 1919.

Everard, J. G., Ph.B.'17, Lafayette Col.; M.S.'35, Pa. State Col.; Supt. of Sch., Huntingdon, Pa., since 1934.

Evingson, Caroline J., B.S.'30, N. Dak. State Col.; Co. Supt. of Sch., Court House, Fargo, N. Dak., since 1923.

Ewan, S. N., Jr., Sc.B.'21, Haverford Col.; A.M.'29, Ph.D.'35, Univ. of Pa.; Lt. Comdr., Naval Officers Procurement, Widener Bldg., Philadelphia, Pa.

Ewing, Dean M., B.S.'22, M.S.'30, Univ. of Ill.; Prin., Community H. S., Crystal Lake, Ill., since 1936.

Ewing, Parmer L., B.S.'30, M.S.'34, Univ. of Ill.; Supt. of Sch., Alton, Ill., since 1942.

Exstrom, Paul E., A.B.'27, State Tchrs. Col., Kearney, Nebr.; Co. Supt. of Sch., North Platte, Nebr., since 1935.

Exton, Elaine, B.S.'33, Columbia Univ.; M.A.'34, Univ. of Southern Calif. Address: The Jefferson Apt., 1200 16th St., N. W., Washington 6, D. C.

Eyman, R. L., B.S.'14, Univ. of Ill.; Ed.D. '28, Univ. of Calif.; Dean, Sch. of Educ., Fla. State Col. for Women, Tallahassee, Fla., since 1937.

Eyman, R. Merle, B.Eng.'20, M.A.'29, Ohio State Univ.; Co. Supt. of Sch., Lancaster, Ohio, since 1928.

Eyring, Edward, A.B.'26, Univ. of Ariz.; M.A.'27, Ph.D.'32, Univ. of Calif.; Pres., New Mexico Highlands Univ., Las Vegas, N. Mex., since 1939.

Eyster, Elvin S., M.S.'31, Ind. Univ.; Prof. of Bus. Admin. and Educ. Dir., U. S. Naval Tr. Sch., Ind. Univ., Bloomington, Ind., since 1941.

F

Fairbanks, Joseph Harrison, M.S.'36, Univ. of Southern Calif.; Supt. of Sch., Morenci, Ariz., since 1939.

Fairchild, R. W., A.B.'14, M.A.'19, Univ. of Mich.; Ph.D.'32, Northwestern Univ.; Pres., Ill. State Normal Univ., Normal, Ill., since 1933.

Fairchild, W. W., A.B.'13, Syracuse Univ.; M.A.'30, Columbia Univ.; Supt. of Sch., Rutland, Vt., since 1921.

Falk, Herbert A., B.A. in Ed.'14, Univ. of Minn.; M.A.'32, Tchrs. Col., Columbia Univ.; Ph.D.'33, Columbia Univ.; Supt. of Sch., Sayville, L. I., N. Y., since 1933.

Falk, Philip H., B.A.'21, M.A.'28, Ph.D.'35, Univ. of Wis.; Supt. of Sch., Madison, Wis., since 1939.

Fallgatter, Florence A., Diploma '12, Iowa State Tchrs. Col., Cedar Falls, Iowa; B.S.'17, Univ. of Minn.; M.A.'27, Tchrs. Col., Columbia Univ.; Head, Home Economics Educ., Iowa State Col., Ames, Iowa, since 1938.

Farley, Belmont Mercer, Ph.D.'29, Columbia Univ.; Dir. of Public Relations, Natl. Educ. Assn., 1201 16th St., N. W., Washington 6, D. C., since 1929.

Farnsworth, Philo T., B.S.'26, M.S.'27, Brigham Young Univ.; Ph.D.'40, Tchrs. Col., Columbia Univ.; Supt., Granite Sch. Dist., 3234 S. State, Salt Lake City, Utah, since 1939.

Farquear, Floyd Emmett, B.S.'20, Miami Univ.; M.A.'21, Univ. of Chicago; Ed.D. '42, Univ. of Texas; Chmn., Dept. of Educ., Texas Col. of Mines, El Paso, Texas, since 1943.

Farrar, Joe, B.S.'22, La. State Univ.; M.A. '28, State Univ. of Iowa; Ph.D.'36, George Peabody Col. for Tchrs.; Pres., La. State Normal Col., Natchitoches, La., since 1941.

Farrell, John Franklin, A.B.'18, Univ. of Mich.; M.Ed.'34, Boston Univ.; Supt. of Sch., Adams, Mass., since 1935.

Fassett, Josephine, Diploma '14, Miami Univ.; B.S., M.A., Univ. of Toledo; Supvr., Oregon Twp. Rural Sch. Dist., Toledo 5, Ohio.

Fast, L. Wade, A.B.'20, A.M.'24, Univ. of Mich.; Supt. of Sch., Mt. Clemens, Mich., since 1919.

Faulkner, Elizabeth, A.B.'85, Univ. of Chicago; Prin., Faulkner Sch. for Girls, 4746 Dorchester Ave., Chicago, Ill., since 1909.

Faust, J. Frank, B.Sc.'15, Susquehanna Univ.; M.A.'28, Columbia Univ.; Ed.D. '35, Pa. State Col.; Supt. of Sch., Chambersburg, Pa., since 1940.

Fawcett, Novice G., B.Sc.'31, Kenyon Col.; M.A.'37, Ohio State Univ.; Supt. of Sch., Bexley, Columbus 9, Ohio, since 1943.

Fedric, A. O., A.B.'38, N. Mex. Highlands Univ.; Co. Supt. of Sch., Clovis, N. Mex., since 1940.

Feik, L. W., B.A.'10, North Central Col.; M.A.'26, Univ. of Wis.; LL.D.'34, Morningside Col.; Supt. of Sch., Sch. Admin. Bldg., Sioux City, Iowa, since 1931.

Feik, Roy William, A.M.'19, Univ. of Ill. Address: Sch. Admin. Bldg., East Chicago, Ind.

Fell, E. E., A.B.'02, Alma Col.; A.M.'17, Columbia Univ.; LL.D.'35, Hope Col.; Supt. of Sch., Holland, Mich., since 1910.

Fellows, Ernest W., A.B.'94, Grinnell Col.; A.M.'11, State Univ. of Iowa; A.M.'17, Tchrs. Col., Columbia Univ.; Supt. of Sch., Gloucester, Mass., since 1921.

Fels, Maurice, A.B.'83, Johns Hopkins Univ.; LL.B.'85, Univ. of Pa. Address: Garden Court, 47th and Pine Sts., Philadelphia, Pa.

Fenerty, Agnes L., Supvr. of Art, H. S., 7215 Yates Ave., Chicago, Ill., since 1937.

Ferguson, Aleck Leroy, B.S.'07, Cornell Col.; M.A.'32, Univ. of Southern Calif:; Deputy Supt. of Sch., Glendale 6, Calif., since 1937.

Ferguson, Arthur W., B.S.'12, Univ. of Pa.; A.M.'20, Lafayette Col.; Ph.D.'24, Univ. of Pa.; Supt. of Sch., York, Pa., since 1930.

*Ferguson, Harold A., A.B.'14, A.M.'16, Clark Univ.; Prin., Montclair H. S., Montclair, N. J., since 1926.

Ferguson, J. T., B.A.'22, M.A.'25, Univ. of Texas; Supt. of Sch., Navasota, Texas, since 1935.

Ferguson, James, A.B.'99, A.M.'01, Leland Stanford Jr. Univ.; Dist. Supt., Jefferson Union H. S., Daly City, Calif., since 1928.

Ferguson, Lamar, A.B.'25, Univ. of Ga.; A.M.'30, Columbia Univ.; A.M.'30, Oglethorpe Univ.; Supt. of Sch., Decatur, Ga., since 1925.

Ferguson, Norris W., B.S.'33, Western Mich. Col. of Educ.; Acting Supt., Wyoming Park Schs., Grand Rapids, Mich., since 1943.

Ferguson, William C., B.S.'16, Col. of William and Mary; Mng. Editor, World Book Co., Yonkers-on-Hudson, N. Y.

Fern, Louis J., Pres., George E. Fern Co., 1252 Elm St., Cincinnati, Ohio.

Ferran, Rose Marie, B.A.'25, M.A.'29, Tulane Univ.; Area Supvr., Kdgn.-Prim. Grades, Pub. Schs., New Orleans, La., since 1943.

Ferrell, Glover B., B.A.'24, Iowa State Tchrs. Col., Cedar Falls, Iowa; M.A.'30, State Univ. of Iowa; Supt. of Sch., Brainerd, Minn., since 1938.

Ferriss, Emery N., Ph.B.'04, Western Col.; M.A.'06, Ph.D.'08, State Univ. of Iowa; Prof. of Rural Educ., Stone Hall, Cornell Univ., Ithaca, N. Y., since 1920.

Fetherston, Roy, B.A.'23, Beloit Col.; M.A. '32, State Univ. of Iowa; Supt. of Sch., Monmouth, Ill., since 1930.

Field, Charles Henry, B.S.'29, Alfred Univ.; M.A.'36, N. Y. State Col. for Tchrs.; Supt. of Sch., Waterford, N. Y., since 1939.

Fielstra, Clarence, Curriculum Coordinator, Pub. Sch., Civic Center, San Diego 1, Calif.

Fieser, James L., LL.D.'42, Ind. Univ., Vice-Chmm., American Natl. Red Cross, Washington, D. C., since 1922.

Fildes, Raymond E., M.A.'29, Univ. of Chicago; Supt. of Sch., Springfield, Ill., since 1936.

Fillers, Herbert D., S.B.'16, Univ. of Chicago; M.A.'28, Columbia Univ.; Supt. of Sch., Wichita Falls, Texas, since 1931.

Finck, Edgar M., Litt.B.'10, M.A.'12, Princeton Univ.; Ph.D.'30, New York Univ.; Supvg. Prin. of Sch., Toms River, N. J., since 1919.

Findley, W. C., A.B.'14, Bellevue Col.; M.A.'25, State Univ. of Iowa; Asst. Supt. of Sch., Des Moines, Iowa, since 1941.

Finley, Elden D., B.S.'23, Knox Col.; M.A.'28, Columbia Univ.; Prin., Community H. S., Delavan, Ill., since 1931.

Finley, Lester M., B.S. in Ed.'23, Ohio State Univ.; M.A.'30, Columbia Univ.; Co. Supt. of Sch., Jefferson, Ohio, since 1938.

Finner, F. F., A.B.'12, M.A.'28, Univ. of Wis.; Supt. of Sch., Sheboygan Falls, Wis., since 1933.

Fischer, Fred C., A.B.'21, Mich. State Normal Col., Ypsilanti, Mich.; M.A.'30, Univ. of Mich.; M.Ed.'40, Mich. State Normal Col.; Co. Supt. of Sch., Detroit, Mich., since 1935.

Fischer, Mrs. Helen H., Ph.B.'19, Univ. of Chicago; M.A.'37, State Univ. of Iowa; Supvr. of Elem. Educ., Pub. Sch., Moline, Ill., since 1943.

Fisher, C. Edward, A.B.'98, St. Lawrence Univ.; A.M.'12, Brown Univ.; Supt. of Sch., Braintree, Mass., since 1921.

Fisher, Leon Oscar, B.S. in Ed.'37, Rutgers Univ.; Supvg. Prin. of Sch., Livingston, N. J., since 1937.

Fisher, Lowell B., Asst. H. S. Visitor, Univ. of Ill., Urbana, Ill., since 1943.

Fisher, Rayburn J., Co. Supt. of Sch., Tuscaloosa, Ala.

*Fitzgerald, James A., B.A.'15, M.A.'24, Univ. of S. Dak.; Ph.D.'31, State Univ. of Iowa. Address: 5 Croydon Dr., Baldwin, N. Y.

Fitzgerald, Joseph A., A.B.'13, A.M.'14, Boston Col.; Supt. of Sch., New Haven, Conn., since 1937.

Fitz Gerald, Mrs. Mary M., 1420 Lake Shore Dr., Chicago 10, Ill.

Fitzpatrick, Jerome M., B.S.'14, Univ. of Vt.; Supt. of Sch., Westbury, L. I., N. Y., since 1925.

Fitzpatrick, Loretta M., Prin., Hutchins Intermediate Sch., 4051 Hazelwood, Detroit, Mich.

Fjelsted, Philip L., B.A.'21, St. Olaf Col.; M.A.'30, Univ. of Minn.; Supt. of Sch., Thief River Falls, Minn., since 1943.

Flaharty, William H., B.S.'28, Franklin and Marshall Col.; Ed.M.'32, Rutgers Univ.; Supvg. Prin. of Twp. Sch., Vineland, N. J., since 1942.

Flanagan, John C., B.S.'29, M.A.'32, Univ. of Wash.; Ph.D.'34, Harvard Univ.; Lt. Col., Hq. AAF, 3242 Gunston Rd., Alexandria, Va.

Flanders, Jesse Knowlton, A.B.'04, Bates Col.; A.M.'17, Stanford Univ.; Ph.D.'26, Columbia Univ. Address: 36 W. Seneca St., Oswego, N. Y.

Flaum Harry, B.A.'10, Col. of the City of New York; LL.B.'13, LL.M.'14, New York Law Sch.; Prin., Pub. Sch. 63, The Bronx, Franklin Ave. and 168th St., New York, N. Y., since 1924.

Fleming, John Allen, B.S. in Ed.'18, Kansas State Tchrs. Col., Pittsburg, Kansas; M.S. in Ed.'24, Univ. of Kansas; Supt. of Sch., Iola, Kansas, since 1933.

Fleming, Oliver A., B.A.'13, Simmons Univ.; Supt. of Sch., Freeport, Texas, since 1920.

Fletcher, Arthur, Educ. Sec., War Finance Div., Treasury Dept., 709 12th St., N. W., Washington, D. C.

Flinn, Virgil L., A.B.'19, W. Va. Univ.; M.A.'28, Ohio State Univ.; Co. Supt. of Sch., Charleston, W. Va., since 1937.

Flinner, Ira A., A.B.'11, A.M.'19, Ed.M.'25, Ed.D.'26, Harvard Univ.; LL.D.'27, Grove City Col.; Educ. Dir., Lake Placid Club Educ. Foundation and Headmaster, Northwood Sch., Lake Placid Club, N. Y., since 1925.

Flora, A. Cline, A.B.'12, Daleville Col.; A.M.'17, Univ. of S. C.; Pres., Natl. Educ. Assn., 1942-43; Supt. of Sch., Columbia, S. C., since 1928.

Flower, Frank R., Diploma '10, Williamson Free Sch. of Mech. Trades; Dir. of Voc. Educ., Pub. Sch., Atlantic City, N. J., since 1913.

Flowers, William R., B.S.'21, M.A.'24, Johns Hopkins Univ.; Asst. Supt. of Sch., 3 E. 25th St., Baltimore 18, Md., since 1924.

Floyd, Oliver R., A.B.'25, M.A.'28, Univ. of Pittsburgh; Ph.D.'31, Univ. of Minn.; Supvg. Prin., Avonworth Union Sch. Dist., Ben Avon, Pittsburgh, Pa., since 1938.

Flurry, Bruce, A.B.'17, M.A.'27, Univ. of Ala.; Supt of Sch., Dothan, Ala., since 1935.

Fly, Murry H., B.A.'20, M.A.'29, Univ. of Texas; Supt. of Sch., Odessa, Texas, since 1924.

Foley, James H., A.B.'31, A.M.'33, Brown Univ.; Secy., Sch. Com., 20 Summer St., Providence, R. I., since 1937.

Foote, John M., M.A.'23, George Peabody Col. for Tchrs.; D.Ed.'36, La. State Univ. Address: U. S. Office of Educ., Washington 25, D. C.

Force, Anna Laura, M.A.'21, Colo. State Tchrs. Col., Greeley, Colo. Address: 2254 Lowell Blvd., Denver 11, Colo.

Force, Doris, Asst. Sales Mgr., Univ. of Chicago Press, 5750 Ellis Ave., Chicago, Ill.

Ford, Herbert L., A.B.'19, Ashland Col.; B.Sc.'20, M.A.'27, Ohio State Univ.; Supt. of Sch., Fostoria, Ohio, since 1937.

Ford, Prentice C., Vice-Pres., American Sch. Pub. Corp., 470 Fourth Ave., New York, N. Y.

Ford, Thomas H., Ph.B.'14, Dickinson Col.; A.M.'25, Univ. of Pa.; Litt.D.'36, Albright Col.; Supt. of Sch.; Reading, Pa., since 1933.

Ford, Willard S., A.B.'15, Lawrence Col.; M.A.'25, Tchrs. Col., Columbia Univ.; Ph.D.'26, Columbia Univ.; Supt. of Sch., Glendale, Calif., since 1938.

Forkner, Hamden L., A.B.'29, M.A.'36, Ph.D.'39, Univ. of Calif.; Prof. of Educ., Tchrs. Col., Columbia Univ., New York 27, N. Y., since 1937.

Forrest, Arthur L., B.S.'26, Dartmouth Col.; Mgr., Pub. Service Promotion, NBC, 30 Rockefeller Plaza, New York 20, N. Y., since 1943.

Forrest, Leland K., B.E.'31, State Tchrs. Col., Eau Claire, Wis.; M.A.'38, State Univ. of Iowa; Supt. of Sch., Elkhorn, Wis., since 1942.

Foster, Charles R., Jr., A.B.'23, Univ. of Pittsburgh; Ed.M.'29, Ed.D.'37, Harvard Univ.; Dean, Sch. of Educ., Univ. of Miami, Coral Gables, Fla., since 1940.

Foster, Frank C., B.S.'16, Colby Col.; B.D.'24, Union Theol. Sem.; M.A.'24, Ph.D.'34, Tchrs. Col., Columbia Univ.; Assoc. Dir., Save the Children Federation, 16 Kenilworth Rd., Asheville, N. C., since 1943.

Foster, Harry V., M.A.'31, Western State Tchrs. Col., Gunnison, Colo.; Supt. of Sch., Montrose, Colo., since 1938.

Foster, Henry L., B.S.'26, Southwest Texas State Tchrs. Col., San Marcos, Texas; Supt. of Sch., Longview, Texas, since 1922.

Foster, Isaac Owen, B.S.'21, M.S.'22, Ph.D.'25, Univ. of Ill.; Assoc. Prof. of Educ., Sch. of Educ., Ind. Univ., Bloomington, Ind., since 1926.

Foster, Luther Hilton, Diploma '07, St. Paul Poly. Inst.; LL.D.'40, Morris Brown Col.; LL.D.'43, Va. Union Univ.; Pres., Va. State Col. for Negroes, Petersburg, Va,. since 1943.

Foster, Talmage D., B.S.'24, M.A.'27, Col. of William and Mary; Co. Supt. of Sch., Waverly, Va., since 1925.

Foster, William W., B.A.'23, Reed Col.; M.A.'31, State Univ. of Iowa; Supt. of Sch., Granite Falls, Wash., since 1939.

Foust, John L., Ph.B. in Ed.'17, Univ. of Chicago; M.A.'27, Tchrs. Col., Columbia Univ.; Supt. of Sch., Owensboro, Ky., since 1921.

Fowler, Burton P., A.B.'07, Syracuse Univ.; A.M.'25, Columbia Univ.; Prin., Germantown Friends Sch., Germantown, Philadelphia, Pa., since 1941.

Fowler, Oscar F., Ph.B.'24, Univ. of Chicago; M.A.'35, Northwestern Univ.; Dist. Supt. of High Schs., 6800 Stewart Ave., Chicago, Ill., since 1937.

Fowler, Wade C., B.S. in Ed.'21, Central Mo. State Tchrs. Col., Warrensburg, Mo.; M.A.'31, Ed.D.'38, Tchrs. Col., Columbia Univ.; Supt. of Sch., Jefferson City, Mo., since 1941.

Fowlkes, John Guy, A.B.'16, Ouachita Col.; A.M.'21, Ph.D.'22, Tchrs. Col., Columbia Univ.; Prof. of Educ., Univ. of Wis., Madison, Wis., since 1927.

Fox, George, B.S.'23, St. John's Col.; Co. Supt. of Sch., Annapolis, Md., since 1916.

Fox, James Harold, A.B.'25, A.M.'26, Univ. of Western Ontario; Ed.M.'36, Ed.D.'37, Harvard Univ.; Dean, Sch. of Educ., George Washington Univ., Washington, D. C., since 1938.

Fox, John F., B.S.'29, Univ. of Mo.; M.A. '31, Ph.D.'36, New York Univ.; Supt. of Sch., East Hartford, Conn., since 1942.

Foy, G. N., A.B.'34, Newberry Col.; Supt. of Sch., Goldville, S. C., since 1929.

Foy, Zed L., A.B.'21, Univ. of S. C.; A.M.'29, Tchrs. Col., Columbia Univ.; Ed.D.'38, Stanford Univ.; Supt. of Sch., Boise, Idaho, since 1940.

Frampton, S. A., B.Sc.'09, Ohio Northern Univ.; A.B.'20, Wittenberg Col.; M.A.'28, Ohio State Univ.; Supt. of Sch., Bellefontaine, Ohio, since 1923.

France, M. Adele, A.B.'00, A.M.'01, Washington Col.; M.A.'23, Tchrs. Col., Columbia Univ.; Litt.D.'42, Washington Col.; Pres., St. Mary's Female Sem. and Jr. Col., St. Mary's City, Md., since 1923.

Francis, George C., B.S. and Ed.M., Boston Univ.; Supt. of Sch., Fitchburg, Mass., since 1938.

Francis, Thomas, B.S.'28, Pa. State Col.; M.A.'33, Columbia Univ.; Co. Supt. of Sch., Scranton, Pa., since 1926.

Franzén, Carl Gustave Frederick, A.B.'08, Univ. of Pa.; M.A.'12, Ph.D.'20, State Univ. of Iowa; Prof. of Sec. Educ., Sch. of Educ., Ind. Univ., Bloomington, Ind., since 1923.

Frasier, George Willard, A.B.'16, Mich. State Normal Col.; A.M.'18, Stanford Univ.; Ph.D.'22, Columbia Univ.; M.Ed., Ypsilanti, Mich.; LL.D., Colo. Col.; LL.D., Univ. of Colo.; Pres., Colo. State Col. of Educ., Greeley, Colo., since 1924.

Frazier, Maude, Supt. of Sch., Las Vegas, Nevada, since 1927.

Frederick, Sister Mary, Ph.D.'34, Univ. of Notre Dame; Pres., Dunbarton Col., Washington, D. C., since 1943.

Freegard, Ruth, Ph.B.'23, Univ. of Chicago; M.A.'30, Tchrs. Col., Columbia Univ.; State Supvr. of Home Economics Educ., State Bd. of Control for Voc. Educ., Lansing, Mich., since 1921.

Freeman, Frank N., B.A.'04, Wesleyan Univ.; M.A.'06, Ph.D.'08, Yale Univ.; Dean, Col. of Educ., Univ. of Calif., Berkeley, Calif., since 1939.

Freeman, H. S., B.A.'19, Morningside Col.; M.A.'34, Univ. of Minn.; Supt. of Sch., Mobridge, S. Dak., since 1929.

Freese, Earl P., B.A.'07, Bates Col.; Supt. of Sch., Bristol, N. H., since 1922.

Freese, Theron, A.B.'32, A.M.'41, Univ. of Southern Calif.; Prin., Eastmont Jr. H. S., Montebello, Calif., since 1941.

Freifeld, George F., B.S.'14, Wesleyan Univ.; M.A.'16, Columbia Univ.; Prin., Abraham Clark H. S., Roselle, N. J., since 1920.

French, Harold P., B.S.'24, N. Y. State Col. for Tchrs., Albany, N. Y.; M.S.'30, Cornell Univ.; Ph.D.'40, New York Univ.; Dist. Supt. of Sch., Loudonville, N. Y., since 1931.

French, Robert B., M.A.'33, Univ. of Mich.; Supt. of Sch., Pontiac, Mich., since 1939.

French, W. C., A.B.'07, Univ. of Okla.; A.M.'24, Univ. of Chicago; Ph.D.'29, New York Univ.; Prof. of Educ., George Washington Univ., Washington, D. C., since 1929.

French, Will, A.B.'12, B.S.'14, Univ. of Kansas; A.M.'22, Ph.D.'33, Tchrs. Col., Columbia Univ.; Acting Supt. of Sch., Long Beach 2, Calif., since 1942.

Fries, H. C., A.B.'20, Bucknell Univ.; A.M.'22, Columbia Univ.; Supvg. Prin. of Sch., South Plainfield, N. J., since 1927.

Fritz, F. Herman, A.B.'09, A.M.'12, Bucknell Univ.; Ed.M.'28, Harvard Univ.; Supt. of Sch., Chester, Pa., since 1934.

Frizzell, Bonner, A.B.'09, Texas Christian Univ.; B.S.'11, Columbia Univ.; LL.D.'37, Texas Christian Univ.; Supt. of Sch., Palestine, Texas, since 1919.

Froelicher, Francis Mitchell, A.B.'13, Haverford Col.; A.M.'21, Johns Hopkins Univ.; LL.D.'37, Colo. Col.; Headmaster, Fountain Valley Sch., Colorado Springs, Colo., since 1930.

Frost, C. A., A.B.'33, Western State Tchrs. Col., Kalamazoo, Mich.; M.A.'38, Univ. of Mich.; Supt., Oakleigh Jr. H. S., Grand Rapids, Mich., since 1928.

Frutchey, F. P., A.B.'22, Ursinus Col.; M.A.'30, Colo. State Tchrs. Col., Greeley, Colo.; Ph.D.'32, Ohio State Univ.; Sr. Educ. Analyst, Extension Service, U. S. Dept. of Agriculture, Washington, D. C., since 1938.

Fuchs, John William, A.B.'20, Univ. of Toledo; M.A.'33, Columbia Univ.; Supvg. Prin. of Sch., Palisades Park, N. J., since 1935.

Fuguitt, G. V., A.M.'34, Univ. of Chicago; Supt. of Sch., Clearwater, Fla., since 1937.

Fulghum, Ruby E., Co. Supt. of Sch., Bisbee, Ariz., since 1930.

Fuller, Albert C., B.A.'11, State Univ. of Iowa; Dir., Bureau of Alumni Affairs and Pub. Sch. Relations, Iowa State Tchrs. Col., Cedar Falls, Iowa, since 1934.

Fuller, C. H. R., Bus. Admin. and Secy. Treas., Bd. of Educ., 155 College St., Toronto 2-B, Canada.

Fuller, Delbert O., Ph.B.'20, Brown Univ.; M.A.'33, Columbia Univ.; Lt. Col., F.A. Headquarters 71, Fourth WAC Tr. Center, Ft. Devens, Mass.

Fuller, Edgar, A.B.'27, Brigham Young Univ.; J.D.'32, Univ. of Chicago; Ed.D. '40, Harvard Univ.; Prin. Educationist, Civil Aeronautics Admin., 3730 McKinley St., N. W., Washington 15, D. C., since 1942.

Fuller, Edward H., A.B.'12, A.M.'16, Bates Col.; M.A.'34, Ed.D.'37, New York Univ.; Supt. of Sch., Darien, Conn., since 1923.

Fuller, Robert J., A.B.'98, A.M.'15, Brown Univ.; Supt. of Sch., Hanover, N. H., since 1928.

Funkhouser, O. W., A.M., Univ. of Chicago. Address: Twp. H. S., Amboy, Ill.

Funston, Augusta Redfield, B.S.'37, M.A.'38, New York Univ.; Prin., Pub. Sch. 37, Jersey City, N. J., since 1934.

Furgeson, Paul F., Supt. of Sch., Centralia, Wash., since 1936.

Furr, C. A., A.B.'20, Loyola Univ.; A.M.'31, Univ. of N. C.; Co. Supt. of Sch., Concord, N. C., since 1939.

Fuszard, Melvin C., B.A.'30, M.A.'37, Univ. of Wis.; Supt. of Sch., Lake Mills, Wis., since 1936.

Futrall, Alma, Co. Supt. of Sch., Marianna, Ark., since 1921.

G

Gable, H. E., B.A.'10, Southwestern Univ.; Supt. of Highland Park Sch., Dallas, Texas, since 1920.

Gabriel, Florence, Ph.B.'25, Univ. of Chicago; M.A.'29, Tchrs. Col., Columbia Univ.; Prin., Malvern and Sussex Schs., Malvern Rd., Shaker Hgts., Ohio, since 1925.

Gaffney, James T., Asst. Supt. of Sch., 228 N. La Salle St., Chicago, Ill., since 1940.

Gaffney, Matthew P., A.B.'12, Colgate Univ.; M.A.'19, Columbia Univ.; Litt. D.'42, Colgate Univ.; Supt., New Trier Twp. H. S., Winnetka, Ill., since 1931.

Gage, Harry Morehouse, A.B.'00, Wooster Col.; A.M.'03, Columbia Univ.; LL.D. '22, Wooster Col.; Pres., Lindenwood Col., St. Charles, Mo., since 1941.

*Gage, Snyder J., A.B.'99, Union Col.; Pd.B.'01, Albany Normal Col.; Supt. of Sch., Newburgh, N. Y., 1922 to 1930 and since 1938.

Gallagher, Buell Gordon, B.A.'25, Carleton Col.; B.D.'29, Union Theol. Seminary; Ph.D.'38, Columbia Univ.; Pres., Talladega Col., Talladega, Ala., since 1933.

Gallagher, Joseph D., A.B.'26, Univ. of Pa.; M.A.'37, New York Univ.; Supt. of Twp. Sch., Hazleton, Pa., since 1938.

Gallagher, M. C., B.A.'18, M.Ed.'42, Mont. State Univ.; Supt. of Sch., Billings, Mont., since 1937.

Gallardo, Jose M., A.B.'22, Park Col.; M.A.'26, Pa. State Col.; Ph.D.'33, Univ. of N. C.; LL.D.'37, Polytech. Inst. of P. R.; Litt.D.'42, Park Col.; Commr. of Educ., San Juan, P. R., since 1937.

Gallington, Ralph O., B.S.'31, Ind. State Tchrs. Col., Terre Haute, Ind.; A.B.'37, Columbia Univ.; Asst. Prof. of Educ., Univ. of Md., College Park, Md., since 1938.

Galloway, Henry Edward, B.A.'27, Union Col.; Supvg. Prin. of Sch., Morrisville, N. Y., since 1939.

Galvin, Sister Eucharista, A.B.'24, Col. of St. Catherine; M.A.'25, Ph.D.'29, Univ. of Chicago. Address: Col. of St. Catherine, St. Paul, Minn.

Gammage, Grady, B.A.'16, M.A.'26, LL.D. '27, Univ. of Ariz.; Ed.D.'40, New York Univ.; Pres., Ariz. State Tchrs. Col., Tempe, Ariz., since 1933.

Gammon, Delore, B.S.'29, State Tchrs. Col., Emporia, Kansas; M.A.'37, Tchrs. Col., Columbia Univ.; Supvr. of Elem. Educ., Pub. Sch., 428 S. Broadway, Wichita 2, Kansas, since 1943.

Gant, George F., A.B.'30, M.A.'31, Univ. of Nebr.; Ph.D.'34, Univ. of Wis.; Dir. of Personnel, Tenn. Valley Authority, Norris, Tenn., since 1937.

Gantz, Ralph M., B.S.'29, Otterbein Col.; M.S.'35, Univ. of Akron; Supt. of Twp. Sch., 2546 Sunbury Rd., Columbus, Ohio, since 1935.

Garcelon, A. B., Ph.B.'02, J.D.'04, Univ. of Chicago; Supt. of Sch., Uxbridge, Mass., since 1928.

Gard, W. L., B.S.'21, M.S.'28, Univ. of Ill.; Supt. of Sch., Beardstown, Ill., since 1928.

Garelle, Augustus C., Supvg. Prin. of Sch., Mattituck, L. I., N. Y.

Garlin, R. E., B.A.'20, M.A.'21, Ph.D.'27, Univ. of Texas; Head, Dept. of Educ., Texas Tech. Col., Lubbock, Texas, since 1943.

Garrett, Leslie, A.B.'31, State Tchrs. Col., West Liberty, W. Va.; M.A.'41, W. Va. Univ.; Co. Supt. of Sch., New Martinsville, W. Va., since 1927.

Garrison, S. C., Ph.D.'19, George Peabody Col. for Tchrs.; Pres., George Peabody Col. for Tchrs., Nashville 4, Tenn., since 1937.

Garver, Harlie, B.S.'14, Hiram Col.; M.A. '26, Columbia Univ.; Supt. of Sch., Hobart, Ind., since 1940.

Garver, V. A., Ph.B.'16, Wooster Col.; M.A.'25, Ohio State Univ.; Supt. of Sch., Rittman, Ohio, since 1925.

Gary, Enos G., B.A.'07, M.A.'24, Univ. of Texas; Prin., Brackenridge H. S., San Antonio, Texas, since 1928.

Gary, John L., B.A.'16, Willamette Univ.; M.Ed.'34, Univ. of Oregon; Supt. of Sch., West Linn, Oregon, since 1919.

Gates, Arthur I., A.B.'14, M.A.'15, Univ. of Calif.; Ph.D.'17, Columbia Univ.; Prof. of Educ., Tchrs. Col., Columbia Univ., New York 27, N. Y., since 1917.

Gates, C. Ray, B.E.'11, State Tchrs. Col., Peru, Nebr.; B.A.'16, Univ. of Nebr.; M.A.'20, Ed.D.'38, Columbia Univ.; Supt. of Sch., Grand Island, Nebr., since 1922.

Gates, Caleb F., Jr., B.A.'26, Princeton Univ.; B.A.'29, M.A.'31, Balliol Col., Oxford, England; Chancellor, Univ. of Denver, Denver, Colo., since 1941.

Gates, Dale W., B.S. in Ed.'28, M.A.'38, Ohio State Univ.; Supt. of Sch., Willard, Ohio, since 1939.

Gatje, George H., Ch.E.'21, Rensselaer Polytech. Inst.; M.A.'24, Ed.D.'41, Columbia Univ.; Supt. of Sch., Bay Shore, N. Y., since 1939.

Gatton, Harper, A.B.'12, Georgetown Col.; A.M.'26, Univ. of Chicago; LL.D.'36, Georgetown Col.; Supt. of Sch., Madisonville, Ky., since 1914.

Gayman, H. E., B.S.'16, Cornell Univ.; M.A.'33, Columbia Univ.; Exec. Secy., Pa. State Educ. Assn., 400 N. Third St., Harrisburg, Pa., since 1939.

*Gecks, Mathilde C., A.B.'22, Harris Tchrs. Col., St. Louis, Mo.; A.M.'26, New York Univ.; Lecturer and Counselor, Harris Tchrs. Col., St. Louis, Mo., since 1940.

Gehman, A. L., A.B.'09, Franklin and Marshall Col.; A.M.'18, Tchrs. Col., Columbia Univ.; Supt. of Springfield Twp. Sch., Chestnut Hill, Philadelphia, Pa., since 1922.

Geiger, Albert J., B.S.'23, M.A.'31, Univ. of Fla.; Ph.D.'33, George Peabody Col. for Tchrs.; Supvg. Prin. of Sch., St. Petersburg, Fla., since 1934.

Geiger, Vincent, B.S.'23, Pa. State Col.; M.A.'28, Tchrs. Col., Columbia Univ.; Supvg. Prin. of Sch., Verona, N. J., since 1938.

Geiss, Newton W., Diploma '09, State Normal Sch., Kutztown, Pa.; A.B.'15, Muhlenberg Col.; A.M.'23, Univ. of Pa.; Asst. Co. Supt. of Sch., Oley, Pa., since 1926.

Geissinger, John B., A.B.'27, Muhlenberg Col.; M.A.'29, Univ. of Pa.; Supvg. Prin. of Sch., North Wales, Pa., since 1940.

Gentry, Frank T., A.B.'16, Tusculum Col.; Supt. of Sch., Erwin, Tenn., since 1928.

Gentry, George H., B.A.'26, Baylor Univ.; M.A.'33, Univ. of Texas; Acting Supt. of Sch. and Pres., Jr. Col., Temple, Texas, since 1939.

George, N. L., B.S. in Ed.'26, Ed.M.'31, Univ. of Okla.; Bus. Mgr., Pub. Sch., Oklahoma City 4, Okla., 1941.

Geppert, O. E., Secy.-Treas., Denoyer-Geppert Co., 5235 Ravenswood Ave., Chicago 40, Ill.

Gerber, Raymond A., B.A.'25, Univ. of Mont.; M.A.'32, Univ. of Wash.; Supt. of Sch., Sidney, Mont., since 1932.

Gerken, Edna A., A.B.'14, Washburn Col.; C.P.H.'26, Mass. Inst. of Tech.; Supvr. of Health Educ., U. S. Office of Indian Affairs, Denver, Colo., since 1935.

*Gerling, Henry J., A.B., LL.B. and P.E.B. '94, A.M.'96, Univ. of Mo.; LL.D.'31, Muskingum Col.; LL.D.'32, Washington Univ.; LL.D.'33, Univ. of Mo. Address: 945 Beverly Ave., Glendale, Mo.

Getsinger, J. W., B.S.'16, Univ. of Ariz.; M.A.'39, Stanford Univ.; Dist. Supt. of Sch., Carmel, Calif., since 1942.

Getter, R. A., M.A.'34, Columbia Univ.; Supt. of Sch., Wilkinsburg, Pa., since 1941.

Geyer, Eldon C., A.B.'25, Univ. of Mich.; M.A.'28, Battle Creek Col.; Supt. of Sch., Battle Creek, Mich., since 1935.

Gibbons, Austin J., A.B.'04, Holy Cross Col., Worcester, Mass.; M.A.'08, LL.D. '36, Seton Hall Col.; Supt. of Sch., Manchester, N. H., since 1938.

Gibbons, Thomas F., A.B.'99, Holy Cross Col.; LL.B.'02, Boston Univ.; Supt. of Sch., Clinton, Mass., since 1915.

Gibbs, Andrew H., A.B.'39, George Wash. Univ.; Chief Educ. Asst. in State Sch. Admin., U. S. Office of Educ., Washington 25, D. C., since 1936.

Gibson, A. B., A.B.'26, Duke Univ.; M.A. '40, Columbia Univ.; Supt. of Sch., Laurinburg, N. C., since 1940.

Gibson, A. J., A.B.'16, W. Va. Univ.; M.A.'20, Columbia Univ.; State Supvr. of H. S., State Dept. of Educ., Charleston, W. Va., since 1933.

Gibson, Charles S., B.S.'29, Syracuse Univ.; Prin., Roosevelt Jr. H. S., Syracuse, N. Y., since 1924.

Gibson, Grant M., A.B.'13, Univ. of Wash.; Supt., Sultan Union H. S., Sultan, Wash., since 1926.

Gibson, Mae S., B.S.'39, Rutgers Univ.; Co. Helping Tch., Freehold, N. J., since 1928.

Gibson, Roy, B.S.'26, M.A.'35, Univ. of Ala.; Co. Supt. of Sch., Ashville, Ala., since 1938.

Giese, William C., B.S.'09, Kalamazoo Col.; B.S.'09, Univ. of Chicago; M.A.'17, Columbia Univ.; Supt. of Sch., Racine, Wis., since 1933.

Gifford, Myrtie, 971 Santa Barbara Rd., Berkeley, Calif.

Gil, Pedro, B.A. in Sc.'17, Univ. of Puerto Rico; Asst. Dir., Div. of Community Service Programs, WPA, San Juan, P. R.

Gilbert, Levi, B.S.'22, Franklin and Marshall Col.; M.A.'29, Univ. of Pa.; D.Ed. '38, Univ. of Pittsburgh. Address: Bd. of Educ., Altoona, Pa.

Gilkeson, A. Crawford, B.S.'05, Va. Poly. Inst.; Div. Supt. of Sch., Staunton, Va., since 1933.

Gill, Normer L., A.B.'30, A.M.'33, Univ. of Miss.; Supt. of Sch., Fernwood, Miss., since 1934.

Gilland, Edwin C., A.B.'07, Lafayette Col.; Supt. of Sch., Red Bank, N. J., since 1920.

Gilland, Thomas M., A.B.'09, Ursinus Col.; A.M.'26, Tchrs. Col., Columbia Univ.; Ph.D.'35, Univ. of Chicago; Dir. of Tr., State Tchrs. Col., California, Pa., since 1931.

Gillespie, Robert H., A.B.'27, Wheaton Col.; M.A.'35, Univ. of Mo.; Dir., Univ. H. S. and Asst. Prof. of Educ., Univ. of Miss., University, Miss., since 1942.

Gillett, Arthur Dudley, B.L.'02, M.A.'07, Univ. of Wis.; LL.D.'31, Northland Col.; Supt. of Sch., Eveleth, Minn., since 1934.

Gilman, Stanwood C., B.S.'33, Boston Univ.; Union Supt. of Sch., Wiscasset, Maine, since 1940.

Gilmer, Ira T., A.B.'05, LL.B.'10, M.A.'36, Univ. of Miss.; Supt. of Sch., Graham, Texas, since 1924.

Gilmore, W. Lee, B.E.'02, M.E.'04, State Tchrs. Col., Slippery Rock, Pa.; A.B.'05, Central Univ.; B.S. and B.S.E.'18, Univ. of Pittsburgh; D.Ped.'32, Webster Univ.; Dist. Supt. of Sch., Oakmont, Pa., since 1916.

Gilpin, Howard H., B.S.'33, Central State Tchrs. Col., Mt. Pleasant, Mich.; Supt. of Sch., Rogers City, Mich., since 1906.

Ginn, Susan J., Dir. of Voc. Guidance, Pub. Sch., 45 Myrtle St., Boston 14, Mass., since 1916.

Givens, Willard E., A.B.'13, Ind. Univ.; M.A.'15, Columbia Univ.; Diploma '16, Union Theol. Sem.; LL.D.'38, Ind. Univ.; Ed.D.'41, Miami Univ.; Exec. Secy., Natl. Educ. Assn., 1201 16th St., N. W., Washington 6, D. C., since 1935.

Glad, Amos W., A.B.'16, Bethany Col., Lindsborg, Kansas; A.M.'24, Univ. of Kansas; Supt. of Sch., Pratt, Kansas, since 1931.

Glann, John D., B.A.'26, M.A.'40, Wash. State Col.; Supt. of Sch., Chehalis, Wash., since 1936.

Glasgow, M. W., A.B.'21, Univ. of Mich.; Ed.M.'33, Ed.D.'37, Univ. of Okla.; Supt. of Sch., Bartlesville, Okla., since 1940.

Glasser, Norman L., A.B.'07, Groves City Col.; A.M.'13, Univ. of Pa.; Supt. of Sch., Carnegie, Pa., since 1926.

*Glenn, Charles B., B.S.'91, M.S.'92, Ala. Poly. Inst.; A.B.'96, Harvard Univ.; LL.D.'18, Univ. of Ala.; Litt.D.'31, Birmingham-Southern Col.; Pres., American Assn. of Sch. Admin., 1937-38; Supt. Emeritus of Sch., 3215 Sterling Rd., Birmingham, Ala., since 1943.

Glenn, Mabelle, B.M.'08, Monmouth Col.; Mus.D.'30, Chicago Musical Col.; Dir. of Music, Pub. Sch., Library Bldg., Kansas City, Mo., since 1921.

Glover, Oscar S., Ph.B.'19, M.A.'24, Univ. of Chicago; Supt. of Edina-Morningside Sch., Minneapolis, Minn., since 1926.

Gluck, Harold, B.S.S.'26, M.S. in Ed.'27, Col. of the City of New York; J.D.'30, J.S.D.'33, New York Univ.; Ph.D.'40, Fordham Univ. Address: W. H. Taft H. S., Bronx, N. Y.

Goddard, V. F., B.A.'13, Maryville Col.; M.A.'28, Univ. of Mich.; Supt. of Sch., Alcoa, Tenn., since 1924.

Godwin, Wendell R., A.B.'26, DePauw Univ.; M.A.'32, Univ. of Chicago; Supt. of Sch., Hutchinson, Kansas, since 1943.

Goetsch, Edward William, Diploma '06, Iowa State Tchrs. Col., Cedar Falls, Iowa; B.A.'10, M.A.'20, Ph.D.'25, State Univ. of Iowa; Prof. of Educ., Iowa State Tchrs. Col., since 1918 and Dir. of Tchr. Placement, Iowa State Tchrs. Col., Cedar Falls, Iowa, since 1928.

Goins, Jesse L., A.B.'25, Univ. of Wyo.; A.M.'31, Univ. of Chicago; Supt. of Sch., Cheyenne, Wyo., since 1938.

Golden, J. B., B.S.'30, West Texas State Tchrs. Col., Canyon, Texas; M.E.'39, Southern Methodist Univ.; Co. Supt. of Sch., Wichita Falls, Texas, since 1935.

Goldring, Cecil C., B.A.'18, Queen's Univ.; M.A.'20, D.Ped.'24, Univ. of Toronto; Supt. of Sch., Toronto, Canada, since 1932.

Goodall, Elizabeth J., A.B.'28, A.M.'37, W. Va. Univ.; Asst. Co. Supt. of Sch., Charleston, W. Va., since 1935.

Goode, Benjamin Clifford, B.A.'19, Univ. of Richmond; M.A.'25, Univ. of Va. Address: 7621 Sweetbrier Rd., Richmond, Va.

Goodell, M. R., Diploma '16, State Normal Sch., River Falls, Wis.; B.S.'34, Ph.M. '36, Univ. of Wis.; Prin., Normal Sch., Columbus, Wis., since 1930.

Goodier, Floyd T., A.B.'03, Colgate Univ.; A.M.'09, Tchrs. Col., Columbia Univ.; Dir. of Integration, Ill. State Normal Univ., Normal, Ill., since 1937.

Goodrich, Lowell Pierce, Supt. of Sch., 1111 N. Tenth St., Milwaukee 1, Wis., since 1943.

Goodwill, G. T., A.B.'29, Univ. of Redlands; M.A.'38, Univ. of Southern Calif.; Supt. of Sch., Needles, Calif., since 1937.

Goodykoontz, Bess, B.A.'20, M.A.'22, State Univ. of Iowa; D.Ped.'35, N. Y. State Col. for Tchrs., Albany, N. Y.; Asst. U. S. Commr. of Educ., Federal Security Agency, Washington 25, D. C., since 1929.

Goold, H. R., B.S.'08, Northwestern Univ.; M.A.'22, Univ. of Wash.; Supt. of Sch., Tacoma 7, Wash., since 1937.

Goold, J. Vernon, A.B.'20, Stanford Univ.; Dist. Supt., Wash. Union H. S., Centerville, Calif., since 1942.

Gordon, Claude T., Diploma '18, State Tchrs. Col., Denton, Texas; B.S.'39, Ill. Inst. of Tech.; Ed.M.'42, De Paul Univ.; Prin., Drexel Sch., Cicero, Ill., since 1933.

Gore, Walter R., A.B.'39, M.A.'40, Univ. of Denver; Supt., Huerfano Co. H. S., Walsenburg, Colo., since 1940.

Gore, William A., A.B.'05, A.M.'08, Univ. of Ill.; Ph.D.'31, New York Univ.; Supt. of Sch., Hempstead, N. Y., since 1932.

Goreham, Wilfred John, A.B.'24, Ill. Wesleyan Univ.; M.A.'33, Univ. of Ill.; Prin., Twp. H. S., Sidell, Ill., since 1927.

Gores, Harold B., B.S.'31, State Tchrs. Col., Bridgewater, Mass.; M.Ed.'38, Harvard Univ.; Asst. Supt. of Sch., Newtonville, Mass., since 1943.

Gorsline, Robert H., B.S.'20, Mich. State Col., East Lansing, Mich.; M.A.'35, Univ. of Mich.; Supt. of Sch., Milford, Mich., since 1933.

Goslin, Willard E., B.S. in Ed.'22, Northeast Mo. State Tchrs. Col., Kirksville, Mo.; A.M.'29, Univ. of Mo.; Supt. of Sch., Webster Groves, Mo., since 1930.

Gossard, Paul, A.B.'21, Ohio State Univ.; M.A.'26, Ph.D.'40, Univ. of Chicago; Supt. of Sch., Bloomington, Ill., since 1938.

Gough, Harry B., B.A.'14, Hamline Univ.; M.A.'28, Univ. of Minn.; Supt. of Sch., St. Cloud, Minn., since 1930.

Gould, Arthur L., A.B.'12, A.M.'13, LL.D., Boston Col.; Supt. of Sch., 15 Beacon St., Boston, Mass., since 1937.

Gowans, Harry W., B.S.'08, M.A.'13, Univ. of Kansas; Ed.D.'38, Univ. of Tulsa; Supt. of Sch., Tulsa, Okla., since 1935.

Goward, Paul F., B.S.'16, Dartmouth Col.; Bus. Mgr., *School Arts Magazine*, Printers Bldg., Worcester, Mass., since 1922.

Grace, Alonzo G., A.B.'17, A.M.'22, Univ. of Minn.; Ph.D.'32, Western Reserve Univ.; State Commr. of Educ., Hartford, Conn., since 1938.

Grace of the Sacred Heart, Sister, Ph.D.'29, Fordham Univ.; Pres., D'Youville Col., Buffalo, N. Y., since 1934.

Grady, Margaret, Prin., John Henry Brown Sch., Dallas, Texas.

Graff, Willard J., B.S.'30, Southwest Mo. State Tchrs. Col., Springfield, Mo.; A.M. '34, Univ. of Mo.; Supt. of Sch., Independence, Kansas, since 1941.

Graham, Frank P., Pres., Univ. of N. C., Chapel Hill, N. C.

Graham, Jessie, Ph.D.'33, Univ. of Southern Calif.; Head Supvr. of Comml. Educ., Pub. Sch., Los Angeles 15, Calif., since 1942.

Gralapp, Arnold L., B.A.'17, Willamette Univ.; M.A.'36, Univ. of Calif.; Supt. of Sch., Klamath Falls, Oregon, since 1941.

Grandchamp, A. D., B.A.'32, Univ. of Wash.; A. M.'43, Univ. of Chicago; Supt. of Sch., Columbia Falls, Mont., since 1941.

Granrud, John, B.A.'17, St. Olaf Col.; M.S. '21, Univ. of Minn.; Ph.D.'24, Tchrs. Col., Columbia Univ.; Supt. of Sch., 32 Spring St., Springfield, Mass., since 1933.

Granskou, Clemens Matthew, D.D.'36, Luther Theol. Sem., St. Paul, Minn.; Pres., St. Olaf Col., Northfield, Minn., since 1943.

Grant, Alfred E., B.S.'23, Tufts Col.; Ed.M. '30, Harvard Univ.; Asst. Supt. of Sch., Cranston, R. I., since 1932.

Grant, Francis V., B.S.'21, Colgate Univ.; Supt. of Sch., Williamstown, Mass., since 1922.

Grant, Mildred, Co. Supt. of Sch., Yreka, Calif.

Graves, Albert D., A.B.'26, A.M.'32, Stanford Univ.; Deputy Supt. of Sch., San Francisco 2, Calif., since 1941.

Graves, Frank Pierrepont, A.M.'90, A.M.'91, Columbia Univ.; Ph.D.'92, Boston Univ.; Litt.D.'97, Heidelberg Col.; LL.D.'97, Hanover Col.; Ph.D.'12, Columbia Univ.; LL.D.'20, Oberlin Col.; L.H.D.'21, Tufts Col.; L.H.D.'22, Colgate Univ.; LL.D.'22, Hobart Col.; LL.D.'22, Hamilton Col.; Litt.D.'23, Univ. of Rochester; LL.D.'26, Union Univ.; LL.D.'28, Alfred Univ.; LL.D.'29, Col. of William and Mary; LL.D.'29, Columbia Univ.; LL.D.'30, Univ. of Mo.; LL.D.'30, Syracuse Univ.; LL.D.'30, Juniata Col.; LL.D.'31, Niagara Univ.; LL.D.'33, Ohio Univ.; LL.D.'33, Fordham Univ.; Litt.D.'35, Canisius Col.; LL.D.'35, St. Bonaventure's Col.; LL.D. '36, Manhattan Col.; LL.D.'37, Univ. of Wyo.; D.C.L.'38, Ursinus Col.; LL.D.'38, George Washington Univ.; LL.D.'38, Houghton Col.; LL.D.'38, Bucknell Univ.; LL.D.'39, Wash. Col.; LL.D.'39, Boston Univ.; LL.D.'39, Western Reserve Univ.; LL.D.'39, Miami Univ.; J.U.D.'40, Univ. of Pa.; LL.D.'40, Bethany Col.; D.C.L.'40, Univ. of the South; LL.D.'40, St. John's Univ.; L.H.D.'40, Yeshiva Col.; LL.D.'40, Univ. of the State of New York; Honorary Life Member, American Assn. of Sch. Admin.; Pres., Univ. of the State of New York and State Commr. of Educ., Albany, N. Y., 1921-1940. Address: 56 S. Swan St., Albany, N. Y.

Graves, S. Monroe, A.B.'02, Colgate Univ.; A.M.'12, Ph.D.'13, Harvard Univ.; Registrar and Prof. of English, Mt. Ida Jr. Col., Newton, Mass. Address: 31 Elm St., Wellesley Hills, Mass.

Gray, Julius Cornelius, B.A.'16, M.S.'29, Univ. of Ark.; Supt. of Sch. and Co. Sch. Examiner, Eudora, Ark., since 1933.

Gray, Reede, B.A.'25, Carleton Col.; M.A. '33, Univ. of Minn.; Supt. of Sch., Redwood Falls, Minn., since 1935.

Gray, William S., S.B.'13, Univ. of Chicago; M.A.'14, Columbia Univ.; Ph.D.'16, Univ. of Chicago; Prof. of Educ., Univ. of Chicago, Chicago, Ill., since 1921.

Green, Charles Sylvester, A.B.'22, Wake Forest Col.; A.M.'24, B.D.'30, Duke Univ.; D.D.'34, Wash. and Lee Univ.; Litt.D.'41, Univ. of S. C.; Adviser in Religious Activities, Duke Univ., Durham, N. C., since 1943.

Green, R. J., B.S.'29, Iowa State Tchrs. Col., Cedar Falls, Iowa; M.A.'38, Columbia Univ.; Supt. of Sch., Greenfield, Iowa, since 1940.

Green, William M., A.B.'23, Colo. State Tchrs. Col.; M.A.'30, Tchrs. Col., Columbia Univ.; LL.D.'39, Texas Christian Univ.; Supt. of Sch., 409 E. Weatherford St., Ft. Worth, Texas, since 1931.

Greenawalt, George L., Ph.B.'21, Univ. of Chicago; M.A.'29, Tchrs. Col., Columbia Univ.; Acting Supt. of Sch., Jackson, Mich., since 1942.

*Greenawalt, William C., A.B.'07, A.M.'12, Franklin and Marshall Col.; Supt. of Sch., Olean, N. Y., 1920-40. Address: 418 W. Market St., Orwigsburg, Pa.

Greenberg, Benjamin B., M.A.'10, New York Univ.; Ed.D.'37, Tchrs. Col., Columbia Univ.; Asst. Supt. of Sch., 110 Livingston St., Brooklyn 2, N. Y., since 1931.

Greene, Channing Hildreth, Ed.M.'33, Univ. of N. H.; Supt. of Sch., Southbridge, Mass., since 1936.

Greene, Charles E., A.B.'10, A.M.'11, Univ. of Denver; A.M.'19, Tchrs. Col., Columbia Univ.; LL.D.'42, Univ. of Denver; Supt. of Sch., 414 14th St., Denver, Colo., since 1939.

Greene, Crawford, A.B. and B.S.'21, Henderson-Brown Col.; M.A.'26, Peabody; Dir. of Sch. Admin., State Dept. of Educ., Little Rock, Ark., since 1941.

Greene, Fred W., A.B.'24, M.Ed.'31, Duke Univ.; Secy., N. C. Educ. Assn., Raleigh, N. C., since 1941.

Greene, Pat H., M.A.'32, Univ. of Texas; Supt. of Sch., Webster, Texas, since 1924.

Greene, William A., A.B.'12, Kansas Wesleyan Univ.; Ed.M.'35, Univ. of Okla. Address: 407 E. Harrison, Guthrie, Okla.

Greenfield, M. LeRoy, A.B.'08, Colgate Univ.; Union Supt. of Sch., Ware, Mass., since 1941.

Greer, Hugh G., B.S.'17, Miss. Col.; A.M.'27, Univ. of Chicago; Co. Supt. of Sch., Monroeville, Ala., since 1930.

Greer, Wilson, B.A.'17, Wesleyan Univ.; M.A.'28, Yale Univ.; Supt. of Sch., Wethersfield, Conn., since 1928.

Greever, A. S., B.A.'87, M.A.'92, Roanoke Col.; Co. Supt. of Sch., Tazewell, Va., since 1917.

Grenia, Lura A., A.B.'16, Univ. of Oregon; Co. Supt. of Sch., Stevenson, Wash., since 1943.

Greve, Anne C., A.B.'29, John Fletcher Col.; M.S.'37, Iowa State Col.; Dean, Kletzing Col., University Park, Iowa, since 1943.

Gribble, Merl E., Ph.B.'24, Lawrence Col.; Ph.M.'35, Univ. of Wis.; Supt. of Sch., Wisconsin Dells, Wis., since 1936.

Gridley, Earl G., A.B.'10, Simpson Col.; Secy.-Treas., Bay Section, Calif. Tchrs. Assn., Berkeley, Calif., since 1929.

Grieder, Calvin, B.A.'27, Univ. of Dubuque; M.A.'36, Ph.D.'38, State Univ. of Iowa; Assoc. Prof. of Sch. Admin., Univ. of Colo., Boulder, Colo., since 1940.

Grieder, Theodore G., A.B.'20, Univ. of Dubuque; A.M.'28, State Univ. of Iowa; Dist. Supt. of Sch., 1120 E. Main St., Ventura, Calif., since 1939.

Grier, B. M., A.B.'16, Erskine Col.; M.A.'28, Univ. of Ga.; Supt. of Sch., Athens, Ga., since 1929.

Griewe, C. S., B.A.'23, Morningside Col.; M.A.'37, Univ. of Colo.; Supt. of Sch., Sibley, Iowa, since 1940.

Griffey, Annie G., Asst. Supt. of Sch., 800 Louisiana St., Little Rock, Ark.

Griffin, Lee H., Ph.B.'16, Univ. of Chicago; Ginn & Co., 2301 Prairie Ave., Chicago, Ill.

Griffin, Margery M., Prin., Clay Sch., 3820 N. 14th St., St. Louis, Mo.

Griffith, Charles E., B.A.'04, Beloit Col.; Co. Supt. of Sch., Toulon, Ill., since 1923.

Grigg, Claud, A.B.'21, M.A.'28, Duke Univ.; Supt. of Sch., Albemarle, N. C., since 1934.

Griggs, Joseph Reagan, B.A.'32, M.A.'39, Texas Tech. Col., Lubbock, Texas; D.Ed. '43, Univ. of Texas; Dir. of Supvn. and Curriculum, State Dept. of Educ., Austin, Texas.

Griggs, William C., A.B.'98, Howard Col.; Supt. of City and Co. Sch., Barton Bldg., Mobile, Ala., since 1927.

Grigsby, Paul A., A.B.'22, Central Col., Fayette, Mo.; A.M.'29, Univ. of Mo.; Supt., Community H. S., Granite City, Ill., since 1932.

Grim, Paul H., B.S.'27, Albright Col.; Supvg. Prin. of North Coventry Schs., Pottstown, Pa., since 1940.

Grim, Paul R., B.S., M.A., Ph.D.'38, Ohio State Univ.; Dir. of Campus Schs. and Student Tchg., Western Wash. Col. of Educ., Bellingham, Wash., since 1942.

Grimes, A. B., B.S.'23, Coe Col.; M.A.'31, State Univ. of Iowa; Supt. of Sch., Monticello, Iowa, since 1928.

Grimes, Leslie K., A.B.'22, A.M.'34, Univ. of Mo.; Supt. of Sch., Eureka, Mo., since 1939.

Grimes, Loyd E., B.S.'28, Southwest Mo. State Tchrs. Col., Springfield, Mo.; A.M. '31, D.Ed.'43, Univ. of Mo.; Asst. State Supt. of Sch., Jefferson City, Mo., since 1943.

Grindle, Thomas S., M.Ed.'24, Harvard Univ.; Supt. of Sch., Lexington, Mass., since 1924.

Gronde, Franklin J., B.S.'11, Bucknell Univ.; M.A.'35, New York Univ.; Supvg. Prin. of Sch., Bradley Beach, N. J., since 1923.

Groner, H. L., Supt of Consol. Sch., Greenbrier, Ark.

Grose, C. Herman, B.S.'16, W. Va. Wesleyan Col.; A.M.'27, Ph.D.'40, Univ. of Pittsburgh; Ped.D.'40, W. Va. Wesleyan Col.; Supt. of Sch., Erie, Pa., since 1935.

Gross, Ira C., B.S.'15, M.S.'17, Susquehanna Univ.; Supvg. Prin. of Southmont Sch., Johnstown, Pa., since 1934.

Gross, John Owen, A.B.'18, Asbury Col.; S.T.B.'21, Boston Univ.; D.D.'30, Asbury Col.; L.H.D.'38, Union Col.; Secy., Dept. of Educ. Institutions, Bd. of Educ., The Methodist Church, 810 Broadway, Nashville 2, Tenn., since 1941.

Grossley, Richard S., B.S.'11, Alcorn Agrl. and Mech. Col. for Negroes; M. A.'36, New York Univ.; Pres., State Col., Dover, Del., since 1923.

Grove, Frank L., A.B.'09, Univ. of Ala.; A.M.'17, Columbia Univ.; Secy., Ala. Educ. Assn., 21 Adams Ave., Montgomery 4, Ala., since 1928.

Grover, Elbridge C., B.S.'14, Harvard Col.; M.A.'20, Tchrs. Col., Columbia Univ.; Ph.D.'25, Sch. of Educ., New York Univ.; Supt. of Sch., Reading, Mass., since 1939.

Grubbs, Mrs. Ethel Harris, B.S.'15, Howard Univ.; A.M.'24, Columbia Univ.; Head, Dept. of Mathematics, H. S., Div. 10 to 13, Pub. Sch., Washington, D. C., since 1927.

Gruenberg, Benjamin C., B.S.'96, Univ. of Minn.; A.M.'08, Ph.D.'11, Columbia Univ. Address: 418 Central Park, W., New York, N. Y.

Gruver, Harvey S., A.B.'02, Otterbein Col.; A.M.'10, Harvard Univ.; Supt. of Sch., Lynn, Mass., since 1923.

Gugle, Marie, A.B.'97, Ohio State Univ.; A.M.'13, Columbia Univ.; Prin., East Sr. H. S., Columbus, Ohio, since 1935.

Gum, B. E., A.B.'31, McKendree Col.; A.M. '38, Univ. of Ill.; Supt. of Sch., Salem, Ill., since 1937.

Gumser, W. W., A.B.'17, Hope Col.; A.M. '26, Univ. of Mich.; Supt. of Sch., Lowell, Mich., since 1926.

Gussner, William S., B.S.'26, Jamestown Col.; M.S. in Ed.'38, Univ. of N. Dak.; Supt. of Sch., Jamestown, N. Dak., since 1939.

Guthridge, Wallace H., Supt. of Sch., Parsons, Kansas.

Gwinn, Joseph Marr, A.B.'02, Univ. of Mo.; A.M.'07, Tchrs. Col., Columbia Univ.; LL.D.'26, Univ. of Mo.; Pres., Dept. of Superintendence, 1927-28; Prof. Emeritus of Educ., San Jose State Col., San Jose, Calif., since 1940. Address: 551 S. Wilson Ave., Pasadena 5, Calif.

Gwynn, John Minor, Ph.D.'35, Yale Univ.; Assoc. Prof. of Educ., Univ. of N. C., Chapel Hill, N. C., since 1927.

H

Haack, Otto, B.S.'25, Univ. of Minn.; B.E. '29, State Tchrs. Col., Bemidji, Minn.; M.S.'33, Univ. of N. Dak.; Supt. of Sch., Pine River, Minn., since 1935.

Haas, Francis B., B.S.'13, Temple Univ.; M.A.'22, Univ. of Pa.; Pd.D.'25, Temple Univ.; LL.D.'34, Juniata Col.; State Supt. of Pub. Instr., Harrisburg, Pa., since 1939.

Hackenberg, J. L., A.B.'20, Susquehanna Univ.; A.M.'29, Pa. State Col.; Supt. of Sch., Hollidaysburg, Pa., since 1941.

Hacker, Ralph E., Sch. Architect, Ft. Lee Trust Bldg., Ft. Lee, N. J.

Hadfield, Albert E., A.B.'24, Hiram Col.; A.M.'32, Tchrs. Col., Columbia Univ.; Supt. of Sch., Maple Hgts., Ohio, since 1938.

Haebich, I. E., B.A.'15, Baldwin-Wallace Col.; M.S.'33, Univ. of Chicago; Supt. of H. S., Riverside, Ill., since 1939.

Hagan, John R., Ph.D.'10, D.D.'14, Urban Col., Rome, Italy; M.A.'27, D.Sc. in Ed.'31, Catholic Univ. of America; Supt. of Catholic Schools, Cleveland, Ohio, since 1921.

Hagen, H. H., A.B.'13, Ohio Wesleyan Univ.; M.A.'34, Northwestern Univ.; Dist. Supt. of Sch., 6130 S. Wolcott Ave., Chicago, Ill., since 1940.

Hager, Walter E., B.S.'16, Univ. of Nebr.; A.M.'27, Ph.D.'31, Columbia Univ.; Pres., Wilson Tchrs. Col., Washington, D. C., since 1941.

Haggard, W. W., B.A.'17, Maryville Col.; M.A.'27, Univ. of Mich.; Ph.D.'37, Univ. of Chicago; Pres., Western Wash. Col. of Educ., Bellingham, Wash., since 1939.

Haisley, Otto W., M.A.'17, Columbia Univ.; Supt. of Sch., Ann Arbor, Mich., since 1924.

Haiston, F. M., B.S.'15, Susquehanna Univ.; M.A.'32, Ph.D.'34, New York Univ.; Supt. of Sch., Pottstown, Pa., since 1934.

Halberg, Anna D., B.S.'22, A.M.'24, Columbia Univ.; Prof. of Educ. and Chmm., Div. of Educ. and Psych., Wilson Tchrs. Col., Washington, D. C., since 1927.

Haldaman, D. H., M.A.'30, Univ. of Mo.; Supt. of Sch., Bismarck, Mo., since 1929.

Hale, Arthur W., A.B.'06, Amherst Col.; Ed.M.'24, Harvard Univ.; Supt. of Sch., Franklin, Mass., since 1918.

Hale, Florence, L.H.D.'32, Colby Col.; Pres., Natl. Edu. Assn., 1931-32; Editor, *The Grade Teacher*, Darien, Conn., since 1927.

Hale, William J., M.A.'14, Lincoln Univ.; LL.D.'36, Wilberforce Univ.; LL.D.'39, Howard Univ.; Pres., Tenn. Agrl. and Industrial State Tchrs. Col., Nashville 8, Tenn., since 1912.

Haley, Harvey H., B.S.'18, Peabody Col.; M.A.'22, Columbia Univ.; Supt. of Sch., Stuttgart, Ark., since 1940.

Haley, Nelle, M.A.'28, Tchrs. Col., Columbia Univ. Address: 620 S. Jefferson Ave., Saginaw, Mich.

Halkyard, Marcita B., Ph.B.'30, A.M.'37, Univ. of Chicago; Genl. Supvr., Pub. Sch., 153 S. Ottawa St., Joliet, Ill., since 1935.

Hall, Chester A., B.S.'26, Southwest Mo. State Tchrs. Col., Springfield, Mo.; M.A.'34, Univ. of Ariz.; Supt. of Sch., Bisbee, Ariz., since 1942.

Hall, John W., B.S.'01, M.A.'02, Tchrs. Col., Columbia Univ.; Prof. Emeritus, Univ. of Nevada, since 1937. Address: 235 W. 10th St., Reno, Nevada.

Hall, Robert C., B.A.'24, Univ. of Wash.; Supt. of Fife Pub. Sch., Tacoma, Wash., since 1937.

Hall, Sidney B., A.B.'18, Col. of William and Mary; M.A.'24, Univ. of Va.; Ed.M. '25, Ed.D.'26, Harvard Univ.; Prof. of Educ., George Washington Univ., Washington, D. C., since 1941.

Hallman, E. B., A.B.'04, Newberry Col.; Acting Supt. of Sch., Spartanburg, N. C., since 1943.

Halter, Millard M., A.B.'21, Central Wesleyan Col.; A.M.'26, Univ. of Mo.; Supt. of Sch., 6301 Wells Ave., Wellston, St. Louis, Mo., since 1939.

Hamilton, Charles Woods, Life Cert.'14, State Normal Sch., Plattsburg, N. Y.; B.C.S.'24, B.S. in Ed.'29, M.A.'32, New York Univ.; Asst. in Sec. Educ., State Dept. of Pub. Instr., Trenton, N. J., since 1936.

Hamilton, Otto T., A.B. and LL.B.'11 Ind. Univ.; A.M.'18, Ph.D.'27, Tchrs. Col., Columbia Univ.; Asst. Prof. of Educ., Extension Div., Ind. Univ., since 1927. Address: Oaklandon, Ind.

Hamilton, William J., Supt. of Sch., Oak Park, Ill., since 1917.

Hamm, Hal W., A.M.'30, Colo. State Col. of Educ.; Dist. Supt., Surprise Valley Union H. S., Cedarville, Calif., since 1941.

Hamm, William G., B.S.'22, M.A.'41, George Peabody Col. for Tchrs.; Supt. of Sch., Huntsville, Ala., since 1928.

Hamner, Herman B., Diploma '09, Southern Univ.; Co. Supt. of Sch., Phenix City, Ala., since 1920.

Hamon, Ray L., B.S.'22, Univ. of Fla.; A.M.'25, George Peabody Col. for Tchrs.; Ph.D.'30, Columbia Univ.; Sr. Specialist in Sch. Plant, U. S. Office of Educ., Washington 25, D. C., since 1943.

Hampton, A. C., A.B.'18, Univ. of Oregon; Supt. of Sch., Astoria, Oregon, since 1925.

Hanawalt, Paul B., A.B.'18, Col. of Puget Sound; M.A.'25, Univ. of Wash.; Supt. of Sch., Puyallup, Wash., since 1930.

Hancher, Virgil M., B.A.'18, J. D.'24, State Univ. of Iowa; B.A.'22, M.A.'27, Oxford Univ.; LL.D.'41, Grinnell Col.; LL.D.'41, St. Ambrose Col.; Pres., State Univ. of Iowa, Iowa City, Iowa, since 1940.

Hand, Harold C., B.A.'24, Macalester Col.; M.A.'30, Univ. of Minn.; Ph.D.'33, Columbia Univ.; Prof. of Educ., Univ. of Md., College Park, Md., since 1940.

Handlin, William C., A.B.'09, Univ. of Ill.; M.A.'28, James Millikin Univ.; Prin., Community H. S., Lincoln, Ill., since 1919.

Handwork, Cora Lacey, Ph.B.'14, Dickinson Col.; M.S.'37, Univ. of Pa.; Supvg. Prin. of Sch., Birdsboro, Pa., since 1935.

Handy, Anson B., B.A.'08, Ed.M.'30, Harvard Univ.; Pres., State Tchrs. Col., Hyannis, Mass., since 1941.

Hanes, W. T., M.A.'38, Texas Tech. Col.; Supt. of Sch., Tahoka, Texas, since 1938.

Hanley, James Lawrence, A.B.'19, Boston Col.; A.M.'20, Brown Univ.; LL.B.'27, Northeastern Univ.; Ed.D.'37, Catholic Tchrs. Col.; D.Ped.'41, Bryant Col.; Supt. of Sch., 20 Summer St., Providence, R. I., since 1937.

Hanna, George W., M.Di.'99, Highland Park Col.; A.B.'18, Des Moines Univ.; Supt. of Sch., Valley City, N. Dak., since 1899.

Hannah, Stanford, B.S.'22, Mont. State Col., Bozeman, Mont.; M.A.'30, Univ. of Calif.; Dist. Supt., Taft Union H. S. and Jr. Col., Taft, Calif., since 1937.

Hanson, Abel A., B.Ed.'30, Ill. State Normal Univ.; M.S.'35, Univ. of Ill.; D.Ed.'41, Columbia Univ.; Acting Supvg. Prin., Union Free Sch. Dist. No. 16, Elmont, N. Y., since 1941.

Hanson, Earl H., A.B.'24, Augustana Col.; M.A.'33, Columbia Univ.; Supt. of Sch., Rock Island, Ill., since 1937.

Hanson, Ernest M., B.S. in Ed.'22, M.A.'27, Univ. of Minn.; Asst. Supt. of Sch., Salt Lake City, Utah, since 1938.

Hanson, W. E., Supt. of Sch., Braham, Minn., since 1936.

Hanson, Warren A., A.B.'09, Harvard Col.; Ph.D.'36, Yale Univ.; Supt. of Sch., New London, Conn., since 1918.

Hapgood, Charles G., M.A.'37, Boston Univ.; Supt. of Sch., Barton, Vt., since 1942.

Hapgood, E. A. T., Diploma '10, Worcester Polytech, Inst.; B.S.'27, M.A.'35, Tchrs. Col., Columbia Univ.; Supt. of Sch., Mount Morris, N. Y., since 1935.

Harbeson, John W., A.B.'11, Univ. of Kansas; M.A.'16, Columbia Univ.; Ph.D.'31, Univ. of Southern Calif.; Prin., Jr. Col., Pasadena, Calif., since 1927.

Harbison, James Wesley, A.B.'27, M.Ed.'43, Duke Univ.; Supt. of Sch., Pinehurst, N. C., since 1938.

Harbo, L. S., B.A.'18, Augsburg Col.; M.A.'32, Univ. of Minn.; Supt. of Sch., Red Wing, Minn., since 1941.

*Hardesty, Cecil D., A.B.'28, Kansas Wesleyan Univ.; M.A. in Ed.'32, Ed.D.'33, Univ. of Southern Calif.; Lt. (J. G.), S.C.-V (s) USNR, Naval Supply Depot, Clearfield, Utah.

Harding, H. P., A.B.'99, Univ. of N. C.; A.M.'32, Columbia Univ.; Supt. of Sch., Charlotte, N. C., since 1913.

Hardy, H. Claude, A.B.'11, Wesleyan Univ.; M.A.'21, Univ. of Rochester; M.A.'23, Syracuse Univ.; Ph.D.'31, New York Univ.; Supt. of Sch., 166 Old Mamaroneck Rd., White Plains, N. Y., since 1934.

Harkins, John M., A.B.'08, Bates Col.; Supt. of Sch., Warren, R. I., since 1941.

Harman, Arthur Fort, Diploma '96, Peabody Normal Col.; LL.D.'24, Univ. of Ala.; B.S.'28, Tchrs. Col., Columbia Univ.; Pres., Ala. Col., Montevallo, Ala., since 1935.

Harman, Milton, Co. Supt. of Sch., Bucyrus, Ohio.

Harmon, George Henry, B.S. and B.A.'04, Bates Col.; Union Supt. of Sch., Raymond, N. H., since 1929.

Harnden, Willard G., A.B.'25, Southwestern Col.; Supt. of Sch., Moxee City, Wash., since 1939.

Harney, Julia C., B.S.'18, M.A.'20, Ph.D.'31, New York Univ.; LL.D.'37, St. Elizabeth's Col.; Asst. Supt. of Sch., Jersey City, N. J., since 1936.

Harney, Thomas E., B.Ed.'27, State Tchrs. Col., Superior, Wis.; M.A.'29, Univ. of Notre Dame; Supt. of Sch., Dunkirk, N. Y., since 1942.

Harper, Thomas B., M.A.'27, New York Univ.; Co. Supt. of Sch., 500 Sixth Ave., Belmar, N. J., since 1936.

Harriman, Edwin J., B.S.'21, M.Ed.'35, Bates Col.; Supt. of Sch., Hudson, Mass., since 1935.

Harrington, H. L., A.B.'15, M.A.'20, Ph.D. '30, Univ. of Mich.; Asst. Supt. of Sch., 1354 Broadway, Detroit 26, Mich., since 1942.

Harris, Franklin S., B.S.'07, Brigham Young Univ.; Ph.D.'11, Cornell Univ.; Pres., Brigham Young Univ., Provo, Utah, since 1921.

Harris, John, B.S.'02, Carleton Col.; Co. Supt. of Sch., Folkston, Ga., since 1924.

Harris, Sterling R., B.S.'24, Utah State Agrl. Col.; Supt. of Sch., Tooele, Utah, since 1940.

Harris, William, A.B.'14, A.M.'23, Univ. of Ill.; Supt. of Sch., Decatur, Ill., since 1926.

Harrison, G. L., A.B.'26, Howard Univ.; B.E.'27, M.A.'29, Univ. of Cincinnati; Ph.D.'36, Ohio State Univ.; Pres., Langston Univ., Langston, Okla., since 1939.

Harrison, W. T., Supt. of Sch., West Point, Ga.

Harriss, E. E., Supt. of Sch., Lombard, Ill.

Harry, David P., Jr., A.B.'16, Swarthmore Col.; A.M.'22, Ph.D.'28, Tchrs. Col., Columbia Univ.; Prof. of Educ., Graduate Sch., Western Reserve Univ., Cleveland, Ohio, since 1937.

Harshbarger, Ernest M., B.S.'34, Univ. of Ill.; Co. Supt. of Sch., Court House, Urbana, Ill., since 1931.

Hart, Frank W., Prof. of Educ., Univ. of Calif., Berkeley, Calif.

Hartley, Byron W., A.B.'12, Univ. of Chicago; M.A.'15, Columbia Univ.; Supt. of Sch., Dover, Del., since 1941.

Hartley, Henry H., B.A.'27, Willamette Univ.; M.A.'40, Univ. of Oregon; Supt. of Sch., Nyssa, Oregon, since 1940.

*Hartman, Albert L., Prin., Edgemont and Watchung Schs., Montclair, N. J.

Hartman, W. Harold, Supt. of Consol. Sch., Jesup, Iowa.

Hartsfield, Loy William, B.A.'25, M.A.'30, Univ. of Texas; Supt. of Sch. and Pres., Jr. Col., Hillsboro, Texas, since 1930.

Hartstein, Jacob I., B.A.'32, Yeshiva Col.; M.S.'33, Col. of the City of New York; M.A.'36, Columbia Univ.; Asst. Prof. of Educ. and Psych., Long Island Univ., New York 33, N. Y., since 1943.

Hartz, David M., A.B.'21, B.S.'25, Wash. Col. of Educ.; Supt. of Sch., Arlington, Wash., since 1929.

Harvin, E. L., B.A.'21, Baylor Univ.; M.A.'26, Univ. of Texas; Dean, Jr. Col., Corpus Christi, Texas, since 1938.

Haskew, L. D., B.Ph.'26, Emory Univ.; M.A.'34, Univ. of Chicago; Ph.D.'41, Univ. of Ga.; Coordinator for Tchr. Educ., Emory Univ., Emory University, Ga., since 1941.

Haskin, Lynn G., B.A.'16, Ripon Col.; M.A.'27, Univ. of Wis.; Supt. of Sch., Sandwich, Ill., since 1926.

Hastings, D. C., B.S.'20, M.S.'31, Univ. of Ark.; Supt. of Sch., Crossett, Ark., since 1906.

Hasty, S. G., B.A.'03, Wake Forest Col.; M.A.'15, Columbia Univ.; Co. Supt. of Sch., Salisbury, N. C., since 1930.

Hatch, H. T., A.B.'22, Western State Col., Gunnison, Colo.; M.A.'30, Univ. of Calif.; Supt. of Sch., Gunnison, Colo., since 1934.

Hatfield, W. Wilbur, A.B.'02, Ill. Col.; Litt.D.'39, Chicago Tchrs. Col.; Head, English Dept., Chicago Tchrs. Col., Chicago, Ill., since 1921.

Hatton, O. C., B.A.'10, M.A.'27, Ohio State Univ.; Supt. of Sch., Akron, Ohio, since 1942.

Haugen, Conrad G., B.A.'21, St. Olaf Col.; M.A.'31, Univ. of Minn.; Supt. of Sch., Wadena, Minn., since 1943.

Haught, D. L., A.B.'18, Salem Col.; A.M. '21, Univ. of Mich.; Ed.D.'34, Univ. of Pittsburgh; Pres., Glenville State Col., Glenville, W. Va., since 1942.

Hauser, Ludwig J., B.A.'19, M.A.'28, Univ. of Minn.; Ed.D.'39, Columbia Univ.; Supt. of Sch., Riverside, Ill., since 1931.

Haussler, A. G., M.A.'41, New York Univ.; Prin., Pekin Com. H. S., Pekin, Ill., since 1942.

Hawk, Rupert Adam, M.A.'34, State Univ. of Iowa; Supt. of Sch., Grinnell, Iowa, since 1937.

Hawke, Oscar T., A.B.'14, A.M.'17, Wittenberg Col.; Co. Supt. of Sch., Springfield, Ohio, since 1922.

Hawkes, Franklin Powers, A.B.'17, Amherst Col.; A.M.'21, Ph.D.'27, Boston Univ.; Supt. of Sch., West Springfield, Mass., since 1940.

Hawkins, Earle T., B.A.'23, Western Md. Col.; M.A.'28, Columbia Univ.; Ph.D.'42, Yale Univ.; State Supvr. of H.S., Lexington Bldg., Baltimore, Md., since 1938.

*Hawkins, George L., A.B.'04, B.S.'07, Univ. of Mo.; Prin., Buder-Kennard Schs., 5319 Lonsdowne Ave., St. Louis, Mo., since 1943.

Hawkins, R. M., B.A.'27, Southwestern Univ.; M.A.'35, Southern Methodist Univ.; D.Ed.'43, Univ. of Texas; Supt. of Sch. and Dir. of Tchr. Tr., Sam Houston State Tchrs. Col., Huntsville, Texas.

Hawley, Ray C., A.B.'24, Morningside Col.; A.M.'33, Univ. of Ill.; Supt. of Sch., Marseilles, Ill., since 1936.

Haworth, C. V., A.B.'08, A.M.'21, Ind. Univ.; Supt. of Sch., Kokomo, Ind., since 1914.

Hawthorne, Lee B., A.B.'03, De Pauw Univ.; B.S.'09, A.M.'32, Univ. of Mo.; Supt. of Sch., Mexico, Mo., since 1917.

Hay, George A. F., A.B.'23, A.M.'27, Colo. State Col. of Educ., Greeley, Colo.; Prin., Ridgewood H. S., Ridgewood, N. J., since 1931.

Hay, Homer William, A.B.'24, M.A.'27, Ed.D.'34, Univ. of Pittsburgh; Supvg. Prin. of Sch., Somerset, Pa., since 1934.

Haycock, Robert L., B.A.'11, M.A.'12, George Washington Univ.; Supt. of Sch., Franklin Admin. Bldg., Washington 5, D. C., since 1943.

Hayes, Eleanor H., B.A.'19, Bates Col.; M.Ed.'29, Harvard Univ.; Dir. of Guidance and Research, Jr. H. S., Belmont, Mass., since 1928.

Haynes, Rufus D., A.B.'30, State Tchrs. Col., Conway, Ark.; M.Ed.'39, Univ. of Mo.; Supt. of Sch., Paragould, Ark., since 1937.

Hays, Jo, Diploma '18, State Tchrs. Col., Shippensburg, Pa.; A.B.'23, Pa. State Col.; Ed.M.'29, Harvard Univ.; Supvg. Prin. of Sch., State College, Pa., since 1927.

Hazel, Floyd M., B.S.'22, Mich. State Col.; M.A.'26, Univ. of Mich.; Supt., Lakeview Consol. Sch., 300 Highland Ave., Battle Creek, Mich., since 1922.

Hazeltine, Howard W., Fremont Sch., San Luis Obispo, Calif.

Hazen, Oliver M., B.A.'27, Univ. of Wash.; Supt. of Sch., Renton, Wash., since 1936.

Head, Roy S., B.S.'11, Univ. of Mich.; Supt. of Godfey-Lee Schools, Grand Rapids, Mich., since 1925.

Headden, Harmon C., B.S.'29, State Tchrs. Col., Memphis, Tenn.; M.A.'30, Columbia Univ.; Dir., Div. of Schoolroom Planning and Transportation, War Memorial Bldg., Nashville 3, Tenn., since 1939.

Healy, Joseph E., A.B.'10, Col. of William and Mary; M.A.'25, Tchrs. Col., Columbia Univ.; Supt., Va. Sch. for the Deaf and the Blind, Staunton, Va., since 1939.

Heath, Cecil N., B.S.'29, Keene Tchrs. Col., Keene, N. H.; Supt. of Sch., Hopkinton, R. I., since 1940.

Heath, George A., B.A.'29, West Texas State Tchrs. Col., Canyon, Texas; M.A.'32, Texas Tech. Col.; Dist. Supt. of Sch., Midland, Texas, since 1941. On military leave since 1943.

Heaton, Kenneth L., A.B.'24, Ind. Univ.; A.M.'26, Boston Univ.; Ph.D.'31, Univ. of Chicago; Prin. Consultant, U. S. Office of Civilian Defense, since 1942. Address: 123 W. Woodbine, Chevy Chase, Md.

Heck, Mrs. Phyllis Mason, Ph.B.'15, Dickinson Col.; M.A.'26, Tchrs. Col., Columbia Univ.; Supvr. of Rural Schools, State Dept. of Pub. Instr., Wilmington, Del., since 1923.

Hedges, C. F., Ph.B.'12, Univ. of Wis.; Supt. of Sch., Neenah, Wis., since 1917.

Hedges, Stoy, B.S.'30, Evansville Col.; M.S.'36, Ind. Univ.; Supt. of Sch., Mt. Vernon, Ind., since 1939.

Hedrick, E. H., A.B.'16, M.A.'29, Univ. of Oregon; Supt. of Sch., Medford, Oregon, since 1925.

Heemstra, Rev. Jacob, A.M.'14, D.D.'39, Hope Col.; Pres., Northwestern Jr. Col., Orange City, Iowa, since 1928.

Heer, Amos L., A.B. and B.Pd.'14, Tri-State Col.; A.M.'21, Tchrs. Col., Columbia Univ.; Ph.D.'26, Ohio State Univ.; Dir. of Tchr. Tr., Kent State Univ., Kent, Ohio, since 1927.

Heffernan, Helen, B.A.'24, M.A.'25, Univ. of Calif.; Chief, Div. of Elem. Educ., State Dept. of Educ., Sacramento, Calif., since 1926.

Heggerston, A. I., B.A.'21, St. Olaf Col.; M.A.'30, Univ. of Minn.; Dir. of Admin. Research, Pub. Sch., Minneapolis, Minn., since 1936.

Hegner, Herman H., Ph.B.'25, Univ. of Wis.; Pres., Pestalozzi Froebel Tchrs. Col., 410 S. Michigan Ave., Chicago, Ill., since 1936.

Heidelberg, H. B., B.A.'03, Millsaps Col.; M.A.'33, Univ. of Mich.; Supt. of Sch., Clarksdale, Miss., since 1905.

Heineman, Mrs. Irene Taylor, B.A.'01, M.A.'02, Univ. of Calif.; Asst. State Supt. of Pub. Instr., Calif. State Bldg., Los Angeles, Calif., since 1931.

Heineman, Mrs. Walter F., A.B.'26, Univ. of Chicago; Member, Bd. of Educ., 9920 S. Hoyne Ave., Chicago, Ill., since 1938.

Heinemann, F. E., B.A.'16, Carleton Col.; M.A.'38, Univ. of Minn.; State Dept. of Educ., State Office Bldg., St. Paul, Minn., since 1942.

Helfer, Philetus M., B.S.'02, Syracuse Univ.; Dist. Supt. of Sch., Marcellus, N. Y., since 1929.

Helms, Walter T., Ph.B.'99, Univ. of Calif.; Supt. of Sch., Richmond, Calif., since 1909.

Hemenway, Homer S., Diploma '12, State Tchrs. Col., Milwaukee, Wis.; Ph.B.'19, Univ. of Wis.; M.A.'27, Tchrs. Col., Columbia Univ.; Supt. of Sch., Shorewood, Milwaukee, Wis., since 1926.

Hempel, Edward C., Ph.B.'08, Brown Univ.; Supt. of Sch., Orange, Mass., since 1929.

Hemstreet, A. Earle, Ph.B. and Ped.B.'11, Syracuse Univ.; M.A.'23, Columbia Univ.; Prin., Riverside Elem. Sch. No. 60, 238 Ontario St., Buffalo, N. Y., since 1936.

Henderson, Barbara, B.S.'28, M.A.'29, Tchrs. Col., Columbia Univ.; Dir. of Intermediate Grades, Pub. Sch., Library Bldg., Kansas City, Mo., since 1929.

Henderson, Frank A., A.B.'07, Tarkio Col.; A.M.'16, Tchrs. Col., Columbia Univ.; Supt. of Sch., Santa Ana, Calif., since 1932.

Henderson, Louis C., B.S.'21, Univ. of Miss.; M.A.'35, Peabody Col.; Supt. of Sch., Harlan, Ky., since 1936.

Henderson, Zach. S., B.S.'22, Piedmont Col.; M.A.'28, Columbia Univ.; Dean, Ga. Tchrs. Col., Collegeboro, Ga., since 1927.

Henkel, A. J., Ph.B.'21, Ph.M.'36, Univ. of Wis.; Supt. of Sch., Portage, Wis., since 1921.

Hennessy, Sister M. Kathleen, A.B.'19, St. Elizabeth Col.; A.M.'25, Columbia Univ.; Head, Dept. of Educ., College of St. Elizabeth, Convent Station, N. J., since 1920.

Henry, D. R., Dist. Supt. of Sch., Ventura, Calif.

Henry, David W., Diploma '09, State Tchrs. Col., Hyannis, Mass.; B.A.'11, Kansas State Tchrs. Col., Emporia, Kansas M.A.'16, Columbia Univ.; Dean, Col. of Educ., Univ. of Toledo, Toledo, Ohio, since 1914.

Henry, N. B., Assoc. Prof. of Educ., Sch. of Educ., Univ. of Chicago, Chicago, Ill.

Henry, William Edward, B.A., Va. Union Univ.; M.A., Univ. of Pa.; Pres., Md. State Tchrs. Col., Bowie, Md., since 1942.

Henzlik, F. E., B.S. in Ed.'16, Central Mo. State Tchrs. Col., Warrensburg, Mo.; M.A.'23, Ph.D.'24, Tchrs. Col., Columbia Univ.; Dean, Tchrs. Col., Univ. of Nebr., Lincoln, Nebr., since 1931.

*Hepner, Walter R., A.B.'13, A.M.'16, Ed.D.'37, Univ. of Southern Calif.; Pres., San Diego State Col., San Diego, Calif., since 1935.

*Herber, Howard T., A.B.'25, Ursinus Col.; A.M.'26, Ph.D.'38, Tchrs. Col., Columbia Univ.; Supt. of Sch., Malverne, L. I., N. Y., since 1931.

Herdeg, Leo G., M.A.'35, Northwestern Univ.; Asst. Supt. of Sch., 228 N. La Salle St., Chicago, Ill., since 1941.

Herlihy, Charles Michael, A.B.'12, A.M.'14, LL.D.'34, Boston Col.; Pres., State Tchrs. Col., Fitchburg, Mass., since 1927.

Herlinger, H. V., Ph.B.'13, Grove City Col.; Supt. of Sch., Mt. Lebanon, Pittsburgh, Pa.

Hermann, Barbara V., B.S. in Ed. and M.A., Tchrs. Col., Fordham Univ. Address: 137 Roosevelt Ave., Carteret, N. J.

Herr, Ben B., A.B.'20, Transylvania Col.; M.A.'23, Columbia Univ.; Bus. Mgr., Pub. Sch., Lexington, Ky., since 1934.

Herr, Benjamin B., A.B.'11, Franklin and Marshall Col.; A.M.'19, Columbia Univ.; Prin., J. P. McCaskey Sr. H. S., Lancaster, Pa., since 1937.

Herr, F. Floyd, M.A.'33, Tchrs. Col., Columbia Univ.; Supt. of Sch., Medicine Lodge, Kansas, since 1935.

Herrick, John H., B.A.'28, M.A.'36, Ohio State Univ.; Dir. of Research, Pub. Sch., 216 E. Ninth St., Cincinnati 2, Ohio, since 1941.

Herrmann, Carl, Jr., Asst. Secy. and Budget Dir., Bd. of Educ., 31 Green St., Newark, N. J., since 1932.

Herron, Harry H., Ph.B.'21, Univ. of Chicago; Registrar, Office Supvr. and Pur. Agt., New Trier Twp. H. S., Winnetka, Ill., since 1922.

Herron, John S., Diploma '08, N. J. State Normal Sch., Trenton, N. J.; B.S.'15, M.A.'18, New York Univ.; Supt. of Sch., Newark 2, N. J., since 1943.

Hershey, Charlie Brown, M.A.'21, Univ. of Ill.; Ed.D.'23, Harvard Univ.; LL.D.'34, Colo. Col.; Dean and Prof. of Educ., Colo. Col., Colorado Springs, Colo., since 1923.

Hertzler, Silas, B.A.'13, Goshen Col.; B.D. '17, Yale Divinity Sch.; M.A.'18, Tchrs. Col., Columbia Univ.; Ph.D.'27, Yale Univ.; Dir., Tchr. Tr. and Dean, Summer Session, Goshen Col., Goshen, Ind., since 1920.

Hess, Frank D., B.S.'25, Univ. of Okla.; M.A.'29, Univ. of Colo.; Supt. of Sch., Drumright, Okla., since 1929.

Hesse, Ernest, B.A.'10, Ohio State Univ.; A.M.'12, Columbia Univ.; World Book Co., Yonkers, N. Y.

Hetherington, Charles George, B.S.'16, Colgate Univ.; M.S.'17, Pa. State Col.; Ph.D. '34, New York Univ.; Supt. of Sch., Auburn, N. Y., since 1937.

Hibbs, M. Gregg, Jr., Diploma '28, M.Ed. '35, Rutgers, Univ.; Supt. of Sch., Bridgeton, N. J., since 1942.

Hibschman, Ralph O., D.Ed., Ohio Northern Univ.; Dir., The Andrews Sch. for Girls, Willoughby, Ohio, since 1929.

Hick, Hugh R., B.S.'03, Denison Univ.; M.A.'23, Tchrs. Col., Columbia Univ.; Supt. of Sch., Cambridge, Ohio, since 1924.

Hickey, Margaret A., LL.B.'28, Kansas City Univ.; Prin., Miss Hickey's Tr. Sch. for Secys., 560 N. Skinker, St. Louis, Mo., since 1932.

Hickey, Philip J., B.S.'18, M.S.'20, Univ. of Wis.; Acting Supt. of Instr., 911 Locust St., St. Louis 1, Mo., since 1942.

Hicks, Robert S., A.B.'21, Occidental Col.; M.A.'32, Univ. of Southern Calif.; Dist. Supt., Union H. S., El Monte, Calif., since 1936.

Hicks, Samuel I., A.B.'24, Univ. of Mich.; M.A.'27, Tchrs. Col., Columbia Univ.; Supt. of Sch., Pearl River, N. Y., since 1932.

Hicks, Weimer K., A.B.'32, Princeton Univ.; M.A.'35, Cornell Univ.; Pres., Wayland Jr. Col. and Academy, Beaver Dam, Wis., since 1943.

Hiebert, Noble, Supt. of Sch., Burr Oak, Kansas.

Higdon, Philip, Co. Supt. of Sch., Eldorado, Kansas, since 1933.

Higgins, Edwin E., B.S. in Ed.'25, Ohio Univ.; M.A.'29, Columbia Univ.; Supt. of Sch., Gallipolis, Ohio, since 1936.

Higgins, Eugene, A.B.'26, Wabash Col.; A.M.'29, Ind. Univ.; LL.B.'38, Ind. Law Sch.; Supt. of Sch., Greenfield, Ind., since 1938.

Highsmith, E. M., Ph.B.'07, A.M.'14, Univ. of N. C.; A.M.'15, Peabody Col.; Ph.D.'23, Univ. of N. C.; Dir., Summer Sch. and Chmn., Div. of Educ., Mercer Univ., Macon, Ga., since 1937.

Hildreth, Earl W., Mgr., Textbook Sales Dept., F. A. Davis Co., 1914 Cherry St., Philadelphia, Pa.

Hill, Clyde M., A.B.'10, Drury Col.; A.M.'15, Ph.D.26, Columbia Univ.; M.A.'28, Yale Univ.; Sterling Prof. of Educ. and Chmn., Dept. of Educ., Yale Univ., New Haven, Conn., since 1926.

Hill, E. N., A.B.'05, A.M.'11, Earlham Col.; A.M.'38, Univ. of Kansas; Supt. of Sch., Humboldt, Kansas, since 1934.

Hill, Henry H., A.B. and M.A.'21, Univ. of Va.; Ph.D.'30, Columbia Univ.; LL.D.'43, Univ. of Pittsburgh; Supt. of Sch., 341 Bellefield Ave., Pittsburgh 13, Pa., since 1942.

Hill, O. E., B.S.'27, Ohio Univ.; M.A.'33, Columbia Univ.; Supt. of Sch., Upper Arlington, Columbus, Ohio, since 1942.

Hill, Walter Henry, B.S.'23, Gettysburg Col.; M.A.'31, Columbia Univ.; Supvg. Prin. of Sch., Swedesboro, N. J., since 1926.

Hilleboe, Guy L., A.B.'20, Univ. of Minn.; A.M.'28, Ph.D.'30, Tchrs. Col., Columbia Univ.; Supvg. Prin. of Sch., Rutherford, N. J., since 1938.

Hillis, C. C., Supt. of Sch., Elwood, Ind., since 1941.

Hills, C. A., Ph.B.'26, Univ. of Wis.; Supt. of Twp. H. S., Rochelle, Ill., since 1930.

Hinderman, R. H., 650 Cherry, Denver, Colo.

Hinkle, Thomas L., Ph.B.'33, Muhlenberg Col.; M.S.'38, Bucknell Univ.; Supt. of Sch., Hazleton, Pa., since 1939.

Hirons, Sidney S., B.S.'40, Southern Ill. State Tchrs. Col.; Co. Supt. of Sch., Mt Vernon, Ill., since 1943.

Hirschler, A. E., B.S.'28, M.S.'38, Univ. of Idaho; Supt. of Sch., Baker, Oregon, since 1938.

Hitch, A. M., A.B.'97, B.S. in Ed.'07, A.M.'34, Univ. of Mo.; Pres., Kemper Military Sch., Boonville, Mo., since 1934.

Hix, Richard Milton, A.B.'30, Univ. of Texas; M.S.'38, Texas Agrl. and Mech. Col.; Supt. of Sch., Hearne, Texas, since 1941.

Hoar, Wendell R., A.B.'28, Chico State Tchrs. Col.; A.M.'34, Col. of the Pacific; Dist. Supt. of Elem. Sch., Tracy, Calif., since 1942.

Hoback, L. T., A.B. and B.S. in Ed.'22, Central Mo. State Tchrs. Col., Warrensburg, Mo.; M.A.'26, Univ. of Mo.; Supt. of Sch., Windsor, Mo., since 1923.

*Hobbs, Edwin G., B.A.'25, N. Mex. State Tchrs. Col., Silver City, N. Mex.; M.A.'36, Univ. of N. Mex.; Capt., Infantry, U. S. Army, Fort Snelling, Minn., since 1942.

*Hodge, Lamont F., A.B.'97, A.M.'21, Pd.D.'26, Colgate Univ. Address: 448 Clinton Ave., Albany, N. Y.

Hodge, Oliver, A.B.'30, Univ. of Tulsa; Ed.M.'33, Ed.D.'37, Univ. of Okla.; Co. Supt. of Sch., Tulsa, Okla., since 1937.

Hodges, J. M., M.A.'31, Univ. of Mo.; Supt. of Sch., Tyler, Texas, since 1926.

Hoech, Arthur A., B.S.'07, Central Wesleyan Col.; B.S. in Ed.'18, M.A.'31, Univ. of Mo.; Supt., Ritenour Consol. Sch. Dist., Overland, Mo., since 1920.

Hoff, Arthur G., B.E.'28, State Tchrs. Col., Superior, Wis.; M.A.'30, State Univ. of Iowa; Ph.D.'38, Univ. of Minn., Supvr. of Tchr. Tr., State Tchrs. Col., La Crosse, Wis., since 1932.

Hoffman, C. A., A.B.'18, Manchester Col.; A.M.'36, Univ. of Mich.; Supt. of Consol. Sch., Walled Lake, Mich., since 1935.

Hoffman, M. Gazelle, B.A.'11, Elmira Col.; M.A.'26, Columbia Univ.; Supt. of Sch., Third Supervisory Dist., Niagara Co., Lewiston, N. Y., since 1915, and Lecturer, N. Y. State Tchrs. Col., Buffalo, N. Y., since 1931.

Hogan, Sister M. Rosemary, M.A.'29, St. Louis Univ.; Dean, Mt. St. Scholastica Col., Atchison, Kansas, since 1940.

Hoglan, John C., M.A.'32, State Univ. of Iowa; Supt. of Sch., Cherokee, Iowa, since 1936.

Hogrefe, Roy A., A.B.'29, Presbyterian Col.; M.A.'37, Univ. of S. C.; Supt. of Sch., Union, S. C., since 1941.

Hoke, Kremer J., B.A.'04, Mt. St. Mary's Col., Emmitsburg, Md.; M.A.'11, Ph.D.'15. Columbia Univ.; Dean, Dept. of Educ. and Dir. of Summer Session, Col. of William and Mary, Williamsburg, Va., since 1920.

Holbert, William R., Ph.B.'14, Lafayette Col.; M.A.'25, Univ. of Pa.; Supvg. Prin. of Sch., North Arlington, N. J., since 1935.

Holbrook, C. Ray, B.Ed.'19, M.A.'22, Univ. of Wash.; Ed.D.'39, Stanford Univ.; Dir., Adult Educ., Pub. Sch., 625 Guinda St., Palo Alto, Calif.

Holden, Ellsworth B., B.S.'23, Mich. State Col.; A.M.'34, Columbia Univ.; Supt. of Sch., St. Joseph, Mich., since 1935.

*Holden, Miles C., The Holden Patent Book Cover Co., 53 Hillman St., Springfield, Mass.

Holland, Kenneth, Office of Inter-American Affairs, Commerce Bldg., Washington, D. C.

Holland, Nicholas S., B.A.'17, Southern Methodist Univ.; A.M.'27, Ed.D'37, Tchrs. Col., Columbia Univ.; Supt. of Sch. and Pres., Lee Jr. Col., Goose Creek, Texas, since 1940.

Hollenbach, Charles R., M.A.'17, Univ. of Pa.; Prin., Sr. H. S., Atlantic City, N. J., since 1939.

Holler, James Carlisle, A.B.'21, Wofford Col.; A.M.'43, Univ. of S. C.; Asst. Supt. of Sch., Anderson, S. C., since 1941.

Hollinger, John Ruhl, Diploma '10, State Tchrs. Col., West Chester, Pa. Address: Hotel Madison, Atlantic City, N. J.

Hollingsworth, Henry T., B.S.'18, Wash. Col.; M.A.'23, Columbia Univ.; LL.B.'28, N. J. Law Sch.; Supt. of Sch., Bloomfield, N. J., since 1942.

Hollingsworth, Milton C., B.A.'13, Roanoke Col.; M.A.'32, Univ. of Va.; Div. Supt. of Sch., Woodstock, Va., since 1940.

Hollister, Harold E., A.B.'17, Middlebury Col.; A.M.'35, N. Y. State Col. for Tchrs., Albany, N. Y.; Dist. Supt. of Sch., White Plains, N. Y., since 1941.

Hollister, Neva W., Pres., Calif. Assn. for Childhood Educ., 4669 Madison Ave., Fresno, Calif.

Hollmeyer, Lewis H., A.B.'20, Hanover Col.; M.A.'37, Tchrs. Col., Columbia Univ.; Prin., Community H. S., Camp Point, Ill., since 1931.

Holloway, Fred G., A.B.'18, Western Md. Col.; B.D.'21, Drew Univ.; LL.D.'36, Dickinson Col.; Pres., Western Md. Col., Westminster, Md., since 1935.

Holloway, George Edward, Jr., Major, U. S. Army, Classification Section, A.G.O., The Infantry Sch., Fort Benning, Ga.

Holloway, H. V., A.B.'95, A.M.'98, Washington Col., Chestertown, Md.; Ph.D.'14, Univ. of Pa.; LL.D.'32, Washington Col., Chestertown, Md.; State Supt. of Pub. Instr., Dover, Del., since 1921.

Holloway, W. J., M.A.'29, Univ. of Texas; Supt. of Sch., Port Neches, Texas, since 1930.

Holly, Tom, Supt. of Sch., Sanderson, Texas.

Holmes, Chester W., S.B.'16, Ed.M.'24, Harvard Univ.; Ed.D.'36, George Washington Univ.; Asst. Supt. of Sch., Washington, D. C., since 1936.

Holmes, Dwight Oliver Wendell, A.B.'01, Howard Univ.; A.M.'15, Ph.D.'34, Columbia Univ.; Pres., Morgan State Col., Baltimore, Md., since 1937.

Holmes, Frank L., B.A. and B.Sc.'29, Univ. of Kansas; M.A.'36, Northwestern Univ.; Supt., Maine Twp. H. S., Des Plaines, Ill., since 1943.

Holmes, Harley W., A.B.'25, Western State Tchrs. Col., Kalamazoo, Mich.; M.A.'35, Albion Col.; Supt. of Sch., Marshall, Mich., since 1929.

Holmes, Henry Wyman, A.B.'03, A.M.'04, Harvard Univ.; Litt.D.'24, Tufts Col.; LL.D.'31, Univ. of Pittsburgh; Litt.D.'33, Rutgers Univ.; LL.D.'36, Franklin and Marshall Col.; Chmn., Com. on Educ. Relations, Harvard Univ., Cambridge, Mass., since 1940.

Holmes, Jay William, A.B.'16, Hiram Col.; M.A.'27, Ohio State Univ.; Prin., Wilbur Wright H. S., Dayton, Ohio, since 1940.

Holmes, Joseph R., B.A.'15, Hendrix Col.; M.A.'25, Tchrs. Col., Columbia Univ.; Supt. of Sch., Muskogee, Okla., since 1931.

Holmes, Margaret Cook, A.B.'15, Adelphi Col.; M.A.'24, Tchrs. Col., Columbia Univ.; Dir. of Kdgns., Pub. Sch., New York, N. Y., since 1935. Address: 136 Cambridge Pl., Brooklyn, N. Y.

*Holmes, William H., A.B.'97, Colby Col.; Ph.D.'10, Clark Univ. Address: The Eastland, Portland, Maine.

Holmstedt, Raleigh W., Prof. of Educ., Ind. Univ., Bloomington, Ind.

Holsinger, Clyde Kagey, A.B.'09, Bridgewater Col.; A.M.'18, George Peabody Col. for Tchrs.; L.H.D.'37, Bridgewater Col.; Div. Supt. of Sch., Richmond, Va., since 1938.

Holsinger, Virgil C., Sr., A.B.'27, Juniata Col.; M.Ed.'37, Univ. of Pittsburgh; Supvg. Prin. of Sch., Millvale, Pa., since 1935.

Holst, Alwyn R., B.A.'20, Hamline Univ.; M.A.'34, Univ. of Minn.; Supt. of Sch., Long Prairie, Minn., since 1943.

Holste, Hilary L., B.S.'21, Capital Univ.; M.E.'36, Univ. of Pittsburgh; Supt. of Sch., Arnold, Pa., since 1936.

Holston, Evelyn Turner, B.S.'20, A.M.'21, Tchrs. Col., Columbia Univ.; Genl. Supvr. of Jr. H. S., 32 Spring St., Springfield, Mass., since 1930.

Holt, E. E., A.B.'26, Wilmington Col.; M.A.'36, Miami Univ.; Supt. of Sch., Marion, Ohio, since 1940.

Holt, Frank E., B.S.'06, Amherst Col.; Ed.M.'29, Harvard Univ.; Supt. of Sch., Whitman, Mass., since 1922.

Holton, Edwin Lee, Diploma '00, Ind. State Tchrs. Col., Terre Haute, Ind.; A.B.'04, Ind. Univ.; Ph.D.'27, Columbia Univ.; Head, Dept. of Educ. and Dean of Summer Sch., Kansas State Col., Manhattan, Kansas, since 1910.

Holtzman, Herbert P., Ph.B.'13, A.M.'16, Dickinson Col.; LL.B.'16, Dickinson Law Sch.; A.M.'23, Univ. of Pa.; Supvg. Prin. of Sch., 718 Reading Ave., West Reading, Pa., since 1924.

*Holy, Thomas C., A.B.'19, Des Moines Univ.; M.A.'22, Ph.D.'24, State Univ. of Iowa; Dir., Bureau of Educ. Research, Ohio State Univ., Columbus, Ohio, since 1942.

Honeycutt, Allison W., A.B.'02, Wake Forest Col.; Supt. of Sch., Chapel Hill, N. C., since 1937.

Hood, Charles E., B.S.'27, Jamestown Col.; M.A.'35, Univ. of Mont.; Supt. of Sch., Big Sandy, Mont., since 1941.

Hook, T. E., C.E.'08, Ohio Northern Univ.; A.B.'14, A.M.'18, Univ. of Mich.; A.M.'34, Tchrs. Col., Columbia Univ.; Supt. of Sch., Troy, Ohio, since 1919.

Hooper, Bertrand, B.S.'30, Boston Univ.; Asst. Supt. of Sch., Medford, Mass., since 1922.

Hoos, Ida M., B.A.'23, Harris Tchrs. Col.; M.A.'26, New York Univ.; Prin., Elem. Sch., 5330 Pershing Ave., St. Louis, Mo., since 1926.

Hope, James H., A.B.'29, Newberry Col.; State Supt. of Educ., Columbia, S. C., since 1923.

Hopkins, Johanna Marie, Diploma '14, Brooklyn Tr. Sch. for Tchrs.; B.S.'37, M.A.'38, New York Univ.; Asst. Dist. Supt. of Sch., Pub. Sch. 92, Bronx, 179th St. and Clinton Ave., Bronx, New York 57, N. Y., since 1943.

Hopkins, John L., A.B.'09, M.A.'12, Hamilton Col.; Ph.D.'37, New York Univ.; Supt. of Sch., Hastings-on-Hudson, N. Y., since 1923.

Hopkins, John W., A.B.'30, M.A.'39, Drake Univ.; Ph.D.'41, Williams Col.; Pres., Williams Col., Berkeley, Calif., since 1938.

Hopkins, L. Thomas, A.B.'10, A.M.'11, Tufts Col.; Ed.D.'22, Harvard Univ.; Prof. of Educ., Tchrs. Col., Columbia Univ., New York 27, N. Y., since 1929.

Hopkins, P. H., B.A.'07, Georgetown Col.; Supt. of Sch., Somerset, Ky., since 1927.

Hopkins, W. Karl, A.B.'06, Univ. of Utah; Supt. of Sch., Ogden, Utah, since 1919.

*Horn, Ernest, B.S.'07, A.M.'08, Univ. of Mo.; Ph.D.'14, Columbia Univ.; Prof. of Educ. and Dir., Univ. Elem. Sch., State Univ. of Iowa, Iowa City, Iowa, since 1915.

Horn, Nelson Paxson, A.B.'16, Mo. Wesleyan Univ.; B.D.'18, Garrett Biblical Inst.; M.A.'19, Northwestern Univ.; D.D.'37, Garrett Biblical Inst.; Pres., Baker Univ., Baldwin, Kansas, since 1936.

Horner, F. G., A.B.'12, Juniata Col.; A.M.'16, Columbia Univ.; Supt. of Sch., Tamaqua, Pa., since 1927.

Horner, Harlan Hoyt, A.B.'01, Univ. of Ill.; A.M.'15, Pd.D.'18, N. Y. State Col. for Tchrs., Albany, N. Y.; LL.D.'33, Alfred Univ.; Secy., Council on Dental Educ. of the American Dental Assn., 212 E. Superior St., Chicago, Ill.

Horner, Meyers B., A.B.'13, Juniata Col.; A.M.'26, Ph.D.'38, Univ. of Pittsburgh; D.S.E.'38, Wash. and Jefferson Col.; Supt. of Sch., Washington, Pa., since 1930.

Horst, Walter, A.B.'16, Olivet Col.; M.A.'26, Univ. of Mich.; Supt. of Sch., Three Rivers, Mich., since 1936.

Horstick, Simon M., B.S.'10, M.A.'23, Ph.D.'31, Univ. of Pa.; Supt. of Sch., Pleasantville, N. J., since 1926.

Hortin, James F., A.B.'30, McKendree Col.; M.A.'36, Univ. of Colo.; Supt. of Sch., Vandalia, Ill., since 1937.

Hosler, Fred W., Ed.D.'38, Columbia Univ.; Supt. of Sch., Allentown, Pa., since 1942.

Hostetler, Ivan P., B.S. in Ed.'19, State Tchrs. Col., Emporia, Kansas; M.A. in Ed.'26, Stanford Univ.; Supt., Miami, Lower Miami, and Inspiration Pub. Sch., Miami, Ariz., since 1934.

Houseman, W. Lynn, B.S.'08, Colgate Univ.; M.A.'21, Tchrs. Col., Columbia Univ.; Supt. of Sch., Geneva, N. Y., since 1926.

Howard, Ervin, A.B.'24, M.A.'27, Univ. of Mich.; Asst. Supt. of Fordson Dist. Sch., Dearborn, Mich., since 1934.

Howard, George, A.B.'12, Davidson Col.; A.M.'22, Ph.D.'24, Columbia Univ.; Capt., U. S. Army, Educ. Adviser, Fourth Service Command, Atlanta, Ga.

Howard, Joseph E., B.S.'15, Central Col., Fayette, Mo.; A.M.'28, Univ. of Mo.; Prin., DeMun Sch., Clayton 5, Mo., since 1927.

Howard, Lowry S., Diploma '13, State Tchrs. Col., Cheney, Wash.; A.B.'17, A.M.'20, Stanford Univ.; Pres., Menlo Sch. and Jr. Col., Menlo Park, Calif., since 1927.

Howard, Marie R., Diploma '10, R. I. Normal Sch.; Prin., Elem. Sch., 29 Modena Ave., Providence, R. I., since 1941.

Howard, Ray W., B.A.'31, M.A.'40, Univ. of Wash.; Supt., Overlake Pub. Schs., Bellevue, Wash., since 1942.

Howe, Homer, B.A.'32, M.A.'33, Univ. of Wash.; Supt. of Sch., Gig Harbor, Wash., since 1942.

Howell, A. H., Diploma '02, State Normal Sch., East Stroudsburg, Pa.; B.S.'27, New York Univ.; Co. Supt. of Sch., Honesdale, Pa., since 1921.

Howell, Charles P., A.B.'20, M.A.'28, Univ. of Okla.; Supt. of Sch., Ponca City, Okla., since 1935.

Howell, Clarence E., B.S.'17, James Millikin Univ.; A.M.'23, Tchrs. Col., Columbia Univ. Address: 252 Parkway Ave., Trenton, N. J.

Howie, Thomas W., B.S.'23, Lafayette Col.; M.S.'31, Temple Univ.; Ed.D.'43, New York Univ.; Supt., Alexis I. duPont Special Sch. Dist., Wilmington 67, Del., since 1936.

Howitt, Weldon E., B.S.'17, M.A.'26, St. Lawrence Univ.; Supvg. Prin. of Sch., Farmingdale, N. Y., since 1919.

Hoy, L. B., B.S.'21, Southeast Mo. State Tchrs. Col. Cape Girardeau, Mo.; A.M.'29, Univ. of Mo.; Supt. of Sch., Gideon, Mo., since 1916.

Hoyt, C. O., Asst. Supt. of Sch., 629 Third St., Des Moines, Iowa.

Hubbard, Frank W., A.B.'22, M.A.'26, Univ. of Calif.; Ph.D.'31, Tchrs. Col., Columbia Univ.; Dir. of Research, Natl. Educ. Assn., 1201 16th St., N. W., Washington 6, D. C., since 1940.

Hubbard, Louis H., B.S.'03, M.A.'18, Univ. of Texas; LL.D.'29, Austin Col.; Ph.D.'30, Univ. of Texas; Pres., Texas State Col. for Women, Denton, Texas, since 1926.

Huchingson, J. E., B.C.S.'14, A.M.'16, Univ. of Denver; LL.D.'36, William Jewell Col.; Pres., Colo. Woman's Col., Denver, Colo., since 1931.

Huey, O. E., B.S.'25, La. Polytech. Inst.; Parish Supt. of Sch., Oak Grove, La., since 1929.

Huff, Leo W., State Life Cert.'17, Central State Normal Sch., Mt. Pleasant, Mich.; A.B.'26, M.A.'29, Univ. of Mich.; Supt. of Sch., Lincoln Park 25, Mich., since 1928.

Huff, Raymond, B.A.'21, Univ. of Texas; M.A.'30, Univ. of Colo.; Supt. of Sch., Clayton, N. Mex., since 1920.

Huff, Z. T., A.B.'25, Baylor Univ.; A.M.'29, Columbia Univ.; Ph.D.'36, Univ. of Texas; Dean, Howard Payne Col., Brownwood, Texas, since 1938.

Hufford, G. N., A.B.'14, Hanover Col.; Ph.D.'36, Univ. of Chicago; Supt. of Sch., Joliet, Ill., since 1936.

Hughes, J. M., A.B.'16, Ind. Univ.; M.A.'22, Columbia Univ.; Ph.D.'24, Univ. of Minn.; Acting Dean, Sch. of Educ., Northwestern Univ., Evanston, Ill., since 1940.

Hughes, John Francis, A.B.'09, Washburn Col.; M.S.'31, Kansas State Tchrs. Col., Pittsburg, Kansas; L.H.D.'34, Washburn Col.; Supt. of Sch., Eldorado, Kansas, since 1926.

Hughes, Otto, A.B.'28, Franklin Col.; A.M.'30, Ind. Univ.; Supt. of Sch., Columbus, Ind., since 1942.

Hughes, R. O., A.B.'00, Brown Univ.; A.M.'24, Univ. of Pittsburgh; L.H.D.'41, Brown Univ.; Dir. of Citizenship and Social Studies, Bd. of Educ., Pittsburgh 13, Pa., since 1939.

Hughey, Allen Harrison, B.A.'03, Vanderbilt; LL.B.'08, George Washington Univ.; Supt. of Sch., Sch. Admin. Bldg., El Paso, Texas, since 1919.

Hughson, Arthur, B.A.'16, M.A.'18, Columbia Univ.; Prin., Lew Wallace Jr. H. S., Brooklyn, N. Y., since 1940.

Hull, Osman R., B.S.'13, M.S.'14, Ph.D.'25, Univ. of Calif.; Prof. of Educ., Univ. of Southern Calif., Los Angeles 7, Calif., since 1924.

Hullihen, Walter, A.B. and A.M.'96, Univ. of Va.; Ph.D.'00, Johns Hopkins Univ.; LL.D.'22, Temple Univ.; Pres., Univ. of Del., Newark, Del., since 1920.

Hulme, George W., A.B.'27, Mercer Univ.; M.A.'38, Univ. of Ala.; Co. Supt. of Sch., Ft. Payne, Ala., since 1933.

Hulton, John G., Supt. of Sch., Latrobe, Pa., since 1929.

Hulvey, J. H., B.A.'26, Univ. of Oregon; Supt. of Sch., Spangle, Wash., since 1935.

Hummel, Edward John, A.B.'13, Univ. of Southern Calif.; A.M.'14, Columbia Univ.; Deputy Supt. of Sch., Beverly Hills, Calif., since 1925.

Humphrey, George Duke, B.A.'29, Blue Mountain Col.; M.A.'31, Univ. of Chicago; Ph.D.'39, Ohio State Univ.; Pres., Miss. State Col., State College, Miss., since 1934.

Hunkins, Ralph V., B.A.'14, Univ. of Nebr.; M.A.'21, Univ. of Chicago; D.Litt.'36, Dakota Wesleyan Univ.; Supt. of Sch., Lead, S. Dak., since 1922.

Hunn, Frank L., A.M.'38, Univ. of Kansas; Prin., Atchison Co. Community H. S. Effingham, Kansas, since 1932.

Hunt, Charles W., A.B.'04, Brown Univ.; A.M.'10, Ph.D.'22, Columbia Univ.; Pres., State Tchrs. Col., Oneonta, N. Y., since 1933.

Hunt, Ernest R., M.A.'29, Univ. of Wash.; Supt. of Sch., Lake Stevens, Wash., since 1931.

Hunt, Harry A., A.B.'01, Col. of William and Mary; Supt. of Sch., Portsmouth, Va., since 1909.

Hunt, Heber U., A.B.'21, Central Col., Fayette, Mo.; A.M.'23, Univ. of Minn.; Ph.D.'39, Univ. of Mo.; Supt. of Sch., Sedalia, Mo., since 1927.

Hunt, Herold C., A.B.'23, A. M.'27, Univ. of Mich.; Ed.D.'40, Tchrs. Col., Columbia Univ.; Supt. of Sch., Kansas City, Mo., since 1940.

Hunt, Lyman C., A.B.'12, Univ. of Vt.; M.A.'38, Columbia Univ.; Supt. of Sch., Burlington, Vt., since 1922.

* Hunt, Rolfe Lanier, B.A.'24, Millsaps Col.; M.A.'27, Ph.D.'37, George Peabody Col. for Tchrs.; Supt. of Sch., Magnolia, Miss., since 1942.

Hunter, Frederick Maurice, A.B.'05, Univ. of Nebr.; A.M.'19, Columbia Univ.; Ed.D.'25, Univ. of Calif.; LL.D.'30, Colo. Col.; LL.D.'32, Univ. of Colo.; LL.D.'39, Univ. of Nebr.; Pres., Natl. Educ. Assn., 1920-21; Chancellor, State System of Higher Educ., Univ. of Oregon, Eugene, Oregon, since 1935.

Hunter, H. Reid, A.B.'11, Duke Univ.; M.A.'15, Columbia Univ.; Ph.D.'37, George Peabody Col. for Tchrs.; Asst. Supt. in charge of High Schs., 561 Lakeshore Drive, N. E., Atlanta, Ga., since 1922.

Hurd, A. W., Ph.B.'06, Hamline Univ.; M.S. '24, Ph.D.'28, Univ. of Minn.; Dir., Instr. Research, Medical Col. of Va., Richmond 19, Va., since 1943.

Huss, Hunter, A.B.'23, Univ. of N. C.; Co. Supt. of Sch., Gastonia, N. C., since 1936.

Hussey, John S., Diploma '00, Ind. State Tchrs. Col., Terre Haute, Ind.; Co. Supt. of Sch., Noblesville, Ind., since 1933.

Huston, Harry, A.B.'05, Southwestern Col., Winfield, Kansas; M.S.'38, Okla. Agrl. and Mech. Col.; Supt. of Sch., Blackwell, Okla., since 1931.

Hutchins, Clayton D., B.A. and B.S.'22, M.A.'27, Ph.D.'38, Ohio State Univ.; Chief, Sch. Bus Section, Office of Defense Transportation, Washington, D. C., since 1942.

Hutchins, George F., B.S.'28, M.S.'33, Univ. of Calif.; Chmn., Science, Radio, and Visual Educ., Pub. Sch., Berkeley, Calif., since 1939.

Hutchins, H. Clifton, B.S.'30, Springfield Col.; M.A.'32, Ph.D.'34, Univ. of Wis.; Prof. of Educ., Willamette Univ., Salem, Oregon, since 1940.

Johnson, Carl G., B.A.'24, State Col. of Wash.; Supt. of Sch., Battle Ground, Wash., since 1938.

Johnson, Charles L., Ph.M.'31, Univ. of Wis.; Supt. of Sch., Dunkirk, Ind., since 1927.

Johnson, Charles S., A.B.'28, M.A.'31, Boston Univ.; Ed.D.'43, New York Univ.; Supvg. Prin. of Sch., Locust Valley, N. Y., since 1943.

Johnson, Charles W., B.S. in Ed.'18, Univ. of Cincinnati; M.A.'29, Ohio State Univ.; Ed.D.'38, Univ. of Cincinnati; Assoc. Prof. of Educ. and Asst. to the Dean, Tchrs. Col., Univ. of Cincinnati, Cincinnati, Ohio, since 1940.

Johnson, D. L., Prin., Beaverhead Co. H. S., Dillon, Mont., since 1941.

Johnson, Eleanor M., Mng. Editor, American Educ. Press, Inc., 400 S. Front St., Columbus, Ohio.

Johnson, Frank Clinton, A.B.'97, Dartmouth Col.; M.A.'06, Columbia Univ.; Supt. of Sch., Ayer, Mass., since 1909.

Johnson, Frank R., A.B.'36, Chico State Col., Chico, Calif.; M.S.'40, Univ. of Southern Calif.; Dist. Supt. of Sch., Guadalupe, Calif., since 1927.

Johnson, G. L. H., A.B. and M.A.'08, Col. of William and Mary; Supt. of Sch., Municipal Bldg., Danville, Va., since 1925.

Johnson, Harry O., A.B.'29, Northern State Tchrs. Col., Marquette, Mich.; M.A.'38, Univ. of Mich.; Supt. of Twp. Sch., Ramsay, Mich., since 1937.

Johnson, J. H., Supt. of Sch., Andalusia, Ala.

Johnson, James G., B.A.'97, Milligan Col.; M.A.'06, Ph.D.'09, Univ. of Va.; Supt. of Sch., Charlottesville, Va., since 1909. Address: Cabell Ave., University, Va.

Johnson, Laurence C., B.S.'10, Ph.D.'16, Univ. of Mich.; Supvg. Prin. of Consol. Sch., Orchard Park, N. Y., since 1927.

Johnson, Leslie W., B.E.'28, State Tchrs. Col., Winona, Minn.; M.A.'34, Columbia Univ.; Dir., Child Accounting and Curriculum, Pub. Sch., Superior, Wis., since 1942.

Johnson, Loaz W., A.B.'28, N. Mex. State Tchrs. Col.; M.A.'31, Univ. of Wyo.; Coordinator of Sec. Educ. and Asst. Co. Supt. of Sch., Oroville, Calif., since 1939.

Johnson, Lowell W., B.A.'15, Highland Park Col.; M.A.'36, Univ. of Wash.; Supt. of Sch., Butte, Mont., since 1938.

Johnson, M. K., A.B.'13, Univ. of Ga.; Co. Supt. of Educ., Union Springs, Ala., since 1927.

Johnson, Milton E., B.A.'24, St. Olaf Col.; M.A.'32, Univ. of Minn.; Supt. of Sch., North St. Paul, Minn., since 1934.

Johnson, Ralph W., B.S.'11, Franklin Col.; M.A.'18, Columbia Univ.; Prin., Sr. H. S., Dubuque, Iowa, since 1926.

Johnson, V. Bernard, A.B.'41, Univ. of Calif.; Dist. Supt. and Prin., Amador Valley Joint Union H. S., Pleasanton, Calif., since 1943.

Johnson, W. F., Supt. of Sch., Spencer, Iowa.

Johnson, Waldo P., Pd.B.'11, Southeast Mo. State Tchrs. Col., Cape Girardeau, Mo.; Pres., Webster Pub. Co., 1808 Washington Ave., St. Louis, Mo.

* Johnson, William H., B.S.'17, M.A.'18, Northwestern Univ.; Ph.D.'23, Univ. of Chicago; Litt.D.'38, John Brown Univ.; LL.D.'39, Chicago Tchrs. Col.; Supt. of Sch., 228 N. La Salle St., Chicago, Ill., since 1936.

Johnston, Mrs. Eula A., B.S.'26, M.A.'38, Tchrs. Col., Columbia Univ.; Supvr. of Elem. Sch., Court House, Chattanooga, Tenn., since 1925.

Johnston, Joseph E., A.B.'02, Furman Univ.; Bus. Mgr. and Treas., Bd. of Educ., 23 Westfield St., Greenville, S. C., since 1934.

Johnston, King, A.B.'20, Emory and Henry Col.; M.A.'27, Columbia Univ.; Co. Supt. of Sch., Pearisburg, Va., since 1936.

Jonas, Russell E., B.S.'31, Northern State Tchrs. Col., Aberdeen, S. Dak.; M.A.'34, Ph.D.'36, State Univ. of Iowa; Pres., Black Hills Tchrs. Col., Spearfish, S. Dak., since 1942.

Jones, Arthur J., A.B.'93, Grinnell Col.; Ph.D.'07, Columbia Univ.; Prof. of Secondary Educ., Sch. of Educ., Univ. of Pa., Philadelphia, Pa., since 1915.

Jones, Burr F., A.B.'07, Colby Col.; A.M.'12, Harvard Univ.; Supt. of Sch., Plymouth, Mass.

Jones, Clifford Bartlett, LL.D.'39, McMurry Col.; LL.D.'40, Texas Tech. Col.; LL.D.'41, Southwestern Univ.; Pres., Texas Tech. Col., Lubbock, Texas, since 1938.

Jones, David Paul, A.B.'29, Wash. and Jefferson Col.; Ed.M.'35, Univ. of Pittsburgh; Supvg. Prin. of Sch., Forest Hills, Pittsburgh, Pa., since 1939.

Jones, Donovan S., B.S.'17, Univ. of Vt.; M.A.'37, Tchrs. Col., Columbia Univ.; Dist. Supt. of Sch., Winchendon, Mass., since 1940.

Jones, Evan E., A.B.'16, Hamilton Col., Clinton, N. Y.; M.A.'25, Tchrs. Col., Columbia Univ.; Supt. of Sch., Port Chester, N. Y., since 1934.

Jones, G. B., B.S.'14, Ottawa Univ.; Supt. of Sch., Clarkdale, Ariz., since 1926.

Jones, George E., Ph.B.'30, Ph.M.'37, Univ. of Wis.; Supt. of Sch., Mayville, Wis., since 1940.

Jones, George Eric, Pres., Atlantic Union Col., South Lancaster, Mass., since 1936.

Jones, Guy M., Asst. Dir. of Textbooks, Bureau of Textbooks and Bldg. Survey, Bd. of Educ., 228 N. La Salle St., Chicago, Ill., since 1935.

Jones, H. W., B.S.'09, Cornell Col.; M.A.'22, Univ. of Calif.; Supt. of Sch., Piedmont, Calif., since 1921.

Jones, Harry Mason, B.S.'18, Syracuse Univ.; Supvg. Prin. of Sch., Wyckoff, N. J., since 1930.

Jones, Howard W., A.B.'20, Hiram Col.; A.M.'30, Western Reserve Univ.; Ped.D. '43, Westminster Col.; Pres., Youngstown Col., Youngstown, Ohio, since 1931.

Jones, J. Fred, B.S.'22, M.Ed.'33, Pa. State Col.; Supt. of Sch. Nanticoke, Pa., since 1941.

Jones, J. Morris, Mng. Editor, The Quarrie Corp., 35 E. Wacker Dr., Chicago, Ill.

Jones, John E., Ph.B.'31, Marquette Univ.; Ph.M.'38, Univ. of Wis.; Supt. of Sch., Cudahy, Wis., since 1938.

Jones, M. G., A.B.'11, Univ. of Mich.; A.M.'29, Tchrs. Col., Columbia Univ.; Dist. Supt. and Prin., Union H. S., Huntington Beach, Calif., since 1919.

Jones, Mary Alice, 234 Venice Blvd., Los Angeles, Calif.

Jones, Paul Reese, B.S. in Ed.'28, State Tchrs. Col., Mansfield, Pa.; M.A.'31, Tchrs. Col., Columbia Univ.; Supvg. Prin. of Sch., Palmyra, N. J., since 1936.

Jones, Ralph B., State Commr. of Educ., Little Rock, Ark.

Jones, W. J., B.S.'29, Univ. of Ala.; M.A. '34, Columbia Univ.; Co. Supt. of Educ., Camden, Ala., since 1923.

Jones, Willard T., A.B.'25, M.A.'30, Syracuse Univ.; Ed.D.'42, Tchrs. Col., Columbia Univ.; Supt. of Sch., Ballston Spa, N. Y., since 1933.

Jones, William Clarence, B.S.'22, East Texas State Tchrs. Col., Commerce, Texas; M.A.'25, Colo. State Col. of Educ.; Ph.D.'31, George Peabody Col. for Tchrs.; Dean of Faculty, Eastern Ky. State Tchrs. Col., Richmond, Ky., since 1931.

Jorgensen, A. N., B.S.'21, Coe Col.; M.A.'25, Ph.D.'27, State Univ. of Iowa; Pres., Univ. of Conn., Storrs, Conn., since 1935.

Josetta, Sister Mary, B.S.'35, St. Xavier Col.; M.S.'36, Ph.D.'39, Univ. of Ill.; Dean, St. Xavier Col., Chicago, Ill., since 1940.

Joyal, Arnold E., A.B.'25, M.A.'26, Ph.D.'31, Univ. of Calif.; Prof. of Educ. Admin., Col. of Educ., Univ. of Md., College Park, Md., since 1940.

Joyce, Charles W., B.S. in Ed.'26, M.A.'35, Univ. of Rochester; Prin., Seneca Sch., Irondequoit, Rochester, N. Y., since 1910.

Judd, Charles Hubbard, A.B.'94, Wesleyan Univ.; Ph.D.'96, Leipzig Univ., Germany; Honorary Life Member, American Assn. of Sch. Admin. Address: 5411 Tilden Rd., Decatur Hgts., Hyattsville, Md.

Julian, Roy B., Diploma '17, Ind. State Tchrs. Col., Terre Haute, Ind.; A.B.'23, Butler Univ.; A.M.'30, Ind. Univ.; Supt. of Sch., Valparaiso, Ind., since 1930.

Justitia, Sister Mary, B.A.'14, Catholic Univ.; M.A.'21, Loyola Univ.; Pres., Mundelein Col., 6363 Sheridan Rd., Chicago, Ill., since 1939.

Jutta, Sister M., A.B.'17, Catholic Univ. of America; A.M.'29, Marquette Univ.; Dean, Alverno Tchrs. Col., 1413 S. Layton Blvd., Milwaukee, Wis., since 1936.

K

Kaderli, Fred, M.A.'28, Univ. of Texas. Address: Box 48, San Marcos, Texas.

Kadesch, J. Stevens, A.B.'10, Ed.M.'30, Clark Univ.; Ed.D.'31, Tufts Col.; Supt. of Sch., Medford, Mass., since 1930.

Kaemmerlen, John T., A.B.'16, A.M.'17, New York Univ.; Supt. of Sch., Hudson, N. Y., since 1938.

Kaiser, Paul L., Diploma '23, State Tchrs. Col., Oshkosh, Wis.; Ph.B.'27, Ripon Col.; Ph.M.'33, Univ. of Wis.; Co. Supt. of Sch., Juneau, Wis., since 1923.

Kaler, James Edward, A.B.'29, M.A.'33, Stanford Univ.; Prin., Jefferson Special Sch., 3016 32nd St., Sacramento, Calif., since 1936.

Kampschroeder, W. C., B.S.'27, M.S.'31, Univ. of Kansas; Supt. of Sch., Eureka, Kansas, since 1937.

Kann, Sister Jean Marie, A.B.'31, Loras Col.; M.A.'33, St. Louis Univ.; Ph.D.'39, Yale Univ.; Pres., Briar Cliff Col., Sioux City, Iowa, since 1943.

Kantner, John N., A.B.'14, Ursinus Col.; A.M.'28, Univ. of Mich.; Supt. of Sch., East Detroit, Mich., since 1930.

Karwowski, Henry, LL.B.'24, Detroit Col. of Law; Member, Bd. of Educ., 12044 Joseph Campau Ave., Hamtramck, Mich., since 1927.

Kaser, Louis J., D.Ed.'35, Rutgers Univ.; Co. Supt. of Sch., Mt. Holly, N. J., since 1916.

Kathcart, Rex, B.B.S.'31, Baylor Univ.; M.E.'41, Agrl. and Mech. Col. of Texas. Address: 518 College Ave., Cleburne, Texas.

Kaufman, Edward E., B.S.'30, McPherson Col.; M.A.'39, Univ. of Mo.; Prin., Rural H. S., Buhler, Kansas.

Kaula, F. Edward, A.B.'04, Tufts Col.; World Book Co., 2126 Prairie Ave., Chicago, Ill.

Kavanah, Gladys Emma, B.S.'10, M.S.'11, Univ. of Maine; Asst. Prin., Bassick H. S., Bridgeport, Conn., since 1929.

Kay, Roy R., B.A.'21, Baylor Univ.; M.A. '27, Univ. of Colo.; Pres., San Marcos Academy, San Marcos, Texas.

Kays, V. C., Diploma '02, Northern Ill. State Tchrs. Col., De Kalb, Ill.; B.A.'06. Univ. of Ill.; B.S.A.'07, M.S.A.'08, N. Mex. Col. of Agrl. and Mech. Arts; Pres. Emeritus, Ark. State Col., Jonesboro, Ark., since 1942.

Kealey, Daniel S., A.B.'14, LL.B.'17, Fordham Univ.; U.S.N.E.'18, Stevens Marine Eng. Sch.; LL.D.'25, Gonzaga Col.; Supt. of Sch., Hoboken, N. J., since 1922.

Kearns, Carroll D., Supt. of Sch., Farrell, Pa.

Keating, Norine B., M.A.'29, N. Y. State Col. for Tchrs., Albany, N. Y.; Supt. of Sch., Green Island, N. Y., since 1936.

Keboch, F. D., A.B.'15, Lebanon Valley Col.; A.M.'25, Univ. of Pittsburgh; Supt. of Sch., 121 Emerson Ave., Aspinwall, Pittsburgh, Pa., since 1917.

Keeler, Fred C., B.A.'07, Univ. of Ill.; Co. Supt. of Sch., Belvidere, Ill., since 1929.

Keenan, Robert C., A.B.'20, J.D.'25, M.Ed. '37, Loyola Univ.; Dist. Supt. of Elem. Sch., 5516 S. Maplewood Ave., Chicago, Ill., since 1941.

Keene, Charles H., A.B.'98, M.D.'02, Harvard; Prof. of Hygiene, Univ. of Buffalo, Buffalo, N. Y., since 1926.

Keener, Edward E., A.B.'14, Piedmont Col.; M.A.'17, George Peabody Col. for Tchrs.; Prin., John Hay Sch., 1018 N. Laramie Ave., Chicago, Ill., since 1935.

Keeney, Albert L., B.A.'29, Univ. of Wyo.; M.A.'35, Columbia Univ.; Supt. of Sch., Superior, Wyo., since 1931.

Kefauver, Grayson N., B.A.'21, Univ. of Ariz.; M.A.'25, Stanford Univ.; Ph.D.'28, Univ of Minn.; Dean, Sch. of Educ., Stanford Univ., Stanford University, Calif., since 1933.

Kehres, Harvey E., A.B.'13, Phillips Univ.; B.S.'22, M.A.'40, Univ. of Wash.; Diploma '41, Eastern Oregon Col. of Educ.; Supt. of Sch., Hunters, Wash., since 1943.

Kehrli, Edwin H., Ph.B.'25, Muhlenberg Col.; M.A.'28, Tchrs. Col., Columbia Univ.; Co. Supt. of Sch., Tunkhannock, Pa., since 1934.

Keister, W. H., Supt. of Sch., Harrisonburg, Va., since 1894.

Keith, Everett Earnest, B.S. in Ed.'29, Southwest Mo. State Tchrs. Col., Springfield, Mo.; M.A.'32, Univ. of Mo.; Exec. Secy., Mo. State Tchrs. Assn., Columbia, Mo., since 1941.

Keliher, Alice Virginia, B.S.'28, M.A.'29, Ph.D.'30, Tchrs. Col., Columbia Univ.; Assoc. Prof. of Educ., New York Univ., New York 7, N. Y., since 1935.

Keller, Anna P., Ph.B.'13, Univ. of Chicago; A.M.'37, De Paul Univ.; Dist. Supt. of Sch., 449 N. Austin Blvd., Chicago, Ill., since 1938.

Keller, Charles P., Ph.B.'96, De Pauw Univ.; Supt. of Sch., Brazil, Ind., since 1914.

Keller, Harold E., A.B.'20, M.A.'22, St. Vincent Col. Address: 349 E. Market St., Marietta, Pa.

Keller, James Albert, Diploma '13, State Tchrs. Col., Florence, Ala.; B.S.'30, George Peabody Col. for Tchrs.; L.H.D. '34, Birmingham-Southern Col.; LL.D.'35, Ala. Polytech. Inst.; M.A.'38, Columbia Univ.; Pres., State Tchrs. Col., Florence, Ala., since 1937.

Keller, Roy E., B.S.'15, Pa. State Col.; Ed.M.'23, Harvard Univ.; Supt. of Sch., Manchester, Mass., since 1928.

Kelley, James F., A.B.'24, Seton Hall Col.; A.M.'26, Ph.D.'35, Univ. of Louvain; Pres., Seton Hall Col., South Orange, N. J., since 1936.

Kelley, Margaret R., State Helping Tchr., Derby, Vt.

Kellogg, E. G., Supt. of Sch., Clintonville, Wis.

Kelly, Francis A., A.B.'24, M.A.'25, Boston Col.; Supt. of Sch., Watertown, Mass., since 1939.

Kelly, Fred J., Ph.D.'14, Columbia Univ.; Chief, Div. of Higher Educ., U. S. Office of Educ., Washington 25, D. C., since 1931.

Kelly, Glenn Kuns, B.A.'16, Franklin Col.; M.A.'28, Univ. of Chicago; Assoc. Prof. of Educ., Lake Forest Col., since 1943. Address: 5746 Drexel Ave., Chicago 37, Ill.

Kelty, Mary G., A.M.'24, Univ. of Chicago. Address: 3512 Rittenhouse St., N. W., Washington, D. C.

Kemmerer, W. W., B.A.'24, Lehigh Univ.; Ph.D.'30, Columbia Univ.; Comptroller and Dir. of Curriculum, Univ. of Houston, Houston, Texas, since 1939.

Kemp, W. W., Ph.D.'12, Tchrs. Col., Columbia Univ.; Univ. of Calif., 405 Hilgard Ave., Los Angeles, Calif.

Kendall, Glenn, A.B.'25, Western Ky. State Tchrs. Col., Bowling Green, Ky.; M.A. '31, Univ. of Ky.; Ed.D.'41, Tchrs. Col., Columbia Univ.; Educ. Service, U. S. Dept. of Justice, Franklin Trust Bldg., Philadelphia, Pa.

Kendall, Glenn M., A.B.'23, M.A.'29, Univ. of Nebr.; Ed.D.'37, Columbia Univ.; Dir. of Educ., Dept. of Correction, Albany, N. Y., since 1936.

Kenerson, Edward H., Ginn & Co., Statler Bldg., Park Square, Boston, Mass.

Kennan, Richard Barnes, B.S. and M.A.'29, Ph.D.'40, Tchrs. Col., Columbia Univ.; Exec. Secy., Maine Tchrs. Assn., 14 Western Ave., Augusta, Maine, since 1940.

Kennedy, E. D., A.B.'31, Central Mich. Col. of Educ.; M.A.'38, Univ. of Mich.; Supt. of Sch., Rochester, Mich., since 1941.

Kennedy, Mark, A.B.'21, M.A.'22, St. Bonaventure Col.; Lect. Glis. S.S.'29, Rome, Italy; Pres., Siena Col., Loudonville, N. Y., since 1943.

Kennedy, Mary A., B.S.'26, M.A.'34, New York Univ.; Asst. Supt. of Sch., 110 Livingston St., Brooklyn 2, N. Y., since 1936.

Kennelly, Sister Antonius, A.B.'26, Col. of St. Catherine; Ph.D.'33, Univ. of Munich; Pres., Col. of St. Catherine, St. Paul, Minn., since 1943.

Kent, Ronald W., A.B.'13, Ind. Univ.; Ph.D.'31, New York Univ.; Asst. Dir., Essex Co. Voc. Schools, Hall of Records, Newark, N. J., since 1925.

Kentopp, Henry Eugene, B.A.'21, Midland Col.; M.A.'30, Univ. of Wis.; D.Ed.'40, Tchrs. Col., Columbia Univ.; Supt. of Sch., East Orange, N. J., since 1936.

Kerlin, Oscar F., B.S.'21, Univ. of Mich.; M.S.'26, Syracuse Univ.; Supt. of Sch., Elmira, N. Y., since 1938.

Kernan, Eva Cecilia, B.S.'31, Tchrs. Col., Columbia Univ.; M.Ed.'40, Rutgers Univ.; Dir. of Guidance and Research, Bd. of Educ., Union, N. J., since 1938.

Kerr, A. G., B.S.'26, Ball State Tchrs. Col., Muncie, Ind.; M.S.'34, Ind. Univ.; Supt. of Sch., Columbia City, Ind., since 1935.

Kerr, E. S., B.S. in Ed.'16, Ohio State Univ.; Supt. of Sch., Salem, Ohio, since 1931.

Kerr, Everett F., A.B.'35, M.A.'40, Univ. of Chicago; Dist. Supt. of Sch., Homewood, Ill., since 1938.

Kerr, W. E., M.A.'34, State Univ. of Iowa; Supt. of Sch., Artesia, N. Mex., since 1928.

Kerschner, E. E., A.B.'23, A.M.'32, Univ. of Pa.; Supvg. Prin. of Sch., Ambler, Pa., since 1935.

Kersey, Vierling, M.A.'19, Univ. of Southern Calif.; LL.D.'29, Whittier Col.; D.Ped. '30, Univ. of Southern Calif.; D.Sc.'41; Supt. of Sch., Los Angeles 15, Calif., since 1937.

Kethley, William Marion, B.A.'14, Miss. Col.; M.A.'25, Tchrs. Col., Columbia Univ.; Pres., Delta State Tchrs. Col., Cleveland, Miss., since 1926.

Ketler, Frank C., A.B.'11, Grove City Col.; A.M.'29, Ph.D.'31, Columbia Univ.; Supt. of Twp. Sch., Elkins Park, Philadelphia, Pa., since 1932.

Kibbe, Delia E., A.M.'21, Univ. of Chicago; State Supvr. of Elem. Sch., State Dept. of Pub. Instr., Madison, Wis., since 1924.

Kietzman, Ben, A.B.'18, North Central Col.; M.Ph.'26, Univ. of Wis.; Supt. of Sch., Canton, Ill., since 1935.

Kimball, Reginald Stevens, A.B.'21, A.M. '22, Brown Univ.; Ed.M.'29, Harvard Univ.; Ed.D.'41, New York Univ. Address: Natl. Educ. Alliance, 184 Emerson Pl., Brooklyn, N. Y.

Kimm, Chester C., B.A. in Ed.'39, Eastern Wash. Col. of Educ.; Co. Supt. of Sch., Wenatchee, Wash., since 1943.

Kimm, Willard I., A.B.'15, Columbia Univ.; H. S. and Col. Dept., Ginn & Co., 70 Fifth Ave., New York, N. Y.

Kinard, Knox, A. B.'31, West Texas State Tchrs. Col., Canyon, Texas; M.A.'41, Univ. of Texas; Supt. of Sch., Hereford, Texas, since 1938.

Kincaid, William A., A.B.'23, Ohio Univ.; M.A.'28, Tchrs. Col., Columbia Univ.; Supt. of Sch., Summit, N. J., since 1941.

King, Dana M., B.S.'21, Greenville Col.; A.M.'30, Cornell Univ.; Supt. of Sch., Hudson Falls, N. Y., since 1938.

King, Harold F., A.B.'14, Bowdoin Col.; A.M.'27, Columbia Univ.; Supt., Coventry Schs., Washington, R. I., since 1941.

King, Harry Brandt, Diploma '13, State Tchrs. Col., Millersville, Pa.; A.B.'17, Franklin and Marshall Col.; A.M.'23, Columbia Univ.; Ph.D.'28, New York Univ.; Asst. State Supt. of Pub. Instr. in charge of Elem. Sch., Dover, Del., since 1922.

King, Herbert Baxter, B.A.'13, Queen's Univ.; M.A.'23, Univ. of British Columbia; B.Paed.'29, Univ. of Toronto; Ph.D. '36, Univ. of Wash.; Chief Insp. of Sch., Dept. of Educ., Victoria, B. C., Canada, since 1939.

King, J. D., Jr., A.B.'36, M.S.'39, Southern Methodist Univ.; Supt. of Sch., Ennis, Texas, since 1943.

King, Lloyd W., A.B.'11, William Jewell Col.; M.A.'32, Univ. of Mo.; Exec. Secy., American Textbook Publishers Inst., 104 E. Circle Dr., Jefferson City, Mo., since 1943.

King, W. P., LL.B.'14, Col. of Law, Cincinnati Univ.; Exec. Secy., Ky. Educ. Assn., Heyburn Bldg., Louisville 2, Ky., since 1933.

Kinley, Frederick L., A.B.'16, Heidelberg Col.; M.A.'28, Ohio State Univ.; Supt. of Sch., Findlay, Ohio, since 1936.

Kintigh, W. B., A.B.'25, York Col.; M.E.'37, Univ. of Kansas; Supt. of Sch., Olathe, Kansas, since 1936.

Kipp, George A., A.B.'13, Ohio State Univ.; Pd.M.'17, New York Univ.; Supvg. Prin. of Sch., Tenafly, N. J., since 1930.

Kirby, David, A.B.'21, Morris Harvey Col.; A.M.'28, W. Va. Univ.; Ped.D.'42, W. Va. Wesleyan Univ.; Dean, Concord Col., Athens, W. Va., since 1942.

Kirk, H. H., A.B.'13, Ohio Wesleyan Univ.; A.M.'26, Columbia Univ.; Supt. of Sch., Fargo, N. Dak., since 1935.

Kirk, Thomas J., Vice-Pres. in charge of Educ. Div., Americana Corp., 2 W. 45th St., New York 19, N. Y.

Kirkland, Denver D., B.A.'28, Northwestern State Col., Alva, Okla.; M.Ed.'33, Univ. of Okla.; Supt. of Sch., McAlester, Okla., since 1941.

Kirkland, Mineola, Ph.B. in Ed.'26, Univ. of Chicago; Ed.M.'32, Harvard Univ.; Supvg. Prin. of Sch., 1106 B St., N. E., Washington, D. C., since 1930.

Kissick, Claude, A.B.'21, Fairmount, Col.; A.M.'31, Univ. of Wis.; Supt. of Sch., Wellington, Kansas, since 1935.

Klager, Benjamin, B.Pd.'15, Mich. State Normal Col., Ypsilanti, Mich.; A.B.'19, M.A.'26, Univ. of Mich.; Supt. of Sch., Bay City, Mich., since 1936.

Klapper, Paul, B.A.'04, Col. of the City of New York; Ph.D.'09, New York Univ.; Pres., Queens Col., Flushing, L. I., N. Y., since 1937.

Klauminzer, Frederick A., B.S.'29, M.Ed.'37, Rutgers Univ.; Dir. of Tr., Southbury Tr. Sch., Southbury, Conn., since 1940.

Klaus, Roland A., B.A.'20, Lawrence Col.; M.A.'27, Univ. of Wis.; Supt. of Sch., Edgerton, Wis., since 1929.

Klein, Arthur J., Ph.D.'16, Columbia Univ.; Dean, Col. of Educ., Ohio State Univ., Columbus, Ohio, since 1937.

Kleinpell, E. H., A.B.'25, State Univ. of Iowa; A.M.'26, Univ. of Chicago; Ph.D. '36, Ohio State Univ.; Pres., State Tchrs. Col., Valley City, N. Dak., since 1942.

Kline, Barton L., B.Sc.'29, Cotner Col.; M.A.'32, Univ. of Nebr.; Supt. of Sch., Gothenburg, Nebr., since 1938.

Klonower, Henry, B.S.'15, M.A.'20, Univ. of Pa.; Pd.D.'36, Ursinus Col.; Dir., Tchr. Educ. and Certification, State Dept. of Pub. Instr., Harrisburg, Pa., since 1920.

Klooster, Henry J., B.A.'17, Emmanuel Missionary Col.; B.S.'30, M.S.'31, Univ. of Chicago; Pres., Pacific Union Col., Angwin, Calif., since 1943.

Klontz, Vernon E., B.A.'17, Univ. of Wis.; A.M.'29, Univ. of Chicago; Supt. of Sch., Janesville, Wis., since 1935.

Kluckhohn, Harvey N., B.A.'21, Des Moines Univ.; M.A.'28, State Univ. of Iowa; Supt. of Sch., Le Mars, Iowa, since 1928.

Knapp, M. L., A.B.'19, Ind. Univ.; A.M.'26, Columbia Univ.; Supt. of Sch., Michigan City, Ind., since 1939.

Knight, Frederic B., A.B.'13, Boston Univ.; A.M.'15, Harvard Univ.; Ph.D.'21, Columbia Univ.; Dir., Div. of Educ. and Applied Psychology, Purdue Univ., West Lafayette, Ind., since 1937.

Knight, Melvin Colby, B.A.'13, Bates Col.; Supt. of Sch., Hyannis, Mass.

Knoblauch, Arthur L., B.S.'29, Mich State Col.; M.A.'33, Univ. of Mich.; Ed.D.'41, Harvard Univ.; Prof. of Educ. Admin. and Dir., Div. of Univ. Exten., Univ. of Conn., Storrs, Conn., since 1943.

Knoelk, William C., A.B.'07, M.A.'25, Univ. of Wis.; Prin., West Division H. S., Milwaukee, Wis., since 1940.

Knowles, Joe C., B.S.'21, Wash. State Col.; Dist. Supt. of Sch., Port Orchard, Wash., since 1923.

Knowles, Robert Reily, B.S.'09, M.A.'27, Univ. of Colo.; Supt. of Sch., Sterling, Colo., since 1929.

Knox, J. H., B.S.'22, The Citadel; M.A.'38, Univ. of Chicago; Supt. of Sch., Salisbury, N. C., since 1934.

Knudsen, Charles W., Ph.D.'27, Univ. of Ill.; Prof. of Sec. Educ., George Peabody Col. for Tchrs., Nashville 4, Tenn., since 1928.

Koch, Harlan C., A.B.'19, Ohio Univ.; M.A.'23, Ph.D.'26, Ohio State Univ.; Asst. Dir., Bureau of Cooperation with Educ. Institutions, since 1934 and Prof. of Educ., Univ. of Mich., Ann Arbor, Mich., since 1939.

Koch, J. Wilbur, A.B.'12, Park Col.; M.A. '30, Ohio State Univ.; Supvr. of Adult Educ., WPA Dist. No. 4, Cleveland, Ohio, since 1941. Address: 266 Jefferson St., Ravenna, Ohio.

Koepke, William Charles, Ph.B.'13, Univ. of Wis.; M.A.'27, Columbia Univ.; Ph.D. '31, Marquette Univ.; Prin., Walker Jr. H. S., Milwaukee, Wis., since 1937.

Koffman, Gladstone, A.B.'15, Union Univ., Jackson, Tenn.; A.M.'28, Univ. of Chicago; Supt. of Sch., Hopkinsville, Ky., since 1932.

Kohler, Katherine M., Dir. of Adult Educ., Pub. Sch., Minneapolis, Minn.

Kolasa, John J., A.B.'23, Harvard Univ.; M.A.'35, Niagara Univ.; Pres., Alliance Col., Cambridge Springs, Pa., since 1937.

Koonce, R. J., B.S.'20, Miss. Col.; M.A.'26, Ind. Univ.; Supt. of Sch., Yazoo City, Miss., since 1932.

Koontz, Norman C., B.A.'09, Grove City Col.; B.A.'11, Yale Col.; M.A.'26, Columbia Univ.; Supt. of Sch., Conneaut, Ohio, since 1938.

Koopman, Philip U., A.B.'31, Central State Tchrs. Col., Mt. Pleasant, Mich.; A.M. '32, Univ. of Mich.; Ed.D.'41, Columbia Univ.; Asst. Supt. of Lower Merion Sch. Dist., Ardmore, Pa., since 1940.

Koos, Frank H., Ph.D.'27, Columbia Univ.; Prof. of Educ. Admin., Pa. State Col., State College, Pa., since 1931.

Koos, Leonard V., A.B.'07, Oberlin Col.; A.M.'15, Ph.D.'16, Univ. of Chicago; Litt.D.'37, Oberlin Col.; Prof. of Sec. Educ., Univ. of Chicago, Chicago Ill., since 1929.

Kopka, M. A., Life Cert.'15, A.B.'21, Mich. State Normal Col.; M.A.'22, Univ. of Mich.; Supt. of Sch., Hamtramck, Mich., since 1935.

Kopp, Charles L., A.B.'09, Gettysburg Col.; A.M.'25, Tchrs. Col., Columbia Univ.; Supt. of Sch., Cumberland, Md., since 1928.

Koppin, Paul G., Jr., Pres., Bd. of Educ., 23717 Piper Ave., East Detroit, Mich.

Korb, O. J., B.S.'18, Kent State Univ.; M.A.'27, Tchrs. Col., Columbia Univ.; Ph.D.'38, Western Reserve Univ.; Supt. of Sch., East Cleveland, Ohio, since 1939.

Kostka, Sister Maria, A.B.'18, Catholic Univ.; A.M.'23, Villanova Col.; Ph.D.'31, Univ. of Pa.; Pres., College of Chestnut Hill, Chestnut Hill, Philadelphia, Pa.

Kramer, Frank H., B.A.'14, Gettysburg Col.; A.M.'16, Ph.D.'20, Univ. of Pa.; Prof. of Educ., Gettysburg Col., Gettysburg, Pa., since 1921.

Kramer, J. Howard, Supt. of Sch., Spearfish, S. Dak.

Kramer, R. L., B.A.'20, Carleton Col.; M.A. '34, Univ. of Wash.; Supt. of Sch., Dawson, Minn., since 1937.

Krantz, LaVern L., B.S.'29, M.A.'30, Univ. of Minn.; Supt. of Sch., Mound, Minn., since 1937.

Kratt, Edwin C., A.B.'24, Linfield Col.; M.A.'29, Stanford Univ.; Asst. Supt. of Sch., Fresno 1, Calif., since 1937.

Krause, Arthur W., B.S.'03, Valparaiso Univ.; A.B.'23, Ind. Univ.; Supt. of Sch., Grand Rapids, Mich., since 1936.

Kraybill, D. B., A.B.'11, Franklin and Marshall Col.; A.M.'16, Columbia Univ.; Ph.D.'27, Pa. State Col.; Dean, W. Va. Inst. of Tech., Montgomery, W. Va., since 1933.

Kretzmann, O. P., S.T.M.'24, Litt.D.'41, Concordia Sem.; Pres., Valparaiso Univ., Valparaiso, Ind., since 1940.

Kroesch, Edward D., Supt. of Sch., Hoisington, Kansas.

Krug, George Henry, B.S.'09, Colgate Univ.; M.A.'31, N. Y. State Col. for Tchrs., Albany, N. Y.; Supt. of Sch., Troy, N. Y., since 1930.

Krug, Marguerite Charlotte, B.S.'29, M.A.'34, Wayne Univ.; Prin., Elem. Sch., 2270 Leslie Ave., Detroit, Mich., since 1933.

Kruschke, Walter F., Ph.M.'38, Univ. of Wis.; Supt. of Sch., Rhinelander, Wis., since 1928.

Kruse, Samuel Andrew, A.B. and B.S. in Ed.'09, Univ. of Mo.; A.M.'15, Univ. of Wis.; Ph.D.'28, George Peabody Col. for Tchrs.; Head, Dept. of Educ., State Tchrs. Col., Cape Girardeau, Mo., since 1915.

Kuefler, Bernard C., M.A.'38, Univ. of Minn.; Supt. of Sch., Forest Lake, Minn., since 1930.

Kuhn, Florence E., M.S.'35, Wayne Univ.; Prin., Hamilton Sch., 14223 Southampton, Detroit, Mich., since 1941.

Kuhn, Ray, A.B.'16, B.Pd.'17, Tri-State Col.; M.A.'27, Columbia Univ.; Supt. of Sch., Plymouth, Ind., since 1930.

*Kulp, Claude L., B.S.'27, Univ. of Rochester; M.A.'30, Cornell Univ.; Supt. of Sch., 117 E Buffalo St., Ithaca, N. Y., since 1930.

Kuntzleman, Oliver C., D.Ed.'36, Temple Univ.; Supt. of Sch., Sunbury, Pa., since 1940.

Kurtz, Clyde W., M.A.'37, Univ. of Wyo.; Supt. of Sch., Evanston, Wyo., since 1941.

Kyle, C. J. M., M.A.'29, George Peabody Col. for Tchrs.; Co. Supt. of Sch., Stuart, Va., since 1941.

Kyle, Roy E., B.S.'24, Col. of William and Mary; M.A.'31, George Peabody Col. for Tchrs.; Div. Supt. of Sch., Hillsville, Va., since 1937.

L

Laidlaw, Arthur J., B.S.'11, St. Lawrence Univ.; M.S.'13, Tchrs. Col., Columbia Univ.; Supt. of Sch., Kingston, N. Y., since 1939.

Lake, Charles H., B.A.'09, M.A.'10, LL.D.'34, Ohio State Univ.; Supt. of Sch., Cleveland, Ohio, since 1933.

Lake, Ernest G., B.A.'29, Univ. of Mont.; Ed.M.'38, Ed.D.'43, Harvard Univ.; Supt. of Sch., Barre, Vt., since 1942.

Lakey, Melvin Dallas, B.A.'23, Cornell Col.; M.A.'33, Tchrs. Col., Columbia Univ.; Supt. of Sch., Fabens, Texas, since 1926.

Lamb, L. H., B.S.'22, Stout Inst.; M.A.'30, Univ. of Mich.; Supt. of Sch., Manitowoc, Wis., since 1943.

Lambert, A. C., Ph.D.'36, Stanford Univ.; Prof. of Educ. Admin. and Dean, Summer Sch., Brigham Young Univ., Provo, Utah, since 1934.

Lambeth, M. T., A.B. in Ed.'26, Univ. of N. C.; M.A.'31, Tchrs. Col., Columbia Univ.; Supt. of Sch., Thomasville, N. C., since 1942.

Lamkin, Uel W., Pres., Natl. Educ. Assn., 1928-29; Pres., Northwest Mo. State Tchrs. Col., Maryville, Mo., since 1921.

Lancaster, Allen H., B.S.'18, Univ. of Ill.; M.S.'38, Univ. of Wis.; Supt. of Sch., Dixon, Ill., since 1932.

Lancaster, Bela Allen, A.B. and A.M.'26, Mercer Univ.; Supt. of Sch., La Grange, Ga., since 1937.

Lancaster, C. E., B.S.'23, M.A.'26, Mercer Univ.; Supt. of Sch., Vidalia, Ga., since 1937.

Lancaster, Dabney S., B.A.'11, Univ. of Va.; M.S.'15, Va. Polytech. Inst.; State Supt. of Pub. Instr., Richmond, Va., since 1941.

Lancaster, J. W., B.Ped.'06, M.S.'13, Univ. of Ky.; Supt. of Sch., Georgetown, Ky., since 1923.

Land, John N., A.B.'07, Franklin and Marshall Col.; A.M.'35, Univ. of Pa.; Supvg. Prin. of Sch., Hamburg, Pa., since 1910.

Landis, Emerson H., A.B.'18, Univ. of Pittsburgh; M.A.'28, Columbia Univ.; D.Ed.'41, Univ. of Dayton; Supt. of Sch., Dayton 2, Ohio, since 1937.

Landis, Ira C., Supt. of Sch., 3450 Ninth St., Riverside, Calif., since 1928.

Landreth, Austin, B.A.'19, Ind. Univ.; M.A.'29, Stanford Univ.; Supt. of Sch., Pendleton, Oregon, since 1929.

Lane, Edward M., B.C.Sc.'25, Univ. of Detroit; Secy. and Bus. Mgr., Bd. of Educ., 1354 Broadway, Detroit 26, Mich., since 1939.

Lane, Mrs. Helen Schick, B.A.'26, M.A.'28, Ph.D.'30, Ohio State Univ.; Prin., Central Inst. for the Deaf, 818 S. Kingshighway, St. Louis 10, Mo., since 1942.

Lang, Andrew J., LL.B.'11, Univ. of Mich.; B.S.'20, A.M.'31, Columbia Univ.; Supt. of Sch., Huron, S. Dak., since 1925.

Lang, Charles E., Ph.B.'15, Univ. of Chicago; M.A.'40, Northwestern Univ.; Prin., Lane Tech. H. S., 2501 W. Addison St., Chicago, Ill., since 1933.

Langwith, J. E., A.B.'13, Southwestern Univ.; M.A.'29, Southern Methodist Univ.; Supt. of Sch., Terrell, Texas, since 1923.

*Langworthy, Harry W., Ph.B.'07, Alfred Univ.; M.A.'25, Columbia Univ. Address: 13 E. Boulevard, Gloversville 16, N. Y.

*Lanier, Raphael O'Hara, A.B.'22, Lincoln Univ.; A.M.'28, Stanford Univ.; D.Ped.'41, Lincoln Univ.; Dean of Instr. and Acting Dir., Div. of Genl. Studies and Educ., Hampton Inst., Hampton, Va., since 1941.

Lanning, George B., B.S.'30, State Tchrs. Col., Emporia, Kansas; M.S.'30, Northwestern Univ.; Supt. of Sch., Wamego, Kansas, since 1939.

Lantz, P. G., A.B.'10, Ind. Univ.; A.M.'13, Univ. of Wis.; Supt. of Tr. Sch., Central State Tchrs. Col., Mt. Pleasant, Mich., since 1923.

Lantz, W. W., A.B.'10, Franklin and Marshall Col.; A.M.'22, Univ. of Pittsburgh; Co. Supt. of Sch., Pittsburgh, Pa., since 1942.

La Perche, Raymond C., B.Sc.'22, R. I. State Col.; Supt. of Smithfield Schs., Farnum Pike, Georgiaville, R. I., since 1938.

Lapham, P. C., A.B.'12, Des Moines Col.; A.M.'16, Univ. of Chicago; Supt. of Sch., Charles City, Iowa, since 1927.

Larsen, Arthur Hoff, B.Ed.'29, State Tchrs. Col., Superior Wis.; Ph.M,'31, Ph.D.'39, Univ. of Wis.; Assoc. Prof. of Educ., Ill. State Normal Univ., Normal, Ill., since 1935.

Larson, Carl E., A.B.'16, Knox Col.; M.A. '28, Univ. of Chicago; Supt. of West Side Sch., Aurora, Ill., since 1935.

LaSalle, Jessie, B.S.'18, A.M.'20, Tchrs. Col., Columbia Univ.; Asst. Supt. of Sch., West Sch., Washington, D. C., since 1923.

Lasher, Norman J., Diploma '15, Ind. State Tchrs. Col., Terre Haute, Ind.; A.B.'20, Marion Col.; M.A.'28, Univ. of Wis.; Supt. of Sch., Seymour, Ind., since 1925.

LaSitis, Joseph, A.B.'28, Bethany Col., Bethany, W. Va.; M.Ed.'40, Univ. of Pittsburgh; Supvg. Prin. of Sch., Emporium, Pa., since 1936.

Latham, Rowland H., B.A. and M.A.'03, Univ. of Va.; Supt. of Sch., Asheville, N. C., since 1934.

Lathan, W. L., A.B.'27, Duke Univ.; Co. Supt. of Sch., Bryson City, N. C., since 1937.

Lau, John A., LL.B.'06, Univ. of Wis.; Ph.B.'18, Univ. of Chicago; Scott, Foresman & Co., 623 S. Wabash Ave., Chicago, Ill.

Laudenslager, E. B., A.B.'21, Swarthmore Col.; A.M.'33, Univ. of Pa.; Supt. of Sch., Hatfield, Pa., since 1922.

Lauderbach, John Calvin, B.A.'20, M.A.'31, Univ. of Southern Calif.; Dist. Supt. of Sch., Chula Vista, Calif., since 1923.

Lauer, John Edwards, B.S.'30, Franklin and Marshall Col.; M.A.'37, New York Univ.; Supt. of Sch., Lansford, Pa., since 1938.

Laughlin, Butler, Diploma '10, Ind. State Normal Sch., Terre Haute, Ind.; A.B.'14, A.M.'16, Ind. Univ.; Prin., Harper H. S. and Prof. of Educ., Lewis Inst., Chicago, Ill., since 1937.

Laurent, Sister Mary, B.A.'31, Col. of St. Catherine; M.A.'39, Univ. of Minn.; Prin., St. Joseph's Academy, St. Paul, Minn., since 1941.

Lawler, Eugene S., Ph.D.'32, Tchrs. Col., Columbia Univ. Address: U. S. Office of Educ., Federal Security Agency, Washington 25, D. C.

Laws, Gertrude, Diploma '08, San Diego State Col.; A.B.'19, Stanford Univ.; M.A.'23, Ph.D.'27, Columbia Univ.; Dir. of Educ. for Women, Pub. Sch., Pasadena, Calif., since 1940.

Lawson, James H., B.S.'16, Univ. of Chicago; Ed.D.'34, Univ. of Pittsburgh; Supt. of Sch., Shaw Avenue Bldg., McKeesport, Pa., since 1935.

Lawson, Oliver C., A.B.'26, M.A.'29, Stanford Univ.; Asst. Supt. of Sch., Berkeley 7, Calif., since 1942.

Lawson, Willie A., A.B.'15, Flora MacDonald Col.; B.S.'27, M.A.'28, George Peabody Col. for Tchrs.; Exec. Secy., Ark. Educ. Assn., Insurance Bldg., Little Rock, Ark., since 1935.

Layton, C. M., B.S. in Ed.'20, M.A.'37, Ohio State Univ.; Supt. of Sch., Wooster, Ohio, since 1932.

Leaden, J. Warren, B.A. in Ed.'36, Univ. of Wash.; Supt. of Sch., Okanogan, Wash., since 1942.

Leamer, Emery W., A.B.'09, Univ. of Nebr.; A.M.'19, Univ. of Chicago; Dir. of Tr., State Tchrs. Col., La Crosse, Wis., since 1925.

Lease, R. A., B.S.'24, M.A.'26, Univ. of Minn.; Supt., Grade and H. S., Sycamore, Ill., since 1928.

Leaver, C. B., Supt. of Sch., Kent City, Mich.

LeBarron, E. H., M.A.'33, Columbia Univ.; Supt. of Sch., Hicksville, N. Y., since 1936.

Lecron, W. R., M.A.'28, Univ. of Pittsburgh; Ed.D.'30, Pa. State Col.; Supt. of Sch., Ashland, Pa., since 1942.

Lee, Alton B., M.Ed.'42, Univ. of Texas; Supt. of Sch., Decatur, Texas, since 1935.

Lee, Amos C., Supt. of Sch., West Des Moines, Iowa.

Lee, Charles A., M.A. in Ed.'31, Univ. of Mo.; Ed.D.'36, Tchrs. Col., Columbia Univ.; Prof. of Educ., Washington Univ., St. Louis, Mo., since 1935.

Lee, Donald, B.Ed.'35, State Tchrs. Col., Whitewater, Wis.; M.A.'39, Northwestern Univ.; Supt. of Sch., Jefferson, Wis., since 1941.

Lee, E. A., A.B.'24, La. State Normal Col., Natchitoches, La.; Parish Supt. of Sch., Natchitoches, La., since 1925.

Lee, Edwin A., B.S.'14, M.A.'15, Ph.D.'32, Columbia Univ.; Prof. of Educ. and Dean, Sch. of Educ., Univ. of Calif., Los Angeles, Calif., since 1940.

Lee, J. Murray, A.B.'26, Occidental Col.; A.M.'28, Ph.D.'34, Tchrs. Col., Columbia Univ.; Dean, Sch. of Educ., State Col. of Wash., Pullman, Wash., since 1941.

*Lee, J. R. E., A.B.'89, A.M.'03, Bishop Col.; LL.D.'17, Wilberforce Univ.; Ped. D.'30, Bishop Col.; LL.D.'38, Howard Univ.; Pres., Fla. Agrl. and Mech. Col. for Negroes, Tallahassee, Fla., since 1924.

Lee, James Allen, Co. Supt. of Educ., Selma, Ala., since 1928.

Lee, L. Tennent, Jr., B.S.'28, Ala. Poly. Inst.; M.A.'38, Univ. of Ala.; Ed.D.'42, Columbia Univ.; Asst. Prof. and Acting Head, Dept. of Educ., Lehigh Univ., Bethlehem, Pa.

Lee, Umphrey, B.A.'14, Trinity Univ.; M.A. '16, Southern Methodist Univ.; D.D.'28, Trinity Univ.; Ph.D.'31, Columbia Univ.; Litt.D.'40, Southwestern; Pres., Southern Methodist Univ., Dallas, Texas, since 1939.

LeFevre, Harold E., A.B.'35, Mich. State Normal Col., Ypsilanti, Mich.; M.A.'41, Wayne Univ.; Supt., Kern Road Pub. Sch., East Detroit, Mich., since 1940.

Lefler, Millard C., B.A.'11, State Tchrs. Col., Peru, Nebr.; M.A.'16, Univ. of Nebr.; Supt. of Sch., Lincoln, Nebr., since 1920.

Lehman, C. W., A.B.'17, Univ. of Nebr.; M.A.'27, Tchrs. Col., Columbia Univ.; Supt. of Sch., Rushville, Nebr., since 1940.

Lehman, Clarence O., B.A.'16, Bluffton Col.; M.A.'25, Ph.D.'29, Ohio State Univ.; Pres., State Tchrs. Col., Potsdam, N. Y., since 1939.

Leidle, Vern V., B.A.'38, Western Wash. Col. of Educ.; Co. Supt. of Sch., Mount Vernon, Wash., since 1941.

Leinbach, Earl G., A.B.'20, Albright Col.; A.M.'25, Yale Univ.; Elgin Academy and Jr. Col., Elgin, Ill.

Leinweber, W. J., A.B.'23, North Central Col.; Supt. of Mooseheart, Mooseheart, Ill., since 1934.

Leister, Leroy L., Ph.B.'17, Muhlenberg Col.; Ed.M.'24, Grad. Sch. of Educ., Harvard Univ.; Supt. of Sch., Waterford, Conn., since 1925.

Lemasters, E. M., B.S. in Ed.'25, Northeast Mo. State Tchrs Col., Kirksville, Mo.; A.M.'29, Univ. of Mo.; Supt. of Riverview Gardens Pub. Schools, St. Louis, Mo., since 1935.

Le May, Sonley Robert, B.A.'14, LL.B.'16, Univ. of Texas; B.S.'22, Agrl. and Mech. Col. of Texas; M.A.'30, George Peabody Col. for Tchrs.; Ph.D.'41, Univ. of Texas; Supt. of Sch., Athens, Texas, since 1922.

Lemmel, W. H., A.B.'22, A.M.'28, State Univ. of Iowa; Ed.D.'40, Columbia Univ.; Supt. of Sch., Wilmington 9, Del., since 1942.

Lemmer, John A., Ph.B.'18, Notre Dame; M.A.'25, Univ. of Mich.; Supt. of Sch., Escanaba, Mich., since 1935.

Leonard, Charles B., Ph.B.'29, Brown Univ.; Supt. of Sch., Little Compton, R. I., since 1938.

Leonard, John I., B.S.'10, Lombard Col.; Ed.D.'42, Fla. Southern Col.; Co. Supt. of Pub. Instr., Court House, West Palm Beach, Fla., since 1936.

Leutner, W. G., Ph.D.'05, Johns Hopkins Univ.; LL.D.'35, Wittenberg Col.; LL.D. '35, Col. of Wooster; LL.D.'37, Oberlin Col.; Pres., Western Reserve Univ., Cleveland, Ohio, since 1934.

Lewandowski, John W., Member, Bd. of Educ., 2627 Casmere, Hamtramck, Mich.

Lewis, B. P., A.B.'18, Univ. of Okla.; M.A. '21, Univ. of Kansas; A.M.'25, Tchrs. Col., Columbia Univ.; Supt. of Sch., Rolla, Mo., since 1924.

Lewis, Charles W., A.B.'02, A.M.'05, Hamilton Col.; Supt. of Sch., Frankfort, N. Y., since 1929.

*Lewis, E. E., A.B.'07, M.A.'09, Stanford Univ.; Ph.D.'20, Columbia Univ.; Prof. of Educ., Ohio State Univ., Columbus, Ohio, since 1926.

Lewis, Mrs. Inez Johnson, A.B.'27, Colo. Col.; A.M.'30, Columbia Univ.; Ed.D.'35, Univ. of Colo.; LL.D.'38, Colo. Col.; State Supt. of Pub. Instr., Denver, Colo., since 1931.

Lewis, James A., B.S.'34, Central State Tchrs. Col., Mt. Pleasant, Mich.; M.A.'38, Univ. of Mich.; Supt. of Sch., Dowagiac, Mich., since 1939.

Lewis, John W., A.B.'17, Colgate Univ.; Asst. Supt. of Sch., 3 E. 25th St., Baltimore 18, Md., since 1927.

Lewis, John W., A.B.'26, Rio Grande Col.; M.E.'40, Wayne Univ.; Supt. of Sch., St. Clair Shores, Mich., since 1942.

Lewis, R. F., B.A.'15, M.A.'28, Univ. of Wis.; Supt. of Sch., Waukesha, Wis., since 1938.

Lewis, Russell A., A.B.'22, Abilene Christian Col.; M.A.'28, Ph.D.'38, Univ. of Texas; Supt. of Sch., Austin, Texas, since 1940.

Libby, Herschel Scott, Diploma '11, State Normal Sch., Farmington, Maine; B.Pd. '16, Univ. of Maine; M.A.'32, New York Univ.; Supt. of Sch., Irvington, N. J., since 1934.

Libby, Richard J., A.M.'19, Univ. of Maine; State Agt. for Rural Educ., State House, Augusta, Maine, since 1923.

Licking, R. Herbert, B.A.'23, M.A.'25, Univ. of Wis.; Supt. of Sch., Ripon, Wis., since 1941.

Lidikay, Donald R., Supt. of Sch., Bonner Springs, Kansas.

Liebendorfer, G. F., Supt. of Sch., Sidney, Nebr., since 1923.

Lieberman, Elias, B.A.'03, Col. of the City of New York; M.A.'06, Ph.D.'11, New York Univ.; Assoc. Supt. of Sch., 110 Livingston St., Brooklyn 2, N. Y., since 1940.

Liggitt, Earle O., B.S.'17, Muskingum Col.; A.M.'27, Ph.D.'42, Univ. of Pittsburgh; Dist. Supt. of Sch., Munhall, Pa., since 1938.

Light, N. Searle, B.A.'08, Yale Univ.; Dir., Bureau of Supvn., State Dept. of Educ., Hartford, Conn., since 1932.

Light, Ray H., A.B.'16, Lebanon Valley Col.; A.M.'23, Columbia Univ.; Supvg. Prin. of Sch., Cornwall, Pa., since 1920.

Light, U. L., B.S.'00, Ohio Northern Univ.; Ph.B.'12, Univ. of Chicago; Supt. of Sch., Barberton, Ohio, since 1913.

Lillibridge, Charles Wesley, B.S.'29, State Tchrs. Col., Mansfield, Pa.; Co. Supt. of Sch., Smethport, Pa., since 1911.

Lind, A. Grace, M.A.'32, Tchrs. Col., Columbia Univ.; Supvg. Prin. of Sch., Div. Five, Emery Sch., Washington, D. C., since 1937.

Lindbergh, Mrs. Evangeline L. L., Honorary Life Member, American Assn. of Sch. Admin. Address: 508 Lakepointe, Detroit, Mich.

Linden, Arthur V., B.S.'33, M.A.'35, Tchrs. Col., Columbia Univ.; Ed.D.'41, Arnold Col.; Assoc. Dir. of Student Personnel, Tchrs. Col., Columbia Univ., New York 27, N. Y., since 1936.

Lindley, A. T., A.B.'25, Earlham Col.; M.S.'32, Butler Univ.; Supt. of Sch., Crown Point, Ind., since 1935.

Lindquist, Rudolph D., A.B.'15, M.A.'22, D.Ed.'36, Univ. of Calif.; Supt. of Sch., Santa Barbara, Calif., since 1943.

Lindsay, James Armour, B.S.'19, M.S.'30, Univ. of Colo.; Ph.D.'33, Columbia Univ.; Assoc. Prof. of Educ., Miss. State Col., State College, Miss., since 1941.

Lindsey, Bob, Jr., B.A.'35, M.A.'40, Univ. of Texas; Supt. of Sch., Roby, Texas, since 1943.

Lindsey, Frank G., B.S. in Ed.'20, New York Univ.; Supvg. Prin. of Dist. Sch., Montrose, N. Y., since 1907.

Lindsey, John Clark, A.B.'19, Univ. of S. Dak.; A.M.'23, Columbia Univ.; LL.D. '29, Yankton Col.; Supt. of Sch., Mitchell, S. Dak., since 1918.

Lindsey, Richard V., B.E.'10, Ill. State Normal Univ., Normal, Ill.; Ph.M.'26, Univ. of Wis.; Supt. of Sch., Galesburg, Ill., since 1938.

Linn, Henry H., A.B.'18, State Tchrs. Col., Peru, Nebr.; M.A.'22, Univ. of Nebr.; M.A.'26, Ph.D.'29, Tchrs. Col., Columbia Univ.; Supt. of Bldgs. and Grounds, Tchrs. Col., Columbia Univ., New York 27, N. Y., since 1937.

Linn, Maynard W., Supt. of Sch., Greenwich, Conn., since 1938.

Linscheid, A., B.S.'12, Fremont Col.; M.A. '20, Univ. of Okla.; Ph.D.'28, Columbia Univ.; Pres., E. Central State Col., Ada, Okla., since 1920.

Linton, John H., A.B.'25, Ohio Wesleyan Univ.; M.A.'32, Univ. of Pittsburgh; Supt. of Sch., Titusville, Pa., since 1938.

Lippitt, Walter O., B.S.'03, Carleton Col.; M.A.'11, Univ. of Minn.; Supt. of Sch., Westwood, N. J., since 1929.

Litherland, J. W., M.A.'37, Univ. of Nebr.; Supt. of Sch., Wayne, Nebr., since 1941.

Litle, L. O., B.S.'26, Southwest Mo. State Tchrs. Col., Springfield, Mo.; A.M.'30, Ed. D.'43, Univ. of Mo.; Supt. of Sch., North Kansas City, Mo., since 1938.

Littel, Charles Lester, A.B.'12, Univ. of Nebr.; M.A.'26, Stanford Univ.; Ed.D.'35, New York Univ.; Pres., Bergen Jr. Col., Teaneck, N. J., since 1933.

Little, Adrian O., A.B.'27, M.A.'30, Ind. Univ.; Co. Supt. of Sch., Huntington, Ind., since 1933.

Little, Mrs. Jack M., Pres., Texas Congress of Parents and Tchrs., 3513 Purdue, Dallas 5, Texas.

Little, John R., Supt. of Sch., Arvada, Colo.

Little, Marsby C., B.S.'28, Gettysburg Col.; M.A.'32, Tchrs. Col., Columbia Univ.; Supt. of Sch., Freeport, Pa., since 1942.

Livengood, William W., A.B.'07, Ind. Univ.; Editor, The American Book Co., 88 Lexington Ave., New York 16, N. Y.

Lloyd, George W., M.A.'28, Clark Univ.; Pres., Mount Vernon Seminary, Washington 16, D. C., since 1936.

Lobban, James A., A.B.'98, Middlebury Col.; A.M.'99, Harvard Grad. Sch.; Acting Supt. of Sch., Webster, Mass., since 1943.

Locke, John F., B.S.'31, Univ. of Cincinnati; Dir., Dept. of Community Relations, Pub. Sch., 216 E. Ninth St., Cincinnati 2, Ohio, since 1938.

Lockhart, Albert V., A.B.'15, Mo. Wesleyan Col.; A.M.'17, Northwestern Univ.; Supt., Twp. H. S., Calumet City, Ill., since 1925.

Lockhart, John C., A.B.'12, Univ. of N. C. Address: Woman's Col., Univ. of N. C., Greensboro, N. C.

Lockwood, Charles M., A.B.'16, Furman Univ.; M.A.'38, Univ. of S. C.; Supt. of Sch., Lancaster, S. C., since 1940.

Lockwood, Charles W., A.B.'26, Univ. of Calif. at Los Angeles; M.A.'30, Univ. of Southern Calif.; Supt. of Sch., Palo Alto, Calif., since 1942.

Lockwood, Luther A., A.B.'17, Ind. State Tchrs. Col.; M.A.'29, Univ. of Chicago; Supt. of Sch., Rushville, Ind., since 1930.

Loftin, J. O., B.A.'23, Southwest Texas State Tchrs. Col., San Marcos, Texas; M.A.'25, Colo. Col. of Educ.; Pres., San Antonio Jr. Col., San Antonio, Texas, since 1941.

Logan, Jack M., A.B.'15, Drake Univ.; M.A. '27, State Univ. of Iowa; Supt. of Sch., East Waterloo, Iowa, since 1933.

Logan, S. R., Supt. of Sch., Winnetka, Ill., since 1943.

Loggins, W. F., M.A.'28, Columbia Univ.; Supt. of Sch., Greenville, S. C., since 1940.

Lohrie, Robert F., Supt. of Sch., Chippewa Falls, Wis., since 1922.

Lomax, Paul S., B.S. in Ed.'17, Univ. of Mo.; Ph.D.'27, New York Univ.; Prof. of Educ. and Head, Dept. of Business Educ., Sch. of Educ., New York Univ., New York 7, N. Y., since 1924.

Long, Clarence M., B.S.'31, Calif. State Tchrs. Col.; M.A.'34, D.Ed.'42, Univ. of Pittsburgh; Co. Supt. of Sch., Kittanning, Pa., since 1942.

Long, Oren E., M.A.'15, Univ. of Mich.; M.A. in Ed.'23, Columbia Univ.; Supt. of Pub. Instr., Honolulu, Hawaii, since 1934.

Longfellow, J. T., B.S.'15, Wash. State Col.; Supt. of Sch., Oregon City, Oregon, since 1933.

Longsdorf, A. J. B., Ph.B.'12, Wooster Col.; A.M.'21, Columbia Univ.; Supt. of Sch., Bluffton, Ohio, since 1925.

Longstreet, R. J., B.S.'16, LL.B.'17, Stetson Univ.; A.M.'32, Duke Univ.; Supvg. Prin. of Sch., Peninsula Sta., Daytona Beach, Fla., since 1920.

Loomis, Arthur K., A.B.'09, Baker Univ.; A.M.'17, Univ. of Kansas; Ph.D.'26, Tchrs. Col., Columbia Univ.; Supt. of Sch., Shaker Heights, Cleveland, Ohio, since 1936.

Loomis, G. F., A.B.'96, A.M.'01, Beloit Col.; Supt. of Sch., Kenosha, Wis., since 1921.

Loomis, Glenn E., A.B.'16, M.S.'25, Olivet Col.; M.A.'30, Univ. of Mich.; Supt. of Sch., Traverse City, Mich., since 1938.

Loomis, Harold V., A.B.'12, Syracuse Univ.; M.A.'26, Tchrs. Col., Columbia Univ.; Supt. of Sch., Ossining, N. Y., since 1932.

Loop, Omer Leslie, A.B.'14, Ind. Univ.; M.A.'27, Univ. of Wis.; Ph.D.'36, Univ. of Minn.; Dean of Men and Acting Dir. of Dem. Sch., State Tchrs. Col., Superior, Wis., since 1919.

Loos, Alfred J., A.B.'10, Grinnell Col.; Prin., Cumberland Sch., Dallas, Texas, since 1936.

Loper, John D., M.A.'15, Univ. of Ariz.; Supt. of Sch., Phoenix, Ariz., since 1909.

Lord, Charles E., A.B.'11, Bates Col.; Supt. of Sch., Camden, Maine, since 1923.

Loring, William R., B.Sc.'18, Mass. State Col.; A.M.'28, Tchrs. Col., Columbia Univ.; Union Supt. of Sch., Sheffield, Mass., since 1941.

Loser, Paul, Ph.B.'13, Muhlenberg Col.; M.A.'25, Tchrs. Col., Columbia Univ.; Litt.D.'41, Muhlenberg Col.; Supt. of Sch., 9 S. Stockton St., Trenton 9, N. J., since 1932.

Loveland, Gilbert, Gen. Editor, Henry Holt & Co., Inc., 257 Fourth Ave., New York, N. Y.

Lovell, V. P., M.S.'36, Ind. Univ.; Secy., Dept. of Educ., Lake Union Conference of Seventh-Day Adventists, Berrien Springs, Mich., since 1940.

Low, Edwin L., Dist. Supt., Alisal Union Sch. Dist., Salinas, Calif.

Lowe, Harold T., B.S.'17, Hobart Col.; M.S.A.'34, R. I. State Col. of Educ.; Litt.D.'36, Hobart Col.; Supt. of Sch., Newport, R. I., since 1931.

Lowe, Wayne L., A.B.'22, Pa. State Col.; Ed.M.'31, Harvard Univ.; Prin., Cazenovia Central Sch., Cazenovia, N. Y., since 1932.

Lowery, M. L., A.B.'08, Denison Univ.; A.M.'14, Columbia Univ.; Ph.D.'24, Univ. of Pa.; Co. Supt. of Sch., Co. Office Bldg., New Brunswick, N. J., since 1925.

*Lowrey, Harvey H., A.B.'17, Central State Tchrs. Col., Mt. Pleasant, Mich.; M.A.'21, Univ. of Mich.; Ph.D.'40, Univ. of Grand Rapids; Supt. of Fordson Schs., Dearborn, Mich., since 1922.

Lowry, Charles Doak, B.S.'08, A.M.'13, Northwestern Univ. Address: 628 Foster St., Evanston, Ill.

Lubbers, C. W., A.B.'25, Hope Col.; M.A. '39, Univ. of Mich.; Supt. of Sch., Plainwell, Mich., since 1941.

Lubbers, Irwin J., A.B.'17, Hope Col.; A.M.'27, Columbia Univ.; Ph.D.'31, Northwestern Univ.; Pres., Central Col., Pella, Iowa, since 1934.

Lubbers, Melvin B., A.B.'27, Hope Col.; M.A.'37, Univ. of Mich.; Supt. of Sch., Zeeland, Mich., since 1942.

Lucas, Homer C., A.B.'20, Ohio Wesleyan Univ.; Ginn & Co., 2315 Arlington Ave., Columbus, Ohio.

Lucia, Sister, B.A.'15, Creighton Univ.; M.A.'29, Notre Dame Univ.; Dean of Studies, Great Falls Col. of Educ., Great Falls, Mont., since 1933.

Ludy, Reginald S., B.A.'32, Coe Col.; M.A. '38, Univ. of Minn.; Dir. of Boarding Sch., Eklutna Voc. Sch., Eklutna, Alaska, since 1942.

Luehring, Frederick W., Ph.B.'05, North Central Col.; Ph.M.'06, Univ. of Chicago; Ph.D.'39, Columbia Univ.; Asst. Dean and Prof. of Physical Educ., Univ. of Pa., Philadelphia, Pa., since 1931.

Lull, Herbert G., A.B.'04, Univ. of Mich.; Ph.D.'12, Univ. of Calif.; Head, Dept. of Educ. and Dir. of Tchr. Tr., State Tchrs. Col., Emporia, Kansas, since 1916.

Lusk, Mrs. Georgia L., State Supt. of Pub. Instr., Santa Fe, N. Mex., since 1931.

Luther, E. W., Ph.B.'30, Ph.M.'35, Univ. of Wis.; Supt. of Sch., Plymouth, Wis., since 1940.

Luther, James F., Supt. of Sch., Delavan, Wis.

Lutz, Charles D., M.A.'32, Univ. of Chicago; Supt. of Sch., Gary, Ind., since 1941.

Lydell, Dwight M., Diploma '17, Chico State Tchrs. Col., Chico, Calif.; Supt. of Sch., Monrovia, Calif., since 1939.

Lyman, Warren B., Ph.B.'06, Yale Univ.; Supt. of Sch., Stoughton, Mass., since 1930.

Lynch, Clyde Alvin, A.B.'18, Lebanon Valley Col.; B.D.'21, Bonebrake Theol. Seminary; A.M.'25, D.D.'26, Lebanon Valley Col.; A.M.'29, Ph.D.'31, Univ. of Pa.; LL.D.'37, Albright Col.; Pres., Lebanon Valley Col., Annville, Pa., since 1932.

Lyon, Gilbert R., B.A.'17, Hamilton Col.; M.A.'28, Tchrs. Col., Columbia Univ.; Supt. of Sch., Norwich, N. Y., since 1938.

Mc

McAndrew, Mary B., B.A.'23, Marywood Col.; M.A.'36, Columbia Univ.; Supt. of Sch., Carbondale, Pa., since 1934.

McBee, Mary Vardrine, B.A.'06, Smith Col.; M.A.'08, Columbia Univ.; Litt.D.'32, Converse Col.; L.H.D.'36, Smith Col.; Litt.D. '37, Furman Univ.; Prin., Ashley Hall, Charleston, S. C., since 1909.

McBride, Guy T., Diploma '07, Southwest Texas State Tchrs. Col., San Marcos, Texas; Supt. of Sch., Boling, Texas, since 1929.

McBride, H. E., B.S.'22, Gettysburg Col.; M.A.'26, Univ. of Md.; Co. Supt. of Sch., Elkton, Md., since 1936.

McCall, H. R., A.M.'29, Univ. of Mo.; Supt. of Sch., Charlotte, Mich.

McCall, W. Morrison, A.B.'23, Westminster Col.; A.M.'26, Ph.D.'30, Univ. of Mo.; Dir., Div. of Instr., State Dept. of Educ., Montgomery 6, Ala., since 1937.

McCallum, Arthur N., B.A.'87, Davidson Col.; Supt. Emeritus of Sch., Austin, Texas, since 1943. Address: 613 W. 32nd, Austin, Texas.

McCarl, D. N., Vice Pres., American Tech. Society, Drexel Ave. at 58th St., Chicago 37, Ill., since 1927.

McCarroll, Emmet Fred, A.B., Otterbein Col.; M.A.'40, Univ. of Mich.; Supt. of Sch., Dennison, Ohio, since 1937.

McCauley, G. Kent, M.A.'32, Colo. State Tchrs. Col.; Supt. of Sch., Las Animas, Colo., since 1929.

McCleary, Mrs. Edith Bender, B.S.'27, Johns Hopkins Univ.; Vice-Prin., Southern H. S., Warren Ave. and William St., Baltimore 30, Md., since 1942.

McClenny, George L., State Supt. of Educ., Topeka, Kansas.

McCluer, F. L., A.B.'16, Westminster Col.; Ph.D.'28, Univ. of Chicago; Pres., Westminster Col., Fulton, Mo., since 1933.

McCluer, V. C., A.B.'18, Westminster Col.; A.M.'29, Washington Univ.; Supt. of Sch., Ferguson, Mo., since 1930.

McClure, Worth, A.B.'08, Simpson Col.; A.M.'20, Univ. of Wash.; LL.D.'32, Col. of Puget Sound; D.Ed.'38, Simpson Col.; D.Ed.'42, Columbia Univ.; Pres., American Assn. of Sch. Admin., 1943-44; Supt. of Sch., Seattle 9, Wash., since 1930.

McCombs, Newell D., A.B.'20, Simpson Col.; M.A.'27, State Univ. of Iowa; Supt. of Sch., Des Moines, Iowa, since 1941.

McComsey, G. Edward, B.S.'27, M.A.'33, Univ. of Pa.; Supt. of Sch., Millville, N. J., since 1938.

McConnell, W. Joseph, B.A.'15, M.A.'18, Univ. of Denver; Ph.D.'25, Columbia Univ.; Pres., North Texas State Tchrs. Col., Denton, Texas, since 1934.

McCook, T. Joseph, A.B.'31, Boston Col.; M.Ed.'34, Boston Univ.; Supt. of Sch., Marlborough, Mass., since 1942.

McCord, George M., B.Ph.'27, M.A.'36, Emory Univ.; Prin., J. C. Murphy Jr. H. S., 1425 Memorial Dr., S. E., Atlanta, Ga., since 1942.

McCormack, R. E., B.S.'21, Oregon State Agrl. Col.; Supt. of Sch., Albany, Oregon, since 1939.

McCormick, George A., A.B.'25, Muskingum Col.; M.Ed.'32, Univ. of Pittsburgh; Supt. of Sch., Beaver, Pa., since 1936.

McCormick, Harold W., Life Cert.'25, Mich. State Normal Col., Ypsilanti, Mich.; A.B. '30, Western Mich. Col.; M.A.'35, Ed.D. '41, Tchrs. Col., Columbia Univ.; Confidential Secy. to Member, Bd. of Educ., New York Pub. Sch., 110 Livingston St., Brooklyn 2, N. Y.

McCormick, L. B., B.S.'24, Mulligan Col.; M.A.'29, George Peabody Col. for Tchrs.; Supt. of Sch., Mullins, S. C., since 1928.

McCoy, John H., M.S. in Ed.'33, Univ. of Southern Calif.; Dir., Santa Ana Jr. Col., Santa Ana, Calif., since 1942.

McCoy, Melvin L., B.A.'18, William Jewell Col.; B.S.'24, Univ. of Mo.; M.A.'31, Tchrs. Col., Columbia Univ.; Supt. of Sch., Wayne, Mich., since 1943.

McCuistion, Ed. T., A.B.'17, Hendrix Col.; M.A.'22, George Peabody Col. for Tchrs.; State Dir. of Negro Schs., State Dept. of Educ., Little Rock, Ark., since 1938.

McCulley, Joseph, B.A., Univ. of Toronto; M.A., Oxford Univ.; Headmaster, Pickering Col., Newmarket, Ontario, Canada, since 1926.

McCullough, Ralph, Supt. of Sch., East Prairie, Mo.

McCully, Donald R., Co. Supt. of Pub. Instr., Kansas City, Kansas, since 1937.

McCunn, Drummond J., A.B.'27, Occidental Col.; M.A.'38, Univ. of Southern Calif.; Asst. Supt. of Sch., 320 E. Walnut St., Pasadena 4, Calif., since 1934.

McDaniel, Bernice, M.A.'29, Univ. of Texas; Supt. of Sch., Denison, Texas, since 1937.

McDermith, Clark Wright, A.B.'29, Ill. Col.; A.M.'34, Univ. of Ill.; Ed.D.'40, Tchrs. Col., Columbia Univ.; Supt. of Sch., Salem, Mass., since 1943.

McDermott, Irene E., B.S.'24, Bethany Col.; M.A.'31, Univ. of Pittsburgh; Sr. Supvr., Home Economics Dept., Bd. of Educ., Pittsburgh, Pa., since 1936.

McDonald, Alexander M., B.Pd.'08, Mich. State Normal Col., Ypsilanti, Mich.; LL.B.'13, Detroit Col. of Law; A.B.'15, M.A.'30, Univ. of Mich. Address: 1411 Coolidge Highway, River Rouge, Mich.

McDonald, Martina, LL.B.'27, Portia Law Sch.; A.B.'38, Calvin Coolidge Col.; State Supvr. of Pub. Sch. Music, State Educ. Bldg., Boston, Mass., since 1936.

McDougall, Richard E. C., A.B.'16, Greenville Col.; M.A.'25, Northwestern Univ.; Ph.D.'43, Ohio State Univ.; Supt. of Sch., Orrville, Ohio, since 1936.

McDowell, C. L., B.A.'21, M.A.'31, State Univ. of Iowa; Supt. of Sch., Eagle Grove, Iowa, since 1931.

McEachen, Howard D., A.B.'25, State Tchrs. Col., Wayne, Nebr.; A.M.'35, Univ. of Nebr.; Supt. of Sch., Pittsburg, Kansas, since 1941.

McElroy, Frank D., A.B.'06, Wabash Col.; A.M.'26, Western Reserve Univ.; Ph.D.'39, Ohio State Univ.; Pres., State Tchrs. Col., Mankato, Minn., since 1930.

McEwan, Lee J., M.A.'33, Columbia Univ.; Supt. of Sch., Binghamton, N. Y., since 1941.

McFarland, Kenneth W., B.S.'27, Kansas State Tchrs. Col.; M.S.'31, Columbia Univ.; Ed.D.'40, Stanford Univ.; Supt. of Sch., Topeka, Kansas, since 1942.

McGaughy, James Ralph, A.B.'12, Park Col.; M.A.'21, Ph.D.'24, Columbia Univ.; Prof. Emeritus of Educ., Tchrs. Col., Columbia Univ., New York, N. Y., since 1941. Address: Route 3, Mt. Gilead, Ohio.

McGee, R. R., A.B.'11, A.M.'15, Univ. of Nebr.; Supt. of Sch., Columbus, Nebr., since 1922.

McGehee, E. G., Jr., Dir., Div. of Negro Educ., State Dept. of Educ., Montgomery, Ala.

McGiboney, J. H., Diploma '15, Young Harris Col.; Co. Supt. of Sch., Carrollton, Ga., since 1937.

McGinnis, W. C., B.S., Univ. of Vt.; A.M., Ph.D., Columbia Univ.; Supt. of Sch., Perth Amboy, N. J., since 1930.

McGlade. Charles A., A,B.'25, M.A.'37, State Col. of Wash.; Supt. of Sch., Pullman, Wash., since 1929.

McGraw, Ernest E., B.S.'38, M.S.'39, Ind. Univ.; Supt. of Sch., Liberty, Ind., since 1943.

McGucken, William J., B.A.'09, Marquette Univ.; M.A.'17, St. Louis Univ.; Ph.D.'27, Univ. of Chicago; Dir., Dept. of Educ. and Regional Dir. of Studies in Col. and H. S. of Mo. Province, St. Louis Univ., St. Louis, Mo., since 1935.

McGuire, J. Carson, B.A.'39, Univ. of British Columbia; Supvg. Prin., Jr.-Sr. H. S., Chilliwack, B. C., Canada, since 1939.

McHale, Kathryn, B.S.'19, A.M.'20, Ph.D.'26, Columbia Univ.; Genl. Dir., American Assn. of Univ. Women, 1634 I St., N. W., Washington, D. C., since 1929.

McHenry, J. P., A.B.'29, W. Va. Univ.; M.Ed.'36, Univ. of Pittsburgh; Co. Supt. of Sch., Wheeling, W. Va., since 1935.

McIntosh, Daniel C., A.B.'13, A.M.'16, Ind. Univ.; B.S.'20, Iowa State Col.; Ph.D.'24, Ind. Univ.; Dean, Grad. Sch. and Prof. of Agrl. Educ., Okla. Agrl. and Mech. Col., Stillwater, Okla., since 1928.

McKay, N. H., M.A.'40, Univ. of Minn. Address: H. S., St. Louis Park, Minn.

McKee, W. Dean, B.A.'13, Monmouth Col.; M.A.'29, State Univ. of Iowa; Supt. of Sch., Shenandoah, Iowa, since 1930.

McKee, Walter T., Diploma '28, State Normal Sch., Florence, Ala.; B.S.'33, M.A.'36, Univ. of Ala.; Asst. Supt. of Sch., Montgomery 5, Ala., since 1942.

McKemy, H. M., M.S.'34, Univ. of Southern Calif.; Supt. of Sch., Tempe, Ariz., since 1934.

McKenney, H. L., B.S.'07, A.B. in Ed.'22, Valparaiso Univ.; A.M. in Ed.'31, Univ. of Cincinnati; Supt. of Sch., Auburn, Ind., since 1923.

McKibben, J. D., B.S.'28, Univ. of Chicago; M.S.'40, Univ. of Ill.; Supt. of Sch., Clinton, Ill., since 1940.

McKinley, F. R., Supt. of Sch., Farmington, N. Mex.

McKnight, W. W., Sr., McKnight and McKnight, Educ. Publishers, 109 W. Market St., Bloomington, Ill.

McKusick, Leon Roy, A.B.'11, Bates Col.; Supt. of Sch., Winsted, Conn., since 1928.

McLaughlin, Inez V., Life Cert. '11, State Normal Sch., Bellingham, Wash.; Co. Supt. of Sch., Port Angeles, Wash., since 1943.

McLaughlin, Sister Mary Aquinas, B.A.'17, Catholic Univ. of America; M.A.'22, Notre Dame Univ.; Ph.D.'30, State Univ. of Iowa; Dean, Briar Cliff Col., Sioux City, Iowa, since 1930.

McLaurin, W. H., B.S.'26, La. Polytech. Inst.; Parish Supt. of Sch., Jonesboro, La., since 1933.

McLean, William, Diploma '13, State Normal Sch., Montclair, N. J.; B.S.'24, M.A. '27, Columbia Univ.; Prin., Mt. Hebron Sch., Upper Montclair, N. J., since 1922.

McLeary, Ralph D., B.S.'24, M.A.'30, Colby Col.; Supt. of Sch., Barrington, R. I., since 1942.

McLeod, Egbert Chappelle, A.B.'17, Claflin Col.; B.D.'20, Gammon Theol. Sem.; S.T.B.'27, M.A.'31, Boston Univ.; LL.D. '43, Claflin Univ.; D.D.'43, Gammon Theol. Sem.; Pres., Wiley Col., Marshall, Texas, since 1942.

McLure, John Rankin, B.S.'11, Univ. of Ala.; M.A.'14, Ph.D.'25, Columbia Univ.; LL.D.'30, Univ. of Ala.; Dean, Col. of Educ., Univ. of Ala., University, Ala., since 1942.

McMichael, R. L., Jr., 441 W. Peachtree St., N. E., Atlanta, Ga.

McMillan, J. C., A.M.'26, Univ. of Chicago; Pres., State Normal and Indus. Sch., Ellendale, N. Dak., since 1936.

McMindes, Maude, Dir. of Sec. Educ., Fort Hays Kansas State Col., Hays, Kansas.

McMonagle, Edward L., A.B.'32, Holy Cross Col.; Supt. of Sch., Madawaska, Maine, since 1939.

McMullen, J. Willard, A.B.'21, Univ. of Del.; M.A.'35, Univ. of Pa.; Supvg. Prin. of Sch., Oxford, Pa., since 1923.

McNary, C. W., A.B.'10, Westminster Col., New Wilmington, Pa.; M.Ed.'37, Univ. of Pittsburgh; Asst. Supt. of Sch., Erie, Pa., since 1939.

McNeel, J. H., B.A.'00, Univ. of Wis.; Prin., H. S., Beloit, Wis., since 1913.

McNickle, T. R., M.A.'34, Univ. of Nebr.; Supt. of Sch., York, Nebr., since 1942.

McNitt, Ernest B., M.Ed.'41, Univ. of Pittsburgh; Supt. of Sch., New Brighton, Pa., since 1943.

McNutt, Franklin H., A.B.'16, A.M.'18, Wittenberg Col.; Ph.D.'32, Ohio State Univ. Address: Women's Col., Univ. of N. C., Greensboro, N. C.

McPherson, Harry M., A.B.'30, M.A.'32, Ed.D.'39, Univ. of Calif.; Dist. Supt., Napa Union H. S., Napa, Calif., since 1940.

McQuilkin, D. E., A.B.'05, A.M.'06, W. Va. Univ.; A.M.'08, Harvard Univ.; Supt. of Sch., Roanoke, Va., since 1918.

McSwain, E. T., A.B.'19, Newberry Col.; M.A.'28, Ed.D.'35, Tchrs. Col., Columbia Univ.; Assoc. Prof. of Educ., Northwestern Univ., Evanston, Ill., since 1935.

McVey, William E., B.S. in Ed.'16, Ohio Univ.; A.M.'19, Univ. of Chicago; Supt., Thornton Twp. H. S. and Jr. Col., Harvey, Ill., since 1919.

M

Mabie, Vern E., A.B.'30, Western State Tchrs. Col., Kalamazoo, Mich.; A.M.'33, Univ. of Mich.; Supt. of Sch., Greenville, Mich., since 1935.

MacArthur, Chase, B.S.'09, Univ. of Maine; M.Ed.'29, Harvard Univ.; Supt. of Sch., Foxboro, Mass., since 1931.

MacCalman, Kenneth R., A.B.'21, Elon Col.; M.A.'29, Tchrs. Col., Columbia Univ.; Supt. of Sch., Nyack, N. Y., since 1931.

MacCorkindale, Hugh N., B.A.'13, Univ. of Toronto; Supt. of Sch., 590 Hamilton St., Vancouver, Canada, since 1933.

Mackenzie, Harold, A.B.'09, Wheaton Col.; A.M.'22, Univ. of Chicago; Supt. of Sch., Savanna, Ill., since 1940.

Mackey, A. B., A.B.'25, Eastern Ky. State Tchrs. Col., Richmond, Ky.; M.A.'26, George Peabody Col. for Tchrs.; LL.D.'41, Northwest Nazarene Col.; Pres., Trevecca Nazarene Col., Nashville 10, Tenn., since 1936.

Mackintosh, Helen K., Ph.D.'31, State Univ. of Iowa; Sr. Specialist in Elem. Educ., U. S. Office of Educ., Washington 25, D. C., since 1938.

MacLaughlin, Marlin V., A.B.'27, Univ. of Maine; Supt. of Sch., Berlin, Conn., since 1941.

MacLean, William P., M.A.'27, Univ. of Chicago; Supt., J. Sterling Morton Schs., Cicero, Ill., since 1939.

MacQuarrie, Archibald E., LL.B.'16, Univ. of Wis.; Prin., Washburn H. S., Wentworth Ave. and W. 49th St., Minneapolis, Minn., since 1924.

MacQuiddy, T. S., B.S.'03, Univ. of Calif.; Dist. Supt. of Sch., Watsonville, Calif., since 1907.

Maddox, John J., A.B.'07, Yale Univ.; M.A.'12, Columbia Univ.; Asst. Supt. of Instr., St. Louis 1, Mo., since 1941.

Maddy, Joseph E., Mus.D.'30, Cincinnati Conservatory of Music; Pres., Natl. Music Camp and Prof. of Radio Music Instr., Univ. of Mich., Ann Arbor, Mich., since 1924.

Madeleine of Jesus, Sister Marie, B.A.'22, M.A.'27, Ph.D.'31, Catholic Univ. of America; Pres. and Dean, Rivier Col., 429 Main, Nashua, N. H., since 1933.

Maier, John V., A.B.'20, A.M.'29, Ed.D.'40, Ind. Univ.; Prin., Wilson Jr. H. S., Muncie, Ind., since 1934.

Malcolm, David J., S.B.'13, Harvard Col.; Supt., North Berkshire Union Sch., since 1930. Address: Charlemont, Mass.

Maline, Rev. Julian L., A.B.'20, A.M.'21, Gonzaga Univ., Spokane, Wash.; Ph.D. '34, Ohio State Univ.; Regional Dir. of Educ., Chicago Province, Jesuit Educ. Assn., West Baden Col., West Baden Springs, Ind., since 1934.

Malloch, James Morrow, A.B.'17, M.A.'20, Univ. of Calif.; G.Th.'33, Church Divinity Sch. of the Pacific; D.D.'43, Col. of the Pacific; Dean, St. James' Cathedral, since 1937 and Mem., Bd. of Educ., Fresno, Calif., since 1941.

Malmquist, M. L., B.A.'23, Gustavus Adolphus Col.; Supt. of Sch., Buhl, Minn., since 1937.

Mann, Albert Z., A.B.'09, De Pauw Univ.; M.A.'11, Univ. of Chicago; Dean, Springfield Col., Springfield, Mass., since 1935.

Mann, J. A., A.B.'28, Evansville Col.; A.M.'34, Univ. of Ill.; Supt. of Sch., Shelbyville, Ill., since 1936.

Mann, John P., B.A.'22, Ripon Col.; M.A.'27, Univ. of Wis.; Supt. of Sch., South Milwaukee, Wis., since 1934.

Mann, Lloyd B., B.A.'09, Hanover Col.; A.M.'33, Ind. Univ.; Supt. of Sch., Beech Grove, Ind., since 1925.

Mann, Sue B., B.A.'22, Texas Wesleyan Col.; M.A.'25, Southern Methodist Univ.; Deputy State Supt. of Educ., Ft. Worth, Texas, since 1941.

Manning, C. G., A.B.'07, Morningside Col.; Supt. of Sch., Lewistown, Mont., since 1920.

Mansur, Frank L., A.B.'10, Brown Univ.; Supt. of Sch., Swampscott, Mass., since 1931.

Manwiller, Charles E., M.A.'27, Ph.D.'34, Univ. of Pittsburgh; Dir. of Research, Pub. Sch., Admin. Bldg., Pittsburgh 13, Pa., since 1940.

Marble, Sarah A., A.B.'12, Smith Col.; Kdgn. Primary Diploma '14, State Normal Sch., Worcester, Mass.; A.M.'24, Tchrs. Col., Columbia Univ.; Primary Supvr., Pub. Sch., Worcester, Mass., since 1937.

Marie, Sister Catharine, A.M.'20, Fordham Univ.; Dean, Col. of Mt. St. Vincent, New York, N. Y., since 1937.

Markman, Frank H., A.B.'11, McKendree Col.; M.A.'28, Univ. of Colo.; Prin., Jersey Twp. H. S., Jerseyville, Ill., since 1921.

Marks, Sallie B., A.B.'23, Southwestern State Tchrs. Col., Weatherford, Okla.; M.A.'25, Tchrs. Col., Columbia Univ. Address: Dept. of Educ., Univ. of Chicago, Chicago, Ill.

Marsh, Daniel L., A.B.'06, A.M.'07, Northwestern Univ.; S.T.B.'08, Boston Univ.; D.D.'13, Grove City Col.; LL.D.'26, Univ. of Pittsburgh; Litt.D.'27, Northwestern Univ.; L.H.D.'29, Cornell Col.; Ph.D.'31, Univ. of Bologna, Italy; Sc.D. in Ed.'34, Iowa Wesleyan Col.; J.U.D.'36, Ill. Wesleyan Univ.; D.C.L.'37, Ohio Northern Univ.; LL.D.'38, Simpson Col.; Litt.D.'39, Portia Law Sch.; LL.D.'41, Univ. of Southern Calif.; N.Ph.D.'41, Nebr. Wesleyan Univ.; LL.D.'43, Dickinson Col.; Pres., Boston Univ., 688 Boylston St., Boston, Mass., since 1926.

Marsh, J. Frank, A.B.'07, A.M.'12, W. Va. Univ.; D.Ped.'26, W. Va. Wesleyan Col.; Pres., Concord Col., Athens, W. Va., since 1929.

Marshall, Farnsworth G., A.B.'03, Bowdoin Col.; Supt. of Sch., Malden, Mass., since 1913.

Marshall, George H., M.A.'29, Univ. of Kansas; Supt. of Sch., Ottawa, Kansas, since 1932.

Marshall, H. A., Supt. of Sch., McColl, S. C.

*Marshall, Robert, B.A.'32, Univ. of Texas; B.S.'34, Agrl. and Indus. Col. of Texas; M.A.'39, Univ. of Texas; Supt. of Sch., Beeville, Texas, since 1935.

Martin, Cecil W., A.B.'25, Ill. Col.; M.S.'31, Univ. of Ill.; Ed.D.'42, Tchrs. Col., Columbia Univ.; Supt. of Sch., Peru, Ill., since 1936.

Martin, Charles L., A.B., Howard Col.; Supt. of Sch., Andalusia, Ala., since 1929.

Martin, Charles William, Ph.D.'30, Univ. of Mo.; Prof. of Educ., Northeast Mo. State Tchrs. Col., Kirksville, Mo., since 1930.

Martin, Mrs. Chester, Supt. of Sch., Opelika, Ala., since 1943.

Martin, Edwin D., A.B.'23, Abilene Christian Col.; M.S.'27, Texas Agrl. and Mech. Col.; Ed.D.'41, Colo. State Col. of Educ.; Capt., U. S. Army, U. S. Armed Forces Institute, Madison, Wis.

Martin, Frederick F., Diploma '07, Central State Tchrs. Col., Edmond, Okla.; B.Pd. '08, Southwest State Tchrs. Col., Springfield, Mo.; B.S.'08, Drury Col., Springfield, Mo.; M.A.'11, Yale Univ.; Supt. of Sch., Chico, Calif., since 1938.

Martin, G. B., M.A.'40, Univ. of Mich.; Supt. of Sch., Caro, Mich., since 1942.

Martin, H. Clay, B.S.'17, A.M.'20, Univ. of Pa. Address: 301 Chews Landing Rd., Haddonfield, N. J.

Martin, H. G., B.S.'08, Univ. of Mo.; Dir., Isaac Delgado Central Trades Sch., 615 City Park Ave., New Orleans, La., since 1920.

Martin, J. A., B.S.'18, Pa. State Col.; M.A. '36, Tchrs. Col., Columbia Univ.; Supvg. Prin. of Sch., Trucksville, Pa., since 1932.

Martin, James Edward, A.B.'12, M.A.'14, Mt. St. Mary's Col.; Supt. of Sch., Central Falls, R. I., since 1930.

Martin, Leland L., B.S.'34, M.E.'39, Texas Tech. Col.; Supt. of Sch., Crane, Texas, since 1940.

Martin, William H., A.B.'09, Bates Col.; M.A.'20, Ph.D.'27, Yale Univ.; Supt. of Sch., Mt. Vernon, N. Y., since 1941.

Marzeciak, Peter, Member, Bd. of Educ., 12001 St. Aubin Ave., Hamtramck, Mich., since 1935.

Mason, Charles C., A.B.'25, Central Wesleyan Col.; A.M.'28, Wash. Univ.; D.Ed. '41, Colo. State Col. of Educ., Greeley, Colo.; Asst. Supt. of Sch., 410 S. Cincinnati, Tulsa, Okla., since 1935.

Mason, Howard F., B.A.'31, Dartmouth Col.; M.Ed.'39, Univ. of N. H.; Union Supt. of Sch., Hillsboro, N. H., since 1942.

Mason, Jesse H., B.A.'15, Ohio Wesleyan Univ.; M.A.'28, Tchrs. Col., Columbia Univ.; D.Ed.'37, Ohio Wesleyan Univ.; Supt. of Sch., Canton, Ohio, since 1928.

Massey, Guy B., Supt. of Sch., Broken Bow, Okla., since 1931.

Matheson, Erroll J., Dist. Supt. of Sch., Springfield, Minn.

Matheson, Martin, Vice-Pres., John Wiley & Sons, Inc., 440 Fourth Ave., New York 16, N. Y.

Matthews, W. E., B.S. in Ed.'26, Central Mo. State Tchrs. Col., Warrensburg, Mo.; M.A. in Ed.'34, Univ. of Mo.; Supt. of Sch., Independence, Mo., since 1938.

Mattox, Clifford, A.B.'25, Univ. of Wash.; M.S.'40, Stanford Univ.; Supvg. Prin. of Sch., Rialto, Calif., since 1939.

Matzen, John M., A.B.'27, A.M.'28, Tchrs. Col., Univ. of Nebr.; A.M.'29, Ph.D.'31, Tchrs. Col., Columbia Univ.; Asst. Prof. of Sch. Admin., Tchrs. Col., Univ. of Nebr., Lincoln, Nebr., since 1931.

Maurer, Harold R., B.S.'24, Col. of Wooster; M.A.'31, Ohio State Univ.; Supt. of Sch., Garfield Hgts., Cleveland, Ohio, since 1932.

Maurice, E. D., A.B.'21, Wittenberg Col.; M.A.'38, Ohio State Univ.; Supt. of Sch., Ashtabula, Ohio, since 1940.

MaWhinney, William T., A.B.'10, Beloit Col.; M.A.'26, Columbia Univ.; Registrar and Office Mgr., General Motors Inst., Flint 2, Mich., since 1927.

Maxwell, Charles F., A.B.'09, Lafayette Col.; A.M.'34, Univ. of Pittsburgh; Co. Supt. of Sch., Greensburg, Pa., since 1930.

Maxwell, G. L., A.B.'17, M.A.'25, Univ. of Calif.; Asst. Secy., Educ. Policies Commn., 1201 16th St., N. W., Washington 6, D. C., since 1939.

Maxwell, J. S., Supt. of Sch., Warrensburg, Mo.

Maxwell, Walter, Exec. Secy., Ariz. Educ. Assn., Security Bldg., Phoenix, Ariz., since 1942.

May, Albert L., B.S.'23, M.A.'33, Peabody Col.; Pres., Perkinston Jr. Col., Perkinston, Miss.

May, Walter M., A.B.'05, A.M.'24, Dartmouth Col.; Deputy State Commr. of Educ., Concord, N. H., since 1919.

Mayberry, Lawrence W., A.B.'01, Univ. of Kansas; A.B. and A.M.'18, Columbia Univ.; D.Ed.'28, Municipal Univ. of Wichita. Address: 1014 Shady Way, Wichita, Kansas.

Mayer, Lewis F., B.A.'20, Col. of Wooster; M.A.'30, Ohio State Univ.; Supt., Fairview Pub. Schs., 4507 W. 213th St., Cleveland, Ohio, since 1921.

Maynard, Milton M., A.B.'08, Univ. of Okla.; M.A.'20, Univ. of Ill.; Prof. of Educ., Monmouth Col., Monmouth, Ill., since 1909.

Meade, John D., Supt. of Sch., Petersburg, Va.

Meade, Mary E., A.B.'18, Hunter Col.; A.M.'26, Columbia Univ.; Ph.D.'35, Fordham Univ. Address: 29 Occident Ave., Staten Island 4, New York, N. Y.

Meadows, A. R., B.S.'26, M.A.'32, Univ. of Ala.; Ph.D.'40, Tchrs. Col., Columbia Univ.; Supvr. of Research and Surveys, State Dept. of Educ., Montgomery 4, Ala., since 1929.

Means, Herbert G., M.E.'02, State Tchrs. Col., Slippery Rock, Pa.; Ph.B.'13, Grove City Col.; M.A.'26, Univ. of Pittsburgh; Ed.D.'40, Geneva Col. Address: Highland Colony, East Liverpool, Ohio.

Mehus, O. Myking, B.A.'16, Augsburg Col.; M.A.'20, Ph.D.'31, Univ. of N. Dak.; Pres., Winona State Tchrs. Col., Winona, Minn., since 1939.

Meisberger, D. T., A.B.'30, Susquehanna Univ.; M.A.'35, Bucknell Univ.; Supt. of Twp. Sch., Shamokin, Pa., since 1940.

Melby, Ernest O., M.A.'26, Ph.D.'28, Univ. of Minn.; Pres., Mont. State Univ., Missoula, Mont., since 1941.

Melcher, George, B.S.'89, M.S.'92, Odessa Col.; A.B.'98, Drury Col.; A.M.'19, Tchrs. Col., Columbia Univ.; LL.D.'23, Mo. Valley Col.; LL.D.'25, Drury Col.; Supt. of Sch., 201 W. 51st St., Kansas City, Mo., 1928-40. Supt. Emeritus, since 1940.

Melchior, D. Montfort, A.B.'02, A.M.'04, Gettysburg Col.; Pd.D.'33, Bucknell Univ.; Supvr. of H. S. Instr., Girard Col., Philadelphia, Pa., since 1928.

Melchior, William T., Ph.D.'23, Columbia Univ.; Prof. of Educ. Supvn. of Instr., Syracuse Univ., Syracuse, N. Y., since 1926.

Mellado, Ramón, B.S.'27, Univ. of Puerto Rico; M.A.'40, Columbia Univ.; Asst. Commr. of Educ., San Juan, P. R., since 1941.

Mellon, E. H., B.S.'23, Ill. Col.; M.S.'32, Univ. of Ill.; Ed.D.'42, Colo. State Col. of Educ.; Supt. of Sch., Champaign, Ill., since 1943.

Mellown, Elgin W., B.S.'25, Birmingham-Southern Col.; M.A.'28, Univ. of Ala.; Co. Supt. of Educ., Livingston, Ala., since 1939.

Melton, Monroe, Diploma '12, Ind. State Tchrs. Col., Terre Haute, Ind.; A.B.'15, Ind. Univ.; A.M.'33, Univ. of Colo.; Supt. of Sch., Normal, Ill., since 1925.

Mendel, Augusta, B.S.'34, New York Univ.; Prin., Sheridan Sch., Bridgeport, Conn.

Mendenhall, Clare, B.A.'32, Univ. of Wash.; M.A.'38, Tchrs. Col., Columbia Univ.; Co. Supt. of Sch., Kelso, Wash., since 1940.

Mendenhall, James E., B.S.'24, Kansas State Tchrs. Col., Pittsburg, Kansas; M.A.'25, Ph.D.'30, Tchrs. Col., Columbia Univ. Address: 5 W. Saul Rd., Kensington, Md.

Mensenkamp, Louis E., A.B.'16, A.M.'22, Univ. of Ill.; Prin., Freeport H. S., Freeport, Ill., since 1940.

Merchant, Claude J., B.S. in Ed. and M.A. '22, Syracuse Univ.; M.A.'23, Tchrs. Col., Columbia Univ.; Ed.D.'37, Rutgers Univ.; Dir. of Educ., N. J State Home for Boys, Jamesburg, N. J., since 1924.

Merideth, George H., B.S.'24, Central Mo. State Tchrs. Col., Warrensburg, Mo.; M.A.'25, Tchrs. Col., Columbia Univ.; Ed.D.'38, Univ. of Southern Calif.; Deputy Supt. of Sch., Pasadena 4, Calif., since 1928.

Merriam, Burr J., Diploma '98, State Normal Sch., Oneonta, N. Y.; B.S.'16, Columbia Univ.; Ed.M.'27, Harvard Univ.; Supt. of Sch., Framingham, Mass., since 1922.

Merrill, Albert W., A.B.'90, Grinnell Col.; M.A.'29, Tchrs. Col., Columbia Univ.; LL.D.'37, Drake Univ.; Ed.D.'40, Grinnell Col.; Acting Supt. of Sch., Dubuque, Iowa, since 1942.

Merrill, George A., A.B.'10, Colgate Univ.; M.A.'14, Columbia Univ.; Supt. of Sch., Hackensack, N. J., since 1937.

Messner, J. C., A.B.'16, Franklin and Marshall Col.; B.D.'19, Eastern Theological Seminary of the Reformed Church in the U. S.; M.A.'24, Columbia Univ.; Supt. of Sch., Harrington, Del., since 1926.

Metcalfe, Tristram Walker, Dean, Col. of Arts and Sciences since 1933 and Pres., Long Island Univ., 300 Pearl St., Brooklyn, N. Y., since 1942.

Metz, Robert C., Diploma '10, State Normal Sch., Bloomsburg, Pa.; M.A.'27, Susquehanna Univ.; M.S.'37, Univ. of Pa.; Supt. of Sch., Ashley, Pa., since 1934.

Meyer, William W., Ph.B.'24, A.M.'32, Univ. of Chicago; Supt. of Sch., Harvard, Ill., since 1926.

Micheals, William H., A.B.'07, Dickinson Col.; A.M.'24, Univ. of Pa.; Supt. of Sch., Media, Pa., since 1920.

Michell, Forrest C., Prin., Lakeview Sch., Oakland, Calif.

Michie, James K., M.A.'36, Univ. of Minn.; Supt. of Sch., Little Falls, Minn., since 1937.

Mickelson, Peter P., A.B.'35, State Tchrs. Col., Mayville, N. Dak.; M.A.'39, Ph.D.'41, Univ. of Colo.; Pres., Trinidad State Jr. Col., Trinidad, Colo., since 1941.

Milam, Carl H., A.B.'07, Univ. of Okla.; LL.D.'34, Southwestern Col.; LL.D.'35, Lawrence Col.; Exec. Secy., American Library Assn., 520 N. Michigan Ave., Chicago, Ill., since 1920.

Miller, Alexander W., A.B.'12, Harvard Univ.; A.M.'22, Columbia Univ.; Supt. of Sch., Glens Falls, N. Y., since 1927.

Miller, C. T., Bus. Mgr., Pub. Sch., 319 W. Barnard St., West Chester, Pa., since 1923.

Miller, Charles A., A.B.'23, Franklin and Marshall Col.; Ed.M.'24, Harvard Univ.; Dist. Supt. of Sch., Lee, Mass., since 1926.

Miller, Charles S., A.B.'13, Allegheny Col.; A.M.'15, Univ. of Pittsburgh; Ph.D.'31, New York Univ. Address: Allegheny Col., Meadville, Pa.

Miller, Chester F., A.B.'07, A.M.'09, McKendree Col.; A.M.'18, Tchrs. Col., Columbia Univ.; Litt.D.'28, McKendree Col.; LL.D. '37, Alma Col.; Supt. of Sch., Saginaw, Mich., since 1928.

Miller, Earl G., M.A.'32, Univ. of Minn.; Supt. of Sch., La Salle, Ill., since 1939.

Miller, Elmer G., B.C.Sc.'15, Bowling Green Business Univ.; M.C.Sc.'18, Capitol Col. of Commerce; D.C.Sc.'27, Duquesne Univ.; Dir. of Commercial Educ. and Handwriting, Pub. Sch., Pittsburgh 17, Pa., since 1912.

Miller, Ernest E., A.B.'17, Goshen Col.; M.A.'29, Ph.D.'39, New York Univ.; Pres., Goshen Col., Goshen, Ind., since 1940.

Miller Franklin A., Supvg. Prin. of Twp. Sch., Geistown, Pa.

Miller, Fred B., B.S.'27, Central Mo. State Tchrs. Col., Warrensburg, Mo.; M.A.'29, St. Louis Univ.; Supt. of Normandy Consolidated Sch. Dist., 6701 Easton Ave., St. Louis, Mo., since 1913.

Miller, George R., Jr., A.B.'15, Lafayette Col.; A.M.'22, Columbia Univ.; Supt. of Sch., Smyrna, Del., since 1937.

Miller, Harry W., B.S.'25, Mich. State Normal Col., Ypsilanti, Mich.; M.A.'33, Univ. of Detroit; Supt. of Sch., Center Line, Mich., since 1926.

Miller, Helen Rose, A.B. in Ed.'24, M.A.'30, Univ. of Mich.; Dir. of Exact Science, Pulaski Sch., Hamtramck, Mich., since 1925.

Miller, John L., A.B.'26, Bates Col.; Ed.M. '29, Harvard Univ.; Supt. of Sch., Great Neck, N. Y., since 1942.

Miller, Norman, S.B.'25, Ed.M.'28, Harvard Univ.; Supt. of Sch., Tyrone, Pa., since 1939.

Miller, Thomas R., Dir. of Off-Campus Tchg., State Tchrs. Col., Potsdam, N. Y.

Miller, Van, A.B.'29, Hastings Col.; M.A. '35, Univ. of Nebr.; D.Ed.'41, Harvard Univ.; Supt. of Sch., Ridgefield, Conn., since 1943.

Miller, W. W., A.B.'22, Goshen Col.; M.A. '28, Ph.D.'39, Ohio State Univ.; Asst. Supt. of Sch., 270 E. State St., Columbus, Ohio, since 1936.

Miller, Ward I., A.B.'14, A.M.'15, Univ. of Denver; Ed.D.'41, Tchrs. Col., Columbia Univ.; Supt. of Eastchester Pub. Sch., Tuckahoe, N. Y., since 1941.

Miller, William P., Co. Supt. of Sch., 2324 Adams Ave., Ogden, Utah.

Millikan, Ben S., A.B.'10, M.A.'12, Baker Univ.; Dist. Supt. of Sch., Covina, Calif., since 1918.

Milliken, Mrs. Gertrude Cornish, B.S.'01, M.A.'27, Middlebury Col.; Prin., House in the Pines, Norton, Mass., since 1911.

Milling, C. L., B.S.'26, Miss. Southern Col.; M.A.'38, George Peabody Col. for Tchrs.; Supt. of Sch., Ruleville, Miss., since 1938.

Millmann, Anna, Diploma '07, State Normal Sch., Milwaukee, Wis.; LL.B.'23, Ph.B.'27, M.E.'41, Marquette Univ.; Prin., Luther Burbank Sch., 6035 W. Adler St., Milwaukee 13, Wis., since 1929.

Mills, DeWitt T., A.B.'17, Otterbein Col.; Diploma '19, Univ. of Grenoble, France; M.A.'38, Ohio State Univ.; Co. Supt. of Sch., Marion, Ohio, since 1931.

Mills, H. L., Diploma '11, Sam Houston State Tchrs. Col., Huntsville, Texas; LL.B.'15, Houston Law Sch.; LL.D.'31, Southwestern Univ.; Bus. Mgr., Independent Sch. Dist., 1600 Washington Ave., Houston, Texas, since 1922.

Milne, John, B.S.'29, Univ. of N. Mex.; M.A.'31, Tchrs. Col., Columbia Univ.; Supt. of Sch., Albuquerque, N. Mex., since 1911.

Minear, Craig P., A.B.'23, Iowa Wesleyan Col.; M.A.'30, State Univ. of Iowa; Exec. Secy., Colo. Educ. Assn., Denver, Colo., since 1944.

Miner, S. Donald, A.B.'20, Middlebury Col.; M.A.'39, Univ. of Vt.; Dist. Supt. of Sch., Orwell, Vt., since 1930.

Misner, Paul J., A.B.'26, Mich. State Normal Col., Ypsilanti, Mich.; A.M.'27, Ph.D. '35, Univ. of Mich.; Supt. of Sch., Glencoe, Ill., since 1935.

Mitchell, A. J., M.A.'36, Univ. of Colo.; Supt. of Sch., Nogales, Ariz., since 1928.

Mitchell, Charles A., A.B.'21, Colby Col.; Ed.M.'25, Harvard Univ.; Supt. of Sch., Easthampton, Mass., since 1940.

Mitchell, Claude, A.B.'12, Susquehanna Univ.; A.M.'25, Ph.D.'31, Univ. of Pittsburgh; Supt. of Sch., West Newton, Pa., since 1918.

Mitchell, David R., A.B.'11, Brigham Young Univ.; Supt. of Sch., American Fork, Utah, since 1938.

Mitchell, S. C., Supt. of Sch., Benton Harbor, Mich., since 1923.

Mitchell, William D., M.A.'38, Univ. of Mo.; Co. Supt. of Sch., Quincy, Ill., since 1935.

Mock, Thomas M., M.S.'32, Univ. of Southern Calif.; Prin., Horace Mann Sch., Beverly Hills, Calif., since 1929.

Moe, George A., Diploma '27, State Tchrs. Col., Moorhead, Minn.; B.S.'35, M.A.'39, Univ. of Minn.; Supt. of Sch., Gilbert, Minn., since 1940.

Moe, Martin P., B.S.'27, Univ. of Minn.; Exec. Secy., Mont. Educ. Assn., Helena, Mont., since 1933.

Moehlman, Arthur B., A.B.'12, A.M.'21, Ph.D.'23, Univ. of Mich.; Prof. of Admin. and Supvr., Sch. of Educ., Univ. of Mich., Ann Arbor, Mich., since 1923 and Editor, The Nation's Schools, since 1932.

Moffett, F. L., B.S.'24, Sam Houston State Tchrs. Col., Huntsville, Texas; M.S.'29, Texas Agrl. and Mech. Col.; Supt. of Sch., Center, Texas, since 1926.

Moffitt, J. C., B.S.'26, M.S.'29, Brigham Young Univ.; Ph.D.'40, Univ. of Chicago; Supt. of Sch., Provo, Utah, since 1937.

Moffitt, Laurence C., B.S.'40, Univ. of Oregon; Co. Supt. of Sch., Eugene, Oregon, since 1932.

Mohr, Lloyd C., B.S.'16, Adrian Col.; M.A. '22, Tchrs. Col., Columbia Univ.; Supt. of Sch., South Haven, Mich., since 1920.

Moll, Richard M., Diploma '05, State Normal Sch., Kutztown, Pa.; A.B.'15, Lebanon Valley Col.; A.M.'25, Univ. of Pa.; Asst. Co. Supt. of Sch., 313 W. Penn Ave., Robesonia, Pa., since 1928.

Monahan, Catherine E., B.S.'31, M.A.'35, Tchrs. Col., Columbia Univ.; Supvr. of Elem. Sch., 20 Summer St., Providence, R. I., since 1927.

Monroe, A. L., M.A.'31, George Peabody Col. for Tchrs.; Supt. of Sch., Moss Point, Miss., since 1929.

Monroe, Frank, Acting Supt. of Sch., Midland, Texas.

Monroe, P. E., A.M.'98, N. C. Col.; D.D.'19, Newberry Col.; Pres., Lenoir-Rhyne Col., Hickory, N. C., since 1934.

Monroe, Walter S., A.B.'05, B.S.'07, A.M.'11, Univ. of Mo.; Ph.D.'15, Univ. of Chicago; Dir., Bureau of Educ. Research, Univ. of Ill., Urbana, Ill., since 1921.

Montel, Kenneth F., Supt. of Sch., Sugar City, Colo.

Montgomery, E. W., A.B.'09, A.M.'13, Ind. Univ.; Supt., Phoenix Union H. S. and Jr. Col., 512 E. Van Buren St., Phoenix, Ariz., since 1925.

Moon, F. D., B.S.'29, Langston Univ.; M.A.'38, Univ. of Chicago; Prin., Douglass Jr.-Sr. H. S., Oklahoma City 4, Okla., since 1940.

Moore, C. H., A.M.'17, George Peabody Col. for Tchrs.; Supt. of Sch., Clarksville, Tenn., since 1927.

Moore, Mrs. Clara, A.B.'32, State Tchrs. Col., San Francisco, Calif.; Prin., Bret Harte Sch., San Francisco 24, Calif., since 1943.

Moore, Clyde B., A.B.'12, Nebr. Wesleyan Univ.; B.Ed.'13, Nebr. State Tchrs. Col., Peru, Nebr.; A.M.'16, Clark Univ.; Ph.D. '24, Columbia Univ.; Prof. of Educ., Stone Hall, Cornell Univ., Ithaca, N. Y., since 1925.

Moore, Harold E., A.B.'24, Ind. State Tchrs. Col., Terre Haute, Ind.; A.M.'29, Ind. Univ.; Dir., Bureau of Tchr. Recommendations, since 1936 and Prin., Univ. Sch., Ind. Univ., Bloomington, Ind., since 1943.

Moore, Harry E., A.B.'22, Central State Col., Edmond, Okla.; M.Ed.'34, Univ. of Okla.; Dist. Supt. of Sch., Garvey, Calif., since 1939.

Moore, Harry L., A.B.'01, Bates Col.; Supt. of Sch., Portsmouth, N. H., since 1925.

Moore, Harry W., Ph.B.'13, M.A.'30, Lafayette Col.; Co. Supt. of Sch., Flemington, N. J., since 1928.

Moore, Hollis Andrew, B.S. in Ed.'27, Southwest Mo. State Tchrs. Col., Springfield, Mo.; M.A.'32, Univ. of Mo.; Supt. of Sch., Kerrville, Texas, since 1935.

Moore, J. Layton, A.B.'23, Wesleyan Univ.; Supvg. Prin. of Sch., Ridley Park, Pa., since 1926.

Moore, Mrs. Jere M., Diploma '99, Ga. State Col. for Women; Co. Supt. of Sch., Oglethorpe, Ga., since 1936.

Moore, John W., B.S.'00, The Citadel; A.M.'13, Col. of Charleston; Supt. of Sch., Florence, S. C., since 1923.

Moore, John Watson, A.B.'12, Davidson Col.; M.Ed.'32, Duke Univ.; Supt. of Sch., Winston-Salem, N. C., since 1933.

Moore, R. H., A.B.'09, Erskine Col.; A.B., Peabody Col.; Supt. of Sch., Jonesboro, Ark., since 1934.

Moore, Raymond, A.B.'20, Lake Forest Col.; Ed.M.'30, Harvard Univ.; Prin., Lake Forest H. S., Lake Forest, Ill., since 1935.

Moorhead, M. R., B.S.'20, M.S.'31, Colo. Agrl. Col.; Supt. of Sch., Glenwood Springs, Colo., since 1931.

Moreland, Jerre F., A.B.'25, Univ. of Colo.; M.A.'30, Colo. Col. of Educ.; Ed.D.'40, Columbia Univ.; Supvg. Prin. of Sch., Florence, N. J., since 1939.

Moreland, Ray M., A.B.'32, Colo. State Col. of Educ.; M.A.'35, Western State Col. Tchr., Pub. Sch., Denver, Colo.

Morelock, H. W., L.I.'02, Peabody Normal Col.; B.A.'03, Univ. of Tenn.; M.A.'18, Harvard Univ.; LL.D.'26, Trinity Univ.; Pres., Sul Ross State Tchrs. Col., Alpine, Texas, since 1923.

Morgan, Barton, B.S.'19, Northeast Mo. State Tchrs. Col., Kirksville, Mo.; M.S. '22, Iowa State Col.; Ph.D.'34, State Univ. of Iowa; Head, Dept. of Voc. Educ., and Dir. of Tchr. Educ., Iowa State Col., Ames, Iowa, since 1936.

Morgan, Clarence B., Supvg. Prin. of Twp. Sch., Gibbstown, N. J.

Morgan, DeWitt S., A.B.'12, Henry Kendall Col.; A.M.'16, Univ. of Wis.; LL.D.'37, De Pauw Univ.; LL.D.'40, Butler Univ.; LL.D.'43, Wabash Col.; Supt. of Sch., 150 N. Meridian St., Indianapolis 4, Ind., since 1937.

Morgan, Mrs. Esthelene W., Prin., Leland Jr. H. S., Chevy Chase, Md.

Morgan, Frank H., M.S.'37, East Texas State Tchrs. Col., Commerce, Texas; Supt. of Sch., Commerce, Texas, since 1935.

Morgan, Frederic Evan, A.B.'19, Wash. Univ.; Ed.M.'32, Harvard Univ.; Pres., The Principia, St. Louis 12, Mo., since 1919.

Morgan, Hugh C., A.B.'15, Dickinson Col.; A.M.'20, Tchrs. Col., Columbia Univ.; Supvg. Prin. of Sch., West Grove, Pa., since 1930.

Morgan, Jesse J., B.S.'26, Dartmouth Col.; Ed.M.'34, Harvard Univ.; Supt. of Sch., Auburn, Mass., since 1942.

Morgan, R. R., A.B.'28, Berea Col.; M.A. '40, Univ. of N. C.; Supt. of Sch., Caroleen, N. C., since 1937.

Morgan, R. S., B.A.'31, Southwest Texas State Tchrs. Col., San Marcos, Texas; M.A.'36, Univ. of Texas; Supt. of Sch., Refugio, Texas, since 1943.

Morgan, Victor, B.S.'17, State Col. of Wash.; Supt. of Sch., Omak, Wash., since 1929.

Morgan, W. G., A.B.'29, Oberlin Col.; A.M. '37, Tchrs. Col., Columbia Univ.; Supt. of Sch., Owego, N. Y., since 1937.

Morgan, William E., Jr., Headmaster, The Principia, 5539 Page Blvd., St. Louis 12, Mo.

Moritz, Irene, Supvr. of Research and Statistics, County Sch., Redwood City, Calif.

Morphet, Edgar L., A.B.'18, Ind. State Tchrs. Col., Terre Haute, Ind.; M.A.'25, Ph.D.'27, Tchrs. Col., Columbia Univ.; Dir. of Admin. and Finance, State Dept. of Educ., Tallahassee, Fla., since 1937.

Morris, Charles A., B.S.'05, Rutgers Col.; Co. Supt. of Sch., Toms River, N. J., since 1906.

Morris, Charles S., Pres., San Mateo Jr. Col., San Mateo, Calif.

Morris, Lyle L., B.S.'20, Drake Univ.; A.M.'26, Ph.D.'30, Tchrs. Col., Columbia Univ.; Commanding Officer, Navy V-12 Unit, Wesleyan Univ., Middletown, Conn., since 1943.

Morris, Lynn D., A.B.'37, Western State Tchrs. Col., Kalamazoo, Mich.; M.A.'40, Univ. of Mich.; Supt. of Sch., Rogers Sch., Grand Rapids, Mich., since 1930.

Morris, M. Ray, B.S. in Ed.'27, Muskingum Col.; B.S. in Bus. Admin.'28, Bliss Col.; M.A.'39, Columbia Univ.; Supt. of Sch., Westerville, Ohio, since 1943.

Morrisett, Lloyd N., A.B.'17, Univ. of Okla.; M.A.'30, Ph.D.'34, Columbia Univ.; Prof. of Educ., Univ. of Calif., Los Angeles, Calif., since 1941.

Morrison, E. A., B.A.'22, Upper Iowa Univ.; M.A.'31, State Univ. of Iowa; Supt. of Twp. Sch., Waterloo, Iowa, since 1932.

Morrison, Harvey A., B.S.'00, A.M.'09, Union Col.; Genl. Secy. of Educ., Seventh Day Adventists Genl. Conference, 6840 Eastern Ave., Takoma Park, D. C., since 1936.

Morrison, Howard D., B.S.'26, Columbia Univ.; M.S.'33, Univ. of Pa.; Supvg. Prin. of Hamilton Twp. Sch., Trenton, N. J., since 1939.

*Morrison, J. Cayce, A.B.'12, Valparaiso Univ.; M.A.'16, Ph.D.'22, Columbia Univ.; LL.D.'32, Alfred Univ.; Asst. Commr. for Research, State Educ. Dept., Albany, N. Y., since 1937.

Morrison, John H., A.B.'26, Ohio Univ.; M.A.'40, Wittenberg Col.; Supt., Northridge Schools, Dayton, Ohio, since 1929.

Morrison, Maria P., Asst. Supt. of Sch., Nashua, N. H., since 1937.

Morrison, Robert H., B.A.'23, Mich. State Normal Col., Ypsilanti, Mich.; M.A.'26, Colo. State Col. of Educ., Greeley, Colo.; Ph.D.'33, Tchrs. Col., Columbia Univ.; State Dir. of Tchr. Educ., State Dept. of Pub. Instr., Trenton, N. J., since 1937.

Morrow, Robert D., B.A.'27, George Wash. Univ.; M.A.'27, Gallaudet Col.; M.A.'41, Univ. of Ariz.; Supt. of Sch., Tucson, Ariz., since 1941.

Morse, Charles Kennedy, Diploma '09, Nebr. State Normal Sch., Peru, Nebr.; A.B.'14, Univ. of Nebr.; A.M.'30, Columbia Univ.; Supvr., Professional Tr., Vocational Rehabilitation, Veterans Admin., Washington, D. C.

Morse, Grant D., Ph.D.'41, New York Univ.; Supt. of Sch., Saugerties, N. Y., since 1927.

Morse, Robert Harry, B.S.'33, M.A.'42, Univ. of S. C.; Dist. Supt. of Sch., North Charleston, S. C., since 1941.

Mort, Paul R., Ph.D.'24, Columbia Univ.; Prof. of Educ., Tchrs. Col., Columbia Univ., New York 27, N. Y., since 1929.

Morton, Jack Robert, B.S.'25, Southwest Texas State Tchrs. Col., San Marcos, Texas; M.A.'31, Univ. of Texas; Ed.D. '40, Tchrs. Col., Columbia Univ.; Dir., Extension Tchg. Service and Prof. of Adult Educ., Miss. State Col., State College, Miss., since 1938.

Morton, William Henry, A.B.'09, York Col.; A.M.'12, Univ. of Nebr.; A.M.'23, Columbia Univ.; Ph.D.'28, Univ. of Nebr.; Dir. of Tchr. Tr., Chmn., Dept. of Sec. Educ., and Prin., Tchrs. Col. H. S., Univ. of Nebr., Lincoln, Nebr., since 1927.

Moseley, Clark C., Diploma '07, State Normal Col., Jacksonville, Ala.; A.B.'11, A.M.'29, Univ. of Ala.; Supt. of Sch., Anniston, Ala., since 1935.

Moseley, Nicholas, B.A.'19, Ph.D.'25, Yale Univ. Address: Snake Rock Farm, Sandy Hook, Conn.

Mosher, E. R., B.A.'03, Univ. of Minn.: A.M.'07, Western Reserve Univ.; Ed.M. '21, Ed.D.'24, Harvard Univ.; Dean, Sch. of Educ., Col. of the City of New York, New York, N. Y., since 1940.

Moshier, Stephen W., B.S.'32, M.A.'36, Tchrs. Col., Columbia Univ.; Supvg. Prin. of Sch., Hawthorne, N. J., since 1939.

Moss, John R., M.A.'32, Columbia Univ.; Supt. of Sch., Paris, Ill., since 1922.

Moss, W. A., A.B.'32, M.A.'36, Univ. of Ga.; Co. Supt. of Sch., Hartwell, Ga., since 1937.

Mott, Hubert, B.S.'19, Wesleyan Univ.; M.A.'33, Cornell Univ.; Supt. of Sch., Pleasantville, N. Y., since 1938.

Moulton, Lloyd W., B.S.'27, Dartmouth Col.; M.A.'35, Tchrs. Col.; Columbia Univ.; Supt. of Sch., Bloomfield, Conn., since 1940.

Moulton, Onsville Joshua, B.A.'14, Bates Col.; Ed.M.'32, Harvard Univ.; Ed.D.'37, New York Univ. Address: Old Corlies Ave., Neptune, N. J.

Mourer, Harry H., Supt. of Sch., Bedford, Ind.

Mowls, J. Nelson, B.S. in Ed.'24, Kent State Univ.; A.M.'28, Ph.D.'37, Univ. of Pittsburgh; Supt. of Sch., Uniontown, Pa., since 1934.

Moyer, Harry C., B.S.'21, Columbia Univ.; Co. Supt. of Sch., Lebanon, Pa., since 1926.

Moyer, James A., B.E.'93, State Tchrs. Col., West Chester, Pa.; S.B.'99, A.M.'04, Harvard Univ.; Dir., Div. of Univ. Extension, State Dept. of Educ., Boston, Mass., since 1915.

Moyers, Edison, A.B.'12, Tabor Col.; M.S. '22, Iowa State Col. of Agr. and Mech. Arts; Supt. of Sch., Guthrie Center, Iowa, since 1935.

Moyle, William D., B.A.'23, Wesleyan Univ.; M.A.'29, Tchrs. Col., Columbia Univ.; Supvg. Prin., Edgemont Sch., Scarsdale, N. Y., since 1937.

Muerman, John Charles, A.B.'10, Wash. State Col.; M.A.'16, Ph.D.'22, George Washington Univ.; Prof. of Rural and Visual Educ., Okla. Agrl. and Mech. Col., Stillwater, Okla., since 1930.

Muir, James N., B.S.'04, Univ. of Pa.; Supt. of Sch., Quincy, Mass., since 1926.

Mulford, Charles W., Schermerhorn Tchrs. Agency, 366 Fifth Ave., New York 1, N. Y.

Mullen, J. O., A.B.'28, M.A.'36, Univ. of Ariz.; Supt. of Sch., Jerome, Ariz., since 1918.

Muller, Mrs. Emma Fleer, Mus.B.'18, Marquette Univ.; S.B.'23, Univ. of Chicago; Dir. of Personnel and Registrar, Chicago Tchrs. Col., Chicago, Ill., since 1938.

Mullins, David W., Assoc. Prof. of Educ., Ala. Polytechnic Inst., Auburn, Ala.

Mullins, R. J., B.Sc.'09, Millsaps Col.; M.A.'30, Univ. of Colo.; Exec. Secy., N. Mex. Educ. Assn., Santa Fe, N. Mex., since 1938.

Mummert, Ira C., B.S.'17, M.A.'25, Susquehanna Univ.; M.A.'33, Columbia Univ.; Supvg. Prin. of Sch., Valley Stream, N. Y., since 1928.

Munro, Paul Merritt, A.B.'10, Emory Univ.; A.M.'23, Ed.D.'41, Columbia Univ.; Supt. of Sch., Columbus, Ga., since 1937.

Munson, Grace E., B.A.'11, Univ. of Nebr.; M.A.'12, Wellesley Col.; Ph.D.'16, Univ. of Nebr.; Dir., Bureau of Child Study, Bd. of Educ., 228 N. La Salle St., Chicago, Ill., since 1935.

Munson, Irving, A.B.'13, Augustana Col.; A.M.'29, Univ. of Ill.; Supt. of Sch., Kankakee, Ill., since 1934.

Munson, J. M., Ph.B.'11, Univ. of Chicago; M.Pd.'13, Mich. State Normal Col., Ypsilanti, Mich.; LL.D.'39, Ashland Col.; D.Ed.'42, Wayne Univ.; Pres., Mich. State Normal Col., Ypsilanti, Mich., since 1933.

Munson, M. C., Supt. of Sch., Luverne, Minn.

Munzenmayer, L. H., Ph.D.'31, Ohio State Univ.; Prof. of Educ. and Dir. of Appointments, Kent State Univ., Kent, Ohio, since 1931.

Murphy, Forrest Windsor, A.B.'17, Transylvania Col.; M.S.'31, Univ. of Ill.; Supt. of Sch., Greenville, Miss., since 1933.

Murphy, J. H., B.S.'25, Univ. of Wis.; M.A.'32, Univ. of Minn.; Supt. of Sch., Rice Lake, Wis., since 1940.

Murphy, Joseph E., A.B.'04, Univ. of Mich.; Supt. of Sch., Hurley, Wis., since 1904.

Murphy, Mary E., Dir., Elizabeth McCormick Memorial Fund, 848 N. Dearborn St., Chicago, Ill.

Murray, A. B., A.B.'27, Bluffton Col.; M.A. '35, Ohio State Univ.; Supt. of Sch., Washington Court House, Ohio, since 1941.

Murray, Leonard C., Diploma '24, B.E.'27, State Tchrs. Col., Moorhead, Minn.; M.A. '34, Univ. of Minn.; Supt. of Sch., Aitkin, Minn., since 1930.

Muse, E. W., B.A.'13, Texas Christian Univ.; Prin., Stephen F. Austin and San Jacinto Sch., Dallas, Texas, since 1941.

Musselman, Fren, A.B.'10, Ind. Univ.; A.M. '16, Columbia Univ.; Dean, Summer Session and Extension, Kent State Univ., Kent, Ohio, since 1924.

Myer, Walter E., A.B.'10, Southwestern Col.; A.M.'13, Univ. of Chicago; LL.D.'34, Southwestern Col.; Dir., Civic Educ. Service, 744 Jackson Pl., N. W., Washington 6, D. C., since 1925.

Myers, Lanning, A.B.'06, Brown Univ.; M.S.'42, Univ. of Pa.; Supt. of Sch., Wildwood, N. J., since 1938.

Myers, M. M., Prin., T. G. Terry Sch., Dallas, Texas.

Myers, Newell Dixon, A.B.'33, Stanford Univ.; M.A.'36, Univ. of Calif.; Dist. Supt. of Sch., Palos Verdes Estates, Calif., since 1939.

Myers, Orvil F., A.B.'18, Ohio Wesleyan Univ.; A.M.'22, Ph.D.'26, Univ. of Chicago; Chmn., Dept. of Psychology and Philosophy, Los Angeles City Col., 855 N. Vermont Ave., Los Angeles, Calif., since 1929.

Mylin, Arthur P., Ph.B.'12, Pd.D.'33, Franklin and Marshall Col.; Co. Supt. of Sch., 353 N. W. End Ave., Lancaster, Pa., since 1922.

N

Nanninga, Simon P., B.S.'16, Kansas State Tchrs. Col.; M.A.'22, Stanford Univ.; Ph.D.'25, Univ. of Calif.; Dean, Col. of Educ. and Dir., Summer Session, Univ. of New Mexico, Albuquerque, N. Mex., since 1925.

Nardin, George F., Editor, Educ. Dept., Houghton Mifflin Co., 2 Park St., Boston, Mass.

Narragon, F. R., B.S. in Ed.'23, Ohio Northern Univ.; M.A.'28, Ohio State Univ.; Supt., Leetonia Exempted Village Sch. Dist., Leetonia, Ohio.

Nash, E. C., B.S.'18, Texas Agrl. and Mech. Col.; M.S.'24, Cornell Univ.; Supt., Amphitheater Schs., Tucson, Ariz., since 1937.

Nash, Harry B., B.A.'14, Dakota Wesleyan Univ.; M.A.'24, Univ. of Minn.; Supt. of Sch., West Allis 14, Wis., since 1933.

Nash, James B., B.S.'30, State Tchrs. Col., Kutztown, Pa.; M.Ed.'38, Pa. State Col.; Supvg. Prin. of Twp. Sch., Cumbola, Pa., since 1936.

Nash, M. A., Chancellor, Okla. State Regents for Higher Educ., Capitol Bldg., Oklahoma City, Okla., since 1943.

Neal, Elma A., B.A.'23, M.A.'26, Columbia Univ.; Asst. Supt. of Sch., San Antonio, Texas, since 1930.

Neal, Mrs. Nell B., Chmn., Affiliated Tchr. Organizations, Embassy Auditorium Bldg., Los Angeles 14, Calif.

Neale, D. E., Santa Fe Bldg., Dallas, Texas.

Neale, Russell F., B.A.'22, Amherst Col.; Mgr., Sch. Dept., McGraw-Hill Book Co., Inc., 330 W. 42nd St., New York 18, N. Y., since 1932.

Nelson, Arnold C., Diploma '14, State Normal Sch., Edinboro, Pa.; B.S. in Ed.'27, Pa. State Col.; M.S. in Ed.'33, Univ. of Ill.; Dist. Supt. of Sch., 257 Euclid Ave., Ridgway, Pa., since 1935.

Nelson, Burton E., B.S.'91, M.S.'95, Western Normal Col., Bushnell, Ill.; Pres., Stout Inst., Menomonie, Wis., since 1923.

Nelson, C. P., M.A.'29, Univ. of Ala.; Supt. of Sch., Troy, Ala., since 1943.

Nelson, Edwin A., Diploma '24, State Tchrs. Col., Fitchburg, Mass.; B.S.'35, Ed. M.'40, Boston Univ.; Supt. of Sch., Brockton, Mass., since 1942.

Nelson, John B., A.B.'19, Wheaton Col.; M.A.'28, Univ. of Chicago; Supt. of Sch., Batavia, Ill., since 1938.

Nelson, M. J., B.A.'16, Luther Col.; M.A.'24, Ph.D.'28, Univ. of Wis.; Dean of the Faculty, Iowa State Tchrs. Col., Cedar Falls, Iowa, since 1934.

Nelson, Milton G., B.S.'24, N. Y. State Col. for Tchrs., Albany, N. Y.; M.S.'25, Ph.D. '27, Cornell Univ.; Dean, New York State Col. for Tchrs., Albany 3, N. Y., since 1933.

Nelson, Stanley F., A.B.'26, A.M.'33, Univ. of Wis.; Acting Prin., H. S., Lake Forest, Ill., since 1943.

Nepomucen, Sister Mary, B.A.'29, Immaculate Heart Col.; Prin., Immaculate Heart H. S., 5515 Franklin Ave., Los Angeles 28, Calif., since 1936.

Neulen, Leon Nelson, A.B.'16, St. Olaf Col.; M.A.'21, Ph.D.'31, Columbia Univ..; Ped. D.'37, Temple Univ.; Supt. of Sch., Camden, N. J., since 1931.

Neulen, Lester N., B.A.'16, St. Olaf Col.; M.A.'23, Ph.D.'28, Columbia Univ.; Supvg. Prin. of Twp. Sch., Teaneck, N. J., since 1928. Address: 360 Warwick Ave., West Englewood, N. J.

Neumann, Otto W., B.E.'43, Central State Tchrs. Col.; Co. Supt. of Sch., Oconto, Wis., since 1940.

Neveln, Edward W., B.S.'23, M.S.'33, Drake Univ.; Supt. of Consol. Sch. Dist., Ankeny, Iowa, since 1921.

Neveln, S. T., A.B.'16, Iowa State Tchrs. Col., Cedar Falls, Iowa; M.A.'34, Univ. of Minn.; Supt. of Sch., Austin, Minn., since 1921.

Neville, Ernest L., Ph.B.'00, Univ. of N. C.; Supt. of Sch., Monroe, La., since 1910.

Newburn, Harry K., B.Ed.'28, Western Ill. State Tchrs. Col., Macomb, Ill.; M.A.'31, Ph.D.'33, State Univ. of Iowa; Dir., Univ. H. S. and Assoc. Prof. of Educ., State Univ. of Iowa, Iowa City, Iowa, since 1938.

Newell, R. W., B.S.'16, Des Moines Col.; M.A.'28, State Univ. of Iowa; Supt. of Sch., Emmetsburg, Iowa, since 1929.

Newenham, R. L., Diploma '17, Western Ill. State Tchrs. Col., Macomb, Ill.; B.S.'26, Univ. of Ill.; M.A.'30, Univ. of Chicago; Supt. of Sch., North Chicago, Ill., since 1926.

Newkirk, Louis V., B.A.'25, M.A.'27, Ph.D. '29, State Univ. of Iowa; Dir. of Indus. Arts, Pub. Sch., 228 N. La Salle St., Chicago, Ill., since 1934.

Newlun, Chester Otto, Ph.D.'29, Columbia Univ.; Pres., State Tchrs. Col., Platteville, Wis., since 1943.

Newman, Derwood A., B.S.'22, Univ. of N. H.; Ed.M.'31, Ed.D.'35, Harvard Univ.; Supt. of Sch., Abington, Mass., since 1940.

Newman, Winifred H., A.B.'29, Marshall Col.; M.A.'36, W. Va. Univ.; Asst. Co. Supt. of Sch., Charleston, W. Va., since 1940.

Newsom, Ralph P., M.A.'30, Colo. Tchrs. Col.; Supt. of Sch., Palacios, Texas, since 1927.

Newton, Arthur E., A.B.'04, A.M.'07, Hamilton Col.; Supt. of Sch., Pershing Blvd., Baldwin, L. I., N. Y., since 1922.

Newton, Ralph, A.B.'97, LL.D.'37, Mercer Univ.; M.S.'41, Univ. of Ga.; Supt. of Sch., Waycross, Ga., since 1928.

Neyhart, Amos Earl, B.S. in Indus. Eng.'21, M.S.'34, Pa. State Col.; Admin. Head, Inst. of Pub. Safety, Pa. State Col., State College, Pa., since 1936.

Nichols, Augusta M., B.S. in Ed.'29, M.Ed.'32, Boston Univ.; Asst. Supt. of Sch., Manchester, N. H., since 1938.

Nichols, Claude Andrew, B.A.'98, Southwestern Univ.; Ph.D.'05, Univ. of Havana, Cuba; Ph.D.'31, Columbia Univ.; Dir., Sch. of Educ., Southern Methodist Univ., Dallas, Texas, since 1928.

Nichols, Mary Belle, B.S. in Ed.'38, Univ. of Ga.; Co. Supt. of Sch., Thomasville, Ga., since 1938.

Nichols, R. Clyde, B.S.'27, M.A.'32, Univ. of Mo.; Supt. of Sch., Miami, Okla., since 1931.

Nichols, R. E., B.S. in Ed.'30, Southeast Mo. State Tchrs. Col., Cape Girardeau, Mo.; M.A.'37, George Peabody Col. for Tchrs.; Supt. of Sch., Malden, Mo., since 1935.

Nicholson, James T., B.S.'16, Mass. State Col.; Vice-Chmn., American Red Cross, Washington, D. C., since 1942.

Nickell, Vernon L., B.E.'29, Ill. State Normal Univ., Normal, Ill.; M.A.'32, Univ. of Ill.; State Supt. of Pub. Instr., Springfield, Ill., since 1943.

Nicklas, Victor C., A.B.'17, Univ. of Pittsburgh; M.A.'23, Columbia Univ.; Supvg. Prin. of Sch., Woodbridge, N. J., since 1933.

Nicolello, Louis L. D., A.B.'29, Syracuse Univ.; M.A.'41, New York Univ.; Supvg. Prin. of Sch., Garwood, N. J., since 1941.

Niergarth, J. Ivan, M.A.'36, Univ. of Mich.; Supt. of Sch., St. Johns, Mich., since 1943.

Nifenecker, Eugene A., B.A.'01, Col. of the City of New York; M.A.'06, Columbia Univ.; Dir. of Reference, Research and Statistics, Pub. Sch., 110 Livingston St., Brooklyn 2, N. Y., since 1920.

Niles, Caleb H., Supt. of Sch., Berlin, N. H.

Nill, Louise K., Prin., Pierce Sch., 6131 Iowa, Detroit, Mich.

Nilsen, William O., B.A.'24, St. Olaf Col.; M.A.'35, Univ. of Minn.; Supt. of Sch., Spring Grove, Minn., since 1934.

Nilssen, Morton O., B.A.'26, Upsala Col.; B.Th.'35, Luther Theol. Sem.; Pres., Waldorf Col., Forest City, Iowa, since 1943.

Nisbet, S. S., A.B.'19, Alma Col.; M.A.'30, Univ. of Mich.; Supt. of Sch., Fremont, Mich., since 1923.

Niven, Henry A., Vice-Pres., L. G. Balfour Co., Attleboro, Mass.

Noar, Gertrude, B.S.'19, M.A.'22, Univ. of Pa.; Prin., Gillespie Jr. H. S., Philadelphia 31, Pa., since 1930.

Noble, Frederick R., A.B.'08, Bates Col.; Ed.M.'26, Harvard Univ.; Supt. of Tr. Schs., State Tchrs. Col., Willimantic, Conn., since 1928.

Noble, Ralph E., A.B.'23, Dartmouth Col.; A.M.'32, Ed.M.'40, Univ. of Vt.; Pd.D.'42, Middlebury Col.; State Commr. of Educ., Montpelier, Vt., since 1940.

Noffsinger, Forest R., A.B.'28, A.M.'29, Ph.D.'33, Ind. Univ.; Educ. Consultant, American Automobile Assn., Washington, D. C., since 1936.

Noonan, Joseph Francis, B.Ped.'10, M.Ped. '11, State Tchrs. Col., Millersville, Pa.; Ph.B.'23, Muhlenberg Col.; M.A.'25, Ph.D. '26, New York Univ.; Pres., State Tchrs. Col., East Stroudsburg, Pa., since 1940.

Norby, Theo J., B.S.'35, M.Ed.'39, Univ. of Oregon; Supt. of Sch., Ashland, Oregon, since 1939.

Norene, A., Bd. of Educ., 320 E. Walnut St., Pasadena 4, Calif.

Normington, Roy T., B.Ed.'23, Central State Tchrs. Col., Stevens Point, Wis.; M.A.'30, Tchrs. Col., Columbia Univ.; Supt. of Sch., Reedsburg, Wis., since 1936.

Norris, Forbes H., A.B.'22, Manchester Col.; Ed.M.'26, Harvard Univ.; Asst. Supt. of Sch., 312 N. Ninth St., Richmond, Va., since 1933.

Norrix, Loy, B.Ed.'28, Southern Ill. State Tchrs. Col., Carbondale, Ill.; A.M.'34, Ph.D.'42, Univ. of Chicago; Supt. of Sch., Kalamazoo 5, Mich., since 1937.

North, Ward T., B.S.'15, Drake Univ.; M.A.'31, Univ. of Minn.; Supt. of Sch., Corydon, Iowa, since 1925.

Norton, Bernard Francis, B.S.'27, Providence Col.; Supt. of Sch., Valley Falls, R. I., since 1935.

Norton, Elbert B., A.B.'23, L.H.D.'42, Birmingham-Southern Col.; LL.D.'42, Ala. Poly. Inst.; State Supt. of Educ., Montgomery, Ala., since 1942.

*Norton, John K., A.B.'16, A.M.'17, Stanford Univ.; Ph.D.'26, Tchrs. Col., Columbia Univ.; Prof. of Educ., since 1931 and Dir., Div. of Organization and Admin. of Educ., Tchrs. Col., Columbia Univ., New York, N. Y., since 1942.

*Norton, La Verne Allen, A.B.'31, Colgate Univ.; M.A.'35, Tchrs. Col., Columbia Univ. Address: 321 Broadway, Dobbs Ferry, N. Y.

Norton, Warren P., A.B.'15, Brown Univ.; A.M.'23, Tchrs. Col. Columbia Univ.; Supt. of Sch., Meadville, Pa., since 1928.

Norwood, Pat H., B.A.'25, East Texas State Tchrs. Col., Commerce, Texas; M.A.'28, George Peabody Col. for Tchrs.; Dir., Pub. Service Bureau, Southwest Texas State Tchrs. Col., San Marcos, Texas, since 1935.

Norwood, W. Howard, B.A.'16, Univ. of Texas; M.A.'36, Tchrs. Col., Columbia Univ.; Supt. of Sch., Corsicana, Texas, since 1931.

Notley, Llewellyn, M.A.'33, Univ. of Texas; Supt. of Sch., Teague, Texas, since 1920.

Notz, Hulda M., M.A.'34, Univ. of Pittsburgh. Address: Box 852, R.F.D. 1, Homestead, Pa.

Nourse, Joseph P., A.B.'97, Leland Stanford Univ. Address: 345 Arguello Blvd., San Francisco, Calif.

Nourse, Laurence G., A.B.'17, Dartmouth Col.; A.M.'20, Harvard Univ.; Supt. of Sch., Norton, Mass., since 1924.

Noyes, Ernest C., A.B.'98, Yale Univ.; A.M.'00, Harvard Univ.; Asst. Co. Supt. of Sch., 5232 Forbes St., Pittsburgh 13, Pa., since 1917.

Nugent, James A., A.B.'98, A.M.'99, St. Peter's Col.; LL.D.'24, Seton Hall Col.; Ph.D.'26, Fordham Univ.; Supt. of Sch., 2 Harrison Ave., Jersey City, N. J., since 1924.

Nugent, M. E., B.A.'10, Carleton Col.; M.A.'26, Ed.D.'30, Univ. of N. Dak.; Dean of Instr., Northern State Tchrs. Col., Aberdeen, S. Dak., since 1932.

Nurnberger, T. S., A.B.'26, M.A.'29, Univ. of Mich.; Supt., Union Sch. Dist. No. 1, St. Louis, Mich.

Nusbaum, Louis, B.S.'08, Ped.D.'30, Temple Univ. Address: Bd. of Educ., The Parkway at 21st, Philadelphia, Pa.

Nuttall, L. John, Jr., B.S.'11, A.M.'12, Ph.D.'30, Columbia Univ.; Supt. of Sch., 440 East First South, Salt Lake City, Utah, since 1932.

Nutter, Olin C., A.B.'24, Morris Harvey Col.; M.A.'33, Univ. of Cincinnati; Co. Supt. of Sch., Huntington, W. Va., since 1938.

Nygaard, E. L., Supt. of Sch., Kenilworth, Ill., since 1923.

Nystrom, Wendell C., A.B.'14, Bethany Col.; A.M.'34, Ph.D.'37, Univ. of Kansas; Asst. Dean, Prof., and Head, Dept. of Educ., Wittenberg Col., Springfield, Ohio, since 1937.

O

Oakes, Ralph G., B.Pd.'18, M.A. in Ed.'28, Univ. of Maine; Union Supt. of Sch., Freeport, Maine, since 1925.

O'Banion, John William, B.A.'17, N. Mex. State Normal Univ.; M.A.'30, Southern Methodist Univ.; LL.D.'41, Texas Christian Univ.; Asst. State Supt. and Dir. of Supvn., State Dept. of Educ., Austin, Texas, since 1932.

Oberholtzer, Edison Ellsworth, Ph.B.'10, M.A.'15, Univ. of Chicago; LL.D.'21, Univ. of Tulsa; Ph.D.'34, Columbia Univ.; Pres., Dept. of Superintendence, 1934-35; Supt. of Sch. and Pres., Univ. of Houston, 1500 Louisiana St., Houston, Texas, since 1924.

O'Brien, George M., B.A.'24, M.A.'31, Univ. of Wis.; Supt. of Sch., Two Rivers, Wis., since 1943.

O'Connell, Rev. Michael J., S.T.D.'26, Collegio Angelico, Rome, Italy; Pres., De Paul Univ., 64 E. Lake St., Chicago, Ill., since 1935.

O'Connor, Mary Elizabeth, B.S. in Ed. and M.E.'25, Boston Univ. Address: 158 Highland St., Taunton, Mass.

Odell, William R., B.S.'27, Univ. of Southern Calif.; M.A.'30, Ph.D.'32, Columbia Univ.; Supt. of Sch., 1025 Second Ave., Oakland 6, Calif., since 1943.

O'Donnell, William F., A.B.'12, Transylvania Col.; M.A.'32, Tchrs. Col., Columbia Univ.; LL.D.'43, Transylvania Col.; Pres., Eastern Ky. State Tchrs. Col., Richmond, Ky., since 1941.

Offerman, Kate M., B.S.'20, State Normal Sch., Bowling Green, Ohio; M.A.'27, Univ. of Chicago; Co. Supt. of Sch., Bowling Green, Ohio, since 1921.

Ogden, Chauncey M., B.S.'17, Colgate Univ.; M.A.'33, New York Univ.; Supt. of Sch., Woodmere, N. Y., since 1940.

O'Halloran, William T., 67 Hilltop Ave., Providence, R. I.

O'Hara, Donald M., Ph.B.'19, Univ. of Chicago; M.A.'29, Univ. of Mich.; Supt. of Sch., East Lansing, Mich., since 1929.

Ojemann, Ralph H., B.S.'23, M.S.'24, Univ. of Ill.; Ph.D.'29, Univ. of Chicago; Research Assoc. Prof., Iowa Child Welfare Research Sta., State Univ. of Iowa, Iowa City, Iowa, since 1929.

O'Keefe, Walter, Sales Mgr., Institutional Dept., Doubleday, Doran & Co., Inc., Garden City, L. I., N. Y.

Oldham, James R. D., A.B.'97, Brown Univ.; Supt. of Sch., East Providence, R. I., since 1911.

Oliver, Stanley C., B.S.'19, M.S.'26, Pa. State Col.; Ph.D.'33, Columbia Univ.; Prof. of Rural Educ., Southwest Mo. State Tchrs. Col., Springfield, Mo., since 1929.

Oliver, T. W., Supt. of Sch., Pikeville, Ky.

Olling, Velma B., B.A.'29, State Col. of Wash.; Co. Supt. of Sch., Okanogan, Wash., since 1939.

Olney, Albert Clyde, B.S.'98, Univ. of Calif.; Marin Jr. Col., Kentfield, Calif.

Olsen, Hans C., A.B.'20, Nebr. State Tchrs. Col., Kearney, Nebr.; A.M.'22, Ph.D.'26, Columbia Univ.; Assoc. Prof. of Educ. and Dir. of Off-Campus Student Tchg., Eastern Ill. State Tchrs. Col., Charleston, Ill., since 1938.

Olson, A. J., A.B.'15, Union Col., Lincoln, Nebr.; M.A.'33, Ohio State Univ.; Prin., Auburn Academy, Auburn, Wash., since 1942.

Olson, H. R., B.S.'23, Oregon State Col.; M.A.'32, Univ. of Calif.; Supt., Delano Joint Union H. S., Delano, Calif., since 1932.

O'Malley, Margaret, B.S.'27, Univ. of Buffalo; Prin., Elem. Sch. No. 66, Tacoma and Parkside Aves., Buffalo, N. Y., since 1909.

Opstad, E. R., A.B.'28, Univ. of Wash.; Supt. of Sch., Fall City, Wash., since 1929.

Opstad, Iver A., B.A.'11, Luther Col.; M.A.'19, State Univ. of Iowa; Supt. of Sch., Iowa City, Iowa, since 1920.

Ormsby, Walter M., B.S.'26, Alfred Univ.; M.A.'30, Tchrs. Col., Columbia Univ.; Dist. Supt. of Sch., Bayport, N. Y., since 1936.

Orr, J. Clyde, B.S.'17, Univ. of Ala.; M.A.'26, Columbia Univ.; Supt. of Sch., Bessemer, Ala., since 1936.

Orr, Milton Lee, B.S.'10, Univ. of Ala.; M.A.'27, Ph.D.'30, George Peabody Col. for Tchrs.; Head, Dept. of Educ., Ala. Col., Montevallo, Ala., since 1922.

Orton, Dwayne, A.B.'26, Univ. of Redlands; A.M.'33, Col. of the Pacific; Dir. of Educ., International Bus. Machines Corp., Endicott, N. Y., since 1942.

Osborne, R. E., B.E.'43, State Col. of Wash.; Supt. of Sch., Colfax, Wash., since 1943.

Ostenberg, Joe W., A.B.'24, Bethany Col.; A.M.'31, Univ. of Kansas; Supt. of Sch., Ellinwood, Kansas, since 1935.

Ostenberg, W. M., A.B.'24, Bethany Col.; A.M.'39, Colo. State Col. of Educ., Greeley, Colo.; Supt. of Sch., Coffeyville, Kansas, since 1942.

Ostrander, Mrs. Fay, Secy., Bd. of Educ., 22135 Hayes Ave., East Detroit, Mich.

Ostwald, Ernest, Pres., Uniforms by Ostwald, Inc., 18 E. 16th St., New York, N. Y., since 1932.

Osuna, Juan José, A.B.'12, Pa. State Col.; A.M.'20, Ph.D.'23, Columbia Univ.; Dean, Col. of Educ., Univ. of Puerto Rico, Rio Piedras, P. R., since 1922.

Ott, Emory D., A.B.'12, Gettysburg Col.; M.A.'25, Columbia Univ.; Supvg. Prin. of Dale Borough Schs., Johnstown, Pa., since 1938.

Ottermann, Charles, B.A.'06, M.A.'08, Univ. of Cincinnati; M.A.'15, Columbia Univ.; Prin., Hughes H. S., Cincinnati, Ohio, since 1941.

Partington, Stephen A., A.B.'29, Wheaton Col.; M.A.'38, Univ. of Mich.; Supt., Wyoming Park Pub. Sch., Grand Rapids, Mich., since 1939. On military leave since 1943.

Parton, Daisy, Assoc. Prof. of Educ., Univ. of Ala., University, Ala.

Partridge, H. R., A.B.'13, Nebr. Wesleyan Univ.; A.M.'33, Univ. of Nebr.; Supt. of Sch., Alliance, Nebr., since 1923.

Patchin, Sydney A., B.A.'14, M.A.'15, Univ. of Minn.; Supt. of Sch., Hibbing, Minn., since 1937.

Pate, W. R., A.B.'17, Univ. of Nebr.; A.M.'29, Columbia Univ.; Pres., State Tchrs. Col., Peru, Nebr., since 1923.

Pate, Wylie G., B.S.'21, Washington and Jefferson Col.; M.A.'26, Univ. of Pa.; Ed.D.'36, Rutgers Univ.; Supvg. Prin. of Twp. Sch., Middletown, N. J., since 1938.

Patricia, Sister Mary, Prin., Immaculate Heart Tr. Sch., Los Angeles, Calif.

Patterson, Harry E., B.S.'29, New York Univ.; Supvg. Prin. of Sch., Oakhurst, N. J., since 1921.

Patterson, Herbert, B.A.'08, M.A.'11, Wesleyan Univ.; M.A.'11, Ph.D.'13, Yale Univ.; Dean of Admin., Okla. Agrl. and Mech. Col., Stillwater, Okla., since 1919.

Patterson, John R., Ph.B.'14, Wooster Col.; M.A.'26, Columbia Univ.; Ph.D.'29, New York Univ.; Supvg. Prin. of Sch., Millburn, N. J., since 1937.

Patterson, O. F., B.S.'25, M.S.'30, Univ. of Ill.; Supt. of Sch., Elgin, Ill., since 1938.

Patterson, R. D., Life Cert. '25, A.B.'28, Northeastern State Tchrs. Col., Tahlequah, Okla.; A.M.'33, Columbia Univ.; Supt. of Sch., Broken Arrow, Okla., since 1933.

Patterson, Ruth, Diploma '04, Tchrs. Col. of Indianapolis; B.S.'33, A.M.'39, Tchrs. Col., Columbia Univ.; Asst. Prof. of Kdgn. Educ. and Supvr. of Kdgn. Student Tchg., Butler Univ., Indianapolis, Ind., since 1930.

Patterson, Weldon M., A.B.'15, Piedmont Col.; Supt. of Sch., Chickamauga, Ga., since 1924.

Patton, D. H., M.A.'31, Univ. of Cincinnati; Asst. Supt. of Sch., Toledo, Ohio, since 1937.

Patton, Fred J., B.A.'24, Willamette Univ.; M.A.'35, Univ. of Oregon; Supt. of Sch., La Grande, Oregon, since 1941.

Paul, Arthur G., A.B.'09, Occidental Col.; Dir., Jr. Col., Riverside, Calif., since 1920.

Paulin, Eugene A., B.S.'09, Univ. of Dayton; M.S.'12, Univ. of Fribourg, Switzerland; Ph.D.'29, Univ. of Texas; Insp. of Sch., Maryhurst Normal, Kirkwood, Mo., since 1929.

Pauly, Frank R., Diploma '14, Central State Tchrs. Col., Edmond, Okla.; B.A.'17, Univ. of Okla.; M.A.'25, Ed.D.'35, Columbia Univ.; Dir. of Research, Bd. of Educ., 410 S. Cincinnati, Tulsa, Okla., since 1929.

Pauly, Irene M., 3533 Market St., San Francisco, Calif.

Paxton, W. A., B.S.'23, Brigham Young Univ.; Co. Supt. of Sch., Fillmore, Utah, since 1931.

Peacock, Clayton W., A.B.'11, Meridian Col.; A.B.'24, Univ. of Ga.; Supt. of Sch., La Fayette, Ga., since 1928.

Pearsall, Carl C., B.S.'24, M.A.'26, Univ. of Pittsburgh; Supt. of Twp. Sch., Irwin, Pa., since 1934.

Pearse, Carroll Gardner, LL.D.'14, N. H. State Col.; Pres., Natl. Educ. Assn., 1911-12. Address: 1721 Ludington Ave., Milwaukee 13, Wis.

Pease, J. E., A.B.'29, Central State Tchrs. Col., Mt. Pleasant, Mich.; M.A.'37, Univ. of Mich.; Supt. of Sch., La Grange, Ill., since 1940.

Pebly, Harry E., A.B.'17, Thiel Col.; M.Ed.'35, Univ. of Pittsburgh; Supt. of Sch., Sharpsville, Pa., since 1927.

Peck, J. R., B.E.'38, Western Ill. State Tchrs. Col., Macomb, Ill.; Co. Supt. of Sch., Galesburg, Ill., since 1939.

Peck, William R., B.A.'16, Holy Cross Col.; M.A.'31, Tchrs. Col., Columbia Univ.; Supt. of Sch., Holyoke, Mass., since 1920.

Pederson, C. A., B.A.'09, Luther Col., Decorah, Iowa; Supt. of Sch., Montevideo, Minn., since 1923.

*Peebles, James F., B.S.'31, Ed.M.'40, Boston Univ.; Union Supt. of Sch., Bourne, Mass., since 1927.

Peet, John Herbert, B.A.'16, Cornell Col.; M.A.'28, Univ. of Chicago; Supt. of Sch., Cedar Falls, Iowa, since 1935.

Pegg, Harold J., A.B.'25, Gettysburg Col.; M.A.'34, Univ. of Wash.; Prin., Roosevelt Jr. H. S., Altoona, Pa., since 1938.

Peik, W. E., B.A.'11, Univ. of Minn.; M.A.'24, Tchrs. Col., Columbia Univ.; Ph.D.'28, Univ. of Minn.; Dean, Col. of Educ., Univ. of Minn., Minneapolis, Minn., since 1938.

Pence, Edith E., B.A.'12, M.A.'13, Univ. of Calif.; Prin., Girls H. S., Scott and Geary Sts., San Francisco, Calif., since 1942.

Pence, W. G., A.B.'12, B.S.'21, Northeast Mo. State Tchrs. Col., Kirksville, Mo.; M.S.'22, Univ. of Chicago; Supt. of Sch., Fairfield, Iowa, since 1927.

Pendergraph, L. B., A.B.'07, Duke Univ.; Supt. of Sch., Mount Airy, N. C., since 1928.

Pendleton, Claud B., A.B.'21, M.A.'22, Univ. of Denver; Prin., Cole Jr. H. S., Denver, Colo., since 1937.

Peregoy, C. G., A.B.'23, Wash. Col.; A.M.'32, W. Va. Univ.; Prin., Woodrow Wilson H. S., Beckley, W. Va., since 1933.

Perepelitza, M. J., A.B.'38, Emmanuel Missionary Col.; Educ. Supt., Wis. Conference of Seventh-Day Adventists, 802 E. Gorham St., Madison, Wis., since 1942.

Perkins, Lawrence B., B.Arch.'30, Cornell Univ. Address: Merchandise Mart, Chicago, Ill.

Perrin, Eugene Allen, M.A.'33, Univ. of Texas; Supt. of Sch., Cameron, Texas, since 1934.

Perrin, H. Ambrose, Ph.B.'12, M.A.'22, Ph.D.'32, Univ. of Chicago; Supt. of Sch., Blue Island, Ill., since 1937.

Perry, Arthur L., B.S.'28, Ed.M.'31, Rutgers Univ.; Supt. of Sch., Rahway, N. J., since 1931.

Perry, Edgar C., B.S.'23, Pa. State Col.; M.A.'29, Univ. of Pa.; Supt. of Sch., Indiana, Pa., since 1938.

Perry, L. J., A.B.'23, Elon Col.; M.A.'33, Univ. of N. C.; Supt. of Sch., Reidsville, N. C., since 1933.

Pesta, Rose A., B.L.'02, M.L.'03, Univ. of Wis.; Prin., Kelvyn Park H. S., Chicago, Ill., since 1933.

Peter, Sister Mary, A.B.'20, St. Clara Col.; A.M.'23, Univ. of Wis.; Ph.D.'34, Columbia Univ.; Pres., Rosary Col., River Forest, Ill., since 1943.

Peters, David W., B.S.'23, Roanoke Col.; M.A.'28, Ph.D.'34, Columbia Univ.; Pres., State Tchrs. Col., Radford, Va., since 1938.

Peters, Edmund Clarke, B.A. and B.S.A.'16, Univ. of Tenn.; M.A.'25, Univ. of Chicago; Pres., Paine Col., Augusta, Ga., since 1929.

Petersen, Otto H. H., B.S.'41, Univ. of Oregon; Co. Supt. of Sch., St. Helens, Oregon, since 1941.

Petersen, Robert G., B.E.'30, State Tchrs. Col., La Crosse, Wis.; M.A.'40, State Univ. of Iowa; Supt. of Sch., Stoughton, Wis., since 1940.

Peterson, Agnes Emelie, A.B., Univ. of Calif.; Prin., John Muir Jr. H. S., Los Angeles, Calif., since 1929.

Petit, L. H., A.B.'10, Campbell Col.; Supt. of Sch., Chanute, Kansas, since 1923.

Petry, D. A., Prin., Pub. Sch., Felton, Del.

Phelps, Benjamin J., A.B.'02, Yale Univ.; A.M.'13, Tchrs. Col., Columbia Univ.; Supt. of Sch., Agawam, Mass., since 1921.

Phelps, Shelton, B.S.'15, Southwest Mo. State Tchrs. Col., Springfield, Mo.; M.A.'16, Ph.D.'19, George Peabody Col. for Tchrs.; Pres., Winthrop Col., Rock Hill, S. C., since 1934.

Philhower, Charles A., B.S.'09, A.M.'12, Dickinson Col.; A.M.'15, Columbia Univ.; Supt. of Sch., Westfield, N. J., since 1917.

Phillips, A. J., A.B.'21, Albion Col.; M.A.'25, Ph.D.'33, Univ. of Mich.; Exec. Secy., Mich. Educ. Assn., Lansing, Mich., since 1936.

Phillips, Claude A., A.M.'10, Univ. of Chicago; Ph.D.'20, George Peabody Col. for Tchrs.; Prof. of Educ., Univ. of Mo., Columbia, Mo., since 1935.

Phillips, Clyde U., B.S.'18, Kansas State Tchrs. Col., Pittsburg, Kansas; A.M.'26, Univ. of Chicago; Supt. of Sch., Hays, Kansas, since 1931.

Phillips, F. R., M.A.'27, Univ. of Mich.; Supt. of Sch., Alma, Mich., since 1926.

Phillips, G. Warren, A.B.'30, De Pauw Univ.; M.S.'35, Ind. Univ.; Supt. of Sch., Griffith, Ind., since 1943.

Phillips, Guy B., A.B.'13, Univ. of N. C.; M.A.'41, Columbia Univ. Address: Univ. of N. C., Chapel Hill, N. C.

Phillips, K. G., A.B.'26, A.M.'42, Univ. of N. C.; Supt. of Sch., Gastonia, N. C., since 1941.

Phillips, Ned, B.A.'26, Wash. State Col.; Supt. of Sch., Naches, Wash., since 1940.

Phipps, Harrie J., B.S.'03, Ed.M.'21, Harvard; Supt. of Sch., Northbridge, Mass., since 1922. Address: Grammar Sch., Whitinsville, Mass.

Phipps, W. E., B.A.'09, Westminster Col., Tehuacana, Texas; M.A.'25, George Peabody Col. for Tchrs.; B.S. and M.S.'36, Univ. of Ark.; Supt. of Sch., Russellville, Ark., since 1938.

Phisterer, Isabel Dewey, A.B.'29, Smith Col.; M.A.'32, Univ. of Wash.; Admin. Dean, Cazenovia Jr. Col., Cazenovia, N. Y., since 1942.

Pickard, Edward E., B.S.'25, Univ. of Pa.; M.S.'30, Temple Univ.; Ed. D.'34, Rutgers Univ. Address: H. S., Cape May, N. J.

Pickering, W. L., A.B.'25, De Pauw Univ.; M.A.'33, Univ. of Ill.; Co. Supt. of Sch., Oregon, Ill., since 1935.

*Pickett, Ralph E., B.S.'17, Columbia Univ.; Ph.D.'24, New York Univ.; Assoc. Dean, Sch. of Educ., New York Univ., New York 7, N. Y., since 1940.

Pierce, A. Lester, B.S.'20, State Tchrs. Col., Superior, Wis.; B.A.'21, Milton Col.; M.A.'26, Notre Dame Univ.; D.Ed.'41, Milton Col.; Dean, Sch. of Educ., Duquesne Univ., Pittsburgh, Pa., since 1941.

Pierce, Arthur Edwin, B.S.'24, Mass. State Col.; Ed.M.'30, Harvard Univ.; Supt. of Sch., Wellesley, Mass., since 1943.

Pierce, Frederick H., Supt. of Sch., Beverly, Mass.

Pierce, Harry L., Supt. of Sch., Mojave, Calif.

Pierce, John F., Prin., Kingsbury Joint Union H. S., Kingsbury, Calif.

Pierce, Mary C., B.A.'33, Eastern Wash. Col. of Educ.; M.A.'42, Wash. State Col.; Co. Supt. of Sch., Ritzville, Wash., since 1943.

Pierre, Sister Mary, M.S.'21, Fordham Univ.; Dean, Col. Misericordia, Dallas, Pa., since 1941.

Pietenpol, H. W., A.B.'07, A.M.'08, Central Col.; A.M.'30, State Univ. of Iowa; LL.D. '41, Central Col.; Dean and Prof. of Math., Central Col., Pella, Iowa, since 1916.

Pilkington, Hartwell Gordon, Ed.B.'27, R. I. Col. of Educ.; Ed.M.'38, Boston Univ.; Prin., Locust Ave. Tr. Sch., Danbury Tchrs. Col., Danbury, Conn., since 1936.

Pillsbury, W. Howard, A.B.'06, Carleton Col.; L.H.D.'39, Union Col.; Pres., American Assn. of Sch. Admin., 1941-42; Supt. of Sch., Schenectady, N. Y., since 1929.

Pitkin, Fred E., A.B.'16, Wesleyan Univ.; M.A.'26, Columbia Univ.; Supt. of Sch., North Andover, Mass., since 1927.

Pitt, Rev. Felix Newton, A.B.'16, A.M.'17, St. Mary's Univ., Baltimore, Md.; Ph.D. '33, Univ. of Fribourg, Switzerland; Supt. of Catholic Sch., 443 S. Fifth St., Louisville, Ky., since 1925.

Pittenger, Lemuel Arthur, A.B.'07, A.M.'08, Ind. Univ.; Litt.D.'32, Taylor Univ.; LL.D.'36, Franklin Col.; LL.D.'37, De Pauw Univ.; Pres. Emeritus, Ball State Tchrs. Col., Muncie, Ind., since 1943.

Pitzner, Eldyn A., B.S. in Ed.'39, Northwestern Univ.; Co. Supt. of Sch., Kenosha, Wis., since 1940.

Plenzke, O. H., A.B.'14, Lawrence Col.; A.M.'24, Univ. of Wis.; Exec. Secy., Wis. Educ. Assn., Madison 3, Wis., since 1934.

Plimpton, Blair, S.B.'30, A.M.'38, Univ. of Chicago; Supt., Countryside Sch., Barrington, Ill.

Plough, K. A., Secy., F. A. Owen Pub. Co., Dansville, N. Y.

Pogreba, A. P., B.S.'31, Univ. of Minn.; Supt. of Sch., Grand Rapids, Minn., since 1933.

Pogue, William Richey, B.S.'30, Monmouth Col.; M.A.'34, State Univ. of Iowa. Address: Pub. Sch., Morris, Minn.

Pollack, Richard S., B.S.'31, Mass. Inst. of Tech.; M.S.'38, Temple Univ.; Supvg. Prin., Lower Camden Co. H. S. Dist., Lindenwold, N. J.

Pollock, Thomas L., B.S.'26, Univ. of Pittsburgh; Supt. of Sch., Charleroi, Pa., since 1912.

Poole, Ralph, A.M.'35, Univ. of Mo.; Supt. of Sch., De Soto, Mo., since 1942.

Poppett, Mrs. Carol R., A.B.'41, Univ. of Redlands; Supvg. Prin., Mission Sch., Redlands, Calif., since 1937.

Porch, Marvin E., A.B.'25, M.S.'29, Ed.D.'35, Temple Univ; Supt. of Sch., Gloucester City, N. J., since 1938.

Porter, Frederick W., B.S.'14, Tufts Col.; Ed.M.'27, Harvard Univ.; Supt. of Sch., Greenfield, Mass., since 1929.

Porter, Merwyn D., A.B.'22, Baker Univ.; M.S.'35, Univ. of Southern Calif.; Supt. of Sch., Holbrook, Ariz., since 1935.

Porterfield, John H., A.B.'25, Pasadena Col.; Prin., McFarland H. S., McFarland, Calif., since 1939.

Porter-Shirley, Carl H., B.S.'27, State Tchrs. Col., Bridgewater, Mass.; Ed.M. '23, R. I. Col. of Educ.; Supt. of Sch., Hingham, Mass.

Portwood, Thomas B., B.S.'19, Kansas State Tchrs. Col., Emporia, Kansas; A.M.'22, Columbia Univ.; Asst. Supt. of Sch., San Antonio, Texas, since 1929.

Poteet, Ernest H., B.A.'21, M.A.'30, Baylor Univ.; Supt. of Sch., Harlingen, Texas.

Poteet, G. F., A.M.'37, Univ. of Va.; Co. Supt. of Sch., Floyd, Va., since 1938.

Pottenger, Mary O., M.Ed.'35, American Internatl. Col.; Genl. Supvr. of Elem. Educ., Pub. Sch., Springfield, Mass., since 1921.

Potter, Floyd A., B.S.'33, M.S. in Ed.'35, Rutgers Univ.; Co. Supt. of Sch., Egg Harbor City, N. J., since 1941.

Potter, J. W., Ph.B.'13, Dickinson Col.; A.M.'23, Columbia Univ.; Supt. of Sch., Carlisle, Pa., since 1927.

Potter, John Milton, A.B.'26, A.M.'30, Ph.D. '35, Harvard Univ.; Pres., Hobart and William Smith Colleges, Geneva, N. Y., since 1942.

Potter, Milton Chase, Ph.B.'95, Albion Col.; M.A.'05, Univ. of Chicago; Litt.D.'13, Univ. of Denver; M.Pd.'14, Mich. State Normal Col., Ypsilanti, Mich.; Pres., Dept. of Superintendence, 1932-33; Supt. Emeritus of Sch., Milwaukee, Wis., since 1943. Address: 2725 N. Prospect, Milwaukee, Wis.

Potwin, R. W., A.B.'10, Univ. of Kansas; A.M.'27, Univ. of Chicago; Supt. of Sch., McPherson, Kansas, since 1915.

Povenmire, Mahlon A., B.Sc. in Ed.'26, M.A. '31, Ohio State Univ.; Supt. of Sch., Galion, Ohio, since 1941.

Powell, Harley J., B.A.'29, State Univ. of Iowa; M.A.'30, Univ. of Wis.; Supt. of Sch., Watertown, Wis., since 1942.

Power, Francis Ray, Diploma '20, Shepherd State Tchrs. Col., Shepherdstown, W. Va.; A.B.'25, W. Va. Univ.; A.M.'29, Columbia Univ.; Asst. State Supt. of Free Sch., Charleston 5, W. Va., since 1933.

Power, Leonard, B.S.'16, Central Mo. State Tchrs. Col., Warrensburg, Mo.; M.A.'27, Univ. of Chicago; Ed.D.'35, Tchrs. Col., Columbia Univ.; Educ. Consultant, 2 W. 45th St., New York 19, N. Y., since 1936.

Power, Thomas F., A.B.'08, Amherst Col.; Supt. of Sch., Worcester 6, Mass., since 1943.

Powers, F. R., A.B.'13, Oberlin Col.; A.M. '20, Tchrs. Col., Columbia Univ.; Supt. of Sch., Amherst, Ohio, since 1918.

Powers, Francis F., B.A.'23, Univ. of Wash.; M.A.'27, Univ. of Oregon; Ph.D.'28, Univ. of Wash.; Dean, Col. of Educ., Univ. of Wash., Seattle 5, Wash., since 1939.

Powers, Guy W., B.S.'11, Univ. of Vt.; Supt. of Sch., Brattleboro, Vt., since 1940.

Powers, Pliny H., B.S.'15, Wilmington Col.; M.A.'26, Tchrs. Col., Columbia Univ.; Ed.D.'41, New York Univ.; Prof. of Educ. and Head, Dept. of Admin. and Supvn., Sch. of Educ., New York Univ., New York 7, N. Y., since 1941.

Powers, Samuel Ralph, Ph.D.'23, Univ. of Minn.; Prof. of Natural Sciences, Tchrs. Col., Columbia Univ., New York 27, N. Y., since 1923.

Powers, Sue M., B.S.'20, George Peabody Col. for Tchrs.; Co. Supt. of Sch., Court House, Memphis 3, Tenn., since 1922.

Powers, T. R., Jr., Supt. of Sch. Dist. No. 68, Vida, Oregon.

Poynter, J. W., A.B.'25, State Tchrs. Col., Peru, Nebr.; Supt. of Sch., Hillsboro, Oregon, since 1937.

Pratt, Charles H., A.B.'08, Bates Col.; A.M. '27, Columbia Univ.; Union Supt. of Sch., Harwick, Mass., since 1930.

Pratt, LeRoy A., A.B.'14, M.A.'28, Univ. of Mich.; Supt. of Sch., Flint, Mich.

Pratt, Milford H., A.B.'27, Univ. of Rochester; A.M.'31, Columbia Univ.; Supvg. Prin. of Sch., Barker, N. Y., since 1930.

Pratt, Orville C., Ph.B.'95, De Pauw Univ.; Pres., Natl. Educ. Assn., 1936-37; Supt. of Sch., Spokane, Wash., 1916-43. Address: Sch. Admin. Bldg., Spokane, Wash.

Pressly, William Cornelius, A.B.'14, Litt.D. '26, Erskine Col.; M.S.'33, N. C. State Col.; Pres., Peace Jr. Col., Raleigh, N. C., since 1926.

Preston, Everett Conant, B.S.'21, Mass. State Col.; Ed.M.'26, Harvard Univ.; Ph.D.'36, Tchrs. Col., Columbia Univ.; Supt. of Sch., Haddonfield, N. J., since 1936.

Preston, Kenneth Frank, A.B.'24, Cornell Univ.; A.M.'29, Columbia Univ.; Supt. of Sch., Great Barrington, Mass.

Prestwood, E. L., A.B.'29, Columbia Univ.; M.A.'39, Lehigh Univ.; Supvg. Prin. of Sch., Slatington, Pa., since 1942.

Preus, O. J. H., B.A.'01, Luther Col.; C.T.'04, Luther Theol. Sem.; D.J.'17, Southwestern Univ.; Pres., Luther Col., Decorah, Iowa, since 1932.

Price, Dave D., Pres., The Economy Co., Oklahoma City, Okla.

Price, Frederick E., S.B.'15, Armour Inst. of Tech.; M.A.'36, Northwestern Univ.; Prin., Tilden Tech. H. S., 4747 S. Union Ave., Chicago, Ill., since 1941.

Price, Malcolm, B.A.'18, Cornell Col.; M.A. '28, Ph.D.'29, State Univ. of Iowa; LL.D. '41, Cornell Col.; Pres., Iowa State Tchrs. Col., Cedar Falls, Iowa, since 1940.

Price, R. H., A.B.'21, Western Reserve Univ.; Ph.D.'33, Ohio State Univ.; Dist. Supt. of Sch., Highland Park, Ill., since 1934.

Price, S. W., Supt. of Sch., Walnut Hill Sch., New Britain, Conn.

Prince, A. E., B.A., Howard Payne Col.; B.S.T., La Grange Sch. of Theol.; D.D., Ewing Col.; Pres., Hannibal-La Grange Col., Hannibal, Mo., since 1941.

Pringle, James N., B.A.'97, Dartmouth Col.; State Commr. of Educ., Concord, N. H., since 1930.

Pringle, Lewis A., A.B.'02, Univ. of Chicago; Supt. of Sch., Harvey, Ill., since 1906.

Procter, C. Dan, Ed.D.'43, Univ. of Okla.; Pres., Okla. Col. for Women, Chickasha, Okla., since 1943.

Proctor, Arthur Marcus, A.B.'10, Duke Univ.; A.M.'22, Ph.D.'30, Tchrs. Col., Columbia Univ.; Prof. of Educ., Duke Univ., Durham, N. C., since 1923.

Prout, F. J., B.L.'06, Ohio Wesleyan Col.; D.Ped.'16, Ohio Univ.; Pres., Bowling Green State Univ., Bowling Green, Ohio, since 1939.

Pruitt, Eugene Watts, M.A.'26, Tchrs. Col., Columbia Univ.; Co. Supt. of Sch., Frederick, Md., since 1932.

Puckett, E. F., B.S.'09, Univ. of Miss.; M.A.'27, George Peabody Col. for Tchrs.; Supt. of Consol. Sch., Crystal Springs, Miss., since 1928.

Puderbaugh, J. Frank, A.B.'17, Dickinson Col.; M.A.'27, Columbia Univ.; Supt. of Sch., Lock Haven, Pa., since 1929.

Puff, Clinton M., A.B.'26, Maryville Col.; Ed.M.'32, Univ. of Pittsburgh; Supt. of Sch., Scottdale, Pa., since 1942.

Puffer, Noble J., B.S.'23, Ill. Wesleyan Univ.; M.A.'32, Northwestern Univ.; Co. Supt. of Sch., 160 N. La Salle St., Chicago, Ill., since 1935.

Puffer, R. A., Ph.B.'09, Kalamazoo Col.; M.A.'14, Univ. of Colo.; Asst. to the Supt. of Sch., 414 14th St., Denver, Colo., since 1924.

Pullen, Thomas Granville, Jr., A.B.'17, Col. of William and Mary; A.M.'25, Ed.D.'40, Tchrs. Col., Columbia Univ.; State Supt. of Sch., Lexington Bldg., Baltimore, Md., since 1942.

Purdy, Ralph D., A.B.'29, Asbury Col.; M.A.'33, Univ. of Ky.; Supt. of Sch., Wellington, Ohio, since 1940.

Putnam, Rex, B.A.'15, M.A.'29, Univ. of Oregon; State Supt. of Pub. Instr., Salem, Oregon, since 1937.

Putnam, Rufus A., B.S.'28, Evansville Col.; M.S.'35, Ind. Univ.; Asst. Supt. in charge of Bus. Affairs, Pub. Sch., Evansville, Ind., since 1928. On military leave since 1943.

Pygman, Clarence Huston, A.B.'28, James Millikin Univ.; M.A.'34, Univ. of Chicago; Supt. of Sch., Maywood, Ill., since 1939.

Pyle, T. V., A.B.'32, Ariz. State Tchrs. Col., Tempe, Ariz.; Prin., Elem. Sch., Buckeye, Ariz., since 1942.

Q

Quackenbush, Everett A., B.S.'07, St. Lawrence Univ.; Dir., Bureau of Sch. Admin., State Dept. of Pub. Instr., Harrisburg, Pa., since 1940.

Quickstad, N. J., B.A.'14, Univ. of Minn.; M.S.'32, Univ. of Chicago; Supt. of Sch., Royal Oak, Mich., since 1932.

Quinn, James Joseph, A.B.'12, Amherst Col.; A.M.'14, Harvard Univ.; Supt. of Sch., Winchester, Mass., since 1923.

Quinn, Maisie E., B.Ed.'37, R. I. Col. of Educ.; Supt. of Sch., West Warwick, R. I., since 1938.

R

Rabe, W. C., B.A.'15, Upper Iowa Univ.; M.A.'35, Univ. of Minn.; Supt. of Sch., Milbank, S. Dak., since 1929.

*Race, Stuart R., A.B.'11, Lafayette Col.; A.M.'27, New York Univ.; Supvg. Prin. of Sch., Newton, N. J., since 1941.

Ragland, Fannie J., Diploma '06, B.A.'08, Miami Univ.; M.A.'14, Columbia Univ.; Supvr., Pub. Sch., 216 E. Ninth St., Cincinnati 29, Ohio, since 1929.

Raines, Vincent, Asst. Secy., Ala. Educ. Assn., 21 Adams Ave., Montgomery 4, Ala.

Raker, William W., B.S.'07, Bucknell Univ.; A.M.'21, Tchrs. Col., Columbia Univ.; Dir. of Laboratory Schs., State Tchrs. Col., Kutztown, Pa., since 1932.

Rall, Edward Everett, M.Di.'95, Iowa State Tchrs. Col., Cedar Falls, Iowa; B.A.'00, State Univ. of Iowa; Ph.D.'03, Yale; Pres., North Central Col., Naperville, Ill., since 1916.

Ralph, Richard J., A.B.'25, Hamilton Col.; Supvg. Prin. of Sch., Clinton, N. Y., since 1943.

Rambo, W. L., B.S.'20, Kansas State Tchrs. Col., Pittsburg, Kansas; M.A.'27, Univ. of Chicago; Supt. of Sch., Paola, Kansas, since 1929.

Ramsey, Harold W., A.B.'27, M.A.'40, Col. of William and Mary; Co. Supt. of Sch., Rocky Mount, Va., since 1927.

Ramsey, James William, A.B.'13, Ouachita Col.; M.A.'21, George Peabody Col. for Tchrs.; Supt. of Sch., Fort Smith, Ark., since 1923.

Ramsey, Ralph L., A.B.'23, Emory Univ.; Dir., State Tchrs. Retirement System, State Capitol, Atlanta, Ga., since 1944.

Ramseyer, Lloyd L., A.B.'24, Bluffton Col.; M.A.'32, Ph.D.'38, Ohio State Univ.; Pres., Bluffton Col., Bluffton, Ohio, since 1938.

Ramy, A. Kirk, B.S.'24, Kansas State Tchrs. Col.; M.S.'30, Univ. of Kansas; Prin., Lowther Jr. H. S., Emporia, Kansas, since 1934.

Rand, Harold T., B.S.'25, Univ. of N. H.; M.Ed.'32, Boston Univ; Union Supt. of Sch., Rochester, N. H., since 1943.

*Rankin, Paul T., A.B.'15, Mich. State Normal Col., Ypsilanti, Mich.; M.A.'21, Ph.D.'26, Univ. of Mich.; Asst. Supt. of Sch. and Asst. Dir., Grad. Sch., Wayne Univ., 1354 Broadway, Detroit 26, Mich., since 1943.

Rasor, A. F., M.A.'33, Univ. of Texas. Address: Route 4, Lubbock, Texas.

Ratchford, A. J., A.B.'25, Susquehanna Univ.; M.A.'34, New York Univ.; Supt. of Sch., Shenandoah, Pa., since 1927.

Rathbun, Franklin Ellsworth, A.B.'05, Western Md. Col.; Co. Supt. of Sch., Court House, Oakland, Md., since 1912.

Rathbun, Mrs. Roy E., Diploma '05, State Normal Sch., Cortland, N. Y.; A.B.'10, M.A. in Ed. '35, Syracuse Univ.; Supt. of Sch. Dist. No. 2, Cincinnatus, N. Y., since 1926.

Rather, A. A., A.B.'16, M.A.'24, Univ. of Mich.; M.Pd.'40, Mich. State Normal Col., Ypsilanti, Mich.; Supt. of Sch., Ionia, Mich., since 1917.

Raubinger, F. M., Supvg. Prin., Passaic Valley H. S., Little Falls, N. J.

Rauer, Frances Moran, Acting Vice-Prin., Everett Jr. H. S., 450 Church St., San Francisco, Calif.

Rausch, Arthur F., Treas., Bd. of Educ., 22757 Rausch, East Detroit, Mich.

Rawlins, Robert E., B.S.'16, Huron Col.; M.A.'29, State Univ. of Iowa; Supt. of Sch., Pierre, S. Dak., since 1918.

Ray, Kenneth C., B.S.'25, Muskingum Col.; M.A.'31, Ohio Univ.; Ph.D.'43, Ohio State Univ.; State Dir. of Educ., State Office Bldg., Columbus, Ohio, since 1941.

Ray, U. E., B.A.'34, Southwest Texas State Tchrs. Col., San Marcos, Texas; Supt. of Sodville Schs., Sinton, Texas, since 1930.

Ray, Mrs. Willie C., A.B.'13, M.A.'30, Transylvania Col.; Supt. of Sch., Shelbyville, Ky., since 1930.

Read, Florence M., A.B.'09, Litt.D.'29, Mt. Holyoke Col.; LL.D.'39, Oberlin Col.; Pres., Spelman Col., Atlanta, Ga., since 1927.

Reagan, Chester L., B.S.'12 M.A.'22, Earlham Col.; Ed.M.'30, Harvard Univ.; Prin., Moorestown Friends' Sch., Moorestown, N. J., since 1925.

Reagan, G. H., Prin., Lida Hooe Sch., Dallas, Texas.

Reals, Willis H., A.B.'16, M.A.'21, Syracuse Univ.; Ph.D.'28, Columbia Univ.; Acting Dean, Wash. Univ., St. Louis, Mo., since 1942.

Reaugh, William L., B.E.'34, Ill. State Normal Univ., Normal, Ill.; M.A.'38, Univ. of Ill.; Supt. of Sch. Dist. 148, Dolton, Ill., since 1941.

Reaves, L. R., B.A.'36, Univ. of Texas; Supt. of Sch., Franklin, Texas, since 1941.

Reavis, George Harve, B.S.'11, Univ. of Mo.; M.A.'16, Ph.D.'20, Columbia Univ.; Asst. Supt. of Sch., Cincinnati, Ohio, since 1938.

Reavis, William C., Ph.B.'08, A.M.'11, Ph.D. '25, Univ. of Chicago; Prof. of Educ., Univ. of Chicago, Chicago, Ill., since 1927.

Rebert, G. Nevin, A.B.'10, Franklin and Marshall Col.; A.M.'25, Ph.D.'29, Univ. of Chicago; Head, Dept. of Educ. and Dir. of Tchr. Tr., Hood Col., Frederick, Md., since 1921.

Redd, George N., Fisk Univ., Nashville 8, Tenn.

Redding, C. D., A.B.'19 Georgetown Col.; M.A.'23, Univ. of Ky.; Supt. of Sch., Frankfort, Ky., since 1939.

Redford, Walter, A.B.'24, M.A.'25, Ph.D.'32, Univ. of Wash.; Pres., Southern Oregon Col. of Educ., Ashland, Oregon, since 1932.

Reed, Albert J., A.B.'18 Washburn Col.; M.A.'36, Univ. of Kansas; Supt. of Sch., Kiowa, Kansas, since 1937.

Reed, Carroll R., B.A.'06, M.A.'14, Harvard Univ.; L.H.D.'35, Carleton Col.; Pres., American Assn. of Sch. Admin., 1940-41; First Asst. Supt. in charge of Elem. Sch., Washington, D. C., since 1943. Address: 9300 Georgia Ave., Silver Spring, Md.

Reed, John McLean, M.A.'31, Ohio State Univ.; Supt. of Sch., Lima, Ohio, since 1937.

Reeder, Edwin H., A.B.'13, M.A.'24, Ph.D. '26, Columbia Univ.; Prof. of Educ., Univ. of Ill., Urbana, Ill., since 1937.

Reeder, Ralph R., B.S.'29, M.A.'40, Univ. of Minn.; Supt. of Sch. Litchfield, Minn., since 1941.

Rees, Conard N., M.A.'37, Univ. of Nebr.; Prin., Takoma Academy, Takoma Park, D. C., since 1940.

Reetz, O. A., B.A.'18, Univ. of Wis.; Supt. of Sch., Shawano, Wis., since 1929.

Reeve, Howard, B.S.'37, M.A.'41, New York Univ.; Supvg. Prin. of Sch., Little Falls, N. J., since 1937.

Reeves, Mrs. Ima Lee, Prin., W. A. Blount Jr. H. S., Pensacola, Fla.

Reeves, J. A., A.B.'20, Carpenter Col.; M.A. '28, Univ. of Wash.; Supt. of Sch., Everett, Wash., since 1939.

Reeves, Stanley N., A.B.'25, Univ. of Fla.; A.M.'28, Ph.D.'32, George Peabody Col. for Tchrs.; Supt. of Sch., York, S. C., since 1942.

Rehmus, Paul A., A.B.'23, M.A.'29, Univ. of Mich.; Supt. of Sch., Lakewood, Ohio, since 1941.

*Reid Charles Frederick, A.B.'23, Colgate Univ.; A.M.'29, Ph.D.'40, Columbia Univ.; Instr., Col. of the City of New York, New York, N. Y., since 1931.

Reid, John M., Secy., Bd. of Educ., Trenton, Mich., since 1937.

Reid, Paul Apperson, A.B.'29, M.A.'38, Univ. of N. C.; Supt. of Sch., Elizabeth City, N. C., since 1941.

Reimold, Orlando S., A.B.'97, Univ. of Mich.; Pres., World Book Co., Yonkers 5, N. Y., since 1933.

Rein, Marion Batchelder, Supvg. Prin. of Sch., Riverside, N. J., since 1923.

Reinecke, Lawrence W., A.B.'35, Univ. of Calif.; M.A.'42 Stanford Univ.; Genl. Supvr., Child Welfare and Attendance, Pub. Sch., Yreka, Calif., since 1941.

Reinertsen, S. G., B.A.'11, St. Olaf Col.; M.A.'21, Univ. of Colo.; Supt. of Sch., Moorhead, Minn., since 1926.

Reinhardt, Emma. Ph.D., Univ. of Ill.; Prof. of Educ. and Head, Dept. of Educ., Eastern Ill. State Tchrs. Col., Charleston, Ill.

Reishus, Victor L., B.A.'27, St. Olaf Col.; M.A.'39, Univ. of Minn.; Supt. of Sch., Biwabik, Minn., since 1941.

Reist, Norman I., A.B.'21, Ottawa Univ.; A.M.'27, Univ. of Kansas; Supvg. Prin. of Sch., Wilmerding, Pa., since 1936.

Reiter, M. R., A.B.'27, Muhlenberg Col.; M.S.'39, Univ. of Pa.; Supvg. Prin. of Sch., Morrisville, Pa., since 1940.

Reller, Theodore L., Ph.D.'33, Yale Univ.; Assoc. Prof. of Educ., Univ. of Pa., Philadelphia, Pa., since 1942.

Remaley, Frank H., A.B.'01, A.M.'09, Ped.D. '42, Otterbein Col. Address: 333 Carnegie Pl., Pittsburgh, Pa.

Remy, Ballard D., Ph.B.'02, Franklin Col., Franklin, Ind.; A.M.'18, Tchrs. Col., Columbia Univ.; Supt. of Sch., Longmeadow 4, Mass., since 1928.

Renne, R. E., B.S.'30, Linfield Col.; Supt. of Sch., Newberg, Oregon, since 1936.

Replogle, Laurence K., A.B.'19, Otterbein Col.; A.M.'24, Columbia Univ.; Asst. Supt. of Sch., 270 E. State St., Columbus, Ohio, since 1936.

Reusser, Walter C., A.B.'20, Upper Iowa Univ.; M.A.'23, Ph.D.'29, State Univ. of Iowa; Dir. of Sch. Admin. and Acting Dean, Col. of Educ., Univ. of Wyo., Laramie, Wyo., since 1924.

Reynolds, Elmer J., B.S. in Ed.'29, Northeast Mo. State Tchrs. Col., Kirksville, Mo.; M.A.'35, D.Ed.'40, Univ. of Mo.; Supt. of Sch., Sweet Springs, Mo., since 1935.

Reynolds, Fordyce Thomas, Ph.B.'00, Brown Univ.; A.M.'20, Columbia Univ.; Supt. of Sch., Gardner, Mass., since 1913.

Reynolds, James J., B.S.'93, Col. of the City of New York; LL.B.'00, New York Univ.; M.A.'01, Columbia Univ.; Asst. Supt. of Sch., Brooklyn, N. Y., since 1916.

Reynolds, O. Edgar, Diploma '14, Ill. State Normal Univ.; A.B.'16, Univ. of Ill.; M.A.'17, Ph.D.'27, Columbia Univ. Address: 430 E. Main St., Annville, Pa.

*Rhett, A. Burnet, B.A. and M.A.'99, Univ. of Va.; LL.D.'35, Col. of Charleston; Supt. of Sch., Charleston, S. C., since 1912.

Rhodes, Chester V., B.A.'31, Col. of Puget Sound; Supt. of Sch., Concrete, Wash., since 1942.

Rhodes, L. H., B.S.'26, West Texas State Tchrs. Col., Canyon, Texas; M.A.'31, Univ. of Colo.; Supt. of Sch., Tucumcari, N. Mex., since 1937.

Rice, Arthur Henry, Certif. '25, A.B.'26, Central Mich. Col. of Educ.; M.A.'34, Univ. of Mich.; Editor, *Mich. Educ. Journal* and Dir. of Publications and Informational Serv., Mich. Educ. Assn., Lansing, Mich., since 1929.

Rice, D. R., B.S.'15, Ohio Northern Univ.; M.A.'28, Tchrs. Col., Columbia Univ.; Supt. of Sch., Mentor, Ohio, since 1924.

Rice, Frederick A., A.B.'08, Cornell Univ.; Pres., Ginn and Co., Statler Bldg., Boston, Mass., since 1942.

Rice, Harry W., M.A.'35, Texas Tech. Col.; Supt. of Sch., Throckmorton, Texas, since 1931.

Rice, John D., A.B.'24, Grand Island Col.; M.A.'30, Tchrs. Col., Columbia Univ.; Supt. of Sch., Kearney, Nebr., since 1942.

Rice, Louis A., B.C.S.'21, B.S. in Ed.'27, M.A.'30, New York Univ.; Prin., Packard Commercial School, 253 Lexington Ave., New York, N. Y., since 1938.

Rice, R. S., Supvg. Prin. of Twp. Sch., Bellevue, Pittsburgh, Pa.

Rich, Dwight H., Prin., Eastern H. S., Lansing, Mich.

Richards, H. L., B.S.'20, B.M.S.'24, Pa. Military Col.; Ph.B.'30, M.A. in Ed.'33, Univ. of Chicago; Supt., Community H. S. Dist. 218, Blue Island, Ill., since 1935.

Richards, W. M., B.Sc.'19, State Tchrs. Col., Emporia, Kansas; M.Sc.'27, Univ. of Kansas; Supt. of Sch., Emporia, Kansas, since 1935.

Richardson, Ira, Ph.B.'97, Central Col., Fayette, Mo.; A.M.'08, Tchrs. Col., Columbia Univ.; Pres., Adams State Tchrs. Col., Alamosa, Colo., since 1925.

Richmond, James Howell, A.B.'07, Univ. of Tenn.; LL.D.'21, Lincoln Memorial Univ.; LL.D.'33, Univ. of Ky.; LL.D.'37, Univ. of Louisville; Pres., Murray State Tchrs. Col., Murray, Ky., since 1936.

Richmond, William, Supt. of Sch., Watervliet, N. Y.

Rickards, James S., A.B.'08, De Pauw Univ.; Exec. Secy., Fla. Educ. Assn., Centennial Bldg., Tallahassee, Fla., since 1929.

Ricker, Daniel J., B. A.'09, Middlebury Col.; Co. Supt. of Sch., Cape May, N. J., since 1941.

Rickert, Glennis H., A.B.'22, Susquehanna Univ.; M.A.'28, Tchrs. Col., Columbia Univ.; Supt. of Sch., Kane, Pa., since 1932.

Ricketts, Ella S., B.S.'30, M.A.'35, New York Univ.; Supvg. Prin. of Sch., Belmar, N. J., since 1936.

Riddering, Albert A., A.B.'18, M.A.'30, Univ. of Mich.; Supt. of Twp. Sch., Melvindale, Mich., since 1928.

Riefling, B. Jeannette, B.S.'11, A.B.'13, Univ. of Mo.; A.M.'20, Columbia Univ. Address: 3907 Conecticut St., St. Louis, Mo.

Rightmire, H. A., B.A.'03, Yale Col.; Mgr., Detergent Dept., Wyandotte Chemicals Corp., J. B. Ford Div., Wyandotte, Mich., since 1935.

Risheberger, Paul A., Prof. of Educ., State Tchrs. Col., Indiana, Pa., since 1936.

Risley, James H., A.B.'07, Ind. Univ.; Ph.M.'10, Univ. of Chicago; LL.D.'42, Colo. Col.; Supt., Sch. Dist. No. 1, Pueblo, Colo., since 1921.

Rissler, S. M., A.B.'21, Central Col., Fayette, Mo.; A.M.'31, Univ. of Mo.; Supt. of Sch., Trenton, Mo., since 1937.

Rittenhouse, Floyd O., B.A.'28, Emmanuel Missionary Col.; M.A.'32, Ohio State Univ.; Dean, Wash. Missionary Col., Takoma Park, D. C., since 1942.

Ritter, E. L., A.B.'14, Ind. Univ.; M.A.'16, Ph.D.'20, State Univ. of Iowa; Prof. of Elem. Educ., Iowa State Tchrs. Col., Cedar Falls, Iowa, since 1921.

Robb, Eugene K., Supvg. Prin. of Sch., Bedford, Pa.

Robb, Ralph, A.B.'11, Ill. Col.; Prin., Community H. S. Dist. No. 116, Clinton, Ill., since 1926.

Robbins, Chester, B.A.'13, Ursinus Col.; A.M.'22, Univ. of Pa.; Deputy State Commr. of Educ., Trenton, N. J., since 1942.

Robbins, Edward Tyler, A.B.'26, Univ. of Texas; M.A.'33, Texas Agrl. and Mech. Col.; Supt. of Sch., Taylor, Texas, since 1935.

Roberts, Alexander C., A.B.'06, Univ. of Wis.; M.A.'17, Ph.D.'22, Univ. of Wash.; Pres., San Francisco State Col., San Francisco, Calif., since 1927.

Roberts, Bertha E., B.Ed.'26, State Tchrs. Col., San Francisco, Calif.; Deputy Supt. of Elem. Sch., Civic Auditorium, San Francisco 2, Calif., since 1919.

Roberts, C. Elmer, B.S.'21, M.S.'32, Univ. of Idaho; State Supt. of Pub. Instr., Boise, Idaho, since 1941.

*Roberts, Edward D., B.A.'99, M.A.'07, Univ. of Cincinnati; M.A.'08, Tchrs. Col., Columbia Univ.; LL.D.'32, Col. of Wooster. Address: 3533 Burch Ave., Cincinnati, Ohio.

Roberts, Gilbert, B.S. in Ed.'18, Kent State Col.; Supt. of Sch., Cuyahoga Falls, Ohio, since 1932.

Roberts, J. Earle, A.B.'12, Washington and Jefferson Col.; M.A.'26, W. Va. Univ.; Supvg. Prin. of Twp. Sch., Point Marion, Pa., since 1926.

Roberts, L. A., M.A.'29, Southern Methodist Univ.; Supt. of Sch., Grand Prairie, Texas, since 1934.

Roberts, Roland, Co. Supt. of Sch., Nicholasville, Ky.

Roberts, Thomas R., Ph.B.'05, Upper Iowa Univ.; Supt. of Sch., Decorah, Iowa, since 1931.

Robertson, David Allan, A.B.'02, Univ. of Chicago; LL.D.'28, George Washington Univ.; Litt.D.'29, Bucknell Univ.; Pres., Goucher Col., Baltimore, Md., since 1930.

Robertson, John W., B.S.'24, M.A.'32, Tchrs. Col., Columbia Univ.; Supvg. Prin., Floral Park Bellerose Sch., Floral Park, N. Y., since 1929.

Robertson, Walter J., A.B.'22, Southwestern Col.; A.M.'34, N. Mex. Highlands Univ.; Supt. of Sch., Las Vegas, N. Mex., since 1941.

Robinson, Berton W., A.B.'24, Western State Tchrs. Col., Kalamazoo, Mich.; A.M.'29, Univ. of Mich.; Supt. of Sch., Hartford, Mich., since 1933.

Robinson, Charles M., B.S.'21, A.M.'24, Boston Univ.; Union Supt. of Sch., Townsend, Mass., since 1941.

Robinson, Ernest L., B.A.'94, M.A.'01, Yale; D.E.'36, Southern Col.; Co. Supt. of Sch., Tampa, Fla., since 1933.

Robinson, J. R., A.B.'09, M.A.'12, Univ. of Ky.; Ph.D.'27, George Peabody Col. for Tchrs.; Registrar, George Peabody Col. for Tchrs., Nashville 4, Tenn., since 1927.

Robinson, J. W., B.A.'38, Univ. of Wash.; Supt. of Sch., Cosmopolis, Wash., since 1943.

Robinson, L. C., A.B.'14, Ed.M.'24, Harvard Univ.; Supt. of Sch., Sandpoint, Idaho, since 1923.

Robinson, Louis C., A.B.'05, Washington Col., Chestertown, Md.; Co. Supt. of Sch., Chestertown, Md., since 1922.

Robinson, Luther B., Co. Supt. of Sch., Lenoir, N. C.

Robinson, Lyman D., Co. Supt. of Sch., McKinney, Texas.

Robinson, Mrs. Margaret R., Member, Bd. of Educ., 1459 San Pablo Ave., Fresno 4, Calif.

Robinson, Ross N., A.B.'15, Carson-Newman Col.; A.B.'19, Univ. of Tenn.; A.M.'21, Columbia Univ.; Supt. of Sch., Kingsport, Tenn., since 1924.

Robinson, W. C., A.B.'25, Ph.B.'34, Washburn Col.; M.A.'38, Tchrs. Col., Columbia Univ.; Supt. of Sch., Abilene, Kansas, since 1940.

Robinson, W. Tate, B.A.'31, St. John's Col., Annapolis, Md.; Ed.B.'36, Univ. of Hawaii; Dir., Div. of Health Educ., Dept. of Pub. Instr., Honolulu, Hawaii, since 1939.

Robison, Roy H., A.B.'24, M.A.'42, Univ. of Ariz.; Asst. Supt. of Sch., Tucson, Ariz., since 1942.

Roch, Jennie, Secy., Orleans Parish Sch. Bd., 703 Carondelet St., New Orleans, La., since 1942.

Rockwell, William M., A.B.'03, A.M.'04, Harvard Univ.; Office Mgr., Educ. Dept., Charles Scribner's Sons, 597 Fifth Ave., New York 17, N. Y., since 1925.

Rodes, Lester A., M.A.'17, Univ. of Pa.; Supvg. Prin. of Sch., South River, N. J., since 1935.

Rodgers, J. Harvey, A.B.'20, Franklin and Marshall Col.; Ed.M.'21, Harvard Univ.; Co. Supt. of Sch., Woodbury, N. J., since 1933.

Roeckner, Lucille, B.A.'30, San Francisco State Tchrs. Col.; Prin., Baywood Sch., San Mateo, Calif., since 1939.

Roeder, J. N., A.B.'17, Franklin and Marshall Col.; A.M.'23, Tchrs. Col., Columbia Univ.; Ph.D.'33, New York Univ.; Supt. of Sch., Palmerton, Pa., since 1926.

Rogers, C. E., A.B.'05, LL.B.'07, Univ. of Chattanooga; M.A.'15, Columbia Univ.; Supt. of Sch., Johnson City, Tenn., since 1938.

Rogers, Charles M., A.B.'13, Miss. Col.; M.A.'31, Texas Technological Col.; Supt. of Sch., Amarillo, Texas, since 1935.

Rogers, Don C., B.A.'16, M.A.'21, Ph.D.'23, State Univ. of Iowa; Dist. Supt. of Sch., 228 N. La Salle St., Chicago, Ill., since 1941.

Rogers, Forest Ray, B.Pd. and A.B.'17, Tri-State Col.; A.M.'23, Ind. Univ.; Supt. of Sch., Carrington, N. Dak., since 1929.

Rogers, James Edward, M.S. in Ed.'08, Univ. of Calif.; Dir., Natl. Physical Educ. Serv. of the Natl. Recreation Assn., 315 Fourth Ave., New York 10, N. Y., since 1925.

Rogers, Lester Burton, Ph.D.'15, Tchrs. Col., Columbia Univ.; Dean, Sch. of Educ. and Dean, Summer Session, Univ. of Southern Calif., Los Angeles 7, Calif., since 1919.

Rogers, T. Guy, B.A.'22, Southwest Texas State Tchrs. Col., San Marcos, Texas; M.A.'27, Univ. of Texas; Prin., Thomas Jefferson H. S., San Antonio, Texas, since 1932.

Rogers, Virgil M., A.B.'21, Wofford Col.; M.A.'24, Western State Col.; Supt. of Sch., River Forest, Ill., since 1940.

Rohan, Benjamin J., A.B.'16, Lawrence Col.; Supt. of Sch., Appleton, Wis., since 1925.

Rohleder, W. C., A.B.'20, M.A.'23, Ohio State Univ.; Supt. of Sch., Grandview Hgts., Columbus, Ohio, since 1927.

Rohrbach, Quincy A. W., A.B.'22, Franklin and Marshall Col.; A.M.'23, Ph.D.'25, Univ. of Pa.; LL.D.'34, Univ. of Pittsburgh; Pres., State Tchrs. Col., Kutztown, Pa., since 1934.

Rohrbough, George Irwin, B.A.'23, W. Va. Wesleyan Col.; M.A.'28, Harvard Univ.; D.Ped.'40, W. Va. Wesleyan Col.; Pres., Monticello Col., Alton, Ill., since 1935.

Rohrbough, R. Virgil, M.A.'41, W. Va. Univ.; Co. Supt. of Sch., Grafton, W. Va., since 1942.

Roland, H. M., A.B.'20, Wake Forest Col.; Co. Supt. of Sch., Wilmington, N. C., since 1936.

Rolfe, John J., B.Ed.'36, State Tchrs. Col., New Britain, Conn.; M.Ed.'39, Bates Col.; Union Supt. of Sch., Hinsdale, Mass., since 1939.

Rolfe, Stanley H., A.B.'09, Bucknell Univ.; A.M.'28, Ed.D.'37, New York Univ. Address: 306 Philadelphia Blvd., Sea Girt, N. J.

Rollins, Arthur S., A.B.'10, Dartmouth Col. Address: Pub. Sch., Rochester, N. H.

Ronnei, Herman L., B.A.'16, Luther Col.; M.A.'30, Tchrs. Col., Columbia Univ.; Supvg. Prin. of Sch., Valhalla, N. Y., since 1930.

Rooney, Rev. Edward B., Ph.D.'31, Gregorian Univ., Rome, Italy; Exec. Dir., Jesuit Educ. Assn., 45 E. 78th St., New York 21, N. Y., since 1937.

Root, Charles C., A.B.'09, Univ. of Mich.; A.M.'17, Univ. of Chicago; M.Pd.'20, Mich. State Normal Col., Ypsilanti, Mich.; Head, Dept. of Educ., State Tchrs. Col., Buffalo, N. Y., since 1917.

Rosa, Irvin E., B.A.'24, Carleton Col.; M.A.'31, Univ. of Chicago; Supt. of Sch., Davenport, Iowa, since 1943.

Rose, Clayton Earl, B.S.'24, Colgate Univ.; M.A.'30, Columbia Univ.; Supt. of Sch., Penn Yan, N. Y., since 1937.

Rose, Junius H., A.B.'13, Duke Univ.; A.M. '26, Columbia Univ.; Supt. of Sch. and Dir., Experimental Sch., East Carolina Tchrs. Col., Greenville, N. C., since 1920.

Rose, Sister M., Ph.D.'38, St. Louis Univ.; Dean, Viterbo Col., La Crosse, Wis.

Roselle, Ernest N., Supt., Tr. Sch., Southbury, Conn., since 1936.

Rosenstengel, William E., B.S. in Ed.'23, Northeast Mo. State Tchrs. Col., Kirksville, Mo.; M.A.'27, Ph.D.'31, Univ. of Mo.; Prof. of Educ., Univ. of N. C., Chapel Hill, N. C., since 1941.

Rosier, Joseph, A.M.'15, Salem Col.; Pres., Natl. Educ. Assn., 1932-33; Pres., Fairmont State Col., Fairmont, W. Va., since 1915.

Ross, Carmon, Ph.B.'05, Lafayette Col.; A.M.'16, Ph.D.'22, Univ. of Pa.; Supt. of Sch., Lansdowne, Pa., since 1941.

Ross, Cecil L., A.M.'32, Columbia Univ.; Ph.D.'37, New York Univ.; Sch. of Educ., Univ. of Miami, Coral Gables, Fla.

Ross, Meta M., Prin., Grayling Sch., Detroit, Mich., since 1930.

Ross, W. A., B.A.'23, North Texas State Tchrs. Col., Denton, Texas; M.A.'38, Texas Christian Univ.; Supt. of Sch., Mineral Wells, Texas, since 1937.

Rossey, Chris C., M.A.'23, Tchrs. Col., Columbia Univ.; Pres., State Tchrs. Col., Jersey City, N. J., since 1940.

Rossing, J. Milton, B.A.'21, Johns Hopkins Univ.; M.S.'32, Univ. of Pa.; Supvg. Prin., Glen-Nor H. S., Glenolden, Pa., since 1930.

Rossman, G. F., Asst. Sales Mgr., Superior Coach Corp., Lima, Ohio, since 1941.

Rossman, John G., A.B.'08, A.M.'11, Franklin and Marshall Col.; A.M.'17, Tchrs. Col., Columbia Univ.; Supt. of Sch., Warren, Pa., since 1934.

Rothgeb, Clyde W., B.S., M.S., State Tchrs. Col., Emporia, Kansas; Prin., Jr.-Sr. H. S., Hays, Kansas.

Rothwell, Angus B., B.E.'30, State Tchrs. Col., Superior, Wis.; M.A.'32, Columbia Univ. Address: Pub. Sch., Superior, Wis.

Roudebush, Earl D., A.B.'12, M.S.'27, Ind. Univ.; Supt. of Sch., Winamac, Ind., since 1925.

Roudebush, George E., B.S. in Ed.'18, Ohio State Univ.; M.A.'23, Tchrs. Col., Columbia Univ.; D.Ed.'40, Ohio Wesleyan Univ.; Supt. of Sch., Columbus, Ohio, since 1937.

Rounds, Charles R., Ph.B.'09, Lebanon Univ.; B.S.'13, Ohio Univ.; M.A.'18, Tchrs. Col., Columbia Univ.; Rand McNally & Co., 2009 Terrace Pl., Nashville 4, Tenn.

Roush, Walden F., A.B.'35, Marshall Col.; Co. Supt. of Sch., Point Pleasant, W. Va., since 1937.

Routt, Forrest V., B.L.'06, Univ. of Calif.; Supt. of Sch., Martinez, Calif., since 1933.

Rowe, John R., A.B.'19, Beloit Col.; M.A. '22, Univ. of Chicago; Educ. Dir., Encyclopaedia Britannica, 20 N. Wacker Dr., Chicago, Ill., since 1941.

Rowe, N. Dean, B.S.'27, M.Ed.'40, Univ. of Vt.; Dist. Supt. of Sch., Johnson, Vt., since 1940.

*Rowland, Albert Lindsay, A.B.'08, Temple Univ.; M.A.'11, Ph.D.'14, Univ. of Pa.; Pres., State Tchrs. Col., Shippensburg, Pa., since 1932.

Rowland, Sydney V., B.S.'14, Temple Univ.; M.A.'21, Univ. of Pa.; Supt. of Twp. Sch., Wayne, Pa., since 1920.

Rowland, W. T., M.A., Henderson Col.; Ph.D., George Peabody Col. for Tchrs.; Supt. of Sch., Lexington, Ky., since 1941.

Roy, Percy A., A.B.'07, Immaculate Conception Col.; A.M.'22, St. Louis Univ.; Ph.D.'25, Woodstock Col.; Pres., Loyola Univ., New Orleans, La., since 1939.

Ruby, A. E., Supt. of Sch., Storm Lake, Iowa.

Rud, Loyal A., B.A.'31, Concordia Col.; M.A.'38, Univ. of Wis.; Supt. of Sch., Morris, Minn., since 1943.

Rufi, John, B.S.'18, Kansas State Tchrs. Col., Emporia, Kansas; M.A.'19, Ph.D.'27, Tchrs. Col., Columbia Univ.; Prof. of Educ., Univ. of Mo., Columbia, Mo., since 1928.

Rugg, Earle U., A.B.'15, A.M.'17, Univ. of Ill.; Ph.D.'23, Columbia Univ.; Head, Div. of Educ., Colo. State Col. of Educ., Greeley, Colo., since 1923.

Ruidl, P. F., A.B.'27, Univ. of Wash.; A.B. '29, Eastern Wash. Col. of Educ.; Supt. of Sch., Bainbridge Island, Winslow, Wash., since 1938.

Rumpel, Harry E., Ph.D.'23, Ripon Col.; Supt., Lincolntown Pub. Sch., Mahtomedi, Minn., since 1928.

Rupert, William Earle, Litt.B.'09, Princeton Univ.; Supvg. Prin. of Consol. Sch., Kennett Souare, Pa., since 1932.

Rusley, O. A., B.A.'16, St. Olaf Col.; Supt. of Sch., Lake Mills, Iowa, since 1923.

Russell, Earle S., B.S.'19, Tchrs. Col., Columbia Univ.; Ed.M.'22, Harvard Univ.; Ph.D.'34, Yale Univ.; Supt. of Sch., Windsor, Conn., since 1934.

Russell, John Dale, A.B.'17, A.M.'24, Ph.D. '31, Ind. Univ.; Prof. of Educ., Univ. of Chicago, Chicago, Ill., since 1931.

Russell, R. W., B.A.'20, Wash. and Lee Univ.; M.A.'38, La. State Univ.; Supt. of Sch., Amite, La., since 1940.

Russell, Ralph D., B.A.'17, Union Univ.; Ph.D.'23, State Univ. of Iowa; Prof. of Sec. Educ., Univ. of Idaho, Moscow, Idaho, since 1926.

Russell, William F., A.B.'10, Cornell Univ.; Ph.D.'14, Columbia Univ.; LL.D.'28, George Washington Univ.; LL.D.'28, Univ. of Pittsburgh; LL.D.'29, Colby Col.; LL.D.'29, Columbia Univ.; Ed.D.'35, Colo. State Col. of Educ., Greeley, Colo.; Paed.D.'39, Sofia; Dean, Tchrs. Col., Columbia Univ., New York 27, N. Y., since 1927.

Rust, Mrs. Lucile, Prof. of Home Economics Educ., Kansas State Col., Manhattan, Kansas.

Rutherford, Kenneth L., A.B.'16, Hobart Col.; M.A.'24, Tchrs. Col., Columbia Univ.; Supvg. Prin. of Sch., Monticello, N. Y., since 1928.

Ryan, Belle M., Asst. Supt. of Sch., City Hall, Omaha, Nebr., since 1920.

Ryan Carl J., B.A.'16, Univ. of Dayton; M.A.'24, Ph.D.'27, Catholic Univ. of America; Supt. of Parochial Sch., Cincinnati, Ohio, since 1932.

Ryan, W. Carson, Jr., A.B.'07, Harvard Univ.; Ph.D.'18, George Washington Univ.; Head, Div. of Educ., Univ. of N. C., Chapel Hill, N. C., since 1940.

Ryle, Walter H., B.S.'19, Northeast Mo. State Tchrs. Col., Kirksville, Mo.; A.M. '27, Ph.D.'30, George Peabody Col. for Tchrs.; Pres., Northeast Mo. State Tchrs. Col., Kirksville, Mo., since 1937.

S

Saam, Theodore, A.M.'03, State Univ. of Iowa; Supt. of Sch., Western Springs, Ill., since 1938.

Sabin, Charles E., Life Diploma '26, N. Y. State Col. for Tchrs., Albany, N. Y.; Supt. of Sch., Watertown, N. Y., since 1933.

Sabine, Harold F., Ph.B.'09, Hamilton Col.; Supt. of Sch., Southampton, N. Y., since 1919.

Sackett, C. H., A.B.'04, A.M.'07, Oberlin Col.; Prin., Southwest H. S., 3125 S. Kingshighway, St. Louis 12, Mo., since 1938.

Sadler, Edward T. N., Diploma '05, State Normal Sch., Bridgewater, Mass.; B.S.'31, Boston Univ.; Supt. of Sch., New Bedford, Mass., since 1942.

Sadlowski, Vincent S., Pres., Bd. of Educ., 12044 Moran, Hamtramck, Mich., since 1941.

Saegert, Joe F., B.A.'08, M.A.'14, Univ. of Texas; Supt. of Sch., Seguin, Texas, since 1920.

St. John, Claude E., Diploma '03, Kansas State Normal Col., Emporia, Kansas; Supt. of Sch., Arkansas City, Kansas, since 1918.

Saiz, Clive M., Jefferson Union H. S., Daly City, Calif.

Salisbury, Robert Kenneth, B.A.'23, M.Sc.'33, Ohio State Univ.; Prin., Greenhills Sch., Greenhills, Cincinnati, Ohio, since 1938.

Salser, Alden, A.B.'16, Southwestern Col.; M.A.'24, Univ. of Chicago; Prin., Horace Mann Sch., Wichita, Kansas.

Saltzman, B. George, LL.B.'27, M.A.'40, Univ. of Colo.; Supt. of Sch., Cortez, Colo., since 1936.

Sampson, William C., Ph.B.'02, Sc.D.'33, Dickinson Col. Address: Pub. Sch., Upper Darby, Pa.

Samuelson, Agnes, M.A.'28, State Univ. of Iowa; Litt.D.'35, Augustana Col., Rock Island, Ill.; Ed.D.'36, MacMurray Col.; Ed.D.'36, Simpson Col.; L.H.D.'36, Luther Col.; LL.D.'37, Tarkio Col.; Pres., Natl. Educ. Assn., 1935-36; Exec. Secy., Iowa State Tchrs. Assn., Des Moines 9, Iowa, since 1939.

Sanborn, Kent L., A.B.'12, Clark Univ.; A.M.'30, Univ. of Colo.; Supt. of Sch., Longmont, Colo., since 1934.

Sanders, Bertram, Vice-Prin., Emmerick Manual Tr. H. S., Indianapolis, Ind.

Sanders, Beverly B., A.B.'27, Mercer Univ.; M.A.'36, Univ. of Ga.; Supt. of Sch., Commerce, Ga., since 1940.

Sanders, Joel L., Diploma '21, State Normal Sch., Troy, Ala.; Co. Supt. of Sch., Troy, Ala., since 1923.

Sanders, Walter F., A.B.'09, A.M.'17, Univ. of Chicago; LL.D.'37, Park Col.; Dean, Park Col., Parkville, Mo., since 1920.

Sanderson, Jesse O., A.B.'24, Duke Univ.; Supt. of Sch., Raleigh, N. C., since 1942.

Sands, Elizabeth, Prin., Kern Avenue Jr. H. S., 4765 E. Fourth St., Los Angeles, Calif.

Sanford, Charles Wilson, B.S.'29, M.S.'30, Ph.D.'33, Univ. of Ill.; Prin., Univ. H. S. and Assoc. Prof. of Educ., Col. of Educ., Univ. of Ill., Urbana, Ill., since 1932.

Sanford, Theodore A., A.B.'22, Centre Col.; M.A.'34, Univ. of Ky.; Supt. of Sch., Henderson, Ky., since 1941.

Sangren, Paul V., A.B.'20, Mich. State Normal Col., Ypsilanti, Mich.; A.M.'22, Ph.D.'26, Univ. of Mich.; Pres., Western Mich. Col. of Educ., Kalamazoo, Mich., since 1936.

Saunders, Carleton M., Ph.B.'29, Yale Col.; M.A.'38, Ed. D.'40, Tchrs. Col., Columbia Univ.; Supvg. Prin. of Twp. Sch., Raritan, N. J., since 1942.

Saunders, Charles Perry, Ph.B.'26, A.M.'37, Univ. of Chicago; Prin., Mozart Sch., 1400 Lake Shore Drive, Chicago, Ill., since 1935.

* Saunders, Joseph H., A.B.'17, Col. of William and Mary; A.M.'24, Univ. of Chicago; LL.D.'33, Central Univ.; Pd.D.'41, Col. of William and Mary; Supt. of Sch., Newport News, Va., since 1921.

Saundle, J. S., A.B.'29, W. Va. State Col.; Asst. Co. Supt. of Sch., Bluefield, W. Va., since 1934.

Saur, Charles C., Supt., Godwin Hgts. Schs., Grand Rapids, Mich.

Sauvain, Walter Howard, A.B.'24, Univ. of N. Dak.; A.M.'25, Ph.D.'34, Columbia Univ.; Asst. Prof. of Educ., Bucknell Univ., Lewisburg, Pa., since 1936.

Savoy, A. Kiger, A.B. in Ed.'29, Howard Univ.; A.M.'34, Columbia Univ.; Asst. Supt. of Sch., Franklin Admin. Bldg., Washington 5, D. C., since 1930.

Sawyer, Edmund Read, B.S.'12, Dartmouth Col.; Ed.M.'34, Boston Univ.; Union Supt. of Sch., East Longmeadow, Mass., since 1941.

Sayles, John M., A.B.'00, Colgate Univ.; Pd.B.'02, N. Y. State Col. for Tchrs., Albany, N. Y.; Pd.D.'37, Colgate Univ.; Pres., N. Y. State Col. for Tchrs., Albany, N. Y., since 1943.

Saylor, Charles F., Diploma '21, State Tchrs. Col., California, Pa.; B.A.'27, M.A.'31, Univ. of Pittsburgh; Supvg. Prin. of Sch., Meyersdale, Pa., since 1932.

Scanlon, Edward J., A.B.'15, Holy Cross Col., Worcester, Mass.; Ed.M.'33, Boston Univ.; Pres., State Tchrs. Col., Westfield, Mass., since 1938.

Scarborough, Homer C., A.B.'20, William Jewell Col.; A.M.'32, State Univ. of Iowa; Supt. of Sch., Great Bend, Kansas, since 1932.

Scarborough, William Acree, A.B.'19, Randolph-Macon Col.; M.A.'21, Univ. of Pa.; Co. Supt. of Sch., Dinwiddie, Va., since 1923.

Schad, Bernard T., B.S.'16, Univ. of Dayton; M.S.'20, Univ. of Fribourg, Switzerland; M.S.E.'27, Ph.D.'35, Univ. of Mich.; Insp. of Sch., Mount St. John, Dayton, Ohio, since 1938.

Schaefer, W. D., Supt. of Sch., Espanola, N. Mex., since 1939.

Schafer, J. J., A.B.'20, M.A.'24, Univ. of Mich.; Supt. of Sch., Midland, Mich., since 1919.

Schafer, Russell E., B.S.'22, Ohio Northern Univ.; M.A.'32, Columbia Univ.; Supt. of Sch., Alliance, Ohio, since 1942.

Schaplowsky, A. B., B.S. in Ed. '25, Univ. of Kansas; M.S. in Ed. '33, Univ. of Idaho; Supt., Ind. Sch. Dist. No. 45, Boise, Idaho, since 1929.

Scheer, Raymond A., B.S.'13, M.S.'14, Lincoln Col.; A.M.'25, Univ. of Wis.; Supt., East Alton-Wood River Com. H. S., Wood River, Ill., since 1942.

Schenk, John F., A.B.'22, Occidental Col.; M.A.'35, Univ. of Oregon; Supt. of Sch., Corvallis, Oregon, since 1938.

Schickler, Clyde K., B.S.'27, Mich. State Col.; M.A.'39, Wayne Univ.; Supt. of Sch., Milan, Mich., since 1942.

Schiebel, Walter J. E., B.S. in M.E.'16, M.A.'32, Univ. of Rochester; Prin., N. R. Crozier Tech. H. S., Dallas, Texas, since 1932.

Schinnerer, Mark C., A.M.'23, Tchrs. Col., Columbia Univ.; Ph.D.'43, Western Reserve Univ.; Asst. Supt. of Sch., Cleveland, Ohio, since 1938.

Schlagle, F. L., B.S.'16, State Tchrs. Col., Emporia, Kansas; M.A.'23, Tchrs. Col., Columbia Univ.; Supt. of Sch., Library Bldg., Kansas City, Kansas, since 1932.

Schlechte, William P., Prin., El Segundo H. S., 640 Main St., El Segundo, Calif.

Schlegel, Albert G. W., A.B.'20, Moravian Col.; A.M.'27, Ed.D.'35, Pa. State Col.; Supvg. Prin. of Sch., Red Lion, Pa., since 1927.

Schlockow, Oswald, Ph.D.'05, New York Univ.; Asst. Supt. of Sch., 141 E. 21st St., Brooklyn, N. Y., since 1927.

Schmidt, Caroline, Co. Supt. of Sch., Albuquerque, N. Mex., since 1941.

Schmidt, Frederick K., B.S.A.'21, Purdue Univ.; M.A.'27, State Univ. of Iowa; Supt. of Sch., Eldora, Iowa, since 1933.

Schmidt, H. W., A.B.'08, Univ. of Minn.; Supvr. of Sch. Bldg. Serv., State Dept. of Pub. Instr., 2117 Rowley Ave., Madison, Wis., since 1919.

Schmitt, Irvin H., B.A.'16, Coe Col.; M.A.'37, State Univ. of Iowa. Address: Pub. School, Davenport, Iowa.

* Schniepp, Albert E., B.A.'24, Central Wesleyan Col.; M.A.'30, Univ. of Mo.; Prin., Community H. S., Chenoa, Ill., since 1937.

Schofield, Charles Edwin, A.B.'17, Univ. of Nebr.; S.T.B.'20, Boston Univ.; D.D.'35, Univ. of Denver; LL.D.'38, Boston Univ.; Pres., Southwestern Col., Winfield, Kansas, since 1942.

Schook, Stanley L., Trustee, Bd. of Educ., 14619 Nine Mile Rd., East Detroit, Mich.

Schooling, H. W., B.S.'36, Southwest Mo. State Tchrs. Col., Springfield, Mo.; A.M. '40, Univ. of Mo.; Supt. of Sch., Hayti, Mo., since 1941.

Schoonmaker, N. B., B.S.'23, Univ. of Minn. Address: City Hall, Minneapolis, Minn.

Schrader, Marlin, B.S.'34, M.S.'37, Kansas State Col.; Supt. of Sch., Council Grove, Kansas, since 1942.

*Schreiber, Paul D., B.S.'12, Bucknell Univ.; Supt. of Sch., Port Washington, N. Y., since 1920.

Schroeder, Elroy H., B.S. in Ed.'26, M.S. in Ed.'35, Univ. of N. Dak.; Supt. of Sch., Grand Forks, N. Dak., since 1933.

Schubert, H. Arthur, B.A.'15, Colgate Univ.; M.A.'27, Tchrs. Col., Columbia Univ.; Supt. of Sch., Lynbrook, N. Y., since 1938.

Schultz, Frederick, Ph.B.'22, Univ. of Chicago; A.M.'24, Columbia Univ.; Supvg. Prin. of Sch., 346 N. Park Ave., Buffalo, N. Y., since 1929.

Schultz, Joseph L., A.B.'24, George Washington Univ.; M.A.'28, Ph.D.'38, Univ. of Pa.; Supvg. Prin. of Sch., Hightstown, N. J., since 1939.

Schultz, Joseph P., Member, Bd. of Educ., 2301 Neibel Ave., Hamtramck, Mich., since 1936.

Schultz, Louis J., M.A.'31, State Univ. of Iowa; Supt. of Sch., Central H. S., Cape Girardeau, Mo., since 1935.

Schwartz, Benjamin F., A.B.'19, Grinnell Col.; S.T.B.'22, Boston Univ.; D.D.'31, Iowa Wesleyan Col.; Chancellor, Nebr. Wesleyan Univ., Lincoln, Nebr., since 1938.

Schweickhard, Philip, B.S. in Ed.'17, Univ. of Chicago; Prin., Amherst Central H. S., Snyder, N. Y., since 1930.

Schwiering, Oscar C., A.B.'09, Iowa Wesleyan Col.; M.A.'16, Univ. of Wyo.; Ph.D.'32, New York Univ.; Dean, Col. of Educ., Univ. of Wyo., Laramie, Wyo., since 1939.

Score, J. N. R., A.B.'14, Scarritt Morrisville Col.; B.D.'16, Emory Univ.; Th.D. '25, Pacific Sch. of Religion; D.D.'31, Centenary Col.; LL.D.'43, Central Col.; Pres., Southwestern Univ., Georgetown, Texas, since 1942.

Scott, Cecil Winfield, A.B. in Ed.'27, A.M. in Ed.'28, Univ. of S. C.; Ph.D.'34, Columbia Univ.; Prof. of Sch. Admin., Univ. of Nebr., Lincoln, Nebr., since 1940.

Scott, Charles E., M.A.'22, Colo. Col. of Educ.; Pres., State Tchrs. Col., Dickinson, N. Dak., since 1939.

Scott, Ermo Houston, A.B.'31, M.A.'36, Univ. of Maine; Prin., State Normal Sch., Castleton, Vt., since 1940.

Scott, Julius E., A.B.'26, Ark. State Tchrs. Col.; M.A.'29, Tchrs. Col., Columbia Univ.; Lt., U.S.N.R., 421 State St., Alma, Mich.

Scott, Walter E., B.Sc.'16, Fort Hays Normal Sch., Hays, Kansas; A.M.'32, Univ. of Nebr.; Supt. of Sch., Fairbury, Nebr., since 1926.

Scott, Willis H., 623 S. Wabash Ave., Chicago, Ill.

Scott, Zenos E., B.S.'19, Evansville Col.; A.M.'13, Tchrs. Col., Columbia Univ.; D.Pd.'22, Evansville Col.; Supt. of Sch., Louisville, Ky., since 1937.

Seabrook, J. W., A.B.'09, Biddle Univ.; A.M. '30, Columbia Univ.; Pres., State Tchrs. Col., Fayetteville, N. C., since 1933.

Seamans, Herbert L., A.B.'13, Fairmount Col.; M.A.'26, Yale Univ.; Dir., Commn. on Educ. Organizations, Natl. Conf. of Christians and Jews, 185 Church St., New Haven 10, Conn., since 1941.

Sears, Jesse Brundage, A.B.'09, Stanford Univ.; Ph.D.'20,• Tchrs. Col., Columbia Univ.; Prof. of Educ., Stanford Univ., Stanford University, Calif., since 1911.

Seay, Maurice F., A.B.'24, A.M.'26, Transylvania Col.; Ph.D.'43, Univ. of Chicago; Dir., Bureau of Sch. Service and Head, Dept. of Sch. Admin., Col. of Educ., Univ. of Ky., Lexington, Ky., since 1937.

Secor, Carl T., M.A.'31, New York Univ.; B.S.'27, State Tchrs. Col., E. Stroudsburg, Pa.; Supvg. Prin. of Sch., East Stroudsburg, Pa., since 1938.

See, Otis A., M.A.'22, Tchrs. Col., Columbia Univ.; Supt. of Sch., Jennings, Mo., since 1925.

Seidel, Charles Franklin, Diploma '08, State Tchrs. Col., Kutztown, Pa.; A.B.'14, Muhlenberg Col.; A.M.'17, Univ. of Pa.; Asst. Supt. of Sch., Allentown, Pa., since 1938.

Selke, George A., B.A.'16, Univ. of Minn.; M.A.'26, Columbia Univ.; Pres., State Tchrs. Col., St. Cloud, Minn., since 1927. On military leave since 1943.

Selleck, Eugene R., Diploma '14, State Normal Sch., Platteville, Wis.; Ph.B.'29, Univ. of Wis.; Ph.M.'32, Northwestern Univ.; Supt. of Sch., Des Plaines, Ill., since 1929.

Sellers, J. M., A.B.'22, Ind. State Tchrs. Col., Terre Haute, Ind.; A.M.'26, Ind. Univ.; Ph.D.'37, Univ. of Chicago; Supt. of Sch., Walkerton, Ind., since 1940.

Sellers, Mary, Prin., James Stephen Hogg Sch., Dallas, Texas.

Sellers, Sandford, Jr., B.S.'13, M.A.'34, Univ. of Chicago; Headmaster, The Elgin Academy, Elgin, Ill., since 1943.

Sellig, George A., Ph.B.'32, Providence Col.; M.A.'37, Tchrs. Col., Columbia Univ. Address: Bartlett H. S., Webster, Mass.

Selover, Jesse, Supvg. Prin. of Sch., Sayreville, N. J., since 1901.

Senour, Alfred C., B.A.'17, Ind. State Tchrs. Col.; M.A.'27, Univ. of Chicago; Supt. of Sch., East Chicago, Ind., since 1943.

Severn, William E., B.S.'22, Allegheny Col.; M.A.'35, Columbia Univ.; Supt. of Sch., Corning, N. Y., since 1929.

Sewell, Nelson B., A.B.'32, M.A.'33, Univ. of Calif.; Prin., Union H. S., Salinas, Calif., since 1942.

*Sexson, John A., B.A.'12, Colo. State Tchrs. Col., Greeley, Colo.; M.A.'19, Univ. of Denver; D.Ed.'34, Colo. State Tchrs. Col., Greeley, Colo.; D.Ed.'38, Univ. of Southern Calif.; Pres., American Assn. of Sch. Admin., 1938-39; Supt. of Sch., 320 E. Walnut St., Pasadena 4, Calif., since 1928.

Sexton, J. W., A.B.'02, Albion Col.; M.A.'12, Univ. of Mich.; LL.D.'35, Albion Col.; Supt. of Sch., Lansing, Mich., since 1916.

Shafer, B. F., M.A.'23, Univ. of Chicago; Supt. of Sch., Freeport, Ill., since 1929.

Shafer, P. F., Supt. of Sch., Macomb, Ill., since 1941.

Shambaugh, J. B., B.S.'19, Franklin and Marshall Col.; Supvg. Prin. of Twp. Sch., Succasunna, N. J., since 1928.

Shangle, C. Paine, B.A.'10, Univ. of Oregon; M.A.'11, Univ. of Wis.; Supt. of Sch., Bellingham, Wash., since 1933.

*Shankland, Sherwood D., A.B.'94, Western Reserve Univ.; A.M.'18, Columbia Univ.; Exec. Secy., American Assn. of Sch. Admin., formerly Dept. of Superintendence, Natl. Educ. Assn., 1201 16th St., N. W., Washington 6, D. C., since 1922.

Shanks, Carl H., A.B.'27, Cedarville Col.; M.A.'38, Miami Univ.; Co. Supt. of Sch., Wilmington, Ohio, since 1932.

Shanley, Dorothy M. M., Secy., Conn. Tchrs. Retirement Bd., State Office Bldg., Hartford, Conn., since 1924.

Sharer, Robert E., A.B.'22, Albion Col.; M.A.'36, Univ. of Mich.; Supt. of Sch., Coldwater, Mich., since 1939.

Sharman, Jackson Roger, B.S.'17, Univ. of Miss.; M.A.'24, Ph.D.'30, Columbia Univ.; Head, Dept. of Physical and Health Educ., Univ. of Ala., University, Ala., since 1937.

Shattuck, George E., Ph.B.'22, Brown Univ.; M.A.'33, New York Univ.; Prin., The Norwich Free Academy, Norwich, Conn., since 1940.

Shattuck, Marquis E., A.B.'12, Albion Col.; M.Ed.'29, Harvard Univ.; Dir. of Language Educ., Pub. Sch., 467 W. Hancock, Detroit, Mich., since 1930.

Shaw, Edwin Adams, B.S.'98, Tufts Col.; A.M.'16, Ph.D.'18, Harvard Univ.; Head, Dept. of Educ., Tufts Col., Tufts College, Mass., since 1927.

Shaw, Homer W., A.B.'30, Okla. Baptist Univ.; B.S.'35, Okla. Agrl. and Mech. Col.; Supt. of Sch., Pawnee, Okla., since 1942.

Shaw, John A., B.A.'19, Wash. and Jefferson Col.; Supt. of Sch., Admin. Bldg., Spokkane, Wash., since 1943.

Shaw, Roger M., B.S.'36, M.S.'38, Univ. of Ill.; Ph.D.'42, Ind. Univ.; Instr. in Educ., Oberlin Col., Oberlin, Ohio, since 1943.

Shaw, William Henry, M.Ed.'33, B.A.'28, Duke Univ.; Supt. of Sch., Sumter, S. C., since 1938.

Shea, James T., B.A.'15, M.A.'24, Univ. of Detroit; Dir. of Curriculum and Research, Bd. of Educ., San Antonio, Texas, since 1922.

Shearer, Fred W., B.A.'03, Amherst Col.; Supt. of Sch., Middletown, Conn., since 1931.

Shearouse, H. Sam, A.B. and M.A.'30, Univ. of Ga.; Supt. of Sch., Griffin, Ga., since 1942.

Shedd, Jesse E., B.A.'18, Iowa State Tchrs. Col., Cedar Falls, Iowa; M.A.'34, State Univ. of Iowa; Supt. of Sch., Scottsbluff, Nebr., since 1939.

Shelburne, C. C., B.S.'27, M.S.'34, Univ. of Va.; Div. Supt. of Sch., Christiansburg, Va., since 1929.

Shelburne, L. F., M.A.'14, Univ. of Va.; Supt. of Sch., Staunton, Va., since 1925.

Sheldon, Donald R., B.S.'27, Kansas State Tchrs. Col.; M.A.'31, Stanford Univ.; Supt. of Sch., Prescott, Ariz., since 1935. On military leave since 1943.

Sheldon, Edwin R., B.S.'26, M.S.'32, State Tchrs. Col., Emporia, Kansas; Supt. of Sch., Burlington, Kansas, since 1942.

Shelton, Frank M., B.S.'99, Mt. Union Col.; M.A.'11, Columbia Univ.; Supvr. of H. S., State Dept. of Educ., Columbus, Ohio, since 1936.

Shelton, Nollie W., B.S.'31, Col. of William and Mary; M.A.'37, Univ. of N. C.; Co. Supt. of Sch., Swan Quarter, N. C., since 1941.

Shepherd, B. L., Asst. Supt. of Sch., 410 S. Cincinnati Ave., Tulsa, Okla.

Shepherd, Rulon T., M.S.'34, Univ. of Southern Calif.; Supt. of Sch., Mesa, Ariz., since 1937.

Shepoiser, L. H., B.A.'32, Iowa State Tchrs. Col.; M.A.'39, State Univ. of Iowa; Supt. of Sch., Independence, Iowa, since 1943.

Sherman, Warren A., A.B.'11, A.M.'16, Brown Univ.; Supt. of Sch., Warwick, R. I., since 1930. Address: Apponaug, R. I.

Shetter, Floyd A., B.S.'30, Bradley Polytech. Inst.; M.A.'37, State Univ. of Iowa; Co. Supt. of Sch., Rock Island, Ill., since 1935.

Shibles, Mark R., Supt. of Sch., Belmont 78, Mass.

Shibley, Arleigh P., B.Ped.'11, Northeast Mo. State Tchrs. Col., Kirksville, Mo.; B.S.'28, Univ. of Southern Calif.; Supt. and Dist. Prin., Mt. Empire Union H. S., Pine Valley, Calif., since 1937.

Shields, D. C., Sales Mgr., Superior Coach Corp., Lima, Ohio.

Shields, Richard A., Ph.B.'12, Dickinson Col.; M.A.'33, New York Univ.; Supt. of Special Sch. Dist., Lewes, Del., since 1928.

Shilling, John, Ph.B.'08, A.M.'10, Dickinson Col.; A.M.'25, Columbia Univ.; D.Sc. in Ed.'33, Dickinson Col.; Asst. Supt. Supt. in charge of Secondary Sch., State Dept. of Pub. Instr., Dover, Del., since 1919.

Shimmin, Irvin A., B.S.'28, Univ. of Calif.; Dist. Supt. and Prin., Le Grand Union H. S., Le Grand, Calif., since 1940.

Shineman, Howard G., A.B.'27, Cornell Univ. Address: Clinton, N. Y.

Shirley, William F., B.A.'07, Wabash Col.; M.A.'21, Columbia Univ.; Supt. of Sch., Marshalltown, Iowa, since 1920.

Shores, Roscoe V., A.B.'10, Central Col.; A.M.'25, Univ. of Wis.; Asst. Supt. of Sch., Library Bldg., Kansas City 6, Mo., since 1930.

Shotwell, Fred C., Ph.B.'16, Lafayette Col.; A.M.'21, Tchrs. Col., Columbia Univ.; Supvg. Prin. of Sch., Franklin, N. J., since 1923.

Shotwell, Harry White, B.A.'21, Syracuse Univ.; A.M.'27, Columbia Univ.; Dir. of Sec. Guidance, Pub. Sch., Union City, N. J., since 1938.

Shoun, H. Maine, B.A.'22, Carson-Newman Col.; Supt. of Sch., Jerome, Idaho, since 1930.

Shows, S. M., A.B.'26, La. State Normal Col., Natchitoches, La.; Parish Supt. of Sch., Mansfield, La., since 1926.

Shrode, Carl, A.B.'16, Swarthmore Col.; M.A.'22, Univ. of Pa.; Prin., Central H. S., Evansville 14, Ind., since 1927.

Shryock, Clara M., B.A.'31, M.Ed.'35, Pa. State Col.; D.Ed.'43, Univ. of Pittsburgh; Asst. Co. Supt. of Sch., Wilmore, Pa., since 1924.

Shuck, Albert C., A.B.'11, A.M.'12, Dickinson Col.; Co. Supt. of Sch., Salem, N. J., since 1931.

Shugart, G. Gardner, A.B.'28, A.M.'33, Univ. of Md.; Co. Supt. of Sch., Upper Marlboro, Md., since 1943.

Shulkey, Bruce C., B.A.'16, Baylor Univ.; M.A.'31, Texas Technological Col.; Asst. Supt. of Sch., Fort Worth, Texas, since 1935.

Sickles, Frederick James, A.B.'08, Syracuse Univ.; A.M.'18, Tchrs. Col., Columbia Univ.; Supt. of Sch., New Brunswick, N. J., since 1923.

Siepert, Albert F., B.S.'13, Tchrs. Col., Columbia Univ.; A.M.'24, Univ. of Chicago; Head, Dept. of Educ., Bradley Polytech. Inst., since 1913; Dir., Placement Bureau, Bradley Polytech. Inst., Peoria, Ill., since 1934.

Sifert, E. R., A.B.'13, Des Moines Univ.; M.A.'26, State Univ. of Iowa; Supt., Proviso Twp. H. S., Maywood, Ill., since 1936.

Silke, Eugene H., A.B.'30, Willamette Univ.; Supt. of Sch., Springfield, Oregon, since 1940.

Silver, Ernest L., B.L.'99, Pd.D.'24, Dartmouth Col.; Pres., Plymouth Tchrs. Col., Plymouth, N. H., since 1911.

Silverwood, Olney J., A.B.'00, Ohio Wesleyan Col.; Supt. of Sch., Ellsworth, Kansas, since 1909.

Simar, Harold O., B.A.'17, Upper Iowa Univ., M.A.'39, Univ. of Southern Calif.; Supt., Inglewood Union H. S. Dist., Inglewood, Calif., since 1939.

Simley, Irvin T., A.B.'11, Luther Col.; M.A.'27, Tchrs. Col., Columbia Univ.; Supt of Sch., South St. Paul, Minn., since 1926.

Simmers, Charles L., A.M.'23, Tchrs. Col., Columbia Univ.; Dir. of Tchr. Educ., State Tchrs. Col., Winona, Minn., since 1923.

Simmons, Harry D., A.B.'24, Univ. of Okla.; M.A.'27, Columbia Univ.; Supt. of Sch., Stillwater, Okla., since 1943.

Simmons, Vernon, B.A.'32, Univ. of Buffalo; Supvg. Prin., Eden Central Sch., Eden, N. Y., since 1940.

Simmons, Wiley, B.S.'40, Loyola Univ.; A.M.'42, Univ. of Chicago; Dist. Supt. of Sch., Simmons Sch., Oak Lawn, Ill., since 1925.

Simms, B. F., B.Ph.'26, B.D.'33, M.A.'39, Emory Univ.; Co. Supt. of Educ., Wedowee, Ala., since 1941.

Simon, H. B., B.S.'11, A.M.'26, Columbia Univ.; Supt. of Sch., Geneva, Nebr., since 1932.

Simplicia, Sister M., A.B.'23, Loyola Univ.; M.A.'27, Univ. of Mo.; Pres., Col. of St. Teresa, Kansas City, Mo., since 1939.

Simpson, Alfred Dexter, A.B.'13, Syracuse Univ.; M.A.'23, Yale Univ.; Ph.D.'27, Columbia Univ.; Prof. of Educ., Grad. Sch. of Educ., Harvard Univ., Cambridge, Mass., since 1940.

Simpson, J. Olen, B.A.'32, Univ. of Wash.; Supt. of Sch., Neah Bay, Wash., since 1941.

Simpson, John Childs, A.M.'11, Randolph-Macon Col.; Pres., Stratford Col., Danville, Va., since 1925.

Simpson, Laurens L., Pres., The Manual Arts Press, 237 N. Monroe St., Peoria 3, Ill.

Simpson, Roy E., M.A.'31, Claremont Colleges; Supt. of Sch., South Pasadena, Calif., since 1940.

Sinclair, John A., A.B.'04, Bates Col.; Union Supt. of Sch., Warner, N. H., since 1925.

Sindelar, J. C., Pres., Beckley-Cardy Co., 1632 Indiana Ave., Chicago 16, Ill.

Singer, Mrs. Mary J., M.A.'32, Tchrs. Col., Columbia Univ.; Prin., Park Sch., Wichita, Kansas, since 1929.

Singleton, Gordon G., B.S.'19, Univ. of Ga.; M.A.'24, Ph.D.'25, Tchrs. Col., Columbia Univ.; Pres., Mary Hardin-Baylor Col., Belton, Texas, since 1937.

Sinnott, Edward A., B.S.'22, M.A.'30, Fordham Univ.; Acting Supt. of Sch., Tuckahoe, N. Y., since 1942.

Sipe, Elmer E., Diploma '12 and '14, State Tchrs. Col., Kutztown, Pa.; Co. Supt. of Sch., Burnham, Pa., since 1930.

Sipple, Leslie B., B.Ped.'11, B.S. in Ed. '14, Northeast Mo. State Tchrs. Col., Kirksville, Mo.; M.A.'29, Columbia Univ.; Dean, Col. of Educ., Univ. of Wichita, Wichita 6, Kansas, since 1929.

Sischo, Doris J., Asst. Co. Supt. of Sch., San Bernardino, Calif.

Skarstedt, Marcus, B.L.S.'11, Univ. of Ill.; Ph.D.'24, Univ. of Calif.; Librn., San Francisco Jr. Col., San Francisco, Calif., since 1940.

• Skean, A. H., B.S.'14, Muhlenberg Col.; Exec. Dir., Convention and Visitors Bureau, Woolworth Bldg., New York 7, N. Y., since 1942.

Skeie, Elmer, Diploma '31, Univ. of N. Dak.; Co. Supt. of Sch., Hardin, Mont., since 1941.

Skidmore, Charles H., M.A.'01, Brigham Young Col.; State Supt. of Pub. Instr., Salt Lake City, Utah, since 1933.

Skiles, James Roy, A.B.'13, Univ. of Ill.; Dist. Supt. of Sch., 1323 Hinman Ave., Evanston, Ill., since 1925.

Skinner, John J., M.A.'06, Upper Iowa Univ.; Sc.B.'25, Univ. of Minn.; Supt. of Sch., Fairmont, Minn., since 1934.

Skustad, George A., B.A.'27, St. Olaf Col.; M.A.'34, Univ. of Minn.; Supt. of Sch., Virginia, Minn., since 1942.

Slade, A. A., A.B.'11, State Univ. of Iowa; Supt. of Sch., Laramie, Wyo., since 1927.

Slade, William, Jr., B.S.'17, Middlebury Col.; M.A.'20, Tchrs. Col., Columbia Univ.; Supt. of Sch., Glendale, Ohio, since 1933.

Slager, Fred C., B.Sc. in Ed.'20, Ohio Northern Univ.; M.A.'22, Ph.D.'36, Ohio State Univ.; Prin., Indianola Jr. H. S., Columbus, Ohio, since 1933.

Slater, Paul R., A.B.'25, Geneva Col.; M.Ed. '39, Univ. of Pittsburgh; Supt. of Sch., Cortland, Ohio, since 1937.

Slobetz, F. B., B.S.'31, Kansas State Tchrs. Col., Pittsburg, Kansas; A.M.'38, Univ. of Mo.; Supt. of Sch., Cabool, Mo., since 1942.

Slocum, Clyde W., Supvg. Prin. of Sch., Haddon Hgts., N. J., since 1942.

*Slonecker, Lyle Nelson, B.S.'24, M.S.'33, Colo. State Col.; Supt. of Sch., Leadville, Colo., since 1937.

Slutz, Frank D., A.B.'04, A.M.'06, Mt. Union Col.; A.M.'11, Harvard Univ.; Litt.D.'15, Univ. of Denver; L.H.D.'28, Mt. Union Col. Address: 16 Lexington Ave., Dayton, Ohio.

Sly, John Fairfield, A.B.'17, Iowa State Tchrs. Col.; A.M.'21, State Univ. of Iowa; Ph.D.'26, Harvard Univ.; Prof. of Politics, Princeton Univ., Princeton, N. J., since 1935.

Smaage, Leon, B.A.'30, Buena Vista Col.; M.A. in Ed.'36, Northwestern Univ.; Dist. Supt. of Sch., Brookfield, Ill., since 1940.

Small, Lowell A., B.S.'27, Kansas Wesleyan Univ.; M.A.'35, Univ. of Colo.; Supt. of Sch., Fort Scott, Kansas, since 1942.

Smart, Clifford H., Supt. of Sch., Auburn Hgts., Mich.

Smith, A. Haven, A.B.'04, Dickinson Col.; Supt. of Sch., Orange, Calif., since 1928.

Smith, Allen C., Supt. of Sch., Quitman, Ga.

Smith, Benjamin L., A.B.'16, M.A.'37, Duke Univ.; Supt. of Sch., Greensboro, N. C., since 1936.

Smith, Bertha, B.S.'29, A.M.'31, Tchrs. Col., Columbia Univ.; Asst. Supt. of Sch., Admin. Bldg., Yonkers, N. Y., since 1911.

Smith, C. C., A.B.'12, Lebanon Valley Col.; A.M.'19, Columbia Univ.; Supt. of Sch., Bridgeport, Pa., since 1932.

Smith, Cale C., B.S.'28, Kansas State Tchrs. Col., Pittsburg, Kansas; M.S.'38, State Univ. of Iowa; Supt. of Sch., Casa Grande, Ariz., since 1942.

Smith, Carl D., B.Hum.'14, Springfield Col.; M.Ed.'25, Harvard Univ.; LL.D.'41, Adrian Col.; Pres., Babson Inst., Babson Park, Mass., since 1935.

Smith, Carleton Blose, A.B.'19, Penn Col.; Supt. of Sch., Pekin, Ill., since 1923.

Smith, Cecil E., Prin., Pub. Sch., Pratt, Kansas.

Smith, Charles Bunyan, B.S.'22, M.A.'27, George Peabody Col. for Tchrs.; D.Ed.'40, Tchrs. Col., Columbia Univ.; Pres., State Tchrs. Col., Troy, Ala., since 1937.

Smith, Charles William, B.S.'30, Howard Col.; Acting Supt. of Sch., Hopewell, Va., since 1942.

Smith, Elmer Francis, B.S.'09, R. I. State Col.; M.A.'21, New York Univ.; Supt. of Sch., Roselle Park, N. J., since 1919.

Smith, Erman S., B.S.'00, Northern Ill. Normal Sch., Dixon, Ill.; Supt. of Sch., Barrington, Ill., since 1908.

Smith, Ethel L., B.S.'14, M.A.'25, Tchrs. Col., Columbia Univ.; Dir., Elem. Educ. and Binet Classes, Admin. Bldg., 9 S. Stockton St., Trenton, N. J., since 1936.

Smith, Ezra E., Co. Supt. of Sch., Riverside, Calif., since 1926.

Smith, Floyd, Ph.B.'25, Ph.M.'32, Univ. of Wis.; Supt. of Sch., Wisconsin Rapids, Wis., since 1936.

Smith, Frank L., B.S.'10, Syracuse Univ.; Supt. of Sch., Lancaster, N. Y., since 1921.

Smith, George A., A.B.'19, Mich. State Normal Col., Ypsilanti, Mich.; A.M.'24, Univ. of Mich.; Supt. of Sch., Plymouth, Mich., since 1918.

Smith, George B., Capt., U. S. Army, Calif.-Ariz. Maneuver Area, APO 180, c/o Postmaster, Los Angeles, Calif.

Smith, George Owen, B.S.'01, Valparaiso Univ.; Supt. of Sch., Princeton, Ill., since 1923.

Smith, Guy D., A.B.'98, Kalamazoo Col.; A.B.'00, Univ. of Chicago; Supt. of City Sch. and of Educ. at State Prison, Stillwater, Minn., since 1924.

Smith, H. P., Supt. of Sch., Toronto, Ohio, since 1941.

Smith, Harold W., A.B.'16, East Texas State Normal Sch., Commerce, Texas; M.A.'30, Univ. of Calif.; Supt. of Grammar Sch., Glendale, Ariz., since 1925.

Smith, Harry Pearse, A.B.'09, A.M.'15, State Univ. of Iowa; Ph.D.'25, Columbia Univ.; Prof. of Educ., Syracuse Univ., since 1927 and Dir. of Research, Pub. Sch., Syracuse, N. Y., since 1928.

Smith, Harvey A., A.B.'14, Franklin and Marshall Col.; A.M.'21, Univ. of Pa.; Ph.D.'30, Columbia Univ.; Supt. of Sch., Lancaster, Pa., since 1938.

Smith, Henry Earl, Ph.B.'20, Ph.M.'28, Univ. of Wis.; Supt. of Sch., Sheboygan, Wis., since 1934.

* Smith, Henry Lester, A.B.'98, A.M.'99, Ind. Univ.; A.M.'10, Ph.D.'16, Columbia Univ.; LL.D.'40, Butler Univ.; Pres. Natl. Educ. Assn., 1934-35; Dean, Sch. of Educ., Ind. Univ., since 1916 and Dir., Bureau of Cooperative Research and Field Service, Ind. Univ., Bloomington, Ind., since 1921.

Smith, Hubert H., A.B.'15, Wabash Col.; M.A.'26, Tchrs. Col., Columbia Univ.; Supvg. Prin. of Sch., Hammonton, N. J., since 1927.

Smith, J. W., B.S.'15, Carroll Col.; M.A.'27, Univ. of Chicago; Supt. of Sch., Bemidji, Minn., since 1929.

Smith, Kenneth E., B.S.'21, Colgate Univ.; M.A.'27, Tchrs. Col., Columbia Univ.; Supt. of Sch., Walden, N. Y., since 1937.

Smith, L. J., B.Sc.'18, Ohio State Univ.; M.Sc.'37, Cornell Univ.; Supt. of Sch., Massillon, Ohio, since 1936.

Smith, Leon O., B.A.'10, M.A.'18, State Univ. of Iowa; Asst. Supt. of Sch., City Hall, Omaha, Nebr., since 1919.

* Smith, Lewis Wilbur, A.B.'02, Denison Univ.; A.M.'13, Ph.D.'19, Univ. of Chicago; LL.D.'28, Denison Univ. Address: 98 Alamo Ave., Berkeley, Calif.

Smith, Marion Lofton, M.A. and B.D.'21, Emory Univ.; Ph.D.'29, Yale Univ.; Pres., Millsaps Col., Jackson, Miss., since 1938.

Smith, Mark, B.S.'15, Clemson Agrl. Col.; LL.D.'39, Mercer Univ.; Co. Supt. of Sch., Macon, Ga., since 1942.

Smith, Max S., A.B.'31, Univ. of Denver; M.A.'35, Univ. of Mich.; Supt. of Sch., North Muskegon 31, Mich., since 1940.

Smith, Nelson C., B.L.'01, Boston Univ.; M.L.'10, Univ. of Calif.; Supvg. Prin. of Sch., Leonia, N. J., since 1921.

Smith, Payson, A.M.'03, Tufts Col.; LL.D. '08, Univ. of Maine; Litt.D.'09, Bates Col.; Litt.D.'11, Bowdoin Col.; D.Ed., R. I. Col. of Educ.; LL.D., Norwich Univ.; LL.D., Northeastern Univ.; LL.D.'35, Springfield Col.; D.Ed., Colby Col.; Pres., Dept. of Superintendence, 1923-24; Lecturer, Sch. of Educ., Univ. of Maine, Orono, Maine.

Smith, Raymond A., A.B.'00, A.M.'04, Butler Col.; B.D.'05, Yale Univ.; Dean, Sch. of Educ., Texas Christian Univ., Fort Worth, Texas, since 1943.

Smith, S. L., B.A.'07, Southwestern; M.A. '18, George Peabody Col. for Tchrs.; D.Ed.'32, Southwestern; Dir. of Pub. Relations, George Peabody Col. for Tchrs., Nashville 4, Tenn., since 1938.

Smith, Sim Joe, A.B.'15, Trinity Univ.; LL.B.'21, Univ. of Texas; M.A.'27, Tchrs. Col., Columbia Univ.; Asst. Supt. of Sch., New Rochelle, N. Y., since 1930.

Smith, Thurber Montgomery, A.B.'13, St. Mary's Col., Leavenworth, Kansas; A.M.'15, LL.B.'16, Loyola Univ., Chicago, Ill.; Ph.D.'31, St. Louis Univ.; Dean, Graduate Sch., St. Louis Univ., St. Louis, Mo., since 1933.

Smith, Vernon G., A.B.'21, Colby Col.; A.M.'29, Tchrs. Col., Columbia Univ.; Supt. of Sch., Scarsdale, N. Y., since 1932.

Smith, Vivian Thomas, A.B.'16, Greenville Col.; A.M.'29, Ph.D.'33, Univ. of Ill.; LL.D. '43, Cornell Col.; Pres., Upper Iowa Univ., Fayette, Iowa, since 1938.

Smith, W. H., B.S.'28, M.S.'29, Cornell Univ.; Acting Pres., Copiah-Lincoln Jr. Col., Wesson, Miss., since 1943.

Smith, Walden T., B.A.'24, Iowa Wesleyan Col.; M.A.'37, State Univ. of Iowa; Supt. of Consol. Sch., Mediapolis, Iowa, since 1936.

Smith, Walter Irvine, A.B.'11, Union Col.; M.A.'17, Whitman Col.; Ed.D.'34, George Wash. Univ. Address: Pacific Union Col., Angwin, Calif.

Smith, William M., A.B.'12, Dickinson Col.; Supt. of Sch., Long Branch, N. J., since 1936.

Snapp, C. V., A.B.'23, M.A.'34, Univ. of Ky.; Supt. of Sch., Jenkins, Ky., since 1929.

Snarr, Otto Welton, A.B.'17, W. Va. Univ.; A.M.'19, Ph.D.'41, Univ. of Chicago; Pres., State Tchrs. Col., Moorhead, Minn., since 1941.

Snead, Joseph Payne, Co. Supt. of Sch., Fork Union, Va.

Snider, R. Nelson, A.B.'22, Ball State Tchrs. Col., Muncie, Ind.; M.A.'30, Columbia Univ.; Prin., South Side H. S., Fort Wayne, Ind., since 1926.

Snow, Carl B., Pub. Sch., Caledonia, Mich.

Snow, Fletcher J., Product Mgr., Sch. Div., American Seating Co., Grand Rapids, Mich.

Snow, Irene, Dist. Supt. of Elem. Sch., Napa, Calif., since 1937.

Snowden, Foster B., Ph.B.'15, Lafayette Col.; M.A.'31, Ed.D.'34, Univ. of Pittsburgh; Supt. of Sch., Jeannette, Pa., since 1938.

Snuggs, William E., B.S.'20, Ala. Poly. Inst.; M.A.'28, Tchrs. Col., Columbia Univ.; Supt. of Sch., Selma, Ala., since 1943.

Snyder, Alfred H., B.S.'29, Grove City Col.; M.Ed.'42, Univ. of Pittsburgh; Acting Supvg. Prin. of Sch., Verona, Pa., since 1940.

Snyder, Franklyn B., A.B.'05, Beloit Col.; M.A.'07, Ph.D.'09, Harvard Univ.; LL.D.'35, Beloit Col.; LL.D.'39, Colby Col.; L.H.D.'39, Northwestern Univ.; LL.D.'40, Univ. of Pittsburgh; Litt.D.'40, Ill. Wesleyan Univ.; LL.D.'41, Wesleyan Univ.; Pres., Northwestern Univ., Evanston, Ill., since 1939.

Snyder, Harold E., Commn. on Tchr. Educ., American Council on Educ., 7203 Harwick Rd., N. W., Washington, D. C.

Snyder, Lewis N., A.B.'16, Gettysburg Col.; A.M.'24, Univ. of Pa.; Supvg. Prin. of Sch., Sellersville, Pa., since 1929.

Snyder, Raymond Hugo, A.B.'12, Ind. Univ.; M.A.'19, Univ. of Chicago; Pres., State Normal Sch., Albion, Idaho, since 1933.

Snyder, Warren P., B.S.'20, Muhlenberg Col.; M.S.'32, Temple Univ.; Supt. of Sch., Bristol, Pa., since 1936.

Soderstrom, LaVern W., M.A.'35, Univ. of Kansas; Supt. of Sch., Lindsborg, Kansas, since 1930.

Soelberg, John, B.S.'25, Univ. of Utah; M.A.'29, Univ. of Calif.; Prin., McClymonds H. S., Oakland, Calif., since 1943.

Solomon, R. W., A.B.'99, Ohio Northern Univ.; Ph.B. in Ed.'15, Univ. of Chicago; Supt. of Sch., Middletown, Ohio, since 1917.

* Somerville, Irwin B., Supt. of Sch., Ridgewood, N. J., since 1931.

Sone, L. L., B.S.'26, West Texas State Tchrs. Col., Canyon, Texas; M.S.'40, Univ. of Southern Calif.; Supt. of Sch., Pampa, Texas, since 1938.

Sorensen R. R., B.S.'15, Carleton Col.; A.M.'24, Columbia Univ.; Supt. of Sch., Tracy, Minn., since 1921.

Sorenson, Herbert, Ph.D.'28, Univ. of Minn.; Pres., Duluth State Col., Duluth, Minn., since 1938.

Souder, Rexford S., Ed.D.'41, Tchrs. Col., Columbia Univ.; Admin. and Research Asst., Pub. Sch., 825 Union St., San Diego 2, Calif., since 1941.

Soule, Howard M., A.B.'29, Univ. of Redlands; M.A.'36, Univ. of Colo.; Prin., Osborn Sch., Phoenix, Ariz., since 1934.

Southerlin, W. B., B.A.'29, Furman Univ.; M.A.'42, Univ. of S. C.; Supt. of Sch., Winnsboro, S. C., since 1943.

Southworth. E. F., Pres., Iroquois Pub. Co., Inc., Chimes Bldg., Syracuse, N. Y.

Spain, Charles L., A.B.'93, M.A.'20, Ph.D.'23, Univ. of Mich. Address: Art Center Apts., 201 Kirby Ave., E., Detroit, Mich.

Spalding, Willard, B.B.A.'26, Boston Univ.; Ed.M.'33, Univ. of N. H.; D.Ed.'42, Harvard Univ.; Supt. of Sch., Portland, Oregon, since 1944.

Sparks, Frank H., A.B.'37, Butler Univ.; A.M., Ph.D.'41, Univ. of Southern Calif.; Pres., Wabash Col., Crawfordsville, Ind., since 1941.

Sparling, E. A., B.S.'16, Northeast Mo. State Tchrs. Col., Kirksville, Mo.; M.A.'32, State Univ. of Iowa; Supt. of Sch., Crystal City, Mo., since 1932.

Spaulding, Frank E., A.B.'89, Amherst Col.; A.M., Ph.D.'94, Leipzig Univ., Germany; LL.D.'20, Amherst Col.; A.M.'20, Yale Univ.; Honorary Life Member, American Assn. of Sch. Admin.; Prof. Emeritus of Educ., Yale Univ., since 1935. Address: 2901 Hill Dr., Los Angeles, Calif.

Speaker, Gaylord M., Supt. of Sch., River Rouge, Mich.

Spearman, C. E., A.B.'32, M.A.'39, Univ. of Ala.; Ed.D.'43, Tchrs. Col., Columbia Univ.; Co. Supt. of Sch., Tuscaloosa, Ala., since 1943.

Spears, Harold, A.B.'24, Wabash Col.; M.A.'31, Ed.D.'39, Tchrs. Col., Columbia Univ.; Prin., Highland Park H. S., Highland Park, Ill., since 1941.

Specht, Clarence W., Ph.B.'28, Xavier Univ.; M.Ed.'33, Univ. of Pittsburgh; Supt. of Sch., Fort Jennings, Ohio, since 1936.

Speer, James B., Sr., B.S.'29, West Texas State Tchrs. Col., Canyon, Texas; M.A. '33, Texas Tech. Col.; Supt. of Sch., Canyon, Texas, since 1938.

Speer, Owen D., A.B.'16, Univ. of Mont.; Supt. of Sch., Deer Lodge, Mont., since 1914.

Speer, R. L., M.A.'33, Univ. of Colo.; Supt. of Sch., Sherman, Texas, since 1937.

Spencer, Mrs. Evelyn, Deputy State Supt. of Pub. Instr., Olympia, Wash., since 1941.

Spencer, Herbert Lincoln, B.S.'21, Carnegie Inst. of Tech.; M.A.'26, Ph.D.'34, Univ. of Pittsburgh; Pres., Pa. Col. for Women, Pittsburgh, Pa., since 1935.

Spencer, Robert R., A.B.'23, Univ. of Hawaii; M.A.'33, Stanford Univ.; Prin., Roosevelt H. S., Honolulu, Hawaii, since 1934.

Spiess, Henry R., A.B.'21, Willamette Univ.; A.M.'30, Stanford Univ.; Supt. of Sch., Antioch, Calif., since 1942.

Spiess, R. J., Supt., Bloomfield Hills Sch., Bloomfield, Mich.

Spikes, L. E., A.B.'24, M.Ed.'34, Duke Univ.; M.A.'39, Columbia Univ.; Ph.D.'42, George Peabody Col. for Tchrs.; Supt. of Sch., Burlington, N. C., since 1936.

Spinas, Andrew, A.B.'30, Humboldt State Col.; Dist. Supt. of Sch., Redwood City, Calif., since 1937.

Spinning, James M., A.B.'13, Univ. of Rochester; Supt. of Sch., 13 Fitzhugh St., S., Rochester 4, N. Y., since 1933.

Sprague, G. A., Supt. of Sch., Sweet Home, Oregon.

Sprague, Harry A., B.S.'14, M.A.'23, Ph.D. '40, Tchrs. Col., Columbia Univ.; Pres., N. J. State Tchrs. Col., Upper Montclair, N. J., since 1927.

Spratt, Elliott C., Sales Mgr., The Hillyard Co., St. Joseph 1, Mo., since 1925.

Spring, Gardiner W., A.B.'15, M.A.'27, Univ. of Calif.; Pres., Chaffey Jr. Col. and Supt. of Chaffey H. S., Ontario, Calif., since 1931.

Sprouse, W. Lloyd, A.B.'21, Ohio Univ.; A M.'28. Ph.D.'40, Ohio State Univ.; Dir., Div. of Instr., State Dept. of Educ., State Office Bldg., Columbus, Ohio, since 1943.

* Spry, Edward W., A.M.'22, Univ. of Rochester; Supt. of Sch., LeRoy, N. Y., since 1928.

Spurr, Ethel M., A.B.'19, Radcliffe Col.; A.M.'24, Columbia Univ.; Prin., Northrop Collegiate Sch., Minneapolis, Minn., since 1933.

Stabler, D. A., A.M.'29, Univ. of Chicago; Supt. of Sch., Otsego, Mich., since 1939.

Stabler, Ernest, B.A.'39, Queen's Univ.; M.A.'43, McGill Univ.; Headmaster, Sir George Williams H. S., Y.M.C.A., 1441 Drummond St., Montreal, Canada, since 1942.

Stabley, Elwood C., A.B.'24, Lebanon Valley Col.; M.A.'31, Univ. of Pa.; Supvg. Prin. of Sch., Unionville, Pa., since 1936.

* Stahl, H. E., A.B.'14, Ind. Univ.; A.M.'18, Tchrs. Col., Columbia Univ.; Supt. of Claymont Special Sch. Dist., Claymont, Del., since 1922.

Stahr, Henry I., A.B.'01, A.M.'04, Franklin and Marshall Col.; D.D.'26, Cornell Univ.; LL.D.'35, Ursinus Col.; Pres., Hood Col., Frederick, Md., since 1934.

Staib, J. R., B.S.'21, State Tchrs. Col., Pittsburg, Kansas; M.S. in Ed.'29, Univ. of Okla.; Supt. of Sch., Hominy, Okla., since 1932.

Staley, A. H., A.B.'01, Univ. of Nebr.; D.Ped.'39, Hastings Col.; Supt. of Sch., Hastings, Nebr., since 1919.

Staley, George R., B.S.'00, Syracuse Univ.; Supt. of Sch., Rome, N. Y., since 1912.

Stanforth, Alva T., B.S.'14, Muskingum Col.; Ph.D.'28, New York Univ.; Supvg. Prin. of Sch., Floral Park, N. Y., since 1932.

Staniford, Paul, A.B.'16, Stanford Univ.; LL.B.'24, Univ. of Calif.; Vice-Pres., Sch. Bd., 1444 M St., Fresno 1, Calif., since 1924.

Stansbury, Verne E., A.B.'19, Southwestern Col., Winfield, Kansas; A.M.'20, Univ. of Chicago; Supt. of Sch., Carroll, Iowa, since 1934.

Stanton, Benjamin F., B.A.'96, Oberlin Col.; M.A.'00, Harvard Univ. Address: 232 Vincent Blvd., Alliance, Ohio.

Staples, Leon C., A.B.'03, Colby Col.; Supt. of Sch., Stamford, Conn., since 1933.

Stark, Harold C., B.S.'19, Mich. State Col.; A.M.'29, Univ. of Mich.; Supt. of Sch., Buchanan, Mich., since 1923.

Starke, Louis E., A.B.'26, Culver-Stockton Col.; A.M.'37, Univ. of Mo.; Supt. of Sch., Morris, Ill., since 1939.

Stateler, C. B., Sales Mgr., A. J. Nystrom & Co., 3333 Elston Ave., Chicago, Ill.

Stearns, Harry Lee, A.B.'22, Dickinson Col.; M.A.'29, Univ. of Pittsburgh; Ph.D.'36, New York Univ.; Supt. of Sch., Woodbury, N. J., since 1935.

Steel, Charles L., Jr., B.S.'19, Muhlenberg Col.; Prin., H. S., Teaneck N. J., since 1933.

Steele, A. G., B.S.'25, Southwestern State Tchrs. Col., Weatherford, Okla.; Ed.M. '33, Univ. of Okla.; Supt. of Sch., Altus, Okla., since 1933.

Steele, Harry J., Dir. of Tr., State Tchrs. Col., Buffalo, N. Y.

Steele, M. E., A.B.'15, Valparaiso Univ.; Ph.B.'27, Univ. of Chicago; M.A.'32, Columbia Univ.; Supt. of Sch., Mendota, Ill., since 1927.

Steele, N. E., B.S.'19, S. Dak. State Col.; M.A.'28, Ph.D.'34, State Univ. of Iowa; Pres., Northern State Tchrs. Col., Aberdeen, S. Dak., since 1939.

Steelhead, Bert F., Prin., Home Sch., Glendale, Calif., since 1943.

Steger, Leonard Andrew, A.B.'27, Iowa State Tchrs. Col., Cedar Falls, Iowa; A.M.'32, State Univ. of Iowa; Supt. of Sch., Ames, Iowa, since 1940.

Stegner, Warren E., B.S.'16, Carleton Col.; M.A.'39, Univ. of Minn.; Supt. of Sch., Miles City, Mont., since 1937.

Steiner, John P., A.B.'23, Southwestern Col.; M.A.'34, Univ. of Kansas; Supt. of Sch., Portales, N. Mex., since 1934. On military leave since 1943.

Steiner, Melvin A., B.A.'09, Col. of Wooster; M.A.'13, Ph.D.'30, Univ. of Pittsburgh; Supvg. Prin. of Sch., Ingram, Pittsburgh, Pa., since 1918.

Steinke, E. L., B.A.'34, M.A.'37, Wash. State Col.; Supt. of Sch., Selah, Wash.

Stellwagen, Herbert Philip, B.S.'98, Univ. of Mich.; M.A.'27, Tchrs. Col., Columbia Univ.; Prin., Soldan H. S., 918 Union Blvd., St. Louis, Mo., since 1929.

Stengle, F. E., A.M.'30, Lebanon Valley Col.; A.M.'33, Univ. of Pa.; Supt. of Sch., Collingdale, Pa., since 1934.

Stephan, Burton, A.B.'24, A.M.'29, Ind. Univ.; Supt. of Sch., Huntington, Ind., since 1941.

Stephens, Ernest, A.B.'10, Dartmouth Col.; Ed.M.'27, Harvard Univ.; Deputy Supt. of Sch., Lynn, Mass., since 1927.

Stephens, Joseph B., B.S.'20, M.A.'31, Univ. of Chicago; Sr. Class Prin., Thornton Twp. H. S., Harvey, Ill., since 1925.

Stephens, Theodore P., A:B.'29, Aurora Col.; A.M.'37, Univ. of Chicago; Pres., Aurora Col., Aurora, Ill., since 1933.

Stern, Bessie C., A.B.'09, Cornell Univ.; Ed.M.'21, Harvard Univ.; Dir., Bureau of Measurements, State Dept. of. Educ., Lexington Bldg., Baltimore, Md., since 1921.

Stetson, G. Arthur, B.S.'19, Allegheny Col.; M.A.'27, Tchrs. Col., Columbia Univ.; D.Ed.'41, Univ. of Pittsburgh; Supt. of Sch., West Chester, Pa., since 1938.

Stevens, Evan Ray, B.S.'18, Kansas State Tchrs. Col., Emporia, Kansas; M.S.'25, Univ. of Kansas; Dean, Jr. Col. and Prin., Sr. H. S., Independence, Kansas, since 1926.

Stevens, Francis L., B.S.'26, Union Col.; M.A.'38, Columbia Univ.; Prin., Pub. Sch., Ballston Lake, N. Y., since 1938.

Stevens, Homer L., A.B.'15, Wittenberg Col.; M.A.'30, Ohio State Univ.; Supt. of Sch., Springfield, Ohio, since 1936.

Stevens, Paul C., A.B.'26, M.A.'36, Univ. of Denver; Supt. of Sch., Wheat Ridge, Colo., since 1934.

Stevens, Theodore G., B.A.'23, Univ. of Wash.; Supt. of Sch., Ridgefield, Wash., since 1938.

Stewart, David H., B.S.'15, Pa. State Col.; A.M.'25, Columbia Univ.; Ph.D.'35, Univ. of Pittsburgh; Supt. of Sch., Dormont, Pa., since 1936.

Stewart, Mrs. E. O., M.A.'36, Colo. State Col. of Educ., Greeley, Colo.; Prin., Woodrow Wilson Elem. Sch., Houston, Texas, since 1919.

Stewart, Harry L., A.B.'24, State Tchrs. Col., Valley City, N. Dak.; Supvg. Prin. of Sch., Oakdale, Pa., since 1924.

Stewart, Lyle, A.B.'24, Simpson Col.; A.M. '30, Univ. of Wash.; Admin. Asst., Pub. Sch., 810 Dexter Ave., Seattle 9, Wash., since 1941.

Stewart, R. E., Sch. Sales Mgr., Underwood Elliott Fisher Co., 1 Park Ave., New York, N. Y.

Stiles, Chester D., A.B.'00, M.A.'09, Williams Col.; Supt. of Sch., Westfield, Mass., since 1918.

Stilwell, H. W., B.A.'09, M.A.'19, Univ. of Texas; Supt. of Sch., Texarkana, Texas, since 1920.

Stinebaugh, Virgil, A.B.'21, Manchester Col.; A.M.'27, Columbia Univ.; Asst. Supt. in charge of Jr. H. S. and Curriculum Studies, Pub. Sch., Indianapolis, Ind., since 1936.

Stock, Earl K., A.B.'19, Gettysburg Col.; M.S.'30, Pa. State Col.; Supvg. Prin. of Sch., Bellefonte, Pa., since 1931.

Stockard, L. V., A.B.'11, A.M.'19, Univ. of Texas; Asst. Supt. of Sch., 6944 Lakewood, Dallas, Texas, since 1938.

Stoddard, Alexander Jerry, B.S.'21, Univ. of Nebr.; M.A.'22, Tchrs. Col., Columbia Univ.; D.Ed.'33, R. I. Col. of Educ.; L.H.D.'39, Beaver Col.; LL.D.'39, Temple Univ.; LL.D.'40, Univ. of Nebr.; L.H.D. '40, Univ. of Pa.; Pres., Dept. of Superintendence, 1935-36; Chmn., Educ. Policies Commn., since 1936; Supt. of Sch., Philadelphia 3, Pa., since 1939.

Stoddard, George D., B.A.'21, Pa. State Col.; Diplôme '23, Univ. of Paris; Ph.D.'25, State Univ. of Iowa; Commr. of Educ., State Educ. Dept., Albany, N. Y., since 1942.

Stoddard, J. A., A.B.'02, Univ. of S. C.; M.A.'24, George Peabody Col. for Tchrs.; LL.D.'30, Presbyterian Col. of S. C.; Prof. of Sec. Educ. and Dir. of Summer Sch., Univ. of S. C., Columbia, S. C., since 1918.

Stoffel, John G., Prin., Richland Co. Rural Normal Sch., Richland Center, Wis.

Stokes, Ella Harrison, B.S.'99, M.A.'01, Ohio Wesleyan Univ.; Ph.D.'10, Univ. of Chicago; Head, Dept. of Educ. and Philosophy, Penn Col., Oskaloosa, Iowa, 1901-1908, and since 1911.

Stokesbary, M. R., M.Sc.'37, Univ. of Southern Calif.; Asst. Supt. of Sch., Alhambra, Calif., since 1938.

Stolz, Herbert R., B.A.'10, M.D.'14, Stanford Univ.; Asst. Supt. of Sch., 1025 Second Ave., Oakland, Calif., since 1935.

Stone, Violet G., Ph.D.'37, Univ. of Southern Calif.; Dir. of Elem. Educ., Pub. Sch., Ventura, Calif., since 1942.

Storey, Bernice L., A.B.'19, Univ. of Pittsburgh; M.A.'29, Tchrs. Col., Columbia Univ.; Ph.D.'36, Univ. of Pittsburgh; Prin., Larimer Elem. Sch., Pittsburgh, Pa., since 1939.

Stover, James D., B.A.'12, M.A.'13, Princeton Univ.; Asst. Supt. of Sch., 216 E. Ninth St., Cincinnati, Ohio, since 1929.

Stowe, A. Monroe, A.M.'04, Northwestern Univ.; A.M.'05, Harvard Univ.; Ph.D.'09, Columbia Univ.; Prof. of Educ., Univ. of N. H., Durham, N. H., since 19_

Stowe, George Ed., B.B.A.'28, Texas Christian Univ.; M.A.'40, Hardin-Simmons Univ.; Supt. of Sch., Mertzon, Texas, since 1942.

Strachan, Lexie, Psychologist, Pub. Sch., Library Bldg., Kansas City 6, Mo.

Stradling, James G., B.E.E.'00, Lafayette Col.; Vice-Pres., The John C. Winston Co., 1006-16 Arch St., Philadelphia, Pa., since 1919.

Strahan, Charles J., Exec. Secy., N. J. Educ. Assn., Stacy-Trent Hotel, Trenton, N. J., since 1943.

Strand, Arthur E., M.A.'35, Univ. of Minn.; Co. Supt. of Sch., Duluth, Minn., since 1943.

Stratton, Mason A., B.S. in Ed.'28, New York Univ.; Dir. of Elem. Schools, 1809 Pacific Ave., Atlantic City, N. J., since 1941.

*Strayer, George D., A.B.'03, Johns Hopkins Univ.; Ph.D.'05, Columbia Univ.; LL.D. '25, Col. of William and Mary; Litt.D.'29, Columbia Univ.; LL.D.'30, Bucknell Univ.; Pres., Natl. Educ. Assn., 1918-19; Honorary Life Member, American Assn. of Sch. Admin.; Prof. Emeritus, Tchrs. Col., Columbia Univ., New York 27, N. Y., since 1943.

*Strayer, George D., Jr., B.S.'27, Princeton Univ.; M.A.'28, Ph.D.'34, Tchrs. Col., Columbia Univ.; Assoc. Prof. of Educ., Sch. of Educ., Ind. Univ., Bloomington, Ind., since 1941.

Street, Claude W., B.S.'06, Carleton Col.; A.M.'12, Univ. of Minn.; Ph.D.'33, Columbia Univ.; Head, Dept. of Educ., State Tchrs. Col., Pittsburg, Kansas, since 1932.

Streitz, Ruth, Ph.B.'21, A.M.'22, Univ. of Chicago; Ph.D.'26, Columbia Univ.; Prof. of Educ., Ohio State Univ., Columbus, Ohio, since 1937.

Strickland, Chester O., M.A.'39, Univ. of Texas; Supt. of Sch., White Deer, Texas, since 1941.

Strickland, Ruth G., B.S.'25, M.A.'32, Tchrs. Col., Columbia Univ.; Ph.D.'38, Columbia Univ.; Asst. Prof. of Educ., Sch. of Educ., Ind. Univ., Bloomington, Ind., since 1939.

Strickler, Robert E., Dist. Prin., 7003 Pernod, St. Louis, Mo.

Stringer, Ralph E., A.M.'25, Univ. of Chicago; Prin., Robinson Twp. H. S., Robinson, Ill., since 1932.

Stringer, Simeon Lafayette, B.S.'00, Southern Normal Univ.; B.A.'02, Western Ky. State Normal Sch., Bowling Green, Ky.; M.A.'28, Univ. of Miss.; Supt., Clara Special Consol. Sch., Clara, Miss.

Stroble, M. D., M.Ed.'36, Univ. of Texas; Supt. of Sch., Poteet, Texas, since 1939.

Strong, Ormond B., Supt. of Sch., 208 Bull St., Savannah, Ga., since 1926.

Strong, Solomon C., Diploma '02, State Normal Sch., East Stroudsburg, Pa.; B.S.'16, New York Univ.; Supt. of Sch., West Orange, N. J., since 1918.

Strong, W. Melvin, B.S.'27, Brigham Young Univ.; M.S.'33, Univ. of Utah; D.Ed.'43, Univ. of Southern Calif.; Dir. of Adult Educ., War Relocation Area, Manzanar, Calif.

Strong, William M., B.S.'13, Tufts Col.; Ed.M.'29, Harvard Univ.; Supt. of Sch., Southington, Conn., since 1934.

Stuart, Alden T., Supt. of Sch., Perry, N. Y.

Stuart, Mrs. Amy E., B.A.'29, M.A.'30, Southern Methodist Univ.; Prin., Maple Lawn Sch., Dallas, Texas, since 1923.

Stuart, Harry G., B.S.'11, Muhlenberg Col.; A.M.'34, Tchrs. Col., Columbia Univ.; Supvg. Prin. of Twp. Sch., Bernardsville, N. J., since 1930.

Stuart, Herman H., A.B.'01, Bates Col.; Supt. of Sch., Melrose, Mass., since 1922.

Stubblefield, G. A., B.S.E.'24, M.S.'31, Univ. of Ark.; Supt. of Sch., Marianna, Ark., since 1939.

Stubbs, G. T., A.B.'26, Southeastern State Tchrs. Col., Durant, Okla.; M.A.'31, Tchrs. Col., Columbia Univ.; Supt. of Sch., Durant, Okla., since 1929.

Studebaker, John W., A.B.'10, Leander Clark Col.; A.M.'17, Columbia Univ.; LL.D.'34, Drake Univ.; LL.D.'38, Muhlenberg Col.; U. S. Commr. of Educ., Federal Security Agency, Washington 25, D. C., since 1934.

Studwell, Harold F., A.M.'27, Columbia Univ.; Ed.D.'39, New York Univ.; Supt. of Sch., East Rockaway, N. Y., since 1925.

Study, Harry P., A.B.'03, Baker Univ.; M.A.'11, Boston Univ.; A.M.'28, Columbia Univ.; Supt. of Sch., Springfield, Mo., since 1924.

Sturm, George N., A.B.'30, Okla. City Univ.; M.Ed.'39, Univ. of Okla.; Prin., Classen H. S., Oklahoma City, Okla., since 1942.

Sturtevant, Merle Alton, B.S.'08, Univ. of Maine; Supt. of Sch., Shrewsbury, Mass., since 1923.

Stutsman, I. E., A.B.'09, State Univ. of Iowa; M.A.'24, Univ. of Denver; Supt. of Sch., San Antonio 3, Texas, since 1939.

Suddath, W. N., B.S. in Ed.'31, Central Mo. State Tchrs. Col., Warrensburg, Mo.; M.Ed.'37, Univ. of Mo.; Supt. of Sch., Desloge, Mo., since 1939.

Sudman, Chester G., B.S.'30, Mich. State Normal Col., Ypsilanti, Mich.; Supt. of Sch., Lapham Sch., Allen Park, Dearborn, Mich., since 1930.

Suerken, Ernst Henry, A.B.'30, A.M.'31, Cornell Univ.; M.A.'42, State Tchrs. Col., Montclair, N. J.; Supvg. Prin., The Children's Village H. S., Dobbs Ferry, N. Y., since 1942.

Suhrie, Ambrose L., Ph.B.'06, John B. Stetson Univ.; A.M.'11, Ph.D.'12, Univ. of Pa.; LL.D.'19, John B. Stetson Univ.; Litt.D. '41, Duquesne Univ.; Consultant to Co-operative Negro Col. Study, State Tchrs. Col., Montgomery, Ala., since 1942.

Sullivan, Walter Caswell, A.B.'17, A.M.'18, Univ. of S. C.; Supt. of Sch., Rock Hill, S. C., since 1938.

Sutton, T. D., A.M., Univ. of Chicago; Prin., Amboy Twp. H. S., Amboy, Ill., since 1943.

Sutton, Willis A., Ph.B.'03, LL.B.'04, Emory Univ.; Ped.D.'23, Oglethorpe Univ.; LL.D.'40, Emory Univ.; Pres., Natl. Educ. Assn., 1930-31; Supt. Emeritus, Atlanta Pub. Sch., and Exec. Secy., Ga. Educ. Assn., Atlanta, Ga., since 1944.

Swaim, Laura Grey, Ed.M.'38, Temple Univ.; Supvg. Prin. of Sch., Maple Shade, N. J., since 1922.

Swain, Carl C., M.A.'18, Columbia Univ.; Pres., State Tchrs. Col., Minot, N. Dak., since 1938.

Swanson, A. M., M.S. in Ed.'22, Univ. of Kansas; Pres., Jr. Col., Kansas City, Mo., since 1939.

Swanson, Walter G., Genl. Mgr., Convention and Tourist Bureau, Civic Auditorium, San Francisco 2, Calif.

Swartz, D. V., A.B.'31, Southwestern Col.; M.A.'38, Univ. of Colo.; Supt. of Sch., Sterling, Kansas, since 1942.

Swartz, George G., Supt. of Sch., Meade, Kansas.

Sweeney, Ellen C., B.S.'36, Boston Univ.; Asst. Supt. of Sch., New Bedford, Mass., since 1942.

Sweeney, Joseph C., A.B.'04, Bates Col.; Supt. of Sch., Burrillville, R. I., since 1910. Address: Harrisville, R. I.

Sweeney, Mary J., 118 26th Ave., San Francisco, Calif.

Sweet, Walter Prescott, B.S.'17, Tufts Col.; Ed.M.'30, Harvard Univ.; Supt. of Sch., Danbury, Conn., since 1941.

Swetman, Ralph Waldo, Ph.B.'07, Hamilton Col.; A.M.'17, Columbia Univ.; Ph.D.'28, Stanford Univ.; Pres., State Tchrs. Col., Oswego, N. Y., since 1933.

Swicker, Harold B., B.A. in Ed.'21, Univ. of Maine; M.A. in Ed.'27, Tchrs. Col., Columbia Univ.; Supt. of Sch., Chester, Mass., since 1930.

Swift, Gordon C., Diploma '06, State Normal Sch., Edinboro, Pa.; A.B.'11, Yale Univ.; A.M.'17, Tchrs. Col., Columbia Univ.; Supt. of Sch., Watertown, Conn., since 1919.

Swigart, Forrest Damon, B.S.'21, Denison Univ.; M.A.'29, Ohio State Univ.; Supt. of Sch., Bellevue, Ohio, since 1942.

Swihart, O. M., A.B.'28, N. Manchester Col.; M.S.'36, Ind. Univ.; Supt. of Sch., Richmond, Ind., since 1942.

Swing, Glenn O., B.A.'16, M.A.'17, Ohio State Univ.; Supt. of Sch., Covington, Ky., since 1927.

Swope, Charles S., A.B.'25, Dickinson Col.; A.M.'30, Univ. of Pa.; Pres., State Tchrs. Col., West Chester, Pa., since 1935.

Sylla, Ben A., Ph.B.'28, M.A.'33, Univ. of Chicago; Supt. of Sch., Chicago Hgts., Ill., since 1933.

Sylvest, Murphy J., Dir. of Tchr. Tr., Southeastern La. Col., Hammond, La.

T

Tallman, Norman O., A.B.'31, Occidental Col.; M.A.'36, Univ. of Southern Calif.; Dir. of Research, Child Welfare and Attendance, Unified Sch. Dist., Montebello, Calif., since 1942.

Tallman, Pearle, A.B.'20, Iowa State Tchrs. Col., Cedar Falls, Iowa; M.A.'28, Columbia Univ.; Asst. Supt. of Sch., Houston, Texas, since 1941.

Tarlton, J. J., A.B.'25, Wake Forest Col.; Co. Supt. of Sch., Rutherfordton, N. C., since 1934.

Tasch, Alcuin W., A.B.'15, M.A.'17, St. Vincent Col.; St. Paul's Rectory, 2124 W. 22nd Pl., Chicago, Ill.

Taylor, H. C., B.S.'18, Bethel Col.; M.A.'29, George Peabody Col. for Tchrs.; Supt. of Sch., Elizabethtown, Ky., since 1931.

Taylor, Harvey L., A.B.'21, Univ. of Utah; M.A.'25, Columbia Univ.; Supt., Mesa Union H. S., Mesa, Ariz., since 1933.

Taylor, I. T., B.Litt.'12, B.A.'14, East Texas Normal Col.; LL.D.'37, Sc.D.'38, Webster Univ.; Co. Supt. of Sch., Edna, Texas, since 1935.

Taylor, J. Carey, B.S.'22, M.A.'27, D.Ed.'30, Johns Hopkins Univ.; Asst. Supt. of Sch., 3 E. 25th St., Baltimore 18, Md., since 1930.

Taylor, James F., A.B.'05, Middlebury Col.; LL.D.'32, Niagara Univ.; Supt. of Sch., Niagara Falls, N. Y., since 1924.

Taylor, John Walter, Co. Supt. of Sch., Ukiah, Calif., since 1935.

Taylor, Louis, B.S.'25, M.A.'27, Ohio State Univ.; Supt. of Sch., Superior, Ariz., since 1942.

Taylor, Paul R., M.S. in Ed.'31, Okla. Agrl. and Mech. Col.; Supt. of Sch., El Reno, Okla., since 1935.

Taylor, Roy E., B.S.'22, Kansas State Tchrs. Col., Pittsburg, Kansas; M.S.'27, Univ. of Kansas; Supt. of Sch., Herculaneum, Mo., since 1924.

Taylor, Walter N., B.S.'97, M.A.'98, Miss. Col.; Exec. Secy., Miss. Educ. Assn., 219 N. President St., Jackson, Miss., since 1921.

Taylor, William S., B.S.'12, Univ. of Ky.; M.S.'13, Univ. of Wis.; Ph.D.'24, Columbia Univ.; Dean, Col. of Educ., Univ. of Ky., Lexington, Ky., since 1923.

Teach, Charles Elden, A.B.'03, A.M.'14, Univ. of Nebr.; Supt. of Sch., San Luis Obispo, Calif., since 1928.

Teichert, John R., B.S. in Ed.'30, Wilmington Col.; Supt. of Sch., Waverly, Ohio, since 1932.

Telford, Marian, Natl. Safety Council, 20 N. Wacker Drive, Chicago, Ill.

Templin, R. J. W., Sc.B.'16, A.M.'19, Bucknell Univ.; Supt. of Sch., West Pittston, Pa., since 1923.

Tennis, G. T., Supt. of Sch., Grass Valley, Calif., since 1943.

Tennyson, Harry L., B.S.'26, Wash. and Jefferson Col.; M.A.'33, Tchrs. Col., Columbia Univ.; Supvg. Prin. of Boro and Twp. Sch., Union H. S., Burgettstown, Pa., since 1938.

Terhune, Beekman R., A.B.'01, Princeton Univ.; A.M.'02, Columbia Univ.; Supt. of Sch., Somerset Sch., North Plainfield, N. J., since 1923.

Terrebonne, L. P., M.A.'29, Ph.D.'40, La. State Univ.; Parish Supt. of Sch., Plaquemine, La., since 1929.

Terrill, Newton E., M.S.'27, State Tchrs. Col., Pittsburg, Kansas; Supt. of Sch., Douglas, Kansas, since 1927.

Terry, W. J., Co. Supt. of Sch., Greensboro, Ala., since 1943.

*Tete, Auguste J., B.E.'06, M.A.'23, Tulane Univ.; Supt. of Sch., New Orleans 12, La., since 1942.

Thackston, John A., A.B.'99, Furman Univ.; Pd.M.'07, Ph.D.'08, New York Univ.; Dean, Col. of Educ., Univ. of Tenn., Knoxville, Tenn., since 1916.

Thalman, John W., A.B.'00, Ohio Wesleyan Univ.; M.A.'23, Tchrs. Col., Columbia Univ.; Supt. of Sec. Sch., Waukegan, Ill., since 1924.

Theisen, W. W., B.Sc.'07, Univ. of Nebr.; A.M.'15, Ph.D.'16, Columbia Univ.; Asst. Supt. of Sch., 1111 N. Tenth St., Milwaukee, Wis., since 1922.

Thibadeau, Charles Raymond, B.S.'19, Bates Col.; Ed.M.'30, Harvard Univ.; Supt. of Sch., Weymouth, Mass., since 1940.

Thomas, D. Everett, M.Ed.'38, Univ. of Mo.; Supt. of Sch., Sarcoxie, Mo., since 1941.

Thomas, Earl D., M.A.'30, Univ. of Chicago; Prin., Pub. Sch., 1835 Tracy, Kansas City, Mo., since 1936.

Thomas, F. C., B.A.'25, Mt. Morris Col.; M.A.'31, Univ. of Ill.; Supt. of Sch., Yorkville, Ill., since 1935.

Thomas, Frank W., A.B.'05, Ind. Univ.; A.M.'10, Univ. of Ill.; Ph.D.'26, Stanford Univ.; Pres., Fresno State Col., Fresno, Calif., since 1927.

Thomas, John Q., Ph.B.'20, Univ. of Chicago; M.A.'33, Stanford Univ.; Supt. of Sch., Flagstaff, Ariz., since 1921.

Thomas, L. Ralston, B.S.'13, Haverford Col.; Ed.M.'25, Harvard Univ.; Sc.D.'43, R. I. Col. of Pharm. and Applied Science; Headmaster, Moses Brown Sch., 257 Hope St., Providence 6, R. I., since 1924.

Thomas, M. Ray, B.A.'26, Univ. of Utah; M.A.'33, Columbia Univ.; Supt. of Sch., St. Anthony, Idaho, since 1935.

Thomas, Maurice J., Supt. of Sch., Rochester, Minn.

Thomas, Wade F., Life Diploma '27, Chico State Tchrs. Col., Chico, Calif.; Dist. Supt. of Sch., San Anselmo, Calif., since 1909.

Thompson, Arthur E., B.A.'15, St. Olaf Col.; State Supt. of Pub. Instr., Bismarck, N. Dak., since 1933.

Thompson, Daly, B.A.'14, Vanderbilt Univ.; M.A.'31, George Peabody Col. for Tchrs.; Supt. of Sch., Franklin, Tenn., since 1929.

Thompson, Edward Merle, A.B.'12, Nebr. Wesleyan Univ.; A.M.'29, Colo. State Tchrs. Col., Greeley, Colo.; Supt. of Sch., Rock Springs, Wyo., since 1925.

Thompson, Fred C., B.S.'10, A.M.'12, New York Univ.; Asst. Supt. of Sch., Paterson, N. J., since 1934.

Thompson, Fred R., M.A.'35, Univ. of Texas; Supt. of Sch., Eagle Pass, Texas, since 1935.

Thompson, French W., A.B.'97, Ark. Col.; B.D.'02, Presbyterian Theol. Sem.; D.D.'20, Daniel Baker Col.; Pres., Greenbrier Col., Lewisburg, W. Va., since 1925.

Thompson, J. Leroy, B.A.'25, Wilmington Col.; M.A.'29, Columbia Univ.; Supt. of Sch., Tarrytown, N. Y., since 1933.

Thompson, James B., B.S.'12, Colby Col.; M.A.'27, Tchrs. Col., Columbia Univ.; Supvg. Prin. of Sch., Ft. Lee, N. J., since 1933.

Thompson, O. Scott, A.B.'04, L.H.D.'39, Lake Forest Univ.; Supt. of Compton Union Dist. Sec. Sch., and Pres., Compton Jr. Col., 601 S. Acacia St., Compton, Calif., since 1916.

Thompson, Paul Lamont, B.A.'18, Emmanuel Missionary Col.; B.D.'32, Colgate-Rochester Divinity Sch.; LL.D.'33, Franklin Col.; Pres., Kalamazoo Col., Kalamazoo, Mich., since 1938.

Thompson, R. W., B.A.'28, M.A.'38, Univ. of Wyo.; Prin., Fremont Co. Voc. H. S., Lander, Wyo., since 1938.

Thompson, Robert S., LL.B.'12, Univ. of Mich.; A.B.'25, Univ. of Denver; Ph.D.'30, Columbia Univ.; Dir. of Tr., State Normal Sch., Fredonia, N. Y., since 1937.

Thompson, Roger M., A.B.'17, Ind. State Normal Sch., Terre Haute, Ind.; A.M.'23, Tchrs. Col., Columbia Univ.; Dir. of Admin., State Dept. of Educ., Hartford, Conn., since 1938.

Thompson, Samuel H., B.S.'06, B.Ped.'07, D.Ped.'11, Valparaiso Univ.; Supvr. of Indian Educ., Washington, D. C., since 1929.

Thordarson, T. W., M.S.'25, North State Col.; State Dir. of Correspondence Study, N. Dak. Agrl. Col., Fargo, N. Dak., since 1925.

Thrash, Joseph Meriwether, Pres., South Ga. Col., College, Ga., since 1919.

Threlkeld, A. L., B.Pd.'11, Northeast Mo. State Tchrs. Col., Kirksville, Mo.; B.S. '19, Univ. of Mo.; A.M.'23, Tchrs. Col., Columbia Univ.; LL.D.'30, Univ. of Denver; Ed.D.'32, Univ. of Colo.; LL.D.'35, Colo. Col.; Pres., Dept. of Superintendence, 1936-37; Supt. of Sch., Montclair, N. J., since 1937.

Thuma, Harold L., A.B.'24, Kansas City Univ.; Supt., Territorial Sch., Palmer, Alaska, since 1933.

Thurston, Lee M., Ph.D.'35, Univ. of Mich.; Prof. of Educ., Univ. of Pittsburgh, Pittsburgh 11, Pa., since 1938.

Tibbetts, Keim Kendall, A.B.'10, Oberlin Col.; A.M.'31, Univ. of Chicago; Supt. of Sch., Wheaton, Ill., since 1928.

Tibbetts, Vinal H., A.B.'14, Colby Col. Address: 69 Plandome Rd., Manhasset, N. Y.

Tibby, Mrs. Ardella Bitner, B.S.'29, M.A.'30, Univ. of Southern Calif.; Supt. of Sch., Compton, Calif., since 1934.

Tidball, Lewis C., A.B.'05, Univ. of Wyo.; M.A.'19, Ph.D.'30, Univ. of Wash.; Pres., Grays Harbor Jr. Col., Aberdeen, Wash., since 1930.

Tidwell, Robert E., B.S.'05, Univ. of Ala.; LL.D.'23, Birmingham-Southern Col.; M.A. '25, Columbia Univ.; LL.D.'27, Univ. of Ala.; Dean of Extension and Prof. of Educ., Univ. of Ala., University, Ala., since 1930.

Tiedeman, Henry George, B.S.'28, Univ. of Minn.; M.A.'33, State Univ. of Iowa; Supt. of Sch., Mountain Iron, Minn., since 1938.

Tieje, Ralph Earle, A.B.'10, A.M.'12, Ph.D. '17, Univ. of Ill.; Pres., Eastern Wash. Col. of Educ., Cheney, Wash., since 1939.

Tierney, Mrs. Hallie M., B.A.'10, Lawrence Col.; Co. Supt. of Sch., Alturas, Calif., since 1935.

Tillman, Frank P., A.B.'13, B.S. in Ed.'16, Univ. of Mo.; M.A.'31, Univ. of Ill.; Supt. of Sch., Kirkwood, Mo., since 1923.

Tilton, John Philip, A.B.'23, Colby Col.; Ed.M.'27, Ed.D.'33, Harvard Univ.; Dean, Grad. Sch., Tufts Col., Medford, Mass., since 1943.

Tiner, Hugh M., B.A.'28, Abilene Christian Col.; M.A.'29, Stanford Univ.; Pres., George Pepperdine Col., Los Angeles, Calif., since 1939.

Tink, Edmund L., B.A.'23, Lawrence Col.; M.A.'27, Ph.D.'29, Tchrs. Col., Columbia Univ.; Supt. of Sch., Kearny, N. J., since 1932.

Tirey, Ralph Noble, A.B.'18, A.M.'28, Ind. Univ.; Pres., State Tchrs. Col., Terre Haute, Ind., since 1934.

Tisdale, Wesley D., A.B.'01, Syracuse Univ.; M.A.'30, Tchrs. Col., Columbia Univ.; Supvg. Prin. of Sch., Ramsey, N. J., since 1907.

Tisinger, Richard M., B.S. in Agrl. Ed.'22, Va. Polytech. Inst.; M.S.'29, Ph.D.'38, Cornell Univ.; Supt. of Indian Educ., Indian Sch., Phoenix, Ariz., since 1931.

Tiss, A. I., A.B.'10, Drake Univ.; M.A.'19, State Univ. of Iowa; Supt. of Sch., Ft. Madison, Iowa, since 1920.

Titus, C. P., Co. Commr. of Sch., Webster Sch. Annex, Escanaba, Mich.

Tobin, John M., A.B.'19, Boston Col.; LL.B.'28, Suffolk Law Sch.; Ed.M.'38, Boston Univ.; Asst. Supt. of Sch., Cambridge, Mass., since 1935.

Tobin, Lillian M., Dist. Supt. of Sch., 433 Aldine Ave., Chicago, Ill., since 1928.

Todd, Glenn Wentworth, B.S. in Ed.'16, State Tchrs. Col., Pittsburg, Kansas; M.A.'26, Univ. of Colo.; Pres., State Normal Sch., Lewiston, Idaho, since 1941.

Todd, Lindsey O., B.S.'25, George Peabody Col. for Tchrs.; M.A.'28, Tchrs. Col., Columbia Univ.; Pres., E. Central Jr. Col., Decatur, Miss., since 1934.

Tollinger, William P., A.B.'27, Swarthmore Col.; M. A.'30, Univ. of Pa.; Supvg. Prin. of Sch., Spring City, Pa., since 1936.

Tope, Donald E., B.A.'28, Western State Col., Gunnison, Colo.; M.A.'29, Ph.D.'34, State Univ. of Iowa; Asst. to the Supt., City Hall, Omaha, Nebr., since 1942.

Touchstone, Thompson Nolan, B.S.'17, Miss. Col.; M.A.'32, George Peabody Col. for Tchrs.; Supt. of Sch., Amory, Miss., since 1938.

Towle, Clifton A., A.B.'99, Bowdoin Col.; Union Supt. of Sch., Exeter, N. H., since 1919.

Towne, Charles Franklin, A.B.'00, Colby Col.; A.M.'16, Brown Univ.; Ed.D.'41, R. I. Col. of Educ.; Deputy Supt. of Sch., 20 Summer St., Providence, R. I., since 1936.

Towne, George L., Pres., The Univ. Pub. Co., 1126 Q St., Lincoln, Nebr.

Townsend, Horace R., A.B.'09, Wilmington Col.; A.B.'10, Haverford Col.; A.M.'11, Harvard Univ.; Commr., Ohio H. S. Athletic Assn., Columbus, Ohio, since 1925,

Trabert, Charles L., A.B.'94, Newberry Col.; LL.B.'99, B.F.'12, Univ. of Minn.; Head, Dept. of Educ., Newberry Col., Newberry, S. C., since 1926.

Trabert, M. A., B.A.'20, Simpson Col.; M.A.'40, State Univ. of Iowa; Supt. of Sch., Knoxville, Iowa, since 1935.

Trabue, M. R., B.A.'11, Northwestern Univ.; M.A.'14, Ph.D.'15, Columbia Univ.; Dean, Sch. of Educ., Pa. State Col., State College, Pa., since 1937.

Tracey, Earle T., A.B.'12, Middlebury Col.; M.A.'39, Univ. of Vt.; Supt. of Sch., Nashua, N. H., since 1931.

Trafton, F. Lester, Supt. of Sch., Claremont, N. H.

Trask, Edwin E., Supt. of Sch., Plainville, Conn.

*Travell, Ira Winthrop, B.A.'90, Williams. Address: Pub. Sch., Ridgewood, N. J.

Travis, Martin B., A.B.'09, A.M.'10, Univ. of Mich.; Ed.M.'31, Harvard Univ.; Supt. of Sch., Hinsdale, Ill., since 1933.

Tremain, Eloise R., B.A.'04, Bryn Mawr Col.; M.A.'27, Lake Forest Col.; Prin., Ferry Hall, Lake Forest, Ill., since 1918.

Tremper, George Nelson, A.B.'01, Univ. of Mich.; M.A.'28, Univ. of Ill.; Prin., Sr. H. S., 6611 Fifth Ave., Kenosha, Wis., since 1911.

Trenholm, H. Councill, A.B.'20, Morehouse Col.; Ph.B.'21, A.M.'25, Univ. of Chicago; LL.D., Allen Univ.; Pres., State Tchrs. Col., Montgomery, Ala., since 1925.

Trent, W. W., A.B.'12, W. Va. Univ.; A.M. '21, Tchrs. Col., Columbia Univ.; Ped.D. '32, Salem Col.; LL.D.'41, Marshall Col.; State Supt. of Free Sch., Charleston, W. Va., since 1933.

Trice, J. A., B.S.E.'32, State Tchrs. Col., Conway, Ark.; M.S.E.'33, Univ. of Ark.; Supt. of Educ., War Relocation Authority, McGehee, Ark., since 1942.

Trillingham, Clinton C., A.B.'21, Southwestern Col.; A.M.'31, Ed.D.'33, Univ. of Southern Calif.; Co. Supt. of Sch., 808 N. Spring, Los Angeles, Calif., since 1942.

Trippensee, Arthur E., B.A.'24, Univ. of Mich.; M.A.'32, Yale Univ.; Supt. of Sch., Medina, N. Y., since 1935.

Trogdon, Vera Wurl, A.B.'30, M.A.'41, Univ. of Denver. Address: 1034 Oak Ave., Redwood City, Calif.

Trowt, B. C., Diploma '21, State Normal Sch., Fitchburg, Mass.; Ed.B.'32, R. I. Col. of Educ.; Supt. of Sch., Narragansett, R. I., since 1933.

Troxel, Oliver L., B.S.'14, North Central Col.; A.M.'22, Ph.D.'26, Univ. of Minn.; Prof. of Educ. Admin., Colo. State Col. of Educ., Greeley, Colo., since 1929.

Truax, Mrs. Grace Greves, B.A.'37, Augustana Col.; Special Lecturer, Augustana Col., Sioux Falls, S. Dak., since 1932. Address: 711 W. 12th St., Sioux Falls, S. Dak.

Truax, James L., B.S.'32, Mich. State Normal Col.; M.S.'39, Wayne Univ.; Supt. of Sch., Van Dyke, Mich., since 1940.

Truby, Charlotte C., M.A.'28, Univ. of Pittsburgh; Prin., Humboldt Sch., Pittsburgh, Pa., since 1932.

Truell, Harold A., B.S.'30, Ed.M.'35, Univ. of N. H.; Supt. of Sch., North Brookfield, Mass., since 1943.

Trueman, George Johnstone, B.A.'02, M.A. '04, Mt. Allison Univ.; Ph.D.'19, Columbia Univ.; D.C.L.'38, Acadia Univ.; Pres., Mt. Allison Univ., Sackville, New Brunswick, Canada, since 1923.

Truscott, Raymond W., A.B.'05, Simpson Col.; Supt. of Sch., Loveland, Colo., since 1912.

Tucker, Major E. W., A.B.'21, Lake Forest Col.; A.M.'35, Ed.D.'41, Univ. of Mo.; Exec. Officer, Kemper Military Sch., Boonville, Mo., since 1921.

Tucker, Everett B., A.B.'05, Vanderbilt Univ.; Pres., Austin Col., Sherman, Texas, since 1931.

Tuggle, L. A., Diploma '93, Westfield Col.; Co. Supt. of Sch., Danville, Ill., since 1923.

Tunem, Alfred, B.A.'24, St. Olaf Col.; M.A.'31, Univ. of Mont.; Supt. of Sch., East Stanwood, Wash., since 1929.

Turley, Ira S., A.B.'13, Ind. Univ.; Pres., Chicago Tchrs. Union, 509 S. Wabash Ave., Chicago, Ill., since 1941.

Turnbull, James L., B.S.'17, Oregon State Col.; Supt. of Sch., Ontario, Oregon, since 1928.

Turner, C. B., M.A.'13, La. State Univ. Parish Bd. of Educ., Baton Rouge, La.

Turner, George W., Pres., Bd. of Educ., 2308 Clay St., Fresno 3, Calif., since 1938.

Turner, H. B., A.B.'03, Hiram Col.; M.A.'31, Columbia Univ.; Supt. of Sch., Warren, Ohio, since 1916.

Turner, Horace F., A.B.'11, Bates Col.; Ed.M.'32, Harvard Univ.; Supt. of Sch., Milton, Mass., since 1926.

Turner, J. Frank, Prin., Stephen J. Hay Sch., Dallas, Texas.

Turner, J. J., B.S.'28, Miss. State Col.; M.A.'42, Univ. of Miss.; Supt. of Sch., Hazlehurst, Miss., since 1940.

Turner, Marie R., A.B.'34, Morehead State Tchrs. Col., Morehead, Ky.; Co. Supt. of Sch., Jackson, Ky., since 1931.

Turner, W. E., A.B.'24, M.S.'31, Univ. of Tenn.; State Dir. of Negro Educ., War Memorial Bldg., Nashville 3, Tenn., since 1930.

Turpen, N. C., Immigration and Naturalization Dept., U. S. Dept. of Justice, U. S. Court House, Buffalo, N. Y.

Turrentine, George Ruford, A.B. and B.S.'09, Henderson State Tchrs. Col., Arkadelphia, Ark.; M.S.'27, Iowa State Col.; Dean and Registrar, Ark. Polytechnic Col., Russellville, Ark., since 1921.

Tuttle, Albert E., A.B. and Ped.B.'15, Syracuse Univ.; M.A.'22, Tchrs. Col., Columbia Univ.; Asst. Supt. of Sch., Mamaroneck, N. Y., since 1936.

Twente, John W., A.M.'16, Univ. of Kansas; A.M.'22, Ph.D.'23, Columbia Univ.; Prof. of Educ., Univ. of Kansas, Lawrence, Kansas, since 1925.

Tyler, Harry Edward, A.B.'20, Doane Col.; M.A.'27, Univ. of Nebr.; Dist. Supt. of Sch., Santa Maria, Calif., since 1943.

Tyler, I. Keith, B.A.'25, Univ. of Nebr.; M.A.'30, Ph.D.'39, Tchrs. Col., Columbia Univ.; Asst. Prof. and Research Assoc., Bureau of Educ. Research, Ohio State Univ., Columbus, Ohio, since 1935.

*Tyler, Ralph W., A.B.'21, Doane Col.; A.M.'23, Univ. of Nebr.; Ph.D.'27, Univ. of Chicago; Chmn., Dept. of Educ., since 1938, and Univ. Examiner, Univ. of Chicago, Chicago, Ill., since 1942.

*Tyler, Tracy F., A.B.'16, Doane Col.; M.A. '23, Univ. of Nebr.; Ph.D.'33, Columbia Univ.; Assoc. Prof. of Educ., Univ. of Minn., Minneapolis, Minn., since 1939.

Tyson, John H., Supt. of Sch., Upper Darby, Pa.

Tyson, Levering, A.B.'10, Gettysburg Col.; A.M.'11, Columbia Univ.; Litt.D.'30, Gettysburg Col.; LL.D.'37, Lehigh Univ.; LL.D.'39, Franklin and Marshall Col.; Pres., Muhlenberg Col., Allentown, Pa., since 1937.

U

Uecker, Lloyd T., B.A.'26, M.A.'37, Univ. of S. Dak.; Supt. of Sch., Vermillion, S. Dak., since 1942.

Ullrich, Felix H., B.S.'24, Univ. of Wis.; M.A.'29, Ph.D.'37, Univ. of Texas; Head, Dept. of Educ., Trinity Univ., Waxahachie, Texas.

Umstattd, James G., B.S. in Ed.'18, M.A.'24, Univ. of Mo.; Ph.D.'30, Univ. of Minn.; Prof. of Sec. Educ., Sch. of Educ., Univ. of Texas, Austin, Texas, since 1938.

Underbrink, H. E., M.A.'31, Univ. of Chicago; Prin., Twp. H. S., Libertyville, Ill., since 1922.

*Underwood, Franklin M., A.B.'02, Univ. of Mo.; A.M.'25, Tchrs. Col., Columbia Univ.; Asst. Supt. of Sch., St. Louis 1, Mo., since 1930.

Ungemach, Dena D., B.S.'08, A.M.'11, Univ. of Pa.; Head, Science Dept., Overbrook Sr. H. S., Philadelphia, Pa., since 1930.

Unruh, H. B., Prin., Pub. Sch., Pratt, Kansas.

Updegraff, Harlan, Ph.B.'94, Cornell Col., Mt. Vernon, Iowa; M.A.'98, Ph.D.'08, Columbia Univ.; LL.D.'26, Syracuse Univ. Address: 1596 E. Mountain St., Pasadena 7, Calif.

Uphill, Jared L. M., B.S., Univ. of Rochester; Diploma, State Normal Sch., Geneseo, N. Y.; Dist. Supt. of Sch., 8 Fairmont Ave., Batavia, N. Y., since 1916.

Upton, Arthur V. G., A.B.'23, W. Va. Wesleyan Col.; A.M.'37, W. Va. Univ.; Ped.D. '38, W. Va. Wesleyan Col.; Co. Supt. of Sch., Clarksburg, W. Va., since 1939.

V

Valentine, R. H., Supt. of Sch., New Castle, Ind.

Valentine, William Robert, A.B.'04, Harvard Univ.; A.M.'29, Columbia Univ.; LL.D.'37, Lincoln Univ.; Prin., N. J. Manual Tr. and Indus. Sch., Bordentown, N. J., since 1915.

Van Alstine, Frank L., B.S.'27, Southwestern State Tchrs. Col., Weatherford, Okla.; M.A.'36, Okla. Agrl. and Mech. Col.; Ph.D.'41, Univ. of Minn.; Assoc. Prof. of Educ., Univ. of Wyo., Laramie, Wyo., since 1943.

Van Anden, Hazel, B.S.'34, M.A.'37, New York Univ.; Supvg. Prin., Quantico Post Sch., Marine Barracks, Quantico, Va., since 1939.

Van Buskirk, David A., A.B.'16, A.M.'23, Univ. of Mich.; Supt. of Sch., Hastings, Mich., since 1923.

Vance, R. R., A.B.'20, A.M.'21, Univ. of Tenn.; Supvr., Div. of H. S., State Dept. of Educ., Nashville 3, Tenn., since 1934.

Vanderhoef, W. Howard, B.S.'16, Colgate Univ.; M.A.'29, Columbia Univ.; Supt. of Sch., Hamburg, N. Y., since 1940.

Vanderlinden, J. S., B.S.'21, M.A.'28, State Univ. of Iowa; Supt. of Sch., Perry, Iowa, since 1935.

Van Heuklom, George E., B.S.'30, M.A.'36, Univ. of Minn.; Supt. of Sch., Glidden, Wis., since 1937.

Van Kleeck, E. R., A.B.'27, N. Y. State Col. for Tchrs., Albany, N. Y.; A.M.'33, Cornell Univ.; Ph.D.'37, Yale Univ.; Asst. State Commr. of Educ.. State Educ. Bldg., Albany, N. Y., since 1941.

Van Loan, Wendell L., Ed.D.'42, Stanford Univ.; Asst. Supt., Vanport City Schs., Portland 17, Oregon, since 1943.

Van Natta, J. A., Ph.B.'21, Univ. of Wis.; Supt. of Sch., Sturgeon Bay, Wis., since 1928.

Van Ness, Carl Condit, A.B.'16, Columbia Univ.; Editor, Educ. Book Dept., D. Appleton Century Co., Inc., 35 W. 32nd St., New York, N. Y., since 1922.

Van Ness, H. J., A.B.'19, Cornell Col., Mt. Vernon, Iowa; M.A.'20, Columbia Univ.; Supt. of Sch., Boone, Iowa, since 1937.

van Patter, V. E., B.S.'12, Dakota Wesleyan Univ.; M.S.'15, Univ. of Wis.; Acting Supt. of Sch., Superior, Wis., since 1943.

Van Putten, M. W., B.A.'17, Hope Col.; M.A.'40, Univ. of Minn.; Supt. of Sch., Aurora, Minn., since 1937.

Van Slyck, Willard N., A.B.'14, A.M.'28, Univ. of Kansas; Prin., Topeka H. S., Topeka, Kansas, since 1928.

Van Voris, Will T., Supt., Union H. S. Dist., San Mateo, Calif.

Van Wyk, A. C., B.A.'26, Hope Col.; M.A. '37, Univ. of N. Dak.; Supt. of Sch., Bismarck, N. Dak., since 1942.

Varney, Charles E., Diploma '15, State Normal Sch., Farmington, Maine; B.S. in Ed.'28, M.Ed.'35, Boston Univ.; Supt. of Sch., Stoneham, Mass., since 1929.

Vastine, Richard B., A.B.'27, Bucknell Univ.; M.A.'34, Tchrs. Col., Columbia Univ.; Prin., Wash. Sch., Union, N. J., since 1943.

Vaughan, F. G., Res. Mgr., Sch. and Library Div., The Grolier Society, Inc., 2 W. 45th St., New York, N. Y.

Vaughan, James P., Ph.B.'07, Univ. of Wis.; Supt. of Sch., Chisholm, Minn., since 1907.

Vaughan, John S., B.A.'24, M.A.'27, Univ. of Okla.; Pres., Northeastern State Col., Tahlequah, Okla., since 1936.

Vaughan, William Hutchinson, A.B.'23, Georgetown Col.; A.M.'27, Ph.D.'37, George Peabody Col. for Tchrs.; Pres., Morehead State Tchrs. Col., Morehead, Ky., since 1940.

Vaughn, E. Otis, Supt. of Sch., Reno, Nev.

Vedder, Ollen M., A.B.'24, Mich. State Normal Col., Ypsilanti, Mich.; M.A.'36, Northwestern Univ.; Supt. of Sch., Hancock, Mich., since 1937.

Veit, Benjamin, B.S.'86, Col. of the City of N. Y.; LL.B.'93, New York Univ. Address: 2431 Healy Ave., Far Rockaway, N. Y.

Velte, Charles Henry, A.B.'14, Hastings Col.; M.A.'29, Univ. of Nebr.; Supt. of Sch., Crete, Nebr., since 1919.

Venn-Watson, A. L., Diploma '25, Univ. of Wash.; Co. Supt. of Sch., Port Orchard, Wash., since 1939.

Vikan, Walter L., B.A.'21, Univ. of N. Dak.; M.Ed.'40, Univ. of Colo.; Supt. of Sch., Brighton, Colo., since 1942.

Viles, N. E., A.M.'30, Ph.D.'34, Univ. of Mo. Address: War Relocation Authority, Washington, D. C.

Vincent, Harold S., A.B.'23, Greenville Col.; A.M.'32, Ohio State Univ.; Asst. Supt. of Sch., Akron, Ohio, since 1937.

Vineyard, Jerry., A.B.'21, William Jewell Col.; A.M.'27, Univ. of Mo.; Supt. of Sch., Nevada, Mo., since 1937.

Vitalis, E. L., B.A.'23, Gustavus Adolphus Col.; Supt. of Sch., St. James, Minn., since 1936.

von Borgesrode, Fred, Ph.D.'27, Univ. of Minn.; Lecturer in Educ., Univ. of Minn., Minneapolis, Minn., since 1937.

Vose, James Wilson, A.B.'03, Williams Col.; Ed.M.'28, Harvard Univ.; A.M.'29, Williams Col.; Supt. of Sch., Marblehead, Mass., since 1934.

Voshall, John Harold, B.Ed.'29, Western Ill. State Tchrs. Col., Macomb, Ill.; M.S. '35, Univ. of Ill.; Supt. of Sch., Pittsfield, Ill., since 1935.

W

Waddell, John F., Ph.B.'20, Ph.M.'28, Univ. of Wis.; Asst. State Supt. of Pub. Instr., Madison, Wis., since 1934.

Wade, John E., B.S.'97, Col. of the City of N. Y.; A.M.'02, Columbia Univ.; Supt. of Sch., 2267 Andrews Ave., New York. N. Y., since 1942.

Wagner, C. K., Ph.G.'17, Philadelphia Col. of Pharmacy; B.S.'25, Muhlenberg Col.; A.M.'28, Univ. of Pa.; Supvg. Prin. of Sch., Sharon Hill, Pa., since 1932.

Wagner, Hobson C., B.S.'22, Albright Col.; M.A.'29, Columbia Univ.; Supt. of Twp. Sch., Berwyn, Pa., since 1941.

Wagner, J. Ernest, B.A.'16, Bradley Polytech. Inst.; M.A.'30, Ph.D.'38, Univ. of Pittsburgh; Supt. of Sch., Johnstown, Pa., since 1940.

Wagner, Jonas E., B.S.'02, M.S.'05, Pa. State Col.; Adviser, Research and Statistics, State Dept. of Pub. Instr., Harrisburg, Pa., since 1938.

Wagner, M. Channing, B.A.'13, Wittenberg Col.; A.M.'23, Columbia Univ.; Asst. Supt. of Sch., 1100 Washington St., Wilmington, Del., since 1929.

* Wagner, Thomas J., A.B.'10, Franklin and Marshall Col.; A.M.'13, Tchrs. Col., Columbia Univ.; Pd.D.'23, New York Univ.; Dean, Blackburn Col., Carlinville, Ill., since 1943.

Wagoner, Lovisa C., Dept. of Child Development, Mills Col., Mills College, Calif.

Wagoner, W. E., Acting Pres., Ball State Tchrs. Col., Muncie, Ind.

Wahl, James Frank, B.A.'20, Hendrix Col.; M.A.'26, George Peabody Col. for Tchrs.; Supt. of Sch., Helena, Ark., since 1928.

Walden, Charles B., Supt. of Sch., Merrill, Wis.

Waldo, Karl D., A.B.'06, Univ. of Ill.; A.M.'14, Univ. of Chicago; Supt. of Sch., East Side, Aurora, Ill., since 1928.

Walk, George E., A.B.'99, Ohio Wesleyan Univ.; A.M.'11, Columbia Univ.; Ph.D.'14, New York Univ.; LL.D.'35, Juniata Col.; Dean, Tchrs. Col., Temple Univ., Philadelphia, Pa., since 1919.

Walker, Deane E., A.B.'22, Tri-State Col.; A.M.'28, Tchrs. Col., Columbia Univ.; Co. Supt. of Sch., Plymouth, Ind., since 1925.

Walker, Earle G., J. B. Lippincott Co., 441 W. Peachtree St., Atlanta, Ga.

Walker, Kirby P., A.B.'22, Southwestern, Memphis, Tenn.; M.A.'34, Univ. of Chicago; Supt. of Sch., Jackson 107, Miss., since 1936.

Walker, Knox, A.B.'15, Mercer Univ.; M.A.'25, Columbia Univ.; Genl. Supvr., Fulton Co. Sch., Atlanta, Ga., since 1930.

Walker, W. L., Dist. Supt. of Sch., Downey, Calif.

Walkotten, George, A.B.'22, Kalamazoo Col.; M.A.'31, Columbia Univ.; Supt. of Sch., Albion, Mich., since 1939.

Wallace, Frederick W., A.B.'04, Bates Col.; Supt. of Sch., Poultney, Vt., since 1924.

Wallace, James D., B.S.'28, Lebanon Valley Col.; Secy., Sch. Dist., 2600 Hoffer St., Penbrook, Pa., since 1936.

Waller, DeWitt, A.B.'11, Epworth Univ.; A.M.'28, Univ. of Mo.; Supt. of Sch., Enid, Okla., since 1933.

* Waller, J. Flint, B.A.'16, Univ. of Va.; M.A.'28, Ph.D.'32, Columbia Univ. Address: 227 Kalorama St., Staunton, Va.

Walshe, Minnie E., Asst. Supt. of Sch., 52 Reef Rd., Fairfield, Conn., since 1922.

Walston, Ernest B., B.S.'29, Univ. of Vt.; Ed.M.'38, Harvard Univ.; Assoc. Headmaster, The Farm and Trades Sch., Thompson's Island, Boston, Mass., since 1943.

Walter, G. A., B.S.'19, Mich. State Tchrs. Col.; M.A.'23, Ph.D.'33, Univ. of Wash.; Supt., Tahoma Consol. Schs., Renton, Wash., since 1934.

Walter, R. B., M.S.'39, Univ. of Southern Calif.; Asst. Co. Supt. of Sch., 240 S. Broadway, Los Angeles, Calif., since 1939.

Walter, Z. M., B.Sc. in Ed.'21, M.A.'23, Ohio State Univ.; Supt. of Sch., Wyoming, Ohio, since 1932.

Walters, Newell B., 2040 S. Columbine St., Denver, Colo.

Walton, L. Arthur, B.S.'20, Ursinus Col.; A.M.'24, Univ. of Pa.; Supvg. Prin. of Sch., Pitman, N. J., since 1941.

Wanamaker, Mrs. Pearl A., B.A.'22, Univ. of Wash.; State Supt. of Pub. Instr., Olympia, Wash., since 1941.

Ward, Charles C., B.S.'18, Bucknell Univ.; M.A.'30, Tchrs. Col., Columbia Univ.; Ph.D.'34, New York Univ.; LL.D.'43, Bucknell Univ.; Pres., State Tchrs. Col., Plattsburg, N. Y., since 1933.

Ward, Mrs. Ethel Saxon, Coordinator, Alameda Co. Sch., Oakland, Calif.

Ward, Forrest S., B.Ped.'10, State Normal Col., Troy, Ala.; B.S.'14, Univ. of Ala.; A.M.'27, Tchrs. Col., Columbia Univ.; Co. Supt. of Sch., Carrollton, Ala., since 1931.

Ward, Mrs. Violet Richardson, Supvr. of Health and Physical Educ., Sch. Admin. Bldg., Berkeley, Calif.

Ward, W. H., A.B.'14, Furman Univ.; Dir., Extension Div., Univ. of S. C., Columbia, S. C., since 1937.

Wardlaw, Joseph C., B.A. and M.A.'95, Emory Univ.; Dir. of Genl. Extension, Univ. System of Ga., Atlanta, Ga., since 1928.

Warfield, Silas T., B.S. in Ed.'20, Ohio Univ.; M.A.'34, Columbia Univ.; Supt. of Sch., Barnesville, Ohio, since 1939.

Warner, Rodney J., B.S.'24, M.A.'29, Ohio State Univ.; Supt. of Sch., Xenia, Ohio, since 1937.

Warren, Arthur E., A.B.'23, Hamilton Col.; M.A.'31, Tchrs. Col., Columbia Univ.; Supt. of Sch., Canandaigua, N. Y., since 1940.

Warren, Carl V., B.S.'23, Hamilton Col.; M.A.'32, Columbia Univ.; Supt. of Sch., Middletown, N. Y., since 1939.

Warren, Curtis E., A.B.'15, Ed.D.'40, Univ. of Southern Calif.; Supt. of Sch., San Francisco 2, Calif., since 1943.

Warren, Julius E., A.B.'10, Dartmouth Col.; M.A.'22, Columbia Univ.; State Commr. of Educ., Boston, Mass., since 1943.

Warren, W. Frank, A.B.'10, Elon Col.; M.A.'11, Univ. of N. C.; Supt. of Sch., Durham, N. C., since 1933.

Warren, Worcester, A.B.'12, Knox Col.; A.M.'21, State Univ. of Iowa; Assoc. Prof. of Educ. Admin., Boston Univ., Boston, Mass., since 1943.

Wasson, Roy J., B.A.'20, Cornell Univ.; M.A.'29, Columbia Univ.; Ph.D.'40, Colo. State Col. of Educ.; Supt. of Sch., Colorado Springs, Colo., since 1942.

Wassung, Frank R., Ph.B.'13, Ph.M.'17, Hamilton Col.; Supt. of Sch., Garden City, N. Y., since 1937.

Waterpool, W. F., B.A.'20, Lawrence Col.; Ph.M.'26, Univ. of Wis.; Supt. of Sch., Marinette, Wis., since 1940.

Watkin, Earl P., Ph.B.'12, Ph.M.'17, Hamilton Col.; M.A.'30, Columbia Univ.; Ed.D. '39, New York Univ.; Supt. of Sch., Ilion, N. Y., since 1923.

Watkins, Richard Henry, B.A.'95, Hampden-Sydney Col.; Supt. of Sch., Laurel, Miss., since 1907.

Watson, Charles Hoyt, A.B.'18, A.M.'23, Univ. of Kansas; LL.D.'41, Whitworth Col.; Pres., Seattle Pacific Col., Seattle 99, Wash., since 1926.

Watson, Floyd B., A.B.'14, Cornell Univ.; Supt. of Sch., South Side H. S., Rockville Centre, N. Y., since 1933.

Watson, G. E., B.A.'21, Lawrence Col.; M.A.'32, Univ. of Wis.; Supt. of Sch., Wauwatosa, Wis., since 1940.

Watson, Homer K., 139 W. 69th St., Los Angeles, Calif.

Watson, Murray H., B.S.'37, Univ. of N. H.; Supt. of Sch., Dover, N. H., since 1943.

Watson, Norman E., A.B.'21, Wabash Col.; A.M.'29, Univ. of Chicago; Ph.D.'42, Northwestern Univ.; Supt. of Sch., Northbrook, Ill., since 1929.

Way, James E., Ph.B.'13, Ohio Northern Univ.; Co. Supt. of Sch., Waverly, Ohio, since 1932.

Weakley, Guy A., A.B.'20, Baker Univ.; Dist. Supt. of Sch., El Centro, Calif.

Weatherred, W. B., B.S.'33, West Texas State Col., Canyon, Texas; Co. Supt. of Sch., Pampa, Texas, since 1935.

Weaver, Lucius Stacy, A.B.'24, Duke Univ.; M.A.'32, Columbia Univ.; Supt. of Sch., Statesville, N. C., since 1941.

Weaver, Philip J., A.B.'34, Duke Univ.; A.M.'37, Univ. of N. C.; Supt. of Sch., Southern Pines, N. C., since 1939.

Weaver, Robert B., A.B.'22, De Pauw Univ.; A.M.'26, Univ. of Chicago; Supt. of Sch., Goshen, Ind., since 1942.

Weaver, W. Donald, Supt. of Twp. Sch., DuBois, Pa.

Webb, Henry P., M.A.'32, Texas Technological Col.; Supt. of Sch., Olton, Texas, since 1921.

Webb, J. O., B.A.'14, Southwestern Univ.; M.A.'24, Univ. of Texas; Asst. Supt. of Sch. in charge of Sec. Educ., Houston, Texas, since 1935.

Webb, Paul E., B.A.'17, Pomona Col.; M.A. '25, Univ. of Southern Calif.; Ph.D.'34, Yale Univ.; Prin., Los Angeles H. S., Los Angeles, Calif., since 1941.

Webb, William E., Mgr., Institutional Promotion, NBC, 30 Rockefeller Plaza, New York, N. Y.

*Webber, Elmer Harrison, Diploma '07, State Normal Sch., Farmington, Maine; B.Pd.'15, Univ. of Maine; A.M.'23, Bates Col. Address: Box 204, Mt. Vernon, Maine.

Weber, C. A., A.B.'24, Ill. Col.; M.A.'29, Univ. of Ill.; Ph.D.'42, Northwestern Univ.; Supt. of Sch., Galva, Ill., since 1931.

Weber, Ernest, A.B.'23, Western State Normal Sch., Kalamazoo, Mich.; M.A.'28, Tchrs. Col., Columbia Univ.; Prin., Tr. Sch., Richland, Mich., since 1923.

Webster, Marjorie Fraser, A.B.'33, George Washington Univ.; M.A.'35, American Univ.; Pres., The Marjorie Webster Sch., Rock Creek Park Estates, Washington, D. C., since 1920.

Wedgeworth, C., M.A.'29, Univ. of Colo.; Supt. of Sch., Perryton, Texas, since 1940.

Weet, Herbert S., B.A.'99, M.A.'01, Univ. of Rochester; Pd.D.'18, New York State Col. for Tchrs., Albany, N. Y.; Litt.D.'33, Univ. of the State of New York; Honorary Life Member, American Assn. of Sch. Admin.; Supt. of Sch., Rochester, N. Y., 1911 to 1934. Address: Univ. of Rochester, Rochester 7, N. Y.

*Weglein, David E., A.B.'97, Johns Hopkins Univ.; A.M.'12, Columbia Univ.; Ph.D. '16, Johns Hopkins Univ.; Supt. of Sch., 3 E. 25th St., Baltimore 18, Md., since 1925.

Wegner, Henry C., Ph.M.'23, Univ. of Wis.; Supt. of Sch., Waupun, Wis., since 1926.

Welch, Dale D., A.B.'21, Univ. of Dubuque; M.A.'28, Cornell Univ.; LL.D.'36, Coe Col.; Pres., Univ. of Dubuque, Dubuque, Iowa, since 1936.

Welch, Earl E., B.A.'25, State Univ. of Iowa; Ph.M.'33, Univ. of Wis.; Editor, Silver Burdett Co., 45 E. 17th St., New York 3, N. Y., since 1941.

Welch, M. W., B.S.'17, Univ. of Mich.; W. M. Welch Mfg. Co., 1515 Sedgwick St., Chicago, Ill.

Welch, William A., LL.B.'27, Suffolk Univ.; A.B.'30, M.A.'31, Boston Col.; Supt. of Sch., Peabody, Mass., since 1933.

Welden, Charles Raines, B.S.'33, M.S.'35, Ala. Polytech. Inst.; Co. Supt. of Sch., Wetumpka, Ala., since 1942.

Welden, James E., Supvr. of Vocational Educ., Pub. Sch., 2400 Kern St., Fresno, Calif.

Wells, Clyde P., Ph.B.'08, Syracuse Univ.; Supt. of Sch., Batavia, N. Y., since 1923.

Wells, George N., Ph.B.'28, M.A.'33, Univ. of Chicago; Supt. of Sch., Elmwood Park, Chicago, Ill., since 1929.

Wells, Guy H., A.B.'15, Mercer Univ.; A.M.'25, Columbia Univ.; Pres., Ga. State Col. for Women, Milledgeville, Ga., since 1934.

Wells, H. B., B.S.'24, A.M.'27, Ind. Univ.; LL.D.'39, Butler Univ.; LL.D.'39, Rose Poly. Inst.; LL.D.'39, De Pauw Univ.; LL.D.'42, Wabash Col.; Pres., Ind. Univ., Bloomington, Ind., since 1938.

Wells, J. Evelyn, A.B.'24, Univ. of Louisville; M.A.'34, Columbia Col.; Asst. Prin., Shawnee H. S., Louisville 3, Ky., since 1930.

Welsh, William Henry, Ped.D.'38, Temple Univ.; Asst. Supt. of Sch., Admin. Bldg., Philadelphia 3, Pa., since 1940.

Wendt, Julius A., B.A.'29, Mont. State Univ.; Supt. of Sch., Cathlamet, Wash., since 1937.

Wenger, Paul, B.A.'25, Bluffton Col.; M.A. '30, Ohio State Univ.; Supt. of Sch., Lancaster, Ohio, since 1938.

Wenner, William E., A.B.'97, Ped.D.'36, Westminster Col., New Wilmington, Pa.; Supt. of Sch., 1 Lake St., Ashtabula Harbor, Ohio, since 1909.

Wesley, Charles H., B.A.'11, Fisk Univ.; M.A.'13, Yale Univ.; Ph.D.'25, Harvard Univ.; Pres., Wilberforce Univ., Wilberforce, Ohio, since 1942.

West, Franklin Lorenzo, B.S.'04, Utah State Agrl. Col.; Ph.D.'11, Univ. of Chicago; Commr. of Educ., Church of Jesus Christ of Latter-Day Saints, Salt Lake City, Utah, since 1935.

West, Glen C., B.S. in Ed.'17, Ohio Univ.; M.A.'28, Columbia Univ. Address: Pub. Sch., Bucyrus, Ohio.

West, Guy A., M.A.'28, Univ. of Colo.; Ed.D.'31, Univ. of Calif.; Prof. of Educ. and Dir. of Research, Chico State Col., Chico, Calif., since 1933.

West, Henry S., A.B.'93, Ph.D.'99, Johns Hopkins Univ.; Emeritus Dean and Prof. of Educ., Univ. of Miami, Fla., since 1942. Address: P. O. Box 53, The Plains, Va.

West, Paul Douglass, Ph.B.'24, Emory Univ.; M.A.'25, Oglethorpe Univ.; M.A. '40, Emory Univ.; Prin., Russell H. S., East Point, Ga., since 1932.

West, Roscoe L., A.B.'14, Ed.M.'23, Harvard Univ.; Pres., State Tchrs. Col., Trenton, N. J., since 1930.

Westcott, H. G., A.B.'14, Syracuse Univ.; M.A.'23, Yale Univ.; Supvg. Prin., Chapman Tech. H. S., New London, Conn., since 1937.

Wetherby, Harold Calvert, A.B.'25, Macalester Col.; M.A.'38, Ohio State Univ.; Supt. of Sch., Continental, Ohio, since 1936.

Weyer, Frank E., Ph.D.'41, Univ. of Nebr.; Dean, Hastings Col., Hastings, Nebr., since 1918.

Wezeman, Frederick H., LL.B. and J.D.'14, John Marshall Law Sch.; B.Sc. in Ed.'22, Lewis Inst.; B.D.'26, Univ. of Chicago; Prin., Chicago Christian H. S., Chicago, Ill., since 1927.

Wharton, Lloyd H., Co. Supt. of Sch., Parkersburg, W. Va.

Wheable, Geoffrey Alfred, B.A.'21, Queen's Univ., Kingston, Ont.; Supt. of Sch., Bd. of Educ., London, Ontario, Canada, since 1925.

Wheat, Leonard B., B.A.'24, Northwestern Univ.; Ph.D.'31, Tchrs. Col., Columbia Univ.; Supt. of Sch., Wichita, Kansas, since 1943.

Wheeler, G. R., B.A.'12, Mercer Univ.; City and Co. Supt. of Sch., Sanford, N. C., since 1930.

Whelan, James F., A.B.'21, A.M.'22, Gonzaga Univ.; A.M. in Ed.'35, St. Louis Univ.; Ph.D.'38, Ohio State Univ.; Prof. of Educ. and Chmn., Dept. of Educ., Loyola Univ., New Orleans, La., since 1937.

Whinnery, John Carroll, B.A.'31, Univ. of Calif. at Los Angeles; M.A.'34, Occidental Col.; Asst. Supt. of Sch., Montebello, Calif., since 1942.

Whinnery, Karl E., Ph.B.'12, Mt. Union Col.; M.A.'15, Univ. of Wis.; Supt. of Sch., Sandusky, Ohio, since 1939.

Whipple, Lucius Albert, B.S.'08, R. I. State Col.; A.M.'28, Brown Univ.; D.S.'40, R. I. Col. of Pharmacy; Ed.D.'40, Providence Catholic Tchrs. Col.; Pres., R. I. Col. of Educ., Providence, R. I., since 1939.

Whitcomb, Mrs. Irene B., A.B.'31, Univ. of Southern Calif.; Supt., West Whittier Dist. Sch., Whittier, Calif., since 1930.

White, Edna N., A.B.'06, Univ. of Ill.; LL.D.'28, Mich. State Col.; D.Ped.'30, N. Y. State Col. for Tchrs., Albany, N. Y.; LL.D.'36, Wayne Univ.; Dir., Merrill-Palmer Sch., 71 Ferry Ave., E., Detroit, Mich., since 1920.

White, Heath E., A.M.'30, Columbia Univ.; Supt. of Sch., Westport, Conn., since 1931.

White, I. E., B.S.'22, Oregon State Col.; M.Ed.'41, Univ. of Mont.; Supt. of Sch., Polson, Mont., since 1932.

White, Joseph Benton, A.B.'27, Wofford Col.; M.A.'32, Duke Univ.; Dir., Div. of Tchr. Educ. and Certif., State Dept. of Educ., Columbia, S. C., since 1941.

White, Lawrence B., Prin., Mark Keppel H. S., Alhambra, Calif.

White, Raymond H., Supt. of Twp. Sch., Abington, Pa., since 1942.

White, Robert, Jr., Ph.B.'29, M.A.'36, Univ. of Chicago; Prin., H. S. and Jr. Col., Burlington, Iowa, since 1938.

White, Robert J., B.A.'11, Univ. of Minn.; M.A.'18, Univ. of Wash.; Asst. Co. Supt. of Sch., Martinez, Calif., since 1921.

White, Roscoe H., A.B.'23, A.M.'26, Univ. of Colo.; Supt. of Sch., Shreveport, La., since 1943.

White, Winton John, A.B.'04, A.M.'05, Univ. of Pa.; Supt. of Sch., Englewood, N. J., since 1918.

Whiteman, Harris, A.B.'31, Western State Tchrs. Col., Kalamazoo, Mich.; M.A.'37, Columbia Univ.; Prin., Jr. H. S., Goshen, Ind., since 1932.

Whiteman, Kelro, B.S.'29, Ball State Tchrs. Col., Muncie, Ind.; M.S.'33, Ind. Univ.; Co. Supt. of Sch., Fort Wayne, Ind., since 1937.

Whiteside, Frederick W., A.B.'12, Univ. of Chicago; Supt. of Sch., Camden, Ark., since 1926.

* Whiteside, Harold C., B.S. in Ed.'24, M.A. '26, Univ. of Pa.; Supt. of Sch., New Castle, Del., since 1939.

Whiting, Gregory W., A.B.'17, Fisk Univ.; M.A.'34, Tchrs. Col., Columbia Univ.; Dean and Dir. of Educ., State Col., Bluefield, W. Va., since 1937.

Whitley, Samuel H., B.L.'01, Trinity Univ.; Litt.D.'25, Austin Col.; M.A.'26, Southern Methodist Univ.; LL.D.'29, Trinity Univ.; Pres., East Texas State Tchrs. Col., Commerce, Texas, since 1924.

Whitman, Willard M., A.B.'09, Harvard Univ.; Supt. of Sch., Marquette, Mich., since 1920.

Whitney, Gerald DeForest, B.S.'17, Carnegie Inst. of Tech.; M.A.'26, Columbia Univ.; D.Sc.'27, Stout Inst.; Assoc. Supt. in charge of Sec. Educ., Admin. Bldg., Pittsburgh 13, Pa., since 1938.

Whitten, W. E., B.A.'23, Howard Payne Col.; M.A.'36, Univ. of Colo.; Supt. of Sch., Brady, Texas, since 1931.

Whittier, Amy Rachel, Diploma '92, Mass. Sch. of Art. Address: 96 Pinckney St., Boston, Mass.

Whittier, C. Taylor, A.B.'36, A.M.'38, Univ. of Chicago; Prin., Monroe Elem. Sch., Davenport, Iowa, since 1943.

Whittinghill, Roscoe T., B.Ped.'03, Univ. of Ky.; A.M.'28, Univ. of Chicago; Supt. of Sch., Hazard, Ky., since 1926.

Whitworth, Sidney E., B.S.'11, Whitworth Col.; A.B.'24, A.M.'31, Univ. of Wash.; Supt. of Sch., Dallas, Oregon, since 1942.

Whitzel, William Russell, A.B.'32, Northwestern State Tchrs. Col., Alva, Okla.; A.M.'36, Colo. State Col. of Educ., Greeley, Colo.; Supt. of Sch., Cherryvale, Kansas, since 1940.

Wichman, J. H., B.A.'14, North Central Col.; M.A.'28, Univ. of Chicago; Supt. of Sch., Northfield, Minn., since 1935.

Wickham, William Terry, A.B.'20, Heidelberg Col.; M.A.'27, Ohio State Univ.; Supt. of Sch., Hamilton, Ohio, since 1943.

Wiedefeld, M. Theresa, B.S.'25, Ed. D.'37, Johns Hopkins Univ.; Pres., State Tchrs. Col., Towson, Md., since 1938.

Wieden, Clifford O. T., B.S.'23, Acadia Univ.; Ed.M.'34, Bates Col.; Prin., Wash. State Normal Sch., Machias, Maine, since 1943.

Wiegman, Fred C., B.A.'24, Midland Col.; B.D.'27, Western Seminary; D.D.'39, Wittenberg Col.; Pres., Midland Col., Fremont, Nebr., since 1938.

Wiethaupt, Mervyn E., Secy. and Treas., Bd. of Educ., 911 Locust St., St. Louis 1, Mo.

Wightman, Clair S., A.B.'20, Syracuse Univ.; M.A.'24, Tchrs. Col., Columbia Univ.; Ph.D.'34, New York Univ.; Pres., State Tchrs. Col., Paterson, N. J., since 1937.

Wightman, Vernon E., Acting Supt. of Sch., Bath, N. Y.

Wigton, Charles E., A.B.'19, Ohio Wesleyan Univ.; M.A.'37, Northwestern Univ.; Supt. of Sch., Oberlin, Ohio, since 1937.

Wikre, L. M., B.A.'18, St. Olaf Col.; M.A. '31, Univ. of Minn.; Supt. of Sch., Crookston, Minn., since 1936.

* Wilber, Mrs. Esther R., 11 Ford Ave., Oneonta, N. Y.

Wilber, H. Z., A.B.'08, Mich. State Normal Col., Ypsilanti, Mich.; A.B.'10, A.M.'11, Univ. of Mich.; Prof. of Educ. and Dir., Dept. of Extension Educ., Mich. State Normal Col., Ypsilanti, Mich., since 1921.

Wilcox, Calvin E., Ed.M.'32, Boston Univ.; Ph.D.'39, Yale Univ.; Supt. of Sch., Dedham, Mass., since 1941.

Wilcox, George Milo, Ph.D.'33, Columbia Univ.; Head, Dept. of Educ., since 1933 and Dean, Youngstown Col., Youngstown 3, Ohio, since 1935.

Wildman, Clyde E., A.B.'13, De Pauw Univ.; S.T.B.'16, Ph.D.'26, Boston Univ.; D.D.'27, Cornell Col.; LL.D.'37, Northeastern Univ.; LL.D.'38, Wabash Col.; S.T.D.'40, Northwestern Univ.; Pres., De Pauw Univ., Greencastle, Ind., since 1936.

Wilemon, Tirey C., A.B.'21, Trinity Univ.; Supt. of Sch., Waxahachie, Texas, since 1935.

Wiley, F. L., A.B. and B.S. in Ed.'05, Univ. of Mo.; A.M.'09, Tchrs. Col., Columbia Univ.; Supt. of Sch., Cleveland Hgts., Ohio, since 1923.

Wiley, H. Orton, Pres., Pasadena Col., Pasadena, Calif.

Wiley, Roy William, B.S.'18, Grove City Col.; M.A.'28, Ed.D.'38, Univ. of Pittsburgh; Supt. of Sch., Butler, Pa., since 1937.

Wiley, Will E., M.A.'25, Stanford Univ.; Dist. Supt. of Sch., Whittier, Calif., since 1934.

Wilkerson, J. A., Supt. of Sch., Rockwall, Texas.

Wilkerson, W. D., Supt. of Sch., Bryan, Texas.

Wilkes, L. L., B.A.'12, M.A.'30, Univ. of Texas; Supt. of Sch., Hubbard, Texas, since 1927.

Wilkins, Alger Bright, A.B.'22, Univ. of N. C.; Co. Supt. of Sch., Fayetteville, N. C., since 1932.

Wilkinson, Benjamin G., A.B.'97, Univ. of Mich.; Ph.D.'08, George Washington Univ.; Pres., Washington Missionary Col., Takoma Park, D. C., since 1936.

Wilkinson, Garnet Crummel, A.B.'02, Oberlin Col.; LL.B.'09, Howard Univ.; M.A.'32, Univ. of Pa.; First Asst. Supt. in charge of Colored Sch., Washington 5, D. C., since 1924.

Willey, Gilbert S., B.S.'20, Univ. of Ill.; Ph.D.'26, Univ. of Wis.; Dir. of Instr., Pub. Sch., 414 14th St., Denver, Colo., since 1939.

Willey, Walter O., Prin., El Rodeo Sch., Beverly Hills, Calif.

Williams, Charl Ormond, D.Litt.'25, Southwestern, Memphis, Tenn.; Dir. of Field Service, Natl. Educ. Assn., 1201 16th St., N. W., Washington 6, D. C., since 1922.

Williams, E. I. F., Ph.B.'14, Heidelberg Col.; A.M.'20, Ph.D.'41, Tchrs. Col., Columbia Univ.; Prof. of Educ., Heidelberg Col., Tiffin, Ohio, since 1915.

Williams, Frank L., M.A.'36, Hardin-Simmons Univ.; Supt. of Sch., Mexia, Texas, since 1936.

Williams, Harold J., B.S.'16, Iowa State Col.; M.A.'30, State Univ. of Iowa; Supt. of Sch., Fort Dodge, Iowa, since 1940.

Williams, J. D., Ed. D.'40, Tchrs. Col., Columbia Univ.; Pres., Marshall Col., Huntington, W. Va., since 1942.

Williams, John Fred, Co. Supt. of Sch., Paintsville, Ky.

Williams, John R., Co. Supt. of Sch., Court House, Painesville, Ohio, since 1931.

Williams, Leroy Everett, B.A.'01, M.A.'26, Bates Col.; Supt. of Sch., Rumford, Maine, since 1916.

Williams, Nat, B.A.'24, Hardin-Simmons Univ.; Supt. of Sch., Ballinger, Texas, since 1939.

Williams, R. H., Prin., Reagan Sr. H. S., Houston, Texas.

Williams, R. L., B.A.'25, Abilene Christian Col.; M.A.'38, D.Ed.'43, Univ. of Texas; Supt. of Sch., Lockhart, Texas, since 1935.

Williams, Ralph J., B.A.'15, Ind. Univ.; M.A.'27, Columbia Univ.; Acting Supt. of Sch., Winona, Minn., since 1942.

Williams, Robert C., Ph.D.'38, State Univ. of Iowa; Acting Pres., State Tchrs. Col., Superior, Wis., since 1943.

Williams, Thomas C., B.S.'15, Va. Military Inst.; M.A.'38, George Washington Univ.; Supt. of Sch., Alexandria, Va., since 1933.

Williamson, Edith E., B.S.'33, M.E.'35, Univ. of Pittsburgh; Prin., Lemington Elem. Sch., Pittsburgh, Pa., since 1909.

Williamson, Pauline Brooks, B.S.'18, Columbia Univ.; Chief, Sch. Health Bureau, Welfare Division, Metropolitan Life Insurance Co., 1 Madison Ave., New York 10, N. Y., since 1925.

Willis, Benjamin C., A.B.'22, George Washington Univ.; A.M.'26, Univ. of Md.; Supt. of Sch., Hagerstown, Md., since 1940.

Williston, Arthur L., S.B.'89, Mass. Inst. of Tech. Address: 986 High St., Dedham, Mass.

Willman, Edward J., A.B.'18, A.M.'24, Univ. of Mich.; Supt. of Sch., Owosso, Mich., since 1921.

Willson, Gordon L., B.A.'25, M.A.'35, Univ. of Wis.; Supt. of Sch., Baraboo, Wis., since 1936.

Wilson, A. M., B.Ed.'32, Ill. State Normal Univ., Normal, Ill.; A.M.'40, Wash. Univ.; Supt. of Sch., Granite City, Ill., since 1933.

Wilson, Alan S., B.A.'29, Ohio Wesleyan Univ.; M.A.'37, Wittenberg Col.; Dir., Hillyer Jr. Col., Hartford, Conn., since 1938.

Wilson, Clara Owsley, A.M.'29, Columbia Univ.; Ph.D.'31, Univ. of Nebr.; Prof. and Chmn., Dept. of Elem. Educ., Univ. of Nebr., Lincoln, Nebr., since 1932.

Wilson, Edgar Ellen, B.S.'38, George Peabody Col. for Tchrs.; Asst. State Supt. of Educ., Austin, Texas, since 1933. Address: 1225 Elder St., Houston, Texas.

Wilson, Frank C., B.A.'29, Col. of Puget Sound; Supt. of Sch., Langley, Wash., since 1942.

Wilson, Glenn T., A.B.'18, Geneva Col.; M.S. in Ed.'34, Univ. of Southern Calif.; Supt. of Sch., La Junta, Colo., since 1934.

Wilson, H. F., A.B.'25, Univ. of Kansas City; M.E.'36, Univ. of Kansas; Supt. of Sch., Fredonia, Kansas, since 1932.

Wilson, Homer C., A.B.'25, Fresno State Col.; M.A.'31, Univ. of Southern Calif.; Supt. of Sch., Fresno, Calif., since 1937.

Wilson, I. Duane, B.A.'23, Univ. of Dubuque; M.A.'31, State Univ. of Iowa; Supt. of Twp. Sch., Savanna, Ill., since 1940.

Wilson, James H., A.B.'13, Sterling Col.; A.M.'28, Univ. of Chicago; Supt. of Sch., Rocky Ford, Colo., since 1924.

Wilson, John R., B.S.'13, Columbia Univ.; Supt. of Sch., Paterson, N. J., since 1906.

Wilson, Lytle Murray, B.S.'27, Bucknell Univ.; M.A.'31, Univ. of Pittsburgh; Supt. of Sch., Aliquippa, Pa., since 1937.

Wilson, Martin L., A.B.'07, Cornell Univ.; M.A.'38, Columbia Univ.; First Asst., James Monroe H. S., Bronx, New York, N. Y., since 1925.

Wilson, Otis E., Dist. Supt. of Sch., Emeryville, Calif.

Wilson, P. E., Acting Supt. of Parish Sch., Jennings, La.

Wilson, Paul S., B.A.'21, Carleton Col.; M.A.'31, Univ. of Minn.; Supt. of Sch., Marshall, Minn., since 1939.

Wilson, R. H., A.B.'23, Alma Col.; M.A.'30, Univ. of Mich.; Supt. of Sch., Alpena, Mich., since 1936.

Wilson, R. M., Supt. of Sch., Rocky Mount, N. C.

Wilson, Theodore Halbert, A.B.'07, A.M.'08, Harvard Univ.; S.T.B.'11, Union Theological Seminary; Ed.M.'28, Ed.D.'35, Harvard Univ.; Pres., Univ. of Baltimore, Baltimore 1, Md., since 1940.

Wilson, W. Harmon, Sales Mgr., South-Western Pub. Co., 201 W. Fourth St., Cincinnati 2, Ohio.

Wilson, Wallace Marvin, B.S.'28, Southwest Mo. State Tchrs. Col., Cape Girardeau, Mo.; M.A.'31, Univ. of Mo.; Supt. of Sch., Centralia, Mo., since 1938.

Wiltse, Earle W., A.B.'22, Nebr. Wesleyan Univ.; A.M.'26, Columbia Univ.; Ph.D.'42, Univ. of Nebr.; Supt. of Sch., McCook, Nebr., since 1942.

Wine, Norman B., A.B.'23, Manchester Col.; A.M.'31, Wittenberg Col.; Asst. Supt. of Sch., Dayton, Ohio, since 1937.

Wingate, Harold C., B.A.'05, Clark Col., Worcester, Mass.; Supt. of Sch., Scituate and Marshfield, Mass., since 1926. Address: Egypt, Mass.

Winger, Paul M., A.B.'27, Manchester Col.; A.M.'34, Ind. Univ.; Supt. of Sch., Sturgis, Mich., since 1939.

Wingo, Charles Enos, B.A.'24, Furman Univ.; M.A.'37, Cornell Univ.; Supt., Argo Com. H. S., Argo, Ill., since 1935.

Winslow, Harry D., A.B.'27, Pa. State Col.; A.M.'28, Ph.D.'35, Tchrs. Col., Columbia Univ.; Supt. of Sch., Park Ridge, Ill., since 1930.

Winslow, Howard L., B.S.'05, Wesleyan Univ.; Union Supt. of Sch., Somersworth, N. H., since 1928.

Winslow, Marion B., B.A.'27, Pacific Col.; M.A.'33, Univ. of Wash.; Supt. of Sch., Grants Pass, Oregon, since 1934.

Winterble, Mrs. Margaret R., M.A.'34, Tchrs. Col., Columbia Univ.; Research Asst., Bd. of Educ., 110 Livingston St., Brooklyn 2, N. Y., since 1930.

Winters, Carl, B.S.'24, Univ. of Utah; Supt. of Sch., Park City, Utah, since 1938.

Winters, Thomas Howard, A.B.'96, Ohio Wesleyan Univ.; A.M.'24, Ph.D.'30, Ohio State Univ.; Prof. of Educ., Rider Col., Trenton 9, N. J., since 1932.

Winther, Adolph I., A.B.'30, Augsburg Col.; Ph.M.'38, Univ. of Wis.; Prin., Marinette County Normal Sch., Marinette, Wis., since 1941.

Wippermann, Edgar George, Ph.B.'22, Ph.M. '30, Ph.D.'41, Univ. of Wis.; Supt. of Sch., Columbus, Wis., since 1933.

Wise, Henry A., B.S.'98, Va. Polytech. Inst.; M.A. and LL.B.'05, Centre Col.; M.A.'11, Univ. of S. C.; Div. Supt. of Sch., Accomac, Va., since 1943.

Wiseman, Clinton R., Ph.D.'28, Univ. of Minn.; Head, Dept. of Educ. and Psych., State Col., Brookings, S. Dak., since 1933.

Wish, Fred D., Jr., A.B.'13, Bowdoin Col.; Supt. of Sch., Hartford, Conn., since 1923.

Wisness, Arthur M., B.A.'14, Luther Col., Decorah, Iowa; M.A.'38, Univ. of Minn.; Supt. of Sch., Willmar, Minn., since 1929.

Wisniewski, Andrew, Member, Bd. of Educ., 9609 Gallagher, Hamtramck, Mich., since 1939.

Witham, Ernest C., B.S.'04, Tufts Col.; M.A.'33, New York Univ.; Prof. of Educ., Rutgers Univ., New Brunswick, N. J., since 1939.

Withers, John W., B.S.'90, B.A.'91, Pd.D.'96, Natl. Normal Univ.; M.A.'02, Ph.D.'04, Yale Univ.; LL.D.'17, Washington Univ.; LL.D.'18, Univ. of Mo.; L.H.D.'38, N. Y. Univ.; Honorary Life Member, American Assn. of Sch. Admin.; Dean Emeritus, Sch. of Educ., New York Univ., New York, N. Y., since 1939. Address: 1813 First Ave., Bradenton, Fla.

Witmeyer, Paul E., A.B.'16, Lebanon Valley Col.; M.A.'23, Tchrs. Col., Columbia Univ.; Ed.D.'38, New York Univ.; Supt. of Sch., Sharon, Pa., since 1941.

Witter, Fred L., A.B.'07, Beloit Col.; Supt. of Sch., Burlington, Wis., since 1912.

Woelfel, Erwin R., Diploma '04, State Tchrs. Col., Mansfield, Pa.; Supt. of Sch., Newark, N. Y., since 1936.

Woellner, Robert Carlton, B.S.'22 Univ. of Cincinnati; M.A.'24, Univ. of Chicago; Assoc. Prof. of Educ. and Exec. Secy., Bd. of Vocational Guidance and Placement, Univ. of Chicago, Chicago, Ill., since 1930.

Woglom, Russell S., Ph.B.'15, Lafayette Col.; M. A.'28, New York Univ.; Ph.D.'35, Webster Univ.; Supvg. Prin. of Sch., High Bridge, N. J., since 1928.

Wohlsen, Paul T., A.B.'21, Muhlenberg Col.; M.A.'31, New York Univ.; Supvg. Prin. of Sch., Valley Stream, N. Y., since 1941.

Wolbach, Charles A., A.B.'18, Lehigh Univ.; M.A.'24, Tchrs. Col., Columbia Univ.; Ph.D.'34, New York Univ.; Supvg. Prin. of Sch., Rumson, N. J., since 1934.

Wolfe, Norman A., B.S.'37, M.A.'39, Wayne Univ.; Supt., Redford Union Sch., Detroit, Mich., since 1941.

Wolfe, William D., A.B.'17, Col. of Emporia; M.A.'30, Univ. of Kansas; D.Ed.'41, Col. of Emporia; Supt. of Sch., Atchison, Kansas, since 1929.

Wood, Charles B., B.A.'14, Univ. of Toronto, Canada; A.M.'24, Tchrs. Col., Columbia Univ.; Registrar, Univ. of British Columbia, Vancouver, B. C., Canada, since 1941.

*Wood, F. Ray, B.S.'26, Southwest Mo. State Tchrs. Col., Springfield, Mo.; A.M. '34, Univ. of Mo.; Supt. of Soh., Bolivar, Mo., since 1931.

Wood, H. A., A.B.'23, Mich. State Normal Col., Ypsilanti, Mich.; M.A.'27, Tchrs. Col., Columbia Univ.; Supt. of Sch., Munising, Mich., since 1925.

Wood, Harry H., Ph.B.'08, Grinnell Col.; Dir., Ginn & Co., 2301 Prairie Ave., Chicago, Ill.

Wood, James M., Ph.B.'01, Central Mo. State Normal Sch., Warrensburg, Mo.; A.B. and B.S. in Ed.'07, Univ. of Mo.; A.M.'11, Columbia Univ.; LL.D.'30, Hiram Col.; Pres., Stephens Col., Columbia, Mo., since 1912.

Wood, Ray G., B.S. in Ed.'22, Ohio Northern Univ.; M.A.'28, Ph.D.'35, Ohio State Univ.; Dir., Ohio Scholarship Tests and Instructional Research, State Dept. of Educ., Columbus, Ohio, since 1932.

Wood, V. H., Co. Supt. of Educ., Russellville, Ala.

Wood, Waldo Emerson, B.A.'15, Central Normal Col.; M.A.'17, Univ. of Wis.; Ph.D.'31, Ind. Univ.; Supt. of Sch., Frankfort, Ind., since 1940.

Woodbury, E. Davis, Supt. of Sch., Natick, Mass.

Woodbury, Kenneth F., B.A.'24, Univ. of Maine; M.A.'33, Tchrs. Col., Columbia Univ.; Supvg. Prin. of Sch., Weehawken, N. J., since 1933.

Woodfield, Arthur G., B.A.'97, Western Md. Col.; Supvg. Prin. of Sch., Hillside, N. J., since 1906.

Woods, Elizabeth L., M.A.'09, Univ. of Oregon; Ph.D.'13, Clark Univ.; Head Supvr., Educ. Research and Guidance, Pub. Sch., Los Angeles, Calif., since 1925.

Woods, L. A., B.A.'19, M.A.'25. LL.D.'33, Baylor Univ.; State Supt. of Pub. Instr., Austin, Texas, since 1933.

Woods, Mrs. Mabel Talley, B.A.'30, Texas State Col. for Women; LL.B.'31, Houston Law Sch.; M.A.'42, Univ. of Houston; Prin., Eastwood Elem. Sch., Houston, Texas, since 1942.

Woods, Miss Quata, B.S.'32, North Texas State Tchrs. Col., Denton, Texas; Prin., Obadiah Knight Sch., Dallas, Texas, since 1942.

Woodside, J. Barnes, A.B.'28, Western Reserve Univ.; M.A.'35, Columbia Univ.; Supt. of Sch., Willoughby, Ohio, since 1940.

Woodson, Wilbert T., A.B.'16, Col. of William and Mary; Div. Supt. of Sch., Fairfax, Va., since 1929.

Workman, David Frank, B.S.'25, Franklin and Marshall Col.; M.A.'29, Columbia Univ.; Supvg. Prin. of Sch., Waldwick, N. J., since 1927.

Workman, John H., A.B.'13, M.A.'32, Ph.D. '35, Univ. of N. C.; Prof. of Social Science, Atlantic Christian Col., Wilson, N. C., since 1941.

Workman, John Hunter, A.B.'02, Univ. of Nashville; M.A.'32, George Peabody Col. for Tchrs.; Supvg. Prin. of Sch., Pensacola, Fla., since 1920.

Worlton, James T., Ed.D.'26, Univ. of Calif.; Asst. Supt. of Sch., Salt Lake City, Utah, since 1920.

*Wright, Arthur Davis, A.B., A.M.'04, Col. of William and Mary; Ed.M.'22, Harvard Univ.; A.M.'27, Dartmouth Col.; Pres., Southern Educ. Foundation, 726 Jackson Pl., N. W., Washington, D. C., since 1931.

Wright, C. Milton, A.B.'06, Western Md. Col.; Co. Supt. of Sch., Bel Air, Md., since 1915.

Wright, C. O., Exec. Secy., Kansas State Tchrs. Assn., 315 W. Tenth, Topeka, Kansas.

Wright, Clark G., Supt. of Elem. Sch. Dist. 108, 542 S. Linden Ave., Highland Park, Ill., since 1914.

Wright, Frank Lee, A.M.'15, Univ. of Wis.; Ed.D.'25, Harvard Univ.; Head, Dept. of Educ., Washington Univ., St. Louis, Mo., since 1924.

Wright, Frank M., A.B.'16, Whittier Col.; A.M.'30, Univ. of Southern Calif.; Dist. Supt. of Sch., El Monte, Calif., since 1925.

Wright, George C., M.A.'36, Northwestern Univ.; Supt. of Sch., Lake Bluff, Ill., since 1941.

Wright, George W., Ed.D., Ed.M., B.S., Rutgers Univ.; Supvg. Prin. of Sch., Glassboro, N. J., since 1937.

Wright, Harold N., Supvr., War Production Tr., Pub. Sch., 1025 Second Ave., Oakland, Calif., since 1940.

Wright, Harry Noble, B.S.'04, Earlham Col.; M.S.'11, Ph.D.'13, Univ. of Calif.; Pres., The City Col., 139th St. and Convent Ave., New York, N. Y., since 1941.

Wright, Howard W., Exec. Secy., La. Tchrs Assn., 418 Florida St., Baton Rouge, La., since 1939.

Wright, Isaac Miles, B.S.'04, Alfred Univ.; Pd.M.'14, Pd.D.'16, New York Univ. Address: 2729 Gordon St., Allentown, Pa.

Wright, J. C., A.B.'27, Drake Univ.; M.A. '36, State Univ. of Iowa. Address: Pub. Sch., Keokuk, Iowa.

Wright, John Herbert, B.A.'18, Southern Methodist Univ.; M.A.'39, Univ. of Calif.; Asst. Prin., Lamar H. S., Houston, Texas, since 1936.

Wright, P. A., B.A.'29, Univ. of Wash.; Supt. of Sch., Snohomish, Wash., since 1924.

Wright, W. C., Bus. Mgr., The Natl. Forum, 417 S. Dearborn St., Chicago, Ill.

Wright, Wendell W., A.B.'16, Ind. State Normal Sch.; A.M.'25, Ph.D.'29, Tchrs. Col., Columbia Univ.; Dean, Jr. Div., Ind. Univ., Bloomington, Ind., since 1941.

Wright, Wilbur W., M.S.'29, Kansas State Col.; Supt., Highland Park Schs., Topeka, Kansas, since 1931.

Wrightstone, J. Wayne, B.S.'25, Univ. of Pa.; M.A.'28, New York Univ.; Ph.D.'33, Tchrs. Col., Columbia Univ.; Asst. Dir., Bureau of Reference, Research, and Statistics, Bd. of Educ., 110 Livingston St., Brooklyn 2, N. Y., since 1940.

Wrinkle, Herbert E., Diploma '15, Southwest Mo. State Tchrs. Col., Springfield, Mo.; A.B.'22, M.S.'31, Univ. of Okla.; State Service Dir., Univ. of Okla., Norman, Okla., since 1942.

Wubben, Horace J., B.A.'17, Colo. Col.; M.A.'32, Univ. of Colo.; Pres., Mesa Col., Grand Junction, Colo., since 1937.

Wyatt, Robert H., M.A.'25, Ind. Univ.; Exec. Secy., Ind. State Tchrs. Assn., Hotel Lincoln, Indianapolis 9, Ind., since 1938.

Wyland, Ray Orion, A.B., Univ. of Ill.; M.A.'29, Ph.D.'34, Columbia Univ.; Dir. of Educ. and Relationships, Boy Scouts of America, 2 Park Ave., New York, N. Y., since 1922.

Wyman, Harry B., B.S.'18, M.A.'27, Ph.D. '31, Ohio State Univ.; Dean, Jr. Col., Phoenix, Ariz., since 1931.

Wynstra, W. S., M.A.'37, Univ. of Wash.; Supt. of Sch., Mt. Vernon, Wash., since 1941.

Y

Yaden, Jessie Linden, M.A.'31, Mercer Univ.; Supt. of Sch., Moultrie, Ga., since 1934.

Yawn, Howard W., B.A.'33, Pa. State Col.; Supvg. Prin. of Sch., Lebanon, Pa., since 1937.

Yeager, William A., A.B.'14, Ursinus Col.; A.M.'18, Ph.D.'29, Univ. of Pa.; Prof. of Educ. and Dir. of Courses in Sch. Admin., Univ. of Pittsburgh, Pittsburgh, Pa., since 1934.

Yeubanks, William Raymond, M.S.'42, Okla. Agrl. and Mech. Col.; Supt. of Sch., Springdale, Ark., since 1942.

Yoakam, G. A., B.A.'10, M.A.'18, Ph.D.'22, State Univ. of Iowa; Prof. of Educ. and Dir. of Courses in Elem. Educ., Univ. of Pittsburgh, Pittsburgh, Pa., since 1923.

Yockey, F. Milton, A.B.'08, Simpson Col.; A.M.'11, Univ. of Wis.; Ed.D.'32, Univ. of Calif.; Prin., Tech. Evening H. S., Oakland, Calif., since 1934.

Yoder, C. M., Pres., State Tchrs. Col., Whitewater, Wis., since 1930.

Yoder, Harry T., A.M.'27, Manchester Col.; M.S. in Ed.'34, Ind. Univ.; Co. Supt. of Sch., Columbia City, Ind., since 1937.

York, George A., B.S. in Ed.'24, Kansas State Tchrs. Col., Pittsburg, Kansas; M.E.'35, Univ. of Kansas; Supt. of Sch., Osawatomie, Kansas, since 1924.

Young, Arthur L., A.B.'04, Brown Univ.; A.M.'30, Yale Univ.; Supt. of Rural Educ., State Dept. of Educ., Essex, Conn., since 1912.

Young, Franklin M., B.S.'26, Otterbein Col.; M.A.'31, Ohio State Univ.; Supt. of Sch., Miamisburg, Ohio, since 1943.

Young, Gordie, M.A.'36, Univ. of Ky.; Asst. State Supt. of Pub. Instr., Frankfort, Ky., since 1928.

Young, Harry H., Secy. and Bus. Mgr., Bd. of Educ., 1809 Pacific Ave., Atlantic City, N. J., since 1894.

Young, James B., B.A.'30, Univ. of Miss.; M.A.'36, Columbia Univ.; Pres., Jones Co. Agrl. H. S. and Jr. Col., Ellisville, Miss., since 1940.

Young, John Adams, Ph.B.'03, A.M.12, Bucknell Univ.; Supt. of Sch., Bridgeport, Conn., since 1941.

Young, John J., A.B.'21, Ind. State Tchrs. Col., Terre Haute, Ind.; M.A.'24, Univ. of Wis.; Ph.D.'35, New York Univ.; Supt. of Sch., Rocky River, Ohio, since 1933.

Young, L. P., B.S.'22, State Tchrs. Col., Emporia, Kansas; A.M.'29, Ph.D.'31, Tchrs. Col., Columbia Univ.; Pres., State Tchrs. Col., Keene, N. H., since 1939.

Young, Oliver O., A.B.'04, Bethany Col.; M.A.'14, Univ. of S. Dak.; Supt., Sch. Dist. No. 69, Skokie, Ill., since 1940.

Young, W. Rankin, B.S.'22, Kansas State Tchrs. Col., Pittsburg, Kansas; M.A.'25, Tchrs. Col., Columbia Univ.; Supt. of Sch., Cleveland, Okla., since 1934.

*Young, William E., A.B.'24, Bates Col.; M.A.'28, Ph.D.'30, State Univ. of Iowa; Dir. of Elem. Educ., State Educ. Dept., Albany, N. Y., since 1938.

Younger, Frank B., B.A.'16, M.A.'36, Lawrence Col.; Supt. of Sch., Menasha, Wis., since 1935.

Youngert, Eugene, A.B.'20, Augustana Col.; M.A.'37, Ed.D.'39, Columbia Univ.; Supt., Oak Park and River Forest Twp. H. S., Oak Park, Ill., since 1941.

Yount, Marvin E., A.B.'11, Concordia Col.; M.A.'43, George Peabody Col. for Tchrs.; Co. Supt. of Sch., Graham, N. C., since 1927.

Z

Zavitz, Edwin Cornell, B.A.'14, Univ. of Mich.; M.A.'31, Tchrs. Col., Columbia Univ.; Headmaster, Sidwell Friends Sch., Washington, D. C., since 1943.

Zeliff, L. A., B.S.'20, A.B.'24, Northwest Mo. State Tchrs. Col., Maryville, Mo.; M.A. '29, Univ. of Mo.; Supt. of Sch., Stanberry, Mo., since 1919.

Zeller, Dale, Assoc. Prof. of Educ., Kansas State Tchrs. Col., Emporia, Kansas.

Zeller, Glenn W., B.Sc.'26, M.A.'32, Ohio State Univ.; Supt. of Sch., Uhrichsville, Ohio, since 1942.

Zellmer, Amil William, A.B.'16, Lawrence Col.; A.M.'28, Columbia Univ.; Supt., Wood County Normal Sch., Wisconsin Rapids, Wis., since 1927.

Zerbe, A. W., Co. Supt. of Sch., Tremont, Pa.

Zieg, Lee O., M.S.'32, Ind. Univ.; Supt. of Sch., Boonville, Ind., since 1942.

Ziegler, L. E., A.B.'20, Univ. of Mo.; A.M. '27, Columbia Univ.; Supt. of Sch., Columbia, Mo., since 1941.

Ziegler, Samuel H., A.B.'10, A.M.'12, Ursinus Col.; Ph.D.'23, Univ. of Pa.; Head, Dept. of Educ., Cedar Crest Col., Allentown, Pa., since 1926.

Zimmerman, J. E., A.B.'29, A.M.'30, Baylor Univ.; Supt. of Sch., Winslow, Ariz., since 1942.

Zinn, W. Roger, A.B.'22, Alma Col.; M.A. '26, Univ. of Mich.; Educ. Counselor on Visual Tr. Aids, The Jam Handy Organization, 2900 E. Grand Blvd., Detroit 11, Mich., since 1942.

Zook, Carl S., A.B.'07, Univ. of Wash.; Prin., Woodmere Sch., Portland 6, Oregon, since 1920.

Zook, George F., A.B.'06, A.M.'07, Univ. of Kansas; Ph.D.'15, Cornell Univ.; Pres., American Council on Educ., 744 Jackson Pl., Washington, D. C., since 1934.

Zuill, Frances L., B.S.'20, M.A.'21, Tchrs. Col., Columbia Univ.; Dir. of Home Economics, Univ. of Wis., Madison, Wis., since 1939.

LIBRARIES, COLLEGES, AND SCHOOLS

Library, Alabama Polytechnic Institute, Auburn, Ala.

General Library, College of Education, University of Arkansas, Fayetteville, Ark.

Library, University of California, Berkeley, Calif.

Teachers Library, Kings County Free Library, Hanford, Calif.

Teachers Library, Board of Education, Long Beach, Calif.

California Test Bureau, Ethel M. Clark, President, 5916 Hollywood Blvd., Los Angeles, Calif.

Division of Library and Textbook Activities, Board of Education, Los Angeles, Calif.

California State Library, Sacramento, Calif.

Professional Reference Library, San Diego, Calif.

San Mateo Union High School District, High School, San Mateo, Calif.

Teachers' Library, County Public Schools, Court House, Santa Barbara, Calif.

Summer School of Education, Bank of Nova Scotia Bldg., Victoria, B. C., Canada.

State Teachers College, Willimantic, Conn.

Library, Rollins College, Winter Park, Fla.

Library, Georgia Teachers College, Collegeboro, Ga.

Albion State Normal School, Albion, Idaho.

Bell & Howell Co., 1801 Larchmont Ave., Chicago, Ill.

F. E. Compton & Co., School Service Department, 1000 N. Dearborn St., Chicago, Ill.

National Safety Council, Education Division, 20 N. Wacker Drive, Chicago, Ill.

Society for Visual Education, Inc., 100 E. Ohio St., Chicago, Ill.

Broadview Academy, La Grange, Ill.

Library, Western Illinois State Teachers College, Macomb, Ill.

Library, University of Illinois, Urbana, Ill.

Primary Council of Indiana, Huntington, Ind.

Library, Purdue University, Lafayette, Ind.

Drake University, Des Moines, Iowa.

Midland Laboratories, C. F. Hillyard, Vice-Pres., 210 Jones St., Dubuque, Iowa.

Director General of Education, Ministry of Education, Baghdad, Iraq.

Kansas State Teachers College, Porter Library, Pittsburg, Kansas.

City Teachers Club, Salina, Kansas.

The McCormick-Mathers Publishing Co., 1501 E. Douglas Ave., Wichita, Kansas.

Stevens Memorial Library, Southwestern Louisiana Institute, Lafayette, La.

Library Department, State Normal College, Natchitoches, La.

Professional Library, Orleans Parish School Board, 1835 Erato St., New Orleans, La.

Morgan State College, Baltimore, Md.

Library, State Teachers College, Fitchburg, Mass.

The Standard Electric Time Co., 89 Logan St., Springfield 2, Mass.

Library, State Teachers College, Worcester, Mass.

Registrar's Office, University of Michigan, Ann Arbor, Mich.

Health Education Club, Detroit Public Schools, 467 W. Hancock, Detroit 1, Mich.

Library, Board of Education, City Hall, Minneapolis, Minn.

Library, State Teachers College, Moorhead, Minn.

Library, State Teachers College, St. Cloud, Minn.

Teachers College, Kansas City, Mo.

Library, Harris Teachers College, 1517 S. Theresa, St. Louis 4, Mo.

St. Louis District, Missouri State Teachers Association, St. Louis, Mo.

St. Louis Public Library, St. Louis, Mo.

Bogota High School, Bogota, N. J.

Bridgeton Public Schools, Bridgeton, N. J.

Board of Education, Hackensack, N. J.

Hackensack Teachers Association, Hackensack, N. J.

Public Schools, Lyndhurst, N. J.

Edgemont School, Montclair, N. J.

Montclair High School, Montclair, N. J.

Montclair Public School Teachers Association, Montclair, N. J.

Watchung School, Montclair, N. J.

Public Library, Newark 2, N. J.

Benjamin Franklin Junior High School, Ridgewood, N. J.

Harrison Avenue Elementary School, Ridgewood, N. J.

Kenilworth Elementary School, Ridgewood, N. J.

Ridgewood High School, Ridgewood, N. J.

Union Street Elementary School, Ridgewood, N. J.

George Washington Elementary School, Ridgewood, N. J.

George Washington Junior High School, Ridgewood, N. J.

Willard Elementary School, Ridgewood, N. J.

Tenafly High School, Tenafly, N. J.

Library, State Teachers College, Trenton, N. J.

Board of Examiners, Board of Education, 110 Livingston St., Brooklyn 2, N. Y.

Brooklyn College, Brooklyn, N. Y.

State Teachers College, Fredonia, N. Y.

Hornell Teachers Association, Hornell, N. Y.

Jamestown Teachers Association, Jamestown, N. Y.

Johnson City Teachers Association, Johnson City, N. Y.

Foley & Edmunds, Inc., 480 Lexington Ave., New York 17, N. Y.

International Business Machines Corp., 590 Madison Ave., New York, N. Y.

National Society for the Prevention of Blindness, New York, N. Y.

Library, New York University, Washington Square, East, New York, N. Y.

Niagara Falls Teachers Association, Niagara Falls, N. Y.

Olean Public Schools, Olean, N. Y.

Port Jervis Public School Teachers, Port Jervis, N. Y.

New York State Association of Elementary Principals, Rochester, N. Y.

Rochester Teachers Association, Rochester, N. Y.

Library, Union College, Schenectady, N. Y.

Federation of Parent-Teacher Associations, Yonkers, N. Y.

School No. 16, Yonkers, N. Y.

Library, State Teachers College, Mayville, N. Dak.

Library, East Carolina Teachers College, Greenville, N. C.

Library, Ohio State University, Columbus, Ohio.

Ohio State Library, Columbus, Ohio.

Oklahoma City Teachers Mutual Organization, Oklahoma City, Okla.

Library, University of Oregon, Eugene, Oregon.

Library, Oregon College of Education, Monmouth, Oregon.

John J. Nesbitt, Inc., State Rd. and Rhawn St., Holmesburg, Philadelphia, Pa.

Drexel Institute of Technology, Philadelphia, Pa.

Educational Test Bureau, Educational Publishers, Inc., 3433 Walnut St., Philadelphia, Pa.

Free Library of Philadelphia, Periodical Department, Middle City District, Philadelphia, Pa.

Administration Library, Public Schools, Bellefield Ave. at Forbes St., Pittsburgh, Pa.

Division of Teacher Education and Certification, J. B. White, Director, State Department of Education, Columbia, S. C.

Library, Eastern State Normal Sch., Madison, S. Dak.

Library, George Peabody College for Teachers, Nashville 4, Tenn.

Library, Hardin-Simmons University, Abilene, Texas.

Jefferson County Education Association, Beaumont, Texas.

W. H. Adamson High School, Dallas, Texas.

Stephen F. Austin School, Dallas, Texas.

James B. Bonham School, Dallas, Texas.

John Henry Brown School, Dallas, Texas.

N. R. Crozier Technical High School, Dallas, Texas.

Cumberland School, Dallas, Texas.

Forest Avenue High School, Dallas, Texas.

Stephen J. Hay School, Dallas, Texas.

James Stephen Hogg School, Dallas, Texas.

Lida Hooe School, Dallas, Texas.

Sam Houston School, Dallas, Texas.

Obadiah Knight School, Dallas, Texas.

Richard Lagow School, Dallas, Texas.

William Lipscomb School, Dallas, Texas.

Maple Lawn School, Dallas, Texas.

North Dallas High School, Dallas, Texas.

San Jacinto School, Dallas, Texas.

Ascher Silberstein School, Dallas, Texas.

Sunset High School, Dallas, Texas.

T. G. Terry School, Dallas, Texas.

William B. Travis School, Dallas, Texas.

Trinity Heights School, Dallas, Texas.

Woodrow Wilson High School, Dallas, Texas.

Library, Texas State College for Women, Denton, Texas.

Library, John Tarleton Agricultural College, Stephenville, Texas.

Library, Central Washington College of Education, Ellensburg, Wash.

Spokane Public Library, Spokane, Wash.

Parkersburg Teachers Association, Parkersburg, W. Va.

Racine Public Library, Racine, Wis.

Library, State Teachers College, Whitewater, Wis.

INDEX OF PERSONS

SUBJECT INDEX

A

Administration of school personnel: autocratic versus democratic, 261-64; basic principles, 258; distribution of teaching load, 268-70; evolving concepts, 256-61; human relations in, 255-79; loyalty, recognition, and promotion, 276-77; need for pay adequate to maintain economic self-respect, 274-75; need for security in employment, 270-74; need for wholesome physical conditions of employment, 275-76; problems of communication, 259; problems of individual effectiveness, 260-61; problems of teamwork, 259-60; retention of teachers, 264-79; selection, appointment, and placement of teachers, 265-68; understanding and participation, 277-79

Adult education, 78, 107, 178

Agricultural Adjustment Act, 226

American Association of School Administrators: executive secretary's report, 329-55; members, 357-451; officers, 328; official records, 327-451; publications cited, 63, 138, 156, 159, 171, 222, 228; yearbook (1945) commission, 345; yearbook (1944) commission, 4

American Council on Education, 184-85

American Institute of Public Opinion, 294

American Revolution, 23

American Youth Commission, 84, 90, 104

Anecdotal records, 287

Armed forces, 65, 69-70, 90-92, 96, 100-102, 134, 143, 255, 285

Aspiration, level of, 31, 46-47, 118-19, 293

Assemblies, 217-18

Atlantic Charter, 24, 220, 231, 283

Attitudes: changes thru education, 182-83, 312-13; measurement of, 296-97, 301-11; teaching civic attitudes, 206-12, 214-19

B

Badges and uniforms, 67

Behavior as an indicator of morale, 285-93

Bibliography, 318-26

Bill of Rights, 110, 218, 220, 231, 252, 316

Boxer indemnity, 22

Boy Scouts, 61, 149, 169, 177

Bulletin boards, 218-19

C

Catholic Youth Association, 140

Census Bureau, 91, 92, 93, 97, 109

Character-forming groups, 148-51, 159-60

Child labor, 93-95

Children, morale of: choice and discrimination, 127-28; conditions favoring, 123-29; ideals and purposes, 128-29; opportunities to experiment, 125-27; self-confidence and responsibility, 124-25; sense of belonging and security, 123-24

Children's Bureau, 94, 142

Citizenship, 71-74, 158, 171-201, 184-85, 203-31, 282-83

Civic attitudes, teaching of, 206-12, 214-19

Civilian Conservation Corps, 18, 80, 92-93

Class and caste, 79, 95-100

Codes, rituals, and songs, 66

Commission on Teacher Education, American Council on Education, 185, 237

Commission on the Relation of School and College, Progressive Education Association, 292, 301, 308-11

Committee for National Morale, 11, 13

Committee on Food Habits, National Research Council, 297

Committee on Public Information (1917-18), 13

Common cause, values, 32, 46-47, 105-106, 117, 121-23, 128-29, 185-89

Community Chest, 72, 264

Community councils, 156, 169

Constitution of the United States, 99, 214-15, 220

Constitution, teaching of, 214-15

Controversial issues, teaching of, 225-28

Cooperative Study in General Education, American Council on Education, 301, 307-308

Counseling and guidance, 59, 107, 280, 313

Crop and Marketing Division, U. S. Department of Agriculture, 142

Curriculum, 107, 186-87, 200-201, 313

D

Declaration of Independence, 99, 189, 220, 231

Delinquency, juvenile, 136, 148-51, 291

Democracy: fellow feeling, 33; five ideals, 32-36; freedom under law, 33; love of truth, 32-33; personal responsibility, 34-35; respect for human dignity, 34

Depth of experience and level of function, 119-21

Discipline and human values, 69-71